Fearless Critic

Praise for the restaurant guides

"Pulls no punches...even icons get goosed."

–Austin American-Statesman

"Deft, unblushing prose...good friends to the honest diner, they call it as they see it."

–T. Susan Chang,
Food & Travel Correspondent,
Boston Globe

"Exceptionally experienced restaurantgoers...knowledgeable and enthusiastic about eating well."

–*Yale Daily News*

"Immensely useful, written with panache, as respectful of 'Roadfood' as of 'fine-dining'...one of the most compelling restaurant guides we've seen."

–Jane and Michael Stern,
Authors, *Roadfood;*
columnists, *Gourmet*

"Not just a useful book—a pleasure to read. The only people who won't find it a pleasure are the owners of some of the really bad restaurants it warns us about."

–David Ball, Professor
Emeritus of French and
Comparative Literature,
Smith College

"Scathing and scintillating."

–*New Haven Register*

Also from Fearless Critic

The Wine Trials 2010: The world's bestselling guide to inexpensive wines, with the 150 winning wines under $15 from the latest vintages

Fearless Critic Austin Restaurant Guide

Fearless Critic Houston Restaurant Guide

Fearless Critic New Haven Restaurant Guide

Fearless Critic Washington DC Restaurant Guide

On fearlesscritic.com

For everyone: sortable lists and ratings, what's open now, new reviews, daily rotating reviews, and more

For subscribers: the entire text of Fearless Critic

Fearless Critic

Portland
Restaurant
Guide

WWW.FEARLESSCRITIC.COM/PORTLAND

First edition, 2010

Printed in the United States of America

10 9 8 7 6 5 4 3 2 1

ISBN 978-1-6081600-4-4

Contents

Fearless Critics

Robin Goldstein, Editor-in-Chief
Alexis Herschkowitsch, Associate Publisher
Erin McReynolds, Managing Editor
Kent Wang, Chief Technology Officer
Justin Yu, Executive Chef
Nat Davis, Wine Director

Associate editors

Rachel Carlson   Pavithra Mahesh
Robbie Newsham

Cover photo

Kim Campbell, Campbell Salgado Studio,
Portland, Oregon / **campbellsalgado.com**

Contributing editors

Andrea Armeni, Barry Goldstein, Jacob Katz, David Menschel, Clare
Murumba, Susan Stubbs, Hal Stubbs, Lu Stubbs

Special thanks

Jennifer Bolen, Ed Cavazos, Leslie Doherty, Julian Faulkner, Andrea
Fleck-Nisbet, Andrew Gajkowski, Rosie Goldstein, Laurel Hoyt, Kurtis
Lowe, Ruby Madren-Britton, Jenny Mandel, David Matt, Jill Owens,
Steven Pace, Michael Powell, Marci Saunders, April Savard, Walter
Schmamp, Giuliano Stiglitz, Frank Tasty, Heather Tietgens, Mike Vago,
Tyce Walters, Walter Weintz, Annick Winokur, Peter Workman, and the
Yale Entrepreneurial Society

About the editorial team

Robin Goldstein is founder of the Fearless Critic series and author of *The Wine Trials*. He has written for 35 *Fodor's* travel guides, from Italy to Mexico to Hong Kong. Robin is a graduate of Harvard University, the Yale Law School, and the French Culinary Institute, and has a WSET advanced wine and spirits certificate.

Alexis Herschkowitsch has written for *The Wine Trials*, five *Fearless Critic* guides, and five *Fodor's* travel guides, from El Salvador to Thailand. Alexis is a graduate of the University of Texas at Austin and has a WSET advanced wine and spirits certificate.

Erin McReynolds worked in the restaurant industry for 10 years. She has an M.F.A. in Creative Writing from Queens University and is a graduate of California State University, Fullerton.

The Fearless Critic Council
of local critics & writers:

Mark Annen, Patrick Coleman, Seamus Campbell, Dianne Derse, Aaron Furmanek, David Jenkins, Adam McGovern, Danielle Tarpley, Reiko Hillyer, Juree Sondker, Heather Watkins, Elliott Young

Ratings and reviews represent a council consensus; no council member is individually responsible for the rating or review of any single restaurant. Differences of opinion are resolved by the editors, and are not necessarily endorsed by individual council members. Fearless Critics and Council members are not allowed to participate in the reviews, ratings, or evaluations of restaurants with which they are or ever have been associated or have any personal ties.

Preface

Portland, Oregon, from stumptown to foodie town, is a story of a green-conscious, hipster, DIY alternative to the bourgeois cosmopolitan dining of big-city America. What has happened in Portland in the last couple of decades is nothing less than a social movement around food, from the restaurant that grows its greens on its roof garden, to the local farm-raised and grass-fed animals, to the vegan, gluten-free eateries.

There's a wide variety of food to be relished in this moderately sized city, but more importantly, creativity, sustainability, and taste count here. The Portland ethic seems to be amazing food at prices even underemployed baristas can afford.

Last year we ran into a couple from North Carolina at Park Kitchen who had come to Portland to sample the restaurants. That restaurants have become a significant draw for food tourists is testament to the place that food has in Portland culture. The North Carolina couple came armed with their *New York Times* article "36 hours in Portland," but the newspaper's food recommendations all centered around downtown and the West side. While there are some innovative, knockout restaurants downtown, including Park Kitchen, Andina, and Ping, the city's most creative endeavors are happening on the east side of the river. And the *Times* didn't even scratch the surface of the amazing immigrant restaurants that do their work in relative obscurity around 82nd Avenue in Portland, and scattered throughout the outskirts of Beaverton and Hillsboro, in non-descript strip malls far from the hipster Portland that New Yorkers seem to find so exotic.

These areas are home to some of America's most vibrant Chinese, Vietnamese, Korean, and Japanese culinary communities, just to name a few. Too many of those restaurants are still making the mistake of assuming that people who come in from outside the community are not interested in trying their weirdest, most traditional work, and instead choose to cover it up by translating only a superficial menu of Americanized dishes into English. Those restaurateurs would do well to visit Pok Pok, the authentic Thai restaurant whose extraordinary popularity proves that Portland is ready for the real deal.

Coffee is also a major food group in Portland. Coffee at Stumptown or Albina Press bears no resemblance to what you get at a Starbucks. The baristas, who regularly win international competitions, prepare each cup with the artisanal care you expect from a Swiss watchmaker, finishing each latte with a careful design made from the foamy milk. They are knowledgeable about the coffee they serve, and they can even tell you where it is produced. Stumptown has direct relationships with cooperative coffee farms in Latin America and Africa.

When a Starbucks opened on Southeast Division a few years ago, anarchists tried to firebomb the building; apparently they needed better training as anarchists, because their firebombs failed to ignite. They were worried that Starbucks would put the worker-owned cooperative Red and Black coffeehouse out of business. Red and Black was eventually forced to move due to increased rents in the neighborhood, but it reopened nearby and is still thriving. Meanwhile, Starbucks recently closed, not due to bomb-throwing anarchists, but due to market forces. With eight independently owned cafés within a few blocks, who needs Starbucks? This is the beauty and irony of Portland: capitalist market competition favors the anarchist worker-owned cooperative over the corporate coffee chain. Milton Friedman is rolling over in his grave.

The artistry that is evident in small restaurants like Le Pigeon, Beast, and Pok Pok represents only the vanguard of a more expansive food movement that has begun to make inroads in the public school system and even in national corporate supermarkets. The success of a food culture should not only be measured by whether a few superb restaurants can satisfy the refined palates of their foodie clienteles, but also by the democratization of the best that bourgeois food culture has to offer.

And everywhere there are signs that the healthy local, organic, and creative food has broken out of its rarefied locales: at your local supermarket, you might find organic produce, gluten-free and organic foods, LEED-certified green architecture, and electric car-charging stations. Our daughter's public elementary school, Atkinson, serves edible flowers from their multicultural garden in the school's cafeteria salad bar. And this is not a fancy public school in a well-heeled neighborhood. Half of its students are eligible for free lunch, meaning that they live in poverty.

Portland has America's best farmer's market, the world's first certified sustainable sushi restaurant, and even a burger chain that cares: Burgerville uses Tillamook cheddar, Oregon beef, Walla Walla sweet onions, and local berries. When the provenance and sustainability of ingredients matters even to a fast-food mini-empire, you know something big is happening.

Speaking of burgers, being a carnivore is cool again in Portland. In an earlier era, outsiders might have assumed that Portland's ecotopian cuisine would be heavy on tofu, granola, and sprouts. Not so these days: lately, the relevant categories seem to be not fauna vs. flora but real vs. processed, artisanal vs. industrial. So although you will be able to sample cashew "pâté" at the Blossoming Lotus vegan restaurant, elsewhere in town you are just as likely to run into poutine, home-made maple ice cream with bacon, pork-bone consommé with poached egg, or chicken-fried chicken livers with preserved-lemon aïoli. Ominvorous indulgence is encouraged here, as long as the animals have been well-treated during their lifetimes.

The bacon-infused Bourbon at Belly Timber, the coconut-water ice cubes at Beaker & Flask, and the kaffir lime leaves at Saucebox are reminders that Portland is also a laboratory for pioneering cocktails. With half the prices and twice the originality of bars in bigger cities, Portland has spoiled us for regular drinks. Portland's "mixologists" are craftspeople who serve up cocktails with ingredients that include beets, sweet pea, wasabi, and wormwood. Such beverages make mango margaritas seem as outdated as acid-washed jeans.

A few months ago, a scruffy couple walked into the Clinton Street movie theater, an independent venture in southeast Portland that tends to show off-beat experimental films about cycling or feminist porn. The couple didn't have any cash to buy their tickets, but they offered the attendant two bell peppers, an onion, and a squash from their community garden instead. The attendant accepted the produce, and the couple entered to watch a John Hughes double feature. Beneath the surface of this city, a thriving barter, dumpster-diving, freegan alternative economy is arising—one that is, in its own way, more life-affirming than the culture of cash.

We are irrationally exuberant about the food in Portland: the quality, the inventiveness, the artistry, the passion. And just as importantly, much of the very best of it can be had for moderate prices. You can also find overpriced restaurants in Portland if you like to spend money for the sake of spending money, but you would be missing the point.

We would be remiss if we didn't remind the readers of this guide of the irony that Portland's superlative restaurant scene is located in a state with the highest hunger rate in the nation—and that much of the spectacular produce is still being harvested by Mexican farm laborers working in Depression-era conditions. Unless and until we all figure out how to feed everyone good, healthy food at affordable prices, the foodie movement will remain an esoteric pursuit of food connoisseurs.

But if any town can turn bourgeois consumption into a true food revolution, Portland is it.

We hope that you enjoy this book, we hope that its suggestions broaden your horizons, and we hope that it encourages you to engage on an even closer level with America's most exciting food scene.

–Reiko Hillyer and Elliott Young

The Fearless Critic system

If you're not familiar with the Fearless Critic style and philosophy, then welcome to a new kind of restaurant guide. Within these pages are 300 relentlessly opinionated full-page reviews of places to eat in the greater Portland area. We do not accept advertising from dining establishments, chefs, or restaurateurs.

We evaluate restaurants incognito, and we pay for our own meals. Most reviews are informed by years of repeat visits by our Fearless Critic panel, a team of local food nerds, chefs, critics, and writers who have been dining intensively in Portland for years.

In order to qualify for inclusion in this book, an establishment must serve food and be relevant to readers, in our judgment, whether for positive or negative reasons. Some restaurants that didn't make the cut for this book will have online reviews posted at **www.fearlesscritic.com/portland**.

But we're also sure that we have also unwittingly omitted many true out-of-the-way gems, and for that we apologize in advance, and encourage you to let us know about them at **fearless@fearlesscritic.com**, so that they might be included in the next edition.

Brutally honest

As you might guess from the name of the book, *Fearless Critic* is brutally honest. We tell you exactly what we'd tell a good friend if she called us up and asked what we *really* thought of a place. Although some have called us "scathing," it is not our goal to stir controversy or insult restaurants.

We do believe, however, that in a world of advertorials and often-indistugishable user-generated review websites, restaurant consumers deserve a hard-nosed advocate that can deliver the unapologetic, unvarnished truth. We hope to help you decide where to eat, and also where *not* to eat. Therein, we believe, lies much of the usefulness of food criticism.

For how is one to choose between two places if both are portrayed in dizzying, worshipful prose? Or if you don't know if the review you're reading is written by a real critic, or by the restaurant owner's brother? And how frustrating is it when you spend a lot of your hard-earned money on a restaurant for a special occasion or date on the strength of what turns out to have been a sugar-coated review?

We aim for a punchy evaluation of a restaurant's strengths and weaknesses that ends with a clear judgment and recommendation. We hope that the money you've spent on this book will save you from wasting hundreds of dollars on boring meals. In short, our duty is to our readers, not to the restaurants.

We don't expect you to agree with everything we say—sometimes, we don't even agree with each other—but we do hope that, now that you've bought the book, you will give us the chance to earn your trust over the course of its 300 reviews. Whether you concur or dissent, we would love to hear from you. It is engaging feedback from readers that makes our jobs worthwhile. Visit us at **fearlesscritic.com** to post your own opinions, or your thoughts on ours.

The rating scale

Two or more numerical ratings are assigned by the panel to each establishment that serves full meals. Ratings are not assigned to bakeries, groceries, markets, sweets shops, or other establishments that don't serve full meals.

Food rating (1 to 10): This is strictly a measure of whether the food on offer is appetizing or objectionable, insipid or delicious. We close our eyes to reputation, price, and puffery when we taste, so don't be surprised to find a greasy spoon outscoring a historic, upscale, sit-down establishment, for one simple reason: the food just tastes better. A food score above 8 constitutes a recommendation; a 9 or above is a high recommendation. Don't expect grade inflation here.

Feel rating (1 to 10): Rather than counting the number of pieces of silverware on the table or the number of minutes and seconds before the food arrives, we ask ourselves a simple question: does being here make us happy? The most emphatic "yes" inspires the highest rating. We don't give out points for tablecloths or tuxedos. We reward warm lighting, comfortable accomodations, a finely realized theme, and a strong sense of place or tradition. The dim glow of candles, dark wood, and old local paraphernalia at your neighborhood dive might just garner more accolades than the proliferation of accoutrements at a stuffy so-called "fine dining" restaurant. "Feel" also integrates service, asking the question of whether you'll love or loathe the prospect of interacting with the people who stand between you and your meal. We don't expect the burger flipper at a greasy spoon to start spouting off elaborate wine adjectives, but if a restaurant's staff is unusually helpful and caring, or extraordinarily enthusiastic and knowledgeable about what's coming out of the kitchen, then the "feel" rating will reflect that. On the flip side, if the staff is consistently indifferent or condescending, then points will be deducted.

Wine, beer, and cocktail ratings (1 to 10): Breadth, care of selection, and price are included in this rating. More points are not necessarily awarded for the sheer number of wines or beers served. The criteria used for these ratings are explained more fully in the "lists" section, where the lists of top wine, beer, and cocktail programs appear.

Geography

We have divided the city of Portland into the neighborhoods delineated below. Outside the city limits, the municipality name (e.g. Beaverton, Tigard, McMinnville, Hillsboro) is listed in lieu of a neighborhood name.

Alberta Arts District: Encompasses the area around NE Alberta Street between NE 15th Avenue to the west and NE 33rd Avenue to the east, NE Ainsworth Street to the north and NE Wygant Street to the south. This includes the neighborhood recently christened the "Fox-Chase Addition."

Belmont: Along SE Belmont Street.

Division/Clinton: Along SE Division Street or SE Clinton Street, not including the 82nd Avenue area.

Downtown: North and east of Interstate 405, west of the Willamette River, and south of West Burnside Street.

East Burnside: Along East Burnside Street, not including the 82nd Avenue area.

82nd Avenue Area: Runs the length of NE and SE 82nd Avenue, including the surrounding area east to Interstate 205, between NE Sandy Boulevard along the north and SE Powell Boulevard to the south, and extending west to SE 80th Avenue.

Far East Portland: East of Interstate 205 and within the Portland city limits.

Hawthorne: Along SE Hawthorne Boulevard, not including the 82nd Avenue Area.

Mississippi Avenue Area: The area between Interstate 5 to the west, N. Williams Avenue to the east, N. Fremont Street to the south, and N. Skidmore Street to the north.

North Portland: East of the Williamette River, north and west of NE Martin Luther King Boulevard, south of the Columbia River, and not including the Mississippi Avenue Area.

Northeast Portland: The area east of NE Martin Luther King Boulevard, north of E. Burnside Street, south of the Columbia River, and not including Alberta Arts or the 82nd Avenue Area.

Northwest Portland: North of W. Burnside Street, west of the Pearl District, east of Forest Park, and not including Old Town Chinatown. This includes the areas that some people refer to as "Nob Hill," the "Alphabet District," NW 21st Street ("Spendy-First"), and NW 23rd Street ("Trendy-Third").

Old Town Chinatown: East of NW Broadway, west and south of the train yards, and north of West Burnside Street.

Pearl District: East of NW 19th Avenue, west of NW Broadway, south of the train yard, and north of West Burnside Street (although some argue the Pearl grows by the minute).

Sellwood: Southwest of SE McLoughlin Boulevard, with the Willamette River to the west, and the Waverly Country Club on its southern border.

Southeast Portland: The area east of the Willamette River, south of East Burnside Street, and not including Belmont, Hawthorne, Division/Clinton, Sellwood, the 82nd Avenue Area, or Far East Portland.

Southwest Portland: West of the Willamette River, south of West Burnside Street, east of Washington City Park, and not including Downtown.

The other stuff on the page

Average dinner price: This dollar value is a guide to how much, on average, you should expect to spend per person on a full dinner at the restaurant, including one alcoholic beverage and a 20% tip (for table-service establishments; we encourage you to tip at coffeeshops and take-out joints too, but we don't figure it into the meal price). At simple take-out places, this might be just a sandwich and a soda; at more elaborate sit-down restaurants, we usually figure in the cost of an appetizer (one for every person) and dessert (one for every two people). If the restaurant pushes bottled water or side dishes on you, we figure that in, too. For alcoholic drinks, too, we are guided by what people generally tend to order—from a beer to a third of a bottle of low-to-midpriced wine. Keep in mind that at the higher-end restaurants, you will generally spend considerably less than the quoted price if you go for lunch, or if you order non-alcoholic drinks instead. Only restaurants that serve full meals and have ratings are eligible for price estimates.

Genre: Every establishment in the *Fearless Critic* book is associated with one or more culinary genres. Our "Lists" section includes a cross-referenced guide to all restaurants by genre. Most genres—e.g. Indian or pizza—are self-explanatory, but some require clarification: **American** covers traditional meat-and-potatoes fare, bar food, breakfast food, comfort food, burgers, greasy spoons, and so on. **Steakhouses** have their own category, as does **Southern** cuisine, which includes soul food, fried chicken, Cajun, and Louisiana Creole cooking. We use the word **modern** (not "New American") to describe the new wave of upmarket cuisine, which draws upon diverse world ingredients and technique. This includes the market-to-table and haute nostalgic restaurants (Adam Platt might call them "haute barnyard") that have become fashionable lately. The **Nuevo Latino** category includes modern versions of Central American, South American, Dominican, Puerto Rican, and Cuban, but not **Mexican,** which has its own category. **Vegefusion** is world fusion cuisine aimed mainly at vegetarian and vegans. **Baked goods** can be sweet or savory. **Groceries** can include unprepared foods of any type. **Coffee,** of course, doesn't apply to any restaurant serving coffee—almost all of them do—but rather to an establishment where that's a particular focus.

Establishment type: We have divided eating establishments into several categories. The largest category is **casual restaurant,** which means a place with waiter service at tables but a generally laid-back atmosphere without much fuss. An **upmarket restaurant** is a place with more elegant, trendy, or special-occasion ambitions. The **counter service** category includes cafeterias, self-service places, and also establishments where you place an order at a counter but it is then brought out to your table. We see a **bar** as an establishment that's fundamentally about serving drinks at heart, but it must serve food to be included (although the kitchen often closes before the doors). **Café** means a place whose primary business is the provision of coffee or tea, but it must serve food of some sort to be included in the book. We've also included several notable **markets**, most of which also serve certain varieties of prepared foods that can be eaten straightaway.

Address: We have included addresses and neighborhood designations for up to three locations, and where feasible, we have indexed additional locations in the Lists section of the book. See pages 6–7 for the delineations of Portland neighborhoods. For chains with more than three locations, consult **www.fearlesscritic.com/portland** for a listing of the others.

Special features: These appear in the middle column of information. By **date-friendly,** we mean establishments that we find particularly romantic in some way—and that doesn't necessarily mean tuxedoed waiters or high prices. We look for warm lighting, good vibes, and a sense of easy fun. **Delivery** can be limited to a certain geographical range or minimum order. **Kid-friendly** doesn't just mean a couple of high chairs in the corner; it means a place where the little ones will actually be happy, whether for culinary reasons or for the availability of special activities or play areas. The **live music** designation includes establishments that have it only on certain days or nights, so call ahead if it's atmospherically important to you. **Outdoor dining** can mean anything from a couple of sidewalk tables to a sprawling beer garden. **Wi-Fi** has to be free to qualify—this is the 21st century, after all. We are particularly careful when choosing which establishments to flag as **veg-friendly.** The designation is not limited to vegetarian-only places, but we look for menus where vegetarians will not just be accommodated—they'll actually have an ample selection.

Fearless Critic quirks

Cooking times: as you might notice within these pages, we prefer most cuts of meat rare or medium-rare, and we prefer our fish and fowl moist and juicy rather than dry and more fully cooked. People who like their meat cooked medium or more should take our comments with a grain of salt.

Seasoning: speaking of salt, our position is that there is no such thing as salting "to taste" in the professional kitchen. As a matter of chemistry, a certain amount of salt is necessary to bring out the complexity in most savory flavors. We believe that expecting customers to add their own salt at the table is as absurd as plopping a salad down in front of a customer with a whole carrot and a peeler. And for some foods, like anything deep-fried, it's already too late to do so.

"Mains": you won't find the word "entrée" here. The word is inherently ambiguous, and particularly confusing to foreigners, as the French word "entrée" means "starter" or "appetizer." We're not sure how "entrée" came to mean a main course in the United States, but here we say "main course," or "main," if that's what we mean.

Fearless feedback

The heart and soul of this endeavor is our belief that the world of restaurant reviewing can be improved by opening outspoken channels of communication between restaurants and their customers. If you have a bad meal, or a great one, tell the restaurant what was right and what was wrong. It can only help. And tell us too; we've set up comments at **www.fearlesscritic.com/portland** so that readers can express agreement or dissent. It doesn't require registration, and you can post anonymously. Our panelists will do their best to respond periodically.

The fine print

This entire book is a work of opinion, and should be understood as such. Any and all judgments rendered upon restaurants within these pages, regardless of tense, are intended as statements of pure opinion. Facts have been thoroughly checked with the restaurants in person, via telephone, and on the restaurants' websites; we have gone to the utmost lengths to ensure that every fact is correct, and that every ingredient in every dish is properly referenced. Any factual errors that nonetheless remain are purely unintentional. That said, menus and plates (not to mention hours of operation) change so frequently at restaurants that any printed book, however new, cannot help but be a bit behind the times. Check in at **www.fearlesscritic.com** for new reviews, updates, discussion boards, and more.

About Fearless Critic Media

Fearless Critic Media is a lean, fiercely independent publishing house founded by Robin Goldstein in 2006 and dedicated to providing useful information in an engaging format. In conjunction with its partner, Workman Publishing Company, Fearless Critic Media publishes relentlessly opinionated, irreverent food and wine books. Look for *The Wine Trials 2010*, our blind-tasting guide to wine under $15, in bookstores and food and wine shops nationwide.

Other Fearless Critic books include the *Fearless Critic Washington DC Restaurant Guide*, the *Fearless Critic Austin Restaurant Guide, 2nd Edition*, the *Fearless Critic New Haven Restaurant Guide,* and the *Fearless Critic Houston Restaurant Guide 2010*, all of which can be bought at powells.com, barnesandnoble.com, amazon.com, bookstores, and retail stores. For all the latest book and distribution information, see **www.fearlesscritic.com**. Fearless Critic books are distributed by **Workman Publishing Company (workman.com)**.

Fearless Critic

Lists

Most delicious

These are Portland's **top 100 kitchens** judged from a **pure food** perspective. Ties are ordered by feel rating.

Rank		Food	Cuisine	Location	Type	Price
1	Beast	9.6	Modern	Alberta Arts District	Upmarket	$90
2	Le Pigeon	9.6	Modern	East Burnside	Upmarket	$70
3	Park Kitchen	9.5	Modern	Pearl District	Upmarket	$50
4	Pok Pok	9.5	Thai	Division/Clinton	Casual	$35
5	Clyde Common	9.4	Modern	Downtown	Upmarket	$45
6	Beaker & Flask	9.3	Modern	Southeast Portland	Casual	$35
7	Ping	9.3	Pan-Asian	Old Town	Casual	$35
8	Apizza Scholls	9.3	Pizza	Hawthorne	Casual	$30
9	Tabla	9.2	Modern	Northeast Portland	Upmarket	$45
10	Thistle	9.2	Modern	McMinnville	Upmarket	$60
11	Paley's Place	9.2	Modern	Northwest Portland	Upmarket	$80
12	Yuzu	9.2	Japanese	Beaverton	Casual	$40
13	Sel Gris	9.2	Modern	Hawthorne	Upmarket	$80
14	DOC	9.1	Italian	Alberta Arts District	Upmarket	$70
15	Clarklewis	9.1	Modern	Southeast Portland	Upmarket	$70
16	Laurelhurst Market	9.1	Modern	Northeast Portland	Casual	$50
17	EaT: An Oyster Bar	9.1	Seafood	Mississippi	Casual	$40
18	Hakatamon	9.1	Japanese	Beaverton	Casual	$30
19	Ocean City Seafood	9.1	Chinese	82nd Avenue Area	Casual	$30
20	Simpatica	9.0	Modern	Southeast Portland	Upmarket	$50
21	Nostrana	9.0	Italian, Pizza	Southeast Portland	Upmarket	$55
22	Little T American Baker	9.0	Baked goods	Division/Clinton	Café	$15
23	Karam Lebanese	9.0	Lebanese	Downtown	Casual	$30
24	Ken's Artisan Pizza	9.0	Pizza	Southeast Portland	Casual	$25
25	Country Korean	9.0	Korean	Beaverton	Casual	$20
26	Taquería 7 Estrellas	9.0	Mexican	Tigard	Casual	$15
27	Best Taste	9.0	Chinese	82nd Avenue Area	Casual	$10
28	Ned Ludd	8.9	Modern	Northeast Portland	Upmarket	$45
29	Castagna	8.9	Modern	Hawthorne	Upmarket	$80
30	Lucky Strike	8.9	Chinese	Far East Portland	Casual	$20
31	Pho An Sandy	8.9	Vietnamese	Northeast Portland	Casual	$15
32	Andina	8.8	Peruvian	Pearl District	Upmarket	$70
33	Branch	8.8	Modern	Alberta Arts District	Casual	$40
34	Lovely Hula Hands	8.8	Modern	Mississippi	Casual	$40
35	Kenny & Zuke's	8.8	Sandwiches	Downtown	Casual	$15
36	DJK Korean BBQ	8.8	Korean	Beaverton	Casual	$25
37	Ten01	8.7	Modern	Pearl District	Upmarket	$70
38	Puerto Marquez	8.7	Mexican	Far East Portland	Casual	$25
39	Queen of Sheba	8.7	Ethiopian	Northeast Portland	Casual	$35
40	JCD Korean Restaurant	8.7	Korean	Beaverton	Casual	$20
41	Spring Restaurant	8.7	Korean	Beaverton	Casual	$15
42	BeWon Korean	8.6	Korean	Northwest Portland	Casual	$35
43	Firehouse	8.6	Pizza, Modern	Northeast Portland	Casual	$35
44	Wildwood	8.6	Modern	Northwest Portland	Upmarket	$70
45	Nicholas Restaurant	8.6	Middle Eastern	Southeast Portland	Casual	$20
46	Pine State Biscuits	8.6	Sandwiches	Belmont	Counter	$15
47	La Sirenita	8.6	Mexican	Multiple locations	Counter	$15
48	Belly Timber	8.5	Modern	Hawthorne	Upmarket	$45
49	East India Co.	8.5	Indian	Downtown	Casual	$40
50	Powell's Seafood	8.5	Chinese	Southeast Portland	Casual	$15
51	Patanegra	8.4	Spanish	Northwest Portland	Upmarket	$50
52	Little Red Bike Café	8.4	Modern	North Portland	Counter	$15
53	Du Kuh Bee	8.4	Korean	Beaverton	Casual	$20
54	Hiroshi Sushi	8.4	Japanese	Pearl District	Upmarket	$50

55	Alba Osteria	8.3	Italian	Southwest Portland	Upmarket	$60
56	Auténtica	8.3	Mexican	Alberta Arts District	Upmarket	$45
57	Pho Oregon	8.3	Vietnamese	82nd Avenue Area	Casual	$15
58	Podnah's Pit	8.3	Barbecue	Northeast Portland	Casual	$25
59	Carafe Bistro	8.2	French	Downtown	Upmarket	$45
60	The Observatory	8.2	Modern	Southeast Portland	Casual	$35
61	Nick's Italian Café	8.2	Italian, Modern	McMinnville	Upmarket	$70
62	Serratto	8.2	Modern	Northwest Portland	Upmarket	$60
63	Tábor	8.2	Czech	Downtown	Food cart	$10
64	The Waffle Window	8.2	Baked goods	Hawthorne	Counter	$10
65	Evoe	8.2	Modern	Hawthorne	Casual	$15
66	Red Onion Thai	8.2	Thai	Northwest Portland	Casual	$30
67	Basha's Mediterranean	8.2	Middle Eastern	Downtown	Food cart	$5
68	Pambiche	8.1	Cuban	Northeast Portland	Casual	$35
69	Syun Izakaya	8.1	Japanese	Hillsboro	Casual	$35
70	Bar Avignon	8.1	Modern	Division/Clinton	Upmarket	$45
71	Caffè Allora	8.1	Italian, Pizza	Pearl District	Casual	$40
72	Good Taste	8.1	Chinese	Multiple locations	Casual	$15
73	Bunk Sandwiches	8.1	Sandwiches	Southeast Portland	Counter	$15
74	Meat Cheese Bread	8.1	Sandwiches	Southeast Portland	Counter	$15
75	Shenzhen	8.1	Chinese	82nd Avenue Area	Casual	$25
76	MetroVino	8.0	Modern	Pearl District	Upmarket	$45
77	Bete-Lukas	8.0	Ethiopian	Division/Clinton	Casual	$35
78	Ken's Artisan Bakery	8.0	Baked goods	Northwest Portland	Café	$15
79	Beijing Hot Pot	8.0	Chinese	82nd Avenue Area	Casual	$20
80	Bijou Café	8.0	American	Downtown	Casual	$25
81	Kenny & Zuke's Sandwich	8.0	Sandwiches	Northwest Portland	Counter	$15
82	Slow Bar	8.0	American	Southeast Portland	Bar	$25
83	Nong's Khao Man Gai	8.0	Thai	Downtown	Food cart	$5
84	Pho Hung	8.0	Vietnamese	Southeast Portland	Casual	$15
85	Gold Garden Seafood	8.0	Chinese	Far East Portland	Casual	$30
86	Yummy Yummy	8.0	Chinese	82nd Avenue Area	Casual	$35
87	Brøder Comfort Food	7.9	Scandinavian	Division/Clinton	Casual	$30
88	Gino's	7.9	Italian, Modern	Sellwood	Casual	$40
89	Vindalho	7.9	Indian	Division/Clinton	Upmarket	$60
90	Original Halibut's	7.9	Seafood	Alberta Arts District	Counter	$20
91	Fratelli Cucina	7.8	Italian	Pearl District	Casual	$40
92	Le Happy	7.8	Crêpes	Northwest Portland	Casual	$15
93	Piazza Italia	7.8	Italian	Pearl District	Casual	$35
94	Lincoln	7.8	Italian, Modern	Mississippi	Upmarket	$50
95	Toro Bravo	7.8	Spanish	Northeast Portland	Upmarket	$45
96	Hot Pot City	7.8	Chinese	Downtown	Casual	$20
97	Caffè Mingo	7.7	Italian	Northwest Portland	Upmarket	$50
98	North 45	7.7	American	Northwest Portland	Bar	$35
99	Besaw's Café	7.7	Modern	Northwest Portland	Casual	$40
100	Echo Restaurant	7.7	Modern	Northeast Portland	Casual	$40

Good vibes

Fearless Critic's feel rating measures the enjoyment we get from the atmosphere and people. Here are the **top 50.** Ties are ordered by food rating.

Rank		Feel	Cuisine	Location	Type	Price
1	Ned Ludd	10	Modern	Northeast Portland	Upmarket	$45
2	McMenamins	10	American	Multiple locations	Casual	$30
3	Tabla	9.5	Modern	Northeast Portland	Upmarket	$45
4	DOC	9.5	Italian	Alberta Arts District	Upmarket	$70
5	Simpatica	9.5	Modern	Southeast Portland	Upmarket	$50
6	Andina	9.5	Peruvian	Pearl District	Upmarket	$70
7	Higgins	9.5	Modern	Downtown	Upmarket	$60
8	Veritable Quandary	9.5	Modern	Downtown	Upmarket	$45
9	The Press Club	9.5	Sandwiches	Division/Clinton	Casual	$20
10	Doug Fir	9.5	American	East Burnside	Bar	$30
11	The Liberty Glass	9.5	American	North Portland	Bar	$20
12	Le Bistro Montage	9.5	Southern	Southeast Portland	Casual	$35
13	Beast	9.0	Modern	Alberta Arts District	Upmarket	$90
14	Beaker & Flask	9.0	Modern	Southeast Portland	Casual	$35
15	Thistle	9.0	Modern	McMinnville	Upmarket	$60
16	Branch	9.0	Modern	Alberta Arts District	Casual	$40
17	Lovely Hula Hands	9.0	Modern	Mississippi	Casual	$40
18	BeWon Korean	9.0	Korean	Northwest Portland	Casual	$35
19	Firehouse	9.0	Pizza, Modern	Northeast Portland	Casual	$35
20	Alba Osteria	9.0	Italian	Southwest Portland	Upmarket	$60
21	Carafe Bistro	9.0	French	Downtown	Upmarket	$45
22	The Observatory	9.0	Modern	Southeast Portland	Casual	$35
23	Pambiche	9.0	Cuban	Northeast Portland	Casual	$35
24	Syun Izakaya	9.0	Japanese	Hillsboro	Casual	$35
25	MetroVino	9.0	Modern	Pearl District	Upmarket	$45
26	Fratelli Cucina	9.0	Italian	Pearl District	Casual	$40
27	Caffè Mingo	9.0	Italian	Northwest Portland	Upmarket	$50
28	North 45	9.0	American	Northwest Portland	Bar	$35
29	Siam Society	9.0	Pan-Asian	Alberta Arts District	Casual	$40
30	Fenouil	9.0	French	Pearl District	Upmarket	$60
31	Bistro Maison	9.0	French	McMinnville	Upmarket	$60
32	The Farm Café	9.0	Modern	East Burnside	Upmarket	$45
33	Gilt Club	9.0	Modern	Old Town	Upmarket	$60
34	La Calaca Comelona	9.0	Mexican	Belmont	Casual	$35
35	Teardrop Lounge	9.0	Modern	Pearl District	Bar	$35
36	Biwa	9.0	Japanese	Southeast Portland	Casual	$35
37	Mother's Bistro & Bar	9.0	American	Downtown	Casual	$40
38	Fats	9.0	British	Alberta Arts District	Casual	$35
39	Portland City Grill	9.0	Steakhouse	Downtown	Upmarket	$70
40	St. Honoré	9.0	Baked goods	Northwest Portland	Café	$15
41	Ciao Vito	9.0	Italian	Alberta Arts District	Casual	$40
42	Living Room Theaters	9.0	Modern	Downtown	Theater	$35
43	Thatch Tiki Bar	9.0	Hawaiian	Northeast Portland	Bar	$30
44	The Tin Shed	9.0	Vegefusion	Alberta Arts District	Casual	$30
45	Sapphire Hotel	9.0	Modern	Hawthorne	Bar	$20
46	Park Kitchen	8.5	Modern	Pearl District	Upmarket	$50
47	Clyde Common	8.5	Modern	Downtown	Upmarket	$45
48	Paley's Place	8.5	Modern	Northwest Portland	Upmarket	$80
49	Yuzu	8.5	Japanese	Beaverton	Casual	$40
50	Clarklewis	8.5	Modern	Southeast Portland	Upmarket	$70

Wine

Fearless Critic's wine ratings, which include sake, consider quality, creativity, value, and depth—in that order. A small but interesting list that is carefully paired with the food might rank higher than a thick, overpriced volume of prestigious producers. We do, however, award extra points for older vintages. Establishments only receive a wine rating if we judge their wine programs to be ambitious or significant. Ties are ordered first by feel rating, then by food rating.

	Name	Cuisine	Location	Type	Price
9.0	Tabla	Modern	Northeast Portland	Upmarket	$45
9.0	Thistle	Modern	McMinnville	Upmarket	$60
9.0	Lovely Hula Hands	Modern	Mississippi	Casual	$40
9.0	Carafe Bistro	French	Downtown	Upmarket	$45
9.0	Paley's Place	Modern	Northwest Portland	Upmarket	$80
9.0	Clarklewis	Modern	Southeast Portland	Upmarket	$70
9.0	Nostrana	Italian, Pizza	Southeast Portland	Upmarket	$55
9.0	Patanegra	Spanish	Northwest Portland	Upmarket	$50
9.0	Noble Rot	Modern	East Burnside	Upmarket	$40
9.0	Le Pigeon	Modern	East Burnside	Upmarket	$70
9.0	Serratto	Modern	Northwest Portland	Upmarket	$60
9.0	Bar Mingo	Italian	Northwest Portland	Casual	$35
9.0	Berlin Inn	German	Southeast Portland	Casual	$40
9.0	Southpark Seafood	Modern, Seafood	Downtown	Casual	$40
9.0	Navarre	Modern	Northeast Portland	Upmarket	$45
8.5	DOC	Italian	Alberta Arts District	Upmarket	$70
8.5	MetroVino	Modern	Pearl District	Upmarket	$45
8.5	Biwa	Japanese, Korean	Southeast Portland	Casual	$35
8.5	Ciao Vito	Italian	Alberta Arts District	Casual	$40
8.5	Park Kitchen	Modern	Pearl District	Upmarket	$50
8.5	Wildwood	Modern	Northwest Portland	Upmarket	$70
8.5	Nick's Italian Café	Italian, Modern	McMinnville	Upmarket	$70
8.5	Bar Avignon	Modern	Division/Clinton	Upmarket	$45
8.5	Gino's	Italian, Modern	Sellwood	Casual	$40
8.5	3 Doors Down Café	Modern	Southeast Portland	Upmarket	$45
8.5	Papa Haydn	Modern	Multiple locations	Upmarket	$50
8.5	Bamboo Sushi	Japanese	Southeast Portland	Upmarket	$40
8.5	Sal's Famous Italian	Italian, Pizza	Northwest Portland	Casual	$35
8.0	Ned Ludd	Modern	Northeast Portland	Upmarket	$45
8.0	Andina	Peruvian	Pearl District	Upmarket	$70
8.0	Beast	Modern	Alberta Arts District	Upmarket	$90
8.0	BeWon Korean	Korean	Northwest Portland	Casual	$35
8.0	Firehouse	Pizza, Modern	Northeast Portland	Casual	$35
8.0	Syun Izakaya	Japanese	Hillsboro	Casual	$35
8.0	Fratelli Cucina	Italian	Pearl District	Casual	$40
8.0	Bistro Maison	French	McMinnville	Upmarket	$60
8.0	Gilt Club	Modern	Old Town	Upmarket	$60
8.0	Clyde Common	Modern	Downtown	Upmarket	$45
8.0	Piazza Italia	Italian	Pearl District	Casual	$35
8.0	Lucy's Table	Modern	Northwest Portland	Upmarket	$50
8.0	Pok Pok	Thai	Division/Clinton	Casual	$35
8.0	Castagna	Modern	Hawthorne	Upmarket	$80
8.0	Ten01	Modern	Pearl District	Upmarket	$70
8.0	Tanuki	Japanese, Korean	Northwest Portland	Casual	$35
8.0	Café Castagna	Modern	Hawthorne	Upmarket	$45

8.0	Nel Centro	Italian	Downtown	Upmarket	$60
8.0	Bastas Trattoria	Italian	Northwest Portland	Upmarket	$45
8.0	Ken's Artisan Pizza	Pizza	Southeast Portland	Casual	$25
8.0	Evoe	Modern	Hawthorne	Casual	$15
8.0	Toro Bravo	Spanish	Northeast Portland	Upmarket	$45
8.0	Justa Pasta	Italian	Northwest Portland	Counter	$15
8.0	23Hoyt	Modern	Northwest Portland	Upmarket	$60
7.5	The Press Club	Sandwiches, Crêpes	Division/Clinton	Casual	$20
7.5	Alba Osteria	Italian	Southwest Portland	Upmarket	$60
7.5	The Farm Café	Modern, Vegefusion	East Burnside	Upmarket	$45
7.5	Yuzu	Japanese	Beaverton	Casual	$40
7.5	Brøder Comfort Food	Scandinavian	Division/Clinton	Casual	$30
7.5	Vindalho	Indian	Division/Clinton	Upmarket	$60
7.5	Besaw's Café	Modern	Northwest Portland	Casual	$40
7.5	Laurelhurst Market	Modern	Northeast Portland	Casual	$50
7.5	Caffè Allora	Italian, Pizza	Pearl District	Casual	$40
7.5	Lincoln	Italian, Modern	Mississippi	Upmarket	$50
7.5	Urban Farmer	Steakhouse	Downtown	Upmarket	$110
7.5	Tastebud	Pizza	Southeast Portland	Casual	$30
7.5	Vita Café	Vegefusion	Alberta Arts District	Casual	$25
7.5	Yakuza Lounge	Japanese	Alberta Arts District	Upmarket	$60
7.5	EaT: An Oyster Bar	Seafood, Southern	Mississippi	Casual	$40
7.5	Silk	Pan-Asian	Pearl District	Upmarket	$40
7.5	Lucca	Italian, Modern	Northeast Portland	Casual	$35
7.5	Apizza Scholls	Pizza	Hawthorne	Casual	$30
7.5	Hakatamon	Japanese	Beaverton	Casual	$30
7.5	Mingo	Italian, Pizza	Beaverton	Upmarket	$50
7.0	Higgins	Modern	Downtown	Upmarket	$60
7.0	Siam Society	Pan-Asian, Thai	Alberta Arts District	Casual	$40
7.0	Fenouil	French, Modern	Pearl District	Upmarket	$60
7.0	Teardrop Lounge	Modern	Pearl District	Bar	$35
7.0	Mother's Bistro & Bar	American	Downtown	Casual	$40
7.0	Iorio	Italian	Hawthorne	Upmarket	$50
7.0	The Country Cat	Modern, Southern	Southeast Portland	Casual	$40
7.0	Driftwood Room	American	Southwest Portland	Bar	$35
7.0	Masu	Japanese	Downtown	Upmarket	$45
7.0	Decarli	Italian, Modern	Beaverton	Upmarket	$50
7.0	Brazil Grill	Brazilian	Southwest Portland	Casual	$40
7.0	RingSide Steakhouse	Steakhouse	Multiple locations	Upmarket	$80
7.0	Morton's	Steakhouse	Downtown	Upmarket	$100
6.5	McMenamins	American	Multiple locations	Casual	$30
6.5	Doug Fir	American	East Burnside	Bar	$30
6.5	Le Bistro Montage	Southern	Southeast Portland	Casual	$35
6.5	The Observatory	Modern	Southeast Portland	Casual	$35
6.5	Equinox	Modern	Northeast Portland	Casual	$40
6.5	Carlyle	Modern	Northwest Portland	Upmarket	$80
6.5	Ruth's Chris	Steakhouse	Downtown	Upmarket	$100
6.5	Vita Café	Vegefusion	Alberta Arts District	Casual	$25
6.5	Lauro Kitchen	Modern	Division/Clinton	Upmarket	$50
6.5	Pastini Pastaria	Italian	Multiple locations	Casual	$25
6.5	Bluehour	Modern	Pearl District	Upmarket	$70
6.0	Echo Restaurant	Modern	Northeast Portland	Casual	$40
6.0	Café Nell	American	Northwest Portland	Casual	$40
6.0	Sel Gris	Modern	Hawthorne	Upmarket	$80
6.0	¡OBA!	Nuevo Latino	Pearl District	Upmarket	$60
6.0	Saburo's	Japanese	Sellwood	Casual	$30
6.0	Bay 13	Seafood	Pearl District	Upmarket	$50
6.0	The Heathman	American	Downtown	Upmarket	$60
5.5	Veritable Quandary	Modern	Downtown	Upmarket	$45
5.0	Portland City Grill	Steakhouse	Downtown	Upmarket	$70
4.5	El Gaucho	Steakhouse	Downtown	Upmarket	$100
4.5	Screen Door	Southern	Southeast Portland	Casual	$35

Beer

Fearless Critic's beer ratings consider the quality and depth of a restaurant's beer program. Establishments only receive a beer rating if we judge their beer programs to be ambitious or significant. Ties are ordered first by feel rating, then by food rating.

	Name	Cuisine	Location	Type	Price
9.5	Horse Brass Pub	British	Belmont	Casual	$25
9.5	Green Dragon	American	Southeast Portland	Casual	$25
9.5	Deschutes Brewery	American	Pearl District	Casual	$25
9.5	Rogue Public House	American	Pearl District	Bar	$25
9.0	North 45	American, Belgian	Northwest Portland	Bar	$35
9.0	Acropolis Club	Steakhouse	Sellwood	Strip club	$15
8.5	Higgins	Modern	Downtown	Upmarket	$60
8.5	Beaker & Flask	Modern	Southeast Portland	Casual	$35
8.5	Teardrop Lounge	Modern	Pearl District	Bar	$35
8.5	Clyde Common	Modern	Downtown	Upmarket	$45
8.5	Bye and Bye	Vegefusion	Northeast Portland	Bar	$30
8.5	Lucky Labrador	American	Multiple locations	Bar	$15
8.5	5th Quadrant	American	Mississippi	Bar	$15
8.5	Berlin Inn	German	Southeast Portland	Casual	$40
8.5	Henry's 12th St. Tavern	American	Pearl District	Upmarket	$40
8.0	Tabla	Modern	Northeast Portland	Upmarket	$45
8.0	The Liberty Glass	American, Italian	North Portland	Bar	$20
8.0	Branch	Modern	Alberta Arts District	Casual	$40
8.0	The Observatory	Modern	Southeast Portland	Casual	$35
8.0	The Farm Café	Modern, Vegefusion	East Burnside	Upmarket	$45
8.0	Fats	British	Alberta Arts District	Casual	$35
8.0	Sapphire Hotel	Modern, Pan-Asian	Hawthorne	Bar	$20
8.0	Clarklewis	Modern	Southeast Portland	Upmarket	$70
8.0	Bar Avignon	Modern	Division/Clinton	Upmarket	$45
8.0	Brøder Comfort Food	Scandinavian	Division/Clinton	Casual	$30
8.0	Gino's	Italian, Modern	Sellwood	Casual	$40
8.0	Pause	American	North Portland	Casual	$35
8.0	Dots Café	American	Division/Clinton	Bar	$20
8.0	The Country Cat	Modern, Southern	Southeast Portland	Casual	$40
8.0	Mississippi Pizza Pub	Pizza	Mississippi	Counter	$20
8.0	Driftwood Room	American	Southwest Portland	Bar	$35
8.0	Vincenté's Pizza	Pizza	Hawthorne	Casual	$20
8.0	Le Pigeon	Modern	East Burnside	Upmarket	$70
8.0	Pok Pok	Thai	Division/Clinton	Casual	$35
8.0	Urban Farmer	Steakhouse	Downtown	Upmarket	$110
8.0	Delta Café	Southern	Southeast Portland	Casual	$35
8.0	Kornblatt's Deli	Sandwiches	Northwest Portland	Casual	$20
8.0	Escape From NY	Pizza	Northwest Portland	Counter	$10
8.0	Apizza Scholls	Pizza	Hawthorne	Casual	$30
8.0	Fire on the Mountain	American	Multiple locations	Counter	$20
8.0	23Hoyt	Modern	Northwest Portland	Upmarket	$60
7.5	Ned Ludd	Modern	Northeast Portland	Upmarket	$45
7.5	Doug Fir	American	East Burnside	Bar	$30
7.5	Firehouse	Pizza, Modern	Northeast Portland	Casual	$35
7.5	Living Room Theaters	Modern	Downtown	Theater	$35
7.5	Besaw's Café	Modern	Northwest Portland	Casual	$40
7.5	Tastebud	Pizza	Southeast Portland	Casual	$30
7.5	EaT: An Oyster Bar	Seafood, Southern	Mississippi	Casual	$40
7.5	Silk	Pan-Asian	Pearl District	Upmarket	$40
7.5	Evoe	Modern	Hawthorne	Casual	$15

7.5	Swagat	Indian	Multiple locations	Casual	$25
7.5	Saburo's	Japanese	Sellwood	Casual	$30
7.5	Bread and Ink Café	American	Hawthorne	Casual	$40
7.0	McMenamins	American	Multiple locations	Casual	$30
7.0	The Press Club	Sandwiches, Crêpes	Division/Clinton	Casual	$20
7.0	Vindalho	Indian	Division/Clinton	Upmarket	$60
7.0	Masu	Japanese	Downtown	Upmarket	$45
7.0	Laurelhurst Market	Modern	Northeast Portland	Casual	$50
7.0	Decarli	Italian, Modern	Beaverton	Upmarket	$50
7.0	Petisco	Sandwiches	Northeast Portland	Casual	$20
7.0	Bernie's	Southern	Alberta Arts District	Casual	$40
7.0	New Old Lompoc	American	Northwest Portland	Casual	$25
7.0	Laughing Planet	Vegefusion	Multiple locations	Counter	$15
7.0	Original Halibut's	Seafood	Alberta Arts District	Counter	$20
7.0	Nob Hill Bar & Grill	American	Northwest Portland	Bar	$20
7.0	Pizzicato	Pizza, Sandwiches	Multiple locations	Counter	$20
6.5	Tube	Vegefusion	Old Town	Bar	$15
6.0	East India Co.	Indian	Downtown	Casual	$40
6.0	Screen Door	Southern	Southeast Portland	Casual	$35
5.5	Ten01	Modern	Pearl District	Upmarket	$70
5.0	Slow Bar	American	Southeast Portland	Bar	$25

Cocktails

Fearless Critic's cocktail ratings value creativity, balance, and complexity. Prestigious name-brand liquors are useless without a staff that knows how to mix them. Our tastes are aligned with the classic cocktail renaissance that's gradually taking hold all over the country. If you like sugary, vodka-based 'tinis, then you'll probably hate our cocktail recommendations. Establishments only receive a cocktails rating if we judge their cocktail programs to be ambitious or significant. Ties are ordered first by feel rating, then by food rating.

	Name	Cuisine	Location	Type	Price
9.5	Beaker & Flask	Modern	Southeast Portland	Casual	$35
9.5	Branch	Modern	Alberta Arts District	Casual	$40
9.5	Teardrop Lounge	Modern	Pearl District	Bar	$35
9.5	Belly Timber	Modern	Hawthorne	Upmarket	$45
9.0	North 45	American, Belgian	Northwest Portland	Bar	$35
9.0	Park Kitchen	Modern	Pearl District	Upmarket	$50
9.0	Clyde Common	Modern	Downtown	Upmarket	$45
9.0	Wildwood	Modern	Northwest Portland	Upmarket	$70
9.0	Driftwood Room	American	Southwest Portland	Bar	$35
9.0	Pok Pok	Thai	Division/Clinton	Casual	$35
9.0	Urban Farmer	Steakhouse	Downtown	Upmarket	$110
9.0	Saucebox	Pan-Asian	Downtown	Bar	$40
8.5	Gilt Club	Modern	Old Town	Upmarket	$60
8.5	Clarklewis	Modern	Southeast Portland	Upmarket	$70
8.5	Delta Café	Southern	Southeast Portland	Casual	$35
8.5	Yakuza Lounge	Japanese	Alberta Arts District	Upmarket	$60
8.5	EaT: An Oyster Bar	Seafood, Southern	Mississippi	Casual	$40
8.0	Tabla	Modern	Northeast Portland	Upmarket	$45
8.0	Andina	Peruvian	Pearl District	Upmarket	$70
8.0	Lovely Hula Hands	Modern	Mississippi	Casual	$40
8.0	Gino's	Italian, Modern	Sellwood	Casual	$40
8.0	Besaw's Café	Modern	Northwest Portland	Casual	$40
8.0	Miss Delta	Southern	Mississippi	Casual	$35
8.0	Equinox	Modern	Northeast Portland	Casual	$40
8.0	McCormick & Schmick's	Seafood, American	Multiple locations	Upmarket	$60
8.0	Toro Bravo	Spanish	Northeast Portland	Upmarket	$45
7.5	Le Bistro Montage	Southern	Southeast Portland	Casual	$35
7.5	Caffè Mingo	Italian	Northwest Portland	Upmarket	$50
7.5	The Farm Café	Modern, Vegefusion	East Burnside	Upmarket	$45
7.5	Thatch Tiki Bar	Hawaiian	Northeast Portland	Bar	$30
7.5	Auténtica	Mexican	Alberta Arts District	Upmarket	$45
7.5	Nuestra Cocina	Mexican	Division/Clinton	Upmarket	$40
7.5	3 Doors Down Café	Modern	Southeast Portland	Upmarket	$45
7.5	The Country Cat	Modern, Southern	Southeast Portland	Casual	$40
7.5	Carlyle	Modern	Northwest Portland	Upmarket	$80
7.5	Decarli	Italian, Modern	Beaverton	Upmarket	$50
7.5	Bar Mingo	Italian	Northwest Portland	Casual	$35
7.5	Tube	Vegefusion	Old Town	Bar	$15
7.5	Westcafé	Modern	Downtown	Casual	$35
7.5	Bamboo Sushi	Japanese	Southeast Portland	Upmarket	$40
7.5	¡OBA!	Nuevo Latino	Pearl District	Upmarket	$60
7.0	The Press Club	Sandwiches, Crêpes	Division/Clinton	Casual	$20
7.0	Doug Fir	American	East Burnside	Bar	$30
7.0	The Observatory	Modern	Southeast Portland	Casual	$35

7.0	Siam Society	Pan-Asian, Thai	Alberta Arts District	Casual	$40
7.0	Bye and Bye	Vegefusion	Northeast Portland	Bar	$30
7.0	Mississippi Pizza Pub	Pizza	Mississippi	Counter	$20
7.0	El Gaucho	Steakhouse	Downtown	Upmarket	$100
7.0	Vita Café	Vegefusion	Alberta Arts District	Casual	$25
7.0	Screen Door	Southern	Southeast Portland	Casual	$35
7.0	Queen of Sheba	Ethiopian	Northeast Portland	Casual	$35
7.0	Vault Martini	Modern	Pearl District	Bar	$35
6.5	Veritable Quandary	Modern	Downtown	Upmarket	$45
6.5	Dots Café	American	Division/Clinton	Bar	$20
6.5	Huber's Restaurant	American	Downtown	Casual	$40
6.5	Swagat	Indian	Multiple locations	Casual	$25
6.0	Ten01	Modern	Pearl District	Upmarket	$70
6.0	Malay Satay Hut	Malaysian	82nd Avenue Area	Casual	$25
6.0	Café Castagna	Modern	Hawthorne	Upmarket	$45
6.0	New Old Lompoc	American	Northwest Portland	Casual	$25
6.0	Everett Street Bistro	Modern	Pearl District	Casual	$35
6.0	East India Co.	Indian	Downtown	Casual	$40
6.0	Lauro Kitchen	Modern	Division/Clinton	Upmarket	$50
5.5	Sapphire Hotel	Modern, Pan-Asian	Hawthorne	Bar	$20
5.5	Vindalho	Indian	Division/Clinton	Upmarket	$60
5.5	Masu	Japanese	Downtown	Upmarket	$45
5.5	Slow Bar	American	Southeast Portland	Bar	$25
5.0	Silk	Pan-Asian	Pearl District	Upmarket	$40
5.0	Bay 13	Seafood	Pearl District	Upmarket	$50
4.5	Living Room Theaters	Modern	Downtown	Theater	$35
4.5	Ruth's Chris	Steakhouse	Downtown	Upmarket	$100

By genre

Places to eat **listed by culinary concept, ranked by food rating**. Establishments that don't serve full meals (e.g. cafés, bakeries, grocery stores) appear as "NR" at the bottom of the list.

American *includes traditional American food, bar food, burgers, greasy-spoon fare, and breakfast food. For creative American or market-to-table cuisine, see "Modern." For steakhouses, Southern cuisine, sandwiches, or baked goods, see those genres.*

8.0	Bijou Café	Downtown	Casual	$25
8.0	Slow Bar	Southeast Portland	Bar	$25
7.7	North 45	Northwest Portland	Bar	$35
7.6	John Street Café	North Portland	Casual	$20
7.4	Pause	North Portland	Casual	$35
7.3	Helser's on Alberta	Alberta Arts District	Casual	$15
7.2	Nob Hill Bar & Grill	Northwest Portland	Bar	$20
7.1	5th Quadrant	Mississippi	Bar	$15
7.1	Detour Café	Division/Clinton	Casual	$15
7.1	Genies	Division/Clinton	Casual	$20
7.1	Mother's Bistro & Bar	Downtown	Casual	$40
7.0	Dots Café	Division/Clinton	Bar	$20
7.0	Zell's An American Café	Belmont	Casual	$20
6.8	Deschutes Brewery	Pearl District	Casual	$25
6.8	Fire on the Mountain	Multiple locations	Counter	$20
6.7	Jam on Hawthorne	Hawthorne	Casual	$25
6.6	Driftwood Room	Southwest Portland	Bar	$35
6.5	Original Pancake House	Southwest Portland	Casual	$15
6.4	Café Nell	Northwest Portland	Casual	$40
6.4	Cricket Café	Belmont	Casual	$20
6.4	Elephants Delicatessen	Multiple locations	Counter	$20
6.4	Green Dragon	Southeast Portland	Casual	$25
6.4	Potato Champion	Hawthorne	Food cart	$5
6.1	Alameda Café	Northeast Portland	Casual	$30
6.1	Doug Fir	East Burnside	Bar	$30
6.1	Gravy	Mississippi	Casual	$25
6.1	Grilled Cheese Grill	Northeast Portland	Food cart	$5
6.0	New Old Lompoc	Northwest Portland	Casual	$25
6.0	Original Hotcake House	Southeast Portland	Casual	$20
5.7	Byways Café	Pearl District	Casual	$15
5.7	Henry's 12th St. Tavern	Pearl District	Upmarket	$40
5.6	Rogue Public House	Pearl District	Bar	$25
5.6	The Heathman	Downtown	Upmarket	$60
5.6	The Tin Shed	Alberta Arts District	Casual	$30
5.4	McCormick & Schmick's	Multiple locations	Upmarket	$60
5.3	Bread and Ink Café	Hawthorne	Casual	$40
5.2	Burgerville	Multiple locations	Counter	$10
5.1	SuperDog	Multiple locations	Counter	$10
5.0	FlavourSpot	Multiple locations	Food cart	$5
4.9	Huber's Restaurant	Downtown	Casual	$40
4.7	Cup & Saucer Café	Multiple locations	Casual	$15
4.7	Jake's	Multiple locations	Upmarket	$50
4.5	The Liberty Glass	North Portland	Bar	$20
4.0	Fat City Café	Multnomah Village	Casual	$20
3.9	McMenamins	Multiple locations	Casual	$30
3.0	Lucky Labrador	Multiple locations	Bar	$15

Baked goods

NR	Albina Press	North Portland	Café
NR	Baker & Spice	Southwest Portland	Counter
NR	Bakery Bar	Multiple locations	Counter
NR	Caffé Umbria	Pearl District	Café
NR	Coffee Time	Northwest Portland	Café
NR	Coffeehouse Northwest	Northwest Portland	Café
NR	Crowsenberg's	Downtown	Café
NR	Cupcake Jones	Pearl District	Counter
NR	FlavourSpot	Multiple locations	Food cart
NR	Fleur de Lis	Northeast Portland	Counter
NR	Grand Central Bakery	Multiple locations	Counter
NR	Ken's Artisan Bakery	Northwest Portland	Café
NR	Little T American Baker	Division/Clinton	Café
NR	Pambiche	Northeast Portland	Casual
NR	Papa Haydn	Multiple locations	Upmarket
NR	Pix Pâtisserie	Multiple locations	Counter
NR	Ristretto Roasters	Multiple locations	Café
NR	St. Honoré	Northwest Portland	Café
NR	Stumptown Roasters	Multiple locations	Café
NR	The Waffle Window	Hawthorne	Counter
NR	Voodoo Doughnut	Multiple locations	Counter
NR	Whiffies Fried Pies	Hawthorne	Food cart

Barbecue

8.3	Podnah's Pit	Northeast Portland	Casual	$25
6.9	Campbell's BBQ	Southeast Portland	Casual	$20
5.0	Russell Street BBQ	Northeast Portland	Casual	$25

Belgian

7.7	North 45	Northwest Portland	Bar	$35

Bosnian

6.9	Ziba's Pitas	Downtown	Food cart	$5

Brazilian

6.5	Brazil Grill	Southwest Portland	Casual	$40

British

7.6	Horse Brass Pub	Belmont	Casual	$25
7.0	Fats	Alberta Arts District	Casual	$35

Chinese

9.1	Ocean City Seafood	82nd Avenue Area	Casual	$30
9.0	Best Taste	82nd Avenue Area	Casual	$10
8.9	Lucky Strike	Far East Portland	Casual	$20
8.5	Powell's Seafood	Southeast Portland	Casual	$15
8.4	Du Kuh Bee	Beaverton	Casual	$20
8.1	Good Taste	Multiple locations	Casual	$15
8.1	Shenzhen	82nd Avenue Area	Casual	$25
8.0	Beijing Hot Pot	82nd Avenue Area	Casual	$20
8.0	Gold Garden Seafood	Far East Portland	Casual	$30
8.0	Yummy Yummy	82nd Avenue Area	Casual	$35
7.8	Hot Pot City	Downtown	Casual	$20
7.6	Wong's King Seafood	82nd Avenue Area	Casual	$45
7.4	Wing Wa BBQ King	82nd Avenue Area	Casual	$20
7.1	Jin Wah	Multiple locations	Casual	$25
6.3	Asian Station Café	Downtown	Food cart	$5

Coffee

NR	Albina Press	North Portland	Café	
NR	Backspace	Old Town	Café	
NR	Barista Café	Pearl District	Café	
NR	Caffé Umbria	Pearl District	Café	
NR	Coffee Time	Northwest Portland	Café	
NR	Coffeehouse Northwest	Northwest Portland	Café	
NR	Crowsenberg's	Downtown	Café	
NR	Ken's Artisan Bakery	Northwest Portland	Café	
NR	Little T American Baker	Division/Clinton	Café	
NR	Ristretto Roasters	Multiple locations	Café	
NR	Spella Caffè	Downtown	Food cart	
NR	St. Honoré	Northwest Portland	Café	
NR	Stumptown Roasters	Multiple locations	Café	
NR	Vivace	Northwest Portland	Café	
NR	World Cup Coffee	Multiple locations	Café	

Crêpes

7.8	Le Happy	Northwest Portland	Casual	$15
6.8	The Press Club	Division/Clinton	Casual	$20
4.8	Vivace	Northwest Portland	Café	$15

Cuban

8.1	Pambiche	Northeast Portland	Casual	$35

Czech

8.2	Tábor	Downtown	Food cart	$10

Dim Sum

9.1	Ocean City Seafood	82nd Avenue Area	Casual	$30
9.0	Best Taste	82nd Avenue Area	Casual	$10
8.1	Shenzhen	82nd Avenue Area	Casual	$25
7.6	Wong's King Seafood	82nd Avenue Area	Casual	$45
7.4	Wing Wa BBQ King	82nd Avenue Area	Casual	$20
7.1	Jin Wah	Multiple locations	Casual	$25

Ethiopian

8.7	Queen of Sheba	Northeast Portland	Casual	$35
8.0	Bete-Lukas	Division/Clinton	Casual	$35
7.7	E'Njoni Café	North Portland	Casual	$30

French

8.2	Carafe Bistro	Downtown	Upmarket	$45
7.5	Fenouil	Pearl District	Upmarket	$60
7.4	Bistro Maison	McMinnville	Upmarket	$60

German

6.6	Altengartz	Downtown	Food cart	$5
6.0	Berlin Inn	Southeast Portland	Casual	$40

Greek

2.9	Eleni's	Multiple locations	Casual	$40

Groceries

NR	City Market	Northwest Portland	Market
NR	Food Fight Grocery	Southeast Portland	Market
NR	Fubonn Supermarket	82nd Avenue Area	Market
NR	Good Neighbor Market	82nd Avenue Area	Market
NR	New Seasons Market	Multiple locations	Market

Groceries *continued*

NR	Pastaworks	Multiple locations	Market
NR	Uwajimaya	Beaverton	Market
NR	Whole Foods Market	Multiple locations	Market

Hawaiian

5.7	Thatch Tiki Bar	Northeast Portland	Bar	$30
4.4	Bamboo Grove	Southwest Portland	Casual	$25

Indian

8.5	East India Co.	Downtown	Casual	$40
7.9	Vindalho	Division/Clinton	Upmarket	$60
7.2	Swagat	Multiple locations	Casual	$25
5.3	Bombay Cricket Club	Hawthorne	Upmarket	$40
2.5	India Chaat House	Downtown	Food cart	$5

Italian

9.1	DOC	Alberta Arts District	Upmarket	$70
9.0	Nostrana	Southeast Portland	Upmarket	$55
8.3	Alba Osteria	Southwest Portland	Upmarket	$60
8.2	Nick's Italian Café	McMinnville	Upmarket	$70
8.1	Caffè Allora	Pearl District	Casual	$40
7.9	Gino's	Sellwood	Casual	$40
7.8	Fratelli Cucina	Pearl District	Casual	$40
7.8	Lincoln	Mississippi	Upmarket	$50
7.8	Piazza Italia	Pearl District	Casual	$35
7.7	Caffè Mingo	Northwest Portland	Upmarket	$50
7.5	Garden State	Sellwood	Food cart	$10
7.2	Decarli	Beaverton	Upmarket	$50
7.0	Nel Centro	Downtown	Upmarket	$60
6.9	Lucca	Northeast Portland	Casual	$35
6.9	Pastini Pastaria	Multiple locations	Casual	$25
6.8	Iorio	Hawthorne	Upmarket	$50
6.8	Justa Pasta	Northwest Portland	Counter	$15
6.8	Portobello	Southeast Portland	Casual	$35
6.5	Sal's Famous Italian	Northwest Portland	Casual	$35
6.4	Bar Mingo	Northwest Portland	Casual	$35
6.2	Ciao Vito	Alberta Arts District	Casual	$40
6.1	Mingo	Beaverton	Upmarket	$50
5.9	Bastas Trattoria	Northwest Portland	Upmarket	$45
4.5	The Liberty Glass	North Portland	Bar	$20
3.6	Pizza Schmizza	Multiple locations	Counter	$25

Japanese

9.2	Yuzu	Beaverton	Casual	$40
9.1	Hakatamon	Beaverton	Casual	$30
8.4	Hiroshi Sushi	Pearl District	Upmarket	$50
8.1	Syun Izakaya	Hillsboro	Casual	$35
7.7	Koji Osakaya	Multiple locations	Casual	$35
7.5	Sorabol	Southeast Portland	Casual	$30
7.3	Tanuki	Northwest Portland	Casual	$35
7.2	Biwa	Southeast Portland	Casual	$35
7.0	Yakuza Lounge	Alberta Arts District	Upmarket	$60
6.6	Bamboo Sushi	Southeast Portland	Upmarket	$40
6.3	Masu	Downtown	Upmarket	$45
5.9	Saburo's	Sellwood	Casual	$30
4.1	Samurai Bento	Downtown	Food cart	$15
NR	Uwajimaya	Beaverton	Market	

Korean

9.0	Country Korean	Beaverton	Casual	$20
8.8	DJK Korean BBQ	Beaverton	Casual	$25
8.7	JCD Korean Restaurant	Beaverton	Casual	$20
8.7	Spring Restaurant	Beaverton	Casual	$15
8.6	BeWon Korean	Northwest Portland	Casual	$35
8.4	Du Kuh Bee	Beaverton	Casual	$20
7.7	Koreana	Beaverton	Casual	$30
7.5	Sorabol	Southeast Portland	Casual	$30
7.4	Hae Rim	Beaverton	Casual	$20
7.4	Nakwon	Beaverton	Casual	$20
7.3	Tanuki	Northwest Portland	Casual	$35
7.2	Biwa	Southeast Portland	Casual	$35
6.7	KOi Fusion	Southwest Portland	Food cart	$5

Lebanese

9.0	Karam Lebanese	Downtown	Casual	$30
6.9	Aladdin's Café	Northeast Portland	Casual	$20
6.0	Madena of the Pearl	Pearl District	Casual	$20
5.4	Arabian Breeze	Northeast Portland	Casual	$25

Malaysian

7.7	Malay Satay Hut	82nd Avenue Area	Casual	$25

Markets

NR	City Market	Northwest Portland	Market
NR	Food Fight Grocery	Southeast Portland	Market
NR	Fubonn Supermarket	82nd Avenue Area	Market
NR	Good Neighbor Market	82nd Avenue Area	Market
NR	New Seasons Market	Multiple locations	Market
NR	Pastaworks	Multiple locations	Market
NR	Sahagún Chocolates	Northwest Portland	Market
NR	Uwajimaya	Beaverton	Market
NR	Whole Foods Market	Multiple locations	Market

Mexican

9.0	Taquería 7 Estrellas	Tigard	Casual	$15
8.7	Puerto Marquez	Far East Portland	Casual	$25
8.6	La Sirenita	Multiple locations	Counter	$15
8.3	Auténtica	Alberta Arts District	Upmarket	$45
7.4	Nuestra Cocina	Division/Clinton	Upmarket	$40
7.3	La Calaca Comelona	Belmont	Casual	$35
7.2	¿Por Qué No?	Multiple locations	Counter	$20
6.7	KOi Fusion	Southwest Portland	Food cart	$5
6.7	La Bonita	Alberta Arts District	Counter	$15
6.0	King Burrito	North Portland	Counter	$10
6.0	Pepino's Mexican Grill	Multiple locations	Counter	$10
4.9	Taquería Los Gorditos	Division/Clinton	Food cart	$5

Middle Eastern

8.6	Nicholas Restaurant	Southeast Portland	Casual	$20
8.2	Basha's Mediterranean	Downtown	Food cart	$5

Modern

9.6	Beast	Alberta Arts District	Upmarket	$90
9.6	Le Pigeon	East Burnside	Upmarket	$70
9.5	Park Kitchen	Pearl District	Upmarket	$50
9.4	Clyde Common	Downtown	Upmarket	$45
9.3	Beaker & Flask	Southeast Portland	Casual	$35
9.2	Paley's Place	Northwest Portland	Upmarket	$80

Modern *continued*

9.2	Sel Gris	Hawthorne	Upmarket	$80
9.2	Tabla	Northeast Portland	Upmarket	$45
9.2	Thistle	McMinnville	Upmarket	$60
9.1	Clarklewis	Southeast Portland	Upmarket	$70
9.1	Laurelhurst Market	Northeast Portland	Casual	$50
9.0	Simpatica	Southeast Portland	Upmarket	$50
8.9	Castagna	Hawthorne	Upmarket	$80
8.9	Ned Ludd	Northeast Portland	Upmarket	$45
8.8	Branch	Alberta Arts District	Casual	$40
8.8	Lovely Hula Hands	Mississippi	Casual	$40
8.7	Ten01	Pearl District	Upmarket	$70
8.6	Firehouse	Northeast Portland	Casual	$35
8.6	Wildwood	Northwest Portland	Upmarket	$70
8.5	Belly Timber	Hawthorne	Upmarket	$45
8.4	Little Red Bike Café	North Portland	Counter	$15
8.2	Evoe	Hawthorne	Casual	$15
8.2	Nick's Italian Café	McMinnville	Upmarket	$70
8.2	Serratto	Northwest Portland	Upmarket	$60
8.2	The Observatory	Southeast Portland	Casual	$35
8.1	Bar Avignon	Division/Clinton	Upmarket	$45
8.0	MetroVino	Pearl District	Upmarket	$45
7.9	Gino's	Sellwood	Casual	$40
7.8	Lincoln	Mississippi	Upmarket	$50
7.7	Besaw's Café	Northwest Portland	Casual	$40
7.7	Echo Restaurant	Northeast Portland	Casual	$40
7.6	Higgins	Downtown	Upmarket	$60
7.6	Urban Farmer	Downtown	Upmarket	$110
7.5	Fenouil	Pearl District	Upmarket	$60
7.4	Lucy's Table	Northwest Portland	Upmarket	$50
7.4	The Farm Café	East Burnside	Upmarket	$45
7.3	Gilt Club	Old Town	Upmarket	$60
7.3	Teardrop Lounge	Pearl District	Bar	$35
7.3	Veritable Quandary	Downtown	Upmarket	$45
7.2	Decarli	Beaverton	Upmarket	$50
7.1	3 Doors Down Café	Southeast Portland	Upmarket	$45
7.1	Café Castagna	Hawthorne	Upmarket	$45
7.1	Southpark Seafood	Downtown	Casual	$40
6.9	Lucca	Northeast Portland	Casual	$35
6.8	Bluehour	Pearl District	Upmarket	$70
6.8	Papa Haydn	Multiple locations	Upmarket	$50
6.7	Navarre	Northeast Portland	Upmarket	$45
6.7	The Country Cat	Southeast Portland	Casual	$40
6.4	Portland City Grill	Downtown	Upmarket	$70
6.4	Vault Martini	Pearl District	Bar	$35
6.2	Equinox	Northeast Portland	Casual	$40
6.1	Noble Rot	East Burnside	Upmarket	$40
6.0	Carlyle	Northwest Portland	Upmarket	$80
5.7	Living Room Theaters	Downtown	Theater	$35
5.6	Everett Street Bistro	Pearl District	Casual	$35
5.5	Lauro Kitchen	Division/Clinton	Upmarket	$50
5.3	23Hoyt	Northwest Portland	Upmarket	$60
5.3	Sapphire Hotel	Hawthorne	Bar	$20
5.0	50 Plates	Pearl District	Upmarket	$40
4.9	Westcafé	Downtown	Casual	$35

Nuevo Latino

8.8	Andina	Pearl District	Upmarket	$70
8.3	Auténtica	Alberta Arts District	Upmarket	$45
8.1	Pambiche	Northeast Portland	Casual	$35
7.4	Nuestra Cocina	Division/Clinton	Upmarket	$40
6.5	¡OBA!	Pearl District	Upmarket	$60

Pan-Asian

9.3	Ping	Old Town	Casual	$35
7.6	Siam Society	Alberta Arts District	Casual	$40
7.0	Silk	Pearl District	Upmarket	$40
6.1	Saucebox	Downtown	Bar	$40
5.7	Thatch Tiki Bar	Northeast Portland	Bar	$30
5.3	Sapphire Hotel	Hawthorne	Bar	$20
4.9	Typhoon!	Multiple locations	Casual	$40
NR	Fubonn Supermarket	82nd Avenue Area	Market	

Peruvian

| 8.8 | Andina | Pearl District | Upmarket | $70 |

Pizza

9.3	Apizza Scholls	Hawthorne	Casual	$30
9.0	Ken's Artisan Pizza	Southeast Portland	Casual	$25
9.0	Nostrana	Southeast Portland	Upmarket	$55
8.6	Firehouse	Northeast Portland	Casual	$35
8.2	Nick's Italian Café	McMinnville	Upmarket	$70
8.1	Caffè Allora	Pearl District	Casual	$40
7.2	Decarli	Beaverton	Upmarket	$50
7.0	Tastebud	Southeast Portland	Casual	$30
6.7	Mississippi Pizza Pub	Mississippi	Counter	$20
6.5	Sal's Famous Italian	Northwest Portland	Casual	$35
6.4	Escape From NY	Northwest Portland	Counter	$10
6.3	Dove Vivi Pizza Deli	Northeast Portland	Casual	$15
6.1	Mingo	Beaverton	Upmarket	$50
5.8	Pizzicato	Multiple locations	Counter	$20
5.8	Vincenté's Pizza	Hawthorne	Casual	$20
3.6	Pizza Schmizza	Multiple locations	Counter	$25

Polish

| 7.6 | Euro Dish | Downtown | Food cart | $10 |

Sandwiches

9.1	Laurelhurst Market	Northeast Portland	Casual	$50
9.0	Little T American Baker	Division/Clinton	Café	$15
8.8	Kenny & Zuke's	Downtown	Casual	$15
8.6	Pine State Biscuits	Belmont	Counter	$15
8.4	Little Red Bike Café	North Portland	Counter	$15
8.2	Evoe	Hawthorne	Casual	$15
8.2	The Waffle Window	Hawthorne	Counter	$10
8.1	Bunk Sandwiches	Southeast Portland	Counter	$15
8.1	Meat Cheese Bread	Southeast Portland	Counter	$15
8.0	Kenny & Zuke's Sandwich	Northwest Portland	Counter	$15
8.0	Ken's Artisan Bakery	Northwest Portland	Café	$15
7.5	Garden State	Sellwood	Food cart	$10
7.4	Kornblatt's Deli	Northwest Portland	Casual	$20
7.0	Brunchbox	Downtown	Food cart	$5
6.9	Petisco	Northeast Portland	Casual	$20
6.8	The Press Club	Division/Clinton	Casual	$20
6.7	Addy's Sandwich Bar	Downtown	Food cart	$10
6.4	Elephants Delicatessen	Multiple locations	Counter	$20
6.3	St. Honoré	Northwest Portland	Café	$15
6.1	Crowsenberg's	Downtown	Café	$15
5.9	Grand Central Bakery	Multiple locations	Counter	$15
5.8	Pizzicato	Multiple locations	Counter	$20
4.8	Vivace	Northwest Portland	Café	$15

Scandinavian

7.9	Brøder Comfort Food	Division/Clinton	Casual	$30

Seafood

9.1	EaT: An Oyster Bar	Mississippi	Casual	$40
9.1	Ocean City Seafood	82nd Avenue Area	Casual	$30
8.5	Powell's Seafood	Southeast Portland	Casual	$15
8.1	Shenzhen	82nd Avenue Area	Casual	$25
8.0	Yummy Yummy	82nd Avenue Area	Casual	$35
7.9	Original Halibut's	Alberta Arts District	Counter	$20
7.6	Wong's King Seafood	82nd Avenue Area	Casual	$45
7.1	Southpark Seafood	Downtown	Casual	$40
5.5	Bay 13	Pearl District	Upmarket	$50
5.4	McCormick & Schmick's	Multiple locations	Upmarket	$60
4.7	Jake's	Multiple locations	Upmarket	$50
NR	Fubonn Supermarket	82nd Avenue Area	Market	
NR	Uwajimaya	Beaverton	Market	

Southern *includes soul food, Cajun, Creole*

9.1	EaT: An Oyster Bar	Mississippi	Casual	$40
8.6	Pine State Biscuits	Belmont	Counter	$15
8.3	Podnah's Pit	Northeast Portland	Casual	$25
7.5	Delta Café	Southeast Portland	Casual	$35
7.3	Screen Door	Southeast Portland	Casual	$35
7.2	Miss Delta	Mississippi	Casual	$35
6.9	Campbell's BBQ	Southeast Portland	Casual	$20
6.7	The Country Cat	Southeast Portland	Casual	$40
6.6	Bernie's	Alberta Arts District	Casual	$40
6.1	Gravy	Mississippi	Casual	$25
5.0	Russell Street BBQ	Northeast Portland	Casual	$25
3.7	Le Bistro Montage	Southeast Portland	Casual	$35

Spanish

8.4	Patanegra	Northwest Portland	Upmarket	$50
7.8	Toro Bravo	Northeast Portland	Upmarket	$45

Steakhouse

9.1	Laurelhurst Market	Northeast Portland	Casual	$50
7.6	Urban Farmer	Downtown	Upmarket	$110
7.5	Ruth's Chris	Downtown	Upmarket	$100
7.3	Morton's	Downtown	Upmarket	$100
7.1	El Gaucho	Downtown	Upmarket	$100
6.7	Acropolis Club	Sellwood	Strip club	$15
6.5	Brazil Grill	Southwest Portland	Casual	$40
6.4	Portland City Grill	Downtown	Upmarket	$70
5.6	RingSide Steakhouse	Multiple locations	Upmarket	$80

Sweets

NR	Cacao Chocolate	Multiple locations	Counter	
NR	Cupcake Jones	Pearl District	Counter	
NR	Pix Pâtisserie	Multiple locations	Counter	
NR	Sahagún Chocolates	Northwest Portland	Market	
NR	Voodoo Doughnut	Multiple locations	Counter	

Thai

9.5	Pok Pok	Division/Clinton	Casual	$35
8.2	Red Onion Thai	Northwest Portland	Casual	$30
8.0	Nong's Khao Man Gai	Downtown	Food cart	$5
7.6	Siam Society	Alberta Arts District	Casual	$40
7.5	Kinara Thai Bistro	Southwest Portland	Casual	$25

Thai *continued*

7.1	Pad Thai Kitchen	Belmont	Casual	$25
6.7	Tara Thai	Northwest Portland	Casual	$25
5.9	Sweet Basil	Multiple locations	Casual	$25
4.9	Typhoon!	Multiple locations	Casual	$40

Vegefusion

7.4	The Farm Café	East Burnside	Upmarket	$45
7.2	Blossoming Lotus	Multiple locations	Casual	$30
7.0	Bye and Bye	Northeast Portland	Bar	$30
7.0	Dots Café	Division/Clinton	Bar	$20
7.0	The Whole Bowl	Multiple locations	Food cart	$5
7.0	Vita Café	Alberta Arts District	Casual	$25
6.8	Portobello	Southeast Portland	Casual	$35
6.6	Papa G's	Division/Clinton	Counter	$20
6.1	Crowsenberg's	Downtown	Café	$15
5.6	The Tin Shed	Alberta Arts District	Casual	$30
5.3	Tube	Old Town	Bar	$15
5.0	Laughing Planet	Multiple locations	Counter	$15
4.1	Paradox Café	Belmont	Casual	$20
NR	Backspace	Old Town	Café	
NR	Food Fight Grocery	Southeast Portland	Market	

Vietnamese

8.9	Pho An Sandy	Northeast Portland	Casual	$15
8.3	Pho Oregon	82nd Avenue Area	Casual	$15
8.0	Pho Hung	Southeast Portland	Casual	$15
7.2	Pho Van	Multiple locations	Casual	$25
7.1	Jin Wah	Multiple locations	Casual	$25
7.0	Silk	Pearl District	Upmarket	$40

By location

Places to eat **listed by neighborhood, suburb, or town, ranked by food rating**. Establishments that don't serve full meals (e.g. cafés, bakeries, grocery stores) appear as "NR" at the bottom of the list.

Alberta Arts District

		Cuisine	Type	Price
9.6	Beast	Modern	Upmarket	$90
9.1	DOC	Italian	Upmarket	$70
8.8	Branch	Modern	Casual	$40
8.6	La Sirenita	Mexican	Counter	$15
8.3	Auténtica	Mexican, Nuevo Latino	Upmarket	$45
7.9	Original Halibut's	Seafood	Counter	$20
7.6	Siam Society	Pan-Asian, Thai	Casual	$40
7.3	Helser's on Alberta	American	Casual	$15
7.0	Fats	British	Casual	$35
7.0	Vita Café	Vegefusion	Casual	$25
7.0	Yakuza Lounge	Japanese	Upmarket	$60
6.7	La Bonita	Mexican	Counter	$15
6.6	Bernie's	Southern	Casual	$40
6.2	Ciao Vito	Italian	Casual	$40
5.6	The Tin Shed	Vegefusion, American	Casual	$30
4.7	Cup & Saucer Café	American	Casual	$15
3.9	McMenamins	American	Casual	$30
NR	New Seasons Market	Groceries	Market	

Beaverton

		Cuisine	Type	Price
9.2	Yuzu	Japanese	Casual	$40
9.1	Hakatamon	Japanese	Casual	$30
9.0	Country Korean	Korean	Casual	$20
8.8	DJK Korean BBQ	Korean	Casual	$25
8.7	JCD Korean Restaurant	Korean	Casual	$20
8.7	Spring Restaurant	Korean	Casual	$15
8.4	Du Kuh Bee	Korean, Chinese	Casual	$20
7.7	Koreana	Korean	Casual	$30
7.4	Hae Rim	Korean	Casual	$20
7.4	Nakwon	Korean	Casual	$20
7.2	Decarli	Italian, Modern, Pizza	Upmarket	$50
7.2	Swagat	Indian	Casual	$25
7.2	Pho Van	Vietnamese	Casual	$25
7.1	Jin Wah	Chinese, Vietnamese	Casual	$25
6.9	Pastini Pastaria	Italian	Casual	$25
6.1	Mingo	Italian, Pizza	Upmarket	$50
5.8	Pizzicato	Pizza, Sandwiches	Counter	$20
5.4	McCormick & Schmick's	Seafood, American	Upmarket	$60
4.9	Typhoon!	Pan-Asian, Thai	Casual	$40
3.6	Pizza Schmizza	Pizza, Italian	Counter	$25
NR	New Seasons Market	Groceries	Market	
NR	Uwajimaya	Groceries, Japanese	Market	
NR	World Cup Coffee	Coffee	Café	

Belmont

		Cuisine	Type	Price
8.6	Pine State Biscuits	Sandwiches, Southern	Counter	$15
7.6	Horse Brass Pub	British	Casual	$25
7.3	La Calaca Comelona	Mexican	Casual	$35
7.1	Pad Thai Kitchen	Thai	Casual	$25
7.0	Zell's An American Café	American	Casual	$20
6.4	Cricket Café	American	Casual	$20

5.0	Laughing Planet	Vegefusion	Counter	$15
4.1	Paradox Café	Vegefusion	Casual	$20
NR	Stumptown Roasters	Coffee, Baked goods	Café	

Division/Clinton

9.5	Pok Pok	Thai	Casual	$35
9.0	Little T American Baker	Baked goods, Sandwiches	Café	$15
8.1	Bar Avignon	Modern	Upmarket	$45
8.0	Bete-Lukas	Ethiopian	Casual	$35
7.9	Brøder Comfort Food	Scandinavian	Casual	$30
7.9	Vindalho	Indian	Upmarket	$60
7.4	Nuestra Cocina	Mexican, Nuevo Latino	Upmarket	$40
7.1	Detour Café	American	Casual	$15
7.1	Genies	American	Casual	$20
7.0	Dots Café	American, Vegefusion	Bar	$20
6.9	Pastini Pastaria	Italian	Casual	$25
6.8	The Press Club	Sandwiches, Crêpes	Casual	$20
6.6	Papa G's	Vegefusion	Counter	$20
5.8	Pizzicato	Pizza, Sandwiches	Counter	$20
5.5	Lauro Kitchen	Modern	Upmarket	$50
4.9	Taquería Los Gorditos	Mexican	Food cart	$5
NR	New Seasons Market	Groceries	Market	
NR	Pix Pâtisserie	Baked goods, Sweets	Counter	
NR	Stumptown Roasters	Coffee, Baked goods	Café	

Downtown

9.4	Clyde Common	Modern	Upmarket	$45
9.0	Karam Lebanese	Lebanese	Casual	$30
8.8	Kenny & Zuke's	Sandwiches	Casual	$15
8.5	East India Co.	Indian	Casual	$40
8.2	Carafe Bistro	French	Upmarket	$45
8.2	Tábor	Czech	Food cart	$10
8.2	Basha's Mediterranean	Middle Eastern	Food cart	$5
8.0	Bijou Café	American	Casual	$25
8.0	Nong's Khao Man Gai	Thai	Food cart	$5
7.8	Hot Pot City	Chinese	Casual	$20
7.7	Koji Osakaya	Japanese	Casual	$35
7.6	Higgins	Modern	Upmarket	$60
7.6	Urban Farmer	Steakhouse, Modern	Upmarket	$110
7.6	Euro Dish	Polish	Food cart	$10
7.5	Ruth's Chris	Steakhouse	Upmarket	$100
7.3	Veritable Quandary	Modern	Upmarket	$45
7.3	Morton's	Steakhouse	Upmarket	$100
7.1	Mother's Bistro & Bar	American	Casual	$40
7.1	El Gaucho	Steakhouse	Upmarket	$100
7.1	Southpark Seafood	Modern, Seafood	Casual	$40
7.0	Brunchbox	Sandwiches	Food cart	$5
7.0	Nel Centro	Italian	Upmarket	$60
7.0	The Whole Bowl	Vegefusion	Food cart	$5
6.9	Ziba's Pitas	Bosnian	Food cart	$5
6.9	Pastini Pastaria	Italian	Casual	$25
6.7	Addy's Sandwich Bar	Sandwiches	Food cart	$10
6.6	Altengartz	German	Food cart	$5
6.4	Portland City Grill	Steakhouse, Modern	Upmarket	$70
6.4	Elephants Delicatessen	American, Sandwiches	Counter	$20
6.3	Masu	Japanese	Upmarket	$45
6.3	Asian Station Café	Chinese	Food cart	$5
6.1	Crowsenberg's	Baked goods, Sandwiches	Café	$15
6.1	Saucebox	Pan-Asian	Bar	$40
5.8	Pizzicato	Pizza, Sandwiches	Counter	$20
5.7	Living Room Theaters	Modern	Theater	$35

Downtown *continued*

5.6	The Heathman	American	Upmarket	$60
5.4	McCormick & Schmick's	Seafood, American	Upmarket	$60
5.1	SuperDog	American	Counter	$10
4.9	Huber's Restaurant	American	Casual	$40
4.9	Typhoon!	Pan-Asian, Thai	Casual	$40
4.9	Westcafé	Modern	Casual	$35
4.7	Jake's	Seafood, American	Upmarket	$50
4.1	Samurai Bento	Japanese	Food cart	$15
3.9	McMenamins	American	Casual	$30
3.6	Pizza Schmizza	Pizza, Italian	Counter	$25
2.5	India Chaat House	Indian	Food cart	$5
NR	Cacao Chocolate	Sweets	Counter	
NR	Spella Caffè	Coffee	Food cart	
NR	Stumptown Roasters	Coffee, Baked goods	Café	
NR	Voodoo Doughnut	Baked goods, Sweets	Counter	

East Burnside

9.6	Le Pigeon	Modern	Upmarket	$70
7.4	The Farm Café	Modern, Vegefusion	Upmarket	$45
6.1	Doug Fir	American	Bar	$30
6.1	Noble Rot	Modern	Upmarket	$40

82nd Avenue Area

9.1	Ocean City Seafood	Chinese, Seafood	Casual	$30
9.0	Best Taste	Chinese, Dim Sum	Casual	$10
8.3	Pho Oregon	Vietnamese	Casual	$15
8.1	Good Taste	Chinese	Casual	$15
8.1	Shenzhen	Chinese, Seafood	Casual	$25
8.0	Beijing Hot Pot	Chinese	Casual	$20
8.0	Yummy Yummy	Chinese, Seafood	Casual	$35
7.7	Malay Satay Hut	Malaysian	Casual	$25
7.7	Koji Osakaya	Japanese	Casual	$35
7.6	Wong's King Seafood	Chinese, Seafood	Casual	$45
7.4	Wing Wa BBQ King	Chinese, Dim Sum	Casual	$20
7.2	Pho Van	Vietnamese	Casual	$25
7.1	Jin Wah	Chinese, Vietnamese	Casual	$25
NR	Fubonn Supermarket	Groceries, Pan-Asian	Market	
NR	Good Neighbor Market	Groceries	Market	

Far East Portland

8.9	Lucky Strike	Chinese	Casual	$20
8.7	Puerto Marquez	Mexican	Casual	$25
8.0	Gold Garden Seafood	Chinese	Casual	$30

Hawthorne

9.3	Apizza Scholls	Pizza	Casual	$30
9.2	Sel Gris	Modern	Upmarket	$80
8.9	Castagna	Modern	Upmarket	$80
8.5	Belly Timber	Modern	Upmarket	$45
8.2	The Waffle Window	Baked goods, Sandwiches	Counter	$10
8.2	Evoe	Modern, Sandwiches	Casual	$15
7.2	¿Por Qué No?	Mexican	Counter	$20
7.2	Pho Van	Vietnamese	Casual	$25
7.1	Café Castagna	Modern	Upmarket	$45
7.0	The Whole Bowl	Vegefusion	Food cart	$5
6.8	Iorio	Italian	Upmarket	$50
6.7	Jam on Hawthorne	American	Casual	$25
6.4	Potato Champion	American	Food cart	$5
6.0	Pepino's Mexican Grill	Mexican	Counter	$10
5.9	Grand Central Bakery	Baked goods, Sandwiches	Counter	$15

Hawthorne *continued*

5.8	Vincenté's Pizza	Pizza	Casual	$20
5.3	Sapphire Hotel	Modern, Pan-Asian	Bar	$20
5.3	Bombay Cricket Club	Indian	Upmarket	$40
5.3	Bread and Ink Café	American	Casual	$40
5.2	Burgerville	American	Counter	$10
4.7	Cup & Saucer Café	American	Casual	$15
3.9	McMenamins	American	Casual	$30
3.0	Lucky Labrador	American	Bar	$15
NR	Pastaworks	Groceries	Market	
NR	Whiffies Fried Pies	Baked goods	Food cart	

Hillsboro

8.1	Syun Izakaya	Japanese	Casual	$35
8.1	Good Taste	Chinese	Casual	$15
7.7	Koji Osakaya	Japanese	Casual	$35
7.2	Swagat	Indian	Casual	$25

McMinnville

9.2	Thistle	Modern	Upmarket	$60
8.2	Nick's Italian Café	Italian, Modern, Pizza	Upmarket	$70
7.4	Bistro Maison	French	Upmarket	$60

Mississippi Ave. Area

9.1	EaT: An Oyster Bar	Seafood, Southern	Casual	$40
8.8	Lovely Hula Hands	Modern	Casual	$40
7.8	Lincoln	Italian, Modern	Upmarket	$50
7.2	Miss Delta	Southern	Casual	$35
7.2	¿Por Qué No?	Mexican	Counter	$20
7.1	5th Quadrant	American	Bar	$15
6.7	Mississippi Pizza Pub	Pizza	Counter	$20
6.1	Gravy	American, Southern	Casual	$25
5.0	Laughing Planet	Vegefusion	Counter	$15
5.0	FlavourSpot	American, Baked goods	Food cart	$5
NR	Pastaworks	Groceries	Market	
NR	Pix Pâtisserie	Baked goods, Sweets	Counter	
NR	Ristretto Roasters	Coffee, Baked goods	Café	

Multnomah Village

5.9	Grand Central Bakery	Baked goods, Sandwiches	Counter	$15
4.0	Fat City Café	American	Casual	$20
3.0	Lucky Labrador	American	Bar	$15

North Portland

8.4	Little Red Bike Café	Modern, Sandwiches	Counter	$15
7.7	E'Njoni Café	Ethiopian	Casual	$30
7.6	John Street Café	American	Casual	$20
7.4	Pause	American	Casual	$35
6.8	Fire on the Mountain	American	Counter	$20
6.0	King Burrito	Mexican	Counter	$10
5.2	Burgerville	American	Counter	$10
5.0	FlavourSpot	American, Baked goods	Food cart	$5
4.7	Cup & Saucer Café	American	Casual	$15
4.5	The Liberty Glass	American, Italian	Bar	$20
NR	Albina Press	Coffee, Baked goods	Café	
NR	New Seasons Market	Groceries	Market	

Northeast Portland

9.2	Tabla	Modern	Upmarket	$45
9.1	Laurelhurst Market	Modern, Steakhouse	Casual	$50

8.9	Ned Ludd	Modern	Upmarket	$45
8.9	Pho An Sandy	Vietnamese	Casual	$15
8.7	Queen of Sheba	Ethiopian	Casual	$35
8.6	Firehouse	Pizza, Modern	Casual	$35
8.3	Podnah's Pit	Barbecue, Southern	Casual	$25
8.1	Pambiche	Cuban, Nuevo Latino	Casual	$35
7.8	Toro Bravo	Spanish	Upmarket	$45
7.7	Echo Restaurant	Modern	Casual	$40
7.7	Koji Osakaya	Japanese	Casual	$35
7.2	Blossoming Lotus	Vegefusion	Casual	$30
7.0	Bye and Bye	Vegefusion	Bar	$30
6.9	Petisco	Sandwiches	Casual	$20
6.9	Aladdin's Café	Lebanese	Casual	$20
6.9	Lucca	Italian, Modern	Casual	$35
6.9	Pastini Pastaria	Italian	Casual	$25
6.7	Navarre	Modern	Upmarket	$45
6.3	Dove Vivi Pizza Deli	Pizza	Casual	$15
6.2	Equinox	Modern	Casual	$40
6.1	Grilled Cheese Grill	American	Food cart	$5
6.1	Alameda Café	American	Casual	$30
5.9	Sweet Basil	Thai	Casual	$25
5.9	Grand Central Bakery	Baked goods, Sandwiches	Counter	$15
5.8	Pizzicato	Pizza, Sandwiches	Counter	$20
5.7	Thatch Tiki Bar	Hawaiian, Pan-Asian	Bar	$30
5.6	RingSide Steakhouse	Steakhouse	Upmarket	$80
5.4	Arabian Breeze	Lebanese	Casual	$25
5.2	Burgerville	American	Counter	$10
5.0	Russell Street BBQ	Barbecue, Southern	Casual	$25
3.6	Pizza Schmizza	Pizza, Italian	Counter	$25
NR	Bakery Bar	Baked goods	Counter	
NR	Fleur de Lis	Baked goods	Counter	
NR	Ristretto Roasters	Coffee, Baked goods	Café	
NR	Voodoo Doughnut	Baked goods, Sweets	Counter	
NR	Whole Foods Market	Groceries	Market	

Northwest Portland

9.2	Paley's Place	Modern	Upmarket	$80
8.6	BeWon Korean	Korean	Casual	$35
8.6	Wildwood	Modern	Upmarket	$70
8.4	Patanegra	Spanish	Upmarket	$50
8.2	Serratto	Modern	Upmarket	$60
8.2	Red Onion Thai	Thai	Casual	$30
8.0	Ken's Artisan Bakery	Baked goods, Sandwiches	Café	$15
8.0	Kenny & Zuke's Sandwich	Sandwiches	Counter	$15
7.8	Le Happy	Crêpes	Casual	$15
7.7	Caffè Mingo	Italian	Upmarket	$50
7.7	North 45	American, Belgian	Bar	$35
7.7	Besaw's Café	Modern	Casual	$40
7.4	Lucy's Table	Modern	Upmarket	$50
7.4	Kornblatt's Deli	Sandwiches	Casual	$20
7.3	Tanuki	Japanese, Korean	Casual	$35
7.2	Nob Hill Bar & Grill	American	Bar	$20
7.2	Swagat	Indian	Casual	$25
6.9	Pastini Pastaria	Italian	Casual	$25
6.8	Papa Haydn	Modern, Baked goods	Upmarket	$50
6.8	Justa Pasta	Italian	Counter	$15
6.7	Tara Thai	Thai	Casual	$25
6.5	Sal's Famous Italian	Italian, Pizza	Casual	$35
6.4	Café Nell	American	Casual	$40
6.4	Bar Mingo	Italian	Casual	$35
6.4	Escape From NY	Pizza	Counter	$10
6.4	Elephants Delicatessen	American, Sandwiches	Counter	$20

Northwest Portland *continued*

6.3	St. Honoré	Baked goods, Sandwiches	Café	$15
6.0	Carlyle	Modern	Upmarket	$80
6.0	New Old Lompoc	American	Casual	$25
6.0	Pepino's Mexican Grill	Mexican	Counter	$10
5.9	Bastas Trattoria	Italian	Upmarket	$45
5.9	Sweet Basil	Thai	Casual	$25
5.9	Grand Central Bakery	Baked goods, Sandwiches	Counter	$15
5.8	Pizzicato	Pizza, Sandwiches	Counter	$20
5.6	RingSide Steakhouse	Steakhouse	Upmarket	$80
5.3	23Hoyt	Modern	Upmarket	$60
5.0	Laughing Planet	Vegefusion	Counter	$15
4.9	Typhoon!	Pan-Asian, Thai	Casual	$40
4.8	Vivace	Sandwiches, Crêpes	Café	$15
3.9	McMenamins	American	Casual	$30
3.6	Pizza Schmizza	Pizza, Italian	Counter	$25
3.0	Lucky Labrador	American	Bar	$15
NR	City Market	Groceries	Market	
NR	Coffee Time	Coffee, Baked goods	Café	
NR	Coffeehouse Northwest	Coffee, Baked goods	Café	
NR	Pastaworks	Groceries	Market	
NR	Sahagún Chocolates	Sweets	Market	
NR	World Cup Coffee	Coffee	Café	

Old Town Chinatown

9.3	Ping	Pan-Asian	Casual	$35
8.1	Good Taste	Chinese	Casual	$15
7.3	Gilt Club	Modern	Upmarket	$60
5.3	Tube	Vegefusion	Bar	$15
NR	Backspace	Coffee, Vegefusion	Café	

Pearl District

9.5	Park Kitchen	Modern	Upmarket	$50
8.8	Andina	Peruvian, Nuevo Latino	Upmarket	$70
8.7	Ten01	Modern	Upmarket	$70
8.4	Hiroshi Sushi	Japanese	Upmarket	$50
8.1	Caffè Allora	Italian, Pizza	Casual	$40
8.0	MetroVino	Modern	Upmarket	$45
7.8	Fratelli Cucina	Italian	Casual	$40
7.8	Piazza Italia	Italian	Casual	$35
7.5	Fenouil	French, Modern	Upmarket	$60
7.3	Teardrop Lounge	Modern	Bar	$35
7.2	Blossoming Lotus	Vegefusion	Casual	$30
7.0	Silk	Pan-Asian, Vietnamese	Upmarket	$40
7.0	The Whole Bowl	Vegefusion	Food cart	$5
6.8	Deschutes Brewery	American	Casual	$25
6.8	Bluehour	Modern	Upmarket	$70
6.5	¡OBA!	Nuevo Latino	Upmarket	$60
6.4	Vault Martini	Modern	Bar	$35
6.0	Madena of the Pearl	Lebanese	Casual	$20
5.7	Byways Café	American	Casual	$15
5.7	Henry's 12th St. Tavern	American	Upmarket	$40
5.6	Everett Street Bistro	Modern	Casual	$35
5.6	Rogue Public House	American	Bar	$25
5.5	Bay 13	Seafood	Upmarket	$50
5.0	Laughing Planet	Vegefusion	Counter	$15
5.0	50 Plates	Modern	Upmarket	$40
3.6	Pizza Schmizza	Pizza, Italian	Counter	$25
2.9	Eleni's	Greek	Casual	$40
NR	Barista Café	Coffee	Café	
NR	Caffè Umbria	Coffee, Baked goods	Café	
NR	Cupcake Jones	Baked goods, Sweets	Counter	

Pearl District *continued*

NR	Whole Foods Market	Groceries	Market
NR	World Cup Coffee	Coffee	Café

Sellwood

8.6	La Sirenita	Mexican	Counter	$15
7.9	Gino's	Italian, Modern	Casual	$40
7.5	Garden State	Italian, Sandwiches	Food cart	$10
6.8	Papa Haydn	Modern, Baked goods	Upmarket	$50
6.7	Acropolis Club	Steakhouse	Strip club	$15
5.9	Saburo's	Japanese	Casual	$30
5.9	Grand Central Bakery	Baked goods, Sandwiches	Counter	$15
5.8	Pizzicato	Pizza, Sandwiches	Counter	$20
2.9	Eleni's	Greek	Casual	$40
NR	New Seasons Market	Groceries	Market	

Southeast Portland *Establishments on Belmont, Clinton, Division, and Hawthorne Streets are listed in the Belmont, Division/Clinton, and Hawthorne neighborhoods*

9.3	Beaker & Flask	Modern	Casual	$35
9.1	Clarklewis	Modern	Upmarket	$70
9.0	Simpatica	Modern	Upmarket	$50
9.0	Nostrana	Italian, Pizza	Upmarket	$55
9.0	Ken's Artisan Pizza	Pizza	Casual	$25
8.6	Nicholas Restaurant	Middle Eastern	Casual	$20
8.5	Powell's Seafood	Chinese, Seafood	Casual	$15
8.2	The Observatory	Modern	Casual	$35
8.1	Bunk Sandwiches	Sandwiches	Counter	$15
8.1	Meat Cheese Bread	Sandwiches	Counter	$15
8.0	Slow Bar	American	Bar	$25
8.0	Pho Hung	Vietnamese	Casual	$15
7.5	Delta Café	Southern	Casual	$35
7.5	Sorabol	Korean, Japanese	Casual	$30
7.3	Screen Door	Southern	Casual	$35
7.2	Biwa	Japanese, Korean	Casual	$35
7.1	3 Doors Down Café	Modern	Upmarket	$45
7.0	Tastebud	Pizza	Casual	$30
6.9	Campbell's BBQ	Barbecue, Southern	Casual	$20
6.8	Portobello	Vegefusion, Italian	Casual	$35
6.8	Fire on the Mountain	American	Counter	$20
6.7	The Country Cat	Modern, Southern	Casual	$40
6.6	Bamboo Sushi	Japanese	Upmarket	$40
6.4	Green Dragon	American	Casual	$25
6.0	Berlin Inn	German	Casual	$40
6.0	Original Hotcake House	American	Casual	$20
5.2	Burgerville	American	Counter	$10
5.0	Laughing Planet	Vegefusion	Counter	$15
3.7	Le Bistro Montage	Southern	Casual	$35
NR	Bakery Bar	Baked goods	Counter	
NR	Food Fight Grocery	Groceries, Vegefusion	Market	
NR	Whole Foods Market	Groceries	Market	

Southwest Portland

8.3	Alba Osteria	Italian	Upmarket	$60
7.7	Koji Osakaya	Japanese	Casual	$35
7.5	Kinara Thai Bistro	Thai	Casual	$25
6.7	KOi Fusion	Mexican, Korean	Food cart	$5
6.6	Driftwood Room	American	Bar	$35
6.5	Brazil Grill	Brazilian, Steakhouse	Casual	$40
6.5	Original Pancake House	American	Casual	$15
6.4	Elephants Delicatessen	American, Sandwiches	Counter	$20
5.0	Laughing Planet	Vegefusion	Counter	$15

Southwest Portland *continued*

4.4	Bamboo Grove	Hawaiian	Casual	$25
3.6	Pizza Schmizza	Pizza, Italian	Counter	$25
NR	Baker & Spice	Baked goods	Counter	

Tigard

9.0	Taquería 7 Estrellas	Mexican	Casual	$15

By special feature

Ranked by food rating. Establishments that don't serve full meals (e.g. cafés, bakeries, grocery stores) appear as "NR" at the bottom of the list.

	Breakfast	Cuisine	Location	Type	Price
9.0	Little T American Baker	Baked goods	Division/Clinton	Café	$15
8.8	Kenny & Zuke's	Sandwiches	Downtown	Casual	$15
8.6	Pine State Biscuits	Sandwiches	Belmont	Counter	$15
8.4	Little Red Bike Café	Modern	North Portland	Counter	$15
8.2	The Waffle Window	Baked goods	Hawthorne	Counter	$10
8.1	Pambiche	Cuban	Northeast Portland	Casual	$35
8.1	Bunk Sandwiches	Sandwiches	Southeast Portland	Counter	$15
8.1	Meat Cheese Bread	Sandwiches	Southeast Portland	Counter	$15
8.0	Ken's Artisan Bakery	Baked goods	Northwest Portland	Café	$15
8.0	Bijou Café	American	Downtown	Casual	$25
7.9	Brøder Comfort Food	Scandinavian	Division/Clinton	Casual	$30
7.7	Besaw's Café	Modern	Northwest Portland	Casual	$40
7.6	Horse Brass Pub	British	Belmont	Casual	$25
7.6	John Street Café	American	North Portland	Casual	$20
7.4	Kornblatt's Deli	Sandwiches	Northwest Portland	Casual	$20
7.3	Helser's on Alberta	American	Alberta Arts District	Casual	$15
7.2	Nob Hill Bar & Grill	American	Northwest Portland	Bar	$20
7.1	Mother's Bistro & Bar	American	Downtown	Casual	$40
7.1	Detour Café	American	Division/Clinton	Casual	$15
7.1	Genies	American	Division/Clinton	Casual	$20
7.0	Zell's An American Café	American	Belmont	Casual	$25
7.0	Vita Café	Vegefusion	Alberta Arts District	Casual	$15
7.0	Brunchbox	Sandwiches	Downtown	Food cart	$5
7.0	Nel Centro	Italian	Downtown	Upmarket	$60
6.8	Papa Haydn	Modern	Multiple locations	Upmarket	$50
6.7	The Country Cat	Modern, Southern	Southeast Portland	Casual	$40
6.7	Acropolis Club	Steakhouse	Sellwood	Strip club	$15
6.7	La Bonita	Mexican	Alberta Arts District	Counter	$15
6.7	Jam on Hawthorne	American	Hawthorne	Casual	$25
6.5	Original Pancake House	American	Southwest Portland	Casual	$15
6.4	Café Nell	American	Northwest Portland	Casual	$40
6.4	Elephants Delicatessen	American	Multiple locations	Counter	$20
6.4	Cricket Café	American	Belmont	Casual	$20
6.3	St. Honoré	Baked goods	Northwest Portland	Café	$15
6.2	Equinox	Modern	Northeast Portland	Casual	$40
6.1	Doug Fir	American	East Burnside	Bar	$30
6.1	Crowsenberg's	Baked goods	Downtown	Café	$15
6.1	Gravy	American, Southern	Mississippi	Casual	$25
6.0	Original Hotcake House	American	Southeast Portland	Casual	$20
5.9	Grand Central Bakery	Baked goods	Multiple locations	Counter	$15
5.7	Byways Café	American	Pearl District	Casual	$15
5.6	The Tin Shed	Vegefusion	Alberta Arts District	Casual	$30
5.6	Everett Street Bistro	Modern	Pearl District	Casual	$35
5.6	The Heathman	American	Downtown	Upmarket	$60
5.3	Bread and Ink Café	American	Hawthorne	Casual	$40
5.2	Burgerville	American	Multiple locations	Counter	$10
5.0	FlavourSpot	American	Multiple locations	Food cart	$5
4.9	Taquería Los Gorditos	Mexican	Division/Clinton	Food cart	$5
4.8	Vivace	Sandwiches, Crêpes	Northwest Portland	Café	$15

Breakfast *continued*

4.7	Cup & Saucer Café	American	Multiple locations	Casual	$15
4.1	Paradox Café	Vegefusion	Belmont	Casual	$20
4.0	Fat City Café	American	Multnomah Village	Casual	$20
NR	Albina Press	Coffee	North Portland	Café	
NR	Baker & Spice	Baked goods	Southwest Portland	Counter	
NR	Bakery Bar	Baked goods	Multiple locations	Counter	
NR	Caffé Umbria	Coffee	Pearl District	Café	
NR	Coffee Time	Coffee	Northwest Portland	Café	
NR	Coffeehouse Northwest	Coffee	Northwest Portland	Café	
NR	Fleur de Lis	Baked goods	Northeast Portland	Counter	
NR	New Seasons Market	Groceries	Multiple locations	Market	
NR	Spella Caffè	Coffee	Downtown	Food cart	
NR	Stumptown Roasters	Coffee	Multiple locations	Café	
NR	Whole Foods Market	Groceries	Multiple locations	Market	

Brunch

9.6	Beast	Modern	Alberta Arts District	Upmarket	$90
9.1	Ocean City Seafood	Chinese, Seafood	82nd Avenue Area	Casual	$30
9.0	Simpatica	Modern	Southeast Portland	Upmarket	$50
9.0	Little T American Baker	Baked goods	Division/Clinton	Café	$15
9.0	Best Taste	Chinese, Dim Sum	82nd Avenue Area	Casual	$10
8.8	Kenny & Zuke's	Sandwiches	Downtown	Casual	$15
8.6	Pine State Biscuits	Sandwiches	Belmont	Counter	$15
8.5	Belly Timber	Modern	Hawthorne	Upmarket	$45
8.4	Little Red Bike Café	Modern	North Portland	Counter	$15
8.3	Auténtica	Mexican	Alberta Arts District	Upmarket	$45
8.3	Podnah's Pit	Barbecue, Southern	Northeast Portland	Casual	$25
8.2	The Waffle Window	Baked goods	Hawthorne	Counter	$10
8.1	Pambiche	Cuban	Northeast Portland	Casual	$35
8.1	Bunk Sandwiches	Sandwiches	Southeast Portland	Counter	$15
8.1	Shenzhen	Chinese, Seafood	82nd Avenue Area	Casual	$25
8.0	Ken's Artisan Bakery	Baked goods	Northwest Portland	Café	$15
8.0	Bijou Café	American	Downtown	Casual	$25
8.0	Kenny & Zuke's Sandwich	Sandwiches	Northwest Portland	Counter	$15
8.0	Gold Garden Seafood	Chinese	Far East Portland	Casual	$30
7.9	Brøder Comfort Food	Scandinavian	Division/Clinton	Casual	$30
7.7	Besaw's Café	Modern	Northwest Portland	Casual	$40
7.7	Echo Restaurant	Modern	Northeast Portland	Casual	$40
7.7	Malay Satay Hut	Malaysian	82nd Avenue Area	Casual	$25
7.6	John Street Café	American	North Portland	Casual	$20
7.6	Wong's King Seafood	Chinese, Seafood	82nd Avenue Area	Casual	$45
7.5	Fenouil	French, Modern	Pearl District	Upmarket	$60
7.5	Delta Café	Southern	Southeast Portland	Casual	$35
7.4	Bistro Maison	French	McMinnville	Upmarket	$60
7.4	Kornblatt's Deli	Sandwiches	Northwest Portland	Casual	$20
7.4	Wing Wa BBQ King	Chinese, Dim Sum	82nd Avenue Area	Casual	$20
7.3	Veritable Quandary	Modern	Downtown	Upmarket	$45
7.3	Helser's on Alberta	American	Alberta Arts District	Casual	$15
7.3	Screen Door	Southern	Southeast Portland	Casual	$35
7.2	Decarli	Italian, Modern	Beaverton	Upmarket	$50
7.2	¿Por Qué No?	Mexican	Multiple locations	Counter	$20
7.1	Mother's Bistro & Bar	American	Downtown	Casual	$40
7.1	Detour Café	American	Division/Clinton	Casual	$15
7.1	Genies	American	Division/Clinton	Casual	$20
7.1	Jin Wah	Chinese	Multiple locations	Casual	$25
7.0	Fats	British	Alberta Arts District	Casual	$35
7.0	Zell's An American Café	American	Belmont	Casual	$20
7.0	Tastebud	Pizza	Southeast Portland	Casual	$30
7.0	Vita Café	Vegefusion	Alberta Arts District	Casual	$25
7.0	Brunchbox	Sandwiches	Downtown	Food cart	$5
7.0	Nel Centro	Italian	Downtown	Upmarket	$60
6.9	Petisco	Sandwiches	Northeast Portland	Casual	$20

Brunch *continued*

6.8	Papa Haydn	Modern	Multiple locations	Upmarket	$50
6.8	Bluehour	Modern	Pearl District	Upmarket	$70
6.7	The Country Cat	Modern, Southern	Southeast Portland	Casual	$40
6.7	Navarre	Modern	Northeast Portland	Upmarket	$45
6.7	Jam on Hawthorne	American	Hawthorne	Casual	$25
6.5	Original Pancake House	American	Southwest Portland	Casual	$15
6.4	Café Nell	American	Northwest Portland	Casual	$40
6.4	Cricket Café	American	Belmont	Casual	$20
6.2	Equinox	Modern	Northeast Portland	Casual	$40
6.1	Crowsenberg's	Baked goods	Downtown	Café	$15
6.1	Gravy	American, Southern	Mississippi	Casual	$25
6.1	Alameda Café	American	Northeast Portland	Casual	$30
6.0	Berlin Inn	German	Southeast Portland	Casual	$40
6.0	Original Hotcake House	American	Southeast Portland	Casual	$20
5.9	Grand Central Bakery	Baked goods	Multiple locations	Counter	$15
5.7	Byways Café	American	Pearl District	Casual	$15
5.6	The Tin Shed	Vegefusion	Alberta Arts District	Casual	$30
5.6	Everett Street Bistro	Modern	Pearl District	Casual	$35
5.6	The Heathman	American	Downtown	Upmarket	$60
5.3	Sapphire Hotel	Modern, Pan-Asian	Hawthorne	Bar	$20
5.3	Bread and Ink Café	American	Hawthorne	Casual	$40
5.0	FlavourSpot	American	Multiple locations	Food cart	$5
4.9	Westcafé	Modern	Downtown	Casual	$35
4.7	Cup & Saucer Café	American	Multiple locations	Casual	$15
4.1	Paradox Café	Vegefusion	Belmont	Casual	$20
4.0	Fat City Café	American	Multnomah Village	Casual	$20
3.7	Le Bistro Montage	Southern	Southeast Portland	Casual	$35

BYO *We consider any restaurant with a corkage fee of $10 or under to be BYO. If there is a wine program, however, it is polite to tip on what you would have spent had you not brought your own. Offering a taste is optional.*

9.1	EaT: An Oyster Bar	Seafood, Southern	Mississippi	Casual	$40
9.0	Karam Lebanese	Lebanese	Downtown	Casual	$30
8.5	Belly Timber	Modern	Hawthorne	Upmarket	$45
8.4	Hiroshi Sushi	Japanese	Pearl District	Upmarket	$50
7.9	Brøder Comfort Food	Scandinavian	Division/Clinton	Casual	$30
7.7	E'Njoni Café	Ethiopian	North Portland	Casual	$30
7.7	Koji Osakaya	Japanese	Multiple locations	Casual	$35
7.6	Siam Society	Pan-Asian, Thai	Alberta Arts District	Casual	$40
7.4	The Farm Café	Modern, Vegefusion	East Burnside	Upmarket	$45
7.4	Nuestra Cocina	Mexican	Division/Clinton	Upmarket	$40
6.9	Campbell's BBQ	Barbecue, Southern	Southeast Portland	Casual	$20
6.8	Justa Pasta	Italian	Northwest Portland	Counter	$15
6.8	Fire on the Mountain	American	Multiple locations	Counter	$20
6.6	Bamboo Sushi	Japanese	Southeast Portland	Upmarket	$40
6.4	Cricket Café	American	Belmont	Casual	$20
6.3	Dove Vivi Pizza Deli	Pizza	Northeast Portland	Casual	$15
6.2	Equinox	Modern	Northeast Portland	Casual	$40
6.0	Berlin Inn	German	Southeast Portland	Casual	$40
6.0	Madena of the Pearl	Lebanese	Pearl District	Casual	$20
4.4	Bamboo Grove	Hawaiian	Southwest Portland	Casual	$25
2.9	Eleni's	Greek	Multiple locations	Casual	$40

Date-friendly

9.6	Beast	Modern	Alberta Arts District	Upmarket	$90
9.6	Le Pigeon	Modern	East Burnside	Upmarket	$70
9.5	Park Kitchen	Modern	Pearl District	Upmarket	$50
9.5	Pok Pok	Thai	Division/Clinton	Casual	$35
9.3	Beaker & Flask	Modern	Southeast Portland	Casual	$35
9.3	Ping	Pan-Asian	Old Town	Casual	$35
9.2	Tabla	Modern	Northeast Portland	Upmarket	$45

Date-friendly *continued*

9.2	Thistle	Modern	McMinnville	Upmarket	$60
9.2	Paley's Place	Modern	Northwest Portland	Upmarket	$80
9.2	Yuzu	Japanese	Beaverton	Casual	$40
9.2	Sel Gris	Modern	Hawthorne	Upmarket	$80
9.1	DOC	Italian	Alberta Arts District	Upmarket	$70
9.1	Clarklewis	Modern	Southeast Portland	Upmarket	$70
9.1	Laurelhurst Market	Modern	Northeast Portland	Casual	$50
9.1	EaT: An Oyster Bar	Seafood, Southern	Mississippi	Casual	$40
9.0	Simpatica	Modern	Southeast Portland	Upmarket	$50
9.0	Nostrana	Italian, Pizza	Southeast Portland	Upmarket	$55
8.9	Ned Ludd	Modern	Northeast Portland	Upmarket	$45
8.9	Castagna	Modern	Hawthorne	Upmarket	$80
8.8	Andina	Peruvian	Pearl District	Upmarket	$70
8.8	Branch	Modern	Alberta Arts District	Casual	$40
8.8	Lovely Hula Hands	Modern	Mississippi	Casual	$40
8.7	Ten01	Modern	Pearl District	Upmarket	$70
8.6	BeWon Korean	Korean	Northwest Portland	Casual	$35
8.6	Firehouse	Pizza, Modern	Northeast Portland	Casual	$35
8.6	Wildwood	Modern	Northwest Portland	Upmarket	$70
8.5	Belly Timber	Modern	Hawthorne	Upmarket	$45
8.5	East India Co.	Indian	Downtown	Casual	$40
8.4	Patanegra	Spanish	Northwest Portland	Upmarket	$50
8.4	Hiroshi Sushi	Japanese	Pearl District	Upmarket	$50
8.3	Alba Osteria	Italian	Southwest Portland	Upmarket	$60
8.3	Auténtica	Mexican	Alberta Arts District	Upmarket	$45
8.2	Carafe Bistro	French	Downtown	Upmarket	$45
8.2	The Observatory	Modern	Southeast Portland	Casual	$35
8.2	Nick's Italian Café	Italian, Modern	McMinnville	Upmarket	$70
8.2	Serratto	Modern	Northwest Portland	Upmarket	$60
8.1	Bar Avignon	Modern	Division/Clinton	Upmarket	$45
8.1	Caffè Allora	Italian, Pizza	Pearl District	Casual	$40
8.0	MetroVino	Modern	Pearl District	Upmarket	$45
8.0	Bete-Lukas	Ethiopian	Division/Clinton	Casual	$35
8.0	Beijing Hot Pot	Chinese	82nd Avenue Area	Casual	$20
8.0	Slow Bar	American	Southeast Portland	Bar	$25
7.9	Brøder Comfort Food	Scandinavian	Division/Clinton	Casual	$30
7.9	Gino's	Italian, Modern	Sellwood	Casual	$40
7.9	Vindalho	Indian	Division/Clinton	Upmarket	$60
7.8	Fratelli Cucina	Italian	Pearl District	Casual	$40
7.8	Le Happy	Crêpes	Northwest Portland	Casual	$15
7.8	Piazza Italia	Italian	Pearl District	Casual	$35
7.8	Lincoln	Italian, Modern	Mississippi	Upmarket	$50
7.8	Toro Bravo	Spanish	Northeast Portland	Upmarket	$45
7.7	Caffè Mingo	Italian	Northwest Portland	Upmarket	$50
7.7	North 45	American, Belgian	Northwest Portland	Bar	$35
7.7	Besaw's Café	Modern	Northwest Portland	Casual	$40
7.6	Higgins	Modern	Downtown	Upmarket	$60
7.6	Siam Society	Pan-Asian, Thai	Alberta Arts District	Casual	$40
7.6	Urban Farmer	Steakhouse	Downtown	Upmarket	$110
7.5	Fenouil	French, Modern	Pearl District	Upmarket	$60
7.5	Ruth's Chris	Steakhouse	Downtown	Upmarket	$100
7.4	Bistro Maison	French	McMinnville	Upmarket	$60
7.4	The Farm Café	Modern, Vegefusion	East Burnside	Upmarket	$45
7.4	Lucy's Table	Modern	Northwest Portland	Upmarket	$50
7.4	Nuestra Cocina	Mexican	Division/Clinton	Upmarket	$40
7.3	Gilt Club	Modern	Old Town	Upmarket	$60
7.3	La Calaca Comelona	Mexican	Belmont	Casual	$35
7.3	Helser's on Alberta	American	Alberta Arts District	Casual	$15
7.2	Biwa	Japanese, Korean	Southeast Portland	Casual	$35
7.2	Miss Delta	Southern	Mississippi	Casual	$35
7.1	Mother's Bistro & Bar	American	Downtown	Casual	$40
7.1	Café Castagna	Modern	Hawthorne	Upmarket	$45

Date-friendly *continued*

7.1	Detour Café	American	Division/Clinton	Casual	$15
7.1	El Gaucho	Steakhouse	Downtown	Upmarket	$100
7.1	5th Quadrant	American	Mississippi	Bar	$15
7.1	Southpark Seafood	Modern, Seafood	Downtown	Casual	$40
7.0	Bye and Bye	Vegefusion	Northeast Portland	Bar	$30
7.0	Dots Café	American	Division/Clinton	Bar	$20
7.0	Tastebud	Pizza	Southeast Portland	Casual	$30
7.0	Yakuza Lounge	Japanese	Alberta Arts District	Upmarket	$60
7.0	Nel Centro	Italian	Downtown	Upmarket	$60
7.0	Silk	Pan-Asian	Pearl District	Upmarket	$40
6.9	Lucca	Italian, Modern	Northeast Portland	Casual	$35
6.8	The Press Club	Sandwiches, Crêpes	Division/Clinton	Casual	$20
6.8	Iorio	Italian	Hawthorne	Upmarket	$50
6.8	Papa Haydn	Modern	Multiple locations	Upmarket	$50
6.8	Deschutes Brewery	American	Pearl District	Casual	$25
6.8	Bluehour	Modern	Pearl District	Upmarket	$70
6.7	Tara Thai	Thai	Northwest Portland	Casual	$25
6.7	Acropolis Club	Steakhouse	Sellwood	Strip club	$15
6.7	Navarre	Modern	Northeast Portland	Upmarket	$45
6.6	Driftwood Room	American	Southwest Portland	Bar	$35
6.6	Bamboo Sushi	Japanese	Southeast Portland	Upmarket	$40
6.5	Brazil Grill	Brazilian	Southwest Portland	Casual	$40
6.5	¡OBA!	Nuevo Latino	Pearl District	Upmarket	$60
6.4	Portland City Grill	Steakhouse	Downtown	Upmarket	$70
6.4	Bar Mingo	Italian	Northwest Portland	Casual	$35
6.4	Vault Martini	Modern	Pearl District	Bar	$35
6.3	Masu	Japanese	Downtown	Upmarket	$45
6.2	Ciao Vito	Italian	Alberta Arts District	Casual	$40
6.2	Equinox	Modern	Northeast Portland	Casual	$40
6.1	Doug Fir	American	East Burnside	Bar	$30
6.1	Noble Rot	Modern	East Burnside	Upmarket	$40
6.1	Saucebox	Pan-Asian	Downtown	Bar	$40
6.1	Mingo	Italian, Pizza	Beaverton	Upmarket	$50
6.0	Carlyle	Modern	Northwest Portland	Upmarket	$80
6.0	Berlin Inn	German	Southeast Portland	Casual	$40
5.9	Bastas Trattoria	Italian	Northwest Portland	Upmarket	$45
5.7	Living Room Theaters	Modern	Downtown	Theater	$35
5.7	Thatch Tiki Bar	Hawaiian	Northeast Portland	Bar	$30
5.6	Everett Street Bistro	Modern	Pearl District	Casual	$35
5.6	RingSide Steakhouse	Steakhouse	Multiple locations	Upmarket	$80
5.5	Lauro Kitchen	Modern	Division/Clinton	Upmarket	$50
5.3	Sapphire Hotel	Modern, Pan-Asian	Hawthorne	Bar	$20
5.3	Tube	Vegefusion	Old Town	Bar	$15
5.3	Bombay Cricket Club	Indian	Hawthorne	Upmarket	$40
5.3	23Hoyt	Modern	Northwest Portland	Upmarket	$60
5.0	50 Plates	Modern	Pearl District	Upmarket	$40
4.9	Huber's Restaurant	American	Downtown	Casual	$40
4.9	Typhoon!	Pan-Asian, Thai	Multiple locations	Casual	$40
4.9	Westcafé	Modern	Downtown	Casual	$35
4.7	Jake's	Seafood, American	Multiple locations	Upmarket	$50
3.9	McMenamins	American	Multiple locations	Casual	$30
3.7	Le Bistro Montage	Southern	Southeast Portland	Casual	$35
3.0	Lucky Labrador	American	Multiple locations	Bar	$15
NR	Backspace	Coffee, Vegefusion	Old Town	Café	
NR	Bakery Bar	Baked goods	Multiple locations	Counter	
NR	Cacao Chocolate	Sweets	Multiple locations	Counter	
NR	Pix Pâtisserie	Baked goods	Multiple locations	Counter	
NR	Sahagún Chocolates	Sweets	Northwest Portland	Market	
NR	Voodoo Doughnut	Baked goods	Multiple locations	Counter	
NR	World Cup Coffee	Coffee	Multiple locations	Café	

Delivery

8.0	Kenny & Zuke's Sandwich	Sandwiches	Northwest Portland	Counter	$15
7.4	Kornblatt's Deli	Sandwiches	Northwest Portland	Casual	$20
6.8	Fire on the Mountain	American	Multiple locations	Counter	$20
6.5	¡OBA!	Nuevo Latino	Pearl District	Upmarket	$60
6.4	Escape From NY	Pizza	Northwest Portland	Counter	$10
6.4	Elephants Delicatessen	American	Multiple locations	Counter	$20
5.8	Vincenté's Pizza	Pizza	Hawthorne	Casual	$20
5.8	Pizzicato	Pizza, Sandwiches	Multiple locations	Counter	$20
3.6	Pizza Schmizza	Pizza, Italian	Multiple locations	Counter	$25
NR	Fleur de Lis	Baked goods	Northeast Portland	Counter	
NR	New Seasons Market	Groceries	Multiple locations	Market	
NR	Pix Pâtisserie	Baked goods	Multiple locations	Counter	

Kid-friendly

9.3	Apizza Scholls	Pizza	Hawthorne	Casual	$30
9.0	Ken's Artisan Pizza	Pizza	Southeast Portland	Casual	$25
8.8	Kenny & Zuke's	Sandwiches	Downtown	Casual	$15
8.7	Puerto Marquez	Mexican	Far East Portland	Casual	$25
8.6	Pine State Biscuits	Sandwiches	Belmont	Counter	$15
8.3	Pho Oregon	Vietnamese	82nd Avenue Area	Casual	$15
8.3	Podnah's Pit	Barbecue, Southern	Northeast Portland	Casual	$25
8.2	The Waffle Window	Baked goods	Hawthorne	Counter	$10
8.1	Bunk Sandwiches	Sandwiches	Southeast Portland	Counter	$15
8.1	Meat Cheese Bread	Sandwiches	Southeast Portland	Counter	$15
8.1	Shenzhen	Chinese, Seafood	82nd Avenue Area	Casual	$25
8.0	Ken's Artisan Bakery	Baked goods	Northwest Portland	Café	$15
8.0	Kenny & Zuke's Sandwich	Sandwiches	Northwest Portland	Counter	$15
8.0	Yummy Yummy	Chinese, Seafood	82nd Avenue Area	Casual	$35
7.9	Original Halibut's	Seafood	Alberta Arts District	Counter	$20
7.7	Besaw's Café	Modern	Northwest Portland	Casual	$40
7.6	John Street Café	American	North Portland	Casual	$20
7.5	Kinara Thai Bistro	Thai	Southwest Portland	Casual	$25
7.4	Pause	American	North Portland	Casual	$35
7.4	Kornblatt's Deli	Sandwiches	Northwest Portland	Casual	$20
7.3	Screen Door	Southern	Southeast Portland	Casual	$35
7.2	Decarli	Italian, Modern	Beaverton	Upmarket	$50
7.2	¿Por Qué No?	Mexican	Multiple locations	Counter	$20
7.1	Detour Café	American	Division/Clinton	Casual	$15
7.0	Vita Café	Vegefusion	Alberta Arts District	Casual	$25
7.0	Brunchbox	Sandwiches	Downtown	Food cart	$5
6.9	Lucca	Italian, Modern	Northeast Portland	Casual	$35
6.9	Pastini Pastaria	Italian	Multiple locations	Casual	$25
6.8	Justa Pasta	Italian	Northwest Portland	Counter	$15
6.8	Fire on the Mountain	American	Multiple locations	Counter	$20
6.7	The Country Cat	Modern, Southern	Southeast Portland	Casual	$40
6.7	Addy's Sandwich Bar	Sandwiches	Downtown	Food cart	$10
6.6	Papa G's	Vegefusion	Division/Clinton	Counter	$20
6.6	Altengartz	German	Downtown	Food cart	$5
6.4	Escape From NY	Pizza	Northwest Portland	Counter	$10
6.4	Elephants Delicatessen	American	Multiple locations	Counter	$20
6.4	Cricket Café	American	Belmont	Casual	$20
6.3	Asian Station Café	Chinese	Downtown	Food cart	$5
6.1	Alameda Café	American	Northeast Portland	Casual	$30
6.0	Original Hotcake House	American	Southeast Portland	Casual	$20
6.0	Pepino's Mexican Grill	Mexican	Multiple locations	Counter	$10
5.9	Sweet Basil	Thai	Multiple locations	Casual	$25
5.9	Grand Central Bakery	Baked goods	Multiple locations	Counter	$15
5.8	Pizzicato	Pizza, Sandwiches	Multiple locations	Counter	$20
5.7	Byways Café	American	Pearl District	Casual	$15
5.6	The Tin Shed	Vegefusion	Alberta Arts District	Casual	$30
5.4	Arabian Breeze	Lebanese	Northeast Portland	Casual	$25
5.2	Burgerville	American	Multiple locations	Counter	$10

Kid-friendly *continued*

5.1	SuperDog	American	Multiple locations	Counter	$10
5.0	Laughing Planet	Vegefusion	Multiple locations	Counter	$15
5.0	FlavourSpot	American	Multiple locations	Food cart	$5
5.0	Russell Street BBQ	Barbecue, Southern	Northeast Portland	Casual	$25
4.9	Huber's Restaurant	American	Downtown	Casual	$40
4.4	Bamboo Grove	Hawaiian	Southwest Portland	Casual	$25
3.9	McMenamins	American	Multiple locations	Casual	$30
3.6	Pizza Schmizza	Pizza, Italian	Multiple locations	Counter	$25
NR	Baker & Spice	Baked goods	Southwest Portland	Counter	
NR	Bakery Bar	Baked goods	Multiple locations	Counter	
NR	Cacao Chocolate	Sweets	Multiple locations	Counter	
NR	Cupcake Jones	Baked goods	Pearl District	Counter	
NR	Fleur de Lis	Baked goods	Northeast Portland	Counter	
NR	New Seasons Market	Groceries	Multiple locations	Market	
NR	World Cup Coffee	Coffee	Multiple locations	Café	

Live music *of any kind, from jazz piano to rock, even occasionally*

9.1	EaT: An Oyster Bar	Seafood, Southern	Mississippi	Casual	$40
8.8	Andina	Peruvian	Pearl District	Upmarket	$70
8.1	Bar Avignon	Modern	Division/Clinton	Upmarket	$45
8.0	Bete-Lukas	Ethiopian	Division/Clinton	Casual	$35
7.8	Fratelli Cucina	Italian	Pearl District	Casual	$40
7.7	North 45	American, Belgian	Northwest Portland	Bar	$35
7.7	Echo Restaurant	Modern	Northeast Portland	Casual	$40
7.7	E'Njoni Café	Ethiopian	North Portland	Casual	$30
7.6	Horse Brass Pub	British	Belmont	Casual	$25
7.5	Fenouil	French, Modern	Pearl District	Upmarket	$60
7.1	El Gaucho	Steakhouse	Downtown	Upmarket	$100
7.0	Nel Centro	Italian	Downtown	Upmarket	$60
6.8	The Press Club	Sandwiches, Crêpes	Division/Clinton	Casual	$20
6.8	Fire on the Mountain	American	Multiple locations	Counter	$20
6.7	Mississippi Pizza Pub	Pizza	Mississippi	Counter	$20
6.6	Papa G's	Vegefusion	Division/Clinton	Counter	$20
6.5	Brazil Grill	Brazilian	Southwest Portland	Casual	$40
6.4	Green Dragon	American	Southeast Portland	Casual	$25
6.1	Doug Fir	American	East Burnside	Bar	$30
6.0	New Old Lompoc	American	Northwest Portland	Casual	$25
5.6	The Tin Shed	Vegefusion	Alberta Arts District	Casual	$30
5.6	The Heathman	American	Downtown	Upmarket	$60
5.5	Bay 13	Seafood	Pearl District	Upmarket	$50
5.3	Sapphire Hotel	Modern, Pan-Asian	Hawthorne	Bar	$20
4.9	Westcafé	Modern	Downtown	Casual	$35
4.4	Bamboo Grove	Hawaiian	Southwest Portland	Casual	$25
3.9	McMenamins	American	Multiple locations	Casual	$30
3.0	Lucky Labrador	American	Multiple locations	Bar	$15
NR	Backspace	Coffee, Vegefusion	Old Town	Café	
NR	Caffé Umbria	Coffee	Pearl District	Café	
NR	Coffee Time	Coffee	Northwest Portland	Café	
NR	Fleur de Lis	Baked goods	Northeast Portland	Counter	
NR	Pix Pâtisserie	Baked goods	Multiple locations	Counter	

Outdoor dining *of any kind, from sidewalk tables to a big backyard patio*

9.5	Park Kitchen	Modern	Pearl District	Upmarket	$50
9.5	Pok Pok	Thai	Division/Clinton	Casual	$35
9.3	Ping	Pan-Asian	Old Town	Casual	$35
9.2	Tabla	Modern	Northeast Portland	Upmarket	$45
9.2	Paley's Place	Modern	Northwest Portland	Upmarket	$80
9.1	DOC	Italian	Alberta Arts District	Upmarket	$70
9.1	Clarklewis	Modern	Southeast Portland	Upmarket	$70
9.1	Laurelhurst Market	Modern	Northeast Portland	Casual	$50
9.1	EaT: An Oyster Bar	Seafood, Southern	Mississippi	Casual	$40

Outdoor dining *continued*

9.0	Nostrana	Italian, Pizza	Southeast Portland	Upmarket	$55
9.0	Little T American Baker	Baked goods	Division/Clinton	Café	$15
9.0	Karam Lebanese	Lebanese	Downtown	Casual	$30
9.0	Ken's Artisan Pizza	Pizza	Southeast Portland	Casual	$25
8.9	Ned Ludd	Modern	Northeast Portland	Upmarket	$45
8.9	Castagna	Modern	Hawthorne	Upmarket	$80
8.8	Andina	Peruvian	Pearl District	Upmarket	$70
8.8	Branch	Modern	Alberta Arts District	Casual	$40
8.8	Lovely Hula Hands	Modern	Mississippi	Casual	$40
8.7	Ten01	Modern	Pearl District	Upmarket	$70
8.6	Firehouse	Pizza, Modern	Northeast Portland	Casual	$35
8.6	Wildwood	Modern	Northwest Portland	Upmarket	$70
8.6	Nicholas Restaurant	Middle Eastern	Southeast Portland	Casual	$20
8.6	Pine State Biscuits	Sandwiches	Belmont	Counter	$15
8.6	La Sirenita	Mexican	Multiple locations	Counter	$15
8.5	Belly Timber	Modern	Hawthorne	Upmarket	$45
8.4	Patanegra	Spanish	Northwest Portland	Upmarket	$50
8.4	Little Red Bike Café	Modern	North Portland	Counter	$15
8.3	Alba Osteria	Italian	Southwest Portland	Upmarket	$60
8.3	Auténtica	Mexican	Alberta Arts District	Upmarket	$45
8.3	Podnah's Pit	Barbecue, Southern	Northeast Portland	Casual	$25
8.2	Carafe Bistro	French	Downtown	Upmarket	$45
8.2	The Observatory	Modern	Southeast Portland	Casual	$35
8.2	Serratto	Modern	Northwest Portland	Upmarket	$60
8.2	Tábor	Czech	Downtown	Food cart	$10
8.2	The Waffle Window	Baked goods	Hawthorne	Counter	$10
8.1	Pambiche	Cuban	Northeast Portland	Casual	$35
8.1	Syun Izakaya	Japanese	Hillsboro	Casual	$35
8.1	Bar Avignon	Modern	Division/Clinton	Upmarket	$45
8.1	Caffè Allora	Italian, Pizza	Pearl District	Casual	$40
8.1	Bunk Sandwiches	Sandwiches	Southeast Portland	Counter	$15
8.1	Meat Cheese Bread	Sandwiches	Southeast Portland	Counter	$15
8.0	MetroVino	Modern	Pearl District	Upmarket	$45
8.0	Ken's Artisan Bakery	Baked goods	Northwest Portland	Café	$15
8.0	Kenny & Zuke's Sandwich	Sandwiches	Northwest Portland	Counter	$15
8.0	Slow Bar	American	Southeast Portland	Bar	$25
8.0	Nong's Khao Man Gai	Thai	Downtown	Food cart	$5
7.9	Brøder Comfort Food	Scandinavian	Division/Clinton	Casual	$30
7.9	Gino's	Italian, Modern	Sellwood	Casual	$40
7.9	Vindalho	Indian	Division/Clinton	Upmarket	$60
7.9	Original Halibut's	Seafood	Alberta Arts District	Counter	$20
7.8	Fratelli Cucina	Italian	Pearl District	Casual	$40
7.8	Le Happy	Crêpes	Northwest Portland	Casual	$15
7.8	Piazza Italia	Italian	Pearl District	Casual	$35
7.7	Caffè Mingo	Italian	Northwest Portland	Upmarket	$50
7.7	North 45	American, Belgian	Northwest Portland	Bar	$35
7.7	Besaw's Café	Modern	Northwest Portland	Casual	$40
7.7	Echo Restaurant	Modern	Northeast Portland	Casual	$40
7.7	E'Njoni Café	Ethiopian	North Portland	Casual	$30
7.6	Siam Society	Pan-Asian, Thai	Alberta Arts District	Casual	$40
7.6	John Street Café	American	North Portland	Casual	$20
7.6	Euro Dish	Polish	Downtown	Food cart	$10
7.6	Wong's King Seafood	Chinese, Seafood	82nd Avenue Area	Casual	$45
7.5	Fenouil	French, Modern	Pearl District	Upmarket	$60
7.5	Delta Café	Southern	Southeast Portland	Casual	$35
7.5	Garden State	Italian, Sandwiches	Sellwood	Food cart	$10
7.4	Bistro Maison	French	McMinnville	Upmarket	$60
7.4	The Farm Café	Modern, Vegefusion	East Burnside	Upmarket	$45
7.4	Lucy's Table	Modern	Northwest Portland	Upmarket	$50
7.4	Nuestra Cocina	Mexican	Division/Clinton	Upmarket	$40
7.4	Pause	American	North Portland	Casual	$35
7.4	Kornblatt's Deli	Sandwiches	Northwest Portland	Casual	$20

Outdoor dining _continued_

7.3	Veritable Quandary	Modern	Downtown	Upmarket	$45
7.3	Gilt Club	Modern	Old Town	Upmarket	$60
7.3	La Calaca Comelona	Mexican	Belmont	Casual	$35
7.3	Teardrop Lounge	Modern	Pearl District	Bar	$35
7.3	Tanuki	Japanese, Korean	Northwest Portland	Casual	$35
7.3	Helser's on Alberta	American	Alberta Arts District	Casual	$15
7.3	Screen Door	Southern	Southeast Portland	Casual	$35
7.3	Morton's	Steakhouse	Downtown	Upmarket	$100
7.2	Biwa	Japanese, Korean	Southeast Portland	Casual	$35
7.2	Decarli	Italian, Modern	Beaverton	Upmarket	$50
7.2	¿Por Qué No?	Mexican	Multiple locations	Counter	$20
7.2	Nob Hill Bar & Grill	American	Northwest Portland	Bar	$20
7.2	Blossoming Lotus	Vegefusion	Multiple locations	Casual	$30
7.1	Mother's Bistro & Bar	American	Downtown	Casual	$40
7.1	Pad Thai Kitchen	Thai	Belmont	Casual	$25
7.1	3 Doors Down Café	Modern	Southeast Portland	Upmarket	$45
7.1	Café Castagna	Modern	Hawthorne	Upmarket	$45
7.1	Detour Café	American	Division/Clinton	Casual	$15
7.1	5th Quadrant	American	Mississippi	Bar	$15
7.1	Southpark Seafood	Modern, Seafood	Downtown	Casual	$40
7.1	Jin Wah	Chinese	Multiple locations	Casual	$25
7.0	Bye and Bye	Vegefusion	Northeast Portland	Bar	$30
7.0	Tastebud	Pizza	Southeast Portland	Casual	$30
7.0	Yakuza Lounge	Japanese	Alberta Arts District	Upmarket	$60
7.0	Brunchbox	Sandwiches	Downtown	Food cart	$5
7.0	Nel Centro	Italian	Downtown	Upmarket	$60
7.0	Silk	Pan-Asian	Pearl District	Upmarket	$40
7.0	The Whole Bowl	Vegefusion	Multiple locations	Food cart	$5
6.9	Petisco	Sandwiches	Northeast Portland	Casual	$20
6.9	Aladdin's Café	Lebanese	Northeast Portland	Casual	$20
6.9	Campbell's BBQ	Barbecue, Southern	Southeast Portland	Casual	$20
6.9	Lucca	Italian, Modern	Northeast Portland	Casual	$35
6.9	Ziba's Pitas	Bosnian	Downtown	Food cart	$5
6.9	Pastini Pastaria	Italian	Multiple locations	Casual	$25
6.8	The Press Club	Sandwiches, Crêpes	Division/Clinton	Casual	$20
6.8	Papa Haydn	Modern	Multiple locations	Upmarket	$50
6.8	Deschutes Brewery	American	Pearl District	Casual	$25
6.8	Justa Pasta	Italian	Northwest Portland	Counter	$15
6.8	Bluehour	Modern	Pearl District	Upmarket	$70
6.8	Fire on the Mountain	American	Multiple locations	Counter	$20
6.7	Mississippi Pizza Pub	Pizza	Mississippi	Counter	$20
6.7	Tara Thai	Thai	Northwest Portland	Casual	$25
6.7	Addy's Sandwich Bar	Sandwiches	Downtown	Food cart	$10
6.7	La Bonita	Mexican	Alberta Arts District	Counter	$15
6.7	Navarre	Modern	Northeast Portland	Upmarket	$45
6.7	Jam on Hawthorne	American	Hawthorne	Casual	$25
6.6	Bernie's	Southern	Alberta Arts District	Casual	$40
6.6	Papa G's	Vegefusion	Division/Clinton	Counter	$20
6.6	Altengartz	German	Downtown	Food cart	$5
6.5	¡OBA!	Nuevo Latino	Pearl District	Upmarket	$60
6.5	Sal's Famous Italian	Italian, Pizza	Northwest Portland	Casual	$35
6.4	Café Nell	American	Northwest Portland	Casual	$40
6.4	Green Dragon	American	Southeast Portland	Casual	$25
6.4	Bar Mingo	Italian	Northwest Portland	Casual	$35
6.4	Escape From NY	Pizza	Northwest Portland	Counter	$10
6.4	Potato Champion	American	Hawthorne	Food cart	$5
6.4	Cricket Café	American	Belmont	Casual	$20
6.4	Vault Martini	Modern	Pearl District	Bar	$35
6.3	St. Honoré	Baked goods	Northwest Portland	Café	$15
6.3	Dove Vivi Pizza Deli	Pizza	Northeast Portland	Casual	$15
6.3	Asian Station Café	Chinese	Downtown	Food cart	$5
6.2	Ciao Vito	Italian	Alberta Arts District	Casual	$40

Outdoor dining *continued*

6.2	Equinox	Modern	Northeast Portland	Casual	$40
6.1	Doug Fir	American	East Burnside	Bar	$30
6.1	Noble Rot	Modern	East Burnside	Upmarket	$40
6.1	Crowsenberg's	Baked goods	Downtown	Café	$15
6.1	Saucebox	Pan-Asian	Downtown	Bar	$40
6.1	Grilled Cheese Grill	American	Northeast Portland	Food cart	$5
6.1	Alameda Café	American	Northeast Portland	Casual	$30
6.1	Mingo	Italian, Pizza	Beaverton	Upmarket	$50
6.0	Carlyle	Modern	Northwest Portland	Upmarket	$80
6.0	Berlin Inn	German	Southeast Portland	Casual	$40
6.0	New Old Lompoc	American	Northwest Portland	Casual	$25
6.0	Madena of the Pearl	Lebanese	Pearl District	Casual	$20
6.0	Pepino's Mexican Grill	Mexican	Multiple locations	Counter	$10
5.9	Bastas Trattoria	Italian	Northwest Portland	Upmarket	$45
5.9	Sweet Basil	Thai	Multiple locations	Casual	$25
5.9	Grand Central Bakery	Baked goods	Multiple locations	Counter	$15
5.8	Vincenté's Pizza	Pizza	Hawthorne	Casual	$20
5.8	Pizzicato	Pizza, Sandwiches	Multiple locations	Counter	$20
5.7	Byways Café	American	Pearl District	Casual	$15
5.7	Henry's 12th St. Tavern	American	Pearl District	Upmarket	$40
5.6	The Tin Shed	Vegefusion	Alberta Arts District	Casual	$30
5.6	Everett Street Bistro	Modern	Pearl District	Casual	$35
5.6	Rogue Public House	American	Pearl District	Bar	$25
5.6	The Heathman	American	Downtown	Upmarket	$60
5.5	Bay 13	Seafood	Pearl District	Upmarket	$50
5.5	Lauro Kitchen	Modern	Division/Clinton	Upmarket	$50
5.4	McCormick & Schmick's	Seafood, American	Multiple locations	Upmarket	$60
5.4	Arabian Breeze	Lebanese	Northeast Portland	Casual	$25
5.3	Sapphire Hotel	Modern, Pan-Asian	Hawthorne	Bar	$20
5.3	Bread and Ink Café	American	Hawthorne	Casual	$40
5.3	23Hoyt	Modern	Northwest Portland	Upmarket	$60
5.2	Burgerville	American	Multiple locations	Counter	$10
5.1	SuperDog	American	Multiple locations	Counter	$10
5.0	Laughing Planet	Vegefusion	Multiple locations	Counter	$15
5.0	FlavourSpot	American	Multiple locations	Food cart	$5
5.0	50 Plates	Modern	Pearl District	Upmarket	$40
5.0	Russell Street BBQ	Barbecue, Southern	Northeast Portland	Casual	$25
4.9	Huber's Restaurant	American	Downtown	Casual	$40
4.9	Typhoon!	Pan-Asian, Thai	Multiple locations	Casual	$40
4.9	Westcafé	Modern	Downtown	Casual	$35
4.9	Taquería Los Gorditos	Mexican	Division/Clinton	Food cart	$5
4.8	Vivace	Sandwiches, Crêpes	Northwest Portland	Café	$15
4.7	Jake's	Seafood, American	Multiple locations	Upmarket	$50
4.7	Cup & Saucer Café	American	Multiple locations	Casual	$15
4.5	The Liberty Glass	American, Italian	North Portland	Bar	$20
4.4	Bamboo Grove	Hawaiian	Southwest Portland	Casual	$25
4.1	Samurai Bento	Japanese	Downtown	Food cart	$15
3.9	McMenamins	American	Multiple locations	Casual	$30
3.6	Pizza Schmizza	Pizza, Italian	Multiple locations	Counter	$25
3.0	Lucky Labrador	American	Multiple locations	Bar	$15
2.5	India Chaat House	Indian	Downtown	Food cart	$5
NR	Albina Press	Coffee	North Portland	Café	
NR	Backspace	Coffee, Vegefusion	Old Town	Café	
NR	Barista Café	Coffee	Pearl District	Café	
NR	Caffé Umbria	Coffee	Pearl District	Café	
NR	Coffee Time	Coffee	Northwest Portland	Café	
NR	Coffeehouse Northwest	Coffee	Northwest Portland	Café	
NR	Fleur de Lis	Baked goods	Northeast Portland	Counter	
NR	Food Fight Grocery	Groceries	Southeast Portland	Market	
NR	New Seasons Market	Groceries	Multiple locations	Market	
NR	Pix Pâtisserie	Baked goods	Multiple locations	Counter	
NR	Ristretto Roasters	Coffee	Multiple locations	Café	

Outdoor dining *continued*

NR	Spella Caffè	Coffee	Downtown	Food cart
NR	Stumptown Roasters	Coffee	Multiple locations	Café
NR	Whiffies Fried Pies	Baked goods	Hawthorne	Food cart

Wi-Fi

9.4	Clyde Common	Modern	Downtown	Upmarket	$45
9.3	Beaker & Flask	Modern	Southeast Portland	Casual	$35
9.0	Little T American Baker	Baked goods	Division/Clinton	Café	$15
9.0	Karam Lebanese	Lebanese	Downtown	Casual	$30
8.8	Andina	Peruvian	Pearl District	Upmarket	$70
8.4	Little Red Bike Café	Modern	North Portland	Counter	$15
8.2	Evoe	Modern	Hawthorne	Casual	$15
8.1	Caffè Allora	Italian, Pizza	Pearl District	Casual	$40
8.1	Bunk Sandwiches	Sandwiches	Southeast Portland	Counter	$15
8.1	Meat Cheese Bread	Sandwiches	Southeast Portland	Counter	$15
7.9	Brøder Comfort Food	Scandinavian	Division/Clinton	Casual	$30
7.7	Besaw's Café	Modern	Northwest Portland	Casual	$40
7.7	E'Njoni Café	Ethiopian	North Portland	Casual	$30
7.5	Fenouil	French, Modern	Pearl District	Upmarket	$60
7.5	Ruth's Chris	Steakhouse	Downtown	Upmarket	$100
7.3	Gilt Club	Modern	Old Town	Upmarket	$60
7.2	Decarli	Italian, Modern	Beaverton	Upmarket	$50
7.1	El Gaucho	Steakhouse	Downtown	Upmarket	$100
7.1	5th Quadrant	American	Mississippi	Bar	$15
7.0	Vita Café	Vegefusion	Alberta Arts District	Casual	$25
7.0	Nel Centro	Italian	Downtown	Upmarket	$60
6.9	Aladdin's Café	Lebanese	Northeast Portland	Casual	$20
6.9	Lucca	Italian, Modern	Northeast Portland	Casual	$35
6.8	The Press Club	Sandwiches, Crêpes	Division/Clinton	Casual	$20
6.7	Navarre	Modern	Northeast Portland	Upmarket	$45
6.6	Driftwood Room	American	Southwest Portland	Bar	$35
6.6	Bamboo Sushi	Japanese	Southeast Portland	Upmarket	$40
6.6	Papa G's	Vegefusion	Division/Clinton	Counter	$20
6.5	¡OBA!	Nuevo Latino	Pearl District	Upmarket	$60
6.4	Bar Mingo	Italian	Northwest Portland	Casual	$35
6.3	Masu	Japanese	Downtown	Upmarket	$45
6.2	Equinox	Modern	Northeast Portland	Casual	$40
6.1	Doug Fir	American	East Burnside	Bar	$30
6.1	Crowsenberg's	Baked goods	Downtown	Café	$15
6.0	Berlin Inn	German	Southeast Portland	Casual	$40
6.0	Madena of the Pearl	Lebanese	Pearl District	Casual	$20
5.7	Living Room Theaters	Modern	Downtown	Theater	$35
5.6	Rogue Public House	American	Pearl District	Bar	$25
5.6	The Heathman	American	Downtown	Upmarket	$60
5.5	Bay 13	Seafood	Pearl District	Upmarket	$50
5.4	Arabian Breeze	Lebanese	Northeast Portland	Casual	$25
5.3	Sapphire Hotel	Modern, Pan-Asian	Hawthorne	Bar	$20
5.2	Burgerville	American	Multiple locations	Counter	$10
5.0	Laughing Planet	Vegefusion	Multiple locations	Counter	$15
5.0	50 Plates	Modern	Pearl District	Upmarket	$40
4.9	Westcafé	Modern	Downtown	Casual	$35
4.8	Vivace	Sandwiches, Crêpes	Northwest Portland	Café	$15
4.4	Bamboo Grove	Hawaiian	Southwest Portland	Casual	$25
4.1	Paradox Café	Vegefusion	Belmont	Casual	$20
3.9	McMenamins	American	Multiple locations	Casual	$30
3.0	Lucky Labrador	American	Multiple locations	Bar	$15
NR	Albina Press	Coffee	North Portland	Café	
NR	Backspace	Coffee, Vegefusion	Old Town	Café	
NR	Bakery Bar	Baked goods	Multiple locations	Counter	
NR	Barista Café	Coffee	Pearl District	Café	
NR	Cacao Chocolate	Sweets	Multiple locations	Counter	
NR	Coffee Time	Coffee	Northwest Portland	Café	

Wi-Fi *continued*

NR	Coffeehouse Northwest	Coffee	Northwest Portland	Café
NR	Ristretto Roasters	Coffee	Multiple locations	Café
NR	Stumptown Roasters	Coffee	Multiple locations	Café
NR	World Cup Coffee	Coffee	Multiple locations	Café

Vegetarian-friendly guide

Places to eat that are **unusually strong in vegetarian options.** This doesn't just mean that there are salads or veggie pastas available; it means that vegetarians will really be happy with the selection at these places. Ranked by **food rating** unless otherwise noted. Establishments that don't serve full meals (e.g. cafés, bakeries, grocery stores) appear as "NR" at the bottom of the list.

All vegetarian-friendly establishments

9.3	Apizza Scholls	Pizza	Hawthorne	Casual	$30
9.1	DOC	Italian	Alberta Arts District	Upmarket	$70
9.0	Nostrana	Italian, Pizza	Southeast Portland	Upmarket	$55
9.0	Little T American Baker	Baked goods	Division/Clinton	Café	$15
9.0	Karam Lebanese	Lebanese	Downtown	Casual	$30
9.0	Ken's Artisan Pizza	Pizza	Southeast Portland	Casual	$25
8.8	Andina	Peruvian	Pearl District	Upmarket	$70
8.7	Queen of Sheba	Ethiopian	Northeast Portland	Casual	$35
8.6	Firehouse	Pizza, Modern	Northeast Portland	Casual	$35
8.6	Nicholas Restaurant	Middle Eastern	Southeast Portland	Casual	$20
8.6	Pine State Biscuits	Sandwiches	Belmont	Counter	$15
8.5	East India Co.	Indian	Downtown	Casual	$40
8.4	Little Red Bike Café	Modern	North Portland	Counter	$15
8.3	Alba Osteria	Italian	Southwest Portland	Upmarket	$60
8.2	Tábor	Czech	Downtown	Food cart	$10
8.2	The Waffle Window	Baked goods	Hawthorne	Counter	$10
8.2	Evoe	Modern	Hawthorne	Casual	$15
8.2	Basha's Mediterranean	Middle Eastern	Downtown	Food cart	$5
8.1	Caffè Allora	Italian, Pizza	Pearl District	Casual	$40
8.1	Bunk Sandwiches	Sandwiches	Southeast Portland	Counter	$15
8.1	Meat Cheese Bread	Sandwiches	Southeast Portland	Counter	$15
8.0	Bete-Lukas	Ethiopian	Division/Clinton	Casual	$35
8.0	Ken's Artisan Bakery	Baked goods	Northwest Portland	Café	$15
8.0	Kenny & Zuke's Sandwich	Sandwiches	Northwest Portland	Counter	$15
7.9	Vindalho	Indian	Division/Clinton	Upmarket	$60
7.8	Fratelli Cucina	Italian	Pearl District	Casual	$40
7.8	Le Happy	Crêpes	Northwest Portland	Casual	$15
7.8	Piazza Italia	Italian	Pearl District	Casual	$35
7.8	Hot Pot City	Chinese	Downtown	Casual	$20
7.7	Caffè Mingo	Italian	Northwest Portland	Upmarket	$50
7.7	E'Njoni Café	Ethiopian	North Portland	Casual	$30
7.6	Siam Society	Pan-Asian, Thai	Alberta Arts District	Casual	$40
7.5	Delta Café	Southern	Southeast Portland	Casual	$35
7.5	Garden State	Italian, Sandwiches	Sellwood	Food cart	$10
7.4	The Farm Café	Modern, Vegefusion	East Burnside	Upmarket	$45
7.2	Biwa	Japanese, Korean	Southeast Portland	Casual	$35
7.2	Swagat	Indian	Multiple locations	Casual	$25
7.2	Blossoming Lotus	Vegefusion	Multiple locations	Casual	$30
7.1	Pad Thai Kitchen	Thai	Belmont	Casual	$25
7.1	Detour Café	American	Division/Clinton	Casual	$15
7.1	5th Quadrant	American	Mississippi	Bar	$15
7.1	Genies	American	Division/Clinton	Casual	$20
7.0	Bye and Bye	Vegefusion	Northeast Portland	Bar	$30
7.0	Dots Café	American	Division/Clinton	Bar	$20

All vegetarian-friendly establishments *continued*

7.0	Tastebud	Pizza	Southeast Portland	Casual	$30
7.0	Vita Café	Vegefusion	Alberta Arts District	Casual	$25
7.0	The Whole Bowl	Vegefusion	Multiple locations	Food cart	$5
6.9	Petisco	Sandwiches	Northeast Portland	Casual	$20
6.9	Aladdin's Café	Lebanese	Northeast Portland	Casual	$20
6.9	Lucca	Italian, Modern	Northeast Portland	Casual	$35
6.9	Ziba's Pitas	Bosnian	Downtown	Food cart	$5
6.9	Pastini Pastaria	Italian	Multiple locations	Casual	$25
6.8	The Press Club	Sandwiches, Crêpes	Division/Clinton	Casual	$20
6.8	Justa Pasta	Italian	Northwest Portland	Counter	$15
6.7	Mississippi Pizza Pub	Pizza	Mississippi	Counter	$20
6.7	KOi Fusion	Mexican, Korean	Southwest Portland	Food cart	$5
6.7	Navarre	Modern	Northeast Portland	Upmarket	$45
6.6	Papa G's	Vegefusion	Division/Clinton	Counter	$20
6.5	¡OBA!	Nuevo Latino	Pearl District	Upmarket	$60
6.4	Escape From NY	Pizza	Northwest Portland	Counter	$10
6.4	Elephants Delicatessen	American	Multiple locations	Counter	$20
6.4	Cricket Café	American	Belmont	Casual	$20
6.3	St. Honoré	Baked goods	Northwest Portland	Café	$15
6.3	Dove Vivi Pizza Deli	Pizza	Northeast Portland	Casual	$15
6.2	Ciao Vito	Italian	Alberta Arts District	Casual	$40
6.2	Equinox	Modern	Northeast Portland	Casual	$40
6.1	Noble Rot	Modern	East Burnside	Upmarket	$40
6.1	Crowsenberg's	Baked goods	Downtown	Café	$15
6.1	Gravy	American, Southern	Mississippi	Casual	$25
6.1	Grilled Cheese Grill	American	Northeast Portland	Food cart	$5
6.0	Berlin Inn	German	Southeast Portland	Casual	$40
6.0	Madena of the Pearl	Lebanese	Pearl District	Casual	$20
6.0	Pepino's Mexican Grill	Mexican	Multiple locations	Counter	$10
6.0	King Burrito	Mexican	North Portland	Counter	$10
5.9	Grand Central Bakery	Baked goods	Multiple locations	Counter	$15
5.8	Vincenté's Pizza	Pizza	Hawthorne	Casual	$20
5.8	Pizzicato	Pizza, Sandwiches	Multiple locations	Counter	$20
5.6	The Tin Shed	Vegefusion	Alberta Arts District	Casual	$30
5.4	Arabian Breeze	Lebanese	Northeast Portland	Casual	$25
5.3	Sapphire Hotel	Modern, Pan-Asian	Hawthorne	Bar	$20
5.3	Tube	Vegefusion	Old Town	Bar	$15
5.3	Bombay Cricket Club	Indian	Hawthorne	Upmarket	$40
5.3	Bread and Ink Café	American	Hawthorne	Casual	$40
5.0	Laughing Planet	Vegefusion	Multiple locations	Counter	$15
4.9	Typhoon!	Pan-Asian, Thai	Multiple locations	Casual	$40
4.9	Taquería Los Gorditos	Mexican	Division/Clinton	Food cart	$5
4.8	Vivace	Sandwiches, Crêpes	Northwest Portland	Café	$15
4.7	Cup & Saucer Café	American	Multiple locations	Casual	$15
4.1	Paradox Café	Vegefusion	Belmont	Casual	$20
3.6	Pizza Schmizza	Pizza, Italian	Multiple locations	Counter	$25
2.5	India Chaat House	Indian	Downtown	Food cart	$5
NR	Albina Press	Coffee	North Portland	Café	
NR	Backspace	Coffee, Vegefusion	Old Town	Café	
NR	Baker & Spice	Baked goods	Southwest Portland	Counter	
NR	Bakery Bar	Baked goods	Multiple locations	Counter	
NR	Cacao Chocolate	Sweets	Multiple locations	Counter	
NR	City Market	Groceries	Northwest Portland	Market	
NR	Coffee Time	Coffee	Northwest Portland	Café	
NR	Coffeehouse Northwest	Coffee	Northwest Portland	Café	
NR	Cupcake Jones	Baked goods	Pearl District	Counter	
NR	Fleur de Lis	Baked goods	Northeast Portland	Counter	
NR	Food Fight Grocery	Groceries	Southeast Portland	Market	
NR	Fubonn Supermarket	Groceries	82nd Avenue Area	Market	
NR	New Seasons Market	Groceries	Multiple locations	Market	
NR	Pastaworks	Groceries	Multiple locations	Market	
NR	Pix Pâtisserie	Baked goods	Multiple locations	Counter	

All vegetarian-friendly establishments *continued*

NR	Ristretto Roasters	Coffee	Multiple locations	Café
NR	Sahagún Chocolates	Sweets	Northwest Portland	Market
NR	Spella Caffè	Coffee	Downtown	Food cart
NR	Stumptown Roasters	Coffee	Multiple locations	Café
NR	Uwajimaya	Groceries, Japanese	Beaverton	Market
NR	Voodoo Doughnut	Baked goods	Multiple locations	Counter
NR	Whole Foods Market	Groceries	Multiple locations	Market
NR	World Cup Coffee	Coffee	Multiple locations	Café

Vegetarian-friendly with top feel ratings

9.5	DOC	Italian	Alberta Arts District	Upmarket	$70
9.5	Andina	Peruvian	Pearl District	Upmarket	$70
9.5	The Press Club	Sandwiches, Crêpes	Division/Clinton	Casual	$20
9.0	Firehouse	Pizza, Modern	Northeast Portland	Casual	$35
9.0	Alba Osteria	Italian	Southwest Portland	Upmarket	$60
9.0	Fratelli Cucina	Italian	Pearl District	Casual	$40
9.0	Caffè Mingo	Italian	Northwest Portland	Upmarket	$50
9.0	Siam Society	Pan-Asian, Thai	Alberta Arts District	Casual	$40
9.0	The Farm Café	Modern, Vegefusion	East Burnside	Upmarket	$45
9.0	Biwa	Japanese, Korean	Southeast Portland	Casual	$35
9.0	St. Honoré	Baked goods	Northwest Portland	Café	$15
9.0	Ciao Vito	Italian	Alberta Arts District	Casual	$40
9.0	The Tin Shed	Vegefusion	Alberta Arts District	Casual	$30
9.0	Sapphire Hotel	Modern, Pan-Asian	Hawthorne	Bar	$20
8.5	Nostrana	Italian, Pizza	Southeast Portland	Upmarket	$55
8.5	Vindalho	Indian	Division/Clinton	Upmarket	$60
8.5	Le Happy	Crêpes	Northwest Portland	Casual	$15
8.5	Piazza Italia	Italian	Pearl District	Casual	$35
8.5	Pad Thai Kitchen	Thai	Belmont	Casual	$25
8.5	Bye and Bye	Vegefusion	Northeast Portland	Bar	$30
8.5	Dots Café	American	Division/Clinton	Bar	$20
8.5	Mississippi Pizza Pub	Pizza	Mississippi	Counter	$20
8.5	Equinox	Modern	Northeast Portland	Casual	$40
8.5	Noble Rot	Modern	East Burnside	Upmarket	$40
8.5	Vincenté's Pizza	Pizza	Hawthorne	Casual	$20
8.0	Little T American Baker	Baked goods	Division/Clinton	Café	$15
8.0	Little Red Bike Café	Modern	North Portland	Counter	$15
8.0	Caffè Allora	Italian, Pizza	Pearl District	Casual	$40
8.0	Bete-Lukas	Ethiopian	Division/Clinton	Casual	$35
8.0	Ken's Artisan Bakery	Baked goods	Northwest Portland	Café	$15
8.0	Delta Café	Southern	Southeast Portland	Casual	$35
8.0	Detour Café	American	Division/Clinton	Casual	$15
8.0	5th Quadrant	American	Mississippi	Bar	$15
8.0	Genies	American	Division/Clinton	Casual	$20
8.0	Tastebud	Pizza	Southeast Portland	Casual	$30
8.0	Vita Café	Vegefusion	Alberta Arts District	Casual	$25
8.0	Petisco	Sandwiches	Northeast Portland	Casual	$20
8.0	Crowsenberg's	Baked goods	Downtown	Café	$15
8.0	Gravy	American, Southern	Mississippi	Casual	$25
8.0	Berlin Inn	German	Southeast Portland	Casual	$40
8.0	Laughing Planet	Vegefusion	Multiple locations	Counter	$15
7.5	Karam Lebanese	Lebanese	Downtown	Casual	$30
7.5	East India Co.	Indian	Downtown	Casual	$40
7.5	Tábor	Czech	Downtown	Food cart	$10
7.5	The Waffle Window	Baked goods	Hawthorne	Counter	$10
7.5	Kenny & Zuke's Sandwich	Sandwiches	Northwest Portland	Counter	$15
7.5	Garden State	Italian, Sandwiches	Sellwood	Food cart	$10
7.5	Aladdin's Café	Lebanese	Northeast Portland	Casual	$20
7.5	Escape From NY	Pizza	Northwest Portland	Counter	$10
7.5	Tube	Vegefusion	Old Town	Bar	$15
7.5	Typhoon!	Pan-Asian, Thai	Multiple locations	Casual	$40
7.5	Cup & Saucer Café	American	Multiple locations	Casual	$15

7.5	Pizza Schmizza	Pizza, Italian	Multiple locations	Counter	$25
7.0	Ken's Artisan Pizza	Pizza	Southeast Portland	Casual	$25
7.0	Nicholas Restaurant	Middle Eastern	Southeast Portland	Casual	$20
7.0	Pine State Biscuits	Sandwiches	Belmont	Counter	$15
7.0	Evoe	Modern	Hawthorne	Casual	$15
7.0	E'Njoni Café	Ethiopian	North Portland	Casual	$30
7.0	Swagat	Indian	Multiple locations	Casual	$25
7.0	Lucca	Italian, Modern	Northeast Portland	Casual	$35
7.0	Ziba's Pitas	Bosnian	Downtown	Food cart	$5
7.0	Justa Pasta	Italian	Northwest Portland	Counter	$15
7.0	¡OBA!	Nuevo Latino	Pearl District	Upmarket	$60
7.0	Grilled Cheese Grill	American	Northeast Portland	Food cart	$5
7.0	Vivace	Sandwiches, Crêpes	Northwest Portland	Café	$15

Vegetarian-friendly and date-friendly

9.1	DOC	Italian	Alberta Arts District	Upmarket	$70
9.0	Nostrana	Italian, Pizza	Southeast Portland	Upmarket	$55
8.8	Andina	Peruvian	Pearl District	Upmarket	$70
8.6	Firehouse	Pizza, Modern	Northeast Portland	Casual	$35
8.5	East India Co.	Indian	Downtown	Casual	$40
8.3	Alba Osteria	Italian	Southwest Portland	Upmarket	$60
8.1	Caffè Allora	Italian, Pizza	Pearl District	Casual	$40
8.0	Bete-Lukas	Ethiopian	Division/Clinton	Casual	$35
7.9	Vindalho	Indian	Division/Clinton	Upmarket	$60
7.8	Fratelli Cucina	Italian	Pearl District	Casual	$40
7.8	Le Happy	Crêpes	Northwest Portland	Casual	$15
7.8	Piazza Italia	Italian	Pearl District	Casual	$35
7.7	Caffè Mingo	Italian	Northwest Portland	Upmarket	$50
7.6	Siam Society	Pan-Asian, Thai	Alberta Arts District	Casual	$40
7.4	The Farm Café	Modern, Vegefusion	East Burnside	Upmarket	$45
7.2	Biwa	Japanese, Korean	Southeast Portland	Casual	$35
7.1	Detour Café	American	Division/Clinton	Casual	$15
7.1	5th Quadrant	American	Mississippi	Bar	$15
7.0	Bye and Bye	Vegefusion	Northeast Portland	Bar	$30
7.0	Dots Café	American	Division/Clinton	Bar	$20
7.0	Tastebud	Pizza	Southeast Portland	Casual	$30
6.9	Lucca	Italian, Modern	Northeast Portland	Casual	$35
6.8	The Press Club	Sandwiches, Crêpes	Division/Clinton	Casual	$20
6.7	Navarre	Modern	Northeast Portland	Upmarket	$45
6.5	¡OBA!	Nuevo Latino	Pearl District	Upmarket	$60
6.2	Ciao Vito	Italian	Alberta Arts District	Casual	$40
6.2	Equinox	Modern	Northeast Portland	Casual	$40
6.1	Noble Rot	Modern	East Burnside	Upmarket	$40
6.0	Berlin Inn	German	Southeast Portland	Casual	$40
5.3	Sapphire Hotel	Modern, Pan-Asian	Hawthorne	Bar	$20
5.3	Tube	Vegefusion	Old Town	Bar	$15
5.3	Bombay Cricket Club	Indian	Hawthorne	Upmarket	$40
4.9	Typhoon!	Pan-Asian, Thai	Multiple locations	Casual	$40
NR	Backspace	Coffee, Vegefusion	Old Town	Café	
NR	Bakery Bar	Baked goods	Multiple locations	Counter	
NR	Cacao Chocolate	Sweets	Multiple locations	Counter	
NR	Pix Pâtisserie	Baked goods	Multiple locations	Counter	
NR	Sahagún Chocolates	Sweets	Northwest Portland	Market	
NR	Voodoo Doughnut	Baked goods	Multiple locations	Counter	
NR	World Cup Coffee	Coffee	Multiple locations	Café	

Vegetarian-friendly and kid-friendly

9.3	Apizza Scholls	Pizza	Hawthorne	Casual	$30
9.0	Ken's Artisan Pizza	Pizza	Southeast Portland	Casual	$25
8.6	Pine State Biscuits	Sandwiches	Belmont	Counter	$15
8.2	The Waffle Window	Baked goods	Hawthorne	Counter	$10

Vegetarian-friendly and kid-friendly _continued_

8.1	Bunk Sandwiches	Sandwiches	Southeast Portland	Counter	$15
8.1	Meat Cheese Bread	Sandwiches	Southeast Portland	Counter	$15
8.0	Ken's Artisan Bakery	Baked goods	Northwest Portland	Café	$15
8.0	Kenny & Zuke's Sandwich	Sandwiches	Northwest Portland	Counter	$15
7.1	Detour Café	American	Division/Clinton	Casual	$15
7.0	Vita Café	Vegefusion	Alberta Arts District	Casual	$25
6.9	Lucca	Italian, Modern	Northeast Portland	Casual	$35
6.9	Pastini Pastaria	Italian	Multiple locations	Casual	$25
6.8	Justa Pasta	Italian	Northwest Portland	Counter	$15
6.6	Papa G's	Vegefusion	Division/Clinton	Counter	$20
6.4	Escape From NY	Pizza	Northwest Portland	Counter	$10
6.4	Elephants Delicatessen	American	Multiple locations	Counter	$20
6.4	Cricket Café	American	Belmont	Casual	$20
6.0	Pepino's Mexican Grill	Mexican	Multiple locations	Counter	$10
5.9	Grand Central Bakery	Baked goods	Multiple locations	Counter	$15
5.8	Pizzicato	Pizza, Sandwiches	Multiple locations	Counter	$20
5.6	The Tin Shed	Vegefusion	Alberta Arts District	Casual	$30
5.4	Arabian Breeze	Lebanese	Northeast Portland	Casual	$25
5.0	Laughing Planet	Vegefusion	Multiple locations	Counter	$15
3.6	Pizza Schmizza	Pizza, Italian	Multiple locations	Counter	$25
NR	Baker & Spice	Baked goods	Southwest Portland	Counter	
NR	Bakery Bar	Baked goods	Multiple locations	Counter	
NR	Cacao Chocolate	Sweets	Multiple locations	Counter	
NR	Cupcake Jones	Baked goods	Pearl District	Counter	
NR	Fleur de Lis	Baked goods	Northeast Portland	Counter	
NR	New Seasons Market	Groceries	Multiple locations	Market	
NR	World Cup Coffee	Coffee	Multiple locations	Café	

Vegetarian-friendly delivery

8.0	Kenny & Zuke's Sandwich	Sandwiches	Northwest Portland	Counter	$15
6.5	¡OBA!	Nuevo Latino	Pearl District	Upmarket	$60
6.4	Escape From NY	Pizza	Northwest Portland	Counter	$10
6.4	Elephants Delicatessen	American	Multiple locations	Counter	$20
5.8	Vincenté's Pizza	Pizza	Hawthorne	Casual	$20
5.8	Pizzicato	Pizza, Sandwiches	Multiple locations	Counter	$20
3.6	Pizza Schmizza	Pizza, Italian	Multiple locations	Counter	$25
NR	Fleur de Lis	Baked goods	Northeast Portland	Counter	
NR	New Seasons Market	Groceries	Multiple locations	Market	
NR	Pix Pâtisserie	Baked goods	Multiple locations	Counter	

What's still open?

This is our late-night guide to Portland food. These places claim to stay open as follows; still, we recommend calling first, as the hours sometimes aren't honored on slow nights. Establishments that don't serve full meals (e.g. cafés, bakeries, grocery stores) appear as "NR" at the bottom of the list.

Weekday food after 10pm

9.4	Clyde Common	Modern	Downtown	Upmarket	$45
9.3	Beaker & Flask	Modern	Southeast Portland	Casual	$35
9.2	Yuzu	Japanese	Beaverton	Casual	$40
9.1	Laurelhurst Market	Modern	Northeast Portland	Casual	$50
9.1	Hakatamon	Japanese	Beaverton	Casual	$30
9.1	Ocean City Seafood	Chinese, Seafood	82nd Avenue Area	Casual	$30
9.0	Country Korean	Korean	Beaverton	Casual	$20
8.8	Branch	Modern	Alberta Arts District	Casual	$40
8.8	DJK Korean BBQ	Korean	Beaverton	Casual	$25
8.7	Puerto Marquez	Mexican	Far East Portland	Casual	$25
8.7	JCD Korean Restaurant	Korean	Beaverton	Casual	$20
8.6	La Sirenita	Mexican	Multiple locations	Counter	$15
8.5	Powell's Seafood	Chinese, Seafood	Southeast Portland	Casual	$15
8.4	Du Kuh Bee	Korean, Chinese	Beaverton	Casual	$20
8.3	Pho Oregon	Vietnamese	82nd Avenue Area	Casual	$15
8.2	The Observatory	Modern	Southeast Portland	Casual	$35
8.1	Bar Avignon	Modern	Division/Clinton	Upmarket	$45
8.1	Shenzhen	Chinese, Seafood	82nd Avenue Area	Casual	$25
8.0	Slow Bar	American	Southeast Portland	Bar	$25
8.0	Gold Garden Seafood	Chinese	Far East Portland	Casual	$30
8.0	Yummy Yummy	Chinese, Seafood	82nd Avenue Area	Casual	$35
7.8	Le Happy	Crêpes	Northwest Portland	Casual	$15
7.7	North 45	American, Belgian	Northwest Portland	Bar	$35
7.7	Echo Restaurant	Modern	Northeast Portland	Casual	$40
7.7	Koji Osakaya	Japanese	Multiple locations	Casual	$35
7.6	Higgins	Modern	Downtown	Upmarket	$60
7.6	Horse Brass Pub	British	Belmont	Casual	$25
7.6	Wong's King Seafood	Chinese, Seafood	82nd Avenue Area	Casual	$45
7.5	Delta Café	Southern	Southeast Portland	Casual	$35
7.5	Sorabol	Korean, Japanese	Southeast Portland	Casual	$30
7.4	The Farm Café	Modern, Vegefusion	East Burnside	Upmarket	$45
7.4	Pause	American	North Portland	Casual	$35
7.4	Wing Wa BBQ King	Chinese, Dim Sum	82nd Avenue Area	Casual	$20
7.3	Gilt Club	Modern	Old Town	Upmarket	$60
7.3	Teardrop Lounge	Modern	Pearl District	Bar	$35
7.2	Biwa	Japanese, Korean	Southeast Portland	Casual	$35
7.2	Nob Hill Bar & Grill	American	Northwest Portland	Bar	$20
7.1	El Gaucho	Steakhouse	Downtown	Upmarket	$100
7.1	5th Quadrant	American	Mississippi	Bar	$15
7.1	Jin Wah	Chinese	Multiple locations	Casual	$25
7.0	Dots Café	American	Division/Clinton	Bar	$20
6.8	The Press Club	Sandwiches, Crêpes	Division/Clinton	Casual	$20
6.8	Deschutes Brewery	American	Pearl District	Casual	$25
6.8	Fire on the Mountain	American	Multiple locations	Counter	$20
6.7	Mississippi Pizza Pub	Pizza	Mississippi	Counter	$20

Weekday food after 10pm *continued*

6.7	Acropolis Club	Steakhouse	Sellwood	Strip club	$15
6.7	Navarre	Modern	Northeast Portland	Upmarket	$45
6.6	Driftwood Room	American	Southwest Portland	Bar	$35
6.4	Portland City Grill	Steakhouse	Downtown	Upmarket	$70
6.4	Bar Mingo	Italian	Northwest Portland	Casual	$35
6.4	Escape From NY	Pizza	Northwest Portland	Counter	$10
6.4	Potato Champion	American	Hawthorne	Food cart	$5
6.4	Vault Martini	Modern	Pearl District	Bar	$35
6.3	Masu	Japanese	Downtown	Upmarket	$45
6.1	Doug Fir	American	East Burnside	Bar	$30
6.1	Noble Rot	Modern	East Burnside	Upmarket	$40
6.1	Saucebox	Pan-Asian	Downtown	Bar	$40
6.0	New Old Lompoc	American	Northwest Portland	Casual	$25
6.0	Original Hotcake House	American	Southeast Portland	Casual	$20
6.0	King Burrito	Mexican	North Portland	Counter	$10
5.8	Vincenté's Pizza	Pizza	Hawthorne	Casual	$20
5.7	Living Room Theaters	Modern	Downtown	Theater	$35
5.7	Thatch Tiki Bar	Hawaiian	Northeast Portland	Bar	$30
5.7	Henry's 12th St. Tavern	American	Pearl District	Upmarket	$40
5.6	RingSide Steakhouse	Steakhouse	Multiple locations	Upmarket	$80
5.6	Rogue Public House	American	Pearl District	Bar	$25
5.4	McCormick & Schmick's	Seafood, American	Multiple locations	Upmarket	$60
5.3	Sapphire Hotel	Modern, Pan-Asian	Hawthorne	Bar	$20
5.3	Tube	Vegefusion	Old Town	Bar	$15
5.3	23Hoyt	Modern	Northwest Portland	Upmarket	$60
5.2	Burgerville	American	Multiple locations	Counter	$10
5.0	50 Plates	Modern	Pearl District	Upmarket	$40
4.9	Huber's Restaurant	American	Downtown	Casual	$40
4.5	The Liberty Glass	American, Italian	North Portland	Bar	$20
3.9	McMenamins	American	Multiple locations	Casual	$30
3.7	Le Bistro Montage	Southern	Southeast Portland	Casual	$35
3.0	Lucky Labrador	American	Multiple locations	Bar	$15
NR	Backspace	Coffee, Vegefusion	Old Town	Café	
NR	Coffee Time	Coffee	Northwest Portland	Café	
NR	Pix Pâtisserie	Baked goods	Multiple locations	Counter	
NR	Voodoo Doughnut	Baked goods	Multiple locations	Counter	
NR	Whiffies Fried Pies	Baked goods	Hawthorne	Food cart	
NR	World Cup Coffee	Coffee	Multiple locations	Café	

Weekday food after 11pm

9.3	Beaker & Flask	Modern	Southeast Portland	Casual	$35
9.2	Yuzu	Japanese	Beaverton	Casual	$40
9.1	Ocean City Seafood	Chinese, Seafood	82nd Avenue Area	Casual	$30
9.0	Country Korean	Korean	Beaverton	Casual	$20
8.8	Branch	Modern	Alberta Arts District	Casual	$40
8.7	JCD Korean Restaurant	Korean	Beaverton	Casual	$20
8.4	Du Kuh Bee	Korean, Chinese	Beaverton	Casual	$20
8.2	The Observatory	Modern	Southeast Portland	Casual	$35
8.1	Shenzhen	Chinese, Seafood	82nd Avenue Area	Casual	$25
8.0	Slow Bar	American	Southeast Portland	Bar	$25
8.0	Gold Garden Seafood	Chinese	Far East Portland	Casual	$30
8.0	Yummy Yummy	Chinese, Seafood	82nd Avenue Area	Casual	$35
7.8	Le Happy	Crêpes	Northwest Portland	Casual	$15
7.7	North 45	American, Belgian	Northwest Portland	Bar	$35
7.7	Echo Restaurant	Modern	Northeast Portland	Casual	$40
7.6	Horse Brass Pub	British	Belmont	Casual	$25
7.5	Delta Café	Southern	Southeast Portland	Casual	$35
7.4	The Farm Café	Modern, Vegefusion	East Burnside	Upmarket	$45
7.4	Pause	American	North Portland	Casual	$35
7.3	Gilt Club	Modern	Old Town	Upmarket	$60
7.3	Teardrop Lounge	Modern	Pearl District	Bar	$35
7.2	Biwa	Japanese, Korean	Southeast Portland	Casual	$35

Weekday food after 11pm *continued*

7.2	Nob Hill Bar & Grill	American	Northwest Portland	Bar	$20
7.1	El Gaucho	Steakhouse	Downtown	Upmarket	$100
7.1	5th Quadrant	American	Mississippi	Bar	$15
7.1	Jin Wah	Chinese	Multiple locations	Casual	$25
7.0	Dots Café	American	Division/Clinton	Bar	$20
6.7	Mississippi Pizza Pub	Pizza	Mississippi	Counter	$20
6.7	Acropolis Club	Steakhouse	Sellwood	Strip club	$15
6.6	Driftwood Room	American	Southwest Portland	Bar	$35
6.4	Portland City Grill	Steakhouse	Downtown	Upmarket	$70
6.4	Bar Mingo	Italian	Northwest Portland	Casual	$35
6.4	Potato Champion	American	Hawthorne	Food cart	$5
6.4	Vault Martini	Modern	Pearl District	Bar	$35
6.1	Doug Fir	American	East Burnside	Bar	$30
6.1	Saucebox	Pan-Asian	Downtown	Bar	$40
6.0	Original Hotcake House	American	Southeast Portland	Casual	$20
5.8	Vincenté's Pizza	Pizza	Hawthorne	Casual	$20
5.7	Living Room Theaters	Modern	Downtown	Theater	$35
5.6	RingSide Steakhouse	Steakhouse	Multiple locations	Upmarket	$80
5.6	Rogue Public House	American	Pearl District	Bar	$25
5.3	Sapphire Hotel	Modern, Pan-Asian	Hawthorne	Bar	$20
5.3	Tube	Vegefusion	Old Town	Bar	$15
4.9	Huber's Restaurant	American	Downtown	Casual	$40
4.5	The Liberty Glass	American, Italian	North Portland	Bar	$20
3.9	McMenamins	American	Multiple locations	Casual	$30
3.7	Le Bistro Montage	Southern	Southeast Portland	Casual	$35
3.0	Lucky Labrador	American	Multiple locations	Bar	$15
NR	Backspace	Coffee, Vegefusion	Old Town	Café	
NR	Coffee Time	Coffee	Northwest Portland	Café	
NR	Pix Pâtisserie	Baked goods	Multiple locations	Counter	
NR	Voodoo Doughnut	Baked goods	Multiple locations	Counter	
NR	Whiffies Fried Pies	Baked goods	Hawthorne	Food cart	

Weekday food after midnight

8.7	JCD Korean Restaurant	Korean	Beaverton	Casual	$20
8.4	Du Kuh Bee	Korean, Chinese	Beaverton	Casual	$20
8.0	Slow Bar	American	Southeast Portland	Bar	$25
8.0	Yummy Yummy	Chinese, Seafood	82nd Avenue Area	Casual	$35
7.8	Le Happy	Crêpes	Northwest Portland	Casual	$15
7.7	Echo Restaurant	Modern	Northeast Portland	Casual	$40
7.6	Horse Brass Pub	British	Belmont	Casual	$25
7.5	Delta Café	Southern	Southeast Portland	Casual	$35
7.4	Pause	American	North Portland	Casual	$35
7.3	Gilt Club	Modern	Old Town	Upmarket	$60
7.3	Teardrop Lounge	Modern	Pearl District	Bar	$35
7.2	Nob Hill Bar & Grill	American	Northwest Portland	Bar	$20
7.0	Dots Café	American	Division/Clinton	Bar	$20
6.7	Acropolis Club	Steakhouse	Sellwood	Strip club	$15
6.4	Potato Champion	American	Hawthorne	Food cart	$5
6.4	Vault Martini	Modern	Pearl District	Bar	$35
6.0	Original Hotcake House	American	Southeast Portland	Casual	$20
5.3	Sapphire Hotel	Modern, Pan-Asian	Hawthorne	Bar	$20
5.3	Tube	Vegefusion	Old Town	Bar	$15
3.7	Le Bistro Montage	Southern	Southeast Portland	Casual	$35
NR	Coffee Time	Coffee	Northwest Portland	Café	
NR	Voodoo Doughnut	Baked goods	Multiple locations	Counter	
NR	Whiffies Fried Pies	Baked goods	Hawthorne	Food cart	

Weekday food after 1am

8.0	Slow Bar	American	Southeast Portland	Bar	$25
8.0	Yummy Yummy	Chinese, Seafood	82nd Avenue Area	Casual	$35
7.7	Echo Restaurant	Modern	Northeast Portland	Casual	$40

Weekday food after 1am *continued*

7.6	Horse Brass Pub	British	Belmont	Casual	$25
7.3	Gilt Club	Modern	Old Town	Upmarket	$60
7.3	Teardrop Lounge	Modern	Pearl District	Bar	$35
7.2	Nob Hill Bar & Grill	American	Northwest Portland	Bar	$20
7.0	Dots Café	American	Division/Clinton	Bar	$20
6.7	Acropolis Club	Steakhouse	Sellwood	Strip club	$15
6.4	Potato Champion	American	Hawthorne	Food cart	$5
6.0	Original Hotcake House	American	Southeast Portland	Casual	$20
5.3	Sapphire Hotel	Modern, Pan-Asian	Hawthorne	Bar	$20
5.3	Tube	Vegefusion	Old Town	Bar	$15
3.7	Le Bistro Montage	Southern	Southeast Portland	Casual	$35
NR	Voodoo Doughnut	Baked goods	Multiple locations	Counter	
NR	Whiffies Fried Pies	Baked goods	Hawthorne	Food cart	

Weekday food after 2am

8.0	Slow Bar	American	Southeast Portland	Bar	$25
7.6	Horse Brass Pub	British	Belmont	Casual	$25
7.2	Nob Hill Bar & Grill	American	Northwest Portland	Bar	$20
6.7	Acropolis Club	Steakhouse	Sellwood	Strip club	$15
6.4	Potato Champion	American	Hawthorne	Food cart	$5
6.0	Original Hotcake House	American	Southeast Portland	Casual	$20
5.3	Tube	Vegefusion	Old Town	Bar	$15
NR	Voodoo Doughnut	Baked goods	Multiple locations	Counter	
NR	Whiffies Fried Pies	Baked goods	Hawthorne	Food cart	

Weekend food after 10pm

9.4	Clyde Common	Modern	Downtown	Upmarket	$45
9.3	Beaker & Flask	Modern	Southeast Portland	Casual	$35
9.2	Paley's Place	Modern	Northwest Portland	Upmarket	$80
9.2	Yuzu	Japanese	Beaverton	Casual	$40
9.2	Sel Gris	Modern	Hawthorne	Upmarket	$80
9.1	Laurelhurst Market	Modern	Northeast Portland	Casual	$50
9.1	EaT: An Oyster Bar	Seafood, Southern	Mississippi	Casual	$40
9.1	Hakatamon	Japanese	Beaverton	Casual	$30
9.1	Ocean City Seafood	Chinese, Seafood	82nd Avenue Area	Casual	$30
9.0	Simpatica	Modern	Southeast Portland	Upmarket	$50
9.0	Nostrana	Italian, Pizza	Southeast Portland	Upmarket	$55
9.0	Country Korean	Korean	Beaverton	Casual	$20
8.8	Andina	Peruvian	Pearl District	Upmarket	$70
8.8	Branch	Modern	Alberta Arts District	Casual	$40
8.8	DJK Korean BBQ	Korean	Beaverton	Casual	$25
8.7	Ten01	Modern	Pearl District	Upmarket	$70
8.7	Puerto Marquez	Mexican	Far East Portland	Casual	$25
8.7	JCD Korean Restaurant	Korean	Beaverton	Casual	$20
8.6	La Sirenita	Mexican	Multiple locations	Counter	$15
8.5	Powell's Seafood	Chinese, Seafood	Southeast Portland	Casual	$15
8.4	Du Kuh Bee	Korean, Chinese	Beaverton	Casual	$20
8.3	Pho Oregon	Vietnamese	82nd Avenue Area	Casual	$15
8.2	The Observatory	Modern	Southeast Portland	Casual	$35
8.2	Serratto	Modern	Northwest Portland	Upmarket	$60
8.1	Pambiche	Cuban	Northeast Portland	Casual	$35
8.1	Syun Izakaya	Japanese	Hillsboro	Casual	$35
8.1	Bar Avignon	Modern	Division/Clinton	Upmarket	$45
8.1	Shenzhen	Chinese, Seafood	82nd Avenue Area	Casual	$25
8.0	Slow Bar	American	Southeast Portland	Bar	$25
8.0	Gold Garden Seafood	Chinese	Far East Portland	Casual	$30
8.0	Yummy Yummy	Chinese, Seafood	82nd Avenue Area	Casual	$35
7.9	Gino's	Italian, Modern	Sellwood	Casual	$40
7.9	Original Halibut's	Seafood	Alberta Arts District	Counter	$20
7.8	Le Happy	Crêpes	Northwest Portland	Casual	$15
7.8	Toro Bravo	Spanish	Northeast Portland	Upmarket	$45

Weekend food after 10pm *continued*

7.7	Caffè Mingo	Italian	Northwest Portland	Upmarket	$50
7.7	North 45	American, Belgian	Northwest Portland	Bar	$35
7.7	Echo Restaurant	Modern	Northeast Portland	Casual	$40
7.7	Koji Osakaya	Japanese	Multiple locations	Casual	$35
7.6	Higgins	Modern	Downtown	Upmarket	$60
7.6	Horse Brass Pub	British	Belmont	Casual	$25
7.6	Urban Farmer	Steakhouse	Downtown	Upmarket	$110
7.6	Wong's King Seafood	Chinese, Seafood	82nd Avenue Area	Casual	$45
7.5	Delta Café	Southern	Southeast Portland	Casual	$35
7.5	Ruth's Chris	Steakhouse	Downtown	Upmarket	$100
7.5	Sorabol	Korean, Japanese	Southeast Portland	Casual	$30
7.4	The Farm Café	Modern, Vegefusion	East Burnside	Upmarket	$45
7.4	Pause	American	North Portland	Casual	$35
7.4	Wing Wa BBQ King	Chinese, Dim Sum	82nd Avenue Area	Casual	$20
7.3	Gilt Club	Modern	Old Town	Upmarket	$60
7.3	Teardrop Lounge	Modern	Pearl District	Bar	$35
7.3	Morton's	Steakhouse	Downtown	Upmarket	$100
7.2	Biwa	Japanese, Korean	Southeast Portland	Casual	$35
7.2	Miss Delta	Southern	Mississippi	Casual	$35
7.2	Decarli	Italian, Modern	Beaverton	Upmarket	$50
7.2	Nob Hill Bar & Grill	American	Northwest Portland	Bar	$20
7.1	Café Castagna	Modern	Hawthorne	Upmarket	$45
7.1	El Gaucho	Steakhouse	Downtown	Upmarket	$100
7.1	5th Quadrant	American	Mississippi	Bar	$15
7.1	Southpark Seafood	Modern, Seafood	Downtown	Casual	$40
7.1	Jin Wah	Chinese	Multiple locations	Casual	$25
7.0	Dots Café	American	Division/Clinton	Bar	$20
6.8	The Press Club	Sandwiches, Crêpes	Division/Clinton	Casual	$20
6.8	Papa Haydn	Modern	Multiple locations	Upmarket	$50
6.8	Deschutes Brewery	American	Pearl District	Casual	$25
6.8	Bluehour	Modern	Pearl District	Upmarket	$70
6.8	Fire on the Mountain	American	Multiple locations	Counter	$20
6.7	Mississippi Pizza Pub	Pizza	Mississippi	Counter	$20
6.7	Acropolis Club	Steakhouse	Sellwood	Strip club	$15
6.7	Navarre	Modern	Northeast Portland	Upmarket	$45
6.6	Driftwood Room	American	Southwest Portland	Bar	$35
6.4	Portland City Grill	Steakhouse	Downtown	Upmarket	$70
6.4	Café Nell	American	Northwest Portland	Casual	$40
6.4	Bar Mingo	Italian	Northwest Portland	Casual	$35
6.4	Escape From NY	Pizza	Northwest Portland	Counter	$10
6.4	Potato Champion	American	Hawthorne	Food cart	$5
6.4	Vault Martini	Modern	Pearl District	Bar	$35
6.3	Masu	Japanese	Downtown	Upmarket	$45
6.1	Doug Fir	American	East Burnside	Bar	$30
6.1	Noble Rot	Modern	East Burnside	Upmarket	$40
6.1	Saucebox	Pan-Asian	Downtown	Bar	$40
6.1	Grilled Cheese Grill	American	Northeast Portland	Food cart	$5
6.0	New Old Lompoc	American	Northwest Portland	Casual	$25
6.0	Original Hotcake House	American	Southeast Portland	Casual	$20
6.0	King Burrito	Mexican	North Portland	Counter	$10
5.9	Bastas Trattoria	Italian	Northwest Portland	Upmarket	$45
5.9	Saburo's	Japanese	Sellwood	Casual	$30
5.8	Vincenté's Pizza	Pizza	Hawthorne	Casual	$20
5.7	Living Room Theaters	Modern	Downtown	Theater	$35
5.7	Thatch Tiki Bar	Hawaiian	Northeast Portland	Bar	$30
5.7	Henry's 12th St. Tavern	American	Pearl District	Upmarket	$40
5.6	RingSide Steakhouse	Steakhouse	Multiple locations	Upmarket	$80
5.6	Rogue Public House	American	Pearl District	Bar	$25
5.6	The Heathman	American	Downtown	Upmarket	$60
5.5	Bay 13	Seafood	Pearl District	Upmarket	$50
5.4	McCormick & Schmick's	Seafood, American	Multiple locations	Upmarket	$60
5.3	Sapphire Hotel	Modern, Pan-Asian	Hawthorne	Bar	$20

Weekend food after 10pm *continued*

5.3	Tube	Vegefusion	Old Town	Bar	$15
5.3	23Hoyt	Modern	Northwest Portland	Upmarket	$60
5.2	Burgerville	American	Multiple locations	Counter	$10
5.0	50 Plates	Modern	Pearl District	Upmarket	$40
4.9	Huber's Restaurant	American	Downtown	Casual	$40
4.8	Vivace	Sandwiches, Crêpes	Northwest Portland	Café	$15
4.7	Jake's	Seafood, American	Multiple locations	Upmarket	$50
4.5	The Liberty Glass	American, Italian	North Portland	Bar	$20
3.9	McMenamins	American	Multiple locations	Casual	$30
3.7	Le Bistro Montage	Southern	Southeast Portland	Casual	$35
3.0	Lucky Labrador	American	Multiple locations	Bar	$15
2.9	Eleni's	Greek	Multiple locations	Casual	$40
NR	Backspace	Coffee, Vegefusion	Old Town	Café	
NR	Coffee Time	Coffee	Northwest Portland	Café	
NR	Pix Pâtisserie	Baked goods	Multiple locations	Counter	
NR	Voodoo Doughnut	Baked goods	Multiple locations	Counter	
NR	Whiffies Fried Pies	Baked goods	Hawthorne	Food cart	
NR	World Cup Coffee	Coffee	Multiple locations	Café	

Weekend food after 11pm

9.4	Clyde Common	Modern	Downtown	Upmarket	$45
9.3	Beaker & Flask	Modern	Southeast Portland	Casual	$35
9.2	Yuzu	Japanese	Beaverton	Casual	$40
9.1	EaT: An Oyster Bar	Seafood, Southern	Mississippi	Casual	$40
9.1	Ocean City Seafood	Chinese, Seafood	82nd Avenue Area	Casual	$30
9.0	Country Korean	Korean	Beaverton	Casual	$20
8.8	Branch	Modern	Alberta Arts District	Casual	$40
8.7	JCD Korean Restaurant	Korean	Beaverton	Casual	$20
8.4	Du Kuh Bee	Korean, Chinese	Beaverton	Casual	$20
8.2	The Observatory	Modern	Southeast Portland	Casual	$35
8.1	Pambiche	Cuban	Northeast Portland	Casual	$35
8.1	Bar Avignon	Modern	Division/Clinton	Upmarket	$45
8.1	Shenzhen	Chinese, Seafood	82nd Avenue Area	Casual	$25
8.0	Slow Bar	American	Southeast Portland	Bar	$25
8.0	Gold Garden Seafood	Chinese	Far East Portland	Casual	$30
7.8	Le Happy	Crêpes	Northwest Portland	Casual	$15
7.7	North 45	American, Belgian	Northwest Portland	Bar	$35
7.7	Echo Restaurant	Modern	Northeast Portland	Casual	$40
7.6	Horse Brass Pub	British	Belmont	Casual	$25
7.5	Delta Café	Southern	Southeast Portland	Casual	$35
7.4	The Farm Café	Modern, Vegefusion	East Burnside	Upmarket	$45
7.4	Pause	American	North Portland	Casual	$35
7.3	Gilt Club	Modern	Old Town	Upmarket	$60
7.3	Teardrop Lounge	Modern	Pearl District	Bar	$35
7.2	Biwa	Japanese, Korean	Southeast Portland	Casual	$35
7.2	Nob Hill Bar & Grill	American	Northwest Portland	Bar	$20
7.1	El Gaucho	Steakhouse	Downtown	Upmarket	$100
7.1	5th Quadrant	American	Mississippi	Bar	$15
7.1	Jin Wah	Chinese	Multiple locations	Casual	$25
7.0	Dots Café	American	Division/Clinton	Bar	$20
6.8	The Press Club	Sandwiches, Crêpes	Division/Clinton	Casual	$20
6.8	Papa Haydn	Modern	Multiple locations	Upmarket	$50
6.8	Deschutes Brewery	American	Pearl District	Casual	$25
6.8	Fire on the Mountain	American	Multiple locations	Counter	$20
6.7	Mississippi Pizza Pub	Pizza	Mississippi	Counter	$20
6.7	Acropolis Club	Steakhouse	Sellwood	Strip club	$15
6.7	Navarre	Modern	Northeast Portland	Upmarket	$45
6.6	Driftwood Room	American	Southwest Portland	Bar	$35
6.4	Portland City Grill	Steakhouse	Downtown	Upmarket	$70
6.4	Café Nell	American	Northwest Portland	Casual	$40
6.4	Bar Mingo	Italian	Northwest Portland	Casual	$35
6.4	Potato Champion	American	Hawthorne	Food cart	$5

Weekend food after 11pm *continued*

6.4	Vault Martini	Modern	Pearl District	Bar	$35
6.3	Masu	Japanese	Downtown	Upmarket	$45
6.1	Doug Fir	American	East Burnside	Bar	$30
6.1	Noble Rot	Modern	East Burnside	Upmarket	$40
6.1	Saucebox	Pan-Asian	Downtown	Bar	$40
6.1	Grilled Cheese Grill	American	Northeast Portland	Food cart	$5
6.0	New Old Lompoc	American	Northwest Portland	Casual	$25
6.0	Original Hotcake House	American	Southeast Portland	Casual	$20
5.8	Vincenté's Pizza	Pizza	Hawthorne	Casual	$20
5.7	Living Room Theaters	Modern	Downtown	Theater	$35
5.7	Henry's 12th St. Tavern	American	Pearl District	Upmarket	$40
5.6	RingSide Steakhouse	Steakhouse	Multiple locations	Upmarket	$80
5.6	Rogue Public House	American	Pearl District	Bar	$25
5.5	Bay 13	Seafood	Pearl District	Upmarket	$50
5.4	McCormick & Schmick's	Seafood, American	Multiple locations	Upmarket	$60
5.3	Sapphire Hotel	Modern, Pan-Asian	Hawthorne	Bar	$20
5.3	Tube	Vegefusion	Old Town	Bar	$15
5.0	50 Plates	Modern	Pearl District	Upmarket	$40
4.9	Huber's Restaurant	American	Downtown	Casual	$40
4.7	Jake's	Seafood, American	Multiple locations	Upmarket	$50
4.5	The Liberty Glass	American, Italian	North Portland	Bar	$20
3.9	McMenamins	American	Multiple locations	Casual	$30
3.7	Le Bistro Montage	Southern	Southeast Portland	Casual	$35
3.0	Lucky Labrador	American	Multiple locations	Bar	$15
NR	Backspace	Coffee, Vegefusion	Old Town	Café	
NR	Coffee Time	Coffee	Northwest Portland	Café	
NR	Pix Pâtisserie	Baked goods	Multiple locations	Counter	
NR	Voodoo Doughnut	Baked goods	Multiple locations	Counter	
NR	Whiffies Fried Pies	Baked goods	Hawthorne	Food cart	

Weekend food after midnight

9.4	Clyde Common	Modern	Downtown	Upmarket	$45
9.3	Beaker & Flask	Modern	Southeast Portland	Casual	$35
9.0	Country Korean	Korean	Beaverton	Casual	$20
8.8	Branch	Modern	Alberta Arts District	Casual	$40
8.7	JCD Korean Restaurant	Korean	Beaverton	Casual	$20
8.4	Du Kuh Bee	Korean, Chinese	Beaverton	Casual	$20
8.0	Slow Bar	American	Southeast Portland	Bar	$25
7.8	Le Happy	Crêpes	Northwest Portland	Casual	$15
7.7	North 45	American, Belgian	Northwest Portland	Bar	$35
7.7	Echo Restaurant	Modern	Northeast Portland	Casual	$40
7.6	Horse Brass Pub	British	Belmont	Casual	$25
7.5	Delta Café	Southern	Southeast Portland	Casual	$35
7.4	Pause	American	North Portland	Casual	$35
7.3	Gilt Club	Modern	Old Town	Upmarket	$60
7.3	Teardrop Lounge	Modern	Pearl District	Bar	$35
7.2	Nob Hill Bar & Grill	American	Northwest Portland	Bar	$20
7.1	El Gaucho	Steakhouse	Downtown	Upmarket	$100
7.1	5th Quadrant	American	Mississippi	Bar	$15
7.0	Dots Café	American	Division/Clinton	Bar	$20
6.7	Mississippi Pizza Pub	Pizza	Mississippi	Counter	$20
6.7	Acropolis Club	Steakhouse	Sellwood	Strip club	$15
6.6	Driftwood Room	American	Southwest Portland	Bar	$35
6.4	Portland City Grill	Steakhouse	Downtown	Upmarket	$70
6.4	Potato Champion	American	Hawthorne	Food cart	$5
6.4	Vault Martini	Modern	Pearl District	Bar	$35
6.1	Doug Fir	American	East Burnside	Bar	$30
6.1	Saucebox	Pan-Asian	Downtown	Bar	$40
6.1	Grilled Cheese Grill	American	Northeast Portland	Food cart	$5
6.0	Original Hotcake House	American	Southeast Portland	Casual	$20
5.7	Living Room Theaters	Modern	Downtown	Theater	$35
5.6	Rogue Public House	American	Pearl District	Bar	$25

Weekend food after midnight *continued*

5.5	Bay 13	Seafood	Pearl District	Upmarket	$50
5.3	Sapphire Hotel	Modern, Pan-Asian	Hawthorne	Bar	$20
5.3	Tube	Vegefusion	Old Town	Bar	$15
4.9	Huber's Restaurant	American	Downtown	Casual	$40
3.9	McMenamins	American	Multiple locations	Casual	$30
3.7	Le Bistro Montage	Southern	Southeast Portland	Casual	$35
NR	Coffee Time	Coffee	Northwest Portland	Café	
NR	Pix Pâtisserie	Baked goods	Multiple locations	Counter	
NR	Voodoo Doughnut	Baked goods	Multiple locations	Counter	
NR	Whiffies Fried Pies	Baked goods	Hawthorne	Food cart	

Weekend food after 1am

9.4	Clyde Common	Modern	Downtown	Upmarket	$45
9.0	Country Korean	Korean	Beaverton	Casual	$20
8.8	Branch	Modern	Alberta Arts District	Casual	$40
8.4	Du Kuh Bee	Korean, Chinese	Beaverton	Casual	$20
8.0	Slow Bar	American	Southeast Portland	Bar	$25
7.8	Le Happy	Crêpes	Northwest Portland	Casual	$15
7.7	Echo Restaurant	Modern	Northeast Portland	Casual	$40
7.6	Horse Brass Pub	British	Belmont	Casual	$25
7.3	Gilt Club	Modern	Old Town	Upmarket	$60
7.3	Teardrop Lounge	Modern	Pearl District	Bar	$35
7.2	Nob Hill Bar & Grill	American	Northwest Portland	Bar	$20
7.0	Dots Café	American	Division/Clinton	Bar	$20
6.7	Acropolis Club	Steakhouse	Sellwood	Strip club	$15
6.4	Potato Champion	American	Hawthorne	Food cart	$5
6.4	Vault Martini	Modern	Pearl District	Bar	$35
6.1	Doug Fir	American	East Burnside	Bar	$30
6.1	Saucebox	Pan-Asian	Downtown	Bar	$40
6.1	Grilled Cheese Grill	American	Northeast Portland	Food cart	$5
6.0	Original Hotcake House	American	Southeast Portland	Casual	$20
5.3	Sapphire Hotel	Modern, Pan-Asian	Hawthorne	Bar	$20
5.3	Tube	Vegefusion	Old Town	Bar	$15
3.7	Le Bistro Montage	Southern	Southeast Portland	Casual	$35
NR	Coffee Time	Coffee	Northwest Portland	Café	
NR	Pix Pâtisserie	Baked goods	Multiple locations	Counter	
NR	Voodoo Doughnut	Baked goods	Multiple locations	Counter	
NR	Whiffies Fried Pies	Baked goods	Hawthorne	Food cart	

Weekend food after 2am

8.0	Slow Bar	American	Southeast Portland	Bar	$25
7.8	Le Happy	Crêpes	Northwest Portland	Casual	$15
7.6	Horse Brass Pub	British	Belmont	Casual	$25
7.2	Nob Hill Bar & Grill	American	Northwest Portland	Bar	$20
6.7	Acropolis Club	Steakhouse	Sellwood	Strip club	$15
6.4	Potato Champion	American	Hawthorne	Food cart	$5
6.1	Grilled Cheese Grill	American	Northeast Portland	Food cart	$5
6.0	Original Hotcake House	American	Southeast Portland	Casual	$20
5.3	Tube	Vegefusion	Old Town	Bar	$15
3.7	Le Bistro Montage	Southern	Southeast Portland	Casual	$35
NR	Voodoo Doughnut	Baked goods	Multiple locations	Counter	
NR	Whiffies Fried Pies	Baked goods	Hawthorne	Food cart	

Top tastes

Apizza amore, Apizza Scholls
Bagel, Kenny & Zuke's Sandwich Works
Barbecued ribs, Podnah's Pit
Beef brisket stew, JCD Korean Restaurant
Black-bean noodles, Du Kuh Bee
Bloody Mary, Besaw's Café
Braised pork belly, Yuzu
Burger, Nob Hill Bar & Grill
Camarones ahogados (raw marinated shrimp), Puerto Marquez
Cappuccino, Spella Caffè
Caramel, Sahagún Chocolates
Causa morada, Andina
Chao long (rice soup with pork blood), Pho Oregon
Chapulines (grasshoppers), La Calaca Comelona
Charcuterie plate, Beast
Cheesus burger, Grilled Cheese Grill
Chicken liver mousse, Ten01
Coffee, Stumptown Roasters
Coho salmon, Clarklewis
Double Dead Guy Ale, Rogue Distillery & Public House
Doughnuts, Voodoo Doughnut
Duck confit, Tabla Mediterranean Bistro
Espresso, Ristretto Roasters
Falafel, Basha's Mediterranean
Fish from the tank, Wong's King Seafood
French fries, Clyde Common
French press coffee, Albina Press
Galbi, DJK Korean BBQ & Shabu Shabu
Goat bil tfeen, Karam Lebanese
Gravlax, Brøder Comfort Food
Grilled cheese, Dots Café
Han jung shik (tasting menu), BeWon Korean
Homemade tagliatelle, DOC
House-made hot dog, Park Kitchen
Ken's Special (pastrami, chopped liver, and cole slaw), Kenny & Zuke's Deli
Lamb crépinette, Wildwood
Ma po tofu, Lucky Strike
Maple breakfast sandwich, Meat Cheese Bread
Meatball sandwich, Bunk Sandwiches
Moules frites, North 45
Nahm dtok (grilled beef salad), Kinara Thai Bistro
Offal, Le Pigeon
Oysters on the half shell, EaT: An Oyster Bar
Painted Hills burger with bacon, white cheddar, and barbecue sauce, Serratto
Pho, Pho An Sandy
Pita, Nicholas Restaurant
Pizza margherita, Ken's Artisan Pizza

Pizza margherita, Nostrana
Pork collar skewers, Ping
Pork rillettes, Branch
Poutine, Potato Champion
Reggie Deluxe, Pine State Biscuits
Roast marrow bones, Paley's Place
Roast suckling pig, Best Taste
Sashimi omakase, Hiroshi Sushi
Scones, Baker & Spice
Slowburger, Slow Bar
Smoked salmon on spelt, Little T American Baker
Som tam (green papaya salad) with raw crab, Pok Pok (Whiskey Soda Lounge)
Soondae guk (blood-sausage stew), Country Korean Restaurant
Sourdough bread, Ken's Artisan Bakery
Steak, Laurelhurst Market
Steamed bait shrimp, Ocean City Seafood
Sweetbreads, Sel Gris
Tacos de lengua, Taquería 7 Estrellas
Three B's Waffle (bacon, brie, basil, and peach jam), The Waffle Window
Tonkotsu ramen, Hakatamon
Vacuum-pot coffee, Barista Café
Viking Quest cocktail, Beaker & Flask
Whole Bowl, The Whole Bowl
Whole trout, Ned Ludd
Xiao long bao (Shanghai soup dumplings), Asian Station Café
YouCanHasCheeseburger, Brunchbox
Younger Special Bitter, Horse Brass Pub

If you're a wine drinker, check out **the world's bestselling guide to wines under $15** from the Fearless Critic editors. Now on sale online and at stores.

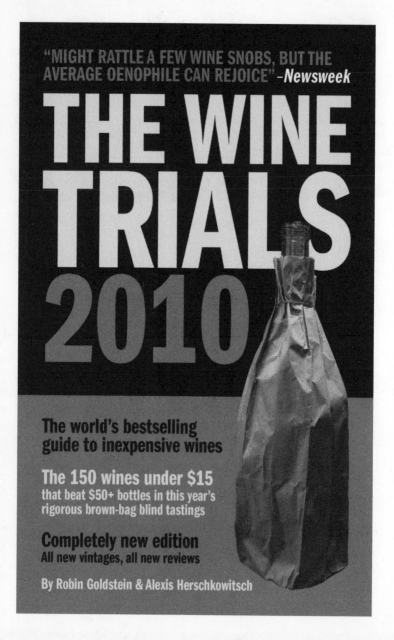

Fearless Critic
Reviews

Acropolis Club

Flesh for fantasy...and $10

6.7	6.5	9.0
Food	Feel	Beer

Steakhouse

Strip club

$15
Price

www.acropolis-portland.com

Mon–Sat 7:30am–2:30am
Sun 11am–2:30am

Bar Beer, wine, liquor
Credit cards Visa, MC, AmEx
Date-friendly

Sellwood
8325 SE McLoughlin Blvd.
(503) 231-9611

Portland, according to Wikipedia, has a higher number of strip clubs per capita than does Las Vegas. We've found some dreadful food at strip clubs, but we've also found some really decent food. Perhaps nowhere is the strip-club food more decent than it is in Portland, and perhaps nowhere in Portland is it more decent than it is at the Acropolis Club.

The trick is being able to go for the $10 steak without bleeding $20 bills the whole time, because if you go far enough, you could end up spending as much as you would for a brilliant Porterhouse...*and* a good bottle of wine...at a more serious steakhouse. Unless, of course, you consider that the formula for measuring the value of your steak includes boobies.

The great thing about the Acropolis, though, is that there's no pressure to bleed bills. The entertainers will actually back off and let you enjoy your ridiculously inexpensive meal. In other words, it is entirely possible to have your steak...and eat it, too.

That isn't to say you won't be able to see gyrating flesh from wherever you sit, and it's commonly felt that the quality of that flesh at Acropolis is at least as high as that of the flesh on your plate. Then again, it is pitch black in there, a lighting that is notoriously flattering. But the mouth doesn't lie—this is pretty good meat (the steak, that is—even if it doesn't actually come from the owner's cattle ranch, as has been sometimes misreported). Sandwiches like French dips and Reubens are huge and cheap, and everything comes with onion rings, fries, baked potato, or salad. There's even a salad bar if your desire for flesh doesn't run to the palate. Breakfast is also good, greasy and filling.

The club's dimmer-than-dim lighting isn't the only great equalizer here. A magnificent collection of 51 beer taps yield just short of a pint each, for $4. $4 for everything. PBR? $4. MGD? $4. Rogue Dead Guy? $4. Rainier? $4. It's surreal, and pretty exciting if you like a bargain.

Dinner and a show? El Gaucho would do well to amp up those tableside antics to justify their sky-high prices. Maybe they could hire these gals to toss the Caesar to "She's Only Seventeen." Then they'd really have something.

Addy's Sandwich Bar

6.7 Food
7.5 Feel

There might be some hype around these sandwiches, but we're not so smitten

Sandwiches

Food cart

$10 Price

www.addyssandwichbar.com

Mon–Fri 11am–3pm

Bar None
Credit cards Visa, MC
Kid-friendly, outdoor dining

Downtown
SW 10th and Alder
(503) 267-0994

Addy's Sandwich Bar, located in one of the lovely slews of food carts downtown, has all the marks of coolness: a minimalist logo of an unevenly drawn red circle; a throwback font with thick black shadowing; and a hipster name: Addy. (Retro names are totally hot—think Ruthie, Grace, Mabelline).

Also at this mobile food station are all the signs that show that it's run by a Portlander who cares: compostable wares, organic veggies that vary based on availability, you know the drill. Oh, and bread from Little T.

The cute ante is upped by a small outdoor wooden porch and counter that add quaintness, while skillfully avoiding kitsch. It's one of the food carts at which we could actually see ourselves lingering. (And that's saying something.) It definitely has an edge over the other food carts with this hipness-cum-coziness.

The buildup continues; at this point, Addy has us expecting some really great grub. There's a pâté de campagne sandwich on the menu, a rare sight in Portland. The delicious fresh baguette from Little T, of course, doesn't disappoint, and the ingredients are fresh. Pickles, fermented in house (if one can really say that), add a lovely briny crunch, but it's the pâté that is the loser. It doesn't quite have that pop that we look for; it leaves us wanting more of those big, porky, fatty flavors of which a good terrine is capable. The whole sandwich ends up slightly disappointing.

Other sandwiches seem carefully thought out, though, such as a duck confit, plum sauce, and shredded cabbage combo or one with ham, Gruyère, and butter. Or you can save your appetite for the delicious, borderline savory dessert sandwich with chocolate, sea salt, and olive oil. Can you really argue with those ingredients?

You might as well try to lodge a case against this place's cuteness.

Aladdin's Café

A good introduction to Lebanese food, and a fine way to satisfy well-established cravings

6.9	7.5
Food	Feel

Lebanese

Casual restaurant

$20
Price

www.aladdinscafe.com

Daily 11am–9pm

Bar Beer, wine
Credit cards Visa, MC, AmEx
Reservations Accepted
Outdoor dining, veg-friendly, Wi-Fi

Northeast Portland
6310 NE 33rd Ave.
(503) 546-7686

Like most good non-European eateries, Aladdin's Café is not about the ambience. Not that there's anything wrong with it; the interior is bright, with multi-colored walls showcasing interesting Middle Eastern and Egyptian artwork. It's just that it's mostly utilitarian, its purpose being to serve food—which it does very well. However, if you can swing it, the small patio area out front with about six tables is a nice place to hang out on a warm evening.

The Lebanese food served here is of the quotidian street-food variety, and priced so reasonably that it's easy to get carried away and order more than you can eat. A very crisp falafel ball with a molten interior snaps as you bite into it. Baba ghanoush is loaded with good eggplant flavor, balanced by tahini and lemon, but isn't as smoky as it could be. Hummus is very smooth and balanced—a bit more processed-tasting than some— but with excellent flavors. Fattoush comes with small chips of toasted pita bread that give it a good crunch, and is finished with sumac, garlic, olive oil, and lemon juice. The tomatoes tend to taste rather industrial, but with good spices. Tabbouleh is nicely spiced and citric, getting a chewy texture from bulgur. But most addictive is safeeha (a Lebanese version of pizza), baked crispy with ground beef, tomatoes, and onions on top—this is also among the cheapest dishes in Portland.

What really sets Aladdin apart is its bright, lively tahini, which integrates into many other dishes in judicious quantities, rather than drenching. We also love the pita bread, which is baked fresh with every order, turning from a round little ball of dough to a wonderfully hot, delicately crispy brown disc that's rushed to your table right out of the oven. The pitas aren't too thick and come nicely browned, making a great foundation for some sandwiches, like lamb shawarma and kofta, both of which are textural wonders redolent of cumin.

This is not a destination restaurant, but it can be quite good. If you are anywhere near the neighborhood or are into Lebanese food, you need to put it on your list.

Alameda Café

A neighborhood bistro that relies on your low expectations to really shine

6.1	6.5
Food	Feel

American Casual restaurant **$30** Price

Mon–Fri 8am–9pm; Sat 8am–2pm, 3pm–9pm; Sun 8am–2pm

Bar Beer, wine, liquor
Credit cards Visa, MC, AmEx
Reservations Accepted
Kid-friendly, outdoor dining

Northeast Portland
4641 NE Fremont St.
(503) 284-5314

Alameda Café comes across, at first, as sort of boring and outdated with its white tablecloths and floral theme. (Sunflowers? Is this the set of *Blossom*?) The bottles-of-wine-as-décor concept has that kind of earnest artlessness you'd get from a couple of kids playing restaurant for their parents.

At brunch, it's hard to argue with French toast made from baguettes dunked in cinnamon-dusted Corn Flakes, or huge and delicious Benedicts, especially at these prices. We find the migas on the menu adorable, even though this is a decidedly Northwest version that wouldn't fly in Texas. (Pepper Jack? Lackaday!) The menu incorporates more Southwest kicks like chorizo and jalapeño this and that, and sells Belgian waffles for less than a fiver. Unfortunately, omelettes can be dense and fluffy one day, dry and crumbly the next. It's popular with families—kids can draw on the paper over the tablecloths. (Translation: don't show up with a hangover.) But there's no excuse for coffee this weak, especially in Portland, and especially when it's Stumptown.

For lunch, you'll find fancy-prosaic items like chicken quesadillas, hand-cut fries, the usual salads, and "Cajun halibut sandwich" with lovely, bright spices. Meatloaf is moist and flavorful, and chicken picatta has a fresh lemon flavor. But again, these are the kinds of dishes kids could make at an after-school cooking class. It's fine, but nothing worth going out of your way for.

At night, as the space becomes more intimate and warmly lit, the otherwise boring food improves slightly to "elegantly outdated." There are careful renditions of classics using local ingredients, like Cascade ribeye with Crater Lake blue-cheese butter; and Carlton Valley pork chop with a baby summer vegetable hash. And then there are not-so-careful preparations like miso-glazed halibut (leave the Asian fusion to the '90s, please).

In any case, any romantic feelings of benevolence toward this unassuming food are whisked away by curt, annoyed servers that will begin to unceremoniously whisk *you* away as soon as they feel they've closed. In the end, Alameda is predominantly a decent brunch spot (for mimosas) if you're in the neighborhood. Just don't expect good service or mind-blowing food, and you'll be all right.

Alba Osteria

A charming, romantic homage to all things Piedmontese

8.3	9.0	7.5
Food	Feel	Wine

Italian

Upmarket restaurant

$60
Price

www.albaosteria.com

Tue–Thu 5:30pm–9pm
Fri–Sat 5:30pm–9:30pm

Bar Beer, wine, liquor
Credit cards Visa, MC, AmEx
Reservations Accepted
Date-friendly, outdoor dining, veg-friendly

Southwest Portland
6440 SW Capitol Hwy.
(503) 977-3045

Alba Osteria, hidden away across the bridge in Hillsdale, is one of those places that you could drive past a million times and not notice. In a narrow building that is occupied on one end by Capitol Coffee House, this authentic Northern Italian restaurant is much more date-friendly than you might expect upon first glance.

Although you park rather unceremoniously in a gravel lot across the street, there are several nooks and crannies inside that allow for private, intimate conversations. Old wood floors, warmed by light spilling in through generous windows, are a charming and homey contrast to crisp white table linens.

The menu is divided, true to form, into antipasti, primi (usually pastas), and secondi (protein-centered plates), with selections rotating somewhat seasonally. You'll start with good bread and recommendations by the knowledgeable staff, which manages to strike that sweet spot between available and hovering.

Of the antipasti, salads are just what you'd expect, nothing more, with top-quality greens and large portions; dressings are balanced but unexciting. Go for more interesting renditions, such as top-quality beef tartare. Classically prepared terrines of duck and pork have been served much too cold, muting their flavors. But the menu changes often enough that it's always a new game.

Alba Osteria does make some of the best pasta we've had outside of Italy. Homemade maltagliati (which means "badly cut"—literally torn) melt in the mouth; agnolotti have paper-thin skin so that the fillings—such as veal, pork, and spinach—burst forth bite after bite; and tajarin, the souvenir pasta of the Langhe, is skillfully cut in long, thin strands. With seasonal porcini, morels, and spring onions, it is a revelation.

Secondi, on the other hand, are a bit of a mixed bag. Meats can be overcooked, but are usually well paired, if a little pricey for what they are. We've had a duck leg confit that was a total train wreck, dry and overcooked, then glazed with too-sweet honey and aged balsamic vinegar; but we've also had a fine, if underwhelming, halibut prep.

The all-Piedmontese wine list is commendable and fairly priced, but we wish there were more older-vintages, as many of these wines are drinking fine, but only at a fraction of their potential. In general, there's a lot of care put into this place. Despite a few missteps, this is a memorable and worthwhile meal, with just the sort of vibe that will bring you back.

Albina Press

Come for a pedagogical experience or just a religious one—either way, this is coffee at its best

Coffee, Baked goods

Café

Daily 6am–8pm

Bar None
Credit cards Visa, MC, AmEx
Outdoor dining, veg-friendly, Wi-Fi

North Portland
4637 North Albina Ave.
(503) 282-5214

Albina Press is like the small-production, biodynamic winery that refuses to oak (or oak much) and is obsessed with terroir-driven juice. These guys are artists; they're passionate and persnickety. Not only do they care about the beans, but also they care about where the beans were harvested and how much the pickers were paid. The coffee must be tamped perfectly, and if the pull or the temperature or the crema is not perfect, they'll dump the shot and start over.

The results are life-changing, even for self-proclaimed coffee snobs, who will find such an intoxicating and yet stimulating blend of aromas, mouthfeel, and flavor that they will never again settle for big bruisers like Starbucks—or coffee that they have to load up with sweeteners and flavored cream in order to make palatable.

When the place isn't slammed, the baristas will walk you through the choices of espresso: Hairbender, Stumptown or Harar. Americanos are lush and translucent and have a great depth. The French press is done with just the right grind to minimize leftover sediment. Cappuccinos are rich, with a buttery mouthfeel and nearly perfect body. The artistry takes visual forms, as well: a latte might have a perfect apple of white and tan floating on a smooth, brown crema. At most serious coffee houses, if you order hot chocolate, you'll get it with a bit of attitude; here, it may come with a perfect rosette.

The interior is inviting, with a laid-back vibe and mellow music. Check out the trophies from the National Barista championships. A bar next to the windows invites contemplation, and there are plenty of regular tables and soft couches to dive into. Free Wi-Fi and a surprising number of electrical outlets lures college students, neighborhood regulars, and newly converted coffee geeks. There are also a dozen blends of Tao of Tea, and the pastries are a step up from the norm in quality and size. But all of this is in mere service of some of America's best coffee.

Altengartz

The food cart post of a sausage empire

6.6 Food

6.0 Feel

German

Food cart **$5** Price

www.germanbratwurst.com

Mon–Fri 11am–2:30pm

Bar None
Credit cards Visa, MC
Kid-friendly, outdoor dining

Downtown
SW 10th and Alder

It's not uncommon to find, in the great American melting pot, unlikely marriages of cuisines. In what we like to call "Modern American" cuisine, there are all sorts of stunted love children, like mango-jalapeño spicy tuna rolls or pesto enchiladas. There are also careful, successful pairings that will have even the most red-blooded Commie appreciating the unrestrained creativity of these kitchen pioneers.

But another thing that America's immigrant communities can provide is a sort of culinary time travel. Academics are offered a look back in time, for instance, at unique pockets of linguistic interest that are preserved all across the country; there are Czech towns in central Texas where residents still speak the language of 1800s Czechoslovakia, which isn't immediately recognizable to a speaker of the modern-day incarnation of the language. And there are communities that have preserved the food not only of another country, but of a distinct period in that country's history.

Such, supposedly, is the case with the family at Altengartz. They left Germany in the late 1800s, and, as the story goes, on a recent pilgrimage back to the motherland, an exhaustive search yielded no sausage quite like theirs. We have a hunch that this lovely little anecdote has more to do with selling sausage than an anthropological inquiry, but we'll bite. The sausage is great at this humble, friendly food cart. Bratwurst have a lovely snap to their casing and a full, meaty flavor. Ask for it without cheese—we find it too distracting, and it's not a move you see too often back in the Old World. Bread isn't the freshest.

This is a bare-bones experience. Those manning the cart are polite, but a bit quiet. Diners are provided with way-too-flimsy plastic tables and chairs. Get it to go if you can, and enjoy.

Should you become hooked, sausages from the Altengartz diaspora are available just about everywhere, in any frozen foods aisle.

Andina

Both the classic and the nouvelle work well
at this sexy, fun take on Peruvian

8.8	9.5	8.0
Food	Feel	Drinks

Peruvian, Nuevo Latino

Upmarket restaurant

$70
Price

www.andinarestaurant.com

Sun–Thu 11:30am–2:30pm,
4pm–9:30pm
Fri–Sat 11:30am–2:30pm,
4pm–10:30pm

Bar Beer, wine, liquor
Credit cards Visa, MC, AmEx
Reservations Essential
Date-friendly, live music, outdoor
dining, veg-friendly, Wi-Fi

Pearl District
1314 NW Glisan St.
(503) 228-9535

With all the yuppies and bright colors and self-aggrandizing chef
accolades in the lobby, this showy restaurant *couldn't* be good—could it?

Andina is the rare upmarket case where the combination works. The
bar area is lively; everyone is having fun and drinking strong cocktails, and
there are warm colors and a bustle. The dining room is a bit more sedate,
but equally warm, and we love the area of outdoor tables on the floor
below, which has the feel of a cute courtyard overlooked by a balcony
within the restaurant.

The menu is divided into "platos criollos" (traditional Peruvian) and
"platos novoandinos" (nouvelle Andean), of which we favor the former:
seco a la norteña (a nicely braised lamb shank), a surprisingly flavorful
vegetarian squash soup, and such. Even when nouvelle creations get
overly elaborate, their execution is generally spot on. There are special
vegetarian and gluten-free menus, as well.

The real highlight, though, is the tapas menu, which centers around
Peruvian with some Spanish conceits. Causa (a sort of molded terrine) is
terrific, whether it's done as morada (made from irresistible purple
potatoes and smoked chicken) or mixta nikkei (with spicy tuna, crab salad,
and fried shrimp—a nod to the sizeable Japanese community in Peru that
has deeply influenced the country's modern cuisine). In the "chicharrón
de langostinos," quinoa batter forms such an impenetrable barrier
between frying oil and jumbo shrimp that it's able to keep the meat
remarkably moist even while obtaining a deeply browned crust. Of the
formidable array of ceviches, we love the simplest: a silky fish of the day,
kissed gently by citrus. Even the most elemental dish on the menu, grilled
asparagus, gets a nice char from the fire and richness from olive oil.

Rare are missteps like piquillo peppers stuffed with barely noticeable
cheese, overcooked jamón serrano, and a quinoa mixture that falls apart
when you cut into it. And although people love the three sauces that
come with bread to begin with, we're not sold; the bread isn't the
freshest, and the sauces tend to be prosaic and oversweet.

The wine list stretches from Old World to New, and is astute and well
priced; there are several good bottles here under $40. There are also
several interesting, if often sweet, Nuevo Latino cocktails. Ask for the
"tortuga"—gin shaken with cucumber, lime, mint, and sugar—with half
the sugar, and you're in for a delicious treat. Or just keep it simple and
stick to sangría, the perfect date drink.

Apizza Scholls

Here, the pie—not the customer—is always right

9.3	6.5	8.0
Food	Feel	Beer

Pizza

Casual restaurant

$30
Price

www.apizzascholls.com

Mon–Sat 5pm–9:30pm
Sun 4pm–8pm

Bar Beer, wine
Credit cards Visa, MC
Reservations Not accepted
Kid-friendly, veg-friendly

Hawthorne
4741 SE Hawthorne Blvd.
(503) 233-1286

We're not sure if this is one of the top pizzerias in America, as some of the food media claim, but Apizza Scholls does make a damned delicious pie, putting to bed the trendy theory that only pizzas cooked in a wood-fired oven are worth getting excited about. This one's fired in a good, old-fashioned American pizza oven—but the operators of the oven seem to achieve high enough temperatures for a beautiful sear on the crust.

The accolades have lured a mighty queue of people; you'll have to wait outside as early as 4:45pm (3:45 on Sundays) if you want to squeeze into the first seating at this no-reservations pizzeria. Who has the time for this? But just when you start to complain that Apizza Scholls has gotten too big for its britches, you taste the pizza.

Keeping it pure and simple, the "Margo-rita" (named for Apizza's beloved long-time waitress) is excellent: creamy, briny whole-milk mozzarella (fior di latte, not bufala), applied in bright white medallions; and tomatoes that are sweet, sweet, sweet. You might, however, choose to add a few chunks of the irresistible house-made fennel sausage. The half-and-half toppings option is popular, especially with so many exciting ingredients made on the premises (hot capicollo, for instance). House-made bacon appears in long strips on a laudable bianca pie with sea salt, extra virgin olive oil, mozzarella, and Pecorino Romano. Regular pizzas are sized for 2-3 people, but solo diners can get half-pizzas (though you can't do these half-and-half).

Wait to be seated in the bar, if you can. The mostly good, mostly cheap Italian wine list is good, but here, we prefer beer. This praiseworthy, succinct list could begin and end with Trumer Pils, a crisp Austrian pilsner that goes perfectly with pizza. It's on tap and, even better, now brewed at a branch in Berkeley, so it's fresher. Local beer is underrepresented on draft, but hoppy IPA isn't the greatest match with pizza. Still, there's plenty of it in the bottle, as well as German wheat beers, and the terrific, fruity Duchesse de Bourgogne.

Service is brusque and distracted—even getting a beer can be an ordeal. And don't expect the doors to open even 30 seconds early. The space is airy, a bit bright, and tables are missing a certain intimacy. It's not a romantic spot. The second room is sleeker and a bit sexier, but nobody comes to Scholls for the vibe. They come to meditate on tomatoes, mozzarella, and crust. (After sweating outside for a long while.)

Arabian Breeze

Neither Arabian nor particularly breezy—just hit-or-miss Lebanese food with none of the perks

Lebanese

Casual restaurant

$25
Price

www.arabianbreezeportland.com

Mon–Thu 11am–9pm
Fri–Sat 11am–10pm
Sun noon–9pm

Bar Beer, wine
Credit cards Visa, MC, AmEx
Reservations Not accepted
Kid-friendly, outdoor dining,
veg-friendly, Wi-Fi

Northeast Portland
3223 NE Broadway
(503) 445-4700

Arabian Breeze: the name conjures up romantic images of desert oases scented with turmeric. This is more like staging Disney's *Aladdin* in a converted basement: low ceilings, lots of bright colors, and positively goofy décor. The center pillars sandwich a long community table, and the fruity smell of smoke from the hookahs upstairs wafts by now and then. Even the long menu is entertaining, with enticing descriptions and pictures of both the usual Lebanese fare and some less common dishes.

Service is friendly but clumsy. Appetizers are routinely delivered with main courses, and water glasses might sit empty for long, parched periods. The cutlery is the cheap, malleable stuff you find in cafeterias.

You do get a lot of food for your money, though. Saj (similar to pita bread) is made fresh and hot off the griddle, draped over a holder on your table. Go ahead and wolf it down—this is something the staff will refill hastily. Kofta is very mild; the meat is juicy, though not particularly lamby. The chicken kebab, on the other hand, is irresistible: two large skewers of moist, tender chicken are served with peppers and onions over a mound of rice and a side of toom (traditional yogurt cheese in a garlic purée). This alone is worth coming back for.

Unfortunately, everything else ranges from average to pathetic. Freekah—smoked, cracked green wheat that is imported from Damascus and cooked with chicken, pine nuts, herbs, and spices—is unique and satisfying, but doesn't blow our skirts up. Salads are just pathetic, with inadequate vegetables, drowned in garlicky dressing. Labna, a thick, fresh yogurt cheese with mint, thyme, and olive oil, comes on a huge plate surrounded by industrial-tasting cucumber and tomato slices; at least you get a lot of it, if that's a good thing. There are several types of stuffed and fried sambousik (traditional turnovers), but these can be heavy, dripping with oil and quickly turning soggy. At best, they tend to be unspiced and boring. Falafel isn't even close to the best around.

If the dishes were nearly as good as their descriptions, we could forgive all other gripes about this place. Certainly, this is a lot of food for the money, and the hookah scent is great. But culinarily, the name remains the most transportive part of the meal.

Asian Station Café

Shanghai soup dumplings—and don't you forget it

<table>
<tr><td>6.3</td><td>5.0</td></tr>
<tr><td>Food</td><td>Feel</td></tr>
</table>

Chinese

Food cart

$5
Price

www.asianstationcafe.com

Mon–Fri 11:30am–2pm

Bar None
Credit cards Visa, MC
Kid-friendly, outdoor dining

Downtown
SW 10th and Alder
(503) 227-5727

The owners of this little stand are passionate about their menu, which they like to think of as Chinese soul food. And as with any of Portland's food carts, it's a great place to see people and mingle. It's also a great place for a progressive dinner or lunch, wandering around and sampling from each cart. But for this leg of your cart crawl, the Shanghai soup dumplings are the only reason to stop; everything else is mediocre.

Seldom available in restaurants, soup dumplings are a unique food item in Portland. The gingery soup broth on the inside is a warm, comforting burst of deliciousness upon biting into the dumpling, followed by a firm meatball of pork within the soupy depths.

The dumplings are served with brightly colored red wine vinegar whose purpose is to add some tangy acidity, but we still find a hint of sweetness in it. The dough is firm and pasty enough to hold the soup inside. Mechanically, it checks out (which is good—a soup dumpling that doesn't remain intact can be a shirt-ruining disaster). Still, it's not the mind-blowing experience you look for. Yet it's still better than anything else here.

Malaysian coconut chicken curry is a bland, mushy mix of chicken, potatoes, and onions, with a surprising—perhaps overbearing—sweetness from the coconut. Its accompanying potstickers cheapen the dish a bit. Dessert roti with cinnamon and sugar are decent, but a bit illustrative of the menu's lack of focus.

By virtue of being an open-air cart, this is indeed street food. But where are the bold, bowl-you-over flavors that Chinese street food is known for? A walk through a hawker center in China is an assault on the senses. Asian Station Café, beyond the soup dumplings, is more of a frustrating tease.

The dumplings take 10 minutes—understandable, as they're steamed to order—but you should only visit this cart if you're a soup-dumpling aficionado with a real craving.

Auténtica

Authentic dishes from Mexico's Pacific coast
that don't always pander to American palates

8.3	8.5	7.5
Food	Feel	Drinks

Mexican, Nuevo Latino

Upmarket restaurant

$45
Price

www.autenticaportland.com

Tue–Fri 11am–2pm, 5pm–10pm
Sat–Sun 10am–2pm, 5pm–
10pm

Bar Beer, wine, liquor
Credit cards Visa, MC, AmEx
Reservations Accepted
Date-friendly, outdoor dining

Alberta Arts District
5507 NE 30th Ave.
(503) 287-7555

This restaurant, in an exploding area of Northeast Portland near the Alberta stretch, self-christened as the "Fox-Chase Addition," has been plagued in the past by poor service and timing issues which deterred a lot of people from experiencing this food, which can be challenging enough as it is. Many dishes are (you guessed it) authentically made in the style found in the Guerrero state of Mexico, home to Acapulco. In this area, they use the pungent, somewhat fetid herb epazote to help control gas. Hey, there's a price for everything.

The airy space seems to pull off a slightly trendy, lively buzz on almost every night, an atmosphere extremely conducive to drinking many margaritas. The menu is fairly static, with occasional specials that are often very good. Portions, as you'd expect, are generous. Meals start with a refreshing, not-too-spicy escabeche of potatoes, carrots, and cauliflower. Guacamole is fresh and balanced—much better than most restaurant versions. Seafood cocktails are a great way to start, especially with tender, toothsome octopus with tomatoes, red onions, and serrano peppers. Out-of-season tomatoes don't help any of the cocktails, but the prawns and scallops are great. Skip the soups—the tortilla in particular is rather wimpy and soggy. Instead, save room for wonderful tamales. The pork version has a deep, vivid red chili sauce; a vegetarian option with poblanos, cream, and that slightly bitter epazote is also good.

Red mole here is one of the better versions in town, complex and intense, with bitter chocolate unifying the several different kinds of dried chilies. On a moist half chicken, it's delicious, as is a smoky chipotle mole. Whole fish is also cooked beautifully, and paired with a sauce that complements, rather than overwhelming.

It's easy to keep picking out winners: a thin flatiron steak, cooked quickly on the flat-top with charro beans, serrano peppers, epazote, and little strips of nopalitos (cactus); or lomitos de puerco, fork-tender pork tenderloin with a green mole of pumpkin seeds and serranos. Less impressive is a cocido de res, slow-cooked beef short ribs that tend to be underseasoned and served in a somewhat bland broth. But the hits vastly outnumber the misses.

Margaritas vary greatly depending on who's making them. On one night they will be perfect; on another the balance will be way off. For the most part, the food here is interesting and well prepared, and gives those used to the standard burrito-and-enchilada plates a foray into real Mexican food. And now that the service and timing issues have improved, we'll be back again and again.

Backspace

A venue with many faces, good vegetarian café fare, Stumptown coffee, and surprisingly little attitude

Coffee, Vegefusion

Café

www.backspace.bz

Mon–Fri 7am–midnight
Sat–Sun 10am–midnight

Bar Beer, wine
Credit cards Visa, MC, AmEx
Date-friendly, live music, outdoor
dining, veg-friendly, Wi-Fi

Old Town Chinatown
115 NW 5th Ave.
(503) 248-2900

Backspace is a techno-playground. An internet café. A coffee lounge. A concert venue. An art gallery. How well it does each of these things varies. It's a cozy, narrowish room that invites hours of lingering, gaming, and general dorking out; but it gets claustrophobic during concerts. The blood-red brick walls are spectacular for showcasing gorgeous, surreal art from locals and friends—not so much for acoustics. The sound quality is a common complaint amongst concertgoers, which is a shame considering the diversity of bands that perform here: DJs, hip hop, math rock, punk, girl/boy-and-guitar/piano, and so on.

   PCs are available for rent by the hour in a secluded, dungeon-like space toward the back, so this is an ideal spot for network gaming. But no one will stink-eye you for just checking emails or lingering for hours. Perhaps the peaceful spirit is owed to the all-vegetarian food served here: serviceable sandwiches made with meat substitutes, salads, black bean and rice bowls, and the like. The reptilian part of the brain is lit up by a number of caffeine drinks, from Stumptown coffees and espressos to Jolt colas and guarana tinctures. And don't come looking for sweet, caramel-white-chocolate-vanilla-mochaccinos—you'll have to get your sugar in the form of Voodoo Donuts, which Backspace often carries.

   To mellow out after a good ten-hour cybertrouncing, there are a handful of taps pouring local brews brewers, and some more in bottle. Wine should just be ignored, as should tea (by Stash). The trick to Backspace is in knowing how to use it. Beware of concerts, and don't think of it as a destination for vegan and vegetarian food; that stuff is just there to fuel hours of "pwning."

Baker & Spice

They can bake it and you can take it—or go to their classes to make it

Baked goods

Counter service

www.bakerandspicebakery.com

Tue–Fri 6am–6pm	**Bar** None	**Southwest Portland**
Sat 7am–6pm	**Credit cards** Visa, MC, AmEx	6330 SW Capitol Hwy.
Sun 7am–3pm	Kid-friendly, veg-friendly	(503) 244-7573

Baker & Spice is everything you want from a bakery. It's warm and friendly, a sweet little place to hang out on snowy days, and it smells like cookies. The pastry cases are framed in wood, and it's totally un-self-conscious. In short, we want to move there.

Its spot next to Starbucks doesn't concern it much—you might even be able to pick up some of the Wi-Fi from next door (but it'll cost you). People are always lined up at this counter for espresso from ZBeanZ, a very local roaster. These are made carefully, as carefully as the coffee cake that is its natural partner—Ginger to its Fred. The moist cake is topped with crunchy sugar and cinnamon, but flaky croissants—like a ham and Gruyère—are just as tempting. Scones are buttery and not too crumbly nor greasy. Granola with yogurt and berries, when in season, is also phenomenal—and sort of almost healthy.

For something unabashedly sweet, try a "Katie Bun," but share: it's too gooey to take down alone (a large drip coffee helps—then you'll be good and high all day long). Bread puddings make good use of bread that's too old to sell—perhaps the most delicious recycling effort in the world. This bread, when fresh, includes baguettes, challah, rye, and ciabatta with black and green olives.

Sandwiches can be chewy and crusty, sometimes jaw-wearingly so. But the fillings are great, like tuna salad with cornichons and dill, or smoked ham and Gruyère with Dijon mustard. Soups change daily and are often a good effort.

And after you've eaten all your nutritious lunch, you may take a lovely cake to go. Whole cakes cost much less than they do at Papa Haydn, and are nearly as good (better, if you prefer your carrot cake sans pineapple—this one is nothing but carrots, raisins, walnuts, and spice). Or head a few doors down to their baking supply store, SweetWares, and learn how to do it yourself.

Bakery Bar

A sweet, secret haven of pastry

Baked goods

Counter service

www.bakerybar.com

Mon–Thu 7am–5pm
Fri 7am–4pm
Hours vary by location

Bar None
Credit cards Visa, MC, AmEx
Date-friendly, kid-friendly,
veg-friendly, Wi-Fi

Southeast Portland
1028 SE Water Ave.
(503) 546-8110

Northeast Portland
2935 NE Glisan St.
(503) 477-7779

Although both branches of this bakery are easy to miss, it would be a shame if you did. Inside the space is bigger than you'd expect, spacious and airy with an open kitchen. Large windows invite light on dark days, and a nice collection of art hangs on the walls. You could probably hang out here for hours, drooling over a selection of pastries and breads from the glass display case.

Those looking for a buzz will be happy to know that the coffee here is from Stumptown. If you order something like a mocha or the caramel-Bourbon latte, it might come with pillowy homemade marshmallows. Compared to the coffee found at most other places in town, the Bakery Bar's flavor actually triumphs over the caramel; the house-made syrup has a woodsy, not overly sweet, Bourbon flavor. Cappuccinos and drip coffees taste just like you would expect from a Stumptown vendor.

Desserts seem to come out of the oven all day long. They tend to be simple, but beautifully decorated, and stay thankfully more toward well balanced than cloyingly sweet. For a gratuitous scheme to make you drool, here's a list of recent offerings: ginger cookies; moist carrot cake; orange-cranberry scones; coconut cakes; cupcakes topped with coconut frosting; coconut cream puffs filled with coconut pastry cream and topped with chocolate ganache and yet more coconut; Linzer tortes with rhubarb and pears (a seasonal dish). Not everything is available at one time, but you can always order custom cakes for weddings and the like.

There are also several good-sized pressed panini, and these are okay— sometimes the spreads overwhelm the other components. But you're only eating these to justify cramming a small cake down your gullet, aren't you? Bakery Bar is one of those places you want to take friends to because it feels like such a secret—a sweet, clandestine affair for which even clarklewis diners sometime slink across the dark street.

Bamboo Grove

4.4 Food   **7.5** Feel

For flourescent-bulb burnout and gray-day doldrums,
greasy pork and teriyaki to hula them away

Hawaiian

Casual restaurant   **$25** Price

Mon–Fri 11am–9pm
Sat noon–9pm
Sun 4pm–8pm

Bar Beer, wine, liquor, BYO
Credit cards Visa, MC, AmEx
Reservations Accepted
Kid-friendly, live music, outdoor
dining, Wi-Fi

Southwest Portland
0515 SW Carolina St.
(503) 977-2771

We're not really that far from Hawaii in terms of mileage, but for weather
and culture, it couldn't get any more different than Portland. And in this
gastronomically impoverished neighborhood, especially on a gray, drizzly
day, Bamboo Grove Hawaiian Grille can sound pretty tempting (just don't
come by on hot days—there's no A/C).

The place is always packed with office types at lunch, especially on
Fridays. But tables turn quickly, owing in part to brusque, efficient service.
Don't expect smiling hulas or anything that excessive; the décor is
surprisingly un-kitschy. There's a surfboard near the daily specials board
and faux bamboo painted on a wall. But head to the back, and you're
totally in Disney's Tiki Room. Sometimes there's even a live ukelele band.

Fridays and Saturdays bring a more benign form of kalua pork, what
you'd associate with a luau. We say "benign" because it's not roasted in a
pit under banana leaves. Here, it's oven roasted with liquid smoke and
Hawaiian salt, which makes for some juicy, delicious, and quite greasy pig.
The sides, a watery macaroni salad and unseasoned sticky rice, are total
throw-aways, but it's cheap and there's plenty of pork.

Let's face it—teriyaki is good. Or it can be, anyway. Foodies sneer at the
gloppy sweet stuff their less genteel friends order at sushi restaurants, and
rightfully so. But this teriyaki has much more soyish umami, and comes on
charred chicken, tough beef, and better pork. Ribs tend to be stringy, but
with pretty addictive sauces; Maui-style ribs are super-sweet, and Korean-
style short ribs are garlicky, though nothing like good, cross-cut galbi.

And third in the Hawaiian food triumvirate—no, not Spam, though it's
here, too—is poke, kind of a marinated-tuna tartare. Bamboo Grove
offers this three ways: with soy and sesame oil (traditional), ginger, or
shoyu. Again, this is just okay, with the traditional being slightly better
than the overbearing shoyu.

Hawaiian food certainly has its place, and it would be nice to see an
ambitious, perhaps Japanese-trained chef come along and temper the
grease and mayonnaise on traditional preparations with some nuance and
sophistication. Bamboo Grove isn't entirely faithful to the best renditions
found in Hawaii. But it's here on gray days, and it's pretty fun.

Bamboo Sushi

Sushi that makes sustainability chic and often delicious

6.6	7.0	8.5
Food	Feel	Wine

Japanese

Upmarket restaurant

$40
Price

www.bamboosushipdx.com

Daily 5pm–10pm

Bar Beer, wine, liquor, BYO
Credit cards Visa, MC, AmEx
Reservations Not accepted
Date-friendly, Wi-Fi

Southeast Portland
310 SE 28th Ave.
(503) 232-5255

Bamboo Sushi holds the distinction of being the first certified sustainable sushi bar in the world. You won't find anything from the Monterey Bay Aquarium's red list here. For fans of buttery toro, beefy bluefin, and unagi, it's time to weigh values against one another. Here, you know that what you order will have been fished responsibly, which also includes treatment of human workers. The freshwater eel industry in Korea, for instance, is riddled with Upton-Sinclairesque worker strife.

But even good intentions can become antagonistic if restaurant owners aren't careful. Bamboo is classy and elemental, all glass and wood and low lighting, and platings are artful—but the service can be spotty. Also, it seems essential to wade through much table-tented dogma and guilt before ever putting that first piece of fish into your mouth. The high-mindedness can get a bit tiresome.

Owing in part to this hyperconsciousness, the sushi here does tend to be some of the freshest in town. Uni is properly served in smaller portions and not super cold; it's buttermilky and briny, like a spray of Pacific surf. Safer tunas like yellowfin, skipjack, and albacore are less full of flavor than blood-rich bluefin, but worth retraining the palate for. Ama ebi (sweet shrimp) is always a rare, glutinous treat, and saba is wonderfully oily.

Wild salmon nigiri has been too lean and underwhelming, and wild hamachi, when in season, has periodically suffered from inelegant cuts; sometimes, it's on the grain and sometimes, as is preferred, against.

Unfortunately, Bamboo Sushi seems to miss its own point by stuffing the majority of the menu with Westernized, muddy-tasting rolls that utterly mask the fish flavors. That Americans pay such a high premium for lower-quality cuts of fish mashed up with spices and mayonnaise must be baffling to economists.

Hot dishes are pretty successful, like soul-warming age dofu made with local Ota bean curd, and decent udon. The sake selection is terrific and diverse, but pricey, too, without a single bottle under $35. At least you get education for your money; the menu has a helpful guide to the levels of rice polishing and quality, as well as region. Apparently, fish aren't the only species being looked out for at this well-meaning and accessible sushi restaurant.

Bar Avignon

Good food and drinks in a simple, chic setting—it's not "just" a bar

8.1	8.5	8.5
Food	Feel	Wine

Modern

Upmarket restaurant

$45
Price

www.baravignon.com

Sun–Thu 4pm–11pm
Fri–Sat 4pm–midnight

Bar Beer, wine, liquor
Credit cards Visa, MC, AmEx
Reservations Not accepted
Date-friendly, live music, outdoor dining

Division/Clinton
2138 SE Division St.
(503) 517-0808

Whenever we see the Casablanca Antique font and its progeny—as we do on the shingle outside Avignon, we get nervous. Is this a popular design affectation that is meant to lure hipsters, or is there sincerity behind this rustic aesthetic? Is it trendy-posing-as-unfussy, or is this bare-bones wine bar effortlessly chic in its simplicity? Then we remember: we're on Division Street. It's most likely the real deal.

And in fact, this wine bar is very hip and hopping these days—for all legitimate reasons. The very cool (but not quite cooler-than-thou) servers are very knowledgeable about wine, more likely to recommend an interesting Grüner than a watery Pinot Grigio. It helps that the selection here is astute and passionate, with as many small-production biodynamic Europeans as there are prestigious bottles of Willamette Pinot Noir. There are few mass-produced cop-outs here, but wine nerds will recognize and appreciate the (mostly) reasonable markups on harder-to-find wines. A small but focused beer list, with almost all locals (including one delicious cask-conditioned), is starting to receive just as much attention as the wine.

Lately, Bar Avignon has been making serious inroads as a restaurant. The food has really developed, with a chef-driven menu focused on local, seasonal produce—everything seems to be made to complement the wines. Great cheeses come from small farms that grass-feed their livestock. Charcuterie boards include wine-cured salumi and excellent chicken-liver mousse. Plump mussels are served with a broth that balances acidic wine and rich cream so beautifully that you'll want to soak up every drop with griddled bread. Speaking of which, Little T supplies the loaves here, which we love on sandwiches.

The décor supports Avignon's slogan, printed on some of the staff's T-shirts: "Just a bar." There are stained concrete floors, exposed pipes, wine racks and boxes, and industrial lighting fixtures kept at an enjoyably dim setting. The baby-blue bar is long and sleek, and the booths are nice—there isn't a bad seat in the joint. A second glance at that sign out front, and we believe this understated, humble, comfortable bar is just as promised.

Bar Mingo

Focus on happy hour at this popular wine-bar offshoot

6.4	8.0	9.0
Food	Feel	Wine

Italian

Casual restaurant

$35
Price

www.barmingonw.com

Sun–Mon 4pm–11pm
Tue–Sat 4pm–midnight

Bar Beer, wine, liquor
Credit cards Visa, MC, AmEx
Reservations Not accepted
Date-friendly, outdoor dining,
Wi-Fi

Northwest Portland
811 NW 21st Ave.
(503) 445-4646

The lower-commitment wing of Caffè Mingo, Bar Mingo started, like Bar Avignon, as a wine-focused venue unconcerned with food. But the bar snacks became so popular—people tend to like the smaller-plate/smaller-price format—that the place expanded the menu and became more of a restaurant. The result is a spot that now glows with quite a buzz.

Much of the menu here is composed of small plates of antipasti, which range from spicy goat cheese to oysters on the half shell to lamb meatballs. Sautéed calamari are tender and wonderful, with a lively freshness coming from lemon and parsley. But even simple antipasti here can trip over themselves, like prosciutto and melon plagued by dull-flavored, graying meat that is cut too thick. Chunky, gamy chicken-liver bruschetta is totally unworkable, cloyingly sweet from Marsala wine and dotted with unnecessary and distractingly salty capers of low quality.

Salads are fine, but pastas are a highlight. The homemade noodles have a gentle toothsomeness; delicate flavor shows through a simple a cacio e pepe, with pecorino and black pepper. Best of all, during happy hour (4–6pm daily), several plates and drinks are just $5 a pop, making for some good bargain eating.

The wine list is a sort of pocket guide to Italian varietals, Northern and Southern, cool climates and warm. A few are even exciting, and all are priced so low that we have to give props. There is a strangely heavy Napa showing, too, but why? Cocktails are decent—you have to appreciate the attempt at real Italian aperitivi. We like the negroni made with Portland's own Aviation gin. But most cocktails are in the sweeter school.

The sidewalk seating outside is nice, but there's more of a fun vibe inside, with warm lighting and a good crowd (if a little yuppie-heavy). It's a place that would be easier to rave about if not for the you're-lucky-if-you-get-a-seat attitude surrounding it. It reminds us of something Yogi Berra once said: "No one goes anymore—it's too crowded."

Barista Café

A turn-of-the-century laboratory brewing more than just a fix

Coffee

Café

www.baristapdx.com

Daily 7am–6pm

Bar None
Credit cards Visa, MC, AmEx
Outdoor dining, Wi-Fi

Pearl District
539 NW 13th Ave.
(503) 274-1211

Barista is a little more Pearl District and a little less indie than former tenant Acorn, but the place is still entirely coffee-geeky. Their beans come not only from the perfunctory Stumptown whizzes, but from equally epicurean roasters in Chicago, Durham, and the Bay Area. Pastries from the excellent Nuvrei also mean business.

The windows of this shabby, old brick building glow warmly in the fog and drizzle of an early morning. There's something about stumbling in here, sans adrenaline and hope, that makes the able hands of your barista no less than mystical. Coffee is, after oil (and sometimes steel and grain), the largest market in the world; it's been shown that people who drink coffee are less likely to commit suicide (*one more day, one more cup*). So no wonder that in Portland—which is the perfect storm between gastronomic obsession and coffee addiction—there are more and more places making coffee with devoted precision and artisanship.

These baristas are generous with their knowledge and passion for coffee; they will patiently offer information to help you choose, and will explain the various processes used to make it (just please don't expect this during rushes—we're in line behind you, and we're on the edge).

Most basic is the French press, done expertly with a uniform grind for the best extraction; then espresso shots of your choice of coffee, pulled short with a fine crema; macchiatos, lattes, and cappuccinos are made with specific espressos to best suit the milk, and don't bring any 2% nonsense in here—it's only whole milk, baby (or soy). From there, you may indulge in a vanilla or mocha latte, but it will be made with organic cane sugar and Guittard chocolate. That's as far from the pure product as they'll go.

But the Ferrari experience comes in the form of a $10 cup of vacuum-pot-brewed coffee. Seeing these glass-and-brass contraptions lined up together reminds us of the workshop of some Victorian mad scientist. This method will drip you a cup so gently (and slowly) that the nuanced flavors all sing clearly, where they are otherwise somewhat pummeled and muffled, even by careful hands. Try a cup, and decide for yourself whether it's worth the money.

Basha's Mediterranean

8.2 Food
6.5 Feel

Good gyros, shawarma, and baba ghanoush—with the falafel to end all falafel

Middle Eastern

Food cart

$5 Price

Mon–Fri 11:30am–4pm

Bar None
Credit cards None
Veg-friendly

Downtown
600 SW Pine St.
No phone

By "Mediterranean" they mean "Middle Eastern"—and many people similarly misuse the terms, despite the fact that the Mediterranean culinary swatch cuts across Morocco and Marseilles to Sicily to Greece and on to Turkey and Lebanon. Basha's menu focuses on the foods of the latter regions, namely the universal dishes shared between them: hummus, kofta, baba ghanoush, and everything else that has three or four different sanctioned spellings.

And—perhaps unsurprising given that this is a food cart that only accepts cash—we've had at Basha's some of the best falafel we've found in Portland. Seriously. Each is made to order with incredible complexity, depth, seasoning, and ideally fried texture. The tangy tzatziki is lovely and hummus is creamy, dense, and flavorful. Even the pita delivers. It's just outstanding; the iconic Mamoun's in New York City could learn a thing or two from this falafel.

Gyros and lamb shawarma can be good or oily, soggy messes, depending on the day. Most things, it seems, are inconsistent, but the falafel is routinely exemplary. A vegan lentil soup is hearty and cheap, served with that good pita bread. Baba ghanoush could be smokier, but it's still satisfying.

Warning: the hours aren't posted. The cart seems to appear and disappear at different hours throughout the week, but as far as we can tell, it's a lunchtime-through-the-afternoon operation. PSU students, consider yourselves lucky.

Bastas Trattoria

Rich impressions of Italian dishes that don't really impress much

5.9	7.5	8.0
Food	Feel	Wine

Italian

Upmarket restaurant

$45
Price

www.bastastrattoria.com

Mon–Thu 5pm–10pm
Fri–Sat 5pm–11pm
Sun 5pm–10pm

Bar Beer, wine, liquor
Credit cards Visa, MC, AmEx
Reservations Accepted
Date-friendly, outdoor dining

Northwest Portland
410 NW 21st Ave.
(503) 274-1572

At first glance, Bastas might seem like a cute, humble Italian trattoria from the *Wall Street* days; not that greed-promoting Gordon Gekko would ever be caught dead in what appears to be a former Tastee Freeze, even if it is dark and charming inside. But what lurks within is very confusing; a lot of vaguely Italian-sounding words that don't amount to much. Even the name is confusing: "Basta" means "enough," as in, "Basta! We're full!" Making it plural just drives this right into non-sequitur territory.

Which is also where the entire menu seems rooted. The hanger steak, we're told, is marinated in a "Tuscan pestino." What the hell is that? All three Google hits for "Tuscan pestino" are reviews of Bastas Trattoria and "pestino" is not an Italian noun. Is it an attempt at a diminutive of "pesto" (which is Ligurian, not Tuscan)? If so, why would you marinate a steak in pesto?

You'll also never find Italians stir frying ginger with wild prawns and squid in a tomato sauce. In fact, the only truly Italian dishes on this menu are arancini (fried saffron-risotto balls that are usually stuffed with cheese or meat ragù); carpaccio; and Bolognese. Everything else is essentially American with misspelled Italian names. We don't dismiss fusion automatically, but grilled pork tenderloin with gnocchi and marsala cream sauce is straight-up Macaroni Grill fare. It's rich enough to make us want to yell…you guessed it. Enoughs!

Regardless of how inauthentic the menu is, service is sincere and accommodating. The wine list features some very good producers, even if they are pretty common big names from Tuscany (home of the pestino) and Piedmont. Everyone will find something to drink within their price range. And these, they can be assured, are thoroughly Italian.

Bay 13

Underwhelming fish in an overhyped urban-chic behemoth

5.5	7.0	6.0
Food	Feel	Wine

Seafood

Upmarket restaurant

$50
Price

www.bay13restaurant.com

Sun–Thu 4pm–10pm
Fri–Sat 4pm–1am

Bar Beer, wine, liquor
Credit cards Visa, MC, AmEx
Reservations Accepted
Live music, outdoor dining, Wi-Fi

Pearl District
701 NW 13th St.
(503) 227-1133

Bay 13 opened in its converted warehouse space to a lot of hullabaloo, much of it self-generated. Its Moana Group owners clearly spent a lot of money renovating this 175-seat beast, which does bring an urban sophistication to an area that is typically a goomba-fest after 8pm. But by focusing on attracting a fickle crowd obsessed with the nouvelle, it may have doomed itself. It's certainly not winning anyone over with its kitchen.

The interior is huge, a monument to the un-Portland ideal that bigger is better. In fact, it's really impressive how a concrete floor, unadorned wood, and exposed brick can feel every bit as corporate-slutty as a velvet-draped steakhouse. There, at least, it would be quieter. No attempts are made to absorb sound here, which rattles uncomfortably off the hard surfaces (at least it used to, when more people would come).

A raw bar fills the front part of this monstrosity. Stick to the good oysters, as sushi attempts are uninspired and average. Although the fish tastes fresh, there is no art to any of it, to the eye or the tongue. Don't expect these to come out before main courses, either—if the sushi bar is backed up, you'll get 'em when you get 'em.

Even the simplest dishes are problematic. A roasted beet salad has come curiously lacking beets, and what few shards there were got overwhelmed by dressing. Caesar salads have often been overdressed. Fish is the focus here, and it is properly cooked, but platings and pairings are off. White fishes have been over-soaked in butter. Tuna has been fine, adorned with grill marks, served with a small ramekin of decent salsa verde. But there is nothing inspired about any of these preps—no innovation, playfulness, or confidence. And no main dish reaches the heights achieved by the humble vegetable sides.

Cocktails are—across the board—unbalanced and weak. The wine list would be fine in a less-savvy town, but here, it reads as careless, knee-jerk, and dull. At any rate, markups are strange—no one should pay $120 for Veuve Clicquot Yellow Label unless a lap dance is involved. It can hardly get any more gauche around here.

Beaker & Flask

Updated comfort food complements
Portland's most exciting cocktails

9.3	9.0	9.5
Food	Feel	Drinks

Modern

Casual restaurant

$35
Price

www.beakerandflask.com

Mon–Wed 5pm–midnight
Thu–Sat 5pm–1am

Bar Beer, wine, liquor
Credit cards Visa, MC
Reservations Accepted
Date-friendly, Wi-Fi

Southeast Portland
727 SE Washington St.
(503) 235-8180

Judging by the name, one would imagine Beaker & Flask to be a cleverly constituted bar and little more. You might surmise that it's got an ambitious cocktail program and an understated hipness. But who knew the food could be so drop-dead gorgeous, too?

Of course, the bar here is whipping up some of the most interesting cocktails in town, making use of *The Gentleman's Companion*, by Charles H. Baker, Jr., of which there's an original copy in the house. Drinks with cheeky names like "Daddy Issues" and "Viking Quest" take classic preparations and turn them on their head; the latter, for instance, mixes Portland's own Krogstad Aquavit with Campari and the wonderfully herbaceous digestif Chinato. This lovely bitter drink will totally wreak havoc on anyone used to drinking sickly sweet Stoli -tinis at outdated clubs, much like, we imagine, a Viking raid would do. That's not to say that you'll find these on the menu; rather, the drinks list changes constantly. Props, also, to an exceedingly well-chosen and succinct selection of local craft beers on tap.

The food is just as outstanding and well conceived, start to finish. Even a simple butter lettuce salad with tarragon is expertly dressed and fresh-tasting. Like the beverages, dishes here play with recognition. A smoked-trout deviled egg encompasses the best of both worlds, with smoky fish and creamy, slightly spicy egg yolk forming as intoxicating a cocktail as anything coming from the bar. Pork rillettes tots come with a mustardy Béarnaise-like sauce, and the tots are so expertly fried that they are elevated well beyond any school-cafeteria associations. Breakfast gets its homage here in Millas, which taste like sweet griddle cakes and come with poached egg, smoky bacon (a bit chewy), Vermont maple syrup, and Tabasco. Even Mexican street-food throwbacks are represented here, as in a corn on the cob with poblano aïoli and grated cheese. Perhaps most indulgent is a mac and cheese with blood sausage and an herb-thyme crust. This and the braised pork belly sandwich, coupled with their late-night availability, draw hungry chefs here like moths to a flame.

The space is chic and dark, with those lovely round banquettes and comely service. This really must be one of the best waitstaffs in Portland—ask their expert advice on food and cocktail orders. They have a knack for making you feel giddily engaged and all warm and fuzzy inside. It's a response that pairs perfectly, by the way, with modernized mac and cheese.

Beast

An intimate ride where the chef is the driver and diners are thrilled to come along

9.6	9.0	8.0
Food	Feel	Wine

Modern

Upmarket restaurant

$90
Price

www.beastpdx.com

Wed–Sat 5:30pm–9:30pm in 2 seatings
Sun 10am–2pm

Bar Wine
Credit cards Visa, MC, AmEx
Reservations Essential
Date-friendly

Alberta Arts District
5425 NE 30th Ave.
(503) 841-6968

Perhaps the most seductive restaurant experience in all of Portland begins in a small, undecorous dining room with a chalkboard wall listing the night's fare. Two large community tables are flanked by uncomfortable chairs; artful graffiti is splayed across the restrooms. Music plays below the vibrant chatter of the full room; candle lighting is low but not dark. From here, you can watch magic emerge from a kitchen whose close proximity to those two tables draws diners into the experience—even thermodynamically: on cold days, the heat from the equipment is great; on hot days, it's an exercise in tolerance.

We count ourselves among those under Beast's spell, in part because it represents such a magnificent rejection of the mistaken notion that the customer is always right (would this fly at a surgeon's office? An auto garage? Then why at a restaurant?). Here, you get only what's being served that night for each course—no substitutions.

Meals generally begin here with a small cup of soup, usually terrific. Cream of asparagus has been an anthem to spring—lush, smooth, and brimming with flavor from herbed crème fraîche and trout roe. Less successful was a carrot soup with Washington mussels and saffron cream, which wound up an overpowering melée of flavors. The charcuterie rotates frequently but has always been impressive, highlighted, perhaps, by a freshly chopped steak tartare with raw quail egg. Foie gras bon-bons come topped with a tiny trembling square of Sauternes gelée.

Comforting mains that center around slow-cooked meats are best, like a feather-light pot pie with tender braised short rib, wild onion, and earthy morels accompanied by glazed turnips and sautéed turnip greens. Rare are the less successful ventures, like miniscule baby lamb chops that required a surgical extraction of meat off the bone, an experience that went from zen-like to unworthy hassle fast.

Subtly complex salads finish you off, and cheeses from the renowned Steve's come with interesting accoutrements like cracked black pepper shortbread, Mars-Venus grapes, and wonderful Champagne-poached apricots. You're strongly encouraged to order the wine pairings, which are well chosen but pricey. We prefer to order by the bottle from a short but very thoughtful list of wines, many of them French.

The costs of dining properly—leaving it up to the kitchen, small portions, unfussy and capable service, and the convivial company of strangers—are high, but we're more bothered that it isn't the norm. This is what's happening *now*. Come and see, America, what the modern restaurant experience should be.

Beijing Hot Pot

It's not the best hot pot experience around, but it may be the friendliest

8.0 Food

7.5 Feel

Chinese

Casual restaurant

$20 Price

www.beijingxiaoguan.com

Mon–Fri 11am–2pm, 5pm–10pm
Sat–Sun 11am–10pm

Bar Beer, wine
Credit cards Visa, MC, AmEx
Reservations Accepted
Date-friendly

82nd Avenue Area
2768 SE 82nd Ave.
(503) 774-2525

Cookertainment. We're officially naming that genre of eating that spans Japan, China, Taiwan, Korea, and Vietnam, inviting diners to barbecue, grill, sauté, and simmer their own meal. In Korean restaurants, there's shabu shabu, and in Chinese and Taiwanese, hot pot. The Taiwanese are now hip to this trend of individual pots, which we love, and which you can find over at Hot Pot City; but Beijing Hot Pot still does it old-school, a style that has its own perks (ever used chopsticks as a flirting device?).

There are also kitchen-prepared dishes like congee and handmade dumplings, but you're here to cookertain yourselves, so just get down to business. The selection of broths isn't as varied here as it is at Hot Pot City—there are two kinds: plain and spicy. Plain is really plain, and spicy still needs some help. Meats are also more limited here, but you can (and should) get lamb, which just tastes grassy and funky, adding some much-needed depth to the broth. But remember to fish these thin cuts out early—overcooked meat is no better when *you* overcook it than when someone else does. Hand-cut noodles are a nice touch here, even if there isn't a terribly interesting array of hot pot ingredients.

The room is stunningly prettier than many other of its ilk, with white tile floors and walls and bright red chairs with skirts. The artwork on the walls feels like something you'd want in your home.

Service is exceedingly friendly and helpful, even when language is a barrier. Luckily, it doesn't take a working knowledge of English to smile and turn down a burner, or point to a dipping sauce and nod, or refill your broth for you when it starts to get low. Cookertainment is the universal language.

Belly Timber

A crowded house that, at its best, can brandish real nouvelle splendor

8.5	7.5	9.5
Food	Feel	Drinks

Modern

Upmarket restaurant

$45
Price

www.bellytimberrestaurant.com

Tue–Thu 5pm–9pm
Fri–Sat 5pm–10pm
Sun 9am–2pm, 5pm–9pm

Bar Beer, wine, liquor, BYO
Credit cards Visa, MC, AmEx
Reservations Accepted
Date-friendly, outdoor dining

Hawthorne
3257 SE Hawthorne Blvd.
(503) 235-3277

We like lively places, but Belly Timber is loud enough to be uncomfortable. Sure, the building looks like a beautiful Victorian house from the outside, but it seems that every inch of space inside has been used to maximize seating. It's nearly impossible not to be involved in your neighbors' conversations. Drop a morsel of food and you'll be fishing it out of their lap. That being said, the service here does go a long way to soothe some of the cramped feelings. And at brunch, do try to grab a patio seat.

The food is often delicious, but the kitchen can struggle with consistency. It's the usual downside to a constantly changing menu: the ups are really up and the downs, though less dramatically down, might be somewhat frequent. House-cured "whole hog" charcuterie is not to be missed. Whether the prep is a ham hock hot pot or a crispy fried whole tail (it's not curly, don't worry), it comes with homemade pickled veggies and three kinds of mustard. Escargots in bone-marrow butter should be divinely rich, but instead take a back seat to a bland chickpea sauce and yellow beets that are lively but curiously paired. Crab cakes have come plump and loaded with lump crabmeat, with an excellent crispness on the outside.

Main dishes are as terse as the selection of small plates, and are equally unpredictable. A pork shoulder chop is superbly cooked and paired with sweet peaches—or apples, when in season—and a savory green like bok choy. However, successful simplicity goes out the window in a flatiron steak, which is often underseasoned and propped up only by an aggressive sauce. French fries are sometimes crisp and sometimes soggy, with a smoky flavor that we'd trade for a balance of salt, pepper, and fresh herbs. The horseradish butter, yet another component of this needlessly complex dish, has little left to do.

Regardless of a few missteps, brunch is a worthwhile meal. It makes good work of never-tiresome salmon Benedict (expertly poached eggs) and bacon-banana French toast. Dreamy!

The cocktails are terrific, made with small-batch ryes and vodkas, absinthe, artisanal bitters, and touches like rhubarb, cinnamon, and cayenne pepper. An Old-Fashioned lists, as its final ingredient, "love." Even when Belly Timber fails, you can taste some of that, at least, in just about every drink and every dish—and even in some of your neighbor's.

Berlin Inn

A quaint Victorian house that's warmed by Bavarian dishes, fondue, and brew

6.0	8.0	9.0
Food	Feel	Wine

German Casual restaurant **$40** Price

Tue–Fri 5pm–9pm
Sat–Sun 10am–3pm, 4pm–9pm

Bar Beer, wine, BYO
Credit cards Visa, MC, AmEx
Reservations Accepted
Date-friendly, outdoor dining,
veg-friendly, Wi-Fi

Southeast Portland
3131 SE 12th Ave.
(503) 236-6761

The Berlin Inn looks as if your elderly Oma decided to start a restaurant in her own home, trading out her sofas for dark wood chairs and tables under tablecloths (not her best ones). Each room is small and cozy, but when it's crowded, it can get beer-hall loud. It's so damned adorable, though, all lace curtains and kitschy German paraphernalia. The outside beer garden does a fine job of keeping the grit and noise of adjacent Powell Boulevard at bay, but just barely. Your dog is welcome, and there's even a menu for him (and vegans, vegetarians, and gluten-free diets are pretty well served here, too).

The food is traditional German (with some liberties taken), the kind of stick-to-your-ribs fare that can keep you from shivering through a cold winter night. Berlin Inn is also a bakery, so cakes are seriously fresh, and pretzels are out of this world.

Brunch is even more popular than dinner, where the highlight seems to be fondue. This is not the fondue of the Swiss; it's sort of a mildish Gouda that doesn't melt down so well, and it relies too heavily on a boost from garlic to make up for its relatively wimpy flavor. A sharp cheddar-and-Doppelbock-beer version is nice, but you may incur palate fatigue after a few morsels. Share these with a large group and move on.

Herring cured in white wine is nice with potato pancakes and onions; so is the competent, if hardly memorable, spätzle. And on and on through the alluring menu: decent renditions, made from scratch. Schnitzels are crispy and satisfying, and sausage performs as expected (even when it's bad, sausage is pretty good). More inconsistent are the specialties, which often sound insanely craveworthy, but are just sort of okay. Sauerkraut isn't quite sauer enough. But it all hits the spot.

The most exciting part of Berlin Inn is the German-centric wine and beer selection. Only a few are on draft, but we love the refreshingly bitter Bitburger, and salute the smaller-batch pilsners, hefeweizens, Dunkels, and Doppelbocks. The wines, which can also be purchased to go from the goofy and dated wine bar (think plastic grapevines and ribbons), are wonderfully priced and offer a comprehensive tour of German and Austrian varietals you don't otherwise see much of. And that kind of experience is really the point of this whole place.

Bernie's

Happy hour is your best bet for Northwestern
takes on Southern comfort food

6.6	8.0	7.0
Food	Feel	Beer

Southern

Casual restaurant

$40
Price

www.berniesbistro.com

Tue–Sat 4pm–10pm
Sun 4pm–9pm

Bar Beer, wine, liquor
Credit cards Visa, MC, AmEx
Reservations Accepted
Outdoor dining

Alberta Arts District
2904 NE Alberta St.
(503) 282-9864

Southern rock is hot, cans of PBR are in, mullets are ironic, and the bigger the 'stache, the sexier. Bernie's, like the general PDX vibe, seems like a reaction against fancy-pants platings and molecular gastronomy. After all, what's more comforting on a rainy Portland night: slowly cooked collard greens with pork fat, or a carrot foam with beet gelée?

The city has no shortage of down-home-chic places that fetishize fried chicken and waffles: Delta Café, Miss Delta, and Screen Door, for instance. Each does a handful of Southern dishes reasonably well, but Bernie's seems to be most on its game when it steers clear of this genre. Blackened catfish is fine, not too muddy but still distinctive enough not to be mistaken for tilapia. But better is wild Alaskan halibut, pan-seared to moist flakiness and given a tart bite from pomegranate and crystallized ginger.

But your bayou cred is seriously called into question when you serve your (albeit nicely crunchy) buttermilk-fried-chicken boneless. Whole chicken pieces, bones and skin and all, lock in the moisture and rock the fat. Boneless fried chicken is for wusses, and serving it will get you kicked out of several states south of the Mason-Dixon line.

Mac and cheese is made with cheddar, as is traditional, but it's missing any sort of crust with caramelized bits. Sweetly, the menu boasts fried pickles as "a little secret treasure from the South." But we wish they were served as spears, which maintain a juicy middle under all that breading rather than the more shriveled slices.

While the Southern dishes aren't totally on the mark, the space is Alberta funky, a great place to spend happy hour. A flower-strewn patio is terrific for large groups sharing $3 happy hour plates of decent fried green tomatoes; fried okra (in appropriately small bites); and Bernie's passable attempt at po' boys. But it's pretty weak to serve bottled beer only; a few taps of Portland's own could be the most authentic thing going here.

Besaw's Café

Charming dinners and popular breakfasts
served in a house older than the hills

7.7	8.5	8.0
Food	Feel	Drinks

Modern

Casual restaurant

$40
Price

www.besaws.com

Mon 7am–3pm
Tue–Fri 7am–10pm
Sat 8am–10pm
Sun 8am–3pm

Bar Beer, wine, liquor
Credit cards Visa, MC, AmEx
Reservations Accepted
Date-friendly, kid-friendly, outdoor
dining, Wi-Fi

Northwest Portland
2301 NW Savier St.
(503) 228-2619

The charming little house known as Besaw's is one of Portland's oldest restaurants. You can even feel the dips in the mahogany bar from the elbows of patrons that have dug into it since the turn of the century. (The previous century.)

Its sunny yellow exterior and striped awning call breakfast seekers all week long. Its lunch and dinner menus change weekly, and aren't exactly ground breaking, but are full of simple dishes like Alaskan cod with cauliflower, preserved lemon, and collards; good burgers; and fresh-tasting salads.

But mostly, people come for what may be the best Benedict in town, good omelettes, and biscuits and gravy. Do not miss the superb "Uncle Earl's" Bloody Mary here, whatever you do. It's kind of redundant to say about a Portland breakfast or brunch: be prepared for long waits. It's a given that there will be a wait at any worthwhile place you go (and many unworthwhile places, as well). At least the hospitable staff at Besaw's will provide you with a cup of free Stumptown coffee while you wait. It is a move like this that keeps a place in business for a hundred years.

There have been accusations that Besaw's highish prices aren't deserved, considering that you can get much better Modern American in town for the same price. But "Recession Buster" menus are gracious, with $6 breakfasts and lunches that cost only a buck or two more than they would in a greasy spoon—and here you've got the added benefit of better ingredients and charming surroundings. Portions aren't all that big, but this is quality over quantity (if you can still manage to afford that).

Wines are more obvious than carefully chosen, with a heavy domestic presence and plenty of Oregon Pinot. There are a few grower-producer Champagnes, however. Only a few beers grace the taps, but these are popular locals, and there are more in bottle with the usual imports. Some Prohibition-era cocktails are made just fine, with minimal strides towards the artisanal (less common liquors, Port-soaked cherries, local berries, and so on).

Mostly, it's just fun to sit someplace where the drink that is now retro fashionable was once brand new.

Best Taste

Meat by the pound in a less-than-charming, gritty space

9.0 Food **3.5** Feel

Chinese, Dim Sum

Casual restaurant **$10** Price

Daily 9am–8pm

Bar None
Credit cards Visa, MC
Reservations Not accepted

82nd Avenue Area
8350 SE Division St.
(503) 771-0812

We're willing to bet that you don't know about this place. If you do, we tip our caps to you. It's little more than a sleazily labeled storefront along a particularly gritty stretch of the 82nd Avenue area that has, in recent decades, turned into Portland's legit Chinatown.

The Chinese have always had a penchant for purveying the most delicious things in places where you'd least expect them—from rickety roadside carts, in blank banquet halls, beneath seamy thickets of urbanity. And so it might not surprise the true Sinophiles that Portland's best Cantonese roast meats are being hacked up behind a counter that comes off as just a bit less sophisticated than the one in front of which you might have once queued up in public school to beg the lunch lady for seconds of franks and beans.

The people here, though, are a great deal nicer than she probably was, although they barely speak English and might well try to convince you to take a pound or two of impossibly juicy roast meat when you really only want a half-pound. (Later, you'll thank them.) Hanging in front of these wizards of barbecue and negotiation—and, really, dominating the décor—are those giant glistening animals, visible from the street, signifiers of meaning beyond their grisly selves, emblems of the fat-worshipping school of modern chef-geekery, the embalmed pig sliced cruelly in two, the duck publicly hanged as if to be punished for some terrible crime.

Roast suckling pig at Best Taste is a study in textural contrasts, crackling skin against a melting layer of fat and some of the juiciest pork flesh into which you are likely to sink your teeth anywhere in Portland. And yet the duck might be even better, with a flavor whose rich finish seems to carry on for minutes, like that of a great wine. There's also an entire menu of noodle soups, rice plates, porridges, even some seafood and dim sum and vaguely Vietnamese dishes. But keep your eyes on the prize: the section of the menu labeled "Barbecue & Soy Meat." It's about $7.50 per pound, and two pounds of it is easily the best $15 you can spend in the city of Portland.

Although almost every Chinese customer (and almost every customer is Chinese) takes a bag of the stuff to go. But if you venture a taste of meat from your plastic bag—before stepping beyond the smudged glass door and back into the grimy reality of the neighborhood—you may quickly forget your mission. You may forget that this bare box is one of the least attractive spaces in the whole city in which to dine. For within that flimsy bag lies the power to turn rickety tables to pools of untold joy, blank walls to expanses of wide-eyed wonder.

Bete-Lukas

Nutritious, totally satisfying, and refreshingly escapist food from the birthplace of humanity

8.0 Food

8.0 Feel

Ethiopian

Casual restaurant

$35 Price

www.bete-lukas.com

Tue–Thu 5pm–9pm
Fri–Sat 5pm–10pm
Sun 5pm–9pm

Bar Beer, wine, liquor
Credit cards Visa, MC
Reservations Accepted
Date-friendly, live music,
veg-friendly

Division/Clinton
2504 SE 50th Ave.
(503) 477-8778

Is there anything in the world so satisfying, so hearty and complex, as spicy, slow-simmered meats, legumes, and vegetables? Ethiopian food is every bit as enjoyable as Indian—and, we'd argue, less frequently homogenized for American palates—yet we never seem to find as many Ethiopian restaurants in a given city (except, perhaps, DC) as Indian.

Bete-Lukas doesn't just satisfy your need for Ethiopian; it takes things to a more elegant level. There are white tablecloths, linen napkins, and lovely water glasses. The service is impeccable, but it's still difficult to shake the fact that the place looks very much like an apartment living room in which the furnishings have been removed and replaced by dining room tables. Track lighting highlights a few Ethiopian artifacts, and sometimes, an African band plays in the background.

If you're a food nerd, the owners of Bete-Lukas are more than happy to help explain the flavors and textures that are happening on your plate (or more accurately, on your fat bed of sourdough injera). It's heartening to see the headdress-clad women in the kitchen cooking with such concentration and zeal. This cuisine is extremely vegetarian-friendly, and variable in heat. Great flavor is teased out of kale, yellow lentils, and eggplant tibs. Doro wot, the national dish of Ethiopia, is a sauce of dried-chile berbere spices and tender chicken drumsticks, with garlic and a hard-boiled egg. It's like sunshine and earth.

Scoop it all up with that spongy injera, whose citrusy-sour freshness complements the bitter greens and hot spices beautifully. Just watch your intake; it expands like a supernova in your stomach. Portions are a little smaller than those we tend to find in shabbier joints, but this is all part of being classy. Besides, it's still plenty filling.

There's a full bar, but don't come expecting genius cocktails; there's some good beer on draft, like Mirror Pond, but the mead-like Ethiopian-style honey wine ends up tasting like little more than oxidation. There are some good wine pairings out there for this type of food, but they're not here. Beer is best, as is the company of the charismatic couple who owns the place. Enjoy their hospitality and nutritious, satisfying food, and you'll have all the high you need.

BeWon Korean

Korean gone underground and upscale

8.6	9.0	8.0
Food	Feel	Wine

Korean

Casual restaurant

$35
Price

www.bewonrestaurant.com

Mon–Thu 11:30am–2:30pm, 5pm–9pm; Fri 11:30am–2:30pm, 5pm–10pm; Sat 5pm–10pm

Bar Wine
Credit cards Visa, MC, AmEx
Reservations Accepted
Date-friendly

Northwest Portland
1203 NW 23rd Ave.
(503) 464-9222

BeWon was King Tae Jong's secret royal garden, a favorite escape for outdoor feasts and celebrations. Down a stairway from bustling Trendy-Third Street and tucked under another floor, this BeWon is also something of a quiet, festive hideaway. The setting is cool and modern, the tables covered with crisp white linens, and the service is some of the most knowledgeable and professional in the city. And, unlike at those divier Korean joints along 82nd Avenue, there's no smoke here to cling to your clothes.

While there is a standard menu, the most fun is the han jung shik, a seven-course tasting meal offered at an incredibly low price (but at least two people at the table must order it). In a total departure from the Korean-restaurant norm, some refreshingly astute wine pairings are available for a little extra, and the prices on these mostly small-production bottles are also ridiculously low.

You'll start the tasting menu with hobak-juk, a bright-orange rice porridge made with three different pumpkins—it's thick and slightly sweet; and samsak gyu-ja-chae, a little salad of three julienned vegetables with mustard dressing, a great, refreshing contrast. Next is gujeolpan, crêpes that you fill with shiitake and black mushrooms, cucumber, carrot, chopped hard-boiled eggs, bean sprouts, and minced beef. Each of these things is an explosive delicacy. Japchae, stir-fried sweet potato noodles, are completely addictive, earthy and not at all sugary, with a few mushrooms and other vegetables adding texture and depth.

We like most of the mains, but the best are daeji bulgogi (spicy pork with onions and scallions), galbi (tender, melting short ribs), and go-deung-uh (broiled mackerel caked in sea salt). A bowl of boiling chi-ge (tofu bean curd stew) is also placed in the middle of the table, surrounded by nine seasonal banchan dishes and rice, making something of a vivid artist's palette. You might be treated to sautéed spinach, fermented black beans, dried squid in chili sauce, thinly sliced dark mushrooms, kimchi, mung bean sprouts, and so on. Your grandmother will be so pleased to see that you're eating enough.

A couple of light digestif courses cap the meal, with barley tea and dduk, a mellow, slightly sticky rice cake that grows on you as you eat it.

Ordering à la carte certainly isn't a bad idea, and the usual suspects are all here, but BeWon's bargain prix-fixe is the optimal way to try the full spectrum of Korean cooking. It's an experience like no other in town.

Bijou Café

Lunch, good—breakfast, better

8.0	7.5
Food	Feel

American

Casual restaurant

$25
Price

Mon–Fri 7am–2pm
Sat–Sun 8am–2pm

Bar Beer, wine
Credit cards Visa, MC
Reservations Not accepted

Downtown
132 SW 3rd Ave.
(503) 222-3187

Perhaps thanks in part to a Frommer's shout-out, Bijou is the darling of a breakfast-crazed town, a sort of down-home girl next door at the moment of her big Hollywood discovery. It looks unassuming in its old brick corner building, with a benign color palette inside that suggests egg whites and butter. The vivid blue sign outside reads, somewhat cheekily, "Bijou, café." Unless that comma was a misprint, it's sort of a hilarious, self-important introduction to what turns out to be a wonderful meal served with little pomp or arrogance.

You'll sit at the old-school counter underneath a chalkboard of specials like bacon-and-blue cheese hash, buttermilk oatmeal pancakes with apple-pear compote, and Greek omelette. Nothing ground breaking here, but, then, breakfast need never be ground breaking. It needs only to invigorate the senses, thicken the blood, and, perhaps, comfort those weary from a night of psychic re-runs. And Bijou performs justly.

Omelettes are deeply yellow, meltingly fluffy, and bursting with quality ingredients, many of which are organic and locally grown. An oyster version receives a lot of press, as does its hash incarnation. And rightfully so: the briny pop of the oyster is still alive and well under its crisp cornmeal breading, paired simply with one of a few strips of sautéed onion and potato, with a bit of fresh herbs. It's rich, flavorful…and expensive. A seasonal chicken-and-apple-sausage hash is good, moist enough to escape that insulation-fiber consistency many hashes can get in less capable hands.

Share one of these and a French toast made with thick, eggy bread from Pearl Bakery. And throw in a compote of seasonal fruit. Pastries are uneven; muffins, like an apple crisp or banana-hazelnut, can range from sublime to stale. Lunch, though, is reliable and hearty, with a standout burger, a terrific mushroom panino, a surprisingly good quesadilla with pumpkin-seed mole, and a tuna melt with all the classic elements except a mid-century Americana over-greasiness.

Bijou is accommodating, but don't bring large groups or antsy children. The feeling in here is grown-up and sedate, yet not really dull. Expect longer waits and an inevitable dip in quality as Bijou, Café becomes Bijou, Tourist Stop. We've seen the once-sincere girl with stars in her eyes slogging herself down the avenue in a torn fur coat one too many times. Hopefully, this one will keep it simple and never forget who her first fans were.

Bistro Maison

Sweet bistro fare and local bounty served up in a wine country cottage

7.4	9.0	8.0
Food	Feel	Wine

French

Upmarket restaurant

$60
Price

www.bistromaison.com

Wed–Thu 11:30am–2pm, 6pm–9pm; Fri 11:30am–2pm, 5pm–9pm; Sat 5pm–9pm; Sun noon–8pm

Bar Beer, wine, liquor
Credit cards Visa, MC, AmEx
Reservations Accepted
Date-friendly, outdoor dining

McMinnville
729 NE 3rd St.
(503) 474-1888

The drive through the Willamette Valley—especially if you take back roads—takes you through idyllic pastures and picturesque old downtowns, most notably McMinnville, home to Bistro Maison, which glows warmly next to an ancient train station. The Bistro's patio is terrific, separated from the street by shady pines, and watched over by a dog named Lily, who sleeps quietly in the corner. Make reservations to guarantee a coveted spot out here. Inside, the lighting and wallpaper match the age of the building. French artwork dots the walls, and light jazz floats through the air. Padded leather chairs surround linen-covered tables.

The wine list is long, if redundant, and full of French and Oregon bottles at all price points (the latter have higher markups). We love how many half-bottle choices there are—especially key if you've got to drive back to Portland.

Service is friendly and efficient, if awkwardly formal at times (staff will read the specials off to you even while you're staring down at them). The chef and his wife often come out to greet tables. It's a meal you want to love before you've even taken a bite.

And, just like when you visit a friend's house for dinner, the food is deeply enjoyable, if not mind-blowing. The kitchen makes good use of seasonal ingredients, like in a soup bursting with summery local corn and Vidalia onion. But a "Caprese" salad of local peaches and mozzarella—while a good idea—may feature impenetrable peaches or chewy and bland mozzarella di bufala. Other salads like Neskowin pepper greens with bacon, local berries, toasted almonds, and triple-cream cow's-milk cheese, have been great.

Mussels and french fries are reliably good here. Carlton Farms thick-cut pork chops are properly cooked to a tender, deep pink, but one preparation of grilled peaches on top *and* a peach sauce was overkill; a different version with mixed berries fared much better. Hanger steak came tender one night, full of inedible tendon on another night.

Desserts bring the meal up a peg, with deftly made profiteroles au chocolat, filled with vanilla bean ice cream, and served with warm chocolate sauce; and a brilliant Napoleon of crispy, flaky layers. It's a sweet note to end on as you contemplate the evening sky, far from the trendy, ambitious restaurants of the city.

Biwa

Have a soul-soothing, hangover-curing, vegan-nourishing, sake-educating good time

7.2	9.0	8.5
Food	Feel	Wine

Japanese, Korean

Casual restaurant

$35
Price

www.biwarestaurant.com

Daily 5pm–midnight

Bar Beer, wine, liquor
Credit cards Visa, MC, AmEx
Reservations Not accepted
Date-friendly, outdoor dining, veg-friendly

Southeast Portland
215 SE 9th Ave.
(503) 239-8830

Izakaya is becoming all the rage in Portland, much to our glee. Not only do we have the authentically divey bars like Tanuki and the accessible, clean places like Syun in Hillsboro, but now there is a smart, modern, upscale version. Where those other two serve inarguably delicious and transportive dishes that call to mind foggy stumbles at midnight through Okinawan streets, Biwa answers Portland's yearning for all the comfort foods from its latitudinal neighbor, noodles, kimchi, yaki, and all.

Although it's sunk into the basement of an old church in a less-heeled neighborhood, with little signage and treacherous steps, Biwa is no dive. It's a cozy but trendy buzzfest, even on a Monday night. Clean lines, an open kitchen, and high wooden booths create an upscale Japanese feel, but unlike at most sushi joints, the lighting is dim and warm. Votives on tables glow warmly in the evening, making this an ideal hideout from the world above.

Izakaya consists of small plates, hot and cold—essentially, Japanese pub grub, meant to be enjoyed with sake. And sake here is the thing. These are, for the most part, well chosen, with a wide range of body, flavor, prefecture, and price points. The menu will provide detailed descriptions, and servers often know their stuff enough to help novices navigate their choices. Cocktails are not worth missing the sake for. If rice wine isn't your thing, the succinct grape wine selection here is equally complementary to the food.

The best work of this kitchen, by far, is the array of noodle dishes. Udon wheat noodles are hand cut and thick, toothsome, and hearty; ramen noodles in meat-based broths are fantastically nourishing. Several different add-ons are available, as well, like hard-boiled egg, seaweed, and pork. Deep-fried daikon-radish kimchi is like a brilliant Korean version of Southern fried pickles. Tofu made by neighboring soy-star Ota is silky, firm, and nutty, and aged miso made by Soy Beam makes for an umami-bomb of a soup.

But consistent problems with oversalting, along with mishandled proteins, bring much of Biwa's menu down. Charcoal-grilled yakitori of chicken thigh, hanger steak, and lamb are competent, but gizzard has come undercooked and spongy-tough. Yukke ("Korean beef tartare") with a quail egg is chewy and salted to oblivion; vinegar-pickled mackerel is too sweet, but not as sweet as the miso scallop, which might as well be dessert. It's the worst izakaya dish in the entire Portland area, curable only by another bottle of dry sake.

Blossoming Lotus

7.2 Food   **6.5** Feel

Surprisingly delicious, wholesome foods served with a side of ohm shanti

Vegefusion

Casual restaurant   **$30** Price

www.blpdx.com

Daily 9am–9pm
Hours vary by location

Bar Beer, wine
Credit cards Visa, MC, AmEx
Reservations Not accepted
Outdoor dining, veg-friendly

Pearl District
925 NW Davis St.
(503) 228-0048

Northeast Portland
1713 NE 15th Ave.
(503) 228-0048

After an hour of downward-facing dogs and warrior poses, the manipura chakra really lights up. Luckily, you can sate it with Blossoming Lotus, an all-organic vegan cafeteria in the lobby of the Yoga Pearl studio. Signs remind you to speak quietly as you order, and the staff isn't exactly gregarious or quick, having probably submerged into a third-eye meditation upon clocking in. A second location in Irvington is slightly more versatile—and the menu does vary slightly between the two—offering casual take-out or lunch and, at night, a somewhat romantic setting in which to eat foods that will leave the reptilian brain dormant. It's the sort of dinner that precedes watching a thoughtful documentary or playing a game of chess; in other words, few babies are conceived on this stuff.

The menu calls to mind the scene in *Annie Hall* where Woody Allen's character, upon arriving in Los Angeles (to which he is seriously allergic), orders "the alfalfa sprouts and a plate of mashed yeast." But everything is surprisingly flavorful. It is a little disconcerting to have the word "live" before so many foods you don't normally associate with having a metabolic process, foods like a "live" taco salad; "live" soup du jour; and even "live" chocolates. It does confuse the benevolent mind, biting into a "live" nacho—does it feel pain? Or is this its dharma? It's all too much to think about. At least you can place some sort of personification on a lobster or a catfish in a tank: It looks like a jerk, ergo, it deserves to be cooked.

But try to swallow your guilt and indulge in a "live" cashew hummus with tomato, cucumber, and flax crackers. It is quite good, every bit worth the life you are taking. Also refreshing and invigorating is a "Salud Salad" with romaine, brown rice, tomato, and avocado dressed with a spicy vinaigrette, that gets enough of a fatty and creamy texture from black beans and cashew "sour cream."

Even meat substitutes like tempeh, which can taste like canvas dyed to look like meat, are pretty delicious. Cheese made with almond milk is subtle, the nuttiness giving lasagne (with tofu ricotta, squash, and a lemon-basil cashew cream) an unexpected dimension.

Follow it up with a kombucha tea (live) or a bottle of Samuel Smith Lager (dead, or at least hopefully through with fermentation), and for dessert, enjoy the sweetness of a Sattvic fullness.

Bluehour

A trendy space where the competent kitchen goes unnoticed and unchallenged

6.8	6.5	6.5
Food	Feel	Wine

Modern

Upmarket restaurant

$70
Price

www.bluehouronline.com

Mon–Thu 11:30am–2:30pm, 5pm–10pm; Fri–Sat 11:30am–2:30pm, 5pm–10:30pm; Sun 10am–3:30pm, 5pm–10pm

Bar Beer, wine, liquor
Credit cards Visa, MC, AmEx
Reservations Accepted
Date-friendly, outdoor dining

Pearl District
250 NW 13th Ave.
(503) 226-3394

Bluehour has the Pearl-trendy thing down, for sure. It's the sort of place we love to hate: high drama and pretense without much distinguishing character. An otherwise warehouse-sized white room is sectioned off by long dark green curtains and there are interesting visual textures here and there, but little else. Don't look to the staff for entertainment or enlightenment—they're polite, but not as food-nerdy or engaged as some more kick-ass servers in town. There's an open kitchen in the back, through which we once saw a whole pig, but the crowd here seems too "Mirror in the Bathroom" to actually notice or care.

That kitchen is absolutely competent at Modern American cuisine, but the food here lacks the excitement that would come from a truly seasonal or an original chef-driven menu. A burger is certainly one of the better in town, but you aren't asked you how you want it cooked—strange for an upscale bistro burger. It does come a tender, unobjectionable medium, with the nice addition of pickled vegetables. Gnocchi with black truffle and fontina cheese is absolutely spot on, with tender and dreamy puffs of potato dough that aren't overwhelmed by the truffle. A crab sandwich, although full of real crabmeat, is a bit disappointing. Especially for the price.

Most un-Portland of all is the way-overpriced beer list. The mark up on local craft beers, as compared to other places in town, is downright brazen. Again, this crowd doesn't much seem to mind. Wines are also annoyingly arranged on the list according to varietal, which is totally incomprehensible. Nevermind that the selection is kind of an (overpriced) afterthought.

Brunch has some attractive options, but again, it's more expensive than anything else around. And for no reason; there's some great execution here, but no soul in this food. It could be a restaurant anywhere. Wake us when it's over.

Bombay Cricket Club

A little bit of fascism and a whole lot of mango-rita color an otherwise dull range of flavors

5.3 Food

6.5 Feel

Indian

Upmarket restaurant

$40 Price

www.bombaycricketclubrestaurant.com

Sun–Thu 5pm–9pm
Fri–Sat 5pm–10pm

Bar Beer, wine, liquor
Credit cards Visa, MC, AmEx
Reservations Accepted
Date-friendly, veg-friendly

Hawthorne
1925 SE Hawthorne Blvd.
(503) 231-0740

Bombay Cricket Club has a reputation for being a bit of a pain in the ass. Be prepared for long waits almost any night of the week; if everyone in your party isn't there, you won't be seated, and your table will be given away if you're late. On busy nights, if you don't have a reservation, you'll be dismissed with a wave of the hand; and if you do manage to get on a list, you'll be forced to wait in the doorway, blocking everyone's way, which just annoys the owner. Don't even think about bringing kids.

Despite all this, the tiny place is packed every night with loud, happy diners (perhaps thrilled that they ran the gauntlet and lived to tell about it).

Once you are seated, however, the service is remarkably patient and helpful. Strangely, the kitchen uses three types of chili to produce heat to your liking: habanero, Thai, or Indian. Medium-hot is right on the money, but very hot is mouth-scalding. One of the much-publicized mango-ritas will help with this (and will get you loaded fast).

Dishes are of the meat-centric variety, although there are a lot of vegetarian options as well. These are not terribly authentic dishes, and stew flavors are often bland. (Maybe the high prices are here to capitalize on the purported dearth of good Indian food about town.) Tandoor items are marinated overnight with yogurt, garlic, and spices, then cooked in the traditional clay oven and served with tomatoes and onions, but the meat can dry out or overcook. Other dishes, from saag to biryani to chana masala are aggressively salted and curried, and their flavors feel homogenous. The one bright spot has been tender lamb shahi, an interesting and complex prep with tomatoes, saffron, ginger, garlic, almonds, raisins, and cilantro.

If you love Draconian seating policies, impatient owners, and paying top dollar for inauthentic, lackluster food, then by all means, come see what the fuss is about. You'll likely find that, after all is said and done, you still don't have a clue.

Branch

Meat is the focus at this über-hip bar

8.8	9.0	9.5
Food	Feel	Drinks

Modern

Casual restaurant

$40
Price

www.branchwhiskeybar.com

Mon, Wed–Thu 5pm–midnight
Fri–Sat 5pm–2am
Sun 5pm–midnight

Bar Beer, wine, liquor
Credit cards Visa, MC, AmEx
Reservations Accepted
Date-friendly, outdoor dining

Alberta Arts District
2926 NE Alberta St.
(503) 206-6266

To call it a "whiskey bar" isn't wrong—it's just misleading. Yes, the simple space—dim yellow lighting, warm orange walls—*is* totally dominated by the bar, and that's where you'll probably want to sit, even if you come to dine. That way you can quiz the barkeeps (who have that Portlandish air of casual cocktail genius) about the extensive bourbon and scotch list; about the secrets behind their excellent Sazerac or their equally excellent "Old Pal" (Buffalo Trace Bourbon, dry vermouth, and Campari, served straight up); about which excellent beers are currently populating the modest four-member tap; or, perhaps, about what goes into their smashing homemade bitters.

But there is real culinary firepower in this kitchen, and in that sense, Branch is really more of a serious gastro-pub than a whiskey bar. Consider the pork rillettes, for instance. At French brasseries, rillettes are generally just a meatier way to butter your bread, a little cold starter to munch on while you contemplate the way the evening will go. At Branch, they burst out of the gate with almost too much energy, bathed in duck fat, redolent of thyme, searingly hot from the oven. Once the dish cools, though, you begin to notice faraway fragrances from an overnight session with baking spices. Is that clove? Is that cinnamon? Are you dreaming?

Speaking of pork and duck, Branch is clearly a part of Portland's meat movement—the band of newly opened restaurants that seem to be reacting against the over-proliferation of gluten-free, vegan-friendly garden-vegetable cuisine in town. Branch's reaction has been particularly extreme: all five of the main courses on its printed menu are made from beef, pork, duck, or some combination of those three. Not even seafood makes the cut. In case you still don't get the point, there's a sign posted: "Hippies use back door." It's particularly funny to see this on Alberta, right across the street from Vita Café.

But this is hardly biker-bar cuisine. For every intense protein, there is a context of subtle undertones. The kitchen seems to have a particular way with duck, as in a duck-confit hash with poached egg, onion, potatoes, and roasted red peppers that's like a smarty-pants take on breakfast; or pan-seared duck livers with bacon. House-made pork sausages and mortadella are feisty and aromatic, and a beef burger with German potato salad hits all the pleasure points. Delicata squash gnocchi prove that the kitchen has a feminine side, too. But that's not to say that they won't direct the ladies toward the whiskey and meat.

As they should.

Brazil Grill

A fun, friendly all-you-can-eat meat extravaganza

6.5	8.0	7.0
Food	Feel	Wine

Brazilian, Steakhouse

Casual restaurant

$40
Price

www.brazilgrillrestaurant.com

Daily 5pm–10pm

Bar Beer, wine, liquor
Credit cards Visa, MC, AmEx
Reservations Accepted
Date-friendly, live music

Southwest Portland
1201 SW 12th Ave.
(503) 222-0002

Brazilian-style churrascarias are a carnivore's paradise, owing their origins to the centuries-old campfire roasts in the Pampa region of southern Brazil. Servers dressed in relatively restrained gaucho outfits (as gaucho outfits go) come to your table with long rotisserie skewers speared with one of many meats: pork loin, tri-tip, flank steak, bacon-wrapped filet mignon, lamb chops, beef short ribs, lamb loin, chicken hearts, and so on.

The space is open and comfortable with dark wood floors, a high ceiling, and bright-orange walls, and the service is friendly and enthusiastic. The large windows and vivid green, red, and yellow sign make the joint easy to spot from the street. The interior sports a full bar at which you can wait for your table. Caipirinhas here are inconsistent, ranging from icy to poorly muddled, with low-quality liquor. A small wine list featuring reasonable markups on well-made domestic, South American, Italian, and Spanish bottles is a better way to go.

You'll start with a salad bar of several interesting selections: a wonderful potato salad; orzo with corn, ham and peas; and so on. Some salad-bar items are better than others, but most are worth trying. (Just don't over-indulge. Meat is ahead.)

When the roaming gauchos bring meat to your table, they'll tell you what cut it is and what sauce, if any, has been used for a marinade. A simple nod of the head and the server will begin cutting off a thin slice. See something at another table you want? Just let someone know and they'll bring it out to you. Don't waste your time on prosaic chicken, but be sure to try picanha, the traditional tri-tip roast. Chicken hearts are wonderful, an explosion of flavor. Even shrimp are cooked beautifully and have wonderful, sweet, smoky flavor.

Every so often, the servers will wander by with caramelly grilled pineapple meant to refresh your palate between courses. For heaven's sake, don't pair it with red wine.

This isn't the best that a churrascaria can be, but it's a good time and worth the money and the, ahem, digestive issues you'll no doubt incur with this level of meat consumption.

Bread and Ink Café

Come for a decent breakfast—or if you've got to get your 1992 on

5.3	6.5	7.5
Food	Feel	Beer

American

Casual restaurant

$40
Price

www.breadandinkcafe.com

Sun–Thu 8am–9pm
Fri–Sat 8am–10pm

Bar Beer, wine, liquor
Credit cards Visa, MC, AmEx
Reservations Accepted
Outdoor dining, veg-friendly

Hawthorne
3610 SE Hawthorne Blvd.
(503) 239-4761

Bread and Ink Café was quite a happening little spot in the '80s and '90s, popular for its cool, understated interior, comfortable green leather chairs, and eclectic art on the walls. Back then, it was still exciting to see a menu that tackled Thailand and Italy in one dinner rush—hey, it was the era of fuchsia and Color Me Badd. The whole country was mired in bad judgment.

These days, people are bemoaning the redesign that has stripped any character from the place, leaving only white tablecloths and an often-snotty attitude. As it was in its heyday, breakfast is the hottest thing going here—breakfast and the Waffle Window around the corner.

Such breakfasts might include homemade bialys and bagels, which are great with smoked trout or lox and all the fixings. Some pretty run-of-the-mill scrambles and omelettes form a backdrop against more exciting-sounding egg enchiladas, but these are more bark than bite. A rather large amount of cumin helps scent the dish, but the texture is too mealy to contrast the salsa, sour cream, and eggs. The result is soupy and boring after a few bites. Still, there's no trouble with classic breakfast staples like Benedicts, blueberry pancakes, and pepper bacon. And if you're a fan of the Waffle Window (reviewed separately), it's here, too.

At lunch and dinner, the basics are done well enough. Mac and cheese comes with a strongly flavored blend of Fontina, cheddar, and parmesan, and a baked crust of herbed bread crumbs. It does the trick, but it's not worth the price.

Beyond that, the menu is a dated wreck. Plates are drizzled with enough zany balsamic reduction to make Jackson Pollock look like Mondrian. Surely something is needed to make "Steak with Peppernade" even look palatable, let alone worth its insane $25 price. Roasted red and green bell peppers, onions, and beef tenderloin with mashed potatoes and "seasonal vegetables"? It translates to the nursing home's fajitas day, sans tortillas, rice, beans, and flavor.

But nothing comes close to the catastrophic "Grilled Curried Chicken," chunks of boneless white meat (yum!) doused in homemade curry with more bell peppers and onions, served on cardamom rice with…you guessed it: "seasonal vegetables." The cardamom would be much better suited to a fruity dish; here it's irritating and domineering. Which is a fitting description of Bread and Ink, in 21st-century Portland.

Brunchbox

You, too, can have a cheeseburger at this Zeitgeisty, over-the-top stand

7.0 Food | **7.5** Feel

Sandwiches

Food cart | **$5** Price

Mon–Fri 8am–4pm

Bar None
Credit cards Visa, MC, AmEx
Kid-friendly, outdoor dining

Downtown
SW 5th Ave. and Stark
(503) 477-3286

It's brunch. In a box. What's not to love? Actually, it's breakfast (served all day every day) and burgers and sandwiches. The great thing about this little fold-up food cart is that it's whatever you want it to be—except dinner.

Breakfast sandwiches come on freshly baked English muffins with your choice of meat, including ham, bacon, soy sausage, and Spam. For those of you who have never had Spam for breakfast (*Spam, Spam, Spam, Spam, Spam, Baked Beans, and Spam*?) you're missing out on a quintessential piece of Americana—Hawaiian Americana, to be exact. They love it about as much as the Brits do.

The appropriately named "omg!" with melty American cheese *and* ham *and* bacon, is what you'll be texting your cardiologist if the grease running down your arm doesn't clog up the keypad first. The "omg!" is also available as a burger, but we don't advise eating this without a will. It would be an incredibly indulgent way to go. Better yet, make it a sure thing with the "Redonkadonk," which is, indeed, as redonky-kong as it gets—a cheeseburger on Texas toast with just about everything. Let's picture this again: fluffy, crispy grilled cheese on Texas toast; then a fried egg; ham; slab o' Spam; crisp bacon; gooey American cheese; and another fluffy, crispy grilled cheese on Texas toast. Cheesus Christ! The amazing part is that this is actually a viable burger, and all the ingredients stay put reasonably well (*you* try busting through two Texas toast grilled cheese sandwiches).

If flirting with hypertension isn't your thing, there are veggie burgers, hot dogs with sauerkraut, and kids' meals. This being Portland, of course, the French-press coffee is roasted by a local farm-friendly company. We love the low prices and, at lunch, things move along more quickly than you'd expect. And if you have a great suggestion for an over-the-top burger, Brunchbox features specials now and then. Now all you need is a triage tent next door.

Brøder Comfort Food

7.9	8.5	8.0
Food	Feel	Beer

Hip, brunchy, airy, and fun—the very essence of Southeast

Scandinavian

Casual restaurant

$30
Price

www.broderpdx.com

Mon–Wed 9am–3pm
Thu–Sat 9am–3pm, 6pm–9:30pm
Sun 9am–3pm

Bar Beer, wine, liquor, BYO
Credit cards Visa, MC
Reservations Accepted
Date-friendly, outdoor dining, Wi-Fi

Division/Clinton
2508 SE Clinton St.
(503) 736-3333

Ah, Sweden. Vikings, herring, and Greta Garbo. Is there anything coming out of this country that isn't cool? Brøder captures the aesthetic and spirit of Scandinavia, with its seamless marriage between minimalist furnishings like robin's-egg-blue aluminum chairs, and the efficient craftsmanship of the kitchen is put on display for all counter patrons to see. It's airy inside with good natural light, and there are a few outdoor tables, as well. Presentations are equally artful, balanced between rustic and eye-catching.

Maybe because of the vulnerability of just-waking humans, breakfast is the most exciting meal here, with quaint boards and trays of homemade breakfast breads, excellent Danish pancakes, and smoked trout hash. Most important is the good, strong coffee. Though Brøder is more often regarded as a sunny breakfast and lunch joint, the hipsters are also filing in for dinner, Thursdays through Saturdays. (The kitchen seems glad to stay open until 10pm on those nights, if you just let them know you're coming.) Service can be a bit distracted, but it's fun to sit at the bar and watch the cooks deftly juggle orders.

As the hinterlands are renowned for their pickling, it's fitting that pickled veggies here are superb, with flavors bright and clear. Pickled beets perk up a well-browned potato pancake, which is by itself slightly underseasoned. A Brøder club sandwich pairs moist, crispy bacon with subtle gravlax, which is interesting—cured surf, meet cured turf—although a superfluous avocado makes it a bit mushy. We'd swap out the avocado for the roe and pickled onions that come on a separate plate. In general, recipes are simple and good, but nothing too exciting—and yes, this food can get exciting. For instance, where's the bleak roe? Swedish meatballs with very rich Sherry cream sauce and lingonberry jam is good, but surprisingly ordinary.

There's a really decent little showing of mostly Old World wines that pair well with this food—Blaufränkisch, sparkling Jura, and so on—and the prices are good, if a little closer to dinner-appropriate than lunch. The beers offer a rare opportunity to traverse not only Belgium and Germany, but all of Scandinavia, as well. There's an Oregonian beer on tap, too, and Portland's own Krogstad Aquavit. It's not hard to see why this place is well loved.

Bunk Sandwiches

8.1	6.0
Food	Feel

Pick a sandwich, any sandwich—and come hungry for flavor and fat

Sandwiches

Counter service

$15
Price

www.bunksandwiches.com

Mon–Sat 8am–3pm

Bar Beer
Credit cards Visa, MC
Kid-friendly, outdoor dining,
veg-friendly, Wi-Fi

Southeast Portland
621 SE Morrison St,
(503) 477-9515

You set the bar pretty low when you call a place "Bunk," and it's especially funny given the warm and confident mustard-and-ketchup-colored walls and ceiling. The checkerboard linoleum floor reminds us of the ubiquitous sandwich dives all over the East Coast, except that this one is clean and the sandwiches are mostly good. A huge chalkboard seems to change every day, so don't get too attached to any one sandwich. Items also get crossed off as ingredients start running out.

Breakfast sandwiches are intensely satisfying, all variations on simple, buttery, flaky biscuits with egg or meat, always with cheese. At lunch, one of our favorite sandwiches features moist, flavorful meatballs that somehow hold together until bitten into, then melt on the tongue. The bread is slightly toasted to stand up against the sauce, which is flavorful and herbaceous without being overpowering. A Spanish sandwich that pairs salt cod with olives and a spicy chorizo is as unusual as it is successful. Roasted eggplant with red pepper, fresh mozzarella, and basil is drizzled with fragrant olive oil and a bit of salt; it's substantive without being too heavy, clean-tasting, and wonderfully aromatic. Again, the hoagie-style bun is the right choice to hold the wet innards.

There's this consistent heaviness here, which can be fine except when it occurs where you'd least expect it, like in a grilled albacore sandwich whose mayonnaise and Swiss cheese are just way too rich. It's saved (just barely) by an add-on of good pickled hot peppers. Even vegetable sandwiches and sides can sometimes whack you over the head with fat; potato salad with bacon and egg is good, but too weighty for lunch. These preps are more conducive to curing insomnia than recharging your batteries on a workday.

Still, the bread here is first-rate and the pressing of the sandwich is done expertly. Ingredients are obviously top quality, and meats are smoked, roasted, and sliced with great care.

Bunk is painfully hip, with bands playing overhead that are out of style as soon as you say their name, and Miller High Life mimosas. Thanks to some zealous reporting by media and bloggers, the waits here can get up to 30 minutes, and the counter service has a certain you-should-feel-lucky-to-be-here attitude (the "Soup Nazi" phenomenon.) But the fervor isn't entirely unwarranted—this is definitely not your dime-a-dozen sandwich joint.

Burgerville

Sort-of-healthy fast food with a sort-of-healthier conscience

5.2	5.5
Food	Feel

American

Counter service

$10
Price

www.burgerville.com

Daily 7am–11pm

Bar None
Credit cards Visa, MC, AmEx
Kid-friendly, outdoor dining, Wi-Fi

Hawthorne
1122 SE Hawthorne Blvd.
(503) 230-0479

North Portland
1135 NE MLK Blvd.
(503) 235-6858

Southeast Portland
3432 SE 25th Ave.
(503) 239-5942

Additional locations
and more features at
www.fearlesscritic.com

A sustainable and local fast food chain that uses seasonal ingredients? Only in the Pacific Northwest. There are about 40 locations from here to Vancouver, but aside from philosophy (which, admittedly, holds a lot of weight these days), we can't figure out what's making them so popular. The burgers are fine, but they're nothing to rave about. There are some unexpected, unusual items like an asparagus sandwich, and fresh berry shakes are good, but they don't stand out that much from other fast-food shakes.

We love that there's a relationship (or the illusion of one, anyway) with local farmers, and that you can read about the source of the apples on an apple-and-peppered-bacon turkey club—we've come a long way from the meat patties of shady origins, Upton Sinclair's portrait of bloody mayhem at meat-processing plants, and genetically treated super-tomatoes. And you have to admire a burger chain that lists its wind power partners on its website.

But Country Natural beef, the stuff they use in McMenamins' serviceable burgers, is only as good as how you grill it and stack it. Burgers at the 'Ville are well done in that fast-food fashion, with nothing to make them taste atypical. There are better burgers all over town. At least your conscience can rest assured that it's antibiotic-and-hormone-free meat. French fries are just—we hate to say it—not as good as McD's. Your best choice of all might be the Pacific-halibut fish sandwich, done exactly how a fast-food fish sandwich should be, all crispy and moist inside. Onion rings, made from Walla Walla onions, are also exemplary.

As for the locations, they're done up with a derivative, corporate-y '50s décor, but the oldest branches are great, with more legit personality. In general, Burgerville has more character than the bigger companies we've grown up with, and that fact, along with a commendable ethic, elevates it above the rest of the fast-food pack.

Bye and Bye

A place of contradictions: meaty vegan food and hipness without hipster attitude

7.0	8.5	8.5
Food	Feel	Beer

Vegefusion

Bar

$30
Price

Mon–Thu 4pm–10pm; Fri 2pm–10pm; Sat–Sun noon–10pm

Bar Beer, wine, liquor
Credit cards Visa, MC, AmEx
Date-friendly, outdoor dining, veg-friendly

Northeast Portland
1011 NE Alberta St.
(503) 281-0537

Bye and Bye is one of a growing number of great-looking lounges that serve food for vegetarians and vegans, but do so without being preachy. In fact, you may not know this is a vegan bar until you get halfway through the menu. Normally, bar food is atrocious but perfect, in a way that only carnivores can really understand; after all, a certain amount of self-loathing mixed with grease and cheese is a fine way to soak up excess alcohol from the blood. So what does bar food amount to for the squeaky-clean consciences of drinking vegans?

Well, nearly the same, as it turns out. A much-heralded "meatball" sub is among the star options here, and it's surprisingly satisfying, even by carnivore standards. Helped out by a spicy marinara, the "meat" has a good, substantial texture and the bread is just beautifully toasted. Another popular choice, a "Weeping Tiger," sandwiches braised tofu, "mayo," tomato, lettuce, and hot jalapeño between slices of good bread, amounting to a spicy, hearty good time. Bowls with collards and barbecue-saucey tofu satisfy a certain down-home craving among those who've no doubt been disowned by their Southern families upon going veg.

The atmosphere is terrific—rustic, dark, and candle-lit, with a cozy patio. A jukebox features some punk, a lot of rockabilly, and a few classic standards. There's a good selection of Portland and international cult favorites on tap, poured into quart-sized mason jars for $6 during happy hour—except the excellent, fruity and lively Duchesse de Bourgogne, which gets its own goblet. There's a lean, focused selection by the bottle, too. Cocktails are somewhat innovative and made with house infusions, but tend toward the sweety-sweet side.

Normally, we rail against the sorts of vegetarian and vegan dishes that rely on fake meat (if you know what a vegetable is capable of, why waste your time?). But this is one of very few cases that actually succeeds. To take advantage of this, you'll have to order your food by 10pm, although the bar stays open until 2:30am, by which point you won't even be able to tell the difference between meat and beer.

Byways Café

A totally retro diner with a few small surprises up its sleeve

5.7 Food **7.5** Feel

American

Casual restaurant

$15 Price

www.bywayscafe.com

Mon–Fri 7am–3pm
Sat–Sun 7:30am–2pm

Bar None
Credit cards Visa, MC, AmEx
Reservations Not accepted
Kid-friendly, outdoor dining

Pearl District
1212 NW Glisan St.
(503) 221-0011

Byways has one of those interchangeable mid-century Americana designs. There's a black-and-white checkered floor, thin wood paneling on the walls, and shelves that house souvenir plates from what could be Lucy and Desi's road trip. There are a few nice-looking benches out front, but if you sit outside, you'll miss the metallic red booths and general sense of "What'll it be, hon?" And don't miss the vintage salt-and-pepper shakers.

The menu is definitely going for the Route-66 feeling. In fact, a burger with a glossy bun and curly-leaf lettuce is exactly the sort served to us on road trips by waitresses in support hose. Which isn't necessarily a bad thing. But the fries are the same, mealy, soulless things that no amount of salting at the table is going to help. Sysco-truck fruit isn't a much better choice of side. But if we're going to get a tuna melt anywhere, it's going to be a place like this; and this one is exactly as butter-crunchy and tuna-casserole-y as it is in our dreams. Limp pickle chips and all.

Both the corned beef sandwich and the Reuben on marbled rye are mediocre—not terribly dry. But certainly not as good as Kenny & Zuke's or Kornblatt's. Corned beef hash, on the other hand, makes for a great, greasy breakfast. Blue-corn pancakes have a nice, creamy grit to them, and French toast is thick and orangey.

Another unexpected touch is the cool mix of music here—some samba, some old-school country, and some Southern rock. We also love the decent Stumptown coffee served here. Granted, it sits on a hot plate. But hey, it's a diner. Sometimes you've got to keep it real.

Cacao Chocolate

Think you've had good hot chocolate? You haven't had good hot chocolate.

Sweets

Counter service

www.cacaodrinkchocolate.com

Mon–Thu 9am–8pm
Fri–Sat 9am–10pm
Sun noon–6pm
Hours vary by location

Bar None
Credit cards Visa, MC, AmEx
Date-friendly, kid-friendly,
veg-friendly, Wi-Fi

Downtown
414 SW 13th Ave.
(503) 241-0656

Downtown
712 SW Salmon St.
(503) 274-9510

If the décor somewhat resembles a paler version of Tiffany's robin's-egg blue-and-brown palette, it's no wonder: what is here is no less delicate. Cacao reminds us of a French dress shop more than a patisserie or café; it's elegant and simple, with colorful presentations assembled atop minimalist furnishings, which you can well imagine are fussed over and straightened after every pawing from curious customers.

The lovely, personable owners will answer questions without being the least bit condescending, and have garnered quite a devoted following with their passion and dedication. Oh yes, and with their drinking chocolate. This is no powdery Swiss Miss, no lumpy and uneven Ghirardelli, even. Drinking chocolate, as opposed to hot chocolate, is thicker, more concentrated, and intense. It's a tradition all over Europe, and the tannic-velvet sensation and deeply earthy, nutty flavor will stay with you for days after sipping.

Of course, there's hot chocolate here, too, but this is also a totally different ball game than what you're used to. There's a seamless integration of milk and chocolate, whether in the darker blend or the lighter one. When the sleet is falling outside at Christmastime, drinking this hot chocolate is nothing less than magical.

Once the caffeine buzz has set in, go on a compromised-judgment shopping spree throughout the rest of the store: chocolate-covered nuts; bite-sized chocolates; bar chocolates; fruity chocolates; dark chocolates; milk chocolates. Trust us, you'll be happy about it later.

Café Castagna

An alluring vibe, hit-or-miss service, and a burger to end all arguments

7.1	8.0	8.0
Food	Feel	Wine

Modern

Upmarket restaurant

$45
Price

www.castagnarestaurant.com

Mon 5pm–10pm; Tue–Thu 11:30am–2pm, 5pm–10pm; Fri–Sat 11:30am–2pm, 5pm–11pm; Sun 5pm–9:30pm

Bar Beer, wine, liquor
Credit cards Visa, MC, AmEx
Reservations Accepted
Date-friendly, outdoor dining

Hawthorne
1758 SE Hawthorne Blvd.
(503) 231-9959

On a warm summer evening, there's something impossibly appealing about this Hawthorne hotspot with its shaded outdoor tables and easy informality. Inside, the open kitchen lights up the very austere, Solaris-like air; it's the sort of place where you'll feel comfortable discussing the extensive, well-chosen, Euro-focused wine list in shorts and flip-flops. Servers generally convey a sense of urban indifference that's a bit un-Portland—and they're positively cold-hearted when it comes to seating you 30 seconds after closing time. On busier nights, it's very hard to get the staff's attention, even to order another drink. On the other hand, they're quite knowledgeable about the menu.

The food here is simple: rustic European classics made regional and modern. A large butter-lettuce salad with chives, tarragon, and vinaigrette royal is a study in subtlety and composition. Bargain-priced arancini (fried risotto balls) are crispy and ooze with fontina. It's hard to argue with the house-made sausages—consistently one of the best choices here—and the Caesar salad is a world-class version, eggy and ridiculously moist without sacrificing crispness.

Often, though, the lighter the dish, the less impressive. Chitarra—here as thin as angel hair—sounds great, with prawns, lemon zest, and agretti, but it's an overcooked, underseasoned failure. Penne with cheese lacks strength and isn't worth the money. Pizzas are creative and decent, but no more.

One thing that draws us back again and again, however, is what may be the best hamburger in the area. The house-made bun is toasted to a slight crunch, and holds in all the juices from a top-notch patty cooked exactly as specified. Even people who don't like pickles have raved over these homemade ones, which are served on the side. The entire ensemble comes with a huge mound of crisp, expertly salted shoestring fries.

Desserts are hit or miss, and cocktails, although balanced and made with freshly squeezed juices, are overpriced for what you get. Skip these. If you're on a date, fair enough, but otherwise it's hard to justify the elaborateness here when you could head across the street and have an equally decent pizza and microbrewski—and sit outside on the same street—for less than half the price at the curiously accented Vincenté's. And they'll let you in at five to midnight without even a murmur.

Café Nell

A charming neighborhood brasserie with adequate food and a generous breakfast

6.4	8.5	6.0
Food	Feel	Wine

American

Casual restaurant

$40
Price

www.cafenell.com

Tue–Fri 7am–10pm
Sat 9am–midnight
Sun 9am–2pm

Bar Beer, wine, liquor
Credit cards Visa, MC, AmEx
Reservations Accepted
Outdoor dining

Northwest Portland
1987 NW Kearney St.
(503) 295-6487

Café Nell is the very definition of charming. In its unassuming residential-neighborhood location, it has that hidden-gem thing going for it. It's elegant but understated, like Catherine Deneuve in blue jeans. There's very little on the walls, and nothing to absorb the clamor when the place is full. Come expecting a lively and loud meal. Lighting is gentle but ample; on calmer nights, it's quite romantic.

Brunch is popular, and once in a while features inventive dishes like a (seasonal) braised lamb hash with a little kick of slightly tart sweetness from kumquats. But mostly it's the usual: hanger steak with eggs is cooked properly to temperature; French toast is correct; house-cured salmon is capable. Many brunch items are also available at a daily breakfast, which is served until the generous hour of 4pm.

The accessible lunch and dinner menu does Pacific Northwest takes on French brasserie dishes, but with some missteps: spiced nuts (served only at happy hour) have a strange aftertaste, grilled shrimp are strangely acidic, and a lamb burger is fine, but on a "brioche" bun that isn't really brioche. Grilled whole trout is good, served simply and well executed. Like most things here, however, it manages to escape sublimity.

The almost-all-domestic wine list is surprisingly clueless for Portland. There are a few reputable producers from the Northwest, but most of the selection seems to be motivated by national press. Still, it's hard to argue with the low markups.

Service can be spotty: sometimes it's bored and distracted; other times, it's friendly and efficient. It isn't that Café Nell is a bad restaurant, it's just not actively good. Few dishes will be memorable, but they will be nourishing, and served in a cute joint perhaps filled with your neighbors, all laughing and talking and having a good time. That—and breakfast at 2pm—is sometimes all we want.

Caffè Allora

Totally legit Italian for the preening Pearl

8.1	8.0	7.5
Food	Feel	Wine

Italian, Pizza

Casual restaurant

$40
Price

www.caffe-allora.com

Mon–Fri 7am–10pm
Sat–Sun 8am–10pm

Bar Beer, wine, liquor
Credit cards Visa, MC, AmEx
Reservations Accepted
Date-friendly, outdoor dining,
veg-friendly, Wi-Fi

Pearl District
504 NW 9th Ave.
(503) 445-4612

Caffè Allora, with its slightly sleek, slightly slick chicness, is wonderfully Euro-trash. The joint is always bustling, and with its pretty waitstaff and outdoor tables full of handsome hair-product models, it could be something straight out of Bergamo or Bologna. It's small and casual, though, unlike more annoying American-style trendy places. It's a good spot for a mid-morning espresso or a work meeting, and during the World Cup, the upstairs area turns into the ultimate fan zone.

Beneath the surface, though, this place is totally legit. There are a dozen different salads, but none of them is the un-Italian Caesar. The inexplicably named "Berlusconi" seduces underage ladies with mozzarella, fennel, tomatoes, white beans, and olives. There's also olive-oil-cured tuna, speck, prosciutto di Parma, and salame salad, which you can order as antipasti or in salads, or on panini at lunch.

Beyond that, about a dozen pastas center on delightfully traditional preparations. Penne all'amatriciana is slowly cooked over a long period to layer the spices and tomato, with pancetta (a worthy substitute for guanciale) imparting a slight smoky richness to the sauce. Better is carbonara, brought to the table hot so that upon arrival, the sauce is still in its formation phase, egg cooking to creaminess in pasta steam, Parmigiano melting.

For an authentic Italian experience, start with an aperitivo from the cocktail list. There aren't many creative drinks here, just classics made with Campari and Prosecco, and a few excellent grappas. If you're a Negroni fan, here's your spot. The wine list gives just a glimpse into Italy's diversity; whites are shackled to a uniform price point, and don't have nearly as much variety as the reds. Still, the mostly northern glasses and bottles are eminently well chosen and fairly priced. Beers are even more succinct, but get the job done (but can we please get a better Italian beer than Peroni? Anyone?).

Portions are authentically European, and there won't be any steak, pizza, or ridiculous lobster ravioli. Every now and then, there's a good fish special, cooked expertly. And although the ambience gets kind of romantic, with tealights on the tables and a sexy minimalism, this is really best thought of as a lunch or extremely simple dinner spot.

Caffè Mingo

A neighborhood restaurant with even food
and service that's worth a wait

7.7	9.0	7.5
Food	Feel	Drinks

Italian

Upmarket restaurant

$50
Price

www.barmingonw.com/caffemingo

Mon–Thu 5pm–10pm
Fri–Sat 5pm–10:30pm
Sun 4:30pm–9:30pm

Bar Beer, wine
Credit cards Visa, MC, AmEx
Reservations Not accepted
Date-friendly, outdoor dining,
veg-friendly

Northwest Portland
807 NW 21st Ave.
(503) 226-4646

Caffè Mingo is a stalwart of the Portland dining scene, a place that's pretty routinely overlooked as the clamor of new and exciting ventures reaches a high crescendo. And while its next-door annex, Bar Mingo, satisfies the casual, trendy crowds, Caffè Mingo maintains a reputation for having more serious food and a superb waitstaff, many of whom have been at Mingo for years. There's actually an homage to every staff member who has worked here in the front of the restaurant, and it's a surprisingly short list. Caffè Mingo must have one of the lowest turnover rates in the business.

It's no surprise, then, on any given night, that servers are incredibly helpful and knowledgeable about the menu and wine list. Unlike next door's Italian fare, which serves as more of a supporting chorus to the wines, these dishes are memorable and impressive. We've had good risotto with sweet, fresh corn and heirloom tomatoes; expertly braised meats; and decent fish specials. The kitchen has shown a particular way with melt-in-your-mouth braised cod. As at Bar Mingo, pastas are made in-house, but they're matched by nearly everything else. This may not be the city's most exciting Italian restaurant, but the execution is generally there.

Just because the restaurant is a bit more dressed up than its popular neighbor doesn't mean that it isn't cozy. Quite the opposite: there's a totally approachable neighborhood vibe here. And where Bar Mingo's wine program is a little…egalitarian, this wine list is restrained and predominantly Italian, with the big stars from Tuscany and Piedmont. A generous corkage fee of only $15 also invites you to bring in some of the bargain Italians not on this list, but remember to be polite and offer your server a taste. (Reward good service in this way, and you'll find more of it around town.)

Reservations aren't accepted for parties of less than six, but if you can't wait, it's nice to know there's always the adjacent overflow bar—even if it won't be quite so splendid.

Caffé Umbria

A little taste of Italy—both in the cup and out

Coffee, Baked goods

Café

www.caffeumbria.com

Sun–Thu 7am–7pm
Fri–Sat 7am–8pm

Bar Beer, wine
Credit cards Visa, MC
Live music, outdoor dining

Pearl District
303 NW 12th Ave.
(503) 241-5300

Caffé Umbria appeared on the scene a few months ago, with all the flash and glamour you'd expect at a major restaurant opening. The thing is, it's just an Italian coffeeshop. But the hype is no wonder, as the Umbria beans are becoming a Pacific-Northwest-wide phenomenon whose ambition seems almost limitless. The company has gained a lot of traction packaging its Seattle coffee and selling it to local restaurants, making it a recognizable name before it ever opened shop here in the Pearl Street district's Casey Building.

Inside, the airy space evokes stylish Italian cafés: exposed-brick walls, gleaming glass cases, lightweight cherry-wood tables, standing bars, and high-quality fixtures throughout. It fits the neighborhood, and might be the only coffeehouse in the area that has a modern feel but isn't part of a huge corporate conglomerate. The lack of free Wi-Fi and big, comfy chairs doesn't encourage laptop use or loitering the way a lot of other places do, but it is a really pleasant place to converse with a live human (remember those?) and fancy yourself a European.

Indeed, you will find authentic Italian espresso here, pulled properly short with a layer of crema on top—it's incredible how hard this can be to find. Drip coffee is far from the city's best, but it's smoother and less burnt-tasting than Starbucks, anyway. Orders to be consumed on premise come in a nice ceramic cup, accompanied by a small chocolate. On busy days the employees behind the counter frequently answer in Italian. Even the music playing overhead fits the Pearl District vibe, but it's never too loud. A large plasma TV is in a nook around the corner, and could be a spectacular place to watch Italian soccer.

Dining options are of the usual pedigree: various scones, pastries, homemade panini, pasta salads, and so on. The gelato is cheap and satisfying and comes in a variety of flavors. Beer and wine are also available. Caffé Umbria is classy, but by no means is it stuffy. Should you ever visit Italy, you'll be glad this is here to satisfy the atmospheric longing you'll have when you return.

Campbell's BBQ

The wood makes the difference—but will the future bring better still?

6.9	7.0
Food	Feel

Barbecue, Southern

Casual restaurant

$20
Price

www.campbellsbbq.com

Tue–Thu 11am–2pm, 5pm–9pm
Fri–Sun 11am–9pm

Bar Beer, wine, BYO
Credit cards Visa, MC, AmEx
Reservations Accepted
Outdoor dining

Southeast Portland
8701 SE Powell Blvd.
(503) 777-9795

In an area that's normally associated with excellent Vietnamese and some of Portland's better Asian food, you may see a sign for "BBQ" and assume that it's Korean. But the look of the place will remedy that right away: a cute, cozy house with a homey, familial set of tables and chairs in several rooms and an unmistakably Southern bent to it. A sign depicts an African-American couple holding ribs and smiling with soul-warming content. A plume of smoke rising from the roof gives you the impression that you could step inside to find this couple rocking back and forth in front of a crackling fire.

In fact, this smiling couple did open Campbell's many moons ago, but sold it in 2006. Since then, there has been some debate over whether or not the food has taken a downturn. It's not at all in doubt that it did change, as barbecue is every bit as unique to its pitmaster as a brushstroke is to its hand.

The menu here is somewhat surprising and includes organic bison and duck along with the essential brisket, pork ribs, chicken, and sausage—and, uniquely, it's all smoked over hardwood. This fact represents a pleasant departure from the many gas-smoked barbecue joints around Portland—even if, perhaps due to the limitations of smoking indoors (as Campbell's does) rather than outdoors, there's not as much knee-weakening smokiness as you'd get at a barbecue shack on some roadside in the Deep South. We've had pieces here that had all the juiciness, the melting globules of fat, and the crackling moments of char that inspire mouths to moan—and also pieces that had none of that. To some extent, it's the luck of the draw.

Sauces are available in a wider array than you would find along that roadside: "Smoky Brown Sugar," hot, less hot, and wimpy. All of these are fine; we prefer the hottest version. For now, Campbell's is still worth a detour. This being Portland, though, some perfectionist barbecue fiend will probably move here one day, open a place of his or her own, and smoke Campbell's—and all of us—out.

Carafe Bistro

| 8.2 | 9.0 | 9.0 |
| Food | Feel | Wine |

A delightfully authentic French bistro where most touches are spot on

French Upmarket restaurant **$45**
Price

www.carafebistro.com

Mon–Fri 11:30am–9pm
Sat 5pm–9pm

Bar Beer, wine, liquor
Credit cards Visa, MC, AmEx
Reservations Accepted
Date-friendly, outdoor dining

Downtown
200 SW Market St.
(503) 248-0004

Carafe may cater largely to a distracted business-lunch and pre-theater crowd, and it may sit in a totally random office-building location. But this is the most finely realized French Brasserie concept in the city, beating the more heralded Fenouil at its own game. The mirrors, the banquettes, the lively din, the French shouts coming from the kitchen—Disney World couldn't do any better of a theming job than this. Even the jostling and rudeness in the bar area at happy hour, when some dishes are spectacularly marked down, seems totally authentic. (Once the appropriate hour strikes, the bar prices double, and the ease of sitting down increases dramatically.)

Granted, there are some very un-Parisian touches. To get to the bathroom, for instance, you have to exit the restaurant, look both ways, cross a parking-garage ramp, and actually enter the garage. And the restaurant's windows (along with the outdoor tables) look out onto that garage on one side and another bland office-building set on the other.

Moules frites—that classic French/Belgian brasserie dish—is pulled off with great skill, with good, plump mussels (the minority slightly stanky, but not in a bad way) sitting in a creamily delicious broth with shallots that is just what it should be, designed exclusively for sopping up with baguette slices. We also love the béchamelicious, if almost absurdly rich, croque monsieur and croque madame.

There's a respectable duck confit, a well-balanced frisée aux lardons, and "lamb stewed in the style of Morocco" (tagine, anyone?) with chickpea fries, a clever integration of the two cultures. Steak frites is done, as it should be, with hanger steak, and the French fries are right on the money. There's steak tartare, oysters on the half-shell, and house-made charcuterie with cornichons, mustard, and grilled levain bread. The bread is from Ken's, and the burger comes on a Ken's bun.

The well-chosen, dogmatic wine list is almost entirely French, and almost entirely great-value. You don't often see 1er Cru Chablis or Pernand-Vergelesses Blanc for under $50 at a wine store, never mind at a restaurant. There are perfectly good French reds (like Fronsac) for under $25, and for dessert, unbelievably well priced Sauternes and Côteaux du Layon.

Because of where it is and how it's positioned, Carafe Bistro might be overlooked by a large swath of the population. We think this is unwarranted, and we think that the concept will soon catch on with a broader audience. Consider yourself warned.

Carlyle

Dated trends stand in for philosophy at this undeniably romantic spot

6.0	8.5	7.5
Food	Feel	Drinks

Modern

Upmarket restaurant

$80
Price

www.carlylerestaurant.com

Mon–Sat 5:30pm–10pm

Bar Beer, wine, liquor
Credit cards Visa, MC, AmEx
Reservations Accepted
Date-friendly, outdoor dining

Northwest Portland
1632 NW Thurman St.
(503) 595-1782

It seems as though every dish at Carlyle is composed in a round ring, then piled impossibly high with other ingredients (all of which tremble with the first touch of a fork, and then scatter wildly across the plate). If it occurs to you that this presentation seems to effectively distract from the actual food making up these sweeping architectures, then you may be on to something.

Undeniably, it is a pleasure to be here in this comfortably small and clubby interior. Some outside tables in good weather make for peaceful, rustic twilight-watching. The unexpected location under the Fremont Bridge makes it feel like a special find, and the lighting is magnificent—no wonder it has a romantic reputation. In fact, the ambience tends to paint a patina of success around a less-than-stellar dinner.

The cocktail program here is solid, though not yet one of the more ambitious and dedicated in town. (To be fair, the bar is set extremely high in Portland). At any rate, it's much more careful and astute than the wine list, which is adequate at best, and peppered with goofy, mass-produced wines like Goats do Roam.

The menu is divided into three sections: tastes, small plates, and principals. But most everything, no matter how artful, is plagued by execution problems. Seared foie gras has come carelessly de-veined, making it stringy and off-putting. On the other hand, sweetbreads with olive oil, crushed potatoes, bacon, and mushrooms have been expertly seared, creamy textured, and full of wonderful flavor.

Some dishes are totally hilarious, like a "ravioli of milk-fed veal" that has come as a single, undercooked raviolo sitting in a pool of sauce that, while very good, obliterated any veal taste, rendering the raviolo obsolete. Calamari is cooked fine but served with awful sauces; a butter-lettuce salad with prosciutto and melon worked together about as well as Congress.

Mains are a total disaster, overcooked and paired with salty, inedible components. Hanger steaks and veals are small and disappointing for their price. Fish tends to be the best choice, especially at lunch, where you might find expertly grilled smoky and moist halibut.

But in general, this place is a crap shoot without the thrill.

Castagna

A talented kitchen and even more talented copy-writers for the menu

8.9	8.0	8.0
Food	Feel	Wine

Modern

Upmarket restaurant

$80
Price

www.castagnarestaurant.com

Wed–Sat 5:30pm–9pm

Bar Beer, wine, liquor
Credit cards Visa, MC, AmEx
Reservations Accepted
Date-friendly, outdoor dining

Hawthorne
1752 SE Hawthorne Blvd.
(503) 231-7373

One of the only things in the world that we like better than delicate radishes with creamy butter is delicate radishes with creamy butter plopped down at our table for free, along with crusty bread, just after we sit down.

That will be the simplest vegetable preparation you'll see at Castagna. Matsutake mushrooms have a lot of hard-wired flavor, but they might meet with pine nuts, garlic, and trout roe, turning something simple and earthy into something bouncier and texturally challenging. But this approach can sometimes go wrong. Delicate Dungeness crab would have been much better off without having been invaded by an unexpectedly sweet-tart lemon foam; it was as if a frozen margarita had been accidentally dumped onto the plate.

Speaking of margaritas, you won't find them here. The craft cocktail program is top-notch, and the wine list is fascinating, even in the $30-to-$35 range—Juliénas, Bourgogne Aligoté, Carmignano, Madiran, Alto Adige Lagrein. That said, there's not a single bottle under $30, which we find pompous.

Speaking of pomposity, our panel is deeply divided over the question of whether or not it is pompous to label a dish not by its principal protein but rather by the vegetable that the chef deems to be the dominant flavor—for example, a menu item is called "onions" when it's really house-cured black cod. Yet, at one visit, a dish entitled "*Cabbage*: halibut, fresh ricotta, whey, savoy cabbage, mustard" really *was*—to its credit—first and foremost about the cabbage (and, perhaps secondly, about the mustard), not about the protein, in the same sense that that's true of the classic hearty Yankee dinner of corned beef and cabbage, whose traditional word order was no doubt intended to make the peasants feel that they were eating more of the precious meat than they really were.

Speaking of peasants, you won't find them here. Order the tasting menu plus wine pairings, and you'll approach three figures per head. With a larger group, it's better to just order a bunch of things (it's all small plates) and pass them around.

At its best, this kitchen can play beautifully at the intersection of sweet and savory. A purée of chestnuts—the restaurant's namesake—stuff agnolotti full of a childlike autumn warmth, while pecorino and prosciutto set it straight with salty seriousness. Bites like that reveal this restaurant's vast potential. Reining in some of the pomp and formality—both in the room and on the plate—might bring it up to the next level.

Ciao Vito

A romantic restaurant with more ups and
downs than a trip through the Cinque Terre

6.2	9.0	8.5
Food	Feel	Wine

Italian

Casual restaurant

$40
Price

www.ciaovito.net

Mon–Sat 5pm–10pm
Sun 5pm–9pm

Bar Beer, wine, liquor
Credit cards Visa, MC, AmEx
Reservations Accepted
Date-friendly, outdoor dining,
veg-friendly

Alberta Arts District
2203 NE Alberta St.
(503) 282-5522

Ciao Vito is a tough place to review. Our panel is split over whether it's
any good. This can only be attributed to the fact that you are guaranteed
to have a different experience every time you go, even when your
ordering is identical.

One consistently enjoyable aspect is the atmosphere; the comfortable
space is done in earth tones, with heavy curtains absorbing noise to
ensure easy conversations. The walls glow softly from the amber light of
early evening; late at night, flattering candlelight prevails. The high-
backed wooden chairs and tables wrap around the kitchen in a
horseshoe, with a large bar on one side and a community table in the
middle. Service is friendly and often knowledgeable.

The wine list covers the whole of the Italian boot and is priced very
fairly—you'll drink very well here for under $40 per bottle. Homemade
infusions make for some very good cocktails, as well. Ciao Vito definitely
has all the makings of a superb date spot, but ordering is like playing a
gustatory Russian Roulette.

The menu is split between Italian salads, pastas, and polentas, and
dishes with more Northwest roots, such as duck, pork chops, and razor
clams. Seasonal ingredients tend to make up the hugely portioned plates.
You could stick with a dependable "antipasti della casa," with
(sometimes) cauliflower, marinated broccoli and beets, and perhaps late-
summer figs to counterpoint the mozzarella and house-cured meats.

After that, all bets are off. On one visit, a Caesar salad was very light
and subtle, but a week later, it was clobbered by lemon; a roasted beet
salad—although always generous—was a bit bland one time, and dressed
wonderfully another. A sugo has had shy, wilting pork one time and
prevalent, proud flavor the next. But crispy duck legs (no longer on the
menu) have been so problematic that their success varies wildly even in
one *plate*: the first leg might be okay and the second soggy. A wretched
sauce that tastes like marsala with a few blueberries thrown in didn't
help, and while the white beans were quite good, the potatoes seemed
like a sad afterthought. However, breaded, pan-fried razor clams do an
excellent tango with sweet red-pepper jam, and calamari seems to be
expertly cooked every time, with just the right amount of crunch.

You can count on one thing: desserts will be boring to awful—either
way, a waste of calories. If Ciao Vito were consistent, we might
recommend it more whole-heartedly. As it is, we can only ask you how
lucky you feel.

City Market

Everything you need for a special dinner under one roof

Groceries

Market

Mon–Sat 9:30am–7pm	**Bar** Beer, wine	**Northwest Portland**
Sun 10am–7pm	**Credit cards** Visa, MC, AmEx	735 NW 21st Ave.
	Veg-friendly	(503) 221-3007

What would you pay to have a great fishmonger, butcher, and fromagerie under one roof? And a Pastaworks, complete with gourmet items, flowers, and wine? Now round that figure up and you have what you'll be dropping at City Market.

The cheese selection here is diverse and wonderful, and properly wrapped and stored (it's a living thing, people—you can't strangle it to death in shrink wrap); the staff is usually quite helpful, if a bit condescending at times. The wine list at Pastaworks is brief, but brilliant—mostly small-production Italian and Spanish wines which are also, as it happens, among the best bargains on the market. A gorgeous display of cured meats, pâté, and sausages from locally raised meats are also wonderful, even if only to look at. And a glittering show of live shellfish is hard not to linger over.

City Market is a reasonable lunch stop, too (lunch and entertainment, perhaps?), with a pretty good sandwich counter. Only avoid the muffuletta, which falls into that frequent muffuletta trap of inedible saltiness. The other sandwiches are pretty good, but pricey. Again, it's about where you are.

It's fun to peruse the prettily packaged ingredients in preparation for a special meal you are making; you certainly couldn't do this all the time, although the farm-fresh eggs are something that, once you've had them, you can't live without. Be prepared for some pretty unfriendly hipper-than-thou attitudes, though, and if you show up too close to closing, scoot around the corner to Trader Joe's, which is no match for this selection, but good in a pinch, and open a full two hours later.

Clarklewis
Welcome back to the big time

9.1	8.5	9.0
Food	Feel	Wine

Modern

Upmarket restaurant

$70
Price

www.clarklewispdx.com

Mon–Thu 11:30am–2pm, 5pm–9pm
Fri 11:30am–2pm, 5pm–10pm
Sat 5pm–10pm

Bar Beer, wine, liquor
Credit cards Visa, MC, AmEx
Reservations Accepted
Date-friendly, outdoor dining

Southeast Portland
1001 SE Water Ave.
(503) 235-2294

For years, Clarklewis was (aside from being one of the original shift-key deniers) perhaps Portland's highest-flying restaurant, an icon that delivered the city to a new culinary era, received loads of national recognition, and was imitated lovingly en masse. But after losing some of the key figures at the helm, the restaurant took a turn for the worse, which caused quite a bit of grumbling.

Our recent visits have indicated that it's absolutely back on track, as exciting as ever, yet refreshingly classic, too. The new kitchen keeps it simple, focusing on making great use of local seafood, local produce, and a wood-burning oven that figures into a lot of the menu. In what still feels like a cutting-edge warehouse space (in what also still feels like a cutting-edge part of town, a surprisingly still-not-really-gentrified industrial area), the service is great, the people are beautiful, and one of PDX's top dining experiences has been restored to its former glory.

The kitchen's deftness is evident in soups like chilled cauliflower with almonds and oregano, which has a luxurious smoothness and depth. Although preps that brandish strong fats do well—e.g. pan-roasted pork belly with polenta, gooseberries, and verjus—the ones that focus more on elemental vegetable flavors do even better, like roasted beets with shaved fennel, Gruyère fritters, pistachios, and cherry vinaigrette.

We've really enjoyed the pastas lately; tagliatelle have come with a well-developed lamb ragù that showed unexpected hints of rosemary. Portland has a way with salmon, and Clarklewis has a way with Portland, so it follows that Clarklewis has a way with salmon. Wild Alaskan Coho salmon is cooked expertly and has been spectacular with haricots verts, sweet onions, roasted red onion, baby tomatoes, and gently mustardy sauce gribiche. And it doesn't stop at fish; a pork shoulder is lovingly roasted in the hearth, with sweet corn, braised fennel, baby turnips, arugula, and roasted hazelnuts.

A thorough and astute liquor selection makes for faithfully rendered classic cocktails. You'll pay a very slight premium on these, but we find the lovely, warm, woodsy space worthwhile. A titillating wine list has a range that protects novices as much as it provides for industry professionals, and at some of the lowest markups we've seen. There are unsung crazy Italian geniuses, small-production Austrian crowd pleasers, and the Alsatian reds and whites that were born to be drunk with fish.

Although Clarklewis is getting to be pretty historic, there isn't a trace of datedness these days. It hasn't been reborn; it has come back home.

Clyde Common

The ultimate Portland scene, chic and trendy and with pretty darn good food, too

9.4	8.5	9.0
Food	Feel	Drinks

Modern

Upmarket restaurant

$45
Price

www.clydecommon.com

Mon–Thu 11:30am–11pm
Fri 11:30am–2am
Sat 6pm–2am
Sun 6pm–11pm

Bar Beer, wine, liquor
Credit cards Visa, MC, AmEx
Reservations Not accepted
Wi-Fi

Downtown
1014 SW Stark St.
(503) 228-3333

Clyde Common is a veritable *Who's Who* of Portland. The downstairs is all community tables; you may find yourself seated between the City Commissioner and the Red Hot Chili Peppers. There are the trendy, the not-so-trendy, the gays, the straights, the socialites, the out-of-towners, the indie-emo rockers. And all of these people seem equally happy in the middle of the buzz. What Clyde Common is certainly not is intimate.

Soaring ceilings and window-walls fill the space with light. An open kitchen allows you to watch the cooks from anywhere in the dining room. A mezzanine wraps two walls, providing a great vantage point to view the crowd below and a slightly quieter atmosphere. Service can be plagued by annoying mishaps. Sometimes, the wait for food is longer than it should be; sometimes one guest's plate arrives ten minutes later than the rest. Orders are often mixed up; refills are scarce, although the waitstaff is certainly professional and experienced.

The menu frequently changes and prices are very reasonable, making it easy to try multiple items and still walk out the door with a pretty small tab. It is difficult to critique specific menu items here because they change so frequently, but we've lately been impressed by a thick, rich sweet-onion soup that showed unexpected depth, and albacore, in a loose interpretation of Niçoise, which had a great vinaigrette and summery pickled wax beans. Excellent french fries, one of the mainstays here, are of the thin school, served with a homemade aïoli and ketchup that tastes of harissa and cumin. Homemade pastas can be a touch overcooked, but are usually sauced well and complemented by unusually light sauces of fresh vegetables and good shaved cheese. Rare are dishes that completely miss the mark, like "Spiced Chickpeas" that were neither spiced nor spicy, but rather soaking in a watery, reddish sauce.

Classic cocktails are done well here, as are artisanal modern creations. The bar uses fresh juices, house-pickled onions, infused vodkas, and so on. The selection of top-shelf liquors is one of the best in town. A handful of well-chosen draft beers is rounded out by bigger celebrities in the bottle. The wine list is excellent, with a good selection of varietals from around the world at good markups. Even when Clyde Common suffers from overhyping, you should make no mistake—this is one of Portland's most brightly shining stars.

Coffee Time

A throwback to a time when coffee was simply a hot caffeinated beverage to be drunk after midnight on a slouchy sofa

Coffee, Baked goods

Café

www.coffeetimeportland.com

Sun–Thu 6:30am–1am
Fri–Sat 6:30am–2am

Bar None
Credit cards Visa, MC
Live music, outdoor dining,
veg-friendly, Wi-Fi

Northwest Portland
712 NW 21st Ave.
(503) 497-1090

Coffee Time's logo is adorably 1970s, with the font and coloring of a grocery-store loaf of bread—something with "Hearth" in the name. Indeed, when these windows glow in the gloom of an early morning, the joint is as hearthy as it gets; there are plenty of places to sit without rubbing elbows with people (grrr, people), and it's open until the hospitable hour of 2am. Who needs vacuum pots and indie-grouchy baristas when you can drink coffee the way God intended it to be drunk: until the wee hours of morning, hunched over a laptop?

The layout is charmingly old and unhip, saying "welcome to my home" with mismatched and threadbare area rugs, multiple rooms with wing-backed recliners, and fake plants. There's even a chessboard painted on a ledge separated by a wall, with an arched window so that the players can see each other (but, alas, cannot break out into a chess-boxing match). There are detailed murals on the walls, worn pews, and gorgeous sidewalk seating. In the '90s, this place was definitely the *shit*.

So what of the coffee? Well, it's unpretentious, to put it gently. This place is more about hanging out, or maybe about playing a game of Dungeons & Dragons in the alcove without being taunted. And if you hate being sneered at by purists who won't make you a mocha, there are two indulgent kinds here: cherry-sweet Black Forest and spicy Mexican. Go ahead with your vanilla-almond-mint-latte self—there's no judgment here. There are also competent panini and pastries.

In a city where coffee is pride, where coffee is science, where coffee is art, it's cool that Coffee Time skips gaily behind the tide, offering you an adorable place to curl up and read with an old-school raspberry mocha, sans attitude.

Coffeehouse Northwest

Bliss found in Portland's *other* most common institution

Coffee, Baked goods

Café

www.coffeehousenorthwest.com

Mon–Fri 6:30am–8pm	**Bar** None	**Northwest Portland**
Sat–Sun 7:30am–8pm	**Credit cards** Visa, MC, AmEx	1951 W. Burnside St.
	Outdoor dining, veg-friendly, Wi-Fi	(503) 248-2133

The only thing sluttier than PDX's proliferation of strip clubs is its proliferation of coffeeshops. A few of these have risen above the others in a sort of Olympian feat of excellence, consistency, nerdiness, and vibe. Coffeehouse Northwest stands with the best. And in this unlikely, ungainly, and inhospitable neighborhood, it *is* the best.

Eons-old exposed brick, even older wood floors, quirky local artwork, simple elements, and clean lines: this is the quintessence of coffee in the Northwestern United States, not just the Northwest of Portland.

Beans are handled beautifully here, some say better than at Stumptown's own annex. The coffee-geek staff explains that espresso is best when pulled between three and six days after the beans have been roasted, and indeed, when pulled ristretto, such as these are, you get an intense, inky, complex sip of the purest bean ecstasy there is. What's more, the top-of-the-line machine is adjusted throughout the day as the temperature and humidity warps and wales.

If the behind-the-scenes magic impresses two senses, the baristas' artful toothpick-drawn designs (in what is less a foam and more a silky lather of milk) seal it for the eye. But the accolades don't end with the coffee; the hot chocolate is also among the best we've ever tasted (on par with Cacao's chocolate-shop brew). Made with single-origin Venezualan cacao, it is creamy and a bit spicy, yet not so rich that you can't take more than two sips. A touch of sea salt adds an extra dimension—on a winter day there's nothing better.

Pastries are provided daily by the excellent Nuvrei, and top-notch granola by Crema Bakery. Seriously, with coffeehouses like these, who needs a lap dance?

The Country Cat

A dose of rusticity and warmth that is often delicious and always worth the money

6.7	8.5	8.0
Food	Feel	Beer

Modern, Southern

Casual restaurant

$40
Price

www.thecountrycat.net

Sun–Thu 9am–2pm, 5pm–9pm
Fri–Sat 9am–2pm, 5pm–10pm

Bar Beer, wine, liquor
Credit cards Visa, MC, AmEx
Reservations Accepted
Kid-friendly

Southeast Portland
7937 SE Stark St.
(503) 408-1414

Country Cat does not try to be an epicurean destination, but rather sets the bar much lower. This is not a restaurant of subtle flavors and cutting-edge techniques. Instead, it welcomes everyone from families to retired folk, and aims to provide good food at reasonable prices. Though the road is sometimes rocky, the Cat has provided some much-needed hospitality in what used to be a somewhat seedy neighborhood.

The space is comfortable, with a large bar that specializes in top-shelf Bourbon drinks (some a bit out of balance), and an excellent, succinct beer list of microbrews on tap (and some macros in bottle). Forget about the perfunctory wine list unless you don't really care—many of these are cheap, anyway. Much of the seating is booths, a nice touch these days when restaurants tend to maximize every available foot of space. A chef's table by the open kitchen is a great place to take in a show.

Several mains are grilled: a mixed pork platter with rolled belly, brined chop, and smoked shoulder; molasses-and-hickory-smoked duck legs; or bacon-wrapped trout. The latter looks like it could be on the cover of *Time Life's Foods of America*, circa 1966. It's no longer on the menu, but it was a textbook example of how to prepare this dish: large, fresh, beautifully cleaned fish, cooked expertly moist and then wrapped in generous strips of crispy bacon. In general, Country Cat seems to excel with fish.

Skillet-fried chicken is a total pleasure—a tower of boneless chicken atop a mound of bacon-braised collard greens. The crunchy exterior is right on, with a spicy, vinegary aftertaste. It comes with a large, fluffy sweet-cream biscuit that tastes like butter. And burgers are good too—thick and juicy—with thin, enjoyable onion rings. But beef has come inedibly dry, despite being completely tender (an impressive feat). Desserts are country-inspired (think plum crostata with butterscotch ice cream), but taste pre-fab.

Country Cat has potential, and is a wonderful asset to the neighborhood. It does put out pretty good food at very good prices, but rarely does much more than that.

Country Korean

A simpler-than-simple, barely-English-speaking find
that serves up soondae without pretense

9.0	5.5
Food	Feel

Korean

Casual restaurant

$20
Price

Mon–Thu 11am–midnight
Fri–Sun 11am–2am

Bar Beer, wine
Credit cards Visa, MC, AmEx
Reservations Not accepted

Beaverton
4130 SW 117th Ave.
No phone

Country Korean Restaurant is a trip. The service is hilariously indifferent, yet endearing. They mean well, but they'll watch Korean TV instead of checking on your table. Almost no English is spoken here, and the only décor consists of posters of scantily clad Korean women and a TV which was, on one visit, tuned to an informative medical show about gout and varicose veins. Gilt Club this is not.

What it is, then, is delicious, authentically made Korean food that's available even at 11pm on a Sunday night (at least we think so—communication isn't the best here, a condition made worse by there being no phone to speak of).

Two stews are particularly notable. One is soondae guk, a delicious pork broth that develops as it sits on the table (so take your time with it) and is full of kidney, tripe, intestine, and drumroll please...amazing soondae, which is aromatic blood sausage studded with glass noodles. Add all of the chili paste served on the side for the best effect. If you're not Korean, they'll try to give you a less spicy version of this stew, so be adamant that you like it spicy. Other soups rock, too, like milky, creamy beef-bone broth (seolleongtang), for example, with dropped egg and stewed, shredded beef strands with a deep, slightly gamy beefiness. It's absolutely addictive, and a great hangover alternative to menudo and pho, if you're looking to switch it up.

The banchan (sides that come at the beginning) are terrific: three deeply fermented, stinky kimchis of cabbage, turnip, and cucumber; a lovely egg custard; savory umami-laced seaweed shreds; and more. You can also get the soondae as a plate (sans soup) with condiments, and that's great, too. Just don't come for the barbecue—that's not the focus here and so it isn't very good. Instead, come to have your soul warmed on chilly days or when you're getting over a cold. Or when you've had quite enough of trendy, engineered dining experiences and serious, professional servers.

After your meal, they'll hook you up with some homemade rice nectar. As if the super-low bill weren't kind enough.

Cricket Café

Good breakfast and relaxed vibes make this crunchy
spot a crazy scene on weekends

6.4 Food
6.0 Feel

American

Casual restaurant

$20 Price

Daily 7:30am–3pm

Bar Beer, wine, liquor, BYO
Credit cards Visa, MC
Reservations Not accepted
Kid-friendly, outdoor dining,
veg-friendly

Belmont
3159 SE Belmont St.
(503) 235-9348

Cricket Café is a hippie-dippie little breakfast spot that's known for long
waits on weekends, packed seating, crazy service, and a vegetarian
breakfast that doesn't taste like compost.

A single bad service experience at a restaurant isn't always so
meaningful; people have bad days, servers come and go. But here, the
sketched-out service is so integral to the persona of Cricket that it
warrants added distinction. Ever heard of The Order of the Arrow in Boy
Scouts? Where they leave you in "the wilderness" with a few survival
basics and you have to find your way back to camp on your own? It's
absolutely like that; if you want something, you will have to build it, make
it, or find it yourself. Generally, weekdays are better than weekends,
when those with seniority rake in the bucks with much less gusto than
their tyro colleagues.

The interior appears to be slowly disintegrating—or is in the process of
being devoured by flies—and slapdashes of color and art brighten
otherwise white walls. A Bloody Mary is like an overgrown garden of
celery, hot peppers, pickled okra, and olives. These are strong and pretty
good. Did we mention strong?

Come on weekends for homemade cinnamon rolls; throughout the
week, there's decadent apple bread, sourdough bread, and biscuits.
Otherwise, the menu is gourmet greasy-spoon. Ingredients are mostly
culled from local sources, so they're often organic and hormone-free.
Bacon is cut thick and cooked expertly. Pancakes are terrific and slightly
crunchy, served with maple syrup. Home fries tend to vary, with the
chunky version being okay and seasoned well. Hash browns are crispier
but in need of ketchup. And the combinations are endless—you can
create your own scrambles, omelettes, and skillets. It's not chef driven or
anything, but breakfast is that one meal where we're fine with being our
own kitchen.

House-roasted coffee is brewed strong, and the place is packed with
everyone from vegan granola types to hungover hipsters still fermenting
from a PBR binge the night before. There are kids and dogs, and it's a
happy place to be, rough edges and all.

Crowsenberg's

A famous coffeeshop that's not as good as it thinks it is

6.1 Food **8.0** Feel

Baked goods, Sandwiches, Vegefusion

Café **$15** Price

Mon–Fri 7:30am–6pm
Sat–Sun 8am–6pm

Bar Beer
Credit cards Visa, MC, AmEx
Outdoor dining, veg-friendly, Wi-Fi

Downtown
923 SW Oak St.
(503) 222-4495

Crowsenberg's Half & Half is a green little spot for coffee and sandwiches with a totally skinny-jeans-indie vibe. The whole block feels terrifically Portland, especially for this otherwise buttoned-up part of downtown. A little sparrow silhouette—part of the nature-as-silhouettes movement denoting hipster status—is stamped on every to-go cup, and latte comes in a yellow ceramic mug emblazoned with a creamy little heart on top.

But this tiny, noisy spot isn't really a coffee mecca. The Courier coffee is fine, but espresso drinks are just so-so, and coffee geeks tend to aggregate over at Spella Caffè on trailer-restaurant row. Still, the drip coffee is very cheap, and the vibe is just want you want when you're on a break from that downtown cubicle zoo to which you've sold your soul. The proliferation of zines from next-door Reading Frenzy will help keep you weird.

Sandwiches look scruffy, like the staff who makes them, and they're bursting with flavor. At breakfast, scrambled eggs and tomatoes are good; for lunch, there's grilled cheese with tomato soup, plus plenty of vegan options like a tempeh, lettuce, and tomato sandwich. Sweets like pies and scones are just what you want. Deviled eggs, those haute-nostalgia darlings, are cheap and tasty. Homemade "Oreos" are cute and tasty in that I-know-what-all-these-ingredients-are sort of way.

Surprisingly, for all this überhipness, there isn't a speck of attitude. It's much more My Morning Jacket than Magnetic Fields. If you understood that reference, then this is your coffeeshop.

Cup & Saucer Café

A longtime standby for breakfast that brings at least one new thing to the table: Cholula

4.7	7.5
Food	Feel

American

Casual restaurant

$15
Price

www.cupandsaucercafe.com

Daily 8am–4pm
Hours vary by location

Bar Beer, wine
Credit cards Visa, MC, AmEx
Reservations Not accepted
Outdoor dining, veg-friendly

Hawthorne
3566 SE Hawthorne Blvd.
(503) 236-6001

Alberta Arts District
3000 NE Killingsworth St.
(503) 287-4427

North Portland
8237 N. Denver Ave.
(503) 247-6011

Cup & Saucer has a cadre of cute cafés, spread throughout the north and east of Portland, each with its own distinct neighborhood feeling. The Denver location sports a clean-cut, modern, and somewhat boring corporate-y vibe; but the Hawthorne shop gets funky with brick, lotus-flower murals, and citrus-colored walls. The location up by Alberta is forest green, with plants and mismatched chairs, looking quite hippie to fit in with this area aesthetic.

These are simple café menus, so there's not much in the way of bells and whistles. At breakfast, scrambles made with eggs or tofu cater to carnivores and vegans alike. Ingredients aren't much better than they are anywhere else, but there are more vegetables than you'll find at other equally shabby diners. Cornmeal pancakes are lightly sweet and gritty, if sometimes undercooked. Challah French toast is always a good thing; and homemade scones add to the charm.

If 20 years in business has taught Cup & Saucer anything, it seems to be: if it ain't broke, don't fix it. Very little has changed in the kitchen; potatoes even taste like they're fried in oil that's been recycled over the years. This wouldn't necessarily be a bad thing; think of it like the solera system used to make sherry, gaining complexity with each top-off. Except for the fact that the potatoes often come to the table shriveled and cold.

If you must come, the Northeast location has a full bar, so at least you can get your Bloody Mary on while you muscle your way through a mediocre breakfast. We do love this easy, eclectic space with its good music. The service can be distracted, but it's a breakfast crew, so while irritating (especially when waiting for coffee), it's no surprise.

Lunch—and dinner at the Southeast store—consists of sandwiches, burgers, soups, and salads, plus the usual avoidable pseudo-Mexican vegetarian fare like gummy black-bean burritos and quesadillas that need lots of help from the Cholula sauce at the tables. Which is pretty cool—who else has Cholula?

How does Cup & Saucer stay in business for two decades with all these better breakfast places springing up around town? Maybe the secret's in the sauce.

Cupcake Jones

They're not perfect, but they're cupcakes—and that seems to be plenty

Baked goods, Sweets

Counter service

www.cupcakejones.net

Mon–Sat 10am–8pm
Sun noon–6pm

Bar None
Credit cards Visa, MC, AmEx
Kid-friendly, veg-friendly

Pearl District
307 NW 10th Ave.
(503) 222-4404

Depending upon whom you ask, the cupcake craze that started when *Sex & the City* filmed an episode outside of the West Village's Magnolia Bakery reached its sweet crescendo maybe two or three years ago. These days, the queues that once reached around Magnolia's block now fit inside the building, and bloggers have declared everything from Whoopie pies to macaroons as "the new cupcake."

But it's still a good business move: we've learned that people can't resist a cupcake. We're fools for anything adorable and miniature, and it's precisely this foolishness that cupcake bakeries seem to depend upon. Even Magnolia Bakery is just decent. Cupcakes don't seem to be under the same pressure to perform as, say, pizza. People tolerate mediocre pizza until a slew of excellent ones are available. In the land of the blind, in other words, the mediocre cupcake is king.

Some of Cupcake Jones's creations actually deserve a place in the upper echelon of baked goods. If you do happen to squeeze inside the elevator-sized space, you'll notice a colorful array from a menu that changes seasonally. That selection, further, rotates daily. You can always find "Pearl," a white velvet cake filled with vanilla bean pastry cream, topped with vanilla buttercream and little, handmade white chocolate pearls. But once you stop squealing about how precious it is, you sort of think, "that's it?" The cake on this one is moist, but dense, and then it's over—only a greasy coat of bland buttercream lingering to remind you. The chocolate version is fairly ordinary, but with a sour-cream chocolate ganache that's much more exciting.

Buttercream here is made with very little salt or sugar, a creative choice that works when the flavor of the cake does enough work. But this is too rare. The most interesting bases, like a delicious pretzel cake (!), have non-buttercream icings anyway; the nondescript cakes work best with both assertive fillings and icings, like a "Peanut Butter 'n' Jelly" with homemade berry jam and peanut-butter icing.

You could certainly do worse. Or you could go home and change what you didn't like about it, make a cupcake to your liking, and go into business. We don't think this cupcake craze is going to disappear any time soon.

Decarli

Good Italian-influenced Northwest food and some killer polenta fries for the Beaver set

7.2	8.0	7.5
Food	Feel	Drinks

Italian, Modern, Pizza

Upmarket restaurant

$50
Price

www.decarlirestaurant.com

Wed–Thu 4:30pm–10pm
Fri–Sat 4:30pm–11pm
Sun 10am–2pm, 5pm–9pm

Bar Beer, wine, liquor
Credit cards Visa, MC, AmEx
Reservations Accepted
Kid-friendly, outdoor dining, Wi-Fi

Beaverton
4545 SW Watson Ave.
(503) 641-3223

Decarli comes on strong with lower-case fonts and Pacific-Northwest-fusion recipes, looking appropriately Beaver-trendy. There's the ever-popular big, open kitchen where you can watch everything being made. There's a hopping yuppie solo-and-couples scene at the bar. But it's also kind of that Place for Ladies Who Drink Wine By The Glass. The vibe works when it's crowded, but when it's empty, it's a little forceful and depressing. It can come across as a bit jarring in the otherwise humble downtown Beaverton.

Despite not having a serious pizza oven, Decarli executes well on pizzette, which have a thin crust and a nice sear. The sauce has the sweet depth that suggests high-end Italian tomatoes. A potato-and-rosemary version is also quite nice, with strong, nutty-stinky taleggio that gives it a distinctly grown-up flavor. People buzz, too, about polenta fries with Gorgonzola butter, and rightfully so. The melted butter is not overwhelmed by pungent cheese, and the fries are fried beautifully, with a nice creamy texture within. Meats like a Carlton Farm pork chop are sometimes overcooked but sauces are usually interesting and paired well. Homemade pastas are competent, sometimes good, sometimes very good.

Happy hour specials are a great deal—two can share a pizzetta for $7. Things don't fill up until after happy hour ends, though, and like we said, this space feels odd when empty. Service is irregular: at its best, it's intrusive and comically efficient; at its worst, you might go half an hour without seeing your server or your drinks, whether the restaurant is busy or not.

The wine list isn't bad, but it's heavy on the New World wines, though there's a decent representation of some of the more prosaic Italians. There are a few decent local craft beers, as well. Cocktails are well made by a serious bartender, and there are more than enough sweet creations, if that's your thing. If you like a lot of spice, try the "Hot and Dirty," a worthy chili-infused vodka martini. *Really* chili-infused.

For upscale, fusiony food, this is Beaverton's best option; but for the price, we'd rather drive into Portland. Or stay right here and grab some great Korean for much less.

Delta Café

White trash gets a little glam—but just a little

7.5	8.0	8.5
Food	Feel	Drinks

Southern

Casual restaurant

$35
Price

www.deltacafeandbar.com

Mon–Fri 4pm–1am
Sat–Sun 9am–2pm, 5pm–1am

Bar Beer, wine, liquor
Credit cards None
Reservations Not accepted
Outdoor dining, veg-friendly

Southeast Portland
4607 SE Woodstock Blvd.
(503) 771-3101

Portland's got no shortage of cool, laid-back restaurants with great bars and a penchant for Southern food. But Delta Café belongs particularly to Reed College students, although it is worth a trip for anyone in the city who loves Pabst Blue Ribbon. (And that's a lot of people.) Here it's given its kitschy due, served by the 40-ounce bottle in a coffee can full of ice.

The chairs are of the same floral, vinyl sort that your grandparents had…before they remodeled. Some walls are Crayola green, while others are covered with eclectic art, with baroque archways between rooms. It's just a fun, visual playground: strings of colored lights; odd hanging lamps; and metallic red booths.

Mac and cheese is certainly cheesy, but there aren't any crusty or even burnt parts for texture. Add a dollop of mashed potatoes with gravy and a few slices of "White Trash Meatloaf," and you're talking a serious case of palate fatigue. Not that there's anything wrong with salt and fat being the predominant flavors in a dish. And there's certainly nothing wrong with the gumbo, whose murky roux is full of smoky and spicy sausage, chicken, and shrimp—or a jambalaya that actually tastes indistinguishable from the gumbo. Something is lost in a vegetarian translation with tofu, but Southern authenticity isn't really the aim at a place that offers a Champagne service for PBR.

The easiest stuff to get right is accomplished best here, like black-eyed peas (eat 'em at New Year's for good luck) and collards. Both are tinny and earthy with a bit of pork fat for flavor (again, a veggie version is offered, but this is perhaps the worst cuisine to attempt herbivorously). Brunch is always a solid bet here, with $1 "Red Beers" ("bloody beers," to others), brioche French toast, smoked brisket hash, and variations on eggs Benedict—all of which are reasonably good and within normal brunch prices.

Some specialty cocktails are made with several alluring homemade infusions of tequila (cilantro!) and Monopolowa vodka (Earl Grey!), great small-batch spirits, and less of a candy-sweet focus. A few beers on tap and more in bottle boast some of the best prices we've seen around. But you can't pay with a credit card, which is awfully strange and inconvenient for a restaurant near a college. They do accept checks, however—do they still make those?

Deschutes Brewery

Okay food, better vibes, and better beer still
at one of Portland's iconic local brewpubs

6.8	**8.0**	**9.5**
Food	Feel	Beer

American

Casual restaurant

$25
Price

www.deschutesbrewery.com

Sun–Mon 11am–10pm	**Bar** Beer, wine, liquor	**Pearl District**
Tue–Thu 11am–11pm	**Credit cards** Visa, MC, AmEx	210 NW 11th Ave.
Fri–Sat 11am–midnight	**Reservations** Not accepted	(503) 296-4906
	Date-friendly, outdoor dining	

Deschutes Brewery has been a staple of Oregon's craft beer scene for two decades, growing in that time to the 12th largest brewery in the country and the Pacific Northwest's third largest craft brewery. Their flagship beers—Mirror Pond Pale Ale and Black Butte Porter—are easily spotted on taplists up and down the West Coast. The brewery operates a pair of pubs in Oregon, one in hometown Bend, and one in the Pearl District of Northwest Portland (two blocks north of Powell's Books).

The space is large and open, given mostly to dining tables, with a modestly sized bar area. Above the bar are windows that give diners a peek into the state-of-the-art, fully automated brewhouse, with gleaming copper kettles and shining stainless pipes. The exposed beams of the old building compete for visual attention, perplexingly, with a grid of heavy pine beams set like a series of open-sided boxes over most of the dining area. The large open area makes for acoustic challenges, as well; when the space is full, conversation can be difficult.

But for those drawn to the beer Deschutes offers, these details are of little consequence. The Deschutes Portland Brewpub offers 18 taps of craft beer heaven: six permanent taps representing the regular production line of Deschutes' bottled beers, and a dozen taps of seasonals (the lightly spiced winter seasonal, Jubelale, is a local favorite), experimental beers, and pub-only offerings.

The food menu is competent, self-impressed, and moderately overpriced. A natural elk burger with gruyère and shallot-thyme aïoli makes an interesting departure from the more typical beef alternative of buffalo. Avocado-tomatillo salsa doesn't prevent a house-made veggie burger from coming off as mushy and bland. In the end, however, the beer's the thing, and this pub has that in pints as well as bottles to go.

Detour Café

This pretty breakfast spot offers homemade bread, build-your-own frittatas, and little attitude

7.1 Food

8.0 Feel

American

Casual restaurant

$15 Price

www.detourcafe.com

Daily 8am–4pm

Bar Beer, wine
Credit cards Visa, MC
Reservations Not accepted
Date-friendly, kid-friendly, outdoor dining, veg-friendly

Division/Clinton
3035 SE Division St.
(503) 234-7499

Is there any phrase sweeter to the American ear than "Breakfast served all day"? Multiply that joy times 10, and you have Portland's obsession with breakfast. Maybe it's the drizzle and chill, maybe it's the constant coffee drinking, but we're a people who must have our breakfast.

Detour Café performs to that end admirably, in true Portland fashion (local, seasonal ingredients; cage-free eggs; hormone-free meats). On the cleaner, nicer end of things, it's kind of the anti-Cricket Café. The staff is friendly, the blossom-and-vine-decorated patio is lovely and inviting, and the inside is clean and colorful. Keep it real with lightweight wooden tables and plastic chairs.

There are also similarities to Cricket: breads here are homemade; serve-yourself Stumptown coffee is available, which reminds us of Cricket's you're-on-your-own-suckers feeling; and vegans and vegetarians are amply provided for. There's an invitation to build your own frittata. You can choose from smoked salmon, goat cheese, two types of cream cheese, Manchego, feta, pepper bacon, Italian sausage, pepperoni (!), hot peppers, basil, spinach, and tomato. But we wish the chef had more to say and the customer less; they should know better than us, right?

Also outstanding is French toast made with Detour's own cardamom bread, soaked in custard and then fried to golden, lovely, and spicy with a topping of warm cherry compote and almonds. Breakfast sandwiches are ample and well balanced, and employ excellent potato bread.

It doesn't end with breakfast, though; lunch sandwiches are simple but wonderful. Albacore with melted cheddar is classic, greasy-spoon satisfying, but not at all greasy-spoon greasy. Salads are full of fresh greens that play off each other's natural flavors and are expertly, carefully dressed. Veggie burgers are made in-house and are superb.

This is how to eat breakfast: on the florid patio of a lime-green little house, with nice people who leave you alone and delicious ingredients put together with care.

DJK Korean BBQ

Forget the shabu shabu—this here is a temple of
superlative BBQ

8.8 Food **6.5** Feel

Korean

Casual restaurant

$25 Price

Daily 11am–10:30pm

Bar Beer, liquor
Credit cards Visa, MC, AmEx
Reservations Not accepted

Beaverton
12275 SW Canyon Rd.
(503) 641-1734

We've seen it before: the unmarked nondescript structure that looks like
nothing from the outside, but houses a morsel of food so deeply
enjoyable that it becomes something of a pilgrimage for its devotees. In
this case, it is not the shabu shabu that draws the masses (even at 10pm
on a Thursday night), but rather DJK's barbecue. Specifically, the galbi.

You name the animal, and DJK will provide its flesh for you to sear and
char yourself, at the table, to your stomach's content: beef, pork, chicken,
and so on. The smell of crackling fat wafts up through the smoke hoods
that sit over each table and hovers over the room like an invisible storm of
grilling meat and onions and garlic. Don't dress too nicely.

Go right for the galbi (short ribs), which are easily some of the best
Portland has to offer. Do not miss these, but do try some other variations
as well—spicy pork galbi are also quite good. Shabu shabu is good, and
it's always fun to cook with hot pots, but it's not your best bet here.

As far as the other elements go, banchan aren't terribly varied or
plentiful; soups and stews are not of the transcendent quality that JCD's
or Country Kitchen's are; and don't come expecting benevolent service.

What you will get is the satisfaction of cooking something spectacular,
even if you can't cook at all. That's worth a little abuse. Just knock it back
with some soju and Hite.

DOC

The dining experience is all Italian, even if
the ingredients are all Pacific Northwest

9.1	9.5	8.5
Food	Feel	Wine

Italian

Upmarket restaurant

$70
Price

www.docpdx.com

Tue–Sat 6pm–9pm

Bar Beer, wine, liquor
Credit cards Visa, MC, AmEx
Reservations Essential
Date-friendly, outdoor dining,
veg-friendly

Alberta Arts District
5519 NE 30th Ave.
(503) 946-8592

DOC is incredibly cozy and inviting. You enter through the kitchen (which
feels a bit naughty), and are seated at one of only a few tables; one table
is communal. From any of these, you can watch all action in the kitchen,
the only source of visual stimulus aside from the food. The minimalist-chic
room has plain cream walls, warm lighting, and a friendly buzz. Service
may not be the most astute, but it is on the ball and very sweet. This is
Portland at its very best.

There's a $50 tasting menu, but the ever-changing regular menu is so
refreshingly small that you can almost get through the whole thing
anyway with two or more people. The smaller number of dishes allows
the kitchen to really focus on each; true to Italian form, these are divided
into three courses: antipasti, primi, and secondi.

On one visit, an antipasto of delicata squash (like pumpkin) with bok
choy and fennel was interesting, even if the bok choy didn't contribute
much beyond nutrition. Balsamic vinegar played off the earthy-sweet
squash nicely. Fried sardines have been absolutely delicious, not too bony,
a bit buttery even. They came with firm, but springy new potatoes and
expertly cooked greens. Risotto is right on, a touch al dente, and it is
usually nicely composed (in one case, with chanterelle mushrooms), but
the number of vegetables can overwhelm the delicateness of the dish.
Tagliatelle are homemade (right in front of you), and might come
adorned, for instance, with big chunks of pork and Southern greens. The
porky-sweet broth is great for sopping up with a spoon or their very good
bread, but it didn't bind at all with the pasta. Also made on the premises
is a loose-packed pork sausage which, when served with poached peach,
burst with loads of interesting flavors. Ricotta pie has also been nice, light
and airy, and with a hint of Meyer lemon.

The wine list is remarkably well chosen, a reasonably priced selection of
lesser-known and smaller-production Italians from truly reputable (not
magazine-hyped) producers. Cheers to that. Many of these are opened
each night and paired with the menu, but this has resulted in a few
tasting oxidized, probably from having been open too long. There's also a
welcome effort at Italian cocktails here, employing digestifs like Campari,
Chinato, and limoncello.

While the constant menu changes may prevent the kitchen from totally
mastering any one dish, this is a brilliant way to have dinner: with
intention focused so keenly on each playful creation, you really feel that
you have not just eaten, but *dined*.

Dots Café

An absolutely classic dive bar for the arty
crowd, with surprisingly good food

7.0	8.5	8.0
Food	Feel	Beer

American, Vegefusion

Bar **$20**
Price

Daily noon–2am

Bar Beer, wine, liquor
Credit cards None
Date-friendly, veg-friendly

Division/Clinton
2521 SE Clinton St.
(503) 235-0203

Dots, with its infamous blue façade and divey-looking sign, is an East Side
staple. The atmosphere is just vintage cool, with velvet wallpaper, stoner
art, and several jewel-toned glass globe lamps giving it a certain 1970s-
harem sort of feel. Eclectic strings of lights and votives on tables are the
main sources of light, so everyone looks darkly sexy in here. In fact, some
of the waitresses may even be Suicide Girls, those pale and tattooed
cybersirens.

It's an absolutely fitting neighborhood hangout, considering that you're
surrounded by both young families and college students, not to mention
the lure of the indie theater across the street. What results is a diverse
crowd—well, diverse within a certain subset of the population.

It wouldn't be at all strange to sit alone at the bar with a beer and a
book, looking aloof and deep; to come to flirt over a game of pool in the
back; or even to gather a group of old dudes for burgers and beers.
About those burgers, they're juicy, and thick; ask for your burger rare if
you want it medium. There's also a totally addictive black-bean burrito.
Nachos are quite decent, as is a buttery grilled cheese, served on retro
red-and-white-checkered paper. Fries are thick and sort of mealy, but the
spicy tofu sauce they're served with is the bee's knees. It's vaguely ma-po-
tofu-ish, but without the zany Szechuan-peppercorn mouth trip.

Overall, the food's much better here than it is at most dives and pubs in
town, if not quite as good as the food at some more ambitious cocktail
bars. Wholesome vegan plates aside, the menu here is still composed of a
certain recognizable bar-food species.

There's a great beer selection, with many locals on draft, and at really
reasonable prices. Cocktails are strong and sweet, though, still as stuck in
the dormitory days as those posters are. And yes, it's cash only, which can
be a real pain in the ass. But then, isn't Dots worth it?

Doug Fir

A sylvan-chic hotel bar and lounge where the shows and décor are the main attractions

6.1	9.5	7.5
Food	Feel	Beer

American

Bar

$30
Price

www.dougfirlounge.com

Sun–Thu 7am–midnight
Fri–Sat 7am–2am

Bar Beer, wine, liquor
Credit cards Visa, MC, AmEx
Date-friendly, live music, outdoor dining, Wi-Fi

East Burnside
830 E. Burnside St.
(503) 231-9663

If you're an indie rocker visiting Portland (and given the statistics, there's a good chance that you are), you're probably staying at the hip-as-shit Jupiter Hotel. It's little more than a renovated mid-century-looking motel with that retro thing in spades, but it's got Doug Fir on its hip, which amps up its cool factor considerably.

This concert-venue-cum-lounge looks like a high-gloss lumberjack hangout, with wood, wood, and more wood, tweaked and sleeked and wavy and wonderful. Imagine living inside a Lincoln Log house as designed by Elroy Jetson. Look for the mounted deer head on acid. Lighting is strategic and harvest-gold colored, and there are several cozy areas in which to hang out, even outside, where the Jupiter's iconic firepits—one of East Burnside's modern landmarks—keep you warm.

The prices on the bar menu (served later than the dinner menu, except Fridays and Saturdays) and during the daily happy hour are fair. You can find a really good burger and a serviceable Caesar (sans anchovies, but you can add smoked salmon or a crab cake—tacky, but hey, what did you expect?). A salmon chowder is surprisingly great, full of red bell pepper, onion, and zucchini. But the menu is generally less retro and more outdated. It's a fine line, you know—one that is drawn in the sand, perhaps, by fish with mango salsa. But derivative as they may be, most of these dishes are mostly pretty enjoyable. Or is it just the atmosphere? Also, who doesn't love cheese fries with ranch dressing at 2am?

You must, at least, come for a drink—but you'll be coming to enjoy the décor more than what's in the glass. These cocktails are still stuck where the mango salsa is: firmly in 1999. Red Bull and everything, in other words. You can get decent renditions of your favorite classic cocktails, but don't expect the level of artisanship you'd find at, say, Beaker & Flask. There's also the standard Portland-hip beer list—locals IPAs and such—plus low-brow-chic Miller High Life on tap, and even lower-brow-chic PBR in the bottle. Wines are passable, with a few very good choices.

Downstairs is where the shows happen, and you should go to one, sooner or later. So often, bar-restaurant concert venues have terrible sound, but Doug Fir is outfitted just beautifully. You can hear everything that happens on stage, for better or worse. It's just a mandatory stop on your tour of Portland—skinny jeans not required.

Dove Vivi Pizza Deli

Religion, politics, and pizza

6.3 Food **6.5** Feel

Pizza

Casual restaurant

$15 Price

www.dovevivipizza.com

Daily 4pm–10pm

Bar Beer, wine, BYO
Credit cards Visa, MC, AmEx
Reservations Not accepted
Outdoor dining, veg-friendly

Northeast Portland
2727 NE Glisan St.
(503) 239-4444

There are three subjects you are never supposed to bring up in polite conversation: religion, politics, and pizza. Not only does it invite bad blood, but you'll have as much success bringing others into your camp as you would single-handedly forging peace between all nations.

Although pizza's epicenter is understood to be Naples, everyone everywhere has their own style, from dough to toppings, to firing method. Pizza is no stranger to loose interpretations, and each version has its own rabid defenders of the faith.

Our panel is split on the subject of deep-dish pizza. Some of us adore it, having grown up on sweetish, buttery crusts that set off the ingredients in a totally comforting, indulgent way. Others call it weighty and unpleasant. Either way, it's really not very healthy; it's basically a casserole with fried edges. It's meant to be eaten in the depths of Chicago, where the excess of cholesterol will protect your organs from subzero winds.

Regardless of whether you're a believer or not, Dove Vivi's rendition of this cornmeal-crust pizza is not nearly as inspiring as it could be. The crust is blonde and bubbly, but vapid. Although the list of available ingredients is impressive (some of them gourmet items like golden chanterelle mushrooms in brandy-shallot-jalapeño sauce—whew!), most of these, especially the vegetables, are mere phantoms of flavor that would benefit from heavier seasoning. Sausage is actually really good, but you kind of want to just peel it off the incoherent pie and eat it separately. We get the feeling this place is less holy temple of pizza and more card-table Tarot reader. We've had better.

Cheers to this place for being so Portland—there are one or two local beers on tap, even. It is, however, kind of irritating that you have to wait with no bar in order to hang out at such a casual spot, although you can nurse a beer and pass the time outside. Inside, it feels like a hip, urban cafeteria with perfunctory table service and a mess-hall bustle. Outdoor tables are essentially in a parking lot illuminated by a heart-shaped sign that no doubt draws the cold and thin—those looking for gooey, golden acceptance.

Driftwood Room

Surprisingly austere food and interesting
cocktails for such a swanky hotel lounge

6.6	8.5	9.0
Food	Feel	Drinks

American

Bar **$35**

Price

www.hoteldeluxeportland.com

Sun–Thu 2pm–11:30pm
Fri–Sat 2pm–midnight

Bar Beer, wine, liquor
Credit cards Visa, MC, AmEx
Date-friendly, Wi-Fi

Southwest Portland
729 SW 15th Ave.
(503) 219-2094

Picture Las Vegas in the late 1960s, just before Sammy Davis, Jr. and
sweaty Elvis ruled the town: waves of ochre velveteen; butter-colored
leather; and brown faux-snakeskin bar bumpers. Artfully placed sconces
leak light gently, helping the opposite sex look ten times better to you; of
course, two dry martinis aren't hurting, either. This is the Driftwood
Room, the swanky cocktail lounge in the shift-key-challenging Hotel
deLuxe.

The food and drinks here are surprisingly understated, given that this is,
after all, a hotel. Cocktails manage to be innovative without any of the
sugary-sweet shortcuts to turn on the lowest common denominators that
might be staying over on any given weeknight. It doesn't hurt that this is
a boutique hotel and therefore subject to a much higher standard, but
we've been relatively disappointed by the food and drinks at Heathman
and Jupiter, which are arguably closer to deLuxe's genre than, say, an
Omni is.

An "Elizabeth Taylor" is a simple and successful "Champagne" cocktail
of crème de violette, with crisp bubbles sending up a faint whiff of spring
violets from which the liqueur is made. Small-batch spirits are employed
to get the point across, like a "Rose City Drop" that adds a gentle kiss of
rose-infused simple syrup to Monopolowa vodka. A simple squirt of fresh
lemon binds and intensifies the flavors. The wine list is decidedly less
accomplished, with virtually no plausible choices by the glass (the only
sparkling option being a $14 Prosecco). But there's an ample selection of
local favorites—plus Guinness—on draft, and a few of the usual mass
markets bottle. But everything costs nearly twice what it does in other
Portland bars. One typical hotel move, for certain.

During generous happy hours (3–6pm and 9pm–close, daily), there are
some great bargains, including a well-edited (but anchovy-less) Caesar, a
good organic burger, and hearty mac and cheese, all for around $5.
Mussels have come more buttery than briny and funky, but a pricey
cheese plate is at least generous, and homemade chicken liver mousse is
hard to argue with. The food isn't groundbreaking, but it is far better
than some other horrific hotel cuisines. Although the atmosphere and
drinks are really the stars of the act here, it's nice that you don't have to
suffer through overwrought, hotellish food to hang out and look good.

Du Kuh Bee

Sincerity and gratitude fill this microscopic handmade-noodle shop

8.4	7.0
Food	Feel

Korean, Chinese

Casual restaurant

$20
Price

Mon–Thu 4pm–1am
Fri–Sat 4pm–2am

Bar Beer, liquor
Credit cards Visa, MC, AmEx
Reservations Not accepted

Beaverton
12590 SW 1st St.
(503) 643-5388

Du Kuh Bee means "lucky" in Korean. You're lucky to be here, yes, but the owner and chef also acts lucky to be doing what he so obviously loves to do. This feeling of gratitude and sincerity is in every dish, both those from his Chinese heritage and those devoted to his Korean-cooking passion.

It's most apparent when you sit at the bar (really, the only place to sit) and watch him hand cut and stretch noodles, performing feats of rhythmic gymnastics before tossing them in a pot of boiling water and then fetching them out while they are still al dente. He then fries these up in a pan of sizzling oil with garlic, garlic, and more garlic (Koreans consume even more garlic than Italians do), plus plenty of chili flakes. All this with a smile or a laughing conversation with patrons. It's so happy it's thought-provoking: what are you doing with *your* life? Are *you* this happy?

Dumplings are also made in house, and are ridiculously cheap. And quite well textured. They do require a little sauce to excite their inner porkiness, however (where's all that garlic now?). Pork makes its way into almost everything here, including vegetable dishes. We do wish kimchi were a little hotter and funkier here; it seems mellowed out for American palates—a rare move in this tiny temple of overachievement. In fact, most dishes suffer from the opposite problem: they're a bit heavy-handed and uniform, trouncing subtleties. Try the dumplings in an earthy soup with odeng (thinly sliced fishcake) to experience them best.

Barbecue performs quite well here, too, even if you don't get to make it yourself (that's often preferable, anyway). Bulgogi is properly charred, with delectable little bits of fat striping through the tender meat; eel is also wonderful, sweet and briny, like the bacon of the sea. Perhaps it's just the soju and beer, or perhaps it's the show in the kitchen. Either way, this place is great, and humbly so.

East India Co.

Elegant, straightforward Northern Indian food that is, for now, the best in the city

8.5	7.5	6.0
Food	Feel	Drinks

Indian

Casual restaurant

$40
Price

www.eastindiacopdx.com

Mon–Sat 11:30am–2pm,
5:30pm–9:30pm

Bar Beer, wine, liquor
Credit cards Visa, MC, AmEx
Reservations Accepted
Date-friendly, veg-friendly

Downtown
821 SW 11th Ave.
(503) 227-8815

Hiding behind the downtown library, sandwiched into a tiny space between an old parking garage and the Dental Building, is East India Co. Although the entrance is inconspicuous, the dining room is intimidating and cavernous, with white tablecloths and candles against a backdrop of warm wood floors, deep aubergine walls, and indirect lighting. Overhead, an eye-catching and oddly roulette-wheelish glass fixture looms. It's somewhat elegant, but not the best design we've seen.

Here you'll find prettier, more careful presentations of Northern Indian food than usual. The slightly higher prices seem motivated by this effort and by the atmosphere; service, on the other hand, doesn't fit. At busier times, tables go unrefilled, guests ungreeted, and waits for food can be awfully long. At best, it's adequate.

Expect instead to be wowed by the kitchen. Samosa chaat has complex flavors, with a hint of mint and coriander. The crust is fairly thin and flaky but a little forgettable. Split a plate of kebabs; they're excellent and not at all dry. The tandoori chicken version is inspired by Kashmiri cayenne, and the fish is flavorful and tender. Aloo gobi is a spicy, alluring mix of cauliflower, potatoes, tomatoes, and ginger.

Lamb does its best work in gosht vindaloo with a mélange of spices, sour vinegar, sweet tamarind, and herbs. Warning: this is hot, even for spice freaks. Lamb chops are better than biryani, where the leaner cut of lamb can be drier. Chicken is usually moist and tender, best in silky makhani, especially when tomatoes are in season.

Cocktails are uninspired and not particularly well executed. The wine selection is cursory and uninformed, with no vintages or vineyards on the list, and we've had several glasses poured from bottles that were open too long. We'd recommend sticking to a draft beer.

Lunches are slightly higher priced than others around town, and the quality definitely isn't as high as it is at dinner. It's fast, though, and a good option if you're sick of mushy buffet standards. We've heard comparisons made between East India and Vindalho, but they have quite different goals. The latter's Indian cuisine is more loosely interpreted and fusion-y. For straight Indian food, East India Company is some of the best around, with a kitchen that obviously cares…even if a manager is sorely needed.

EaT: An Oyster Bar

Slurp and sip your way to happiness at this charming, dedicated bar

9.1	7.5	8.5
Food	Feel	Drinks

Seafood, Southern

Casual restaurant

$40
Price

www.eatoysterbar.com

Sun–Thu 11:30am–10pm
Fri–Sat 11:30am–midnight

Bar Beer, wine, liquor, BYO
Credit cards Visa, MC
Reservations Not accepted
Date-friendly, live music, outdoor dining

Mississippi Ave. Area
3808 N. Williams Ave.
(503) 281-1222

This place gets wildly mixed reviews, but we don't understand why. It's a charming, sincere place that is dedicated to all things oyster (and Louisiana, it seems). And those things oyster are absolutely world-class. What's not to love?

The space is casual and airy, with French-blue walls and some fleur-de-lis details that are more dear than pushy. It's super laid-back, but this is no dingy shuck shack: it's got clean lines, high ceilings, and large windows. You can sidle up to the white tile bar and eat oysters there, but few people do. Despite the neighborhood, the crowd here is slightly less hipsterish than at the nearby cafés and New Lompoc brewery. On a lazy Sunday, the sidewalk tables are just ideal. Service is inexplicably slow but friendly, too. You can see the passion for oysters that underlies the attitude of the place. Beware: closing times are more of a guideline than a hard-and-fast rule. Don't cut it too close.

Fresh oysters are delivered several times per week, coming in mostly from the Pacific Northwest—Washington, Oregon, and British Columbia—and some from Prince Edward Island and thereabouts. Check the ever-changing chalkboard for what's in. These are well chosen and shucked, leaving just about the purest, cleanest liquor you can slurp. Take advantage of Portland's ostreacentric location here by eating fresher and cheaper oysters than almost anywhere else in the country.

If raw's not for you, fried oysters have an ideal crisp-creamy textural counterpoint, with a lovely cornmeal crust; they remind you why fried oysters are one of the most delicious things in the world. They come served in a po' boy, but on request, you can get them on their own for $2 a pop. Fried pickles are a bit disappointing, too salty and oily. Étouffées and gumbos are competent, but hardly the main event.

There's a small draft selection, plus the Abita line, in honor of Louisiana. Wines are succinct and to the point, well chosen for oyster pairings, and decently priced. Of course, an oyster bar must have a good, spicy Bloody Mary, and this one is made from house-infused chili-spiked vodka. A competent Sazerac and other craft cocktails (Absinthe fetish alert) are made here, as well. Sometimes, EaT shows movies and games on TV—next time the Saints play, this is our place.

Echo Restaurant

A no-frills neighborhood holdout that's steadily improving

7.7	8.5	6.0
Food	Feel	Wine

Modern

Casual restaurant

$40
Price

www.echorestaurant.com

Daily 4:30pm–2am

Bar Beer, wine, liquor
Credit cards Visa, MC, AmEx
Reservations Not accepted
Live music, outdoor dining

Northeast Portland
2225 NE MLK Blvd.
(503) 460-3246

Echo is one of those places that flies a bit beneath the radar, turning out decent food that doesn't seek to make headlines, or challenge anyone's palate. It doesn't underachieve so much as undershoot, which is evident even in the simple, cool space. In fact, this building once housed a brothel, around the turn of the last century. Large windows spill light into the room, and a patio is kind of back-alley cool, sheltered on one side by ragged bamboo plants and on the other by an old brick wall that still bears the painted standard of some past incarnation.

When it first opened, Echo was pretty spectacular, but as commonly happens, the consistency and quality just tanked. It seems to have lately hit another stride, and we've had some classic dishes that, again, break no new ground, but are judiciously prepared, like, on one visit, a juicy roasted pork loin justly paired with an onion-fennel confit sweetened slightly by apple, or green beans cooked gently enough not to lose their snap. Mac and cheese with cavatappi pasta is a smart rendition, with the small corkscrew shape ideal for holding the lush white cheddar and the addition of spicy andouille sausage and baked bread crumbs making for a textural hoedown.

The wine list is short and mechanical, with either New World or New World-style wines, none very interesting, but most hard to argue with. With all of them available by the glass, we recommend that you ask your server to direct you to whichever ones were opened that evening—there's a good chance that some will be a few days old.

Vintage cocktails sound promising, but are made with bottom-shelf liquors. Compared to what else is available in the city, we don't have much confidence in these. Take, for instance, the Dark and Stormy, which should be made from Gosling's Black Seal rum and ginger beer. It's got as much bite as it has bittersweetness. Here, a lighter-style rum is substituted, even though Gosling's is used behind the bar for other cocktails. Why on earth do that? And then instead of ginger beer, the bar uses ginger ale, which is much sweeter and gentler. The end result? More like Overcast With A Mild Drizzle.

But for now, it suits mild-mannered Echo just fine.

El Gaucho

Inconsistent steaks and high prices help make obvious nomenclature jokes

7.1	8.0	7.0
Food	Feel	Drinks

Steakhouse

Upmarket restaurant

$100
Price

www.elgaucho.com

Mon–Thu 5pm–midnight
Fri–Sat 5pm–1am
Sun 5pm–11pm

Bar Beer, wine, liquor
Credit cards Visa, MC, AmEx
Reservations Accepted
Date-friendly, live music, Wi-Fi

Downtown
319 SW Broadway
(503) 227-8794

Let's not bury the lead here: there's a real danger in charging this much for dinner and naming your restaurant something that rhymes perfectly with "El Gouge-o." A lot about El Gaucho sounds promising, at first; this four-branch chain hails from the Pacific Northwest and aims for something between Morton's and an Argentine steakhouse, grilling dry-aged beef over coals and dressing its staff in preposterous gaucho costumes. But although some members of our panel have had good experiences here, for most of us, the food and execution just can't justify the prices.

The décor is as expected—rich, dark, and sleek. Live jazz fills in the silences between tinkling glasses and silverware as tuxedo-clad waiters scurry by with carts for tableside Caesar salads, the darkness punctuated by an occasional burst of flame from a bananas Foster in the making. The bar is equally prototypical-classy, and some better deals are had here. We do love the cigar room, though, whose sweet tobacco smell sometimes escapes in tendrils to your table.

As for the dry-aged beef, it's inconsistently cooked. The char on some cuts is wonderfully crisp, but a totally flavorless six-ounce filet is not at all worthwhile. Plus, despite how good it is, the smallest NY strip is not worth $49—where are we, Vegas? Sides are fairly large, and in summer, roasted sweet corn with chipotle honey butter is outstanding. Grilled asparagus with béarnaise is also reliable, but don't bother with overbearing scalloped potatoes (unless that's all you're eating for three days). Worse still are french fries and the classic iceberg wedge salad, which doesn't have enough blue-cheese edge to it. Interestingly, there's nothing remotely Argentine on the menu.

The wine list is more interesting than the ones at most national-chain steakhouses, but it is also amazingly overpriced, with some bottles over three times retail. The reasonable $20 corkage is a better way to go (we rarely see this option at a steakhouse). The liquor selection is great, with many ryes and local spirits, but cocktails suffer from SMS (Steakhouse Mark-up Syndrome), especially one that employs Perrier-Jouet Grand Brut. Why? It might consider using Cava and *not* costing $40.

It may be fun to watch bananas Foster prepared tableside, but this does nothing for its execution. It can't get hot enough this way, and the barely melted brown sugar leaves a grainy texture in the mouth. In fact, dining here reminds us a lot of old-school dinner theater, where the food is not the point. There, too, you pay way too much for the antics and scenery.

Eleni's

2.9 Food

3.0 Feel

Rude service and bad food is only charming when there's a lovely view of the Mediterranean

Greek

Casual restaurant

$40 Price

www.elenisrestaurant.com

Tue–Thu 5pm–10pm
Fri–Sat 5pm–11pm

Bar Beer, wine, liquor, BYO
Credit cards Visa, MC, AmEx
Reservations Accepted

Pearl District
112 NW 9th Ave.
(503) 227-2158

Sellwood
7712 SE 13th Ave.
(503) 230-2165

Both branches of Eleni's upscale Greek duo look warm and modern, vaguely suggesting a European bistro, but at 6:30pm on a Thursday, it's mostly empty. This once-lauded restaurant has had some troubling reviews for a while now, and after a meal here, it's no wonder.

Assuming the interesting Greek or reliable Oregon wine you order is out of stock (chances look good), your server may bring you one you didn't ask for and begin to open it without checking with you. But don't balk or dare ask for a taste, or you'll get eye-rolling and sulking.

A marked lack of hospitality characterizes not just the service, which has been intensely spiteful on several visits, but also the portion sizes, which are shockingly small for the price—not normally a complaint we make if the food is spectacular, but an insult with execution this clumsy. With the exception of warm stuffed grape leaves full of rice, dill, mint, scallions, pine nuts, and golden raisins, dishes are routinely botched.

Grilled eggplant has come severely undercooked, stuffed with cold but well-spiced Cascade Natural ground beef that had almost none of the advertised feta. Another dish sees four thumb-sized, horribly overcooked tiger prawns drowning in a syrupy-sweet cream sherry sauce. It's a lazy prep with no finesse, for the same price you'd be charged for an excellent dish at a more capable restaurant.

And although the menu magnanimously offers to cook several dishes vegan or gluten-free, asking your server may result in a disgusted look and a refusal with no explanations or suggestions. Clearly on your own, you might opt for mixed greens with tomatoes, English cucumber, peppers, mushrooms, avocado, onions and currants dressed in a honey balsamic vinaigrette, which would serve you well, but avoid at all costs another vegan/gluten-free dish of radicchio, spinach and chard sautéed with a combination of three rices that all manage to taste exactly like Rice-a-Roni, gummy and overcooked with the nondescript flavors of a grocery-store spice mix. Although the dish's gigande beans are cooked well, nothing works together, and it's unfinishable.

It's really such a shame, as Portland could do with a nice Greek restaurant (not just gyros—there are plenty of those around town). But in every truly pertinent respect, Eleni's is far from nice.

Elephants Delicatessen

A deli and specialty store with many faces

6.4	6.5
Food	Feel

American, Sandwiches

Counter service

$20
Price

www.elephantsdeli.com

Daily 7am–8:30pm

Bar Beer, wine, liquor
Credit cards Visa, MC, AmEx
Delivery, kid-friendly, veg-friendly

Downtown
625 SW 5th Ave.
(503) 467-4084

Southwest Portland
812 SW Park Ave.
(503) 546-3166

Northwest Portland
115 NW 22nd Ave.
(503) 299-6304

Elephants knows no bounds. It's a deli, a gourmet specialty foods store, a caterer, a happy hour spot, and sort of a supper club. There are a few different locations, including a food cart (Elephants on Wheels). Every Monday night, in the garden room, there's a prix-fixe dinner by the fireplace, including beer, wine, and cocktails. What isn't Elephants? Cheap.

But many of the prepared foods are fantastic, especially soups like tomato-orange; a creamy chicken and vegetable called Mama Leon's; and Elephant Cure, a spicy, gingery version of chicken soup. Hot dishes like mac-and-cheese and casseroles are well loved and pretty good, even if that's only because they're loaded with cheese and butter. There's little invention, little nuance, but a big blast of flavor.

The breads aren't the best in town, but they're better than the average sandwich shop's. A hoisin-pork sandwich on homemade walnut bread is unexpectedly good, with moist, sweet pork. But a turkey Reuben misses the point completely. Baked goods like cookies, scones, and muffins leave something to be desired. Salads routinely come with a side of that's it? But choose wisely and you'll do well.

The wine selection is diverse, if a bit marked up over the norm. Grower-producer Champagnes, reputable Northwest producers, and a brief index of Old World classics are all here. There's a full bar at the 22nd Avenue location, with happy hour specials. It's not the sexiest place in town to hang out, but there it is.

The deli will even deliver sack lunches to your office. If we're going to spend the money, we'd still rather go to City Market for our specialty shopping, but we like the lunch much better here. At all of its "heres."

Equinox

An inviting patio and a creative menu that
sometimes translates to the plate

6.2	8.5	8.0
Food	Feel	Drinks

Modern

Casual restaurant

$40
Price

www.equinoxrestaurantpdx.com

Tue–Fri 4pm–9pm
Sat 9am–2pm, 5pm–10pm
Sun 9am–2pm

Bar Beer, wine, liquor, BYO
Credit cards Visa, MC, AmEx
Reservations Accepted
Date-friendly, outdoor dining,
veg-friendly, Wi-Fi

Northeast Portland
830 N. Shaver St.
(503) 460-3333

Equinox is one of those places people are loath to criticize. We suspect
that the reason is the patio; it's spacious, with lots of tables, each with its
own colorful umbrella. In cold weather, there are plenty of gas heaters
and warm flagstones under your feet to reflect the heat of the day as the
light wanes. It's one of the best outdoor dining spaces in Portland. The
inside of the restaurant is pretty nice, too. One entire side opens up on
warm days, and there are large skylights and a wall of glass channeling a
flood of natural light.

But a restaurant is the sum of many factors. Service has historically been
a problem here, both clueless and unapologetic, even on slower nights.
Specialty cocktails vary wildly from night to night, ranging from balanced
to off-key.

More troubling is the execution of the innovative menu, perhaps due to
its ambitious globetrotting (with sometimes as many as four regional
influences in a single dish.) Some descriptions give us pause—almost as
much pause as the oddly Mario Puzo-ish font in the logo.

Salads (called "Weeds" here—cheeky!) aren't terribly unique, but,
perhaps uncoincidentally, they work best. We especially like a plate of
beets and fennel-blood-orange vinaigrette, and another of pan-seared
chèvre cakes with roasted Bosc pears and lemon-mint vinaigrette. In a
move that's sort of pandering and lame, you can add tofu, grilled chicken,
smoked salmon, or shrimp to any of the salads.

A small selection of pastas is straightforward and quite nice. But mains
are problematic. Vegetarian "Oaxacan" enchiladas are full of good
spaghetti squash, queso fresco, and spinach, but red mole is monotonous
and oversalted. A grilled hanger steak, though nicely flavored, has come
so unevenly cooked that, sliced on the plate, some pieces were almost
raw, while others were completely overcooked.

We appreciate that the restaurant is built from recycled materials and
that it uses renewable energy, local produce, organic meats, wild seafood,
and cage-free eggs. The patio is an incredibly nice place to have brunch.
But for a restaurant to be this popular and yet still so topsy-turvy, we have
to wonder: is there better still to come for this progressive restaurant?

Escape From NY

Pizza for drunk, undiscerning, homesick New Yorkers

6.4	7.5	8.0
Food	Feel	Beer

Pizza

Counter service

$10
Price

Daily 11:30am–11pm

Bar Beer
Credit cards None
Delivery, kid-friendly, outdoor dining, veg-friendly

Northwest Portland
622 NW 23rd Ave.
(503) 227-5423

Escape From New York Pizza is a great place to meet people. It's small, cozy, and smells like a pizzeria should, like sweet dough baking and tangy tomato sauce simmering. Friendly staff makes great conversation with patrons at the counter. It's totally laid back and relaxed.

In other words, it's nothing like New York.

New York's streets are full of mediocre late-night stands tossing slices onto paper plates. So although the atmosphere here is certainly an escape from New York, the pizza is right on the money. To be clear, it doesn't resemble New York's better, more ambitious pizzerias—not the coal-fired-versus-wood-fired-sparring Brooklyners and East Villagers, anyway. And don't mistake New York pizza for New Haven pizza, which is entirely different. This pizza chooses to stay out of all those battles by baking in a simple gas-fired oven.

For this reason, the crust wildly varies from being thin and crunchy to flaccid and undercooked. The tomato sauce is a bit too sweet, but the cheese is melty and greasy and when you fold it, it funnels all the mozzarella ooze into your mouth—in other words, like a standard, forgettable, feed-me-I'm-drunk pizza should. Stick to pepperoni, which is going to be salty, but at least has something going on; mushroom and cheese slices are pretty dull. Vegetables seem to be of the Sysco-truck variety, pink tomatoes and vapid bell peppers, and such.

There are some inhospitable elements that might be more charming if the pizza were better, like a cash-only policy and no free refills on soda. We do love the beer selection, though—half a dozen on draft and the same in bottle, mostly local micros and a few standard domestics. And the well-worn checkerboard linoleum, old-school red stools, and eccentric murals are great.

Now if we could just do something about this jovial attitude, damn it.

Euro Dish

A little yellow Polish food cart serving up one of Portland's most transportive experiences

7.6 Food

7.5 Feel

Polish

Food cart

$10 Price

Mon–Fri 11am–6pm

Bar None
Credit cards None
Outdoor dining

Downtown
SW 10th Ave. & Alder
(971) 344-3704

This jaunty buggy is, as far as we can tell, the only Polish food cart in Portland. It's also perhaps the best in its particular food-cart zone. It's not quite for lunch rush quickies; there's more of a slow-food mentality here. A friendly, older Polish woman will make your food. You will wait a bit for it. And it will be so very worth it.

Some tables set up around the area are surrounded by bushes and trees, giving the whole thing a sort of pleasant village feel. You know, as far as food carts go. There are colorful pictures of all the foods you can order, so if you don't know what Polish food entails, you won't feel so lost.

You can play it safe with potato-and-cheese-curd pierogi, made with unleavened dough and served with a little sour cream. Get these in addition to "Hunters stew," an absolutely soul-soothing blend of pulled pork, sausage, and sauerkraut. Bratwurst tastes correct, with a nice snap to it. Stuffed cabbage might be a little challenging for newbies—it's mushy, but in a good way, filled with meat and spices and rice, then covered in a sweet and spicy tomato sauce. There is also wonderful schnitzel (a tender, lightly breaded, fried pork cutlet), beef goulash, chicken paprikash, and blintzes. Everything is, of course, hearty, so beware of over-ordering (it's hard not to).

There's something so lovely about sitting out here, next to the tiny yellow shack and smelling the cabbage and sausage, tasting the love and care put into every dish. It's certainly the closest to Eastern Europe that you can come while standing on a Portland sidewalk.

Everett Street Bistro

5.6 Food **8.0** Feel **6.0** Drinks

Big portions and big flavors that don't always work

Modern

Casual restaurant

$35 Price

www.everettstreetbistro.com

Sun–Mon 8am–3pm
Tue–Sat 8am–3pm, 5pm–10pm

Bar Beer, wine, liquor
Credit cards Visa, MC, AmEx
Reservations Accepted
Date-friendly, outdoor dining

Pearl District
1140 NW Everett St.
(503) 467-4990

Everett Street Bistro sports white woodwork, attractive café tables, woven chairs, and tiled surfaces, aiming for an airy French look—which is mostly carried off. The gleaming glass case of pastries also kind of gives it away. Large windows let in lots of daylight, and it's great for pretty-people watching.

But where a French bistro has a more focused, succinct menu, this one goes overboard trying to have something for everyone. And portions are huge. In other words, it's too American to be European. The result is a dilution of success; many things are fine, but that's it.

And it's hard to escape the pretentiousness of calling it a "Composed Seafood Salad." If it were a legitimate French salade composée, to which this seems to be a reference, it would be a lot more interesting than this mediocre rendition; it's really more of a ceviche, with citrus and avocado. But we've rarely seen a ceviche approach this sky-high price.

Unable to leave well enough alone, the kitchen wallops pasty french fries with mouth-burning whole roasted garlic. Grand Marnier French toast is soaked in custard, and is candy sweet, if that's your thing. Scrambles are pretty forgettable, which we could understand at a cheaper, shabbier café or diner. But when people come to a gleaming, Old-World-charming so-called "bistro," don't they want to recall having eaten there?

French onion soup is fine, but even the comforting saltiness of the broth can't make the high price feel worthwhile—not when you can get a bowl of pho that's three times bigger for less.

Classic cocktails are made with the *right* ingredients, but not the *best* ingredients; in a city full of fresh-squeezed juices, homemade simple syrups, and small-batch bitters in a variety of flavors, this literal translation feels kind of outdated. Not that we condone fussing with a Manhattan, but this bar is all about martini glasses and sugar rims. These days, it's hard to take anyone seriously who uses Midori in house cocktails.

Given that the place only opened a few years ago, Everett's mentality seems markedly out of step with the ambitious kitchens and bars all over town trying to make simple food better, and for less. Here, almost exactly the opposite seems to be the goal. And good luck figuring out which menus are served at which hours. For that matter, good luck even being seated; on slow nights, the kitchen will close early, leaving those who show up at 9:40pm in the awkward position of either having to go elsewhere or risk pissing off the staff. We'll take our chances elsewhere.

Evoe

A simple gourmet deli brought to you by the
excellent market Pastaworks

8.2	7.0	8.0
Food	Feel	Wine

Modern, Sandwiches

Casual restaurant

$15
Price

www.pastaworks.com/evoe

Wed–Sun noon–6:30pm

Bar Beer, wine
Credit cards Visa, MC, AmEx
Reservations Not accepted
Veg-friendly, Wi-Fi

Hawthorne
3731 SE Hawthorne Blvd.
(503) 232-1010

Evoe (a-voe, as in *Evoe! O Bacchus, thus began the song...*) is the dine-in option brought to you by the Pastaworks market. It's something of a more sophisticated deli, serving small plates, salads, and sandwiches made from ingredients found on the attached market's shelves. If you're lucky, you can sit at the counter and watch your meal come together, start to finish. You might see the chef leave his post to gather more fresh produce from next door for your meal. Otherwise, you're relegated to stools that are taller than the tables, forcing you to hunch uncomfortably over your plate.

But it's informal in that changing-chalkboard sort of way, and you can tell that a lot of sincerity and dedication goes into the food here. The menu features whatever is in that day, simple preparations that showcase the fresh, natural flavors of the ingredients: sliced delicata squash with good olive oil and sea salt and chopped hazelnuts; a beet salad with walnuts and homemade crème fraîche; pork belly with garrafón (large white lima) beans, peppers, and tomatoes.

Sandwiches on bread from Grand Central and Pearl are delicious and simple. They're not the punk-rock or haute-nostalgic versions that titillate the followers of Bunk and Meat Cheese Bread, but rather calmer classics like chicken salad on brioche (made in house) and a pickle-spicy muffuletta. We appreciate the simple, rustic European plates like French breakfast radishes with butter and deviled eggs, and can never get enough of boquerones, which are fleshy, citrusy Omega-3 bombs.

At what operates primarily as a lunch place, it's strange to see this many wines by the glass. The selection is well edited and thorough, with some excellent, affordable producers of which we don't see much around town. Or you can choose from the beer and wine sold at Pastaworks.

On all accounts, it's a great idea for Pastaworks to have Evoe prepare so well the ingredients that it sells; it's hard to resist the urge to raid the market's shelves after your lunch so you can recreate your meal at home. Or try to, anyway.

E'Njoni Café

Rich, complex, and satisfying vegetables lie behind this dull-looking storefront

7.7	7.0
Food	Feel

Ethiopian

Casual restaurant

$30
Price

www.enjonicafe.com

Tue–Fri 11:30am–3pm, 5pm–9pm
Sat–Sun noon–10pm

Bar Beer, wine, BYO
Credit cards Visa, MC
Reservations Accepted
Live music, outdoor dining, veg-friendly, Wi-Fi

North Portland
910 N. Killingsworth St.
(503) 286-1401

The people behind E'Njoni are actually Eritrean. Eritrea—like Ethiopia—was occupied by Italian forces for the first half of the 20th century, before being annexed by Ethiopia for a time, and the cuisines are similar, although they vary with respect to the level of residual Mediterranean influence. Some Eritrean restaurants carry pasta dishes and sandwiches, along with a few flavors that made their way down the Red Sea, like baba ghanoush with pita bread.

E'Njoni's is perhaps the strangest setup we've ever encountered for an East African restaurant: a pristine storefront on a block of quaint, polished shops and cafés. It looks, with its sandwich board and outside tables and chairs, more like a chain sandwich shop than an Ethiopian restaurant, which we more often find carved out of the bottom floor of a homely building, or magically cheering up an otherwise grungy and ramshackle space. Once you get past the placid exterior of E'Njoni, though, there are warmer signs of culture: pepper-red walls; some artifacts here and there; and the smiling owners visiting guests at their tables.

Ethiopian food comes to mind when we feel frustrated by the abundance of gross, boring meat substitutes that constitute many restaurants' vegetarian programs. For around 10 bucks, you can have a platter sampling each of the delicious vegetarian dishes available here. If you love Indian or Southern food, you'll take to this easily: collard greens (somehow more flavorful here without pork than most versions of the classic meaty prep); spicy red lentils; tender, seductive eggplant; and curried okra. Scoop everything up with spongy injera bread, made with teff, one of those wonder grains full of absorbable iron, calcium, and amino acids. In fact, it is one of the few glutinous foods safe for celiac sufferers. Be somewhat sparing, as it expands in the stomach.

Meat eaters are also well served here, especially with alitcha zigni, in which lamb on the bone is slowly simmered to tenderness with complex chili and garlic flavors and a bit of spice. Oddly, the menu doesn't list doro wat, one of the most popular Ethiopian dishes in the US. Instead, "dorho tibs" has unappealing chicken—breast cubes (rather than the whole drumstick)—to accompany the hard-boiled egg. But the berbere spices are abundant and the red stew thick and oniony.

It's not the best version of this cuisine, but it's up there, plus it's pretty darn cute.

The Farm Café

Great, if you're in the neighborhood or just love a quirky, romantic vibe

7.4	9.0	8.0
Food	Feel	Beer

Modern, Vegefusion

Upmarket restaurant

$45
Price

www.thefarmcafe.com

Daily 5pm–11:30pm

Bar Beer, wine, liquor, BYO
Credit cards Visa, MC, AmEx
Reservations Accepted
Date-friendly, outdoor dining,
veg-friendly

East Burnside
10 SE 7th Ave.
(503) 736-3276

Farm Café is a cute, mostly vegetarian restaurant in a charming Victorian-style house that's full of quirks: the host sits right in the middle of the front dining room at an old desk, and once you've signed in, you walk through the kitchen to find a cozy L-shaped bar in the back. The décor is subtle, warm, and full of modern-yet-rustic elements like amber-tinted chandeliers that remind us a bit of jellyfish. It's a great place for dates, between the conversation starters and flattering lighting.

In warmer weather, a colorfully lit patio is a spectacular place to sip on too-sweet blood orange margaritas (we've given up on finding a good margarita in the Northwest), or better, sparkling cocktails like "The Goldenrod," whose little bubbles send up whiffs of Saint-Germain elderflower liqueur and orange peel. The wine list is full of some of the region's best, and the draft selection comes in as wide a range as hoppy locals can get.

Happy hour is briefer than twilight, from 5pm–6:30pm, but if you can squeeze in, chicken wings with Farmstead blue cheese sauce are a good snack, spicy, with a vinegary bite that is softened slightly by the creamy cheese. A $2 seasonally changing cup of soup has to be one of the best deals in town. We've been thoroughly satisfied by a velvety delicata squash. Avoid hand-cut fries that can taste dry and chewy, as though they were fried ahead of time for the happy hour rush.

On the regular menu, an herb-crusted tofu with "mushroom Marsala" is heralded for its vegetarian heartiness, but succumbs to that unfortunate haphazard-pan-world veggieness. Although the breaded tofu is texturally right on, we find the overly thymey potatoes annoying and the sauce bland. Fish is also prominently featured on this short menu, and rightfully so. Pan-fried Idaho trout has come expertly cooked, whole, so that the bones help the flesh retain every drop of moisture. A simple dusting of coarse sea salt and an accoutrement of roasted winter vegetables (parsnips, carrots, and Brussels sprouts) was ideal.

Don't skip a fabulous "Sunken Chocolate Soufflé," a dense, dark chocolate cake with a molten center that, when broken and mixed, makes more of a pudding than a soufflé (which totally works in its favor). A topping of homemade coffee ice cream gives it an amazing finish.

Le Pigeon this may not be, but it's a terrific second choice when the first one's too busy.

Fat City Café

Fat City: A Drama in One Scene

4.0	7.5
Food	Feel

American

Casual restaurant

$20
Price

www.fatcitycafe.net

Daily 6:30am–3pm

Bar None
Credit cards Visa, MC, AmEx
Reservations Not accepted

Multnomah Village
7820 SW Capitol Hwy.
(503) 245-5457

Setting: 1987, Portland, OR. A greasy spoon in the historic Multnomah Village neighborhood. Route 66 signs pepper the walls, as do T-shirts advertising "Fat City." A Coca-Cola ceiling fan spins overhead. A counter seats an old man in a John Deere cap. A zaftig and aging Waitress scratches her head with a pencil as she takes an order from a young couple in a corner booth. The sounds of clinking silverware, sizzling bacon, short-order cooks ringing the bell now and then. Two middle-aged men sit in a center booth with mugs of coffee. They are Police Chief Jim Davis and Mayor Bud Clark. Davis is clearly rattled. Clark is preoccupied with sugaring and creaming his coffee.

Clark: I love this place. Crap for coffee, but I keep coming anyway.

Davis (leaning forward): Listen, I know why you called me here.

The Waitress approaches, a plate in each hand.

Waitress: Who had the corned beef hash? (Clark motions. She drops the plate unceremoniously in front of him and the other in front of Davis. She winks at Davis.) And the cinnamon roll. Extra sweet. (Davis watches her saunter off.)

Clark: This corned beef smells exactly like my dog's food. Tastes like it, too.

Davis: Listen, Bud, I know you know about the audit…

Clark: How hard is it to fry an egg? Jesus, we got one overeasy egg here and the other one is rock solid.

Davis: But I had the right to know what was being said about me and my team.

Clark (Smacking a bottle of Heinz ketchup over his plate): But I love this place, you know. The pork chops are like hockey pucks and I one time had this french fry still frozen right in the middle…

Davis: Will you listen to me? I'm trying to explain myself here.

Clark: Sometimes, you can love a place even when it's a total screw-up. Because that's what it's supposed to be, a screw-up. You don't expect a whole lot, you don't get a whole lot, and no one goes home unhappy. (He looks at Davis, points the ketchup bottle at him.) You had no authority to go over my head like that.

Davis: Read my lips: yes I do have the authority.

Clark: Read my lips: you're fired.

Davis stands. The two men stare long and hard at each other. Davis turns sharply and leaves. Clark reaches across the table and rips off some of Davis's untouched cinnamon roll and eats it, nodding.

Clark (Shaking his head): That's a good goddamned cinnamon roll.

Fats

Lovely pub grub, beer, and...what else might you need?

7.0	9.0	8.0
Food	Feel	Beer

British

Casual restaurant

$35
Price

www.fatspdx.com

Mon, Wed–Fri 4pm–9:30pm
Sat–Sun 10am–2pm, 4pm–
9:30pm

Bar Beer, wine, liquor
Credit cards Visa, MC, AmEx
Reservations Not accepted

Alberta Arts District
2930 NE Killingsworth St.
(503) 206-8261

You might love the name of this brand-new British restaurant. You also might hate it. Either way, the intention seems to be to engage with the innard-glorifying culinary avant-garde while slyly acknowledging the days when overeating wasn't such a hot-button issue.

The same might be said for Fats' entire concept. The gleamingly renovated restaurant—bar in back, beautiful beer taps effortlessly marrying the British with the Oregonian, floor-to-ceiling windows, all of it just a bit too cool for school—is situated in what the restaurant group refers to as the "Fox-Chase Addition," a gentrifying little intersection of NE 30th Ave. and NE Killingsworth, just north of the Alberta Arts District, which scores the place even more trendy points.

Even more tellingly, Fats is owned by the same hip-dining tycoon as nearby Beast, Yakuza, and DOC, and it clearly forms part of the defiant meat movement that is sweeping Portland. This menu is unapologetically food-nerdy, which means that it honors the sort of British nose-to-tail cuisine that, after decades as the pathetic loser of the culinary world, is suddenly in fashion.

Bangers and mash, for instance, has been heroically recast into the mainstream of this new culinary order—not just at Fats, but all over the place—for its relentlessly traditional protein-and-starchness. The dish is well executed here—sausage is juicy, mashed potatoes speak cleanly and clearly. We're delighted by the authentic appearance of the London pub food par excellence: chicken tikka masala.

Looking beyond British borders to other places where the Queen appears on the currency, Fats has also jumped on the poutine bandwagon. Poutine is one of those lesser-known preparations from lesser-known regions—in this case, Québec—that have been elevated to cult status by virtue of their audacious levels of fat, cholesterol, and calories. That's not to say that poutine isn't a delicious indulgence; it always has been. It's simply to say that the sudden popularity of the dish is laughably faddish. Fats' version tries to do too much with it, however, replacing the classic cheese curds with goat cheese, dressing the fries with bacon and poached egg, making it even more overrich than real poutine—and less satisfying. Bone marrow on toast is also overwrought, this time by a salty excess of capers.

Sexy modern trends work better when more careful execution is there.

Fenouil

The décor balances warmth and coolness,
perhaps better than the kitchen does

7.5	9.0	7.0
Food	Feel	Wine

French, Modern

Upmarket restaurant

$60
Price

www.fenouilinthepearl.com

Mon–Fri 5pm–9pm
Sat–Sun 9am–9pm

Bar Beer, wine, liquor
Credit cards Visa, MC, AmEx
Reservations Accepted
Date-friendly, live music, outdoor
dining, Wi-Fi

Pearl District
900 NW 11th Ave.
(503) 525-2225

Fenouil rises like a glacier against the Pearl District square, all white and glass and silver. Tiny lights in the trees add to the wintry effect. Fireplaces, wood floors, and a tin ceiling try for coziness, but the sheer size of the space—the limestone pillars, the magnificent French tapestry, and the vaulted ceiling—are decidedly American. In fact, while you're sitting in one of the padded armchairs in the mezzanine, it hits you: this might well be the French Brasserie Adventure at Epcot.

On the plate, this revelation is alternately affirmed and blown away. Salads are forgettable, but don't miss the French onion soup, with its buttery, caramelized onions and silky, beefy base. Frog's legs, no longer on the menu, have seemed like a waste of a good frog. If you're going to cook nature's cutest amphibian, don't deep fry it beyond recognition and serve it in a bagna cauda that's gelatinous by the time it gets to the table.

In fact, temperature is a persistent problem at Fenouil. Due to the distance from the kitchen to many tables in the enormous space (especially upstairs), dishes often arrive cool. Yet upon sending a dish back, we've had it return seemingly just thrown back on the grill (thus overcooking it) re-plated. This has happened at several different visits.

Were temperature not an issue, we'd find this food mostly successful, if a little soulless, like a steady reproduction of a Matisse. Black cod has been traditionally treated well. Wood-fired duck breast has been smoky and tender. Prunes stewed in Armagnac have been well-executed and enjoyable, as have seared sea scallops with a smoked bacon-leek fondue and verjus.

The lengthy wine list would be even better if it focused all its efforts in France; as it is, few French bottles here under $100 are very exciting. And a French chef would commit hari kari before sending out desserts as average-tasting (but pretty) as these.

Word has it that the 8,500-square-foot interior was designed by KL Design group for several million dollars. It's pretty, but you have to wonder: if they were trying for the ideal venue in which to honor French cuisine, did they get their money's worth?

Did you?

5th Quadrant

A classic neighborhood hangout that sets the bar high for pub food and homemade brews

7.1	8.0	8.5
Food	Feel	Beer

American

Bar

$15
Price

www.newoldlompoc.com

Mon–Thu 11am–midnight
Fri–Sat 11am–1am
Sun 11am–11pm

Bar Beer, wine, liquor
Credit cards Visa, MC
Date-friendly, outdoor dining,
veg-friendly, Wi-Fi

Mississippi Ave. Area
3901-B N. Williams Ave.
(503) 288-3996

Owned by the folks behind Old Lompoc, 5th Quadrant shares a corner with the irresistible Pix Pâtisserie. Its high ceilings of old exposed wood beams and rough concrete floor show its roots as a car repair shop. The roll-up garage door is still in place, although it's been replaced by a newer version that opens up onto a patio on nice days. The overall feeling is warm in the winter, but open and airy in the summer, with plenty of room for larger parties.

Portions are generous and rather upscale...for pub food, anyway. A "5th Quadrant Salad" comes loaded with sweet roasted beets, crunchy hazelnuts, creamy Gorgonzola, fresh greens, and an excellent, balanced orange vinaigrette. An Italian chopped salad in basil vinaigrette is also good, with lots of interesting flavors and textures, but don't bother with the bland Caesar.

Sandwiches are the mainstay here; all come with your choice of soup, salad, fries, or coleslaw. The soups are serviceable, and fries can be slightly mealy, but a good sprinkling of sea salt on top gives little explosive bursts to every bite. The burger is better than most other pub versions: a thick half-pound patty topped with all the normal accoutrements and your choice of smoked Gouda, Swiss, or Tillamook cheddar. Juices run out every time you take a bite, so hold it over the large mound of fries, which will soak up all that goodness. A barbecue pork sandwich is a worthy effort—if hardly world-class—piled high and demonstrating the right balance of vinegary cole slaw.

After 5pm, there are a few more mains available, among them a standard serving of meatloaf on a mound of mashed potatoes, with sautéed vegetables and gravy. Surprisingly, there are quite a few good vegetarian options here: some of the better pub eggplant parmigiana around, or a well-balanced Portobello sandwich with roasted red peppers and spicy remoulade.

Beer, of course, is the star here. There's a wide selection for all tastes, including seasonal beers, some guest microbrews, and mostly house brews—like the culty Lompoc Strong—on draft. Of all the Lompoc locations, this one might just be the most inviting and neighborly.

50 Plates

This trendy concept-kitchen produces more sound-bites than sound bites

5.0	6.5
Food	Feel

Modern

Upmarket restaurant

$40
Price

www.50plates.com

Sun–Thu 11:30am–11pm
Fri–Sat 11:30am–midnight

Bar Beer, wine, liquor
Credit cards Visa, MC, AmEx
Reservations Accepted
Date-friendly, outdoor dining,
Wi-Fi

Pearl District
333 NW 13th Ave.
(503) 228-5050

There is something incredibly unnerving about 50 Plates. We're all for nostalgia and down-home cooking and county-fair food made sophisticated, but when you start talking about grandmothers and Route 66 while looking exactly like a West Elm, you lose us.

It still manages to feel comfortable, despite the glaring white tables, the overly strategic lighting, and the pricey arrangements that our own grandmothers would have clucked their tongues at as "wasteful, and ugly besides." In other words, it's totally at home in the too-cool Pearl, but not reflective of anyone's childhood homes. The bar tends to be more successful in fitting into its trendy, chic design; the bartenders are astute and seem to have fun making the drinks, so people tend to have fun drinking them.

The bar is also a great place to spend happy hour, with so many whimsical sliders (who doesn't love a whimsical slider?) on the menu. They sure do get the blood pumping when you first order them: a fried-chicken-and-waffles slider? A Carolina pulled pork version for $2.50? Kobe, Tillamook cheddar, and tomato jam?

But if everything sounds like the perfect marriage of sentimental flavors in exciting new forms (much like we imagine the business plan for 50 Plates sounded), that's because it is merely that: a sound bite. There is no sense of a great chef behind the scenes, just concepts and gimmicks.

A "Sam Ward," for instance, named for what the menu deems "New York's first 'foodie'," has an alluring-sounding sherry cream and roasted mushroom sauce over challah toast (funny, Sam doesn't *look* Jewish), but on the palate, it comes off like undersalted cream of mushroom soup over eggy toast. Sam would never advocate this kind of blandness. Fries are good, crispy, and hand cut, with a homemade ketchup that is wonderfully light and fresh and not overly sweet and salty like the bottled stuff. But when a menu this large and this titillating only sees a handful of dishes through to delicious fruition, we have to call its bluff.

Fire on the Mountain

6.8 | 6.5 | 8.0
Food | Feel | Beer

A tasty world of wings and beer

American

Counter service

$20
Price

www.portlandwings.com

Sun–Thu 11am–11pm
Fri–Sat 11am–midnight

Bar Beer, wine, BYO
Credit cards Visa, MC, AmEx
Reservations Not accepted
Delivery, kid-friendly, live music,
outdoor dining

Southeast Portland
1708 E. Burnside St.
(503) 230-9464

North Portland
4225 N. Interstate Ave.
(503) 280-9464

Although Buffalo has the mythos of making normally ignored chicken wings a staple of the bar-goer's diet, legend has it that Fire on the Mountain is the first Portland institution to make wings the center of attention. True to Pac-Northwest form, it has a staunch commitment to using biodegradable, sustainable, and renewable materials. Even the fryer oil (trans-fat free) is donated to a local co-op after it's used. Beef comes from Painted Hills ranch. We're not sure where the wings are from (Buffalo, perhaps?), but they are pretty huge and meaty.

The Burnside location has high ceilings and lots of light by day, but it's not necessarily charming. There are picnic tables to sit at communally, a stage upon which bands frequently play, and lots of television sets. Go with a group or to watch a game; you just order at the counter, and the wings are brought out to you in orders of anywhere from 6 to 250.

And these are some of the best wings we've ever had on any coast. They're tender, *maybe* with a bit too much sauce, but we can understand why they're so zealous with it. All sauces are made in house and include a Bourbon chipotle; a Jamaican jerk; raspberry habanero; lime cilantro; sweet BBQ; spicy peanut; the vaguely Mexican El Jefe; and, of course, the classic Buffalo sauce in four degrees of heat. Most of these are balanced and all are pretty addictive. It's a good thing you can purchase them in bottles to go.

Sweet potato fries are also terrific, although sandwiches are just okay. We don't really believe in boneless chicken wings here—their coatings tend to get mushy.

Local microbrews flow from the taps here, and they're wonderfully priced, especially at happy hour (6–10pm daily), when they're only $2 a pint. There's even a late-night happy hour, just for an hour. Can you eat 250 wings in an hour?

We'd like to help you try.

Firehouse

Wood-fired meats and pizzas in a feel-good brick space

8.6	9.0	8.0
Food	Feel	Wine

Pizza, Modern

Casual restaurant

$35
Price

www.firehousepdx.com

Wed–Sun 5pm–10pm

Bar Beer, wine, liquor
Credit cards Visa, MC, AmEx
Reservations Accepted
Date-friendly, outdoor dining, veg-friendly

Northeast Portland
711 NE Dekum St.
(503) 954-1702

As you can guess from the name, Firehouse is situated in a converted fire station of red brick with terrific, almost Art-Deco charcoal-colored designs on its face. Inside, exposed wood beams and the glowing hearth of a brick pizza oven are rustic touches, and a garden out back grows whatever ingredients the kitchen can use. The atmosphere is just terrific; people return faithfully, it seems, for the ambience alone. The walls are covered with black and white photos of old firemen.

Waits can get long, as the space is pretty small. Service can be clumsy, but it's also friendly and familial; can you get mad when your Aunt Joan spills wine on your purse? (No, but she can offer to comp it.)

That wood-fired brick oven is used to good effect, making a thin, golden crust with some nice blackish blisters. This authentically Italian-style pizza gets sparse toppings of great quality, as is custom, and the effect is spot on with a melting middle. San Marzano tomatoes impart an earthy sweetness, and homemade sausage is fennely and spectacular.

Pizzas are the highlight, but they form the mere minority of the menu. Cherry peppers stuffed with mozzarella and anchovies are a good appetizer, but grow tiresome if not shared; hanger steak is cooked properly to temperature, but is underseasoned; and fried cauliflower with lemony crème fraîche is a rare treat in town. The wood oven is also used quite successfully for Coho salmon, mussels, and rotisserie chicken. Some dishes feel more worthwhile than others, but in a group of three or more, you can try a good variety and have a terrific time for relatively little money.

There are some very able-bodied beers on draft, and more microbrews and British ales in bottle, and a Belgian framboise, all at wonderfully low markups. A very succinct wine list is resourceful and smart, with bargain-priced Old World bottles that are better made than many more expensive wines out there.

If the photographs on these walls speak to a sense of nostalgia and a reverence for dedication, then Firehouse follows through on that promise in the kitchen, too.

FlavourSpot

The spot for waffles...and bacon...together

5.0 Food   **7.5** Feel

American, Baked goods

Food cart   **$5** Price

www.flavourspot.com

Mon–Fri 6:30am–2pm
Sat–Sun 8am–3pm
Hours vary by location

North Portland
2310 N. Lombard St.
(503) 289-9866

Bar None
Credit cards Visa, MC
Kid-friendly, outdoor dining

Mississippi Ave. Area
Mississippi and NE Fremont
(503) 282-9866

American waffles—as long as they're not the frozen kind—tend to exist within a limited range of quality, bracketed between the slightly more moist and the slightly more dry, between the slightly sweeter and the slightly saltier. It's comfort food. Sure, you'll find the occasional Liège waffle here and there, served in its sticky glory by an obsessive Europhile, but that's the rare exception to the homogeneous waffle rule.

Given waffles' genetic similarity, it's surprising that so many establishments stick to the one-dimensional sugaring-up school of waffle improvement—maple syrup, corn-syrup-based imitators, fresh fruit—instead of hamming them up with savories. It's a shame, because the salty and umami aspects of pork products, eggs, and pungent cheeses can spin a great deal more complexity from the simple waffle. Why is the bacon waffle still the exception to the rule, the almost-exclusive domain of certain fast-foody pancake-house chains and only the most avant-garde of comfort-food throwback joints?

FlavourSpot, one of whose two branches sits on an emerging end of Mississippi, is one of the rare establishments that gets the genius of the pork-plus-waffle formula. There's a very Portlandy food-cart feeling to the freestanding garage-sized, sided, sleek-wood-fenced structure. The more sophisticated the city's food-cart culture becomes, the more the line blurs between food cart and sit-down restaurant. This one's hard to classify.

The menu's so-called "waffle sandwiches" or "dutch tacos" are basically waffles folded over fillings and half-wrapped in foil. The menu evokes that of a crêperie. All of this is very exciting, which makes the frequent execution problems all the more frustrating.

Waffles often come out overcooked, too dry, or too cool, and fillings too often fail, whether for dryness, toughness, or lack of integration. Melted cheese has been oozy but sparse; Black Forest ham has been leathery; bacon and sausage have lacked the juices and dripping fats that you hope for. The sausage can be nicely set off by maple butter—a good idea even if it gets a bit more hype than it deserves. Ironically, given our rant, some of the sweet waffles—Nutella, for instance—eclipse the savories, perhaps because they require fewer ingredients and less expertise.

Still, it's hard to argue with a decent waffle—there's your bracket theory again. And the picnic tables are a perfectly pleasant place to while away the day. It's hard to argue with that either.

Fleur de Lis

The coffee's just okay, but the freshly baked goods keep us coming back

Baked goods

Counter service

Tue–Fri 7am–6pm
Sat–Sun 8am–3pm

Bar None
Credit cards Visa, MC, AmEx
Delivery, kid-friendly, live music,
outdoor dining, veg-friendly

Northeast Portland
3930 NE Hancock St.
(503) 459-4887

You can somehow tell that Fleur de Lis Bakery used to be a library: tall floor-to-ceiling windows allow light to spill into the cavernous room and there is an array of comfortable tables and chairs, a mix of two- and four-tops, plus a few large tables and some couches. It feels like a place where you ought to be studying or reading. Instead of the yeasty-mildewy smell of old books, however, the yeasty-sweet smell of fresh-baked breads and pastries fills the air, emanating from a small kitchen in the corner.

For its size, the kitchen turns out a great array of goods. It supplies its excellent bread (multi-grain rolls, olive ciabatta, and addictive levain) to many sandwich shops in town.

Stumptown provides the coffee here, and while simple drip is good, the espresso drinks need work. Maybe a tutorial from Albina Press is in order. Better is the variety of tempting pastries: airy little apple puffs; zingy rhubarb tarts; and wonderful scones—maybe the best in town—such as orange-currant, fennel-raisin, and blueberry. The almond ring is a winner, exactly the way it should taste, on an expertly made crust. Croissants are flaky, light, and buttery without being oily; pain au chocolat has a ribbon of excellent bittersweet chocolate running through it. Then there are walnut pecan rolls, cinnamon rolls, pecan coffee cake, apple mazurka, and so on. Of course, the selection is much better if you get there early in the day.

If your glucose level feels a little high, there are also good sandwiches, including a house-roasted pork loin with decent cheese, roasted onions, thinly sliced beets, and a very light coating of mayonnaise on fresh, soft bread. Black Forest ham is worthy. There is also a soup du jour—once a rustic tomato-basil.

The staff seems to be made up of family and friends; people who believe in the place. But let's get one thing straight: unlike librarians, they will *not* be busing your table after you.

Food Fight Grocery

Vegan as f@#*!!

Groceries, Vegefusion

Market

www.foodfightgrocery.com

Daily 10am–8pm

Bar None
Credit cards Visa, MC, AmEx
Outdoor dining, veg-friendly

Southeast Portland
1217 SE Stark St.
(503) 233-3910

Food Fight Grocery is more than just a vegan market—it's a community outreach center, dealing in social conscience as much as in soy cheese. Some events at the market have included screenings of documentaries, parties in which letters of support are written to imprisoned animal rights activists, and monthly bike rides to a vegan dinner somewhere in town. Fans include dreamboat artist Kurt Halsey, who recently designed a shirt for Food Fight depicting a precious cartoon lamb wondering, "What kind of asshole eats a lamb?" We do, and now we feel terrible about it—one shirt, please.

Actually, for a bunch of people whose reptilian brains are so rarely lit up by a mouthful of flesh, Food Fight is refreshingly punk, bringing a level of Henry-Rollins-like energy to veganism. The sign out front sticks it to the Geo-driving-hippie days of animal-friendly lifestyles by declaring the store is "open every fucking day." Where once the object was to guilt non-vegans into this way of life, the new approach—which is working on us, anyway—seems to be scaring the bejesus out of them.

But step inside the store and the Spree-candy-colored walls and hand-drawn signs suggest that this sort of tongue-in-cheek heckling comes from a place of great heart. After all, these are people who demand a world in which no creature suffers for man's appetite for food, prestige, vanity…even sex. Allergic to latex but horrified at the idea of a lambskin condom? Food Fight's got your back.

Also, you can find vegan items many people don't realize are even made vegan: marshmallows, jerky, and pet food. Yes, pet food. Veterinarian and philosophical concerns aside, it's there, and although the prices are a touch high, by shopping here, you're making a locally conscious move as well as a cruelty-free one. Oh, the good feelings!

Fratelli Cucina

The focus here might be on your date or the food, depending on the night

7.8	9.0	8.0
Food	Feel	Wine

Italian

Casual restaurant

$40
Price

www.fratellicucina.com

Sun–Thu 5pm–9pm
Fri–Sat 5pm–10pm

Bar Beer, wine, liquor
Credit cards Visa, MC, AmEx
Reservations Accepted
Date-friendly, live music, outdoor dining, veg-friendly

Pearl District
1230 NW Hoyt St.
(503) 241-8800

Fratelli has that cool, secretive thing going for it. Hidden on a side street, it's only given away by its orange door and small sign. Inside that door is what might be one of the most romantic restaurants in Portland. You enter through a narrow, brightly colored hallway. If necessary, you can wait for a table in the small bar area, next to the open kitchen. In the bright light of an early summer evening, the dining room is fairly ordinary, but once it gets dark, it becomes much more dramatic. Weathered-looking concrete walls are softened by floor-to-ceiling drapes that also absorb the sound. Old wooden tables and chairs with well-placed area rugs add to the effect. Dim candle-lighting makes for a deeply intimate space.

The menu changes by season, making use of local produce wherever it can. But execution is less than consistent. Celeriac and potato gnocchi with blue cheese, pine nuts, and Napa cabbage, a dish no longer on the menu, has been heavy and comforting, if a notch too salty. Risotti are usually superb. One version had a bright, fresh basil flavor, just like a good pesto. On another night, it was an oven-baked prep with mascarpone cheese and deeply fragrant truffle oil, which we found really annoying.

Pastas are a mixed bag. On one visit, a special featuring delicate orecchiette and smoky, good pancetta was the best dish of the night. Another night, beef ravioli drowned in a very heavy, soupy sauce. The beef was odd-tasting and choked by a fair amount of connective tissue—virtually inedible. When filled with smoked chicken and goat cheese, however, the well-made ravioli worked beautifully.

Although good-quality local meats are used, they're often overcooked, such as a Carlton Farms pork loin in an ineffectual pomegranate sauce. And while a duck with roasted rhubarb and black currant demi-glace had an interesting combination of flavors, it, too, was overdone. (At press time, neither duck nor pork were on the menu.)

Wines are interesting and very reasonably priced, highlighting various regions of Italy. Rare is the bottle over $40, and the staff is exceedingly knowledgeable about the choices. Desserts are as inconsistent as everything else.

We really want to like this place. It's lovely, friendly, and the kitchen clearly cares about what it does. It's just that the food won't exactly steal focus from your date. Maybe that's not such a bad thing.

Fubonn Supermarket

An Asian megamart that has its pros and cons—but at what prices!

Groceries, Pan-Asian, Seafood

Market

www.fubonn.com

Daily 9am–8pm

Bar Beer, wine
Credit cards Visa, MC
Veg-friendly

82nd Avenue Area
2850 SE 82nd Ave.
(503) 517-8899

This galaxy-sized supermarket in the heart of Chinatown is a bit of a pain. It's in an out-of-the-way neighborhood to which you usually only go for a good bowl of pho. The service is legendary for being rude (bring cash if you plan to only pick up a few things; there's a draconian minimum policy). And there's that distinctive seafood-and-organ-meat smell to contend with. But once you're used to it (it's *nothing* compared to the smell of China's fish markets in summer—consider it a breath of authenticity), there are aisles upon aisles of Chinese and Southeast Asian ingredients to tempt and inspire you.

Japanese goods aren't well represented here—for that, go to Beaverton's lovely, but also very expensive Uwajimaya—but almost every other major Asian cuisine is represented here: Thai, Laotian, Vietnamese, Korean, Malaysian, and Indonesian. And if it seems like everything is laid out in an utterly random, chaotic way, it's not exactly true; aisles are grouped by region, so you may find duplicates of certain products.

Produce is decent, but be prepared for dirt and bugs—there aren't the fancy timed sprayers that American stores employ to keep things looking glossy and creepy-crawly free. Some prepared foods, like banh mi, are pretty good, but not worth a stop if you aren't shopping here. Have lunch at Malay Satay Hut, inside the same mall, or next door's Koji Osakaya instead.

Meat and seafood selections are perfunctory, and leave something to be desired—especially if you're concerned with cruelty-free, sustainable fishing and ranching. And keep in mind that not much English is spoken here. Just point and try to work it out (imagine you're vacationing in China).

And don't forget to roam around the cheap housewares for some fun dishware and odd utensils, and to peruse the toiletries aisle for eccentric packaging.

Garden State

A tiny trailer serving great Italian street food and sandwiches

7.5 Food

7.5 Feel

Italian, Sandwiches

Food cart

$10 Price

www.gardenstatecart.com

Daily 11am–3:30pm

Bar None
Credit cards None
Outdoor dining, veg-friendly

Sellwood
SE 13th Ave. and SE Lexington St.
(503) 705-5273

Garden State is a thimble of a food cart, but it turns out Italian street food that's big on flavor. The little aluminum trailer is typically simple, with just a few tables and chairs in its gravel lot and a cooler of sodas and waters. This mostly residential part of Sellwood makes for a friendly neighborhood ambience, as well a postprandial walk to some of the coolest antique stores in the city.

Vegetarians will find just as much to love here as will meatier appetites. Arancini, a Sicilian dish, are golf-ball-sized spheres of fried saffrony risotto, each filled with an oozy dollop of mozzarella and surprisingly free of grease. A meaty ragù or vegetarian tomato sauce is served on the side so you can opt for meat or no meat. A fried chickpea "fillet" works well on a sandwich of crusty but yielding ciabatta bread with a carrot-radish slaw, lemony-garlicky aïoli, and gently sweet delicata squash.

Some sandwiches flirt with cross-culturalism, including a plentiful meatball sub with nicely toasted edges and a spicy tomato sauce. A "Cuban Vacation," a take on the cubano, is packed with slow-cooked, shredded pork and a tangy green-tomato chutney. Mustard and sour cream help to moisten the pork so the ciabatta is nice and soaked by the last bite.

Soups change frequently, and salads can be added for just a few bucks more. Chickpea fries are also terrific and, at just a couple bucks a pop, one of the best deals in town.

This would be a great meal anywhere in the city, but this stretch of Sellwood is particularly lucky to have it for refueling while antiquing.

Genies

A friendly rock-and-roll vibe to accompany some decent breakfast favorites

7.1	8.0
Food	Feel

American

Casual restaurant

$20
Price

www.geniescafepdx.com

Daily 8am–3pm

Bar Beer, wine, liquor
Credit cards Visa, MC, AmEx
Reservations Not accepted
Veg-friendly

Division/Clinton
1109 SE Division Street
(503) 445-9777

Genies Café (spelled correctly, as in a gaggle of genies) is a tatted-up and dressed-down breakfast and lunch spot with strong Bloody Marys; well-made cappuccinos served in cute, white cups; and serviceable food. The look of the place is pretty nonspecific, benign enough not to aggravate any hangovers. It's nice, but not crisp and corporate-looking; shabby, but not dirty.

Local ingredients make up the all-American dishes here: Viande sausages and hams; farm-fresh, cage-free eggs; Carlton Farms applewood-smoked bacon; Stumptown Coffee; and so forth. The result is something that's familiar, but capable of excellence if the kitchen is on that day. Eggs Benedict come in a few variations, including vegetarian ones, and are usually expertly poached with a lightly citrusy homemade hollandaise. But scrambles can be runny and sloppy, with some elements a little undercooked. Spicy roasted potatoes are a crapshoot, sometimes hot and sometimes old and cold.

The staff will totally accommodate you if that's the case, but you might be tempted just to shut up and put up so as not to inconvenience them. Not because they're rude; quite the opposite. Servers are mellow, but sincerely personable. In fact, these likeable girls probably get a lot of Facebook friend requests from stalky customers. Don't be that stalky customer.

Even sweeter than the service is French toast made with ciabatta, which can get rubbery; it's a lot of work for a morning meal. Opt instead for silky griddle cakes, especially the version with local toasted hazelnuts and chocolate chips. The texture is as much fun as the lightly sweet, nutty taste. If you like Nutella but the idea of eating a thick glob of it for breakfast turns you off, this is the cake for you.

At lunch, a burger is good (better ordered medium-rare). A roasted-veggie-and-Portobello sandwich manages to be neither slimy nor messy, held together by some cream cheese. We'd still rather something other than the spongy focaccia bread it comes on, but it's fine. Homemade daily-changing soups like creamy corn chowder are even better, as are large salads full of fresh ingredients.

Bloody Marys are practically salads, full of extra celery, hot peppers, and green olives. Beyond this, there's a lot of fruity sweetness on the cocktail menu. An "Emergen-C Elixir" is total nonsense, as the energy-dampening and immunosuppressive effects of orange vodka cancel out the popular multivitamin powder. But if you take things like this too seriously, then Genies isn't for you, anyway.

Gilt Club

An over-the-top atmosphere where the late-night food is better than you'd expect

7.3	9.0	8.5
Food	Feel	Drinks

Modern

Upmarket restaurant

$60
Price

www.giltclub.com

Mon–Sat 5pm–2am

Bar Beer, wine, liquor
Credit cards Visa, MC, AmEx
Reservations Accepted
Date-friendly, outdoor dining,
Wi-Fi

Old Town Chinatown
306 NW Broadway
(503) 222-4458

Gilt Club tries to be many things to many people. Its great beverage program and David Lynchish fetish for red drapes make it a popular lounge, and the late-night availability of ambitious dishes makes it a foodie-night-owl hangout. Nice-looking sidewalk tables are a pleasant, low-key place to imbibe cocktails made with homemade bitters and infusions, but you can also head inside for a dramatic, upscale dining experience. The ostentatious décor is a little Vegas-slutty with its undulating lines, a flat-screen TV over the bar, and oversized booths, but we dig the unusual, bold accents such as chandeliers that look like snare drums blooming from a vine.

In fact, the propensity for making diners feel overwhelmed yet wealthy—like an heiress on LSD—is in every move, from the comically enormous menus that pile up at tiny two-tops, to a daunting selection of small plates that combine trendy ingredients with local ones. Most of these are better than you'd expect from a place that is packed at 1am, yet they hardly compete with those at Portland's more reputable upmarket restaurants.

A beet salad, at one visit, was a little pedestrian, but it came dressed with a superlative pear vinaigrette. French fries are addictive, properly thin, crispy, and well salted. Their accompanying mango-red pepper ketchup was gimmicky and sweet; better is the replacement of roasted garlic aïoli. Meats are generally well executed, like flatiron steak and (seasonal) venison chops, though the latter has come with a Bing cherry sauce that overwhelmed their natural, lightly sweet flavor. Accompaniments are superb, though, like Brussels sprouts and an apple-sweet potato purée. Their burger, made with local beef, is among the best late night choices in Portland, moist and flavorful.

Seafood is sometimes less impressive. Pan-seared Alaskan halibut has come dry and overcooked atop a cold tarragon-French-bean salad with brown butter, and smothered in a dense sprinkling of chopped hazelnuts. It was a melée in which no flavors won. The latest prep is olive-oil poached with a "bouillabaisse" of tomato water, shellfish, garlic fingerling potatoes, leeks, basil oil, and saffron aïoli—another busy dish.

Everything from classic craft cocktails to modern twists are well executed, even if tableside shaking is a misguided practice. A good selection of well-made wines and beers is reasonably priced. Plus, you can indulge in foie gras after most other restaurants have closed. How rich is *that*?

Gino's

A cozy, kitschy neighborhood restaurant with heritage

7.9	8.5	8.5
Food	Feel	Wine

Italian, Modern

Casual restaurant

$40
Price

www.ginossellwood.com

Mon–Thu 4pm–10pm
Fri–Sat 4pm–11pm
Sun 4pm–9pm

Bar Beer, wine, liquor
Credit cards Visa, MC, AmEx
Reservations Accepted
Date-friendly, outdoor dining

Sellwood
8051 SE 13th Ave.
(503) 233-4613

Even though it's only been around since 1996, Gino's reminds us of the old-school Italian-American joints that have peppered New England and the tri-state for decades. The red-sauce, red-checkered-tablecloth look is endearing, but usually a sign that the most authentically Italian element you can expect to find will be on the wine list.

The craftsman feel of this cozy little joint really fits the Sellwood neighborhood. The old, ornate bar was salvaged by the owners from Back East—for a good story, ask about it. You could certainly bring a date here, but only if he or she appreciates florid kitsch.

Although this is a menu of American conceits like Caesar salad and cioppino, the former comes with a fearless load of garlic and the latter isn't that far removed from seafood stews that vary regionally around the Mediterranean. This one is pleasantly surprising, less watery than some more mundane versions, loaded with seafood and saffron. We still prefer the more intense broth in a starter of mussels, which you will want to sop up with lots of extra bread.

Other dishes have even less to do with Italian cuisine, but are great in their own right. Dry-aged, free-range steaks are seasoned and cooked as well as they would be at a respectable steakhouse, and gleefully underpriced. Do take advantage. Sustainable fish are aptly paired with interesting flavors like a chutney of green olives, celery, and apples. Don't miss "Grandma Jean's," a comforting stew of tomatoes, pork rib meat, beef, and pepperoni. It's every bit as charming as a grandmotherly invention, and without any need for polite nods and tight-lipped smiles. Besides, when in Rome…

We appreciate the very thorough list of Italian wines—from the big regions like Piedmont and Tuscany, mostly—with low markups. Beers on tap cover all the niches from Guinness to Bud to local brews; and classic cocktails are done competently. In a refreshingly authentic move, Gino's resists the urge to make a bitter negroni sweeter.

While Gino's advertises itself with enough Italian words and sentiments about family history to make it seem legit, that's not really the point; it finds plenty more legitimacy in making delicious the cuisine of Italian immigrants, tweaked and altered for the New World.

Gold Garden Seafood

Flopping fresh seafood in an authentically Chinese space

8.0	6.0
Food	Feel

Chinese

Casual restaurant

$30
Price

Mon–Fri 10am–midnight
Sat–Sun 9:30am–midnight

Bar Beer, wine
Credit cards Visa, MC
Reservations Accepted

Far East Portland
1818 SE 122nd Ave.
(503) 777-3399

This excellent Cantonese restaurant, which relocated from the space now occupied by the also-excellent Ocean City, suffers from the classic plight of Chinese food in America: segregation between the English-speaking minority and the Chinese-speaking majority, and the resulting obfuscation of the kitchen's best work from those not in the loop.

Gold Garden's cavernous modern room is standard for the genre, with fish tanks full of lobsters and crabs, big round banquet-style tables, and gaudy (by American standards) displays of gilded dragons and purple felt. The staff doesn't speak much English, but they're friendly enough. Dim sum carts roll around even on weekdays.

The problem is, if you come for lunch, you'll be handed a totally lame English-language menu full of Chinese-American dishes that (for good reason) aren't even translated into Chinese. Turn your attention, instead, to the secret Chinese menus that (for no good reason) aren't translated into English; these are posted on the back wall next to the fish tanks and on an easel to the left of the door when you walk in. You'll have to ask the staff to translate for you, and they'll probably do so poorly.

But hidden treasures await there. The day's offerings might be headlined by a dish of duck's blood congealed into deep brown rectangles of slightly metallic, offal-y goodness, offset by scallion and generous slices of fragrant garlic; or stir-fried lobster from the tank, served atop big, thick rolls of tightly wound rice noodle. The dish isn't perfect; the rice noodles have a slight vegetable-oil sheen, and the lobster's glaze is a bit glutinous (too much cornstarch in the dredge?), but the meat is wonderfully tender and the price is beyond reasonable. You might also find pork casserole with pickled greens; abalone and mushroom with vegetable; or Dungeness crab from the tank covered with mountains of deep brown fried garlic slices, as it is often served in Hong Kong.

The printed menu is so extensive that you never know what's fresh or what's available, but at least it's translated, and it's full of hard-to-find treats as geoduck two ways (the first course steamed, the second braised with garlic or XO sauce); braised pigeon; jellyfish with soy sauce. Winter melon, fish maw, pork intestine, mustard greens, and salted egg all work their ways into the spectacular array of soups. An entire half-page of the menu is devoted to conch, a half-page to duck; and yet another half-page to sea cucumber and abalone.

Not all of this is good, but Gold Garden is a rare treat in the Portland area—a chance, for a night, to eat as the Chinese do.

Good Neighbor Market

A legit Russian gastronom in the Asian part of town

Groceries

Market

Mon–Sat 10am–9pm
Sun 11am–7pm

Bar None
Credit cards Visa, MC

82nd Avenue Area
4107 SE 82nd Ave.
(503) 771-5171

Good Neighbor is a lovely Russian market, its wares enough to overwhelm anyone who's spent time in the motherland with nostalgia. From the gruff staff (not mean, or rude, just gruff, and just like you find in Russia) to the Cyrillic writing that peppers the place, this is the real deal. And what's great about Good Neighbor is that the shop is engaging in much more than wholesale merchandising; some goods, including five types of bread, are made here on the premises.

And how about these prices? At last check, sour cabbage was being sold at 29 cents per pound.

Tvorog, commonly—though not particularly helpfully—translated as farmer's cheese, is delightful, slightly sweet and texturally just right. Ryazhenka, a cooked cultured milk, is also in the refrigerator, and it's thought by many Russians to be a healthier alternative to cheese and the like. Speaking of cheese, there's a very large selection here. Butter is exciting, too, with four different brands from Russia available. And they've got Kiev cake (don't feel too guilty if you skip this one).

Adjika, a flavoring paste commonly used in the Caucuses, is an exciting find; its main ingredients are hot peppers, garlic, and a number of other savory herbs like (surprise, surprise) dill. There's also kvas, an only slightly alcoholic beverage made from the fermentation of rye bread.

But the real magic is found in the glass case of smoked fishes; there are at least ten types, including some succulent herring. Dried whole fish is another treat, best with a beer to counteract the saltiness. Malossol caviar is surprisingly affordable at $38 per tin.

But, whatever you do, don't miss the Borjomi, a bottled water from Georgian springs that's gently fizzy and just a bit salty. Many, ourselves included, swear by it as a hangover-kicker.

Good Taste

Look past the Cantonese-American classics for some healing, hearty fare

8.1	6.5
Food	Feel

Chinese

Casual restaurant

$15
Price

Daily 10am–8pm
Hours vary by location

Bar None
Credit cards Visa, MC
Reservations Not accepted

Old Town Chinatown
18 NW 4th Ave.
(503) 223-3838

82nd Avenue Area
8220 SE Harrison St.
(503) 788-6909

Hillsboro
7525 SE Tualatin Valley Hwy.
(503) 718-7452

This busy little fledgling empire of family-run restaurants is growing perhaps faster than it can handle. Its newest location in Hillsboro is plagued by befuddled staff and sloppy service. Some dishes sit in the window for a good long while, congealing under the heat of the lights and getting good and…seasoned. At the Old Town Chinatown location, lunch crowds pack into crammed-together tables, and everything flows very smoothly. But at off-hours, both the neighborhood and restaurant feel like a depressing ghost town.

Nonetheless, it's a total Chinese hit, beginning with the great porridges. This is decidedly Cantonese-style congee, like a soupy risotto, best with more strongly flavored meats like tripe and barbecued duck, and even better with a salty, funky preserved egg. Cold and hungry and feeling generally blah? This will fix you right up.

Stay away from General Tso's and chow mein; these mid-century Chinese-American dishes rear their ugly heads here. But we won't even rate Good Taste based on these, because even the menu lets you know the main events are the subtle and heavenly soups, which might feature homemade wontons, scallion, and a restrained sheen of chicken fat. Barbecued pork and duck are good, though. But best of all are the soul-warming soups. On a cold night, you're in good hands.

Grand Central Bakery

Serviceable sandwiches served with warm bread and chilly service

Baked goods, Sandwiches

Counter service

$15
Price

www.grandcentralbakery.com

Mon–Fri 7am–7pm
Sat–Sun 7am–6pm
Hours vary by location

Bar None
Credit cards Visa, MC, AmEx
Kid-friendly, outdoor dining, veg-friendly

Northeast Portland
1444 NE Weidler St.
(503) 288-1614

Northwest Portland
2249 NW York St.
(503) 235-6323

Northeast Portland
714 N. Fremont St.
(503) 546-5311

Additional locations
and more features at
www.fearlesscritic.com

There are a few elite bakeries in Portland supplying several restaurants with their breads, and Grand Central is one of them. It's got about a half dozen of its own stores throughout Portland, and a few more at the farmer's markets; it's even a presence in Seattle. All locations feel pretty warm, if a little chain-ish, but perhaps owing to its expansion, the bakery seems to have lost some of its personality. Attitude is a constant complaint at some locations, and we've seen customers get kicked out at exactly 6pm.

Compared to the breathtaking breads at Ken's and Pearl, other bakeries famous for their widespread availability in acclaimed Portland restaurants, Grand Central's are just good. They make for some okay sandwiches, and some strangely substandard ones, as well. Breakfast is troubling, with a ham-and-cheese croissant that has been served unfortunately cold, with an overly sweet honey-mustard sauce and a snotty retort when asked for it warmed up; another time, a breakfast sandwich seemed to be more roll than egg and bacon. But "Jammers," flaky biscuits filled with homemade jam, are undeniably addictive.

Grilled cheese is best, but chicken salad and even regular turkey sandwiches are skimpy on fillings. Which is just insulting when you're creeping towards the $10 mark for lunch. And while leek and Gruyère tarts are quite good, sweets like macaroons and cookies are a bit tough and unremarkable. Homemade soups are often great, though.

Despite its relative mediocrity, Grand Central has garnered a loyal following, which it doesn't seem to appreciate—at least, the service staff doesn't. We can tolerate pretty good bread, but we can't stand it served so cold(ly).

Gravy

A hipster homage to the greasy spoon

6.1	8.0
Food	Feel

American, Southern

Casual restaurant

$25
Price

Daily 8am–3pm

Bar Beer, wine, liquor
Credit cards Visa, MC, AmEx
Reservations Not accepted
Veg-friendly

Mississippi Ave. Area
3957 N. Mississippi Ave.
(503) 287-8800

Sweet, genteel Gravy used to have an accordion player, which helped give it one of the best breakfast vibes in the city. Now you'll just have to settle for the fact that it features local, organic produce to make hearty, veg-friendly breakfast and lunch classics.

If none of this gets you, maybe the décor will. The walls host really intriguing art from locals, and an eclectic array of textiles and paraphernalia. The staff is Mississippi cool, which means they often get the job done, but won't always do it with a smile.

Which is a good thing for Gravy, because the bulk of its dishes are just so-so. Even interesting-sounding scrambles are clumsy, coming as a huge pile of watery eggs and bland cheese. Those with tomatoes are particularly troublesome. But the eponymous breakfast element here is a flavorful brown version that isn't too heavy, with lots of salty, crumbled sausage and airy biscuits. Even the veggie version is quite good. Hash browns are wonderfully crunchy on the outside, fried as a nest with a middle that can be undercooked.

Generally, it's a pretty high-calorie place: omelettes with sausage gravy; an unusual (and unnecessary) fatty ribeye steak and eggs; and chicken-fried steak and eggs. Oatmeal brûlée is as sweet as it sounds, but damned good if you're in that mood. You can build your own egg dishes from a wide array of veggies and cheeses, and you could even substitute tofu, but then you'd be missing the point of Gravy.

Bloody Marys here are strong and good, and the Mississippi crowd lines up on weekends to replenish its permanent BAC levels, which makes for great indie-fashion watching and scruffy-beard evaluating. With Gravy at the center of this neighborhood's breakfast universe, we have to wonder how everyone fits into those skinny jeans.

Green Dragon

An unsung beer hero, with some of the best craft brews in the city

6.4 Food

8.5 Feel

9.5 Beer

American

Casual restaurant

$25 Price

www.pdxgreendragon.com

Sun–Wed 11am–9pm
Thu–Sat 11am–10pm

Bar Beer, wine, liquor
Credit cards Visa, MC, AmEx
Reservations Accepted
Live music, outdoor dining

Southeast Portland
928 SE 9th Ave.
(503) 517-0606

Since Portland's Green Dragon Bistro and Brewpub opened in 2007, it has become an integral part of the craft beer scene, serving a steadily changing menu of beers on 19 taps. The space is divided into a small restaurant side and a large converted warehouse. In the warehouse, there are two bars—a main bar and a secondary bar that's used for the pub's frequent special events. The bar space also hosts a shuffleboard table and several well-maintained pinball machines. Brewing operations have recently commenced, but as of this writing are not yet a regular part of the bar's offerings.

In 2008, the pub was purchased by the Eugene-based Rogue Brewery (who also operate an eponymous restaurant in Northwest Portland) over the objections of a minority owner; the resulting dust-up in local media and beer-culture blogs is a testament to the niche the Green Dragon had found for itself. A year later, there is little evidence of the transfer. While the menu has shifted from Dutch- and Belgian-themed cuisine to a vaguely Southern approach, the tap list retains its characteristic diversity—on our last visit, only a single tap was pouring Rogue's fine Old Crustacean barley wine.

The tap selection is international and covers a wider range of styles than most serious beer destinations. Strong ales and barley wines seem to get a significant portion of the list; it's not uncommon for a third or more of the beers offered to be served in 8-ounce pours instead of pints. Taps change with sufficient frequency that no attempt is made to print the list; a half-dozen chalkboards around the venue list current selections as well as the next ten or so beers "on deck."

Food is unimaginative, but it's a passable accompaniment in its secondary role supporting the beer list. Belgian-style fries can't compare to those offered by the nearby Potato Champion food cart, but make a solid contribution to the selection of $3 happy hour/late night plates.

Visitors should be aware that the Green Dragon regularly hosts beer-culture events and meetings; these events frequently feature rare or new brews and can draw large crowds. While the bar is spacious enough (and often even expanded to the back bar) to accomodate a standing-room-only crowd of drinkers, the staffing levels for table service and food preparation are not always adequate, and food service can be a frustrating and slow affair.

Grilled Cheese Grill

The elemental pleasure of one of America's most time-tested recipes

6.1 Food | **7.0** Feel

American

Food cart | **$5** Price

www.grilledcheesegrill.com

Tue–Thu 11:30am–9pm
Fri–Sat 11:30am–2:30am
Sun 11:30am–3:30pm

Bar None
Credit cards Visa, MC
Outdoor dining, veg-friendly

Northeast Portland
1027 NE Alberta Ave.
(503) 206-8959

We're not sure how to call this...establishment. It's definitely not a brick-and-mortar type of place; nor is it exactly a food cart. Rather, it's a bus. Which is what ultimately takes the experience of eating a grilled cheese sandwich as a grown adult to a new level.

Now, imagine that you're sitting out in front of in this (albeit stationary) bus, eating a grilled cheese sandwich, and working on a pretty nice buzz. The Grilled Cheese Grill is open until 2:30am on weekends, leaving enough time for Portland's bar-going population to squeeze in some food after last call—and any experienced drinker will know that nothing sops up excess alcohol like grease, bread, and cheese.

The grasp these guys have on the humor of said situation is evident in their nomenclature of the "classic" grilled cheese sandwiches. There's the "Kindergartner," their name for a simple grilled cheese; the "Pre-Schooler," which comes with the crusts cut off (whose only value is the name—the culinary concept doesn't make any sense); and the "First Grader," with your choice of add-on, such as avocado or bacon.

Our complaint, however, is with the choice of cheese (which is a pretty important choice after all). The "Gabby" comes with cheddar, colby, jack, swiss, and mozzarella cheeses, but they don't blend well; the mozzarella turns out too stringy, stealing thunder from the cheddar. Bread is the best part, as it gets an ideal buttered browning from the griddle.

A cup of tomato soup will set you back $2.50, but the nostalgia is worth it. Remember the days when Mom made grilled cheese and you dipped it in your soup? For some, it was decades ago, but it's a combo that still works.

Um, and there's also the issue of the "Cheesus Burger," which is just like any other burger, except that, instead of being sandwiched in between two buns, the meat patty is held together by two grilled cheese sandwiches. Heart-attack jokes aside, this is actually the best thing on the menu. Sometimes keeping it over the top beats keeping it simple.

Hae Rim

Approachable, safe Korean, but Beaverton can be even better

7.4 Food   **7.5** Feel

Korean

Casual restaurant   **$20** Price

Mon–Sat 11am–10pm
Sun 1pm–9pm

Bar Beer, wine
Credit cards Visa, MC
Reservations Accepted

Beaverton
11729 SW Beaverton-
Hillsdale Hwy.
(503) 671-9725

Maybe by virtue of being lauded by local media and perhaps, too, because of its highly trafficked Beaverton Town Square mall location, this place has more of a mixed white-and-Korean clientele than some of the better, more interesting Korean restaurants in Beaverton. It's cute and cozy, lined with soothing wood, but nothing about the atmosphere is particularly enticing. It stays cleanly in the inexpensive-ethnic genre.

With no pretenses of stylishness, the draw here is strictly the Korean food, which newcomers find surprisingly accessible, once they accept that most everything is a stew, porridge, soup, cake, or barbecued meat. Pickled and fermented items in the banchan tend to grow on patrons, who love having anything free to munch on while they wait for their orders. It's a delicious and wonderfully inexpensive cuisine—qualities that are going to generate success for nearly any hole in the wall. But as Korean restaurants go, this one is just somewhere between serviceable and pretty good.

There are some welcome menu highlights: rich samgyub kimchi bokum (stir-fried pork belly with kimchi and tofu), competent preparations of stir-fried octopus and dduk mandoogook (rice-cake-and-dumpling soup), altang (codfish egg in hot-and-spicy stew), and doenjang chigae (soybean-paste soup). The barbecue seems an afterthought—avoid it—but mul nang myun (cold noodles in beef broth) and bibim nang myun (spicy buckwheat noodles) are good. The lunch menu pares the already-short selection down to its most Americanized core.

In general, we sense a little hesitation here to make anything as spicy as you say you want it. Bulgogi is sweet, with little kick to it. Even kimchi is toned down a bit. Hae Rim would be great for Portland Korean, but in Beaverton, you can do better than this.

The Heathman

If it walks like a hotel restaurant and quacks like a hotel restaurant...

5.6	6.5	6.0
Food	Feel	Wine

American

Upmarket restaurant

$60
Price

www.heathmanrestaurantandbar.com

Mon–Thu 6:30am–11am,
11:30am–2pm, 5pm–10pm
Fri 6:30am–11am, 11:30am–
2pm, 5pm–11pm
Sat 7am–2pm, 5pm–11pm
Sun 7am–2pm, 5pm–10pm

Bar Beer, wine, liquor
Credit cards Visa, MC, AmEx
Reservations Accepted
Live music, outdoor dining, Wi-Fi

Downtown
1001 SW Broadway Ave.
(503) 790-7752

The Marble Bar. The Tea Court. The Mezzanine Gallery. We're not sure which has more rooms, the Heathman Hotel or its very typical restaurant. In the latter half of the week, the mahogany-paneled tea room and lounge hosts live jazz, and is a much cooler place to spend the later-night happy hour. The other dining areas are generic and stuffy, and the crowd is, ahem, distinguished—the sort of folks who like their soup reheated beyond all reason and flavor. Its bread and butter also seems to be business luncheons. Everyone seems to enjoy the blazing, unflattering lighting (in the main room), white tablecloths, and somewhat haughty service.

Hotel restaurant kitchens are notoriously plagued with excessive turnover—talented cooks and chefs grow bored quickly, their hands tied by the vitriolic attitude that hotels seem to have toward the avant-garde and risky. We're not sure if that's the case here, but the food follows a familiar pattern. The menu reads like a greatest hits album: it pleases the accountants, but it has no art.

The only time the Heathman isn't overpriced and overrated is during its daily happy hour, when it offers over two dozen of its dishes at a sizeable discount. The bistro fare, like Dungeness crab deviled eggs, is best here. Salads are decent, and brunch is just what you would expect from a hotel: classy-looking, classy-sounding, and pretty forgettable. Oysters are well shucked, and meats are cooked to proper temperatures, but platings are generally boring and overwrought, with a copious amount of creamy sauce and butter. Not that there's anything wrong with butter, but with little balance of flavors, it just tastes heavy and monotonous.

Bring Aunt Gladys for a high tea from local microroaster Fonté. She'll love the tiny cucumber sandwiches and pâté, the buttery scones and moist opera cake. Or enjoy some free live jazz with apéritifs and sherries, both of which are better chosen than the rest of the wine list, which is overpriced and boring. And having this many dessert wines by the glass guarantees a high rate of oxidized, stale pours, so don't get too excited. In fact, it's best not to get excited at all; it might upset the rest of the crowd.

Helser's on Alberta

Quail eggs, good friends, and easy listening—now that's breakfast

7.3	7.5
Food	Feel

American

Casual restaurant

$15
Price

www.helsersonalberta.com

Daily 7am–3pm

Bar Beer, wine, liquor
Credit cards Visa, MC
Reservations Accepted
Date-friendly, outdoor dining

Alberta Arts District
1538 NE Alberta St.
(503) 281-1477

It's hard not to curse appreciatively while reading Helser's menu: Dutch baby, sweet-potato hash, Scotch quail eggs. Do you know how hard it is to find a good Scotch quail egg these days? There's a reason so many people love to take out-of-town visitors here. Well, there are many reasons, actually.

For one thing, it's hard to find a place this friendly for breakfast. For another thing, the space just works. It may not look like much from the outside, in its mint-green-and-tomato-colored brick building or from the inside, for that matter, where it's equally minimalist, with beige walls and a few bamboo plants. And the easy-listening soundtrack is a little uneventful. But it's spacious, which means you won't be sitting on your neighbor's lap like you do at so many other breakfast joints. This is breakfast the easy way.

Most dishes on this menu sound terrific, look rustic and homemade, and taste just fine. A perfectly poached egg is a thing of rare beauty and skill. The ones here are quivering pearls that burst eagerly with warm yolk just a second after being prodded. They can top hashes of lightly seasoned potatoes, cooked to a slight crispness with no overcooked stragglers. They're also perched atop Benedicts, like a moist and creamy smoked salmon version that costs half what it would elsewhere.

Balance these out with sweeter breakfast items like pear-and-havarti pie, brioche French toast soaked in vanilla and cinnamon, and a Dutch baby, baked for 20 minutes to a crispy, deflated balloon of egg fluff, lemon zest, and powdered sugar. Just put butter and lemon on it and nothing else. If the version at Original Pancake House is legendary, this one is an admirable attempt.

But where else can you find Scotch eggs anymore? True, these quail eggs are sometimes too hard-boiled, and wrapped in bratwurst instead of spicy sausage, but the light-handed fry on them is just right. We wish we could get them with a sweetish mustard, which could make them downright addictive.

For a breakfast-crazy town that's seen it all, it's amazing that there aren't more places taking all the hard-to-find favorites and putting their best qualities together. And while we're dreaming, a patio would be great.

Henry's 12th St. Tavern

5.7	7.5	8.5
Food	Feel	Beer

The beer trumps the food at this not-so-Portland institution

American

Upmarket restaurant

$40
Price

www.henrystavern.com

Sun–Thu 11am–11pm
Fri–Sat 11am–midnight

Bar Beer, wine, liquor
Credit cards Visa, MC, AmEx
Reservations Accepted
Outdoor dining

Pearl District
10 NW 12th Ave.
(503) 227-5320

This iconic restaurant-lounge-beer-bar attracts an extremely faithful crowd of Pearl District guppies—that is, half goombas and half yuppies—night after night after night. Its popularity is hardly a surprise, because there is much to like about Henry's: 100 beer taps, most of them local (although the highly touted cider selection disappoints with oversweetness); a glow-in-the-dark vibe; cute boys and girls; and a barroom with real buzz, in spite of the cheeseball house-pop music. And the more hushed restaurant space next door, with great big booths, an open kitchen, and a furtive balcony upstairs, has its own, different charm.

All that said, the *real* reason for the popularity of Henry's is the ridiculously cheap happy-hour bar menu, which is a gift to the Pearl. Beer-cheese soup? $2. A personal-sized pepperoni-and-sausage pizza? $3. A huge baking dish of decent mac and cheese? $2. And happy hour is liberally defined here, so this bargain menu is also available all day Sunday and every day after 10pm. In a tough economy, to dine at these prices in a place that feels even halfway lively and sleek is pretty compelling.

But don't let those facts delude you into thinking that the food is great, because it's not. A cheeseburger, the classic bar dish, comes in a pleasantly oniony roll, but its patty is too thin, and it comes cooked slightly beyond temp, without enough cheese. Still, there's a pleasant beefiness to the beef. Order it with a side of crispy onion rings, which come as a huge, impressive tower.

"Reuben rolls"—like pastrami-and-sauerkraut spring rolls—are a clever idea that fails, missing the compelling melted-Swiss-ness of an actual Reuben sandwich. Instead, the cheese in these rolls is barely perceptible. And deep-frying Reuben ingredients in a wonton skin makes it even more unhealthy than the original, yet simultaneously less satisfying, too. A gloopy Russian-dressing dip adds little.

Over in the main dining room, things get even trickier as the prices go up. An eight-ounce filet mignon with butter, oven-roasted vegetables, and fries is a terrible waste of $35, and chicken with mozzarella and Madeira is just a bad recipe, start to finish, a jumble of mismatched textures and excessive sweetness. And you should know better than to order a dish called "yakisoba garlic noodles" or "Mongolian beef" at an "American Bar & Grill." More direct recipes like meatloaf and fish and chips fare much better. But here, as at the bar, the burger is not what it should be. You're better off hanging out in the other room, because things taste better when they're almost free.

Higgins

A versatile, fun place for good bistro fare and
a brilliant beer selection

7.6	9.5	8.5
Food	Feel	Beer

Modern

Upmarket restaurant

$60
Price

www.higgins.ypguides.net

Mon–Fri 11:30am–10:30pm
Sat–Sun 5pm–10:30pm

Bar Beer, wine, liquor
Credit cards Visa, MC, AmEx
Reservations Accepted
Date-friendly

Downtown
1239 SW Broadway
(503) 222-9070

Higgins is an absolute Portland classic—it's really fun, with a warmly lit interior that aptly walks the line between old-school and old-man. Which, when you think about it, is quite a feat. The dining room bustles with energy, but we prefer the bar in the other room (which serves a bar menu in addition to the regular restaurant menu) because it's so unabashedly time-warpy. A pressed-tin ceiling holds up mahogany-paneled walls (or dusty green, in the other room), and large windows around the kitchen allow for a kind of peep show. The waitstaff is legendary, in an old-world kind of way.

There's an admirable commitment to sustainable, local foods, and Higgins sources directly from farms wherever it can. Plus, the restaurant grows its own vegetables and herbs. How does this all translate onto the plate? Well, it's good. But did we mention how much fun this place is? Just wait until we get to the beer.

Menus change weekly and seasonally, but you can always find Higgins' "famous" open-faced sandwich of house-made pastrami, onions, and sharp white cheddar—yet it's not the kitchen's best work, nor is it even in our top ten for pastrami sandwiches. Mussels are good, but some broth renditions are better than others. Once, they came over-sweetened, tilting too far away from nature's will. A plate of smoked fish was competent, but unremarkable, with only the halibut really standing out.

"Broiled, freshly ground and spiced sirloin on a toasted hearth-baked roll" is an adorable way of saying "cheeseburger." But after a bite, we understand why all the pomp. It's juicy and moist and flavored unlike any old cheeseburger. Anywhere else, this would be pretentious, but here, it's just good ol' Higgins.

The wine list is composed of Northwest and French wines, but features more monotonous-tasting large productions than you'd expect from a place that asserts its commitment to the small and sincere. Almost nothing is under $40. More exciting is the beer selection, which includes Northwest micros, Belgians, British, German, Canadian, Dutch, and so on. About a dozen are on tap, and all are priced fairly.

All of this makes for one jam-packed, lively happy hour scene that rages on until midnight. Yet we also wouldn't think twice about having a romantic anniversary here. Such is the magic of Higgins.

Hiroshi Sushi

The sushi bar is unbeatable, if you avoid the fusion flops and service misfires

8.4 Food **6.5** Feel

Japanese

Upmarket restaurant **$50** Price

Mon 5:30pm–9:30pm; Tue–Fri 11:30am–2pm, 5:30pm–9:30pm; Sat 5:30pm–9:30pm

Bar Beer, wine, liquor, BYO
Credit cards Visa, MC, AmEx
Reservations Accepted
Date-friendly

Pearl District
926 NW 10th Ave.
(503) 619-0580

Hiroshi is elegant and minimalist, which here translates to boring and antiseptic. The floors are hardwood and the lines are simple, but the lone source of visual stimulation comes from a school of silvery metallic fish arranged on the plain wall. Otherwise, it's a bit like the lunch cafeteria at a nice department store. Sit at the sushi bar and chat up the chefs for best results—and that goes for food, too. But it is kind of luck of the draw with regards to which sushi chef you sit in front of; you don't get the same experience with the head guy as you do with the others.

If you do sit at a table, be prepared for variable service; some servers are knowledgeable and attentive while others are forgetful and largely absent. The food can often take an inordinately long time to come out.

Here, as with any other sushi place, you want to order omakase. But how exciting the choices are will vary with your chef. It helps to assert your love of uni gonads and fish heads. Nigiri sushi is mostly successful, fresh-tasting, and, crucially, served at the proper temperature, with judiciously vinegared sushi rice. Wild hamachi belly melts in the mouth, and madai (which is translated alternately as black snapper or sea bream) is astoundingly light and fresh. Cuttlefish, an option at one visit, was served with a shiso leaf whose flavor overwhelmed it somewhat, but the texture was good and bouncy without being cumbersome. Sea urchin is buttermilky and smooth.

Eating bluefin toro may not help us sleep at night—there's just so darn little of it left—but here it's done such justice, such a properly silky square of umami-fat, that we are willing to swallow the guilt (just not much of it). A zuke, or soup, of tuna tartare with dried egg, seaweed, and miso broth is great, and a lightly torched spicy salmon roll is pretty good. But stray too far beyond the traditional and it just gets annoying. We're really unimpressed with the attempts at fusion here, for which you pay a mighty big premium. And the problem is that ordinary omakase might well bring some of those fusion disasters. Try emphasizing the "classic sushi" when you order. Desserts are no better.

Decent nigiri, yes. A full-stop restaurant firing on all cylinders, no.

Horse Brass Pub

Feel yourself British at this lovely pub

7.6	8.5	9.5
Food	Feel	Beer

British

Casual restaurant

$25
Price

www.horsebrass.com

Mon–Fri 11am–2:30am
Sat–Sun 9am–2:30am

Bar Beer, wine, liquor
Credit cards Visa, MC, AmEx
Reservations Not accepted
Live music

Belmont
4534 SE Belmont St.
(503) 232-2202

The Horse Brass Pub is a Portland institution for the soccer-and-darts crowd, offering staple British pub food in a fairly authentic style, alongside a few dozen taps and several decades' worth of lingering tobacco smoke. The dark wood and dense accumulation of British signage make this the ideal place to sit and watch English Premier League football matches—at least for those who can appreciate the carefully maintained anti-atmosphere, which is a casualty of Oregon's adoption of non-smoking laws, even in the darkest and dankest of taverns.

Highlights of the menu include the requisite fish and chips, freshly composed pot pies (turkey, chicken, beef and mushroom, and steak and kidney), scotch eggs, and for vegetarians, a well-composed ploughman's lunch of bread, cheeses, apple, and pickles. The fare is relentlessly authentic: drop in on weekend mornings for a full (and we mean full) English breakfast of potatoes, tomatoes, eggs, bangers, bacon, and beans.

If the food is conventional Brit comfort, the beer list is what makes the Horse Brass a noteworthy corner of Portland. Publican Don Younger, who celebrated his 33rd anniversary as the bar's owner in 2009, has been a gruff but enthusiastic leader of Oregon's craft beer movement since its first days, and it's not uncommon to find specially brewed beers on the tap list (try Rogue's Younger Special Bitter). Staff are well versed in the deep tap list and admirably manage to stay on top of the constant rotations.

Younger also co-founded the nearby Belmont Station, formerly located next door to the pub but now situated a few blocks north on Stark Street. Belmont Station offers one of the deepest selections of beer and cider in Portland (which essentially puts it in competition with the rest of the country), along with a selection of British cuisine essentials like Marmite, PG Tips, and Brown Sauce.

Hot Pot City

A rich variety of soup stuff that you don't even have to share with anyone

7.8 Food **6.5** Feel

Chinese

Casual restaurant

$20 Price

Daily 11:30am–4pm, 5pm–9:30pm

Bar None
Credit cards Visa, MC
Reservations Not accepted
Veg-friendly

Downtown
1975 SW 1st Ave.
(503) 224-6696

Hot Pot City is based on the Taiwanese fad of individual hot pots. A Nobel Peace Prize may be in order just for the number of chopstick fights this concept has broken up. It's cheap and delicious, and now you don't have to share or fight over the last morsel in the broth. What's not to love?

Its proximity to PSU makes this a popular spot for starving students or those on the mend, far from their mother's chicken noodle soup; but it draws all ages and ethnicities. No surprise, it's in a strip mall with an easy-to-spot sign out front. Inside, there are potted plants and bamboo-reed screens, giving the stained ceiling tiles a vaguely transportive look. A long, well-stocked buffet takes up one wall and is full of all your hot-pot ingredient needs, and those you didn't even know you needed.

You first choose your soup base: vegetarian, beef stock, spicy Korean with kimchi, hot lemongrass Thai, or a ma la version full of Szechuan peppercorns and hot chilies. There's even a totally authentic preserved-egg-and-cilantro broth that's exquisitely funky once you get into it. Then, head to the buffet with a bowl to pile stuff in (you can keep going back). Choose from: wafer-thin slices of beef, chicken, pork, or lamb; meatballs; boneless dark-meat chicken marinated in ginger, onion, and soy sauce; offal; and seafood. There's also tofu, fresh and frozen (freezing tofu turns it spongy and toothsome, like the tofu in some popular Thai dishes, stir-fries, and so on).

Vegetables are pretty seasonal and quite fresh. These come in an impressive range of options, as well, and include mung beans, squash, mushrooms (several kinds), bitter melon, and kimchi. Don't ignore delicacies like head-on shrimp, whelks, squid, scallops still in their shells, raw quail egg and preserved duck egg. It's a total adventure. Pile some on, but just know these cost a little extra.

Then cook, remembering to put veggies in first, as they need more time than meats do. Add eggs and noodles at the very end. Then scoop it out into a bowl. The staff will keep watch on your hot pot, refilling whenever needed and offering tips, which are always welcome.

We'd tell you to ignore the Americanized standards, which are greasy and unremarkable, but then, we doubt anyone would come here for reasons unrelated to the hot pot.

Huber's Restaurant

A museum of Americana dining, in all its glory and shame

4.9	8.0	6.5
Food	Feel	Drinks

American

Casual restaurant

$40
Price

www.hubers.com

Mon–Thu 11:30am–midnight
Fri–Sat 11:30am–1am
Sun 4pm–11pm

Bar Beer, wine, liquor
Credit cards Visa, MC, AmEx
Reservations Accepted
Date-friendly, kid-friendly, outdoor dining

Downtown
411 SW 3rd Ave.
(503) 228-5686

Huber's is the oldest restaurant in Portland, and has done a fine job maintaining the charm of the earliest of its thirteen decades, especially in the back bar: handsome, dark-wood paneling; Gothic arches that jettison the ceiling into an elegant curve reminiscent of New York's famed Oyster Bar at Grand Central; skylights overhead with a distinctly Art Deco pattern.

Old-timey still are the sartorial conceits of the capable bartenders, who wear vests and arm garters as they pour drinks with a flourish. Behind them, you might catch a glimpse of the turn-of-the-century cash register, a weighty and formidable bronze hulk next to the glowing flat screen of a computer terminal.

The latter decades of Huber's life are also apparent, in less-flattering forms. The tables and chairs evoke a 1980s pizza parlor; the front room is nondescript in that 1990s sort of way; plates are of the thick, cheap Denny's-circa-1970 variety. But it is what's on the plates that represents the past that we want to deny more fervently: bland nursing-home vegetables ("du jour"!) and rice pilaf; uninspired and saucy mid-century TV dinners like "Turkey Florentine"; even that tacky little sprig of curly parsley, which could be retro chic if it weren't garnishing a mushy breaded cutlet swimming in salty goo.

But if you grew up in America, you'll recognize—perhaps fondly—the Thanksgiving homage played out on this menu all year long. Turkey, baked ham, sage dressing, mashed potatoes, yams, and cranberry sauce? A plate of this sends a single, nostalgic tear trickling down our cheeks, like ratatouille does to the impenetrable Anton Ego, melting all cynicism. The flavors are totally competent and familiar; we admit we are won over.

Or come for the "Spanish Coffee," a strong and delicious concoction of Kahlua, 151, triple sec, and coffee with fresh grated nutmeg that is lit up at your table. It's an event that out-of-town visitors will find absolutely winning (we should hope so, for the nearly $10 ticket price). And as the flames whoosh for one second toward the vaulted ceiling, illuminating briefly the portrait of founder Jim Louie gleefully wielding a carving knife, you understand what it is—and has been for a hundred years—to be an American.

India Chaat House

In this amusing (and sad) War of the Roses, nobody wins

2.5 Food

5.0 Feel

Indian

Food cart

$5 Price

Mon–Sat 11am–7pm

Bar None
Credit cards Visa, MC
Outdoor dining, veg-friendly

Downtown
804 SW 12th St.
(503) 241-7944

As the story goes, this is the famous original truck run by an Indian couple who split acrimoniously. Until then, people really quite enjoyed it. Then, there was a split; the husband went to India; and upon returning, he found that his ex had opened Bombay Chaat House, another truck right by his. At this point, FOX might have picked it up for a hilarious sitcom rife with colorful "ethnic" characters and called it something like "Naansense." But, alas, the husband did what anyone might do in this case: he sold the thing.

In a free-market economy, as the theory goes, competition is supposed to drive up quality and drive down prices. Well, at least half the prediction has come true: the cost here could hardly be any lower. When we discuss the quality of these two carts, though, we remind ourselves of an old couple complaining about their respective ailments.

At both, we've had substandard Southern Indian food, but here, we've had absolutely soggy pakora—some of the worst of our lives; clumpy, boring white rice; a vegetable curry dominated by cauliflower that tasted vaguely winey and fermented, like mushrooms à la grecque; and aloo saag that was ruined by the starchiness of overcooked, crumbly potato blending in with the spinach. Yellow dal is somehow absolutely tasteless. Even naan (if it hasn't run out) is yeasty and undercooked. The list goes on.

We feel bad for anyone coming here with no previous exposure to the wonderful flavors and textures of all-vegetarian South Indian cuisine. It can be better, we assure you. The seating area here is nicer, and the tendrils of incense are a little transportive (and can substitute for the food's lack of flavor), but really, you're better off leaving the parking lot. The free Chai tea is a nice gesture, but it doesn't make this cart worthwhile, nor does the promise of dramatic tension. We say that your safest bet is to avoid both of these chaat carts—the story's the only thing in this parking lot with any good flavor.

Iorio

Italian with heart and a commitment to all things local

6.8	8.5	7.0
Food	Feel	Wine

Italian

Upmarket restaurant

$50
Price

www.ioriorestaurant.com

Tue–Sat 5pm–9pm

Bar Beer, wine, liquor
Credit cards Visa, MC, AmEx
Reservations Accepted
Date-friendly

Hawthorne
912 SE Hawthorne Blvd.
(503) 445-4716

Iorio, so named after the matriach of this family, is a self-described "southern Italian" restaurant. We're not fans of this habit of dividing Italy along north/south lines; many people seem to be under the impression that red-sauce Italian-American (e.g. spaghetti and meatballs) is Southern Italian—it's not—or that Italian protein mains like saucy veal chops are Northern Italian—they're not.

Regardless, this is a warm, romantic eatery, not such a far cry from what you'd find in Italy today (north *or* south!), that serves simple, yet elegantly prepared fare. Iorio is not out to impress with esoteric design; rather, it allows the food to take center stage. Red walls and artwork create a cozy, enveloped feeling, while a bar in the back offers a slightly less formal seating option. The dining room only has 12 tables, so make sure to have a reservation in place. And Iorio herself? Her wedding photos are displayed in an alcove.

Service is attentive and friendly—it's not uncommon to see the chef making the rounds to ensure that everything was satisfactory. Wine offerings are reasonably priced, but it's not an extensive list. That said, we must applaud them for their focus on Willamette Valley wines from Portland's backyard.

Despite the restaurant's proclaimed vegetarian friendliness, the offerings tend toward meats and cream sauces, as in a recent soup of the day: cream of Brussels sprouts. In general, the menu tends towards heavy foods, such as a hearty and generous lamb ragout.

Calamari (billed as "wild-caught") are unspectacular, their preserved-lemon aïoli not quite living up to its promise in prose. A recent fish-of-the-day prep was delicate cod, richly sauced, yet not overpowering. This we give a thumbs up. We like the generous cheese plate, which comes with delicious fruit condiments. But thumbs down to focaccia, which is dry, disappointing, and processed-tasting, like what you find at an airport café. Its accompanying pumpkin butternut squash spread is inventive, but not enough to save it.

Iorio does make accomodations for gluten-free diets, and what they call "age appropriate" requests (Get your NC-17 food here! It's barely legal...). Prices are a bit high for this part of Portland, but they're still reasonable. Buon appetito.

Jake's

Two fun, festive seafood experiences that couldn't be
more touristy if they sold postcards

4.7	8.5
Food	Feel

Seafood, American

Upmarket restaurant

$50
Price

www.mccormickandschmicks.com

Mon–Thu 11:30am–10pm
Fri–Sat 11:30am–midnight
Sun 3pm–10pm
Hours vary by location

Bar Beer, wine, liquor
Credit cards Visa, MC, AmEx
Reservations Accepted
Date-friendly, outdoor dining

Downtown
611 SW 10th Ave.
(503) 220-1850

Downtown
401 SW 12th Ave.
(503) 226-1419

At first blush, you might not notice that Jake's Grill and Jake's Famous
Crawfish form parts of the McCormick & Schmick's chain. That's not quite
as terrible a fact as it might sound: McCormick's is one of the least of
chain evils, and the company actually makes some effort to source fish
locally. Plus, they have a penchant for theming. The two Jake's branches
have a fun old-school vibe, with clubby dark woods, tablecloths, older
male waiters, and brass accents. They're the sorts of places into which, on
a cold day, visitors to town are easily lured by promises of warm air and
caricatured local nostalgia.

One of the branches, Jake's Grill, is located on the bottom floor of the
historic Governor's Hotel and looks absolutely charming from the outside,
like an above-ground Cheers. Inside, though, the carpet is unmistakably
hotelesque, busy and in dark hues, and a huge sepia-tone mural depicts a
placid, friendly scene between Native Americans and what appears to be
Davy Crockett. Jake's Crawfish, meanwhile, is kind of San-Francisco-
Fisherman's-Wharf precious. It's cozier and less opulent, but with just as
much wood and stained glass. The bar is old-timey and well stocked. Your
bow-tied bartender can mix up a classic martini (gin, of course) just as
well as he can a goofy, gross appletini. It's the sort of diplomatic
hospitality required of touristy places like these.

And touristy it is: overcooked, underwhelming, and remarkably
overpriced seafood. Everything has this tacky "meat and two veg" sheen
to it, which is especially disappointing when you discover the two veg
appear to be of the Green Giant variety. Over-buttered, wilting green
beans and julienned carrots, and the like. Skip the fish fillet preps at all
costs; shellfish tends to perform better here, and that's really part of the
show anyway. Crack open a whole Dungeness crab, served only at the
Jake's Crawfish location, which looks like a heaping red monster trying to
feed itself on your bland white rice. (Have at it, crab.) And what fun it is
to delight your tablemates by ripping tails off the boiled crawfish and
imploring them to try sucking the heads.

The whole scene looks like a good time, and indeed it might be. As
long as you go for the escapist theming and not for great seafood (or a
great bargain), you'll be all right. Even if you're not, Jake's—it seems from
the continuous stream of tourist business—certainly will be.

Jam on Hawthorne

<table>
<tr><td>6.7</td><td>1.0</td></tr>
<tr><td>Food</td><td>Feel</td></tr>
</table>

A good breakfast (or so-so lunch) if you can put up
with the rude staff

American

Casual restaurant

$25
Price

Daily 7:30am–3pm

Bar Beer, wine, liquor
Credit cards Visa, MC, AmEx
Reservations Not accepted
Outdoor dining

Hawthorne
2239 SE Hawthorne Blvd.
(503) 234-4790

The name of this neighborhood breakfast spot may refer to a condiment,
but it makes us think of something else: the eternally snarled traffic in this
neighborhood breakfast spot, which, when combined with a consistently
bad attitude from the restaurant's staff, can conjure seething anger from
the good hearts of even the most docile customers.

When those poor, innocent people show up to a half-empty restaurant,
they're not seated; instead, they're instructed to sign their name on a
clipboard full of preschool-type admonishments ("We beg you to wait for
us to clean and set your table BEFORE you sit down"), and told in no
uncertain terms to obey the no-smoking-type sign ("DO NOT BLOCK
DOORWAY; Please wait outside or in the hallway") and get the hell out of
their way for five, 10, 20, maybe 30 minutes. From outside or the hallway,
they watch while that waiter casually froths milk; tries to figure out the
computer system; tightens the caps on ketchup squeeze bottles; or
gossips with the waitress about what happened at the bar last night. The
peanut gallery is overcome with incredulous gestures toward the four or
five empty tables dining room, discussions over whether or not to walk
away in protest, Panglossian ruminations over whether, if this was really
the breakfast spot they'd heard such good things about, this could really
be the best of all possible worlds.

The restaurant is also evidently too cheap to hire a busboy, forcing the
servers to do everything themselves. This has other side effects: orders
frequently come out wrong; monumental crashes and spills are routine;
after endless battles to get more coffee, customers wander over to the
coffee station and do it themselves. Each of these things can be forgiven,
but the callous indifference can't. Challenge your waiter when he messes
up your order, and he might well accuse you of remembering wrong.
Even children are treated as adversaries. It's truly remarkable.

The kitchen's strength—and it's a big one—is in the lovely, creamy,
complex egg scrambles, which are better still with a squeeze of the
vinegary Aardvark hot sauce. Almost as well executed, if slightly
underseasoned, is the pancake of crispy hash browns. Lunch mains are
less impressive, though, and spelt toast—about which we are generally
excited—is a disappointment, a dead ringer for packaged whole wheat.

But it doesn't matter how good or bad the food is when you're treated
this way at a restaurant—not as a customer, but as a supplicant. Jam is
probably responsible for ruining the pleasant Sunday morning mood of
more Portlanders, over the years, than any other. We'd rather starve than
dine like this.

JCD Korean Restaurant

8.7 Food   **5.0** Feel

Don't be fooled by the humble strip-mall digs—this is a real pork palace

Korean

Casual restaurant

$20 Price

Mon–Sat 5pm–1am
Sun 4pm–11pm

Bar Beer, liquor
Credit cards Visa, MC, AmEx
Reservations Accepted

Beaverton
3492 SW Cedar HIlls Blvd.
(503) 644-7378

This little Beaverton gem is barely recognizable as a restaurant; there's hardly a word printed in English on the sign. Its full name is Jang Choong Dong Wang Jok Bal, which translates roughly to "Jang Choong Dong's Pig Hock Palace." We understand shortening it to JCD, but to us, it will always be "Pig Hock Palace."

Upon arrival, you will surely think you're at the wrong place; the restaurant is sandwiched between a video store and an extremely odd sushi joint, in the same shopping plaza as Noho's Hawaiian. But inside there's a certain charm to the place. It's been recently remodeled, and the wooden booths have a dingy elegance. The windows are covered well enough to shield you from the strip-mall parking lot.

This is not the place for Korean barbecue; rather, they do superlative soups, stews, and spicy dishes, headlined by a delicious beef-brisket stew whose deep, complex broth comes from long, slow cooking. A spicy-pork-neck-and-potato stew is also profound and invigorating, with no odd bits of cartilage or bone to contend with. Pajaeon, seafood pancake, is also terrific, full of fresh-tasting chunks of shrimp and squid. A traditional fermented soybean paste soup, daen jang jigae, might be challenging for newcomers, but if you love full frontal umami exposure, you'll be a fan. Also addictive are soondae (tender blood sausage studded with rice noodles and infused with aromatics) and dokboki, toothsome rice cakes in a spicy goo.

Banchan are generous and all are good. To drink, there's Hite (Korean beer) and Korea's more famous rice-based spirit, soju. The place often hops on weekend nights, and parking can be challenging. Don't expect great service, especially on those nights. But do come expecting some powerful pig hocks. What else would you expect from a place that looks like this?

Jin Wah

Half-Vietnamese, half-Chinese, full-on cranky

7.1	3.0
Food	Feel

Chinese, Vietnamese, Dim Sum   Casual restaurant

$25
Price

Daily 11am–midnight

Bar Beer, wine
Credit cards Visa, MC
Reservations Accepted
Outdoor dining

82nd Avenue Area
801 SE Powell Blvd.
(503) 788-3113

Beaverton
4021 SW 117th Ave.
(503) 641-2852

Jin Wah is a pretty popular joint. Its two locations attract people in droves, and it's managed to earn itself a good name around town. One outpost is in Beaverton, and the other is in Portland's mecca of good Asian food along 82nd Avenue. And we don't mean good in a General-Tso's kind of way; we mean good in a live-seafood-plucked-straight-from-the-tank sort of way.

Jin Wah's menu is divided into Chinese on one side and Vietnamese on the other. We recommend that you pay more attention to the Chinese side, especially the hot-pot section. That's what locals in the know order; it's a warm, soothing bowl of stew chock full of meats. And don't miss the tanks of live Dungeness crabs. Pick one, the staff will pluck it out, and you can enjoy.

In fact, this kitchen is very strong with seafood all around. Salt-and-pepper squid is a real winner, texturally just right—neither chewy nor burnt. The seasoning is aggressive, and we mean that in the best way possible. The staff is quick to recommend it to you, and look around—just about every group has at least one order of it on their table. Fried fish is delicate and delectable.

Many people also come for the dim sum service, but we're not converts. The selection could stand to be much broader, and flagging down a cart is about as easy as hailing a cab in New York City in the middle of a thunderstorm.

Bubble tea (if you're into that) is an afterthought here; there might be a lot of flavors, but none of them is particularly good. The worst part of your experience here will be dealing with the sour staff. They're an unfriendly bunch, often given to treating you like a criminal for having walked in. Perhaps their bad attitude comes from working in such a dull space, where décor is non-existent. Just keep your eyes on your hot pot.

John Street Café

Simple, fresh, surprisingly good breakfast—if you can find it and get there on time

7.6 Food | **8.5** Feel

American

Casual restaurant | **$20** Price

Wed–Fri 7am–2:30pm
Sat–Sun 7:30am–2:30pm

Bar Beer, wine
Credit cards Visa, MC, AmEx
Reservations Not accepted
Kid-friendly, outdoor dining

North Portland
8338 N. Lombard St.
(503) 247-1061

Sometimes you're up at the tippy-top of Portland, practically to the state line, and you've gotta have brunch. Usually, a lack of options creates a desperation that can make restaurants seem better than they are (the same goes for romantic partners), but happily, John Street Café stands up on its own merits.

The understated, cute little space is very North Portland, and a lush garden with umbrella-shaded tables is a wonderful place to sit in summer. Even though it seems off the beaten path, the place is just as busy for breakfast as any other place in town—which seems strange, given that the hours here are impossible to remember. Breakfast is available until 11am Wednesdays through Fridays, noon on Saturdays, and 2:30pm on Sundays.

Provided you do make it during that brief window, you won't get anything fussy or fusion-y here, just simple, well-prepared food that's neither greasy nor Southern fetishist. It's not for the Mississippi hangover crowd, in other words. But pancakes are large and fluffy, like a currant-and-toasted-filbert version that's bright, nutty, and fun to chew. Omelettes are super-simple, and the best of these, a "Bacavo," has a sinful, fatty-salty blend of bacon, avocado, jack and blue cheese. It's a great way to kick off a day of hiking around Forest Park.

Lunch is succinct but sweetly outdated. A blackened snapper sandwich is fine, but festive-looking bow-tie pasta are maltreated by mundane, tinny black olives and squash. It reminds us of wedding food. Stick to sandwiches like a Reuben whose reputation precedes it—and almost wholly deservedly. It's still hard to find a Reuben as sour and creamy as you'd get in a good deli, but when you're this far away from one, it's not a bad substitute.

John Street is a happy place, yes, but it's most worthwhile if you're already up here; otherwise, maybe only make the trip if you have ladies in big hats staying with you. We doubt they'll "get" Tin Shed.

Justa Pasta

For a simple, everyday Italian-American place, this is justa fine

6.8	7.0	8.0
Food	Feel	Wine

Italian

Counter service

$15
Price

www.justapasta.com

Mon–Fri 11:30am–3pm,
4:30pm–9pm
Sat–Sun 4:30pm–9pm

Bar Beer, wine, BYO
Credit cards Visa, MC, AmEx
Kid-friendly, outdoor dining,
veg-friendly

Northwest Portland
1326 NW 19th Ave.
(503) 243-2249

Justa Pasta started out as a fresh-pasta maker for local restaurants, purveying to quite a few of the better kitchens in the area. Over time, it opened a to-go window, serving pastas with a choice of sauce and a bit of bread. It has since expanded into a full restaurant that still makes its own pasta, and whose sauces are more of the Italian-American conceit (alfredos and such), but it does so with local, organic ingredients while keeping prices ridiculously low.

The minimalist dining room is padded with red-and-sage-colored batting that keeps the noise level down. On the wall is a daffodil-shaped light fixture; illuminated tulip shapes hang over the tables. It's pretty, but don't expect anything fancy; order at the counter just inside the front door and choose your table. They'll bring your food to you.

The Italian-American menu has pretty much stayed the same for years: three or four salads, a soup or two, eight pastas, and eight ravioli dishes. A lasagne special, a chicken special, and a few other options are always available. A Caesar salad changes pretty much daily, depending on who's working, but it is consistently a garlic-bomb. Soups, like a Yukon Gold potato-leek version drizzled with pesto olive oil, are good and satisfying.

Carbonara here has been less than traditional, with refreshingly light sauce that has lots of smoky bacon flavor. A simpler garlic-chili oil paste showcases the fresh noodles best. Italian sausage and provolone with fire-roasted bell pepper sauce provides a nice contrast between the spiciness of the sausage, the smooth cheese, and the smokiness of the red peppers.

Ravioli can have great flavor, although it's often too thick. Of the fillings, eggplant has been quite nice, the flavor pushing its way through the sauce. Penne with Painted Hills beef Bolognese is a good effort, especially for the price, but the sauce is cooked much too quickly so has little depth.

The mostly Italian wine list is impressive for this kind of place, and the markups are terrifically low. The staff behind the counter is familiar with the characteristics and can help you with your choice, but the bottles tend to be better than the glasses. While this isn't the best pasta in Portland, it stands head and shoulders above anything similarly priced in the area.

Karam Lebanese

The best place in town to sample one of the world's most alluring and complex cuisines

9.0 Food

7.5 Feel

Lebanese

Casual restaurant

$30 Price

www.karamrestaurant.com

Mon–Sat 11am–9pm

Bar Beer, wine, liquor, BYO
Credit cards Visa, MC, AmEx
Reservations Accepted
Outdoor dining, veg-friendly, Wi-Fi

Downtown
316 SW Stark St.
(503) 223-0830

Portland is lucky to have a variety of Lebanese establishments, some quite good, and some downright terrible. Karam, meaning "generous," is perhaps the best of them all. Its unexpected, incongruous space is a completely transportive oasis. The authentic, complex food even makes you forget the cheesy faux ruins painted on the walls.

And yes, the portions are as generous as the name suggests, but beware: they seem to take it a bit personally if you don't take all your leftovers home. And if you're a novice to Middle Eastern cuisine, don't worry, the waitstaff is more than happy to help you through the long menu and give suggestions.

Vegetarians will be at home in any Lebanese restaurant. Veggie mezza are a great way to start, regardless of your experience level. You get small plates of tabbouleh; a balanced hummus with just enough lemon and garlic; moist, delicate grape leaves; smoky baba ghanoush; and the best falafel in town, with a crunchy crust and a terrific spiced filling that holds its shape. For something a bit more Mediterranean, try batenjan mekle—thin, grilled slices of eggplant in olive oil and lemon juice topped with garlic, parsley, and feta, served with tahini. Kibbeh nayee is an interesting mix of bulghur wheat, onions, garlic, and tomatoes, but it's sort of mealy—not for everyone.

There are also plenty of meat options available. Meat masawat includes everything in the veggie mezze, plus moist, spicy kofta kebab, as well as chicken and lamb shawarmas. We can't decide which kibbeh we like better: the one filled with beef, onions, and pine nuts, or the version with grilled ground beef, onions, spices, homemade yogurt, mint, and garlic. Goat is spectacular, slowly simmered to deep tenderness. Ask for it "bil tfeen" (cooked in red wine), topped with garlic, vinegar, and pine nuts, and served with cracked bulgur wheat, chickpeas, and potatoes. If you've never had goat before, you'll fall in love with it here.

Karam has a full bar with some interesting choices, like a cocktail made with arak, an anisey liquor distilled from sundry-palm sap and dates. You'll want to sip this one slowly. Rose syrup is common in desserts and drinks here, like fun sodas also flavored with jallab (a date-molasses syrup), tamarind, or mulberry. Turkish coffee is sumptuous and muddy, and an excellent way to finish this wonderful tour of Lebanese delights.

Kenny & Zuke's Deli

8.8 Food
8.0 Feel

A faithful rendition of New York deli classics, with one of the city's best non-alcoholic drink lists

Sandwiches

Casual restaurant **$15** Price

www.kennyandzukes.com

Mon–Thu 7am–8pm
Fri 7am–9pm
Sat 8am–9pm
Sun 8am–8pm

Bar Beer, wine
Credit cards Visa, MC
Reservations Accepted
Kid-friendly

Downtown
1038 SW Stark St.
(503) 222-3354

Right next to the industrial-chic Ace Hotel and scenester heaven Clyde Common, Kenny & Zuke's is an unassuming and bustling New York-style deli that is, well, just what it should be. The walls of exposed brick and floor-to-high-ceiling windows give a bright, airy feel to the place, and the fontage is fun and playfully retro. It's thankfully resisted the temptation to shove images of Manhattan down patrons' throats, resorting instead to a credibility that is stuffed between slices of bread.

The best sandwich order here has got to be "Ken's Special": pastrami, chopped liver, and cole slaw. The cole slaw is sweet, but not like "it's cabbage—let's cover it up!" This is a much more grown-up version, with layers of earthy cabbage flavor and vinegary tartness. The hot, tender pastrami is quite smoky around the edges, reminding us of Texas's famous barbecued brisket. Its saltiness is absorbed beautifully by ferrous, creamy chopped liver. The Reuben is also very good, piled high with smoky, tender pastrami, melty Swiss, and crisp, tart sauerkraut. Even the dressing manages to stay inside the toasted bread, which is an impressive feat in itself. But we're disappointed by the rye bread. It's authentic (in that in NYC you often don't get good rye at delis either), but why not do better?

German-style potato salad, that staple side dish of any deli worth its salt, is excellent, with balanced acidity coming from a bit of lemon. And the pickles that come with every sandwich are delightfully sour. The selection of sodas here is as astute as a top-notch wine list would be at a French bistro: Mexican Coke and Pepsi; Sioux City Sarsparilla; Boylan's Birch Beer; and totally NYC-authentic Dr. Brown's (pastrami is to Dr. Brown's Cel-Ray Soda as rack of lamb is to Bordeaux).

Bialys, knishes, and bagels are terrific, and you can also get your rugelach, noodle kugel, and challah on here. The menu is dotted with helpful asterisks to guide vegetarians through the tower-of-meat choices. Pints of draft beer are only $2.50 during happy hour (3–6pm on weekdays), which is almost a redundancy here. After all, Kenny & Zuke's is a case study in making people happy.

Kenny & Zuke's Sandwich

8.0 Food   **7.5** Feel

Don't call it #2—the offshoot of the downtown deli has its own thing going on

Sandwiches

Counter service   **$15** Price

www.kennyandzukes.com

Mon–Fri 11am–8pm
Sat–Sun 9am–8pm

Bar Beer
Credit cards Visa, MC
Delivery, kid-friendly, outdoor dining, veg-friendly

Northwest Portland
2376 NW Thurman St.
(503) 954-1737

This outpost of Kenny & Zuke's Deli downtown is quite different. For one thing, there are none of the Jewish-deli classics like tongue or chopped liver here (although there is a Reuben, available as a "slider," which is being far too humble—it's nearly a full-sized sandwich). Lunch gets quite busy. Tables are packed somewhat tightly, but the high ceilings and large windows keep it from becoming claustrophobic. Despite its bursting-at-the-seamsness, there's an easy neighborhood vibe.

This branch's menu is more of a UN of sandwiches: a Chicago Italian beef; a Cuban; a Southwestern pseudo-torta; and a few others. Bread comes fresh from Grand Central, and can get just a tad dry later in the day. Several of the toppings are made at the downtown Kenny & Zuke's, like giardiniera, which sweetly and gently peppers up the Chicago's tender beef. It's not a dead-on impression, but it captures the spirit just fine. The "Hood River" is little more than a fancy turkey sandwich, with Granny Smith apple and Tillamook cheddar, but not toasted to integrate all the fine flavors.

Bread becomes something of a nuisance in the torta and Cubano, where crusty, thick rustic bread outdoes the flavors of the fillings, and does a number on the jaw. Its unyielding cruelty works best on a meatball hero, whose oozy cheese and spot-on tomato sauce needs to be reined in.

Bagels are baked on-site. They're flat out the best in Portland, and along with good lox and cream cheese, they form the basis for the brunch, which comes with the mandatory Stumptown coffee. A couple of outdoor tables are available, but good luck snagging one in nice weather—it's a great place to people-watch.

There is the same impressive selection of sodas as there is at Kenny & Zuke's downtown—nearly every reputable root beer, ginger ale, cream- and fruity-soda producer imaginable. There isn't much in the way of beer here—just a couple of taps. The plan is to use the cavernous back area as a live music venue, in which case Kenny & Zuke's will need more in the way of suds. But the food would have the honor of becoming the best concert fare in Portland.

Ken's Artisan Bakery

8.0	8.0
Food	Feel

If the bread were this good at Communion, we'd all be Catholic

Baked goods, Sandwiches, Coffee

Café **$15**
Price

www.kensartisan.com

Mon–Sat 7am–6pm
Sun 8am–5pm

Bar Beer, wine
Credit cards Visa, MC
Kid-friendly, outdoor dining,
veg-friendly

Northwest Portland
338 NW 21st Ave.
(503) 248-2202

When you walk in the front door of Ken's, a dizzying array of colors and shapes greets you from the glass case. Fluorescent macaroons, a rainbow of tarts, and caramel-colored croissants fight for your attention. On a nice day, large windows let in light and a breeze. The walls are painted in different shades of blue and yellow, making it feel more spacious than it really is. This really reminds us of a French bakery, even more so than the Disneyish version at St. Honoré. Inside and out are plenty of nice tables at which to indulge in some of the finest bread in town.

Made using some of the best flours, French sea salt, and—even more important—hours and hours of patience, Ken's dough ferments slowly, developing great flavor and complexity. Sourdough is inspiring; the crust shatters, giving way to a rush of tangy piquancy, a perfect synergy of ingredients. This is what bread should taste like. You can also find pain rustique, a walnut baguette, huge crown loafs, country boule, Parisian baguette, and many other delicious types, depending on the day.

Given all this superlative bread, of course, sandwiches made here are wonderful. Pulled pork is loaded with lots of tender, moist meat and a somewhat sweet barbecue sauce. The accompanying slaw complements the sandwich with lots of raisins and a little bit of fresh thyme. A croque monsieur is filled with little waves of ham, Gruyère, béchamel, and more of that fresh thyme, all on a thin slice of fresh country bread. It's outstanding, as is a braised and roasted beef sandwich with caramelized onions. All come with a bit of lightly dressed greens or a few tart, bursting blueberries.

The pastries are more of a mixed bag, unless you come early in the morning or on Saturdays, when they're made fresh all day long. Some macaroons can be cloyingly sweet, and amandines are just pretty good—both can be stale-tasting at times. But croissants are marvelously layered and buttery, yet somehow never greasy. Pick one with Valrhona chocolate for an amazing foil to your Mr. Espresso coffee (which is good, not great) and watch the parade of chic Portland pass by, oh so jealous of you.

Ken's Artisan Pizza

9.0	7.0	8.0
Food	Feel	Wine

A pizzeria with one foot in Naples and the other in Portland

Pizza

Casual restaurant

$25
Price

www.kensartisan.com

Tue–Sat 5pm–10pm

Bar Beer, wine
Credit cards Visa, MC
Reservations Not accepted
Kid-friendly, outdoor dining,
veg-friendly

Southeast Portland
304 SE 28th Ave.
(503) 517-9951

Ken's Artisan Pizza is the very definition of neighborhood-friendly. This corner space has huge windows that open up to the street, so that the outdoor and indoor diners are barely separated. It's always bustling, with people lined up waiting for a table at 6:30pm on a Wednesday. Some tables in the back are away from the buzz, but in a lonely way—the bar is better. The walls are bare, and the sole source of décor is exposed wood beams and wooden tables.

Everyone is drawn by Neapolitan-style pizza wood-fired in a brick oven at such high heat that it imparts a firm crust with deep char. The tomato sauce is naturally sweet, with circles of cheese that are well integrated and don't slip and slide off as you lift each slice. The pizza also somehow manages to avoid sogginess. When a margherita is ordered with arugula, it comes with a huge mound of greenery on top, just thrown on when the pizza is done cooking; this may rub some people the wrong way, but it's done in Italy like this because arugula loses its spicy kick when it's cooked even briefly. The tables have little bowls of coarse salt and chili flakes.

There are also delicious lamb pita sandwiches and a smoked trout salad, which is a good way to start. For a pizza joint, this is a very ambitious wine list. We love that there are nine rosés—it certainly puts finer restaurants to shame in this regard, and rosé is one of the better wines to have with pizza, if you must have wine. There are also some surprising apparitions like a $75 Alsatian Riesling. Italophiles favor beer, though, and there are four on draft.

The fact that the beams overhead were salvaged from the old Big Dipper roller coaster ride at Jantzen Beach is just plain cool. There are pictures of the ride in the back of the restaurant. It's this kind of sentimentality, perhaps, that makes these people take the time and effort to learn how to make pizza the way the Italians do—and to source nine different rosés for the list. And it's why Ken's is one of Portland's favorite pizzerias.

Kinara Thai Bistro

This tiny Thai powerhouse turns out authenticity, if not consistency

7.5	7.0
Food	Feel

Thai

Casual restaurant

$25
Price

www.kinarathai.com

Mon–Thu 11am–9pm
Fri 11am–9:30pm
Sat 3pm–9:30pm

Bar Beer, wine
Credit cards Visa, MC, AmEx
Reservations Accepted
Kid-friendly

Southwest Portland
1126 SW 18th Ave.
(503) 227-5161

It seems like there are hundreds of Thai restaurants in Portland with little to differentiate them. Sugary pad Thai, dried-out meat, and curry paste from a jar seem to be the norm. Yet we're always pleasantly surprised by Kinara Thai Bistro. It uses local and sustainable produce in its cooking and corn-oil-based compostable containers for their to-go items. These things alone set the place above most Thai restaurants in Portland.

Kinara's duck rolls sound terrible at first (flour tortilla? Hoisin sauce?)—and certainly aren't Thai—but are worth ordering. The flavors are bright and fresh and the textural interplay between the crispy duck and the other ingredients is just terrific. Another hilarious menu description, "vegetarian dumplings with a saccharine soy sauce," belies the fact that the small, light dumplings, stuffed with crunchy vegetables—again, more Chinese than Thai—are not sweet at all. In fact, you can make out every vegetable inside of each, especially if you go light on the average-tasting dipping sauce. We're hesitant to try "calamari Chardonnay," but we should know by now that we're in good hands.

Nahm dtok, grilled beef salad, is the best we've tried in Portland. It's one hell of a feat to accomplish, considering that the ingredients include mixed greens, radicchio, carrots, onions, scallions, cucumbers, bell peppers, grilled sirloin, coriander, mint, and toasted rice. If any of the components were overused, the entire salad would be thrown off, but this salad shows great balance. Kinara's beef is of excellent quality, a cut above most Thai restaurants—tender, moist, and with just the right amount of fat.

Pad Thai, that dish of falsely reported authenticity that's usually just dessert in an American-sweet-tooth-pandering noodle dish, is much better balanced here than usual, although on some visits it's been ordinary and muted. Pad kee mao is also more authentic than the norm, with fat rice noodles, basil, bell peppers, onions, tomatoes, garlic, and Thai chili.

Kinara offers your choice of brown rice or jasmine rice with the stew dishes. Panang curry has a rich flavor, medium heat, and lots of complexity that builds as you eat. Beef massaman runs a close second to Siam Society's version, while green curry is just average.

The only significant problem here is consistency. We've had the same dish turn out completely different over two nights. But when it's on, it's really on. The restaurant is small, but perhaps understaffed. On second thought, maybe we shouldn't tell you how good it is, or we'll never get our food.

King Burrito

Stuff yourself royally on the cheap

6.0	4.5
Food	Feel

Mexican   Counter service   **$10**
Price

Daily 10am–11pm

Bar None
Credit cards Visa, MC, AmEx
Veg-friendly

North Portland
2924 N. Lombard St.
(503) 283-9757

King Burrito is a nondescript little strip-mall joint whose grungy character is often mistaken for excellence. That's not to say that it's bad—it's good enough, really. It's just that when we become skeptical of anything too clean or corporate-looking, we run the risk of making the opposite mistake, the mistake of assuming that just because a place is grungy, it's good.

That's not always true, and here, we don't really get the prodigious buzz. The burritos are approximately the size of a newborn human infant, but tempt us to reenact that infamous scene in *Anchorman* in which Will Ferrell tosses it out the window, half done. Finish one, and you are likely to be useless the rest of the day. As the common wisdom goes, you're in optimal form when you're a little tired and a little hungry.

The "King Burrito" contains a whole chile relleno plus steak and some good pepper flavor, but is not spicy enough to stave off boredom after a few bites. Tacos are much better, featuring such authentic choices of meat as cabeza and lengua, which tend to be moist and tender, and best when garnished simply with cilantro and onion. Carnitas can be a bit dry but are flavorful, if needing some help from hot sauce, which you have to ask for.

On weekends, there's offal-y, healing menudo for hangovers. There are plenty of vegetarian options here as well, and these are passable, if uninspiring (Mexican cuisine isn't at all inherently vegetarian). If you live in the area, you could do much worse.

KOi Fusion

Check Twitter for the whereabouts and whenabouts of this fiercely followed Korean taco truck

6.7	6.0
Food	Feel

Mexican, Korean

Food cart

$5
Price

www.koifusionpdx.com

Mon–Sat 8:30am–6pm
Sun 10am–5pm

Bar None
Credit cards Visa, MC, AmEx
Veg-friendly

Southwest Portland
Check Twitter
(503) 997-6654

Korea and Mexico. At first glance, you might think one has absolutely nothing to do with the other. But both cuisines love charred meat, garlic, and chili spice. Plus, have you ever wrapped bulgogi in a taco? KOi Fusion has.

And they're not the first, either. There's a taco truck in Los Angeles called Kogi Korean BBQ To Go that moves around the city, Twittering its location daily to hordes of drooling fiends. Word has it that KOi Fusion has some loose connection to the L.A. Kogi, and it does emulate this marketing tool as well as the menu. The service can be incredibly slow when they get slammed with a crowd of people, taking as long as 20-25 minutes for a couple of tacos.

But we're not entirely sold. The idea is great, but the execution is just not as good as it could be. The homemade corn tortillas (props for homemade tortillas) can be dry and chewy, depending on how long ago they were made. Stick to the marinated meats, as tofu tends to be severely underseasoned. Still, it can be hard to tell which meat is which; after dressing them, they all sort of taste similar, negating the differences between bulgogi and the fattier, juicier galbi (short rib). Spicy pork is pretty good; it's not at all like al pastor, but is rather entirely its own thing, sliced thinly and with a thicker sweetness. In general, the heat is dialed way down, as it is at Mexican taco trucks that have learned Americans are control freaks. Here you can add your own from squeeze bottles.

"Seoul Sliders" are okay. These are a little rich (and big), and would benefit from a kimchi condiment, which seems only natural.

Ultimately, this is great late-night drinking food on the weekends, when it's open until 2am. That is, if you can designate a sober person to troll Twitter for you. And, of course, to drive you there.

Koji Osakaya

A legitimate, if somewhat chain-y, Japanese comfort food venture

7.7	5.0
Food	Feel

Japanese

Casual restaurant

$35
Price

www.koji.com

Daily 11:30am–11pm
Hours vary by location

Bar Beer, wine, liquor, BYO
Credit cards Visa, MC, AmEx
Reservations Not accepted

Downtown
606 SW Broadway
(503) 294-1169

Northeast Portland
1502 NE Weidler St.
(503) 280-0992

Southwest Portland
10100 SW Barbur Blvd.
(503) 977-3100

Additional locations
and more features at
www.fearlesscritic.com

The first hint that this growing Portland-area chain might be something more than the usual effort at to be vaguely Japanese is the mathematical LaTeX font used in the menu layout: it's a questionable move from the graphic design/aesthetic point of view, but a sign of total Japanese legitimacy. The second good sign is the geographical distribution of Koji Osakaya branches: with the exception of downtown Portland, they seem to plop down in the Asian neighborhoods of the fringes and suburbs, clearly not catering to a white-only clientele.

The atmosphere varies from branch to branch; the downtown location is a total dive, like a diner with the sort of open kitchen that predates the charming kind. Elsewhere, the furnishings are more modern and the décor more refined, but that's not necessarily a good thing. The space often feels generic and perfunctory, like the service.

Although there's a fair bit of raw fish on the menu and at the sushi bar, that doesn't seem to be the focus of Koji. But if you can overlook the proliferation of weirdo maki, you can enjoy some really excellent fish, here, especially in nigiri form. Albacore and hirame (halibut) have been consistently silky and delicious; sushi chefs will let you know what's freshest. This is worlds above the quality of your local sushi joint.

Shishamo (capelin, or smelt) broiled to a deep char come four whole fish to a plate, the approximate size of steak fries; they need a few squeezes of lemon to come into their own with an interesting, challenging fish flavor. Cold zaru soba (buckwheat noodles), served with a subtly sweet soy-based dipping sauce along with shredded radish, scallion, and nori, always hit the spot; it's a dish that's not as easy to find around town as it should be. We like the noodles a bit less cooked than they are here, but Koji's still have a happy resilience and a refreshing sodium kick from the sauce.

One of the more popular orders here is one of the many versions of the combination dinner, often with broiled fish or meat or a well-executed tonkatsu (breaded, fried pork fillet). It's all well executed, convenient, cheap, and, in general, just the kind of comfort food that's actually aimed at—and appeals to—the local Japanese population. That difference can hardly be overstated.

There's exactly one great sake; beer is scarcely better, but you can have a nice Erath Pinot Gris, enjoy the low prices and the good food, and feel a bit more Japanese than usual.

Koreana

Great, cheap Korean food that's worth leaving the city for

7.7 Food   **6.5** Feel

Korean

Casual restaurant   **$30** Price

Mon–Sat 11am–10pm
Sun noon–10pm

Bar Beer, wine
Credit cards Visa, MC
Reservations Not accepted

Beaverton
9955 SW Beaverton
Hillsdale Hwy.
(503) 646-7767

Normally, advertisements are a negative signal for restaurant quality, but this Korean restaurant along a strip center in Beaverton advertises in the local Korean-language newspaper, which cuts the other way. Given the feeling of the streetside entrance—it's adjacent to a row of stuccoish-and-tinted-window retail spaces that are vaguely evocative of 1960s Latin American sprawl—you might think you're going to a mediocre orthodontist rather than a good Korean restaurant. But the inside is small, unassuming, and wood-paneled; it's laid-back and easy, but terrible for a date.

There's tableside BBQ, and the galbi (short ribs) are very tender and juicy, but that's not really the focus of this menu; the bigger turn-ons are a good array of seafood soups, e.g. ah gu tang (steamed monkfish soup); soon dubu (rich, soft tofu soup with kimchi) and kkakdugi (radish-cube kimchi); and yeom so jun gol (black goat casserole with vegetables); broiled mackerel, alta mackerel, and yellow croaker. We're always delighted to see seolleongtang (beef-bone broth with sliced beef and noodles) on the menu; it's a milky treat underappreciated by Americans. In Oregon's colder months, this soup is like a warm blanket for your sides.

The prices here are a steal, much lower than downtown PDX standards. Servers are friendly and helpful, willing to explain anything on the menu to newcomers (in broken English), and always ready to refill the banchan at your table. These range from salted tiny fish to spicy potatoes and kimchi to pickled bean sprouts, and are good enough to tempt you into stuffing yourself before dinner comes—beware. Since each table comes with a gas grill, tables can't really be pushed together—come as a group of four or fewer; even with that manageable number, you might find yourself fighting over ingredients.

Koreana isn't the best Korean we've found in the area, but it's consistently good and a fair amount of fun—for this little money, how many other places can claim to offer the same?

Kornblatt's Deli

Straightforward Jewish-style deli food and
good sodas and beer—what more is there?

7.4	7.5	8.0
Food	Feel	Beer

Sandwiches

Casual restaurant

$20
Price

www.kornblattsdeli.com

Mon–Thu 7am–8pm
Fri 7am–9pm
Sat 7:30am–9pm
Sun 7:30am–8pm

Bar Beer, liquor
Credit cards Visa, MC, AmEx
Reservations Not accepted
Delivery, kid-friendly, outdoor
dining

Northwest Portland
628 NW 23rd Ave.
(503) 242-0055

Kornblatt's Deli is a good place for breakfast and a pretty classic lunch
spot. Kenny and Zuke's may be a bit more glamorous, but in a certain
sense, Kornblatt's comes a bit closer to duplicating the grungier NYC
aesthetic. You've got your linoleum floors, your big windows facing the
street, your mirrors to look in. The chairs are comfortable, the booths
cozy. Servers are no-nonsense, friendly, and accommodating. What more
could you want?

Perhaps the most universally loved element of Kornblatt's is the freshly
made bagels. Properly fluffy and available in several different flavors,
these make a great breakfast with smoked salmon, pickled herring, and
whitefish salad flown in from NYC each week. Other breakfasts include
real shaved corned-beef hash; challah French toast; and some big, decent
omelettes. Blintzes are better with compotes and stewed fruits, but these
are decent, with preserves and sour cream. Matzoh brei is a scramble of
that Passover staple and eggs, fried in butter, that you won't find
elsewhere in the city.

More famous are mile-high sandwiches made with quality pastrami and
corned beef. These are not as dripping and fatty as some well-loved
renditions, in fact sometimes seeming a little dry, but a Reuben's dressing
helps bring it all together. Tuna salad is also terrific. There are usually
pickles on all the tables, and salads and sides are generous. Of these,
mayonnaise-y salads like potato and macaroni are refreshingly restrained,
but some might find them dry. Kosher beef franks are also delicious, with
a little snap and a lot of juice. Matzoh-ball soup does the trick, even if it's
not as good as some versions, and cabbage borscht is an undeniable
pleasure, especially in cold weather.

There are about half a dozen great local brews on tap here, and a few
rudimentary cocktails for breakfast (Bloody Marys, Greyhounds, and the
like) but none are particularly outstanding. Dr. Brown's make his
mandatory appearance, but espresso drinks are far from the high bar set
by serious coffee places in town. But, then, there aren't many New York
delis with good coffee, either.

La Bonita

Mexican food that's not the most authentic—but it tries hard to convince you otherwise

6.7	6.0
Food	Feel

Mexican

Counter service

$15
Price

Daily 10am–10pm	**Bar** None	**Alberta Arts District**
	Credit cards Visa, MC	2839 NE Alberta St.
	Outdoor dining	(503) 281-3662

If not for the fact that there's better Mexican food a few doors down Alberta, La Bonita would be a godsend. The ladies at the counter beneath the big chalkboard are friendly, and the airy space feels easy and comfortable, even if the wooden tables and chairs feel too dark by day, empty and depressing by night. There are some nice touches on the menu: crumbly queso cotija; tacos de lengua (tongue) and properly gamy machaca (dried beef, a specialty of the states of Tamaulipas and Nuevo León in northeast Mexico); tripe-rich menudo and porky pozole; sweet horchata (rice milk) and tart agua de jamaica (hibiscus infusion).

But La Bonita makes too many compromises on its menu, accommodating the dumbest of dumbed-down recipes, and bringing down the level of the whole operation as a result. We're not talking Tex-Mex—oh no, Tex-Mex is a respectable cuisine. We've got no problem with a good breakfast burrito or melty cheddar-cheese enchilada. No, we're talking a different kind of dumbed-down here: Mexican food for wusses. That means veggie burritos (black beans, rice, cheese, pico de gallo, and lettuce—any Mexican peasant would be appalled), nachos, fajita-veggie tamales, or dried-out shredded beef chimichangas.

The taco al pastor, one of our litmus tests for Mexican, is just okay here; although happily unencumbered by a surfeit of pineapple—a frequent problem with al pastor—these chunks of pork come out a bit tough, and need to be helped along by lots of onions, cilantro, and healthy doses of the well-executed red and green salsas that come in squeeze bottles. You'll find yourself relying on those squeeze bottles a lot in this restaurant, which speaks poorly of the meats but well of the salsas.

Above all, we favor breakfast at La Bonita. Skip the breakfast burrito and head straight for huevos con chorizo—that bright red, oily Mexican sausage scrambled into three eggs, the ultimate comfort food when paired with rice, beans, and warm tortillas. Or try chilaquiles, which are executed reasonably well.

"Food for the people," waxes the menu, "as authentic as Mexican gets." In this country, unfortunately, those are two contradictory statements. When the people want veggie-fajita tamales and wimpy, overcooked pork chunks, the great restaurant is the one that resists the tyranny of the majority.

La Calaca Comelona

A fun Mexican spot where the food is exciting, if not always what it should be

7.3 Food

9.0 Feel

Mexican

Casual restaurant

$35 Price

www.lacalacacomelona.com

Mon–Sat 5:30pm–9pm

Bar Beer, wine, liquor
Credit cards Visa, MC, AmEx
Reservations Not accepted
Date-friendly, outdoor dining

Belmont
2304 SE Belmont St.
(503) 239-9675

La Calaca Comelona ("The Hungry Skeleton") has—by a fair margin—the most exciting menu of any Mexican restaurant in Portland. The multi-roomed restaurant feels like a folk art gallery, with deep red walls and evocative Mexiphernalia everywhere. Gentle yellow light emanates from spiky hanging sun lanterns; Day of the Dead skeletons are sprawled across the ceiling; piñatas watch over the room. The bar in back could easily have been transplanted from a Mexican beach town.

The obsession with authenticity is codified in an essay on La Calaca Comelona's menu about why burritos aren't served, and it's spot-on. In Mexico, the only thing actually called a "burrito" is a thinly rolled tortilla around machaca, with no other fillings, and it's mostly found in Sonora. (The big, stuffed burrito is a California invention. Not that there's anything wrong with California inventions.)

The menu follows through on the promise of escapism. Chiles en nogada, one of our favorite traditional Mexican preps, are made well here, employing smoky pasilla peppers rather than poblanos. We also appreciate the appearance of taquitos dorados de requesón (crispy taquitos with soft white cheese and epazote leaf), and chapulines (grilled grasshoppers) with chili flakes, lime juice, and tortillas. We like "manita de nopal con camarón," a plate of teensy-weensy shrimp resting on a bed of credible cactus strips that get a nicely un-slimy char.

Unfortunately, there are frequent execution problems here, beginning with the sickly-sweet margarita, which tastes mostly of sour mix. The cocktail list is excessively tropical-umbrella-ish, full of sweet-tooth drinks like the "afrodisiaco"—tequila, rum, orange juice, and grenadine. We got quite excited about the appearance of enchiladas morelianas on the menu—we were hoping for that characteristic deep red smokiness that comes from guajillo chile—but La Calaca's version was overloaded with tasteless cabbage, nacho-style pickled jalapeños, dry chunks of chicken, and low-quality sour cream; the dish, although enormous, just didn't have any punch to it. Green mole en pipián, made with pasilla, is a better choice, but we question the overuse of bell peppers and lettuce.

Keep it simple, and you're better off. Plain cheese quesadillas are made from fresh corn tortillas, as they should be, and they're the real deal. Ditto for sopes. You could just come for a drink, and have a great time. Even if the execution in the kitchen often doesn't live up to the promise of the menu, La Calaca is the sort of place that just lures you back again and again for its festive and authentic charm. And grasshoppers.

La Sirenita

It's not the best, but the salsa bar is a wonder

8.6 Food **5.5** Feel

Mexican

Counter service **$15** Price

Daily 10am–11pm

Bar None
Credit cards Visa, MC
Outdoor dining

Alberta Arts District
2817 NE Alberta St.
(503) 335-8283

Sellwood
8029 SE 17th Ave.
(503) 234-3280

Impressive Mexican kitchens often occupy humble digs, and La Sirenita is one of the city's most impressive and most humble.

Entering this cozy space is like walking into a simple family kitchen. Spanish is as welcome as English. The menu is short and sweet; La Sirenita manages to stay focused, unlike the long, meandering, Mexican-American menu at La Bonita, the inferior competitor down Alberta (which nonetheless manages, somehow, to be more popular—ah, the wisdom of the masses).

The meats that fill La Sirenita's tacos are very traditional and very good: juicy tacos al pastor have just a faint kiss of pineapple, as they should; tacos de cabeza (head cheese) are surprisingly meaty, delicious, and probably the best around unless you crave them super-gamy (they're not here). Carnitas are moist and rich, too, whether in a taco or a California-style super-stuffed burrito, which they do quite well. We're also fans of La Sirenita's mole verde.

There's not much of an attempt at décor beyond the brick-trimmed archways. There's a roll of paper towels on each table, a Gatorade-like water dispenser, and cafeteria-style tables and chairs. The most attractive interior element might be the long wooden beams that hang a few inches below the ceiling, spanning its length. But don't come here for dinner. That would be no fun.

Still, humble as it may be, La Sirenita provides more atmosphere than most places at this level of Mexican taco-meat execution. Getting tacos de lengua or al pastor this authentic is something we generally associate with a taco stand off a highway somewhere. Here, at least, you can sit down and spend quality time at the salsa bar.

In fact, "salsa bar" is really an understatement—it's a great condiment bar with pickled vegetables in escabeche, several different types of hot pepper, great homemade salsas, and other goodies. Make good use of the bar, and you'll wind up with the best-dressed tacos in the city.

Laughing Planet

Consume PNDs in a nutty place with a very sound conscience

5.0	8.0	7.0
Food	Feel	Beer

Vegefusion

Counter service

$15
Price

www.laughingplanetcafe.com

Daily 11am–10pm
Hours vary by location

Bar Beer
Credit cards Visa, MC
Kid-friendly, outdoor dining, veg-friendly, Wi-Fi

Pearl District
721 NW 9th Ave.
(503) 505-5020

Northwest Portland
922 NW 21st Ave.
(503) 445-1319

Mississippi Ave. Area
3765 N. Mississippi Ave.
(503) 467-4146

Additional locations
and more features at
www.fearlesscritic.com

It's hard not to like Laughing Planet. It's like the Pee-Wee Herman of fast-food joints. Each location is uniquely wacky; the business actually has a "Creation Myth," and it refers to its main product, burritos, as PND (Portable Nutrition Devices).

According to Laughing Planet's website, the business plan came about when a burrito constellation was beheld in the Southern Sky. Yes, it's like that. And this sweet playfulness is apparent in the décor, which looks like Frank Zappa's take on a toy store. Wildly colorful, cozy and eclectic, and not at all corporate looking (not even in that trying-too-hard Ben & Jerry's kind of way), the cafés feature charming outdoor seating and plenty to look and laugh at.

More serious is the commitment to health and ecology here. Laughing Planet gets its ingredients and materials from a commissary, thus reducing delivery trucks and mileage; composting and recycling is regularly practiced; and locally sourced meats and produce are used wherever plausible.

Burritos taste fresh, but that's it. Chicken could do with more seasoning, and homemade mole has none of the depth of which dried chilies are capable. The result, for the most part, is merely benign—until you get to the ill-advised and convoluted "International-style burritos." For instance, a particularly awful "Thai Me Up"; Thai curry peanut sauce is already reprehensible on a salad, so why would anyone put it with bland brown rice, bland "Steamed Asian veggies," and…pico de gallo? It's as disastrous as it sounds, intensely sweet and tomatoey and odd.

Stick to the "mission-style" burrito, or the bowls, whose compositions work much better when they aren't jammed into a huge, tough tortilla. "Spanky's Bowl" is actually decent, with melted Tillamook cheddar, mashed potatoes, sweet corn, and broccoli. Wash it down with fresh-squeezed juices or a small selection of local microbrews on tap.

No one ever seems to crave a Laughing Planet burrito; they usually choose one out of convenience. But all other things beings equal, why not pick the fast food that leaves the smallest carbon footprint?

Laurelhurst Market

A promising new shout-out to the nose-to-tail crowd

9.1	8.0	7.5
Food	Feel	Wine

Modern, Steakhouse

Casual restaurant

$50
Price

www.laurelhurstmarket.com

Daily 11am–11pm

Bar Beer, wine, liquor
Credit cards Visa, MC, AmEx
Reservations Accepted
Date-friendly, outdoor dining

Northeast Portland
3155 E. Burnside St.
(503) 206-3097

Laurelhurst Market has some serious foodie cred: it's run by the same folks who've created a stir with Simpatica Dining Hall and Viande Meats. This butcher shop and casual steakhouse might look totally informal, but it's serious about food. At lunchtime, the only seating is outdoors; otherwise, the dining room is closed and the service is counter and take-out only (from 10am-7pm daily). For dinner (5-11pm daily), you'll enjoy a nice open space with a butcher in the front, wood beams, modern lighting, and a long bar that's kind of right in everyone's way. Expect long waits, even on a Sunday, thanks to some glowing press.

Service is gracious and efficient, if a bit harried in the storm. Homemade charcuterie steals the show here, with a venison country pâté whose mild flavor works great with the toothsome pistachios. Sopressata is also excellent, and rabbit rillettes are aptly paired, one time with pickled strawberries.

At lunch, there's an assortment of sandwiches, of which the best include a very smoky turkey; juicy porchetta; and very rare roast beef. Some have unexpected condiments like harissa and preserved lemon. The bread is impeccable. In fact, with the exception of useless iceberg lettuce, everything about these sandwiches is fantastic.

At dinner, meat is definitely the point. Steaks vary daily; the day's cut might include a "bavette" (or "flap"), whose intensely meaty flavor and across-the-grain tenderness put it somewhere in the area of a flank. Steaks are seasoned just right and overshadow their fries, which are thick and can come a bit lukewarm. Brussels sprouts have come overcooked and oversalted, but that problem doesn't seem to extend to many of the other sides.

Try not to stray too much: large, sweet shrimp have come unevenly cooked, served on grits with artichokes, mussels, and pancetta. A simpler chicken seared under a brick gets an ideally crisp skin while the meat retains all its moisture.

A wine list is totally appropriate to the steak aspect of the cuisine, if a little short on exciting options; the beer is especially dismal for such a food-forward endeavor. But most details are accounted for, like Stumptown coffee and a very solid, if somewhat derivative dulce de leche cheesecake. It melts in the mouth and is, refreshingly, not too sweet—a successful throwback to vintage steakhouse desserts that doesn't lose Laurelhurst's modern sense of restraint. Continuing in that vein—and keeping the prices refreshingly low compared with the more pretentious steakhouses—will certainly keep the accolades coming.

Lauro Kitchen

A slick, swanky jack-of-all-(Mediterranean) trades, master of none

5.5	7.0	6.5
Food	Feel	Wine

Modern

Upmarket restaurant

$50
Price

www.laurokitchen.com

Mon 5pm–9pm; Tue–Thu
11:30am–2:30pm, 5pm–9pm;
Fri–Sat 11:30am–2:30pm,
5pm–10pm; Sun 5pm–9pm

Bar Beer, wine, liquor
Credit cards Visa, MC, AmEx
Reservations Accepted
Date-friendly, outdoor dining

Division/Clinton
3377 SE Division St.
(503) 239-7000

Lauro Kitchen feels like a chain, or at least part of a big restaurant group. It's very slick and trendy, not really in the spirit of the very cool, anti-corporate neighborhood it's in. That's not to say it isn't a nice place to be; huge windows look out upon the street and the lighting is magnanimous, coming from red-hued Lego-like lighting fixtures overhead. It's just too big to be intimate, and there's too much self-promotion going on to invite adoration.

The staff is friendly, if less food-nerdy than other Portland staffs. We can't totally blame them—"Mediterranean" is a broad, somewhat vague cuisine to serve, ranging from southern Spain and Morocco, eastward through France and southern Italy, and into Turkey and Greece. Add to that list Pacific-Northwest-style cooking (local ingredients in creative but non-locale-specific platings) and you have a plan that looks good on paper, but whose lack of focus invites mediocre renditions of everything. Jack of all trades, master of none.

Take the pizza oven, which is fancy, but gas-burning; the resulting pizzas aren't terrible, but they don't get enough sear because the pizza oven isn't hot enough (it's kept around 600°, about 300 degrees lower than a proper pizza oven should be). Plus they're taken out too soon, and are much too cheesy. Spanish patatas bravas can be wonderful, but here they're butchered, dry and mealy like frozen-and-reheated steak fries, and served with a bland marinara-ish sauce and a mayonnaisey aïoli with little garlic flavor. Mussels are cooked in the pizza oven in an amusing clamshell contraption, but they disappoint, too; the broth doesn't get all funky-mussel-wonderful, and an onion-and-pepper mix doesn't do much.

Fish and meat mains aren't a lot better. The Middle Eastern end is represented less well by chicken tagine that is irresponsibly shoved into the pizza oven with no lid, drying it out.

The wine selection, much of which is (unusually) offered by the quarter- or half-carafe, is decent—including many lesser-known wines that go well with "Mediterranean" food—but this broad a cuisine type could support a much more exciting range. Markups are high, too, so the selection is limited further. Cocktails attempt to keep up with the artisanal movement, but you can see a vodka-happy -tini urge here that's only thinly disguised with infusions. Lauro is not a bad restaurant, but in this great food city, why bother?

Le Bistro Montage

3.7	9.5	7.5
Food	Feel	Drinks

Don't come for the blah attempts at down-home cuisine—come because you *can*

Southern

Casual restaurant

$35
Price

www.montageportland.com

Mon 6pm–2am; Tue–Thu
11:30am–2pm, 6pm–2am; Fri
11:30am–2pm, 6pm–4am; Sat
10am–1:30pm, 6pm–4am; Sun
10am–1:30pm, 6pm–2am

Bar Beer, wine, liquor
Credit cards Visa, MC
Reservations Not accepted
Date-friendly

Southeast Portland
301 SE Morrison St.
(503) 234-1324

Le Bistro Montage claims that it's a "one of a kind place where, when you step in the door, you're not quite sure where you are. Its quirky décor, including huge paintings, a poster pulled off the Berlin Wall, decadent fresh flowers, tin cans pounded into the floor, and long, linen-covered tables, creates an atmosphere that draws all types and guarantees a great time." Well, they're on the money there; we have no clue what they're going for. And we don't care, either. Where else in Portland—or in America, for that matter—can you have a candlelit meal at 3:30 in the morning?

This place can't take itself too seriously, especially with the annoying post-bar crowd tripping all over each other. It's in a cool, edgy neighborhood, so between 10pm and midnight on a weekend, expect a wait, but don't fret—they've built (or forged, seemingly, out of every object found in Portland's alleyways) La Merde, a hilarious lounge in which to wait for your table.

Sure, this is a hell of a fun place to be, but where the food is concerned, almost everything fails. Overwrought macaroni and cheese variations (including a Spam version) are the best thing here, but even that is slightly dissociated. Don't even try the "Green Eggs and Spam," in which Spam and pesto are sort of "scrambled" over cheese grits. Yikes. Cajun and Creole attempts like jambalaya are just wimpy. You'd never get away with roux this bland near the Mississippi, and fried gator, although they have it in Louisiana, is just gimmicky here. You may as well be eating Popeye's "popcorn chicken." And you know better than to order the fusion pastas.

The wine list is weird, sailing freely from entry-level wines from great producers to grocery-store giants. Rare is the bottle over $40, which makes us happy. Cocktails are seasonal and fun, if a little on the sweet side; someone here must be an investor in Godiva chocolate liqueur.

Essentially, Le Bistro Montage is like any amusement where food is an afterthought: a museum, a zoo, a strip club. Just come and enjoy being awake and alive with others in the wee hours. And if you've been drinking, by all means, Spam it up.

Le Happy

A late-night sweet (or savory) rendez-vous

7.8	8.5
Food	Feel

Crêpes

Casual restaurant

$15
Price

www.lehappy.com

Mon–Thu 5pm–1am
Fri 5pm–2:30am
Sat 6pm–2:30am

Bar Beer, wine, liquor
Credit cards Visa, MC
Reservations Not accepted
Date-friendly, outdoor dining,
veg-friendly

Northwest Portland
1011 NW 16th Ave.
(503) 226-1258

How do you not love a place like Le Happy? One, the name. Two, it's absolutely adorable from the outside, with little white lights and a sort of scruffy, rustic look like a yellow Cinema Paradiso. Three, inside, it's filled with friendly servers, delighted diners, and groups playing any number of provided board games in dim reddish lighting into the wee hours.

The menu is loaded with crêpes. Teeming with them. A page of savory and a page of sweet, with about three dozen different ingredients for mixing and matching. Sriracha, cilantro, and tofu? Gotcha covered. Coconut cream, banana, and Grand Marnier? No sweat. There are even reasonably priced sirloin steaks and a few salads to round out your meal.

This is an ideal crêpe, spread super-thin on a searingly hot crêpe pan, then deftly lifted to sizzle in a pat of butter until it caramelizes and crisps at the edges, while its fillings sizzle away on the griddle next to it. Cheese melts into the pores, and the whole thing folds away all meat juices and sauces, trapping them for bite after bite.

"Le Trash Blanc" is clever, pairing a bacon-and-cheddar crêpe with a can of PBR. But we love "Le Jambon Jambon," with ham, bacon, Gruyère, tomato, green onion, and Sriracha. A smoked-salmon version is also spectacular. Of course, you've got to finish with dessert, and with Nutella on the board, how does anyone order anything else? If you can, end the night with the Spectac, flambéed tableside like a Suzette, but with Nutella and banana instead of orange marmalade.

The wine list is sort of disappointing for what it could be. It's perfectly appropriate to be this terse, but few are interesting or well suited to the flavors. But we'll gladly take the Sidre Doux pear cider, which is a magic pairing with just about anything, sweet or savory. There are a couple of beers on tap, and a few more in bottle.

Totally Portlandesque, fun, delicious, and affordable, Le Happy is all it promises to be. Plus they serve at ridiculous hours of the night. If only they'd open for breakfast.

Le Pigeon

Yes, it's as good as you've heard

9.6	8.0	9.0
Food	Feel	Wine

Modern

Upmarket restaurant

$70
Price

www.lepigeon.com

Mon–Sat 5pm–10pm
Sun 5pm–9pm

Bar Beer, wine
Credit cards Visa, MC, AmEx
Reservations Essential
Date-friendly

East Burnside
738 E. Burnside St.
(503) 546-8796

For most of the country, the frequent references to Le Pigeon were the first indications of Portland's up-and-coming status as a dining city. For a few years now, gastrotourists and locals have streamed in to see what all the fuss is about. And a lot of them have been turned away; years after its emergence, this remains perhaps the toughest reservation in town.

It's fitting then that the restaurant is set up, almost theatrically, around an open kitchen; a handful of farmhouse-style tables and a chef's counter are equally good places from which to ooh and ahh (not that that's the intention here). On nice days, there are a couple of tables outside. Some old chandeliers provide plenty of light and, with vintage-looking chairs, make for a quaint, charming spot. It's a place you'll be equally comfortable taking a few friends or a romantic date.

Everything is local, organic, and free-range. The wine list is excellent, loaded with food-loving, lighter-bodied, exciting wines from lesser-known regions; Belgian and local beers on draft change frequently. And the markups for wine and beer are as humble as the atmosphere.

The menu changes weekly, but it frequently dallies with chef candy like marrow, organ meats, and face. Ears, cheeks, tongue, you name it. Preparations are innovative and astute: ideally crispy-creamy sweetbreads with pickled strawberries; refreshing, summery cucumber gazpacho with a single, revelatory grilled prawn in the middle; gently cooked squab with duck-fat-poached potatoes and marrow crostini.

Even a seemingly boring main like fennel chicken with carrots is a work of art, with masterfully crisp skin and a breathtaking balance of sweet onion confit and carrots. Or a quotidian flatiron steak that is canonized with its spot-on cooking and bed of truffled greens, and a topping of the most addictive semolina-crusted onion rings you'll ever have.

But you're here, so why not go whole hog? It's hard to argue with delicious lamb's tongue potato salad, or surprisingly tender calf hearts, even if you're squeamish. A much-publicized dessert of sweet cornbread with apricots, topped with crispy bacon, honey, and maple ice cream is every bit the gustatory nirvana it is cracked up to be.

Le Pigeon is not perfect. Some dishes are ill conceived, like a "foie pb&j" that winds up as a messy mélee of strong flavors, or a dish of salty pork belly with a so-so onion aïoli and some average tempura-fried beans. But we'll take this over passionless, cynical menus full of time-tested safe bets. Besides, everyone knows: to make a really damned good omelette, you've got to break some eggs.

The Liberty Glass

Have a pint with the cool kids (but skip the forgettable cocktails)

American, Italian

4.5	9.5	8.0
Food	Feel	Beer

Bar **$20**
Price

Daily 6pm–midnight

Bar Beer, wine, liquor
Credit cards Visa, MC, AmEx
Outdoor dining

North Portland
938 N. Cook St.
(503) 517-9931

Everyone might just be a bit cooler than you at this beautiful little old house on the very end of the gentrified stretch of Mississippi. They're cooler than us, anyway. But maybe you're cooler than us, too, in which case you might be as cool as the Liberty Glass crowd. By "cool," of course, we mean Portland cool, which means skinny-multi-tattooed-attractive-young-activist-possibly-vegan-but-definitely-arriving-on-a-bicycle cool.

The house that is Liberty Glass is damn cool, too. Descending Mississippi toward the water, in your car or on your bike, after passing Flavor Spot #1 on your left, a house will appear beneath you to your right. Immediately before that house, a winding side street will fork off Mississippi to the right. You've got to take that street. The problem is that by the time the house—never mind the Liberty Glass sign—comes into clear view, you've already missed it, and you're squealing into a private driveway. Then you're turning around, and heading (more slowly, this time) up Mississippi, and making the turn properly this time. Unless you're one of the cool kids, of course, in which case the turn was second nature.

The space here is simply brilliant. It's like someone's super-cute living room turned into a bar full of beautiful, fun people, pouring great local pilsners and IPAs from the tap, serving good craft cocktails, and serving food too. And that's not to mention the delights of the front porch, which is even fun in winter weather because of the little wood-burning fireplace set up at ground level.

As for the food, well...maybe cool doesn't always translate to delicious. The menu is a classic smattering of the worst hits of vegan cuisine, plus some pretty bad non-vegan dishes, too—watery, mushy linguine with meatballs and tomato sauce, for instance. The simplest things, like cheddar biscuits, are best, but there's not much good to report on here. Better would be to dine somewhere else on Mississippi and come here afterward, stick to the good local beer selection and the reasonably priced cocktails, and absorb the classic Portland atmosphere.

The food stops coming a bit before midnight, but in the case of this food, you probably won't mind. This isn't a food place; it's a great local bar that satisfies people's needs when they get the late-night munchies, such that they can continue drinking here instead of having to depart for elsewhere. When you see the place, you'll understand why that's so important.

Lincoln

Interesting preps that have more promise on the page than the palate

7.8	8.0	7.5
Food	Feel	Wine

Italian, Modern

Upmarket restaurant

$50
Price

www.lincolnpdx.com

Tue–Sat 5:30pm–9pm

Bar Beer, wine, liquor
Credit cards Visa, MC, AmEx
Reservations Accepted
Date-friendly

Mississippi Ave. Area
3808 N. Williams Ave.
(503) 288-6200

Lincoln is a big, beautiful space; tall windows let in tons of light by day, which is replaced by a gentle, warm glow by night. There's a fun buzz at peak times when the place gets loud, but not too loud. When the restaurant is slow, it still manages to be inviting, the warm staff more than happy to chat with you and give you recommendations. Even a meal at the bar is quite nice, as you feel incorporated into the coziness of it all, not like an alcoholic who's more interested in the liquid component of his dinner.

But the solubles here are pretty recommendable. The cocktail list has some eye-catching selections, the lightest of which, on a recent visit, was the Elderflower Gimlet. Gin, Saint-Germain, lime juice, and simple syrup worked harmoniously to make this drink go down easy, yet it avoided any sticky sweetness. "El Diablo," with tequila, lime juice, crème de cassis, and ginger ale, while heavier, still slides down the gullet with relative ease. The wine list is serviceable, and, refreshingly, most bottles will cost you less than $50. Largely French, it seems a bit unfocused, but mostly well chosen. The beer selection is also a bit scattered—mediocre at best, but subpar for Portland.

On to the grub. Amongst starters, we really like Spanish-influenced crispy eggplant with blue cheese dressing. The frying technique is spot on, making these little discs addictive, and their dip adds depth, creaminess, and that lovely fungusy flavor. Baked hen eggs, on a recent visit, were ordered by just about every table in the house, and they are indeed good. And creamy. A dish of tagliatelle with pork ragù, sage, and pecorino romano, on the other hand, was plagued with textural problems; the pasta was slightly overcooked and a little slippery, making it almost impossible to compose a bite with both pasta and pork. The meat was nicely cooked and deeply flavored, although slightly undersalted.

Prices can creep a little high, but if you tell yourself that it's a premium for the pretty space and pretty people, it's more worth it.

Little Red Bike Café

A plucky, sincere little café that's hard not to like

8.4 Food **8.0** Feel

Modern, Sandwiches

Counter service **$15** Price

www.littleredbikecafe.com

Tue–Sat 8am–2pm
Sun 9am–2pm

Bar Beer, wine, liquor
Credit cards Visa, MC, AmEx
Outdoor dining, veg-friendly, Wi-Fi

North Portland
4823 N. Lombard St.
(503) 289-0120

As many self-published authors know, if you want to create a fan base before your book goes to press, start a blog. This is what the owners of Little Red Bike Café did, and the result was an eager crowd on opening day that already felt as if they were intimates, confidants, and—most advantageously—predisposed to loving the place. Every otherwise-griped-about misstep, each potentially damning shortcoming, was washed away by the rose glow of goodwill generated by the adorable musings and confessions that humanized the restaurant's tender early days. Which is not to say the love isn't earned. One blog post debates whether bagels should be toasted, a sign of passion and dedication that makes this café stand out from the crowd.

The interior of the jaunty turquoise storefront is gently festooned with bicycle paraphernalia—there's even an air pump for bicyclists in need of a boost. Otherwise, it's quite spare. You order at the counter (or bike-through window) and sit at simple tables and chairs adorned only with Tapatío bottles and napkins. A wooden bar with stools faces the street, and although the traffic here isn't particularly interesting, it does invite overcast-day musings.

What the menu offers sounds pretty typical, but it's tweaked up a notch in complexity and excellence. For breakfast, a "Paper Boy" is a simple fried-egg sandwich elevated above the mundane with the addition of Beecher's Flagship cheese on freshly baked ciabatta. Add caramelized onions and pasilla pepper aïoli and you have a "ZooBomb." Others benefit from homemade apple butter or fig jam to give them added interest. Three-egg scrambles—like one with Cypress Grove chèvre, fresh herbs, homemade tomato jam, and multi-grain toast—will set you right without setting you back. Fleur de Lis pastries, croissants, and scones are also available, including some downright addictive sticky buns.

At lunch, toasted sandwiches come with your choice of chips or a much-better-than-average salad of organic dressed greens. Even prosaic turkey becomes special and texturally intriguing with bacon, homemade onion relish, Beecher's cheese, sun-dried-tomato mayonnaise, and apple slices. A grilled cheese sandwich is given depth with just a kiss of white-truffle oil and some decent brie and jack cheese. But best of all is roast beef, thick and moist with wonderful caramelized onions, roasted tomatoes, crumbled blue cheese, and rosemary aïoli.

All this for about $10, including a good coffee. Blog or no blog, we're followers.

Little T American Baker

9.0 Food   **8.0** Feel

Look beyond the stark, modern space for a timeless warmth from the hearth

Baked goods, Sandwiches, Coffee

Café   **$15** Price

www.littletbaker.com

Mon–Sat 7am–5pm
Sun 8am–2pm

Bar Beer
Credit cards Visa, MC, AmEx
Outdoor dining, veg-friendly, Wi-Fi

Division/Clinton
2600 SE Division St.
(503) 238-3458

The Pacific Northwest coffeeshop is an image burned deep in the minds of people everywhere (wherever *Singles* was released, anyway). It's hard not to think of concrete floors that are strewn with papers, threadbare couches you don't want to inspect too closely, skinny and beautiful baristas, and the sound of grinding beans and sizzling foam wands absorbed by an endless array of local art mounted on exposed brick walls.

Although Little T is more of a bakery than a coffeeshop, it shatters these expectations in a very Scandinavian way while still fulfilling its coffeeshop charge. The stainless steel is terrific at ricocheting noises back at human ears in that sort of psychically jarring way that drives you to seek therapy, and the floors—polished to a high shine—are strangely devoid of crumbs and dried mocha latte splatters. But the flowing wall of wood is downright lovely, and the minimalism is strangely soothing, perhaps because it's pulled off with such brilliant attention to detail.

Above all, Little T focuses on the product of the only hearth it need concern itself with, and the bread fiends who sit peacefully at angular hardwood tables have no complaints (except, perhaps, for the one lonely power outlet).

The freshly baked bread here is uniformly excellent, no matter what type. A wonderful brown slice of spelt bread, which plays here like a Danish brown bread, is served with wild smoked Coho salmon, scallion crème fraîche, and dill; it's one of the most perfect breakfasts or lunches in Portland. The heavier "Cowgirl Toast" is equally impressive, with an egg fried right inside of a cakey Sally Lunn with grilled bacon and cheddar cheese. A fruit spelt roll is absolutely amazing, the crust working in slightly charred harmony with a confit of farm-fresh berries.

The breads also take lunch sandwiches to the next level. An Italian grinder on seeded hoagie is sheer joy with provolone and a brilliant pepper salad. Even a simple turkey breast sandwich is superlative on this 7-grain carrot bread with cream cheese and apple chutney.

It's been said that man cannot live by bread alone, but after visiting Little T, we don't know how we ever lived without it. In light of the food and friendly service, this stark space is actually about as warm as it gets.

Living Room Theaters

5.7 Food 9.0 Feel 7.5 Beer

Take part in an ongoing market survey at this corporate movie-theater-restaurant concept

Modern   Theater $35
                                       Price

www.livingroomtheaters.com

Mon–Fri 11:30am–midnight
Sat–Sun 11:30am–1am

Bar Beer, wine, liquor
Credit cards Visa, MC, AmEx
Reservations Accepted
Date-friendly, Wi-Fi

Downtown
341 SW 10th Ave.
(971) 222-2010

The dine-in movie theater is a fashionable business model around the country these days, and Miami-based Living Room Theaters has invested millions in an effort to capitalize on it. Their website, weighed down by armies of ® and TM symbols, is laughably corporate. According to the *Portland Business Journal*, the firm's executives "consider the Portland project a prototype for a national chain…which cities the firm plans to open depends on ongoing market surveys."

Even this smarmy MBA-case-study attitude can't kill the fun concept. The idea is that, first, you buy a movie ticket; next, you relax with a drink in the airy, glass-panelled, soaring bar, which comes complete with mod wood paneling, loungey seating, and a smile-glued-on-the-face waitstaff; and, finally, you order a meal (10 minutes or more before the show starts) to be delivered to your movie-theater seat. The compact beer selection is serviceable—clean local Pilsners, Oregon-centric stouts and IPAs and such—but cocktails are boring and sweet, Miami-style. And keep in mind that this fun is meant for adults—after 4:30pm all patrons must be of legal drinking age. The films shown here are much better than the Hollywood norm—you'll see more Paul Giamatti than Tom Hanks, and even some small-time indie films without national distribution. The seats are great, too. If Cinemark is coach, this is business-class moviegoing.

Unfortunately, good filmic taste doesn't translate to good culinary taste. This menu plays no better than *Angels & Demons*, skimming the globe's surface without penetrating its soul. You'll find ill-executed spicy tuna hand rolls, vaguely Middle Eastern snack platters, and a pressed sandwich that seems to have been formulated by throwing darts at a purveyor's ingredient list. Red bell pepper—possibly America's most overused ingredient—sauces prosciutto-wrapped chicken (the prosciutto cooked to leather) with "sautéed vegetables and angel hair pasta"; this sort of recipe was euthanized from most menus around 1997.

A dish dubbed "Spanish Style Tortilla," with "golden new potatoes and "aged manchego," is "layered with egg custard and slow-baked." Translation: it's a dissociated stack of ingredients, including prosciutto (cooked to uselessness, yet again), that totally misses the charm of a real Spanish tortilla, in which the egg sets together with onion, potato, and olive oil to spin off a new flavor that's better than its sum of parts. Living Room® Theaters should confiscate this chef's undeserved creative license, 86 his adjectives, and send him to reform school at Living Room®'s Miami corporate HQ, where the company's board of directors should already be hard at work studying remedial community relations.

Lovely Hula Hands

A refinement of space, design, and food in a pretty pink package

8.8	9.0	9.0
Food	Feel	Wine

Modern

Casual restaurant

$40
Price

www.lovelyhulahands.com

Tue–Sun 5pm–10pm

Bar Beer, wine, liquor
Credit cards Visa, MC, AmEx
Reservations Not accepted
Date-friendly, outdoor dining

Mississippi Ave. Area
4057 N. Mississippi Ave.
(503) 445-9910

Lovely Hula Hands is adorable. As the wordless sign out front portends, elegant and grandmotherly touches are everywhere, from pinky-coral walls to vintage lamps with handpainted detail to mismatched china. The two-story, early-20th-century brick building helps add to the feeling that you're over to a very stylish and old-world friend's house for dinner. A shaded patio outside hung with festive paper lanterns is a charming place to sit with a drink on warm evenings.

These drinks might include appropriately vintage cocktails, some with twists involving interesting and somewhat rare ingredients. "Talulah's Bathwater" is popular, with a pomegranate molasses, tequila, fresh lime, and sugar. Local spirits like Aviation gin, New Deal vodka, and Clear Creek pear brandy are used to good effect, even if the drinks do err on the side of sweetness.

A succinct, ever-changing menu focuses on carefully constructed dishes employing lots of local ingredients. Soups are satisfying and intensely flavored, sometimes because of elements like spicy sausage or bacon, but often thanks to profuse salting. The kitchen's keen knowledge of different lettuces makes for some simple salads that are stunning in their results. Although pear, brie, and candied pecans are hardly novel components, it's sheer alchemy to pair them with lightly bitter radicchio.

A small-but-hearty soufflé with leeks and goat cheese, which we sampled at one visit, was showstopping, with an expert sauté of wild mushrooms, spinach, carrots, and cippolini. Carlton Farms pork shoulder has come cooked to deep tenderness. Sometimes it's been served in a shimmering, dark brown sauce with bursts of fig flavor; other times, with red wine and prunes, root vegetables, and Anson Mills corn grits. Both have made ideal dinners on cold fall and winter nights.

The cheapest main on the menu, a simple burger, is better than most: a generous patty, slightly seasoned, with the meat cooked ideally to temperature. It's best with cheddar, as a blue-cheese-and-caramelized-onion version is a bit too heavy. The accompanying french fries, served with the skin still on, are crisp and nicely salted.

Desserts are few but judicious, straying little from the classic preparations that have proven so successful. These nearly share the attention to detail that the décor does. A wine list is beautifully composed for this food, filled with bargains from excellent, lesser-heralded Old World regions, smaller Burgundian producers, and even a few cru Beaujolais. Now that's our kind of accurate.

Lucca

It's nice—you know, if you like that sort of thing

6.9	7.0	7.5
Food	Feel	Wine

Italian, Modern

Casual restaurant

$35
Price

www.luccapdx.com

Tue–Thu 11:30am–9pm
Fri 11:30am–10pm
Sat 5pm–10pm
Sun 10am–2pm, 5pm–9pm

Bar Beer, wine, liquor
Credit cards Visa, MC, AmEx
Reservations Accepted
Date-friendly, kid-friendly, outdoor
dining, veg-friendly, Wi-Fi

Northeast Portland
3449 NE 24th Ave.
(503) 287-7372

Lucca is warm and classy, with a cool basket-weave ceiling and unique lighting fixtures. The walls are earthy orange and green, and the sleek bar makes an attempt with glass pendant lamps and ceramic art.

That said, Lucca is like an uninteresting woman in a beautiful dress. Most of the food here is neither good nor bad—it just sits there smiling, with little to say. Tails & Trotters pork shoulder, slow-roasted in milk with rosemary white beans, is exactly like it sounds, nothing more. Not a single layer of interest or intrigue. Even those of us who can't shut up about food are speechless, stuttering through vapid conversation starters with our food like "Say, is that fennel? Neat."

Maybe because of its accessibility (read: dullness), Lucca is big with families who are hip to the fact that Olive Garden is an inexcusable waste of money. It's the kind of place that will please the older folks, too. Groups with small kiddos tend to be sequestered to the more private back of the room, which is a deal that works out for all parties. Adults will appreciate the plethora of decent glasses for $8 and under, while the blithe Italian-American menu has something for everyone: serviceable pizzas; tender-roasted cod with melted leeks, shaved fennel and lemony Yukon Gold potatoes; capably cooked steaks with creamy polenta; and so on.

Even desserts are just kind of…there. There's nothing wrong with them, nothing memorable, either. A warm lemon soufflé pudding is bright and kind of pretty. Profiteroles, on the other hand, taste like they have grocery store ice cream in their middles. The kids won't mind.

Ultimately, Lucaa is about having a nice plate of pasta that you don't have to clean up later, and the civility of cloth napkins. No more, no less.

Lucky Labrador

A superb brewpub where beer is king—food is just there to help with the BACs

3.0	8.5	8.5
Food	Feel	Beer

American

Bar **$15**
Price

www.luckylab.com

Mon–Sat 11am–midnight
Sun noon–10pm
Hours vary by location

Bar Beer, wine
Credit cards Visa, MC
Date-friendly, live music, outdoor dining, Wi-Fi

Northwest Portland
1945 NW Quimby St.
(503) 517-4352

Hawthorne
915 SE Hawthorne Blvd.
(503) 236-3555

Multnomah Village
7675 SW Capitol Hwy.
(503) 244-2537

This cavernous, wood-beamed barn of a space along a gentrifying stretch of Southeast Hawthorne, and its siblings elsewhere in town, epitomize all that's cool about Portland: great, local, interesting craft beer (e.g. barrel-aged Red Baron), with one rotating into the cask for conditioning and aging; a crowd that effortlessly blends the hippie, blue-collar, and bike-zealot sets; and the superskinny, tattooed, vaguely stoned beer pourer whose disaffected attitude just makes you want him more, like in *The Rules*.

Unfortunately, the food is a total afterthought. It's hard to decide which is more boring: the soup and sandwich recipes might have well have been copied from a Betty Crocker cookbook—if not for the extensive, unsuccessful attempts to appeal to vegetarians (in which hummus is about the only interesting ingredient). A "three-cheese meltdown," for instance, combines Swiss, cheddar, pepper jack, mushrooms, peppers, and salsa on Italian white bread. Who knew vegetarian food could be so unhealthy, too? Aside from the decent ciabatta, expect low-end-supermarket-quality ingredients: flavorless turkey, watery romaine, underripe tomatoes. And you know better than to dare try something called "Thai salad" here, but why doesn't Labrador know better than to serve it? And how about those ridged junk-food potato chips? Wake up, dudes—Portland went kettle-cooked, like, decades ago.

Just come for the beer, or their own root beer, which is also quite good. They cask condition some of their ales so they ferment naturally, without the use of carbon dioxide, resulting in a smoother consistency that allows the flavors to show through better. If that's not your thing, a nitrogen tap produces some creamier ales with more bubbles than the cask-conditioned ones. Mondays and Tuesdays, one or more of the locations has great specials. The staff is well-versed in their different brews and can help you explore. And bring your dog—everyone else does. Word has it that they, too, love beer.

Lucky Strike

Light up with Szechuan peppers and chili oil in this out-of-the-way little gem

8.9	5.0
Food	Feel

Chinese

Casual restaurant

$20
Price

Mon–Fri 6pm–10pm
Sat–Sun noon–10pm

Bar Beer, wine
Credit cards Visa, MC
Reservations Not accepted

Far East Portland
12306 SE Powell Blvd.
(503) 206-8292

Of all the Chinese regional cuisines, Szechuan is the one you are most likely to be ushered away from, even by the people who run the restaurant. Ask for a menu, and you'll be handed some broken-English list of take-out standards. Ask for the "real" menu, and you will have to pass a brief interview about what you're looking for, if you know what you're getting into, and whether you're qualified to get into it. It's understandable, since the staff have probably had one too many kung pao eaters insist they like it spicy, only to return the dish in a tearful huff after it tries to extricate every drop of liquid from their face.

It's chili peppers, not Szechuan peppercorns, that make you a fire-breathing dragon. The peppercorns are just plain fun; they're a total tongue trip. Their flavor is hard to describe and harder to forget: if Hell grew chamomile flowers and dried them for tea, it would taste like this. Bite into one and you'll be alarmed (not but hurt) when it bites back. First, your tongue goes numb. And then comes the drool. Your mouth waters and waters and—speaking of water—when you drink some, it tastes unbelievably like tin and menthol. We have devoured plates full of Szechuan peppercorns just to trip out on the water.

So venture out, far, far off the beaten path to this forgotten corner of Portland and tuck inside this tiny hovel, which is thankfully so dark you can't see how badly it needs a makeover and a cleaning. Wait with the many, many other huddled masses for a table. When the server comes, don't let them pressure you into sickly sweet and tarry Guinness-braised ribs. Say "ma po tofu." Say "lion's head." Say "husband and wife" (we won't name this dish's ingredients, lest they dissuade you). Say "drunken chicken," so named because you'll make yourself drunk trying to extinguish the flames with beer. Lion's head isn't as scary as it sounds; it's actually a garlicky, tender and incredibly flavorful pork meatball. Noodle soup with pork and Chinese broccoli is also a little bit of heaven and a little bit of hell.

Sure, you'll encounter long wait times, the odd closure here and there, and the somewhat inconsistent balance of peppercorn to spice to oil to garlic. But with so few Szechuan options in Portland (Shenzhen only offers some of these dishes), Lucky Strike is worth the minor inconveniences.

Lucy's Table

This grande dame still holds a lot of sway, some of it deserved

7.4	8.5	8.0
Food	Feel	Wine

Modern

Upmarket restaurant

$50
Price

www.lucystable.com

Mon–Thu 5pm–9:30pm
Fri–Sat 5pm–10pm

Bar Beer, wine, liquor
Credit cards Visa, MC, AmEx
Reservations Accepted
Date-friendly, outdoor dining

Northwest Portland
704 NW 21st Ave.
(503) 226-6126

Lucy's Table is unnervingly quiet. There's absolutely no music, and everyone speaks in hushed tones. It's also kept really dark, with heavy velvet drapes and small votives on each table. To some people, this might make for an ideal date situation, but we think it's a spectacular place to wait out a migraine. Or grieve.

If it seems that the entire restaurant has taken a monastic vow of silence, that may be because of the religious experience afforded by a small plate of goat cheese ravioli bathed in brown butter; the only racket associated with Lucy's tends to revolve around singing its praises. And for good reason: the pasta is ideally toothsome, with plenty of savory, creamy goat cheese in every bite. The brown butter is gently sweet and nutty, complementing the tart chèvre.

Other than that, we're lukewarm on the food here. The menu has always seemed somewhat geriatric compared to others in town. While the whippersnappers are cooking nose-to-tail dishes, dabbling in organ meats, and curing their own charcuterie with a punk-rock fervor, Lucy's is like the grande dame looking dazed and wondering what's so wrong with just being nice. Not much, it turns out, but it's still got that high-school-prom feel, or like this is an ideal place to take the in-laws.

A recent chef change hasn't yet improved what has long been a disjointed, vaguely Mediterranean-influenced program. Pomegranate-glazed ribs are hard to argue with, not too sickly sweet and cooked to a docile texture. Expertly cooked halibut is paired with pork belly. But some clumsy moves are still made here, like watery bruschetta; poorly shucked oysters; and a decidedly un-paella-ish rabbit paella with Arborio rice, haricots verts, currants, and fennel. By this loose definition, they may as well call it risotto.

One of the best things about Lucy's Table is its excellent wine list, which combines extraordinarily low markups with wonderful breadth across regions and grape varietals. Tourino Notarpanaro from Puglia in southern Italy for $27, for instance, is one of the best wine buys in the city.

We recommend coming for happy hour, which is endearingly called "Social Hour"—it offers some great deals on food and a more lively crowd. If you plan to come later in the night, make a reservation; if it's slow, the kitchen will start closing down as early as 9pm. Ultimately, this is a decent restaurant without any compelling reason to keep you coming back.

Madena of the Pearl

6.0 Food **6.5** Feel

Inconsistent but well-known Lebanese in a town full of better options

Lebanese

Casual restaurant

$20 Price

www.madenaofthepearl.com

Mon–Thu 11am–7pm
Fri–Sat 11am–9pm

Bar Beer, wine, BYO
Credit cards Visa, MC, AmEx
Reservations Not accepted
Outdoor dining, veg-friendly, Wi-Fi

Pearl District
432 NW 11th Ave.
(503) 231-1000

You know you are nearing Madena when the air is suddenly redolent with spices. Unfortunately, the promise in the air doesn't always reflect in the food that comes to your table.

Located in the Gregory Building, it is a tiny place of five tables for two—more, on sunny days when they can put tables outside. This is, by definition, a hole in the wall; it's nothing fancy, just basic concrete walls adorned with bright artwork. The music swings between Taylor Dane and Flock of Seagulls. The atmosphere is less than transportive.

So is the food any good? Depends on the day. At best, they seem to be merely passable. Baba ganoush is garlicky and smoky, a smooth purée of eggplant, olive oil, and garlic served with a serviceable flatbread. Hummus is nothing special. Falafel is a bit dry with a spice blend that can sometimes be way oversalted. It doesn't really compare to versions in some of the other restaurants in town. Grape leaves also fail to stand out from those found at many other places in town.

A mezza platter is available at dinner and includes a sampler of all of these plus tabbouleh, but the kitchen seems to be out of at least one of the listed items at any given time. On hot days, fattoush salad is refreshing and filling, with romaine, cucumber, tomato, radish, green onion, sumac, garlic, baked pita, fresh mint, and lemon-olive oil dressing. Tender chicken shawarma has a wonderful blend of cinnamon, nutmeg, cloves, allspice, garlic, and green cardamom over basmati rice, accompanied by fresh sweet onion coated with yet more spice mix. When the restaurant first opened, Madena's version was pretty good. Lately, however, it's been dry and short on flavor. The beef version is pretty much the same, cooked until there is no juice left in it. The spice mix is not distributed evenly, leaving some bites spiced and others with little flavor at all.

In fact, the only consistency we've found here has been inconsistency. One week, a dish will be pretty decent, and the next, there will be way too much cardamom/lemon/salt/you name it. Although this restaurant has been open for several years, it doesn't seem to be getting any better; if anything, it's getting worse.

Malay Satay Hut

Quite good Malaysian in an okay setting

7.7	8.0	6.0
Food	Feel	Drinks

Malaysian

Casual restaurant

$25
Price

www.malaysatayhut.com

Mon–Fri 11:30am–2:30pm, 5pm–10pm
Sat–Sun noon–3pm, 5pm–10pm

Bar Beer, wine, liquor
Credit cards Visa, MC, AmEx
Reservations Not accepted

82nd Avenue Area
2850 SE 82nd Ave.
(503) 771-7888

People make a big deal about the Southeast Asian cuisine in San Francisco, Los Angeles, and New York, but the Southeast Asian culinary community in the Pacific Northwest really stands up to any of those. And it doesn't end with Vietnamese and Thai. Malay Satay Hut—which is quickly turning into a mini-empire in the region, with two branches in the Seattle area and now one in the Fubonn Center, along Portland's Asian restaurant row—brings in stellar cuisine from all over Malaysia and, in many cases, Singapore's Straits as well.

Although the restaurant is part of a mall, you can diminish that effect by entering streetside. Anyway, the dining room is escapist enough to make you forget it. This is a finely realized interior, with Malaysian conceits everywhere. The bar has a tiki-ish aspect, with a simulated-outdoor bamboo roof. Large swaths of wall are covered by giant photos of KL's Petronas Towers, a vegetable market, and other tourist-office-type fare, but they fit in, somehow. Tables toward the back of the room are festive and almost romantic, in a mallish kind of way. And then there are the tanks in which the live crabs live. That's exciting.

Roti canai, the buttery flatbread that's one of Malaysia's most magnificent achievements, comes out less gheelicious here than it sometimes does, but its curry-and-potato gravy, although a bit grainy, has a flavor that's right on the money.

Don't stop there. Colorful treasures are strewn across this helpfully illustrated menu: moist Hainanese chicken rice; curried squid; Singapore-style chili crab, hoisted from the tank and turned into a messy indulgence. There's also decent dim sum—headlined by sweet, doughy baked barbecued-pork buns, fried seaweed rolls, stewed tripe, beef stomach, chicken feet, and pan-fried taro or turnip cake—but this is not the best place in Portland for dim sum. Stick to the Malaysian fare if you make this particular Fubonn trek.

Cocktails, like the bar's décor, are in the tiki-bar school of thought—if you're not in the mood for a sugar rush, it's better to stick to the very basic beer and wine selection.

Masu

You can't hope to escape the sugar—you can only hope to contain it

6.3	8.5	7.0
Food	Feel	Wine

Japanese

Upmarket restaurant

$45
Price

www.masusushi.com

Mon–Thu 11:30am–11pm
Fri 11:30am–midnight
Sat 5pm–midnight
Sun 5pm–10pm

Bar Beer, wine, liquor
Credit cards Visa, MC, AmEx
Reservations Accepted
Date-friendly, Wi-Fi

Downtown
406 SW 13th Ave.
(503) 221-6278

In a departure from neighborhood norms, the staff at this ultra-hip second-floor Pearl District Japanese restaurant is universally friendly. We also enjoy the space, which boasts a lovely view through enormous factory windows over the warehouses to treetops and street scenes. The atmosphere is best in the evenings with warm, reddish lighting and a lively buzz. A big bar in the center is a bit random, but breaks up the soaring space well. There's much to look at, between mod Austin-Powers-ish lounge furniture and a big, colorful mural of a sumo wrestler getting a tattoo from a woman the size of his bicep. If you get a chance, check out the bad-ass hand dryer in the bathroom.

If the setting is as sweet as sugar, then that sugar leaks out into seemingly every corner of this restaurant, even in the driest-sounding cocktails, like the "Makers Cup." That would be a clever mix of Maker's Mark, muddled cucumber, and fresh-squeezed lemon-lime juice that's unfortunately served over unneeded ginger ale, which cheapens the whole gig. A "Jessies' Girl" (is this a gay-friendly nod to two moms named Jessie?) sounds like the least sweet cocktail, described as a "smoky martini" with Monopolowa, Suntory whiskey, and olives, but the Suntory contributes rum-like sweetness.

The sushi and cooked Japanese food don't fail miserably, nor do they quite meet expectations. An amuse-bouche of vinegary, unusually tender octopus salad with cucumbers, at a recent visit, had a clear dressing as sweet as dessert, with black sesame seeds contributing little more than color and the occasional crunch.

Fluke and yellowtail sashimi come out clean and inoffensive, without a lot of flavor or particular silkiness. Salmon is fatty and rich, perhaps the best in the raw-fish lineup. Tuna is light, fruity, and fresh enough. In short, this is all standard; it's unremarkable in every way. There's nothing memorable. Yes, there are some harder-to-find pieces—Dungeness crab, Arctic surf clam, bluefin toro—but this isn't the best place in town to get them.

Agedashi tofu can be a beautiful thing when done right, but here, the bean curd is denser and mealier than expected, and once again, there's sugar galore in the dashi-based broth, which lacks the back notes of better Japanese stocks. Bonito flakes contribute little of their intended umami. The menu continues with unnecessary Kobe beef and such, but there's just more disappointment ahead, even with the lovely view.

McCormick & Schmick's

Just-okay seafood in an ever-growing chain

5.4	7.5	8.0
Food	Feel	Drinks

Seafood, American

Upmarket restaurant

$60
Price

www.mccormickandschmicks.com

Sun–Thu 11:30am–11pm
Fri–Sat 11:30am–midnight
Hours vary by location

Bar Beer, wine, liquor
Credit cards Visa, MC, AmEx
Reservations Accepted
Outdoor dining

Downtown
309 SW Montgomery St.
(503) 220-1865

Beaverton
9945 SW Beaverton Hillsdale Hwy.
(503) 643-1322

Even if you love to hate upscale chain restaurants, it's hard to hate this entry from the Pacific Northwest. For one thing, they serve local fish. Not exclusively, but it's still a more conscientious effort than one might expect.

McCormick's serves up reasonably priced, competent preparations of sockeye salmon, spotted prawns, Dungeness crab, razor clams, and so on. Your mother makes an unexpected appearance on the plate in the form of sides like bitter asparagus and useless carrot slices, but your childhood ghosts will be exorcised, because she's powerless to make you eat them.

Another good reason not to hate McCormick & Schmick's is the happy-hour deal at the dark-wood bar tables—and we actually prefer their pubby atmosphere to the more sedate, generic main dining room. There are over a dozen ever-changing draft beers and several local microbrews. Not just from 4-6:30pm, but at some locations during the Euro-Argentine dinner hours of 9-11pm—they give away giant appetizer plates for two, three, or four bucks: fried calamari, seafood tostadas, salmon cakes, and so on. The half-pound cheeseburger is one of the cheapest dinners in town. Don't expect service, though—what's attentive in the dining room turns disastrous in the bar.

Seasonal raw oysters have come sandy, the result of sloppy cleaning and shucking. As for those fried calamari, they're very salty, not quite rubbery but not quite tender, and their sauces are subpar; it's best with a simple squeeze of lemon or dash of malt vinegar, whose acidity balances out the salt. It's not worth anywhere near its rather high price.

In an effort to appease the lowest common denominator, this restaurant dilutes its quality by crowding the menu with too many losers: Fettuccine alfredo? Cioppino (sold here as "San Francisco Seafood Stew")? The latter is a preparation we've never understood; watery and bland, it's the worst offense to seafood since the Bikini Atoll nuclear tests.

Chains will be chains. But this one fits Portland's locavore scene a little better than the others.

McMenamins

This funky, theatrical pub-grub-hotel-music empire needs its own guidebook

3.9	10	7.0
Food	Feel	Beer

American

Casual restaurant

$30
Price

www.mcmenamins.com

Mon–Thu 11am–midnight
Fri–Sat 11am–1am
Sun noon–midnight
Hours vary by location

Bar Beer, wine, liquor
Credit cards Visa, MC, AmEx
Reservations Accepted
Date-friendly, kid-friendly, live music, outdoor dining, Wi-Fi

Downtown
1526 SW 10th Ave.
(503) 497-0160

Northwest Portland
432 NW 21st Ave.
(503) 223-3184

Hawthorne
3702 SE Hawthorne Blvd.
(503) 236-9234

Alberta Arts District
5736 NE 33rd Ave.
(503) 249-3983

No review could possibly do justice to this magical mystery tour throughout Portland's past, a funky, fantastical network with colonies at the Blue Moon, Barley Mill, St. John's Pub, and many more. If it was ever an old movie house or stage theater, McMenamins has saved it from destruction and renovated it, turning it into a three-ring circus of food, drink, and entertainment that flows seamlessly from interior to exterior.

Care is taken to preserve the unique, vintage character of each place. Blue Moon is huge and has billiards. The Back Stage at the Baghdad Theatre is bigger—five stories high—and the façade out front is fantastically old school. Market Street Pub has a heavenly patio and a turn-of-the-century copper bar. McMinnville's Hotel Oregon is by far the coolest place to stay in wine country. Current runs of movies are shown at several locations, for only $3 and a beer.

And this is the next bit of genius: that beer will come from a massive lineup of McMenamins' own microbrews, plus a guest tap or two. There are no casks, that we've found, anyway, but there's usually something on nitro at the brewpubs. These are mostly IPAs, pale ales, stouts, and porters, and lean toward the hoppier side. None are particularly outstanding, but it goes further: wine comes from yet another McMenamins venue, its Edgefield winery. Unlike the venues, the wines are nearly indistinguishable from each other, and drinkable, no more than that. Think it stops there? There are McMenamins distilleries that provide much of the liquor. What's next, McMenamins furnishings?

For all this effort and pride, the food, which is pretty uniform from venue to venue, is just your garden-variety American bar grub. Burgers are best, made with Country Natural beef (not owned by McMenamins—we checked), but such a special Portland restaurant is missing such a big opportunity to do something special with the food, too. Are you listening, McMenamins? We feel like we speak for half of Portland when we ask: why can't you replace the TGI Friday's-level kitchen food with something that actually honors Portland's exciting culinary culture?

Still, if you've ever strolled the inspiring grounds of the hotel/restaurant/theater/art gallery/bar-commune-Fantasyland Kennedy School, you'll know that the costs of admission are well worth it. Long live McMenamins.

Meat Cheese Bread

8.1 | 6.0
Food | Feel

This creative, excellent sandwich shop begs the question: how did we ever live without the BLB?

Sandwiches

Counter service

$15
Price

www.meatcheesebread.com

Mon–Sat 7am–7pm

Bar Beer, wine
Credit cards Visa, MC, AmEx
Kid-friendly, outdoor dining,
veg-friendly, Wi-Fi

Southeast Portland
1406 SE Stark St.
(503) 234-1700

As far as sandwiches are concerned, Portland has quickly gone from a town with hardly any decent options to an embarrassment of riches. The secret ingredient that is setting these shops apart is the staff, who is passionate about making the best damn sandwich possible. This leads to innovation and a competitiveness of execution that just benefits everyone. In the case of Meat Cheese Bread, these may include thoughtful combinations of average ingredients like Granny Smith apples, honey butter, and brie; or it may mean raising the bar of the standard sloppy Joe (no longer on the menu) by using a pork-belly Bolognese on a house-made roll.

One can't help but make the comparison between Meat Cheese Bread (MCB) and Bunk. We like both, but for different reasons. Bunk has a nostalgic dive appeal, whereas MCB feels cleaner and brighter. Bunk tends to use more prestigious ingredients, but MCB seems to prefer to use standard ingredients in more interesting ways. Fear not, there is room in this economy for both.

A breakfast burrito full of smoky green chilies, cheddar cheese, scrambled eggs and hash browns makes a delicious amalgam that has generated a passionate following. Maple bread pudding is another favorite morning choice, made with shaved fennel, spicy cheddar, and piquant sausage. This is a terrific breakfast, rich and satisfying, full of diverse textures and flavors—it's one of the best breakfast sandwiches in Portland.

Park Kitchen's flank steak salad has been reincarnated as a sandwich here. Moist, thinly sliced tender flank steak is piled high with pickled red onions, blue cheese mayo, greens and piquant vinaigrette. But nothing beats MCB's take on a BLT, in which tomatoes are replaced, out of season, with golden beets. This BLB is brilliant, with grilled Grand Central sourdough holding in thick slices of smoky Nueskies bacon. Peppery dribbles of bacon fat run across the beets and down into the bread, giving everything a rich meaty taste. A light aïoli adds a final layer of flavor. It is hard to order anything else once you've had this.

A small selection of beer and wine is available, including Double Mountain Brewery on tap, along with a nice group of sodas. Portland may be a sandwich paradise, but MCB has a niche all its own.

MetroVino

Don't be turned off by the slick name and
trendy look; pleasant surprises abound

8.0	9.0	8.5
Food	Feel	Wine

Modern

Upmarket restaurant

$45
Price

www.metrovinopdx.com

Mon–Sat 5:30pm–9pm

Bar Beer, wine, liquor
Credit cards Visa, MC, AmEx
Reservations Accepted
Date-friendly, outdoor dining

Pearl District
1139 NW 11th Ave.
(503) 517-7778

MetroVino does everything better than you'd expect from a wine bar
that's a bit…Enomatic. That's the name for the machines that preserve
wine for longer than would be possible otherwise, reducing inventory risk
and enabling expensive wines to be poured by the glass, in 5.25-ounce
and 1.75-ounce servings. The machines reside safely behind the bar in the
able hands of the personable, passionate, knowledgeable bar staff, with
occasional ringers. (Not that a $300 bottle offers any better value at $20
per taste, but at least you're limiting your exposure.)

Although the wine program is well conceived (lots of unheralded
appellations and small producers), we do wish wine prices were lower.
$34.50 for a glass of Paul Pernot 2007 1er Cru Folatières Puligny-
Montrachet (retail price per bottle: $70) or $22.50 for a glass of Vietti
2005 Barolo Castiglione (retail price per bottle: $45) aren't absurd from a
markup perspective, but they are from a sanity-check perspective.

MetroVino's vibe is modern to the core, with floor-to-ceiling windows
overlooking the city streets and Portland's urban eco-marsh, Tanner
Springs Park, but there's an unpretentious un-Pearlishness to the place.
An eclectic mix plays while science-lab-ish lamps swing about, mimicking
old-school clear-glass incandescent lightbulbs; and a friendly buzz
pervades, even on a Monday night.

Equally modern are the vaguely Italian-inspired American restaurant
menu and bar menu (the latter is quite inexpensive: $6–$13 for big
portions). Craft cheeses are interesting. More interesting still are Roman-
style tripe stew with tomato, pecorino, and mint; roasted marrow bones;
and an appearance of raclette, one of the unsung heroes of the fondue
world. Less classy, though, is the lame, populist employment of
"edamame" in a purée that decks out "salmon gravlax bruschetta."

We've been pleasantly surprised by shrimp "ceviche," done with spicy,
delightfully tender, teensy-weensy shrimp, and ripe avocado slices
properly seasoned with kosher salt—an oft-overlooked step. Surprising,
too, are pork ribs glazed with hoisin, whose syrupy character is balanced
by a healthy char and globules of delicious fat lurking on the underside of
the bones. Add the "kimchi bean sprouts," which actually deliver with
some heat and pickle flavor, and you've got a Utopian version of Chinese-
American spare ribs in a somewhat Utopian version of a trendy wine bar.

Mingo

Suburban Italian that probably tries harder than it needs to

6.1	6.5	7.5
Food	Feel	Wine

Italian, Pizza

Upmarket restaurant

$50
Price

www.mingowest.com

Mon 5pm–9pm; Tue–Fri
11:30am–2:30pm; Tue–Thu
5pm–9pm; Fri 11:30am–
2:30pm, 5pm–10pm; Sat 5pm–
9:30pm; Sun 5pm–9pm

Bar Beer, wine
Credit cards Visa, MC, AmEx
Reservations Accepted
Date-friendly, outdoor dining

Beaverton
12600 SW Crescent St.
(503) 646-6464

The suburban arm belonging to the successful Bar Mingo and Caffè Mingo is, perhaps unsurprisingly, also the more generic and corporate one. There are some commendable attempts at legitimacy, but they're foiled by an apparent temptation to give into mainstream American demands. While there's no goofy and totally un-Italian Caesar salad on the menu, a "Mingo" is nearly identical, but without any of the anchovy that makes this salad interesting. The menu is divided in primi and secondi (as well as pizza, insalata, and "lunch"), but none of the primi are the pasta and rice-based dishes that Italy considers primi; these appear instead in large portions on the secondi.

In other words, it's a typical Italian-American restaurant posing as an authentic one. Which isn't necessarily the problem—it just explains why everything has that intense burst of heavy-handed flavor, a hallmark-suburban, ham-fisted approach to Italian that includes large chunks of meat covered in sauce, instead of being refined and integrated into it.

For example, pork scaloppine is served over seared polenta and then covered in a mushroom-Madeira sauce; the dish is thick and salty—which some people will love—but it's completely incapable of complexity and subtlety. Grilled salmon with sage cream sauce and butternut squash is a valid ticket item, but this is hardly "simple Italian," as Mingo advertises.

The charade goes too far with a "Mingo Burger," holding firm to any claim of Italianness it can by boasting Piedmont beef; if every bite of this burger smells a little like the jet fuel required to get it over the Atlantic and across the continent, its sheer needlessness ought to make it unbearable. Italians wouldn't brag about Piedmont beef—they'd import American or Argentine beef first. This is still the eco-conscious Northwest: all things being equal, why not use local, free-range beef with much less of a blatant carbon footprint?

Perhaps this is shooting fish in a barrel. After all, looking around this sterile, design-firm-born place, not much is surprising.

Miss Delta

Sweeter than it is soulful, this Miss is a real charmer

7.2	8.5	8.0
Food	Feel	Drinks

Southern

Casual restaurant

$35
Price

missdeltapdx.net

Sun–Thu 5pm–10pm
Fri–Sat 5pm–11pm

Bar Beer, wine, liquor
Credit cards Visa, MC, AmEx
Reservations Not accepted
Date-friendly

Mississippi Ave. Area
3950 N. Mississippi Ave.
(503) 287-7629

Miss Delta is absolutely charming, like a good Southern lady ought to be, in a long narrow room with exposed brick and old-timey lighting fixtures. It could look almost exactly like many Portland coffeehouses, in fact, if not for the open kitchen in the back and the terse antiquey bar running through the middle of the room.

And if the atmosphere is quintessential Portland but not remotely Mississippi-soul-food, the food tends to follow suit. It's charming, and often beautifully executed, but missing the layers of sweat and pork and time and mud that seem to only exist south of the Mason-Dixon line. Fried okra is cut into rings here, lightly breaded with a cornmeal crust and flash fried. They're not greasy, nor are they well seasoned. And though the portion is hearty, no one east of the Colorado would dare charge this much for an order of them. Dorothy, we're still planted solidly in the Northwest.

Otherwise, dishes slant towards the Carolinas, where vinegar lurks in every bite. Sautéed greens have too much of it if you get the vegetarian version; they really need the pork to balance them out. And these are cooked to a nice al dente, which you won't see much of around the Delta, nor will you see this wacky Caesar salad. Is there a Portland city tax imposed on restaurants that don't include a Caesar?

Fried chicken, even when made well, can elude sublimity. All the flavor is in the skin and coating, with the flesh turning out bland, if not fibrous and chewy. Miss Delta's Draper chicken pieces are large, so the cooking is a bit uneven, though the shell is crackling and caramelized. It still feels more like novelty, though. Better is a blackened catfish, very fresh and not too blackened or too salty; it is a home run with its accompanying horseradish remoulade. This fish would make any Cajun proud.

There are about six sides to choose from: mac and cheese is creamy and satisfying, but missing that sublime crusty texture; black-eyed peas need a few splashes of that Tabasco; red beans and rice are just bland and mushy; cornbread has none of the natural corn sweetness of Southern bread, nor the guilty-pleasure sugary sweetness of Yankee bread.

Miss Delta satisfies a Northern craving for Southern food, so it's often crowded. Service is friendly and portions are generous, but the familiar soulful flavors just aren't there. Even a mint julep is made with soda water rather than still water, creating a curious mouthfeel. It's not bad, but it's just not the mint julep of the South.

Mississippi Pizza Pub

6.7	8.5	8.0
Food	Feel	Beer

Pizza and spelling bees—what could be better?

Pizza

Counter service

$20
Price

www.mississippipizza.com

Sun–Thu 11am–midnight
Fri–Sat 11am–1am

Bar Beer, wine, liquor
Credit cards Visa, MC, AmEx
Reservations Not accepted
Live music, outdoor dining,
veg-friendly

Mississippi Ave. Area
3552 N. Mississippi Ave.
(503) 288-3231

The loveable, laid-back atmosphere at Mississippi Pizza Pub goes a long way toward obscuring any shortcomings—perhaps unsurprising, given how great the ambience tends to be at most Mississippi-area eateries. There's a comfortable dining room that invites lingering. Live music plays nearly every night, and the bands are some of Portland's more reputable. This isn't the ideal venue in which to see them, but we're not complaining. But perhaps coolest of all, you can sign up for weekly spelling bees, which are a total must-see (or do) for any Portlander or visitor. There's one for adults and one for kiddos, and these aren't wussy bees, either. One winning word was "oophagous" (egg-eating).

If the cute pea-green building and its straw awnings, hippie-ish stained glass sign, and alluring sounds of revelry don't draw you in, the aromas will. Curiously, few pizzerias in Portland smell like they should; this one is filled with the warm, sweet, and yeasty notes of baking flour and melting cheese.

Perhaps most significantly, there are gluten-free and vegan pizzas available, as well as regular pizzas. The crusts aren't super-thin and charred, but the taste is enjoyable enough—or is it just the happy vibes we're tasting? Ingredients are of the standard variety, with the most "gourmet" choices falling along the lines of sun-dried tomatoes, kalamata olives, and artichoke hearts.

Within the pizzeria is the Atlantis Lounge, a totally maritime-kitschy-adorable place to drink some sweet, tropical elixirs, although savories are done pretty well here, too. An "Argonaut" has the makings of a good Bourbon cocktail, but ask them to go easy on the soda, which can water it down too much. There are 12 taps of good beer, many local microbrews (and the ironic-hip PBR), and a couple are even gluten free.

While we wouldn't suggest a trip here for the regular pizza, those with gluten intolerances will be well served. And if you live in the neighborhood, this is a great hangout. Brush up on your vocab and try out for a T-shirt that's proud but not at all braggy—kind of like Mississippi Pizza Pub.

Morton's

The smoothest ship in the steakhouse business

7.3	6.0	7.0
Food	Feel	Wine

Steakhouse

Upmarket restaurant

$100
Price

www.mortons.com

Mon–Thu 5:30pm–10pm
Fri 5:30pm–11pm
Sat 5pm–11pm
Sun 5pm–10pm

Bar Beer, wine, liquor
Credit cards Visa, MC, AmEx
Reservations Accepted
Outdoor dining

Downtown
213 SW Clay Street.
(503) 248-2100

One of the best meals we've ever had at a chain restaurant, anywhere in the world, was at the Morton's in Singapore. To get those Prime cuts of beef there from the American Midwest would have taken Singapore Airlines' new A380 about 19 hours. The steakhouse décor (corporate luxe, plush booths, dark and elegant, you know the drill) and impeccable service were identical to their counterparts anywhere else. The execution was as good, or better, than it is in Chicago—and Singapore is hardly a city where they're used to broiling steaks at 1800°. That's how smoothly the Morton's machine is running at the moment, although all of these high-priced steakhouses have been threatened by the economy.

One of the trademarks here is the plastic-wrapped beef ritual, wherein your server shows you all the different raw cuts of meat, covered in what looks like Saran wrap, as you're ordering. The idea is to let you choose your Prime weapon, although this steakhouse version of the tableside guacamole routine tends to make at least someone at the table squirm with squeamishness. (There's always someone that loves meat but wants to deny that it ever consisted of living muscle.)

It's pretty hard to go wrong here, except if you consider the effect on your wallet. The only steakhouse chain in town that compares to Morton's is Ruth's Chris. Outback is too modest (and in trouble). Morton's does have one failing: we prefer the funkier flavor of dry-aged beef to the wet-aged version that they settle for. Regardless, three decades after its opening, this remains a genre-defying—or perhaps new-genre-defining—restaurant in the history of the American chain.

And you pay the price. You're best off experiencing all of this with an expense account at your disposal. After all, everyone else in the restaurant seems to be doing so.

Mother's Bistro & Bar

7.1	9.0	7.0
Food	Feel	Wine

Eat your green beans and keep your mouth shut

American

Casual restaurant

$40
Price

www.mothersbistro.com

Tue–Thu 7am–2:30pm, 5:30pm–9pm; Fri 7am–2:30pm, 5pm–10pm; Sat 9am–2:30pm, 5pm–10pm; Sun 9am–2:30pm

Bar Beer, wine, liquor
Credit cards Visa, MC, AmEx
Reservations Accepted
Date-friendly, outdoor dining

Downtown
212 SW Stark St.
(503) 464-1122

Mother's needs a good cleaning. Empty tables full of dirty dishes surround you. Several tables of patrons are looking around, wondering where their food or checks are. Your own empty dishes sit untouched next to your newly dropped plates. Despite the name, make no mistake: your mother doesn't work here.

The inside feels like a hybrid of a shabby-chic diner and a baroque ballroom. Crystal chandeliers and Versailles wallpaper frame a counter riddled with Tabasco bottles and ordinary salt-and-pepper shakers. High cream-colored walls full of artfully mismatched paintings, and enormous windows with diaphanous white curtains loom over dressed tables full of dishes that are plated like they would be at home: no towers, no scattered brunoise of herbs around the rim, and no pretense.

People are fiercely protective of this place. Any attempts to hold it accountable for its shortcomings have frequently been met with wrath. We've seen this happen in other cities at restaurants that also have "Mother" in the name. Don't underestimate the power of the subconscious.

The truth is, many dishes here are competent, nothing more. One time, a pulled pork sandwich with honey-mustard barbecue sauce was bland and rather mushy. A finely ground hamburger has all the basic building blocks, but not much in the flavor department. French fries are better, thin and crisp, with the skins left on (that's where all the nutrition is, your mom would point out).

We come for matzoh ball soup, made with a nice chicken-fat flavor and a huge matzoh ball in the middle. It's the best thing we've had here. Hand-made pierogi were very light on one visit, but with so little potato filling, they were overpowered by the dough. Denver macaroni and cheese with ham, pepper, onions, and cheddar cheese is strictly middle-American, a huge portion on bow-tie pasta and with no crust. Sometimes, it comes with bacon and a dollop of sour cream, but it's underwhelming and a bit gummy.

Breakfast is a huge draw here, when light fills the room and everyone's standards a little lower. It's not that anything here is bad, it's just that most of the dishes you would expect to find in, again, the home of your friends and family, where sentiment puts everything into a rose-tinted context. When you're paying for it, and your mama didn't make it, you just kind of wonder what the big deal is.

Nakwon

Focus on stews and soups at this popular Korean hole in the wall

7.4 Food

6.5 Feel

Korean

Casual restaurant

$20 Price

Mon–Fri 11am–9pm; Sat–Sun 11:30am–2:30pm, 5pm–9pm

Bar Beer, wine, liquor
Credit cards Visa, MC
Reservations Accepted

Beaverton
4600 SW Watson Ave.
(503) 646-9382

Where ethnic foods are concerned, we tend to have the best food experiences in places that are hard to find and where the atmosphere is really nothing special. Head to the middle of picturesque Beaverton, look for a one-story brick warehouse-looking edifice, and you're probably at Nakwon. At lunch and dinner, this space gets jam-packed with a mixed crowd of hipsters, families, and college students. Even at off-hours when the lively bustle calms, it's got a warmer atmosphere than that of many of its competitors.

Service is working at its limit, which means you're mostly on your own. Don't ask for advice or help—this is where you go once you've graduated from Korean novicehood. But don't panic and settle for barbecue, bulgogi, and the like. These things tend to be dry and gristly here. There are some Beaverton Korean restaurants where barbecue is the focus, and this isn't one of them. Instead, say these words: dduk boki (pronounced "duk"). It's the most fun your mouth will have, a chewy little rice cake with spicy dipping sauce. Also start by sharing some pajeon, seafood pancake, full of scallops, scallions, shrimp, and squid.

Follow this up with soon dubu, soft and hearty tofu stews served in stone pots—especially soon dubu jjigae, which is a little spicier. Naengmyeon is also very good, with thin, nicely resilient noodles. If you're feeling under the weather or hungover, any of these stone pots will cure ya.

The selection of banchan is great here; in fact, it's sometimes even better than the main dishes. Kimchi is right on the money, hot and pickle-puckery. And it goes perfectly with a bottle of Hite. When it comes to good Korean, leave it to Beaverton (sorry).

Navarre

The farm-fresh ingredients and good wine are appreciated, even if the service isn't

6.7	5.5	9.0
Food	Feel	Wine

Modern

Upmarket restaurant

$45
Price

www.navarreportland.blogspot.com

Mon–Thu 4:30pm–10:30pm
Fri 11:30am–11:30pm
Sat 9:30am–11:30pm
Sun 9:30am–10:30pm

Bar Beer, wine
Credit cards Visa, MC, AmEx
Reservations Essential
Date-friendly, outdoor dining,
veg-friendly, Wi-Fi

Northeast Portland
10 NE 28th Ave.
(503) 232-3555

We really want to love Navarre, given the concept: small plates of local ingredients, a chef-driven menu, and a "just leave it to us" option (which we always prefer). It's small yet airy inside, with an open kitchen and a rustic shabbiness—a good place for a casual date, especially outside on the sidewalk's tiny wrought-iron tables.

The problem is, although atmosphere is fun, the staff is standoffish and inattentive. Trying to order a second round of drinks or a dessert wine is like trying to get an autograph from a famous person—like they're doing you a huge favor. Worse still, you can often expect long waits.

There is obvious humility and care in this food. It's commonly held in kitchens that most of the work of cooking is done in the fields and at the market; the rest is just staying out of the way. This creed is exemplified in a dish of farm-fresh radishes whose prickly flavor is rendered gentle by French butter. New potatoes cooked with vinegar, white wine, and spices are a fascinating pleasure, too. But "staying out of the way" can be taken a bit too literally here. On one visit, a kohlrabi salad with feta and blueberry was made up of components whose sum was worse than its parts.

Meats are regularly overcooked here, whether halibut or chicken (in the latter case, it has been to the point of being inedible). Or it's just not a good cut, as a rare-plus lamb loin that was too sinewy and chewy to be enjoyable, despite the great fennel with which it was paired. Desserts are a must here, like a delicious cornbread-like peach-bottom cake with apricot, and, when in season, a precious cherry pie with homemade whipped cream.

The succinct, focused wine list matches the unfussy food here beautifully. Almost none of it is New World, there are no knee-jerk choices here, and all wines are priced low. But with more than 50 by-the-glass selections, it's almost a given that some bottles will have been open too long. (In most cases, a huge glass selection is a detriment, not a bragging right.)

Given the iffy food and the snobbish service, we hesitate to recommend Navarre wholeheartedly. Still, we know heart when we see it, and we've got to say: cheers to that.

Ned Ludd

Locavore dishes that often charm, and an artfully rustic vibe that always does

8.9	10	8.0
Food	Feel	Wine

Modern

Upmarket restaurant

$45
Price

www.nedluddpdx.com

Thu–Mon 5pm–10pm

Bar Beer, wine, liquor
Credit cards Visa, MC
Reservations Essential
Date-friendly, outdoor dining

Northeast Portland
3925 NE Martin Luther
King Jr Blvd.
(503) 288-6900

The name Ned Ludd conjures up simplicity, a reticent nostalgia, and a deep mistrust of anything too modern or fabricated. It's just the right name for this place: the staff is food-nerdy, but not pretentious; the servers care as much as the kitchen does, and can talk at length about each of the dishes, some of which are made using vegetables grown in a garden out back. The tiny space is cozy and farmhousish, with sacks of this and kegs of that, a wood pile, and plank wooden bars and tables at which to stand or sit. Vivid lime-green walls and shabby-chic chandeliers lend hipness to the rusticity. Part of the kitchen is open to the dining area, and the chef/owner is generally hanging out there the entire time interacting with customers.

If the accolades ended there, we'd still think this a terribly fun and romantic place to be, but the food makes it a spectacular experience, even when not every dish works. You'll find seasonal preps here that are neither fussy nor boring: an ideal balance of originality, modernity, and simplicity. In summer, barbecue is served at the seating area out front, and includes things like an absolutely delicious cheeseburger cooked over applewood. A beer brat is good and juicy, if a bit overwhelmed by too much dry bread. Ned's rendition of a Carolina-style pulled pork sandwich tastes right (if a little dry), with a good smokiness that's hard to find in this part of the world.

In the main dining room, you might find a wonderful plate of heirloom tomatoes with goat cheese, cucumbers, bright tarragon, and a kiss of chili. A gratin of green beans, zucchini, and mushrooms is like a comfort-food casserole—a better version of dinner at auntie's house. "Meat pie," with lamb and pork, is a bit underseasoned, not the kitchen's best work, but the puff pastry is beautifully executed. A whole trout, blackened and crusted in the brick oven, retains a very moist flesh within, and is served in a delicious prep with tons of lemon and dill.

The wine list is small and precise, with both local producers and food-loving bottles from abroad, all at wonderfully low prices, and the $10 corkage is generous. A tight, succinct selection of local beers on draft has every bit as much careful economy as a drawing on the head of a pin. In the balance, this is one of our very favorite places in the city to dine.

Nel Centro

A few moments make this hotel restaurant stand out from all the others

7.0	7.5	8.0
Food	Feel	Wine

Italian

Upmarket restaurant

$60
Price

www.nelcentro.com

Mon–Thu 6:30am–10:30am,
11:30am–2:30pm, 5pm–9pm
Fri 6:30am–10:30am,
11:30am–2:30pm, 5pm–10pm
Sat 7:30am–11:30am, 5pm–10pm
Sun 8am–2pm, 5pm–9pm

Bar Beer, wine, liquor
Credit cards Visa, MC, AmEx
Reservations Accepted
Date-friendly, live music, outdoor dining, Wi-Fi

Downtown
Hotel Modera
1408 SW 6th Ave.
(503) 484-1099

The newest child of the Vindalho-Lauro Café family, Nel Centro is an ambitious attempt at authentic Italian food: homemade pasta, Euro style, beautiful courtyard.

There's something about each member of this restaurant group that feels studied, a touch obsequious. In many other cities this would just be good business, but in Portland, this soundness is undermined by the risk taking, passion, and intense focus of our best restaurants. Next to something audacious like Pok Pok or Beast, these ventures seem sort of...cynical.

Of course, good business means procuring talent: the excellent breads, pastas, and desserts are made by a Pearl Bakery veteran, and they're the best performers here; the wine program works academically and practically at all price points, with little underachievement; there's a small but ample selection of microbrews on draft and a few of the world's better bottles. Cocktails remain a weakness for this clutch of establishments: some dress as classics but are reluctant to cast off the reliable wardrobe of the –tini age.

Some hesitation is apparent even in the color scheme of the restaurant where various shapes and colors of blown-glass lamps (a proven crowd pleaser since the 1990s) offset a primarily brown palette: brown booths, brown carpet, brown ceiling, brown pillars, and, yes, brown art. The patio of fire pits in the Hotel Modera courtyard is very nice, but at no time do you ever forget you're in a hotel restaurant.

We've been dazzled by a salad of raw zucchini and shaved carpaccio with fresh mint shining through. Bucatini have come perfectly al dente, with a well-developed tomato sauce and deep, rich lamb meatballs. A roast pork sandwich, however, is dry and lacking good pork-fat flavor, and relies heavily upon an overly sweet marmalade. Proteins like grilled wild salmon, braised beef, and rotisserie chicken are generally expertly cooked, but elements of each dish have come oversalted to the point of inedibility. Pizza is not great, with a spurious, pasty crust the color of uncooked dough: what's that visible brick oven being used for?

Desserts are more consistent; it would be criminal to miss an exemplary Scharffen Berger soufflé or a lavender-scented crème brûlée brilliantly complemented by pistachio macaroons. In the end, though, our panel is split on Nel Centro—probably because the restaurant is so unpredictable.

New Old Lompoc

This popular, somewhat historic tavern has
slightly better food than you'd expect

6.0	8.0	7.0
Food	Feel	Beer

American

Casual restaurant

$25
Price

www.newoldlompoc.com

Sun–Thu 11am–11pm
Fri–Sat 11am–midnight

Bar Beer, wine, liquor
Credit cards Visa, MC, AmEx
Reservations Not accepted
Live music, outdoor dining

Northwest Portland
1616 NW 23rd Ave.
(503) 225-1855

The Lompoc Brewery is responsible for some great little beer-drinking
establishments around town: Hedge House down on SE Division Street,
5th Quadrant (reviewed in this book), and Oaks Bottom, plus the Sidebar
tasting room. The name comes from an old W.C. Fields/Mae West movie
in which "Old Lompoc House" was a sort of saloon and hotel. This space
was a popular watering hole in the mid century, and you can feel the
history in the wainscoting, old-wood-smelling booths, and a residual
mural left on the back porch under kitschy plastic grapevines. Picnic
benches make up the seating both within and without, and these all get
filled up, especially during Tuesday's trivia nights.

Happy hour is a frequent event here, with food specials from 3–6pm
(and again, briefly, from 10–11pm) Tuesdays through Fridays; all
weekend, there are drink specials, but not food discounts. Still, it's not
that great a bargain; greasy bar food like Buffalo chicken wings, chicken
tenders with mealy fries, and nachos cost around $6, which is what many
better happy hour menus are charging for better food. But if you're here,
it's probably mainly for the vibe and the beer, which has its fans among
the hop-and malt-loving drinkers. Lompoc beers come in three distinct
varieties: hoppy, hoppier, and hoppy/malty. But there's an okay draft
range here: a chocolatey, creamy stout served on the nitro tap is thick,
but too sweet; some rotating guest taps feature lighter regional beers like
Widmer Hefeweizen and Caldera Pilsner.

Avoid the cocktails, which lean toward the gimmicky and sweet side;
after all, this food is much better suited to beer. There's a decent French
onion soup, some fresh and large salads, and a good array of sandwiches
including a lightly fried halibut that's surprisingly not greasy. Mac and
cheese is kind of bland, with pepper jack and cheddar; it's better with
andouille sausage and bell peppers, but still not something we'd ever pay
this much for. In fact, all of the food is overpriced for what it is.

Nevertheless, people come to watch games on the TV, carouse with
friends in a cool, pubby atmosphere, compete in trivia, and—you know
what?—it grows on you.

New Seasons Market

In a city of high-minded markets, here is a local success story

Groceries   Market

www.newseasonsmarket.com

Daily 8am–10pm

Bar Beer, wine
Credit cards Visa, MC, AmEx
Delivery, kid-friendly, outdoor
dining, veg-friendly

Division/Clinton
1954 SE Division St.
(503) 445-2888

North Portland
6400 N. Interstate Ave.
(503) 467-4777

Alberta Arts District
5320 NE 33rd Ave.
(503) 288-3838

Additional locations
and more features at
www.fearlesscritic.com

New Seasons is Portland's homegrown sustainable, natural, local-ingredients superstore, the local boy made good. There are weekly deals on everything from beers and wines, mostly domestic and locally crafted with some imports; pre-made deli items; local produce; and handmade sausages and regionally sourced seafood. There's a great little selection of top-quality homestuffs like knives and cookware, and these go on sale from time to time, as well, making for some great gift sourcing. A cheese selection is wrapped properly and lorded over by knowledgeable, passionate people who will explain it all.

Bulk flours, rices, lentils, granolas, dried fruits, nuts, and spices is impressive, and a great deal compared to the boxed and bagged stuff you can find in even the cheapest chain grocery stores. There are also tastings—mushrooms, wines, apples, you name it—and classes. It's quite reasonable to grab some breakfast from the bakery or a sandwich made from top ingredients. Breads are made in-house, and you can choose from several different kinds and create virtually any combination of fillings you desire.

And you needn't be well off to shop here: sometimes there's a big box full of free day-old bread, various produce, and so on. Nor do you have to leave the house: New Seasons will deliver from orders made online. This may very well be, as each store's loopy cursive claims, "The friendliest place in town."

Nicholas Restaurant

A tiny, intensely popular spot serving intense flavors on the cheap

8.6	7.0
Food	Feel

Middle Eastern

Casual restaurant

$20
Price

www.nicholasrestaurant.com

Mon–Sat 11am–9pm
Sun noon–9pm

Bar None
Credit cards None
Reservations Not accepted
Outdoor dining, veg-friendly

Southeast Portland
318 SE Grand Ave.
(503) 235-5123

Call us persnickety, but we're always encouraged when a Middle Eastern restaurant doesn't refer to itself "Mediterranean," which is a nebulous and often inaccurate cuisine type. It usually refers to the dishes of lands once covered by the southern penumbra of the Ottoman Empire, but it can technically include cuisines that are now totally distinct, like Moroccan, Italian, and Greek.

What these misleadingly named eateries are usually referring to is a menu much like the one at Nicholas, a mostly Lebanese spread that includes falafel, mezze platters, and the ubiquitous Greek gyro. In other words, foods that turn us on, even in their most Americanized renditions. But the ones here *really* turn us on.

Nicholas is a terrific place for families and groups, as servings are large and dishes are really designed to offset each other. But you won't drop a huge amount of coin here, either: a mezze platter can fill up two people, not to mention the fact that it's a much more delicious and complex vegetarian option than the tofurkey, fake-bacon, and barbecued-tempeh disasters vegetarians are sometimes forced to contend with elsewhere. You get refreshing, minty tabbouleh; creamy, slightly funky hummus; smoky baba ghanoush; and anything else you would want to try here, all on one spectacular plate.

There's a generous and energetic vibe about this place, and people line up at peak hours to squeeze into the humble, tiny restaurant to eat flavorful, moist shawarma with a creamy tahini sauce; gyros that are properly lamby and bright with some of the best tzatziki in the city; and falafel that, while not quite as transcendent as some we've tasted from Basha's ("Mediterranean") food cart, is still superb in both flavor and texture. The *pièce de résistance* here is the pita bread, billowy and warm. It's wrapped around everything, used as a utensil, and generally adored. Finish up with an intense Turkish coffee, just like the Ottomans did.

Nick's Italian Café

8.2	8.5	8.5
Food	Feel	Wine

After a reinvention, Nick's is still one of our best wine country restaurants

Italian, Modern, Pizza

Upmarket restaurant

$70
Price

www.nicksitaliancafe.com

Tue–Sat 11:30am–2pm,
5:30pm–9pm

Bar Beer, wine, liquor
Credit cards Visa, MC, AmEx
Reservations Accepted
Date-friendly

McMinnville
521 NE 3rd St.
(503) 434-4471

Nick's Italian Café is an institution, having watched the Willamette Valley wine scene explode, having been through ups and downs, having been splayed across the pages of the once-glorious *Saveur* like some sort of reverse-world pin-up wherein the older and more forgotten you were, the better.

But like any good icon, it has recently undergone an overhaul, and is now better than ever. For a long time, if you were touring wineries in the Willamette Valley the only decent place to eat in McMinnville was Nick's. Now, of course, there's Thistle. There's still the dinerish counter, booths and tables of dark wood with white tablecloths, charmingly casual mix-and-match plates and silverware.

The main focus here, as you can see through the semi-open kitchen, is the wood-fired oven. Here, pizzas are cooked with quite thin crusts, but at slightly too low a temperature to achieve good blistering. Still, they're quite good, with a terrific, balanced sauce and the right amount of cheese. We like sausage best, but alto try getting the basic flatbread (with no sauce or cheese) and adding anchovy and egg.

Salads are nice and fresh, made from local ingredients. Shallot-laced vinaigrette is very faithfully French; fresh Dungeness crab with pickled beets and goat cheese isn't, and it's lovely. It's a lively and fun combination. Ravioli with sage butter is spot on, with spinach and a hint of citrus.

Items frequently change, which is also a relatively new development in Nick's life. A duck involtino, ground and stuffed into a thin layer of its own tender meat, has been wonderfully autumnal with a celery root purée and earthy roasted shallots. Pan-seared sole has come with a lovely anchovy-caper butter and tender baby kale, although the fish was a bit overcooked. Notoriously difficult monkfish, on the other hand, has come beautifully moist and beefy.

Dessert is all grown up, too. We've had a spectacular black-pepper gelato topped with syrupy, vinegary saba. Likewise, the wine list has done nothing but improve over the years. Ask the servers for suggestions; they are knowledgeable and passionate. It's rare, but always a great treat, to see a restaurant get better with age.

Nob Hill Bar & Grill

7.2	7.0	7.0
Food	Feel	Beer

One of Portland's oldest bars charms with its great burger and vintage sass

American

Bar **$20**
Price

www.nobhillbg.ypguides.net

Daily 8am–2:30am

Bar Beer, wine, liquor
Credit cards Visa, MC, AmEx
Outdoor dining

Northwest Portland
937 NW 23rd Ave.
(503) 274-9616

Nob Hill Bar & Grill is like a museum of American bar culture. In its turn-of-the-century Victorian house in a historic neighborhood, it looks and feels like a slice of some other time. With wood paneling, a stale smoke smell, and several television sets, this funky dive is a great place to watch sports with a pitcher of beer, or to play Keno (Keno!) while the adorably surly waitstaff move with the unhurried deliberateness of those who've seen it all. They might even make you down a glass of water before serving you another drink. It's very Flo and Mel.

The food here is all pretty standard bar fare, except for one thing: delicious burgers, which are not to be missed. They're made in the greasy-spoon fashion: a quarter-pound patty done medium-well, charry, juicy, and with melted cheese settling into its little nooks. It's precious, though, to call Thousand Island dressing "secret sauce." (Kind of like when McDonald's named it "special sauce" on the Big Mac.) This burger couldn't get any more old-timey American than it would if you ate it in a Ford Fairlane. Mealy steak fries, though, taste like they're of the frozen variety; opt instead for tots (tots!). Breakfast is harmless; again, it's like anything you'd find in a diner—greasy and better with booze.

For Portland, the beer selection is good but not great. There are only a few taps, and little of it is exciting, but for a dive bar, it does the trick. Don't even think about getting cute with cocktails here.

While the rest of the city gets hoity-toity with local this and that, daily changing menus, artfully industrial spaces, and artisanal cocktails, it's nice to know that there's one place in town keeping it old school.

Noble Rot

A noble effort where the wine and space are concerned, with food playing just a bit part

6.1	8.5	9.0
Food	Feel	Wine

Modern

Upmarket restaurant

$40
Price

www.noblerotpdx.com

Mon–Thu 5pm–11pm
Fri–Sat 5pm–midnight

Bar Beer, wine, liquor
Credit cards Visa, MC, AmEx
Reservations Not accepted
Date-friendly, outdoor dining,
veg-friendly

East Burnside
1111 E. Burnside St.
(503) 233-1999

Noble rot—a disease called botrytis—is one of the most beautiful things that can happen to a grape, causing grapes to partially raisinate for a sweet, concentrated juice with briny funkiness. It is what makes Sauternes, and it is what makes for one pretty commendable wine program.

On the fourth floor of a tomato-red building where Rocket used to be, Noble Rot's space is beautiful, with an array of discs—some metal and some made of swirling, colored glass—hanging from the ceiling. There's a long bar, several textiled booths, and a large terrace that looks out upon the city lights. It is one of Portland's most scenic restaurants. The 1980s glass-box skyline can feel a bit soulless on some nights, which, in turn, nudges the interior décor just this side of sterile. Truthfully, we kind of miss the old cave-like location. But this new space is classy and comfortable.

Noble Rot makes one of the best burgers in the city—juicy, thick, and beautifully choreographed with the bun and condiments. Bravo. Other than that, we're just not that excited by the food. The menu is succinct, as befits a wine bar, but good wine deserves the right food. Charcuterie and cheese make some attempts towards this end, but there's a disproportionate number of panini. Everything else is pretty overpriced; on a recent visit we paid way too much for herb dumplings—mushy ones at that—even if they *did* contain white truffle.

Perhaps the fancy new digs require a price hike, but the surroundings raise culinary expectations as well. And where Rocket may have been a bit too esoteric, at least it was creative. It's hard to get excited over run-of-the-mill mac and cheese.

As for the main event, it's pretty hard to argue with this wine list. It's a sommelier's playground in the Old World selection: grower-producer Champagne; cru Burgundy; a brief tour of Riesling; and so on. Yet the New World offerings are careful and astute, too. At all price points (but more of them very low), there are exciting options for industry folks, new aficionados, and people who don't care what it is so long as it's good.

We don't generally recommend flights—they're a surefire way to dump old product, so the diner gets stale wine—but here, that's not a persistent problem. Just be sure to ask. And while you're at it, ask to see the roof garden, which is accessible via a private staircase. It's one of the most spectacular views of the city, anywhere.

Nong's Khao Man Gai

Elevating the humble chicken to heights unknown

8.0	6.5
Food	Feel

Thai

Food cart **$5** Price

www.khaomangai.com

Mon–Fri 10am–2pm

Bar None
Credit cards None
Outdoor dining

Downtown
SW 10th and Alder
(971) 255-3480

This is our favorite food cart in Portland. The operation has won us over with its simplicity. This kitchen does one dish, and does it excellently: chicken and rice.

You might consider the dish Hainanese or you might consider it Thai, but it's also similar to street food you might find in the Straits (Singapore or Malaysia), Vietnam, or, really, anywhere in Southeast Asia. They've really got the Southeast Asian street food gig down, more than any other food cart in the PDX area.

One of the most authentic (and green) little touches is the lack of a plate. Instead, the skinless chicken breast, after having been gently boiled in a gingery stock, is sliced up and slapped on paper and hoisted out to you with a delicious soy-garlic-ginger-and-chili dipping sauce, along with soup made from bland but insides-warming vegetable stock and some chunks of Chinese winter squash. For a buck extra, they'll add chicken livers to the pile of tender, moist chicken breast for a more intense flavor experience. Which we highly recommend.

But the truly amazing thing is how carefully the chicken is cooked. We've had far too much overcooked breast meat in our time, so to find such a moist, tender version really makes us happy. It's like rediscovering a new protein.

Skip the underwhelming Vietnamese coffee, which is pretty much the opposite of an intense flavor experience. Juices pack a bit more punch, as in palm or lychee versions.

The good flavors, good people, and uniquely authentic experience elevate Nong's to the very top of the food-cart ladder.

North 45

A friendly, updated pub with a Belgian fetish

7.7	9.0	9.0
Food	Feel	Beer

American, Belgian

Bar **$35**
Price

www.north45pub.com

Mon–Thu 4pm–midnight
Fri 4pm–1am
Sat noon–1am
Sun noon–midnight

Bar Beer, wine, liquor
Credit cards Visa, MC, AmEx
Date-friendly, live music, outdoor dining

Northwest Portland
517 NW 21st Ave.
(503) 248-6317

"Gastropub" is a word that gets tossed about too freely, and often winds up denoting an uptight, pretentious place with sugary drinks and boring food. What we picture is closer to North 45: the inside is full of dark cherry wood and some stained glass details, with faux marble topping the tables; a tented, heated sidewalk patio full of benches sometimes gets impromptu performances from the chef's band (but closes at 10pm per a neighborhood ordinance). St. Paddy's Day is huge here, as is Oktoberfest and any other holiday in which beer drinking is celebrated. It's just a festive, fun, casual place that cares about pairing food and quality beer. In other words, a real gastropub.

There are only half a dozen taps, mostly for seasonally changing or local brews, and sometimes one for a Belgian guest spot. Most Belgians are in the bottle, but the range is impressive. All five of the Trappist beers currently available in the States are here, as well as Lambics, Sours, Saisons, and Tripels. What's more, North 45 cares enough to serve these beers in Belgian beer glasses, which have wide enough bowls for aeration. You will have to give up a shoe as collateral, though; these things don't come cheap.

To pair with these excellent Belgians, there's a selection of moules frites with globetrotting broths. We most like a small bowl of plump, healthy mussels in a light broth of white wine, garlic, and pancetta. A touch of roasted-shallot sweetness adds depth. Suggested beer pairings on the menu are astute, and frites are seasoned to match the mussels: coconut-lemongrass mussels get curry-dusted frites; Amaretto-cream mussels are paired with Old Bay-seasoned frites; the pancetta-shallot version comes with salted frites with fresh herbs; and so on. These are all pretty pricey for the portion size, but they're very good.

Other than that, it's pretty standard upscale bar fare. We normally balk at "Asian" anything on a menu, but these tangy calamari are just fine. A selection of sliders, including petit filet and fried chicken, are good and filling. Happy hour is all night on Monday, after 11pm on Wednesday, and daily from 4–6pm; during these times, most things (but not the mussels) are under $6.

Just as accomplished as the Belgian selection is a cocktail menu with some award-winning talent behind it. Bitters, digestifs, and egg whites are used to gently tweak classic recipes intelligently and carefully. Cheers to that.

Nostrana

This classy Italian joint, Portland-style, is
quietly serving some of the city's best pizza

9.0	8.5	9.0
Food	Feel	Wine

Italian, Pizza

Upmarket restaurant

$55
Price

www.nostrana.com

Mon–Thu 11:30am–2pm, 5pm–
10pm; Fri 11:30am–2pm, 5pm–
11pm; Sat 5pm–11pm; Sun
5pm–10pm

Bar Beer, wine, liquor
Credit cards Visa, MC, AmEx
Reservations Accepted
Date-friendly, outdoor dining,
veg-friendly

Southeast Portland
1401 SE Morrison St.
(503) 234-2427

The inside of Nostrana feels sylvan, with slender panels of warm-hued
wood reaching to the high ceilings and naked tables of dark wood filling
the space. From many of these you can see an open kitchen with a
glowing brick oven; dimly lit chandeliers look vaguely branchlike and cork
floors help absorb sound. The whole look is surprisingly elegant for its
modern-strip-mall surroundings (which you will curse if you choose to sit
outside). While the vibe is definitely relaxed (sometimes too relaxed,
where service is concerned), a night here feels like a special occasion.

The menu is laid out in an authentically Italian format—antipasti, primi,
secondi—but there's a recognizable Pacific Northwest presence
throughout; you'll find local cheeses, beets, and squash, mussel stew, and
expertly grilled halibut. There's a certain tongue-in-cheek downmarketing
of the dish descriptions, like the "Caesar-style" dressing that adorns a
lovely salad of radicchio, Parmigiano-Reggiano, and rosemary-and-sage
croutons. This is Portland's answer, perhaps, to the pretentious upscale
Italian restaurants of the 1990s—a food-nerd restaurant positioning itself
as something *more*, not less, accessible than it really is. How modern.

You should come ready to deal with some service hiccups—but they're
forgiven with your first taste of house-made charcuterie or one of the
fleeting seasonal plates, like a small (and expensive) dish of chanterelle
mushrooms prepared three ways. Aside from the stunning $60 fiorentina
for two, meat-centered secondi like tagliata (sliced flatiron steak with
arugula—an underrated prep) are surprisingly affordable.

But the star of the show here is the pizza. Where many places make a
big deal about using a wood-fired (or, worse, "wood stone") oven but
don't keep it hot enough to blister the crust, Nostrana's pizza, made from
naturally leavened dough, is closer to the gold Italian standard. A
margherita is made properly, with spare discs of creamy, slightly briny
house-made mozzarella and a fresh, vibrant tomato sauce.

Wines that have been "curated" (according to the list—okay, that's a
bit pretentious) are well chosen. This is one of the city's best Italian wine
lists, with unusually good representation of unsung regions like Valle
d'Aosta, Trentino and Abruzzo; great breadth in Piedmont and Tuscany;
and, in some cases, vintages going back to the mid-1990s. There's also a
restrained, somewhat perfunctory selection of Oregon's greats.

This isn't just a wonderful addition to Portland's Italian-restaurant
landscape; it's one of the most exciting new kitchens in the entire city.

Nuestra Cocina

You might get better from a hole in the wall, but you'd miss out on this vibe

7.4	8.5	7.5
Food	Feel	Drinks

Mexican, Nuevo Latino

Upmarket restaurant

$40
Price

www.nuestra-cocina.com

Tue–Sat 5pm–10pm

Bar Beer, wine, liquor, BYO
Credit cards Visa, MC, AmEx
Reservations Not accepted
Date-friendly, outdoor dining

Division/Clinton
2135 SE Division St.
(503) 232-2135

Sometimes you lose your sense of perspective when you hit up against restaurant concepts that are just inherently a shitload of fun. Tricked-out nouvelle Southwestern/Mexican is one of those concepts. How can you argue with good margaritas made with plenty of chile-de-arbol-spiked tequila? With a lovely outdoor patio and a bustling-to-the-bursting-point interior, or a festive open kitchen? With a private "mole room," in deep, burnished reds and browns?

Nuestra Cocina's menu changes seasonally, but you might start with a good salad of nopales (cactus), whose signature sliminess is tempered on the grill. Grated manchego sprinkled on top is a nice idea for the dish, too, and a mild salsa verde is welcome, although its luster is somewhat diminished when it reappears on barbacoa de cordero con salsa verde (lamb shoulder braised in banana leaf, a bit lean but tender and juicy, and better still when you discover another, sweeter, red sauce hiding in the back of the leaf). Carne asada, a tenderized slab of meat that's marinated to bright redness, has a lot of flavor, and its beer-laced beans are better still, but a shredded-pork chile relleno tastes too sweet, and enchiladas are dry and flavor-poor; more spice would help.

In general, this kitchen has a timid hand with chilies. Dishes described as spicy aren't. Even the hot sauce on the table isn't. Now that Portland's got its Nuevo Mexicano place, is it too much to ask for a bit of heat to go with it?

But we're suckers for the good, tart "Cocina Especial" margarita, although the basic version is too lemonadey. And the prices are great; too often, upscale margaritas are an excuse to charge almost $20. Not here. Plus, Tecate on tap is a fun thing to have. Nuestra Cocina can get quite busy, and reservations are not accepted, but if you can swing it, sit at the chef's table for a great view of the action—for instance you can watch tortillas being made to order. Not everything here will be as good as some renditions you'll find at cheaper dives, but this is sincere food made with care and experience. After a couple of margaritas, you'll appreciate it even more.

¡OBA!

Don't miss the tableside show, in which a margarita gets shaken while you get taken

6.5	7.0	7.5
Food	Feel	Drinks

Nuevo Latino

Upmarket restaurant

$60
Price

www.obarestaurant.com

Sun–Mon 5pm–9pm
Tue–Thu 5pm–9:30pm
Fri–Sat 5pm–10pm

Bar Beer, wine, liquor
Credit cards Visa, MC, AmEx
Reservations Accepted
Date-friendly, delivery, outdoor dining, veg-friendly, Wi-Fi

Pearl District
555 NW 12th Ave.
(503) 228-6161

¡OBA! is a common recommendation by luxury-hotel concierges, who probably suppose—and rightly so—that out-of-towners will identify its flashy, overexerted décor and florid descriptions as a fancy event worth every dollar. Imagine a culinary Cirque du Soleil, but less culinary.

The set decoration is similar: dramatic uplighting; random geometric shapes in jewel tones; walls painted in candy colors; architectural lines forming confusing, Escheresque optical illusions; and water goblets are a whimsical cobalt blue. This visual shock and awe—what could it be trying to accomplish?

This may be Portland's only well-advertised attempt at Nuevo Latino, but it's hardly a new concept. It's just one that tends to fall into the same mire that other upscale fusion concepts do—namely, overwrought, fussy dishes that have lots of financial (but little spiritual) impact. According to ¡OBA!'s website: "we begin with the cultures and cuisines of the Caribbean and Cuba, go through South and Central America, up through Mexico to my roots in the American Southwest, interpreting these foods so that they may be enjoyed by people in the Northwest."

If the exhaustive list of regions that will be appearing in tonight's performance doesn't worry you, the phrase "interpreting these foods" should. This means you will be eating sweet, creamy, intense dishes meant to play to a crowd that, the restaurant assumes, doesn't have a palate for Latin flavors. Some might point to the dearth of great, authentic Mexican food in the Northwest as proof that that's a valid assumption, but still…so what? Why not introduce Portland to outstanding food from just a few of those several regions (like Andina has done), instead of slapping them all together in one overbearing dish?

Arroz frito with coconut rice, ginger, cilantro, and fried plantains is so sweet that it wears on you, like an episode of "Friends." In fact, several of these dishes feel like they should come with a laugh track; certainly one is called for in a "certified Angus® prime rib" that costs $39 for 14 ounces. Granted, it's smoked on a mesquite rotisserie, but after the chipotle horseradish cream sauce, we're wondering why we didn't just spend the same amount on a naked, awesome dry-aged ribeye somewhere else.

But don't worry about any of these baroque dishes blowing your palate—most of the wines on this list will do that well before you take the first bite.

The Observatory

A cool space in which to hang out and sample slightly otherwordly flavors

8.2	9.0	8.0
Food	Feel	Beer

Modern

Casual restaurant

$35
Price

www.theobservatorypdx.com

Sun–Mon 3pm–10pm
Tue–Sat 3pm–midnight

Bar Beer, wine, liquor
Credit cards Visa, MC, AmEx
Reservations Not accepted
Date-friendly, outdoor dining

Southeast Portland
8115 SE Stark St.
(503) 445-6284

The Observatory has all the makings of a hip place to hang out and eat: it's located in a once-sketchy area that's gentrifying from other well-loved restaurants; it's cleverly designed and full of conversation pieces; the cocktail menu is infusion-crazy; and dinner is surprisingly good and affordable.

First, consider the décor, which is just a lot of fun. Cable-and-bulb light fixtures descend from the ceiling like War of the Worlds creatures; turn-of-the-century-style furnishings make for a cool but understated lounge space; 12-pointed stars glow throughout rooms painted in shades of blue.

The dinner menu would be somewhat prosaic if not for the elegant inclusion of some exciting Ashkenazi flavors. Smoked whitefish salad doesn't appear on just any modern menu, you know. And this one is good, in a smallish portion with dense crackers and house-pickled vegetables. Smoked trout salad with hard-boiled eggs, potatoes, green beans, olives, and tomatoes makes for a sort of improved Niçoise combination that we can't get enough of. A paprika-dusted potato pancake, served with sustainably fished snapper cooked to an ideal moist flakiness, is nice with wilted (not melted) peppery greens and a citrusy sorrel aïoli.

About those Southeast Asian influences: this is not a rampant misuse of buzzword ingredients like lemongrass, coconut, and Thai this and that; it's rather a considerate (dare we say it) fusion that makes sense. Mussels in a ginger-sake broth with cilantro and basil, for instance. Be warned: this is a rather small portion. But the mussels are plump and huge and the price is right. Savory fry bread makes a popular vessel for the broth, but share with your tablemates; this is the calorie-happy dish that, in 2005, was famously accused of causing rampant obesity in Native Americans.

The average wine list seems to have been subjugated in favor of a slightly more interesting beer selection that includes a few locals on draft and some decent imports in bottle. Cocktails are more of a focus here, made with every infusion you can imagine: Thai-chili-infused vodka; hibiscus-and-açai-infused tequila; rhubarb-infused Cachaça; and so on. But is all the fuss suspicious or just playful? The answer lies, for us, in a "Santorini Martini" in which a dirty martini is made even more convoluted with a sweetening balsamic vinegar, and then garnished with kalamata and feta-stuffed green olives.

Zoiks. At least the kitchen understands that less is more.

Ocean City Seafood

9.1 Food
6.0 Feel

Better vibes, better seafood, and better dim sum—
better get it while you can

Chinese, Seafood, Dim Sum

Casual restaurant

$30 Price

www.oceancityportland.com

Daily 9:30am–midnight

Bar Beer, wine, liquor
Credit cards Visa, MC, AmEx
Reservations Accepted

82nd Avenue Area
3016 SE 82nd Ave.
(503) 771-2299

Ocean City is often compared to Wong's King. Both places serve Cantonese food, including seafood fresh from the tanks and dim sum. Both places are huge and full of round banquet-like tables, but are a little tattered around the edges. Both places are brightly lit, but lively and bustling.

But that's where the similarities end. This more obscure, humbler restaurant stands heads and shoulders above Wong's King. A quick look around the dining room might give you a clue as to why: they're actually catering mostly to the local Chinese population. You'll see entire extended Chinese families here, spanning three or even four generations, coming for dim sum or spectacular seafood. Back over at Wong's King, all the hype has turned the place into more of a white-people trap, and the food has suffered.

We would normally never recommend starting dim sum with a sweet dish, but don't miss the so-called "pineapple buns" whenever they come out of the oven. The buns aren't so named because they are made with pineapples—they just look like them. These treats are a festival of irresistibly yeasty, undercooked dough and creamy yellow goodness. Chicken feet are great, meaty and tender, and dumplings are also wonderful. There's a nearly perfect version of sautéed greens here, as earthy and garlicky as they are tender, with a noticeable kiss of fire from the wok. Pork barbecue is just average, but average pork barbecue isn't a bad thing.

And then comes the pièce de résistance: live bait shrimp taken from the tank and gently steamed to ethereal sweetness. Or choose a whole bass, steamed with ginger and soy, a silky delight.

The staff here is friendly and helpful, and you won't usually have to wait. There's no pomp and circumstance—just a sincere Cantonese effort. Given time, the crowds will get hip to this fact, and the waits will get longer. Hopefully, Ocean City will also resist the downhill turn that tends to come with popularity.

Original Halibut's

Fish and chips taken to the max

7.9	7.5	7.0
Food	Feel	Beer

Seafood

Counter service

$20
Price

Sun–Thu 11:30am–10pm
Fri–Sat 11:30am–11pm

Bar Beer, wine, liquor
Credit cards Visa, MC, AmEx
Kid-friendly, outdoor dining

Alberta Arts District
2525 NE Alberta St.
(503) 808-9600

This small restaurant is made up of a smaller room with maybe seven tables under sky-blue walls and ceiling fans, and a second, larger space next door. It's kitschy and comfortable. On nice days, there are tables out front where you can watch Alberta traffic go by. Everything is served in paper cups or red-checked paper in baskets, which totally reminds us of Monterey's Fisherman's Wharf. Ah, nostalgia!

A fish of the day (often rock cod) always graces the menu, as well as giant tiger prawns, Alaskan halibut, Alaskan Salmon, Southern catfish, and Alaskan true cod. Everything comes in two portion sizes with thick, medium-crisp fries. In a move that's above and beyond the call of duty, lobster tails with sweet potato fries are also available, as are Dungeness crab cakes.

A canola-corn oil blend gives the lightly coated fish a crunchy crust with a remarkably moist flesh. The juice runs down your chin as you bite into it. Tartar sauce is simple and mellow, complementing rather then competing with the fish. Malt vinegar gives it that little extra zing, but isn't totally required, as it is at other blander fish-and-chips places. A smaller portion here will satisfy a lunch urge, but for dinner, go larger.

If you're craving something less fried, homemade clam chowder is really good (worth the highish price), full of chunks of potato and plump clams, and creamy. A nice bacon flavor rounds it out. You can get a combo with this soup and a bay or giant prawn cocktail with some corn on the cob and even a slice of zingy key lime pie.

The few beers on tap are appropriate, if unimaginative: an IPA, a Pabst, a wheat beer, and Anchor Steam. But how about some nice British bitters and ales? Why not pour something British to pair with such a great British contribution to the culinary world?

Original Hotcake House

6.0 Food

8.0 Feel

A mandatory midnight mass for hash

American

Casual restaurant

$20 Price

24 hours

Bar None
Credit cards Visa, MC
Reservations Not accepted
Kid-friendly

Southeast Portland
1002 SE Powell Blvd.
(503) 236-7402

Original Hotcake House is to Portland's rowdy post-bar late-night dining scene what CBGB was to 1970s New York City music. It predates that decade by several more, though, claiming a 60-plus-year run as Portland's go-to spot for midnight breakfast and 3am steak. The high neon sign outside is totally retro-Vegas. It's easy to see even from the backseat of a cab, with double vision and everything.

Whether you're only in town to see a show or you're a longtime local, chances are good you'll end up here in the wee hours, rubbing elbows with the stumbling, the tattooed, the mohawked, the loud—not quite the dregs of society, like you might expect from watching movies. Come at 5:30pm, and you might find a Steve Buscemi look-alike cowering in a stained booth, enjoying a greasy burger and fries. There's something distinctly Tom Waits-ish about this place, and we hope it never changes.

Breakfast is the main event here—breakfast anytime, of course. Eggs come with tons of meat: thick ham slices, greasy bacon, and a cup of crumbled chorizo. The hotcakes are good and the syrup is not; the hash browns are shredded and crispy on the outside, and squishy inside. Cheese isn't just on the omelette—there's a side of omelette with your cheese. It's awesome.

The coffee is strong, burning and getting gross on a hotplate for hours (unless the place is busy, in which case it's more likely to be fresh). You can watch short-order cooks move with the impressive automation of one of those top-hatted drinking birds; and there's a jukebox of old-school jams. A thick coat of grease captures years of dust and probably even the houseplants in the place are weather-proof from it.

About those steaks: listen, this isn't a Morton's or anything. You get what you pay for, which isn't much. If you want it medium-rare, order it rare. If your heart hurts, you can chew on a side salad of crisp, cool iceberg lettuce with a cherry tomato rolling around in it like some accidentally dropped thing. This is the comfort food of America, the good, the bad, and the ugly, all rolled into one.

Original Pancake House

6.5 Food **6.0** Feel

Two words: bacon waffle

American

Casual restaurant **$15** Price

www.originalpancakehouse.com

Wed–Sun 7am–3pm

Bar None
Credit cards None
Reservations Not accepted

Southwest Portland
8601 SW 24th Ave.
(503) 246-9007

Start with "IHOP." Remove "I" and the hokiness. Add in "independently owned and operated." Finally, anagramize. Now you've got the Original Pancake House. OPH is renowned for its gargantuan selection of breakfasts, especially in the griddle-cake area. In fact, some say that OPH wrote the recipe book for IHOP, who is usually the sole purveyor of potato pancakes and blintzes in any given town.

Let's get to the point: bacon waffle! Why is this not a breakfast staple everywhere? It does the work for you. Pigs in blankets are also sumptuous here, but how are you ever going to decide when faced with two pages of sheer temptation? Consider crêpes filled with fruit and cream; pancakes made with berries, nuts, chocolate chips, or bananas; or corned beef hash (which could be better). But the claim to OPH's national fame is the "Dutch Baby," a monstrosity of dough, butter, and powdered sugar for which you wait almost half an hour. It's worth it, though. With a little squeeze of lemon and a puff-popping forkful, you've descended into a trance-like state of ecstasy. Don't let the Americana wholesomeness fool you. These people are sinister geniuses.

Portland is the proud birthplace of OPH and its Dutch Baby, so it's obvious where its blue-roofed contemporary stands among this populace. The old house and country-kitsch décor are so inviting and nostalgic; you can expect a wait on weekends, but tables turn quickly.

And OPH only serves breakfast, so if you want dinner, maybe that's when you could go to IHOP. You know, if you miss it.

Pad Thai Kitchen

7.1 Food **8.5** Feel

Some of the city's best Thai-American dishes in a warm, hip spot

Thai

Casual restaurant **$25** Price

Mon–Thu 11am–3pm, 5pm–9:30pm; Fri 11am–3pm, 5pm–10pm; Sat–Sun noon–10pm

Bar Beer, wine
Credit cards Visa, MC, AmEx
Reservations Accepted
Outdoor dining, veg-friendly

Belmont
2309 SE Belmont St.
(503) 232-8766

When will the madness end? When will real Thai food be readily available all over the United States?

Because as it is now, there are only a handful of restaurants in the entire country serving legit Thai food to non-Thai customers (Pok Pok being one of them). So Portlanders are lucky. But get out of our little oasis, and head east, say, to Omaha, Nebraska, and you're totally out of luck.

Part of this green-curry-with-chicken problem is that non-savvy travelers are duped into believing that Thai food is indeed sticky-sweet pad Thai and milky coconut curries by the fact that you can find this stuff in…Thailand. All over tourist areas in Thailand, establishments have popped up hawking sweet noodles and bland curries to foreigners, perpetuating this myth.

None of this is to say that Thai-American food is bad. It's just important to note the difference between the centuries-old cuisine of a country, and a new—dare we say—fusion of that food with American's fondness for sugar and distaste for spice.

In the case of Pad Thai Kitchen, the name puts it all out there, so we know better than to go in expecting flash-fried ants or fire-roasted snakehead fish stuffed with lemongrass. Yet, we have been pleasantly surprised by touches that elevate Pad Thai Kitchen above your average noodle house. Kaffir lime leaf, an ambassador Thai spice, works its tasty way into some dishes here.

And the eponymous pad Thai isn't half bad, as this kitchen has reined in, to some extent, the sweetness that has become rampant in the dish. Pumpkin curry is immensely popular, but we find it too one-dimensional.

All in all, we understand the appeal of this place. They do a better job than most at making the atmosphere chill, a place you'd want to linger in. There's warm light, the buzz of people, and a certain hipness. This is nothing like the boring cafeteria-like rooms with royal accoutrements that you have come to expect from Thai-American. As such, the place is always packed, making it very lively. Servers flit about, deftly balancing too many plates of food.

But ultimately it's Thai-American, no more. For real Thai food, go to Pok Pok.

Paley's Place

A superlative experience with no bells and
whistles, just great food and vibes every time

9.2	8.5	9.0
Food	Feel	Wine

Modern

Upmarket restaurant

$80
Price

www.paleysplace.net

Mon–Thu 5:30pm–10pm
Fri–Sat 5:30pm–11pm
Sun 5pm–10pm

Bar Beer, wine, liquor
Credit cards Visa, MC, AmEx
Reservations Accepted
Date-friendly, outdoor dining

Northwest Portland
1204 NW 21st Ave.
(503) 243-2403

Paley's Place is considered by many to be the one that started it all, this Portland restaurant scene. Its James Beard-award-winning chef and owner raised the bar high, inspiring a generation of young chefs to open their own restaurants, each seeking the level of all-around excellence achieved by Paley's.

Of course, this converted Victorian house is nearly always crowded with people who are very happy to be there, and there is the camaraderie between strangers at nearby tables that eating great food can bring. The menu uses local and organic ingredients, and dishes are consistently, reliably outstanding.

In fact, it's not unusual for your meal to be so stunning that you and your tablemates fall silent for a few bites. Even simple salads are so gently dressed, with such fresh and vivid natural flavors, that they are enchanting. Poppyseed-crusted albacore with olive and chickpea purée is not over-the-top unusual, but it's playfully coaxed into another place by Middle Eastern nuances. Roast marrow bones are sinfully delicious, and roasted sweet beets with horseradish cream is an exercise in restraint, contrast, and harmony. Meats are cooked beautifully, though some platings are less inspired than others. But rare is the flaw here, and a good time is always had.

For dessert, we've had an amazing tres leches cake with (seasonal) Oregon strawberry sauce. Even a simple crème brûlée is exemplary. A selection of well-made cheeses, both domestic and imported, is broad and inviting.

The wine list, like the food, takes few chances, but is appropriate and well chosen, with bottles from France and Oregon in an American-food-friendly range of varietals. Markups are reasonable, and the price range allows something good for every wallet size. Cocktails are of the nostalgic set, and expertly done. The nice selection of single-malt Scotches and digestifs is welcome and unusual for non-bar-scene restaurants in town.

Our quibbles with Paley's are minor. The constantly ringing phone at the front gets annoying, and some servers can act a bit pretentious, but it hardly affects the great mood that a night here will put you in. It's casual, but not a place you can probably afford to come very often. Save it for people you really care about, because there aren't many better meals in Portland

Pambiche

A cheery Caribbean vibe and legit dishes made with amor

8.1	9.0
Food	Feel

Cuban, Nuevo Latino

Casual restaurant

$35
Price

www.pambiche.com

Sun–Thu 7am–10pm
Fri–Sat 7am–midnight

Bar Beer, wine
Credit cards Visa, MC, AmEx
Reservations Not accepted
Outdoor dining

Northeast Portland
2811 NE Glisan St.
(503) 233-0511

Cuba has captured and held the American imagination since it was concealed behind the Iron Curtain several decades ago. It has since given us an immortal and iconic dictator, surreptitiously smoked cigars, Buena Vista Social Club, and Reinaldo Arenas. From inside its arcane shroud, the country remains, visually, pretty unchanged since the mid-century, as evidenced in its slew of American classic cars, mottled and fading rainbow-colored façades, and refreshing lack of Big Macs.

Pambiche exemplifies the colorful charm of Cuba, or at least America's romantic ideal of it. The exterior is unmistakable, a screaming purple, yellow, pink, and aqua paint job on a Victorian building. Faux-vintage posters invite you to "revolutionize your morning," and this is a really cheery, bustling breakfast scene. A main draw here is the bakery, which puts out some excellent Cuban pastries. A variety of eight minis—from coconut-ginger biscuits to rum-raisin cakes to passion fruit muffins with chocolate chips—comes in a basket for only $8.

A Cuban take on the classic tortilla española gets plantains instead of potatoes, but the same bell pepper, olive oil, and onion treatment. It's much denser and bigger than what you'd find in a tapas bar, of course, but the flavors all mix together for a great, shareable breakfast. There are over a dozen more choices, some with Creole touches and some with more Spanish and Italian influences.

At lunch and dinner, empanadas are great and fairly cheap, especially one filled with a simple picadillo that sports herby beef, potatoes, and vegetables. The shell is crisp, but relenting, and the insides steamy and good. Red beans with rice and smoked ham is impeccable, as are salads, like a traditional beet salad with lightly bitter watercress. An orange vinaigrette also perks up ripe, creamy avocado in the excellent ensalada de aguacate.

There's very little emphasis on alcohol here, save for a decent and very small selection of Spanish and Latin American reds that's well chosen for the low price point. A few rudimentary sherries are quite nice. More the point here are fun espresso drinks, fruit juices, and old-school, cane-sugar sodas.

Best of all, Pambiche's proximity to Laurelhurst means following up dinner with a $3 trip inside America's own Art-Deco past. How much more cultured can it get?

Papa G's

The herbivore's dilemmas are few at this plucky, eco-conscious little deli

6.6	6.5
Food	Feel

Vegefusion

Counter service

$20
Price

www.papagees.com

Daily 11am–9pm

Bar Beer, wine
Credit cards Visa, MC
Kid-friendly, live music, outdoor dining, veg-friendly, Wi-Fi

Division/Clinton
2314 SE Division St.
(503) 235-0244

Papa G's advertises itself as "the most organic restaurant in Portland," and this may in fact be the case. It certainly looks the part, all granola and crunch. Service is friendly in this kind of I-want-to-buy-the-world-(an-organic)-Coke sort of way. There's more smiling and laughter out on the lightly island-themed, pleasant patio; all those reptilian brains are gleefully dormant without the smell of roasting flesh in the air.

Your main dishes are assembled by the server from a buffet line, making it feel a bit like you're getting meat-and-three, but without the meat. Carnivores are surprised to find they really don't miss it here, though. Usually, our go-to for vegetarian cuisine is South Indian or Middle Eastern, in which vegetable dishes are made complex and evocative, as opposed to being composed of sorry cardboard-like meat substitutes. But here, vegetarians and vegans are treated to a globe's worth of influences. And everything is organic, mostly coming directly from small farms.

There's an Italianish play on raw zucchini, which is julienned like spaghetti and served in fragrant basil sauce. Kale and carrots simmered in coconut milk has a nice Southeast Asian thing going on. Spaghetti squash, when in season, is mildly and naturally sweet, which really allows the vegetable to show through in a way that butter-and-sugar recipes don't. Whole-grain rice accompanies Indian-like soups like a yellow dal (that tastes more like a potato curry). Even the missteps feel healthful: several dishes, like black beans and brown rice, are undersalted. Your tongue may be bored, but your kidneys, liver, and heart will absolutely love it.

No stone is left unturned (or unsustainable). The cooler has some good organic teas, sodas, and juices; papa's also makes its own seasoned tofus, which are sold here and at markets around town; and for dessert, Turtle Mountain's dairy-free So Delicious coconut milk ice cream bars satisfy a sweet tooth without any funny stuff involved. Organic beers and wines are available, too—at which point Papa G's will be the uncontested, undisputed super-really-most organic restaurant in Portland.

Papa Haydn

Life is short—eat dessert first

6.8	8.5	8.5
Food	Feel	Wine

Modern, Baked goods

Upmarket restaurant

$50
Price

www.papahaydn.com

Mon–Thu 11:30am–10pm
Fri–Sat 11:30am–midnight
Sun 10am–10pm
Hours vary by location

Bar Beer, wine, liquor
Credit cards Visa, MC, AmEx
Reservations Accepted
Date-friendly, outdoor dining

Northwest Portland
701 NW 23rd Ave.
(503) 228-7317

Sellwood
5829 SE Milwaukie Ave.
(503) 232-9440

Papa Haydn is like a much more likeable Portland version of Cheesecake Factory. The menu is not quite as lengthy nor as globetrotting, but it is pretty nondescript. It's really just a reason to feel like dessert has been earned. Hotellish mains abound, like eggplant parmesan, fettucine alfredo disguised as something called a "Hunter's Pasta" (where did they hunt for this, an Olive Garden?), and a $15 chicken Caesar salad. Mostly older folks and visitors get suckered into this unremarkable dinner. Everyone else comes for one reason and one reason only: dessert.

If you're taking dessert to go, like many do, you'll enjoy some of the nicest, most attentive counter service in the city. Even sweeter is a carrot cake with an ideal ratio of hearty, moist cake to buttery cream-cheese icing. Little bits of pineapple, coconut, and cinnamon give you plenty to think about, while three layers of frosting—plus the outside—shut your brain down entirely. A pretty banana-coconut-cream pie has some extra zing from a rich espresso ganache; meringues, mousses, and panna cottas are impossibly airy, like clouds of fruit, egg, and chocolate.

Any chance you get to purchase a whole one of these beauties, do it (with 24 hours' notice). A Marjolaine is particularly artful: layers of toasted hazelnut-praline cream formed into balls and topped with more layers of chocolate and hazelnut meringue. What results is a study in black and off-white, stripes and spheres, all topped with dainty mint leaves and flowers. It makes a terrific dinner party gift, although no one will want to cut into it. Most cakes are $45 and serve upwards of about 12, so it's still a better deal than ordering it in the restaurant.

The Sellwood location does all the baking for both stores, but the frozen desserts are over at the west side only. The west Papa Haydn also adjoins Jo Bar and Rotisserie, which gets the benefit of a wood-fired oven in which pizzas and chicken are cooked. These are more worth the trouble than dinner next door. A shared wine list is long—perhaps longer than it needs to be; some of it is good, especially Alsatian, Loire Valley, and a few Central Coast bottles; some of it is not so good, but all are a steal.

If we were rating this place solely on its dessert, it would get a 9.0. Maybe Papa Haydn should consider cutting its ballasts and soaring into its sweet, sweet destiny.

Paradox Café

Being vegetarian shouldn't mean making these kinds of compromises

4.1	4.5
Food	Feel

Vegefusion

Casual restaurant

$20
Price

www.paradoxorganiccafe.com

Mon–Sat 8am–9pm
Sun 8am–3pm

Bar None
Credit cards Visa, MC
Reservations Not accepted
Veg-friendly, Wi-Fi

Belmont
3439 SE Belmont St.
(503) 232-7508

What at first sounds like just a terrible name for a restaurant—something that brings to mind a late '80s coffee venture from a bunch of grad students—makes more sense once you look at the menu. Paradox Café is trying to make vegan food that actually tastes good even to carnivores. Why? Because it believes sincerely in offering healthful eating to all people, which is hard to argue with. It seeks to prepare organic and locally made meat substitutes like tofu and tempeh with organic and seasonal produce, mostly dairy-free sauces and breads, free-range eggs, and any other blissed-out, well-meaning, platitudinous ingredients it can find.

Of course, this transcendental attitude bleeds over into everything else, starting with the shabby retro-diner atmosphere and its Formica tables, space-age pendant lamps, and funky blue booths with rips and scuffs. It's pretty dinge-tastic, just like a diner, which is impressive for a place with relatively little bacon. Service is also super-chill, even when you need it not to be.

But we tend to take issue with vegetarian places that focus on meat substitutes. It seems insulting to the brilliant things vegetables and lentils and grains are capable of. South Indian food, along with a lot of Middle Eastern and Ethiopian dishes, are a much tastier testament to the viability of a vegetarian epicure than soy "meats," which often fall into the classic traps: a dry vegan sausage patty, for instance, or off-puttingly sweet and spicy sauces trying to fluff tempeh up into something your palate will enjoy.

It's not just the meat substitutes that we have a beef with; most of the kitchen's work with tempeh and tofu leave something to be desired. Corn cakes and eggless French toast are mealy, although the latter gets a boost from orange juice. Oat waffles will be fine for someone who has never enjoyed the original, and biscuits with bland almond gravy are just a terrible idea, even if you never have had the pork-sausage-infused version.

All-vegetable dishes are done best here. The better ones are unencumbered by all those heavy sauces that seem apologetic and unconfident. But in the balance, there are just too many great vegetarian meals to be had in Portland to keep coming here. In this day and age, Paradox's unimaginative menu and clunky execution is just as outdated as its name.

Park Kitchen

If the Portland School becomes a culinary catch-phrase, this will be its footnote

9.5	8.5	9.0
Food	Feel	Drinks

Modern

Upmarket restaurant

$50
Price

www.parkkitchen.com

Mon–Fri 11:30am–2pm, 5pm–9pm
Sat 5pm–9pm

Bar Beer, wine, liquor
Credit cards Visa, MC, AmEx
Reservations Essential
Date-friendly, outdoor dining

Pearl District
422 NW 8th Ave.
(503) 223-7275

If Portland is the great postmodern restaurant city, then Park Kitchen is its great postmodern restaurant, unique in its ability to reach across the divisions that mark this gastronomic era, almost singular in its ability to touch—sometimes along the arc of a single dish—the locavores and the hedonists, the eco-watchdogs and the offal fiends.

Consider a simple chilled soup that showed up on a recent lunch menu at Park Kitchen. It was a match of the simple—local beets, bright yogurt—with the profane–bracing chili pepper, gnarls of fatty oxtail. Yet it was also a mini-essay on culinary postmodernism–a movement that's marked by a newfound appreciation, sometimes to fetishistic proportions, of the foods that the world's poor have long taken for granted. For generations, Russian peasants have found comfort and sustenance in borscht, while their counterparts in the Caribbean have found it—as we now do too—hanging off the ass of one of the barnyard's least elegant animals.

Consider a piece of sturgeon—another fish long written off by the elite—cooked as delicately as can be imagined, as moist and squeaky as bluefin tuna sashimi, then bedded on refried black beans and bright yellow peppers. It is a dish that quietly turns fusion into something far more sophisticated and subtle than last decade's seared tuna with wasabi mashed potatoes. Or consider a plate of chestnut gnocchi, with all the warmth of the northern Italian street-food stand, a precious gift in Portland's rainy winter; a delicate, aromatic house-made hot dog; or a parsnip soup with almonds and caperberries, a daring recipe that relies on exquisite balance.

Even the location is symbolic—one foot is planted firmly in the trendy Pearl, while the other wiggles its toes in the grass of the North Park. In warm weather, the front doors open onto a verdant patio overlooking the garden blocks. Inside, the space is always intimate, with the kitchen very much a part of the room. At night, votives keep things romantically dark.

This restaurant is not for everyone. Portions are small, and the price is not. Every meal is an unknown quantity, and not every risk taken by the kitchen succeeds. But we feel that the adventure justifies the cost. And the bartenders are as dedicated and innovative as the kitchen. A cocktail that one day comes with pear liqueur might the next day be made with pear purée instead. The price-diverse wine list combines a dizzying Pacific Northwest selection with a playful, astute Old World globe-trot.

On the crest of a new wave, Park Kitchen is indisputable proof of Portland's relevance. The capitals of Europe can keep their Michelin-three-star palaces. We dare them to try making one of *these*.

Pastaworks

A tempting treasure trove of gourmet and specialty goods and a wine selection to top it all

Groceries

Market

www.pastaworks.com

Mon–Sat 9:30am–7pm
Sun 10am–7pm
Hours vary by location

Bar Beer, wine
Credit cards Visa, MC, AmEx
Veg-friendly

Northwest Portland
735 NW 21st Ave.
(503) 221-3002

Mississippi Ave. Area
4212 N. Mississippi Ave.
(503) 445-1303

Hawthorne
3735 SE Hawthorne Blvd.
(503) 232-1010

Pastaworks, a favorite of many gourmands, has stores in the City Market (reviewed separately) as well as the ever-hip Mississippi, and—perhaps best of all—a Hawthorne location with an attached eatery, Evoe. Don't expect to find great bargains here; the point is that there are many imports and specialty foods made in-house that deservedly command higher prices. Produce is expensive, but it comes from local farms, and it's of the highest quality.

This is a spectacular place to find Italian wines, from the value bottles of unsung regions to the superstars from Tuscany and Piedmont. They are all chosen with great care, and there's a special zeal reserved for those funky little rule breakers, the farmers who make exciting terroir-driven wines regardless of how Robert Parker feels about them. This same care and passion extends to a broad Spanish selection, as well as a few French and excellent local wines.

There are a number of imported and Pastaworks-made pastas, including several different types of ravioli stuffed with seasonal ingredients. A beautifully edited array of cheeses from both the US and abroad are well cared for, and can be explained expertly to you while you enjoy a sample. Just try not to drool over cured meats and sausages, also made in-store. Sausage comes in all styles: spicy Italian, chorizo, bratwurst, merguez, and Northern Italian. There's also guanciale (great for amatriciana), andouille for gumbo, and duck confit for risotto. How are you not heading over there right this instant?

And if, while shopping, you get too hungry to wait for dinner, try some prepared foods like lemony, delicious stuffed grape leaves. Or if you're at the Hawthorne location, cruise next door to Evoe for a great sandwich made with Pastaworks goods.

Pastini Pastaria

Surprisingly good Italian-American food from a chain with local motions

6.9	6.5	6.5
Food	Feel	Wine

Italian

Casual restaurant

$25
Price

www.pastini.net

Mon–Thu 11:30am–9pm
Fri–Sat 11:30am–10pm
Sun 4pm–9pm
Hours vary by location

Bar Beer, wine, liquor
Credit cards Visa, MC, AmEx
Reservations Accepted
Kid-friendly, outdoor dining,
veg-friendly

Downtown
911 SW Taylor St.
(503) 863-5188

Northwest Portland
1506 NW 23rd Ave.
(503) 595-1205

Northeast Portland
1426 NE Broadway
(503) 288-4300

Additional locations
and more features at
www.fearlesscritic.com

Sometimes you want a totally authentic Italian experience, and sometimes you just want a good plate of the sort of pasta you grew up with. For those times, there's Pastini Pastaria. It's a locally owned mini-chain, which fact should quell any anxieties about supporting soulless corporations. For as much as we might want to poo-poo anything not handmade or sourced from local farmers, we can't argue with this Italian-American food.

The branches of this restaurant have a cozy feel, despite being pretty large. Part of this is due to the seating in raised alcoves, which allows for a bit of privacy. The branches all share dark woods and a clean modern look, which does bring to mind a sort of Starbucks aesthetic—nice, but generic and predictable.

But before you start making Olive Garden comparisons, make no mistake: these people know pasta. Noodles are never overcooked, and there is an effort to produce more than just lowest-common-denominator food, even if it isn't always the most authentic. A Caprese salad comes with cow's milk mozzarella, sun-dried tomatoes, basil, and kalamata olives; the menu hilariously winks, "what you'd be eating on the Isle of Capri." We'll take that as tongue-in-cheek. Make no mistake, these are purely American reinventions of Italian food: spaghetti with meatballs, chicken piccata, and the like—but it's satisfying and under $10 a pop. Lamb sugo may not have as much depth and complexity as some other more expensive meat sauces in town, but it beats anything comparable in this price range.

There's a good variety on the menu besides pasta, as well, and plenty of vegetarian choices. Perhaps to remind diners that this is still a Portland-owned venture, Pearl Bakery bread is served, and there's a selection of perfunctory regional microbrews and wines, as well as some okay Italians.

Leave it to a Portland-based venture to do Italian-American chain food better than anyone else is doing it.

Patanegra

Worthy tapas served with an authentically relaxed vibe

8.4	8.5	9.0
Food	Feel	Wine

Spanish

Upmarket restaurant

$50
Price

www.patanegra-restaurant.com

Mon 5pm–9pm
Tue–Sat 5pm–10pm

Bar Beer, wine
Credit cards Visa, MC, AmEx
Reservations Accepted
Date-friendly, outdoor dining

Northwest Portland
1818 NW 23rd Pl.
(503) 227-7282

Patanegra tends to become an overflow for the exceedingly popular Toro Bravo, whose waits can skyrocket into the hour-and-a-half range. And it seems to know it, too, leveraging its relative slowness to provide more personable (and more authentically Spanish-style) service than you might otherwise get at crazy-busy and trendy Toro Bravo—and better food, too.

The space is very urban-chic, with black banquettes and tables; the walls are a mottling of vivid red, orange, and yellow. It's totally comfortable and pretty sexy. Stemware is clunky and thick and water glasses no doubt share a bar code with those found at many greasy spoons, but the lack of fuss is appropriate, given the humble bar origins of this cuisine.

True to form, the menu is divided into hot and cold tapas, some much larger paellas for two, and a few salads. And if Toro Bravo seems to bring a Modern American innovation to tapas, there is little straying here. Morcilla (blood sausage) is pleasant, black and oniony with a crisp casing. Prawns sautéed in olive oil and garlic are big and juicy, with a ton of flavor. Tortilla española, arguably the most misunderstood Spanish dish in America, is less dense and overcooked than ones we've had at Toro Bravo—but both miss the sublimely integrated execution that exceeds the sum of its parts.

We are lukewarm on these paellas, which come in a good variety, but are uniformly oversalted, killing the subtleties of the saffron and—in arroz negro—the sweet smokiness of squid ink. For their high price, you certainly fill your belly, but that's not necessarily why you come to a tapas joint. For better seafood preps, stick to pungent, briny little boquerones and properly grilled, if oily, octopus.

The wine list is thorough, but may be disconcerting for newcomers to Spanish wine: there's a confusing, wild variation in fonts and sizes that doesn't follow any geographical or typical line of logic; unhelpful regional lumping without distinction between significantly different DOs; and a pretty good number of landmines mixed willy-nilly among some big winners. When in doubt, stick to the older-school Rioja producers, lovely bargains from Ribera del Duero, and a great selection of Lustau sherry. Or ask your server—they are quite knowledgeable and sincere. We'll take our tapas here, and let the suckers wait at Toro Bravo.

Pause

Comfort food served in a space that's hipper than your grandma's

7.4	8.5	8.0
Food	Feel	Beer

American

Casual restaurant

$35
Price

Mon–Sat 11:30am–1am
Sun noon–midnight

Bar Beer, wine, liquor
Credit cards Visa, MC, AmEx
Reservations Not accepted
Kid-friendly, outdoor dining

North Portland
5101 N. Interstate Ave.
(971) 230-0705

This airy, high-ceilinged, gently upmarket restaurant/bar just across the tracks from the western edge of the Mississippi hip strip is probably one of Portland's coolest restaurants full of kids. Why bother with those big, boring family restaurants when you can take your kids here? You can sip one of the exceedingly well-chosen brews, including one on cask (at our last visit, it was a delicious fresh-hopped local IPA) while you bring the high chair on over and expose the kids to avant-garde art, Portland-style—cool local photos, moddish print hanging lamps, exposed pipes, and industrial ceilings.

And that's not all: Visit two or three times, and Pause will turn into your own personal Cheers—a place where everyone knows your name.

The burger (and its younger and cheaper brother, the slider) is a popular order here, and it's an absolute champion if you're a fan of the fresh-off-the-backyard-grill flavor profile. The meat is juicy even when cooked to medium, and it's beautifully seasoned from within. The burger gains complexity from the addition of pickled red onions that are sweet with baking spice, pickles that are fragrant with curry powder, and buns that are supermarket-style but beautifully toasted to form a welcome textural counterpoint. Add bacon? Hell yeah. Add blue cheese? Nah—stick with the Tillamook cheddar.

The frequently changing menu centers around the burger's genre—simple American comfort food, well executed: deep-fried chicken drumsticks confit, perhaps, or macaroni and cheese plus sausage added. The kitchen continues in the backyard-barbecue theme by making good use of a smoker out back, which might contribute its talents to a sandwich of smoked tri-tip steak or smoked pastrami. Latino influences show up, too, in pozole, a pressed Cuban sandwich, and ancho-braised short ribs with favette pasta and cotija cheese. Perhaps in recognition of the fact that pork chops aren't smoked often enough, Pause does this and does it well, inviting braised pork belly and choucroute (the Alsatian version of sauerkraut) to the party too. In a "snack" (read: small plate) variant of that same combination, house-made sausage substitutes for the pork chop, with equally impressive results.

This is one of the most promising signs that the Alberta buzz is extending outward—and in an altogether pleasant way.

Pepino's Mexican Grill

6.0 Food **5.5** Feel

Sweet and intense—if entirely inauthentic—renditions of Cal-Mex and Tex-Mex dishes

Mexican

Counter service **$10** Price

www.pepinos.org

Daily 11am–10pm

Bar Beer
Credit cards Visa, MC, AmEx
Kid-friendly, outdoor dining,
veg-friendly

Northwest Portland
914 NW 23rd Ave.
(503) 226-9600

Hawthorne
3832 SE Hawthorne Blvd.
(503) 236-5000

Even among demanding food snobs, Pepino's is a regular standby for a cheap weeknight meal. They won't hesitate to tell you (the food snobs, not the people at Pepino's) that Portland's Mexican scene is sorely lacking, which makes the food here seem more exceptional than it might be in, say, Los Angeles. In other words, this is one of the better options in town, which isn't saying a lot.

Part of that success is owed to the fresh flavors of its Cal-Mex menu, particularly grilled fish tacos with crunchy cabbage, cucumbers, and a lightly spicy chipotle mayonnaise. But the Tex-Mex here won't be winning over any Lone Star transplants (barbecue is more often a successful venture up here); enchiladas taste sort of thawed out and mass produced.

For vegetarians, little is impressive. Veggie burritos are flavorless, their flavor-poor beans failing to make up for the lack of lardy depth. They're also plagued with a wateriness that becomes more unmanageable the more vegetables are involved. Meat burritos are full of intensely flavored sauces, some of which are pretty delicious, albeit too sweet (the name "Sweet Tequila" kind of gives it away). But putting barbecue sauce on a burrito just reminds us of what Wolfgang Puck did to pizza in the 1990s. If you like those, you'll dig this.

Stick to the simpler, more authentic dishes like rotisserie chicken with salsa fresca. The skin is flavorful and crispy, with sometimes dry but often good meat inside. And for the love of dios, please avoid the whole-wheat tortilla. If the flour tortillas are somewhat dry and gummy, the whole-wheat ones taste industrial and cardboardy.

The atmosphere is certainly festive, with the bright colors and relative dinginess of a more promising Mexican eatery. There are some beers on draft that go above and beyond the typical Mexican selection, including a few locals. But no margaritas?

For better authentic food, head around the corner to ¿Por Qué No? or better yet, a taco truck. But if you have to get your sweet Thai burrito on, then this is your place.

Petisco

A cute, intimate little place for sandwiches
and salads with a fruity white sangria

6.9	8.0	7.0
Food	Feel	Beer

Sandwiches

Casual restaurant

$20
Price

www.petiscopdx.com

Mon 10am–2pm
Tue–Fri 10am–10pm
Sat 9am–10pm
Sun 9am–2pm

Bar Beer, wine
Credit cards Visa, MC, AmEx
Reservations Not accepted
Outdoor dining, veg-friendly

Northeast Portland
1411 NE Broadway
(503) 360-1048

Petisco offers more than just sandwiches, although they are its main focus. It bills itself as a "little slice of Europe," which is a broad enough claim to be somewhat correct. The place is absolutely tiny and all wood, like a bistro or café in France or Italy; there's a chalkboard listing the daily specials and beer taps. Low, soft lighting glows from candles; there's usually just one server running around, but he or she is personable and accommodating, and seems to remember who you are even after just one visit. If you're dining solo, you might be offered some reading material.

The level of care mostly extends to the food as well. High-quality meats and cheeses go into every sandwich. A prosciutto panino with fresh mozzarella, tomato, and basil is simple and done well. The "Angry Sicilian" with salami and hot capicola and sopressata is deliciously spicy. Bread comes from Fleur de Lis bakery.

There are also salads, like roasted beet and a Niçoise that's got pickled green beans, which gives an added tinge of interest. The tuna salad reminds us a little of a 1970s-Southern-California preparation, but it's totally comforting and refreshing. A Caprese-style salad would be much better without the sweet balsamic vinegar, which is never used in the Italian rendition, and for good reason. Some daily specials like flank steak suggest that some expansion is in the works.

Petisco also takes a stab at brunch, with a short menu of vaguely Continental-style eggs: eggs cooked with prosciutto (which might as well be bacon—why waste prosciutto by cooking it?); eggs with goat cheese and vegetables; eggs with chorizo and onions, and so forth. Pain perdu needs a considerable soak before the baguette is tender enough to chew, and it's pretty boring with just average maple syrup and aerosol whipped cream.

Stick to charming, candlelit sandwich dinners on the tiny, leafy patio. There's a delicious white sangría infused with guava and passion fruit purées, and served ice cold. Most of the wine is lodged firmly in the New World, which doesn't do justice to the cuisine. Beers are only by bottle and can, but include many local micros.

It's a cute place. Not terribly serious, but cute.

Pho An Sandy

8.9 Food **4.5** Feel

Great pho and other Vietnamese delights served in a modest relic of a dying strip-mall era

Vietnamese

Casual restaurant

$15 Price

www.phoansandy.com

Daily 9am–9pm

Bar None
Credit cards Visa, MC
Reservations Not accepted

Northeast Portland
6236 NE Sandy Blvd.
(503) 281-2990

Firing on all cylinders in this ex-fast food spot in the middle of a 1950s suburban strip of Sandy Boulevard is Pho An Sandy. The shape of this straw-colored building suggests it may very well have been a Pizza Hut long ago, but now it reminds us a little of the Lego version of Angkor Wat. Call it guilt by association. Inside, it's every bit as humble as you'd expect a pho place to be, with slurping audible throughout. Service is friendly and there are some attempts at ambience (a plant), but this ultimately feels like a bright, sterile fast food restaurant.

The magic happens in the bowl. To coax a pho broth into this sort of perfumed state is a true feat. The complex broth gets better with every sip. Get the "Pho An Sandy" and be ready for a sensory barrage: perfectly al dente rice noodles, tender slices of round steak (ask for the "steak on the side," which means it comes raw, you put it in the broth yourself, and you cook it for just a second, à la fondue), deeply beefy flank steak, fatty brisket, tendon (again, beef flavor squared), tripe (not as challenging as you'd expect), and beef meatballs (delicious), plus the fresh mint and basil and crisp bean sprouts. The total effect is absolutely stunning.

Also good are bo kho (rich beef stew with French bread), rice plates like com dac biet (broken rice with barbecued pork, pork skin, and an egg-pork patty), and other seriously authentic Vietnamese dishes. Crêpes come thin and eggy, with a good crackly sear in places. There really isn't a bad dish on this entire unassuming menu.

Still, you might ultimately end up back at the pho. It might just be unparalleled in this town.

Pho Hung

Safe ground for new pho fans

8.0	6.5
Food	Feel

Vietnamese

Casual restaurant

$15
Price

www.pho-hung.com

Daily 9am–9pm

Bar None
Credit cards Visa, MC, AmEx
Reservations Not accepted

Southeast Portland
4717 SE Powell Blvd.
(503) 775-3170

In the pho world, you never see websites. Nor dining rooms that are both clean *and* pretty (it's relative). Pho Hung features both, as well as a glowing sign high in the sky. It calls to us on rainy, dark days.

So it's located between Pho Vans, which is never a triumphant thing, as Pho Van's broth is a pretty strong contender; but it's far enough from the exemplary Pho An Sandy and Pho Oregon to end any possible detour discussions. Pho Hung's broth is good in its own right, with a beefy depth, but it doesn't quite go into that intoxicating realm of anise and clove that we get from the city's top phos. Bun is also pretty good here, served with generous helpings of bean sprouts, basil, mint, and lime. A barbecue pork and shrimp version is especially uplifting on a hot day, when the refreshing and vivid flavors perk up the blood.

But back to that nice décor issue—something about the studied track lighting here makes it unsurprising (but no less discouraging) to see the menu divide its pho up into "For Beginners" and "Adventurer's Choice." It's kind of wishy-washy. We prefer to have our tripe and tendon laid out with an authentic nonchalance; like, hey Westerners, get over it. Maybe for this reason, bun bo Hue has no mention of congealed pork blood. Everything feels rounded off for mass appeal, which means it loses its appeal to hardcore Vietnamese-food lovers.

But if you're just here for some noodle soup and vermicelli bowls, you won't be disappointed. Vegetarians won't have much to do here; salad rolls are appropriately named—they taste like lettuce (and the sweet-spicy peanut sauce you dip them in). Vegetable noodle soups are much less flavorful.

No, sorry. This is strictly for meat eaters and beef-broth slurpers. Especially those lost between Pho Vans and too far south for the best.

Pho Oregon

A broth so good, it encourages a chorus of noisy slurpers

8.3 | **7.0**
Food | Feel

Vietnamese

Casual restaurant

$15
Price

Mon–Sat 10:30am–10:30pm

Bar Beer
Credit cards Visa, MC
Reservations Not accepted
Kid-friendly

82nd Avenue Area
2518 NE 82nd Ave.
(503) 262-8816

Many people remember Pho Oregon fondly from its besteepled Sandy Boulevard location, which has since become the even more excellent Pho An Sandy. Pho Oregon's 82nd Avenue incarnation is more like a huge mess hall, and it sounds like one, too. Even at 2:30pm on a Sunday, it's full of people—all, rather encouragingly, seem to be of Asian descent.

The space is fairly standard and utilitarian, with predictable, but modern furnishings that make it look much nicer than Pho An Sandy. The high ceilings and about forty tables of lacquered granite serve as noise amplifiers, sending conversations and slurping noises orbiting around the room. There's a vaguely pan-Asian look to the accessories: an array of Chinese-looking vases with colorful flowers; watercolors of pagodas; and porcelain statues.

Pho is always good, but try the many other Vietnamese specialties on the menu, especially bo la lot. This is a South Vietnamese street food we rarely see: ground beef wrapped with pepper leaves that you can wrap with mint, cilantro, and jalapeño in rice paper and dip in fish sauce. Skip the pedestrian "Salad Rolls," also known as fresh spring rolls, which are cursed with romaine lettuce and bland, overcooked chicken and pasty shrimp. The peanut sauce has an unexpected kick, which is nice.

For something more challenging, try the alluring and complex chao long—rice soup with coagulated pork blood (like bits of soft sausage), liver, heart, and minced pork. We guarantee that upon consumption of a bowl of this, whatever's wrong with you—emotional, physical, or mental—will seem to vanish.

But if you stick to pho, we don't blame you: this broth is outstanding, with strong aromatics of beef, clove, and anise. Order it with fatty brisket to impart more flavor, and tripe for a funky offal element; meatballs have quite a lot of gristle in them, but rare eye round steak is good. Noodles are fine, if a bit overcooked. Overall, Pho An Sandy's pho is a little better, but Pho Oregon's broth, by itself, is king.

To drink, there are the usual beers in bottle, and for dessert, bubble tea and smoothies in a slew of flavors like durian, avocado, and jackfruit. Or just do what we do and have another bowl of broth.

Pho Van

Once upon a time in Portland...

Vietnamese

Casual restaurant   **$25** Price

www.phovanrestaurant.com

Sun–Thu 10am–9:30pm
Fri–Sat 10am–10pm
Hours vary by location

82nd Avenue Area
1919 SE 82nd Ave.
(503) 788-5244

Bar Beer, wine
Credit cards Visa, MC
Reservations Accepted

Beaverton
11651 SW Beaverton Hillsdale Hwy.
(503) 627-0822

Hawthorne
3404 SE Hawthorne Blvd.
(503) 230-1474

It's the oldest story in the book: small Vietnamese restaurant gets "discovered" by local media…small Vietnamese restaurant expands to other branches…now-not-so-small Vietnamese restaurant chain solidifies reputation in media as go-to place in its culinary category…

…Now-verging-on-quite-large ethnic restaurant chain continues to expand, diluting quality…chain launches line of glossy supermarket-style condiments and sauces with big photo of smiling chef on label…one of those condiments is actually fish sauce, but it's humorously renamed "house special dipping sauce"…

…Chain opens bumbling upscale branch aimed at see-and-be-seen Pearl district crowd (we'll deal with Silk in its own review), which struggles…original branches lose their small-time charm and turn corporate, now re-furnished with upmarket-restaurant-catalog interior and nonstop soundtrack of elevator music that drives away some of its most faithful customers…those people defect to two superior restaurants elsewhere in the Portland area, Pho An Sandy and Pho Oregon…

…Pho Van staff refuses, upon request, to serve the thinly sliced steak pieces for the pho raw on the side, so that they can be dunked into the broth for a mere second and eaten rare, as they should be eaten…yet staff at Pho An Sandy and Pho Oregon will still do this…why won't Pho Van, is beef of insufficient quality?…after a sort of negotiation, Pho Van staff might agree to place steak "on top of the broth," but when bowl arrives, meat has already cooked to toughness…

…and the condiments are skimpy, composed (in the case of the small bowl) of a mere sprig of basil, handful of bean sprouts, and three measly slices of japaleño, whereas superior pho joints serve their bowls accompanied with a plate overflowing with herbs and vegetables…

…still, pho isn't half-bad, noodles taste good, fatty brisket is satisfying, broth is aromatic and rich, and it's hard to argue with seven-course beef, one of whose courses is fragrant with kaffir lime, or with whole roasted catfish for two…but that catfish is priced at a very corporate $29.95…and in the end, there are now just better, cheaper options out there, and, unless you're an elevator music fan, there's no remaining reason to patronize this Vietnamese restaurant over its smaller competitors…

…until they get famous, too, at which point the oldest story in the book starts again.

Piazza Italia

A charming, lively restaurant with one foot in the New World and one in the Old

7.8	8.5	8.0
Food	Feel	Wine

Italian

Casual restaurant

$35
Price

www.piazzaportland.com

Mon–Sat noon–10pm
Sun noon–8pm

Bar Beer, wine
Credit cards Visa, MC, AmEx
Reservations Accepted
Date-friendly, outdoor dining,
veg-friendly

Pearl District
1129 NW Johnson St.
(503) 478-0619

This great Old World place feels like just like a trattoria in Rome, complete with an absolutely charming, older, full-blooded Italian owner who like to dance with guests and staff to big band music. There are TV sets everywhere (World Cup alert!) and kitschy Italian items, but instead of looking like a tragic Buco di Beppo, it's both authentic *and* gimmicky. Sidewalk tables, when candlelit, are totally romantic.

Many of the servers are the owner's children, and seem to really respond to the personalities of their tables. They can be exceedingly friendly or chilly and impersonal—think of them as living, reacting Rorschach tests. As an integral part of the ambience, they're often entertaining, putting on acts to amuse diners (or, perhaps, themselves). Despite the festive atmosphere, however, food service is uneven. Larger parties might see dishes come out five minutes apart.

The food consists of the more classically recognizable Italian dishes, mostly pastas: pomodoro; arrabbiata; amatriciana; lasagne al forno, made (as it should be) with béchamel; and fresh and simple linguine with clams. You won't find anchovies, lamb, or whole roasted branzino here. But while the pastas are of the ilk popular with mid-century Americans, they aren't done in that heavy-handed fashion. They are lighter and more subtle.

A Bolognese sauce is delicious, cooked slowly to infuse all the elements, but it's served with big rigatoni instead of tagliatelle ribbons, changing the textural balance.

Bresaola and prosciutto di Parma (not always available) are fine antipasti, and thankfully, melons aren't served out of season. It's hard to argue with the classic, good salads—you may not find bufala on the Caprese, but you won't find a silly non–Italian Caesar either.

The mostly-Italian wine list includes Barolos, Barbarescos, Brunellos and every other super-priced celebrity DOC poised on the lips of American diners, but there are also some great-value wines from lesser known regions. It's not a carefully chosen list so much as a perfunctory one, but like everything else here, it portrays Italy in a flattering if somewhat exaggerated light.

Pine State Biscuits

A tiny place serving a tiny menu of biscuit sandwiches of epic proportion and mass appeal

8.6 Food

7.0 Feel

Sandwiches, Southern

Counter service

$15 Price

www.pinestatebiscuits.com

Daily 7am–2pm

Bar None
Credit cards Visa, MC, AmEx
Kid-friendly, outdoor dining, veg-friendly

Belmont
3640 SE Belmont St.
(503) 236-3346

Portland is crazy for Pine State Biscuits, as evidenced by the long lines outside their farmer's market booth over the years. Even the *Esquire* food editors have deemed Pine State's "Reggie Deluxe" one of the best sandwiches in America, a fact that chick-headed goofball Guy Frieri latched on to for his obnoxious Food Network show. But we won't hold that against them.

This cheery restaurant looks like a piece of treated pine covered in a thick blanket of moss. A retro, tinny sign out front completes an alluring picture. How can you not be drawn in? It's like a darling patisserie that you'd stumble upon in a Grimm Brothers fairy tale. Inside, it's teeny, with only a few tables wedged in and a counter for tightly packed seating. If you eat these drippy, fatty, lardy biscuits often enough, you're going to have to use a shoehorn to get to the counter.

The menu is the sort that makes people who are really into food giddy. That "Reggie Deluxe" has chicken fried expertly for this composition—not so thick and crunchy as to overwhelm with the biscuit, but not at all soggy. There's also thick bacon, melty cheddar cheese, and a fried egg. A meatless "Regina" sees braised collard greens and an ample dowsing of Texas Pete's hot sauce. The "McIsley" has that fried chicken with pickles, mustard, and honey—a spectacular balance that's like having your tongue lightly bitten while frenching. Another vegetarian treat, a "Moneyball" is topped with shiitake-mushroom gravy with egg inside. It's savory and drippy.

And that's essentially it for the sandwiches. Of course, to best experience the buttermilky, slightly salty goodness of these biscuits, you can get a simple "biscuit and spread," with either butter and honey, fruit and whipped cream, or a homemade pimento spread made with chèvre (what tang!). Oniony hash browns and excellent grits are available to round out the meal, and there's Stumptown Coffee, "gourmet" chocolate milk, sweet tea, and Cheerwine sodas to drink. When you're through, call for an airlift to the nearest hammock.

Ping

The grilled creatures of Vietnamese and Thai street
food carts, but with all the comforts of modernity

9.3	8.0
Food	Feel

Pan-Asian

Casual restaurant

$35
Price

www.pingpdx.com

Mon–Fri 11am–10pm
Sat 5pm–10pm

Bar Beer, wine, liquor
Credit cards Visa, MC, AmEx
Reservations Not accepted
Date-friendly, outdoor dining

Old Town Chinatown
102 NW 4th Ave.
(503) 229-7464

The term "pan-Asian" usually brings to mind corporate, dramatic spaces
situated in newfangled shopping centers and a legion of sugary sweet
dishes with indistinct countries of origin. But Ping is quite a different
animal. For one thing, its vibe is dark and intimate, like a hidden Tokyo
izakaya or a watering hole in colonial Saigon. A narrow room with a
warm wood floor and a picture window facing the sidewalk. Some chairs
line up at the kitchen counter, which is lit warmly from above by draping
light fixtures that evoke traditional sushi curtains (which are thought to
refer to the hanging strips of cloth many Japanese sushi street carts
featured as communal napkins, before modern sushi was ever brought
indoors).

Indeed, Ping does specialize in the street foods of Vietnam and
Thailand, though less of the latter. Ping is to Vietnamese what sister
restaurant Pok Pok is (predominantly) to Thai, bringing to Portland those
quotidian delights that have evaded Americanized Southeast Asian menus
in favor of family-friendly, dumbed-down Chinese-American variations.
On a cold night, Ping is soul-warming and nourishing; on a warm one,
you can close your eyes and listen to the banging and clanging of
lightweight pots and bowls, chase the peppery heat down your gullet
with some cold beers, and imagine you are in Chiang Mai, the culinary
heart of Thailand in the Ping River Valley.

The menu consists of noodles, fried cake dishes, rolls, and finger foods,
but the main focus here is on grilled meat, including offal. Some fantastic
skewers include chicken liver, chicken heart, pork collar, baby octopus
(almost too spicy to handle), and a host of others. These come two per
order and are so cheap, you can—and should—sample much of the
bounty. Other legit street foods include delicious roast duck leg in
noodles; Thai-style dried cuttlefish; and Macanese pork-chop sandwiches
in soft buns, flavored with nothing but their own fatty drippings. With
"snacks" like deep-fried tiny fish and Chinese egg steeped in black tea for
$2 a pop, how can you stop ordering?

It's terrific to have a sincere countereffort to the cynical accountant-
driven chains that have deceived American palates for so long. And what
a welcome addition to what had been a fading stretch of Chinatown. If
this is what the new Chinatown is becoming, then we're all for it.

Pix Pâtisserie

Gorgeous superlative pastries and brilliant spirits in a funky wonderland

Baked goods, Sweets

Counter service

www.pixpatisserie.com

Sun–Thu 10am–midnight
Fri–Sat 10am–2am
Hours vary by location

Bar Beer, wine, liquor
Credit cards Visa, MC, AmEx
Date-friendly, delivery, live music,
outdoor dining, veg-friendly

Mississippi Ave. Area
3901 N. Williams Ave.
(503) 282-6539

Division/Clinton
3402 SE Division St.
(503) 232-4407

Portland is a city of unabashed culinary freaks and geniuses, picking up whatever cuisine speaks to them and running full speed in the direction of excellence with a half-mad grin of dopey love the way Brett Favre—bless his heart—still carries a football. Pix Pâtisserie is the very epitome of this passion and greatness, and it puts perhaps every other American pâtisserie to shame.

Where to begin? With the eclectic, absolutely charming shops; the perfect-with-pastries Belgian beer and Lambic selection; the top-shelf liqueurs, apéritifs, and dessert wines; or with fun and innovative events like Dessert Dim Sum, make-your-own-dessert nights, actually challenging gastronomic trivia, and weekly movies?

Let's begin with the pastries, since we're dying to explain them—or let's try to, anyway, as the description of these beauties would elude even Keats. These are creamy tarts covered with vivid, glossy fruits; a flawless orange-vanilla crème brûlée floating on top of a glazed chocolate mousse topped with a Cointreau génoise and caramelized hazelnuts; and a classic gâteau topped with cream puffs, Grand Marnier, and vanilla crème Chantilly. Each looks more opulent than the one before it—you scarcely want to put a dent in it with timid licks, at first, before succumbing to a full-on, eyes-closed, moaning bite.

This is the part that gets us: the flavor and texture on these desserts actually follows through. They're not at all cardboardy and stiff or undersweetened—or overly sweet. These taste as French as they look. Perhaps most beloved here are macaroons, whose variety of Easter-egg colors and flavors inspire Proustian memories: blueberry, pistachio, rose, tawny Port, passionfruit. The list—and rainbow of colors—goes on, and makes for one lovely gift box or tower, which you can order as a wedding cake substitute.

We could hang out forever in these cafés as well; our favorite is the North Williams location, which features little windows in its red-velvet wallpaper that you can peer through to watch the magic happen in the kitchen. Pix also makes its own delectable ice creams, which can be plopped in a lambic or beer to make one mighty fine grown-up float.

If solids aren't your thing, drink equally precious Clear Creek eaux-de-vie, Jacopo Poli Merlot grappa, or Lustau Palo Cortado sherry.

Pizza Schmizza

An unbeatable marketing campaign and attitude can't save bad pizza

3.6 Food

7.5 Feel

Pizza, Italian

Counter service

$25 Price

www.schmizza.com

Mon–Sat 11am–9pm
Sun 11am–8pm

Bar Beer, wine
Credit cards Visa, MC, AmEx
Delivery, kid-friendly, outdoor
dining, veg-friendly

Pearl District
1036 NW Glisan St.
(503) 546-8162

Southwest Portland
732 SW Yamhill St.
(503) 227-0888

Downtown
512 SW Taylor St.
(503) 445-6274

Additional locations
and more features at
www.fearlesscritic.com

Pizza Schmizzas are everywhere, and the ad campaign is pretty cute. We've all enjoyed the "Vote Schmizza for Dinner" posters, snarky commercials, and even professionally printed signs for panhandlers to hold reading: "Pizza Schmizza paid me to hold this sign instead of asking for money." Pizza Schmizza fits right in to the smart, self-conscious, counter-culture zeitgeist of Portland surprisingly well for a chain whose logo has an outer glow effect.

But what the pizza has in exposure it lacks in execution. This is a decidedly fat, doughy, smooshy, throw-away crust. Ingredients come in a slew of '90s-"gourmet" choices like artichoke hearts, sun-dried tomatoes, and spinach. To help distract from the lack of good crust, sauce, and cheese, why not pile on steak and potatoes with sour cream? It tastes like you'd expect—like something you want to scrape off a pizza and eat by itself on a plate.

A "Greek veggie" ingredient combo is better suited for this ho-hum, too-architecturally stable pie, but that's only because feta makes everything seem better. And what's up with the plain, canned black olives instead of kalamata? Even the '90s had those.

It can get much worse. Perhaps the worst atrocity ever committed by a man named Wolfgang (and that's a lot, considering Wolfgang Peterson's films), the Thai pizza, is given a sickly-sweet seat at the table alongside other disasters like "sweet 'n' sour" chicken with pineapple and sesame seeds. If you like Hawaiian pizzas but tend to take the ham off and substitute candy, then you'll love this.

In addition to schmizza, there's schpasta. Don't spend the premium on alligator sausage here—it tastes like regular sausage. It will bite, though, in a chipotle cream sauce with chicken over noodles. But where it bites is not so great. Is there maybe a Mylanta pizza we could get with that?

Pizzicato

One of the better chain delivery pizza
options in town

5.8	6.5	7.0
Food	Feel	Beer

Pizza, Sandwiches

Counter service

$20
Price

www.pizzicatopizza.com

Mon–Fri 11am–9pm
Sat noon–10pm
Sun noon–8pm
Hours vary by location

Bar Beer, wine
Credit cards Visa, MC, AmEx
Delivery, kid-friendly, outdoor
dining, veg-friendly

Downtown
705 SW Alder St.
(503) 226-1007

Northwest Portland
505 NW 23rd Ave.
(503) 242-0023

Northeast Portland
2811 E. Burnside St.
(503) 236-6045

Additional locations
and more features at
www.fearlesscritic.com

Pizzicato is a pretty successful chain of non-hokey pizza parlors that run
down the length of I-5 from Vancouver to San Diego, but it all started
right here in Portland in 1989.

What can we say? Pizzicato's not bad for chain pizza. The dough is
made daily and baked to a nice, thin crust. It holds up to reheating. Good
ingredients are used, like heirloom tomatoes and fresh mozzarella; the
fennel sausage is high quality. Of course, the range of ingredients is all
over the gourmet spectrum: lamb sausage, sun-dried tomatoes, artichoke
hearts, and even (shudder) tzatziki. There's the forgettable "Thai" pizza,
with sweet peanut sauce and chicken or shrimp. But stick to the basics for
best results. A margherita doesn't use great mozzarella, but nor does it
heap on the tomato sauce (it comes with fresh tomatoes; you have to ask
for sauce, but it's better this way).

Salads and panini are also reasonably good for a chain, although quite
pricey. A Caprese is totally crazy, though, with balsamic vinegar and sun-
dried tomatoes and other totally unnecessary ingredients you don't
normally see. And to pay this much money for roasted garlic cloves and a
bit of Gorgonzola is even crazier.

Forget about wine here—it's a lost cause; a few local beers in bottle are
better with this pizza anyway, and there are often a couple of craft beers
on tap. Thomas Kemper sodas, like vanilla cream, are also ideal pizza
partners.

Although the insides of the Pizzicatos certainly feel like a slightly nicer
version of a massive chain restaurant—catalog-style furnishings,
unflattering light—there's sometimes a pleasant array of outdoor seating.
And some even deliver, which is better. In fact, of all your delivered-pizza
options, this might be your best.

Podnah's Pit

Some of the best barbecue in the west...

8.3 Food

6.0 Feel

Barbecue, Southern

Casual restaurant

$25 Price

www.podnahspit.com

Tue–Fri 11am–9pm
Sat–Sun 9am–9pm

Bar Beer
Credit cards Visa, MC, AmEx
Reservations Not accepted
Kid-friendly, outdoor dining

Northeast Portland
1469 NE Prescott St.
(503) 281-3700

Podnah's is about as far from a fancy restaurant as you can get. Its only sign is a small sandwich board on the sidewalk. (Just look for the steamy windows next to the Mexican market.) If you don't get there early, be prepared to wait; and if you get there late, be prepared to be told they have run out of many items.

The room is long and narrow with concrete floors and Formica tables; old photographs pepper the walls. Don't miss the specials on the chalkboard. There are a few beers on tap, and a good selection of others available by the bottle, along with lots of more unusual sodas.

Now let's get down to it: first of all, there's lamb, which is a delightful barbecue anomaly. Then there's moist, delicious pulled pork, vinegary in the North Carolina style. And then there's candy for homesick Texans, in the form of smoked brisket made with Strawberry Farms beef; it's got a crispy, smoky bark of char around the edges and needs no sauce (though there is some, if you'd like).

Ribs (continuing around America, this time to Tennessee and Missouri) are dry-rubbed, and have a good balance of meat and fat. They're also properly smoky and outstanding on their own. Specials come and go, usually on Friday or Saturday nights. One week, we had a wonderful prime rib, which had been smoked for hours to render all that fat, absorbing its flavor into the flesh.

Sides are serviceable: collards, cole slaw, pit barbecue beans, potato salad, and so on. Cornbread has an occasional off night, where it is too dry, or the texture is too cake-like. Pecan pie is wonderful, with a buttery crust and toothsome pecans. Get some to go. You'll be hungry again one day.

It's true that this barbecue probably wouldn't compete with the best in Texas Hill Country, nor Memphis, nor Lexington, North Carolina, but come on—barbecue is a fiercely regional thing. In those places, smokers are passed down as heirlooms and recipes are guarded closely. For Portland, this is as good as it gets, and the Southerners are sure happy to have it.

Pok Pok

For foodie pilgrims, this mecca of flavor and heat is unparalleled

9.5	8.0	9.0
Food	Feel	Drinks

Thai

Casual restaurant

$35
Price

www.pokpokpdx.com

Mon–Fri 11:30am–10pm
Sat–Sun 5pm–10pm

Bar Beer, wine, liquor
Credit cards Visa, MC, AmEx
Reservations Not accepted
Date-friendly, outdoor dining

Division/Clinton
3226 SE Division St.
(503) 232-1387

Thailand is littered with roadside restaurants, rickety places that are miniature conventions of smells and flavors, shacks that are shoddily constructed and not particularly clean. They're places in which to throw back whiskey sodas, listen to some tunes, and eat food so spicy it makes you sweat. Perhaps nowhere in America is this scene more accurately reconstructed than it is at Pok Pok's Whiskey Soda Lounge.

The main lounge downstairs is cozy and divey, with low ceilings. An upstairs dining room accommodates larger parties and is a bit more formal; the driveway/patio area is open for table service on warm days, with Pok Pok's to-go shack above it. Wherever you want to sit, be prepared to wait an hour or more.

Cocktails are more balanced and exotic than what you'd be likely to find in Thailand, including a delicious tamarind whiskey sour with lime, palm sugar, and Bourbon, and a salty plum vodka collins that's as refreshing as an oyster mignonette. Bitburger and Lagunitas IPA are on draft.

A seasonally rotating menu generally focuses on the Northern Thai regions of Isan and Chiang Mai. There is also some Vietnamese crossover in this cuisine. You won't find many recognizable food-court dishes here. If you haven't spent serious time in Thailand (and outside touristy areas), forget everything you think you know, and experience what Thai food really is (and then wonder why on earth no one else is doing this): lime, chili, fish sauce, fermented shrimp paste. Sour, spicy, salty, umami. Amazing. If you're stuck, defer to your knowledgeable server—the one in the mohom shirt.

Pok Pok presses its own coconut juice, which shines in khao soi, with house-made curry paste, chicken on the bone, mustard greens, shallots, dried shrimp, crispy yellow noodles, and chili paste. It is, as James Lipton would say, a revelation.

That sense of wonder continues, dish after dish: grilled boar collar in evocative chili-lime sauce; whole roast chicken; and so on. People go crazy for Ike's Vietnamese fish sauce wings, which are fiery, sweet, and fun, but certainly not the best thing here. It's the dishes with the most disconcerting descriptions that are best—the ones that unmoor you from familiar textures and flavors: stewed pork leg with pickled mustard greens; som tam (green papaya salad with raw crab) glowing nuclear-red with heat; or cha ca la vong, a catfish dish made famous in Hanoi. Just give in to the good pain of Portland's most intense chilies.

¿Por Qué No?

A little dose of rustic, vibrant Mexican culture lives on in a Pacific-Northwest-hipster favorite

7.2 **8.0**
Food   Feel

Mexican

Counter service   **$20**
Price

www.porquenotacos.com

Sun–Thu 11am–9:30pm
Fri–Sat 11am–10pm

Bar Beer, wine, liquor
Credit cards Visa, MC
Kid-friendly, outdoor dining

Mississippi Ave. Area
3524 N. Mississippi Ave.
(503) 467-4149

Hawthorne
4635 SE Hawthorne Blvd.
(503) 954-3138

The original ¿Por Qué No? location is in a small converted basement garage with tables inside and out. Sitting under an umbrella at a sidewalk table and sipping a Negra Modelo, it might occur to you how closely this resembles a Los Angeles beachside taquería. It's artistically shabby, with eclectic found objects decorating the colorful walls and making up the furnishings, and the service is way chill. We half expect to feel gritty sand beneath our feet whenever we visit.

This plucky little venture is the fruit of a Portland backpacker's trip to the heart of Michoacán, and the foods served there—from the Pacific Ocean east into the interior—are done a fair amount of justice here. Despite some claims that this is a yuppie magnet, we've found both locations to be melting pots of people from all walks of life. It's hip, yes, but what place with great vibes and low prices isn't?

After a wobbly start, this kitchen really found its footing, and now produces pretty reliably good tacos, guacamole, ceviches, and tamales, using local meat and produce. Tortillas are made fresh by hand all day long, and are terrific.

Guacamole has big chunks of avocado, onions, and cilantro, with a fine acidity and saltiness. Carnitas are carefully cooked, though better paired with a spunky salsa verde than their pallid smoky chipotle sauce. Fish tacos are usually excellent, full of nice pieces of moist fish, cabbage, and strips of ripe mango. Occasionally, though, you can get smaller pieces of fish that don't have as much flavor. Ceviche is vivacious, full of line-caught fish and sweet, fresh shrimp.

Brunch options include pancakes with plantains and organic maple syrup, huevos rancheros, chilaquiles, and tinga with eggs—all dirt cheap. A daily happy hour features beers and tacos for just a few bucks a piece, strong margaritas, cheap rum-spiked aguas frescas, and delicious red and white sangrías. But it gets so crowded that you might have to go enjoy them on the curb, or sweating in a corner next to a Virgen de Guadalupe figurine on a bright green wall. Which is about as close to the real deal as it gets.

Portland City Grill

A wayfaring menu and stunning views that are more dizzying at full price

6.4	9.0	5.0
Food	Feel	Wine

Steakhouse, Modern

Upmarket restaurant

$70
Price

www.portlandcitygrill.com

Mon–Thu 11am–midnight
Fri 11am–1am
Sat 4pm–1am
Sun 4pm–11pm

Bar Beer, wine, liquor
Credit cards Visa, MC, AmEx
Reservations Accepted
Date-friendly

Downtown
111 SW 5th Ave.
(503) 450-0030

Three words: view, view, view. People love it, they come for it, they pay a premium for it. Portland City Grill is perched on the top floor of the US Bancorp Tower, or "Big Pink," named for its pink granite exterior. From here, you can see the entire city and the Cascades. Only the Wells Fargo Building is taller, by ten feet.

Thanks to the view, this restaurant is intensely popular during happy hour, with a somewhat egalitarian cross-section of Portland's population: indie hipsters and yuppies; old and young; rich and poor. If someone else is paying, it's even easier to love, but prices from 4:30pm–6:30pm and 10pm–midnight (all day on Sunday) are surprisingly affordable.

Even though experience has conditioned us to flinch whenever we see a menu this globetrotting—rarely does anyone master Japanese preps and risotto in one kitchen—we're a little impressed by the competence here. Even sushi is good: fresh and not too thickly cut. Of course, if you order a California roll, you won't get anything to stop the presses for. But at $3, it's cheaper and better tasting than your grocery-store lunch staple. Better is furikake-crusted ahi tuna, the wonderfully umami flavors of seaweed, dashi, and glutamate taking this overrated fish high enough to negate the need for the "firecracker aïoli" that comes with it.

But we'd caution against ordering any of this off the regular menu—for the price, you can do much better at Japanese restaurants around town. Kung pao calamari is only palatable at $6, and "teriyaki chicken rice paper spring rolls" served with "Thai dipping sauce" (which is it?) are never good, no matter the price. We'd rather pay $3 to eat our napkins.

On the regular menu, avoid anything that pits nebulous words like "Thai," "Hoisin," and "Asian" against Euro-American dishes. Where we would commend an expert conjoining of spices, herbs, and chilies in otherwise French preparations, this is more akin to dumping a one-dimensional sauce impersonating all those flavors onto a dull piece of chicken or pork. Dry-aged steaks are good, but they ought to be better for the high prices they command. Again, we suspect that the glittering land out your window has something to do with it.

An offensively overpriced and unimaginative wine list appears to have been culled exclusively from *Wine Spectator* lists—something we rarely see in Portland. Perhaps being up this high has put the restaurant out of touch with what's going on in the city below.

Portobello

Focus on the little things at this temple to health and all things right

6.8 Food

7.5 Feel

Vegefusion, Italian

Casual restaurant

$35 Price

www.portobellopdx.com

Tue–Sat 5:30pm–9pm

Bar Beer, wine
Credit cards Visa, MC
Reservations Essential

Southeast Portland
2001 SE 11th Ave.
(503) 754-5993

Veganism, according to Wikipedia (we know, we know…), is "a diet and lifestyle that seeks to exclude the use of animals for food, clothing, or any other purpose…the most common reasons for becoming a vegan are ethical commitment or moral conviction concerning animal rights, the environment, human health, and spiritual or religious concerns."

Not unsurprisingly, it seems that carnivores aren't stumbling over one another to become vegan so as to have richer gustatory lives. In many parts of the country, if you don't eat any animal products, then you ain't eating out at a restaurant. (At least not in a non-embarrassing way or as some sort of a lettuce-eating spectacle.)

That's why it's refreshing to see places like Portobello, a self-billed vegan trattoria. This being Portland, the restaurant scene is ahead of the curve in matters of progressive eating, so not only do places like this exist, but they serve serviceable food.

A meal at Portobello is, from start to finish, a relaxed and civilized endeavor. Your waitress might be a soft-spoken woman who seems totally happy to be at work. The interior is quaint and rustic, a feeling mirrored by the little touches like wine that is served in small water glasses—a far cry from Riedel.

For starters, or as the menu says, "to share," the simple Little T slab with olive oil and sea salt delivers elemental pleasure, while a beet-and-mushroom tartare is full of big, earthy flavor. Its texture is nice—not too fine, not too rough. The same goes for a truffle-oil-laced mushroom pâté.

While those preps just involve arranging inherently vegan ingredients into a pretty dish, the lasagne Bolognese, on a recent visit, was the biggest feat of them all. Tempeh and cashew cream participated in a culinary sleight of hand. The end result, however, was a fairly dry heap of pasta that, animal byproducts or not, was a fairly poor version of an Italian classic.

You'll leave Portobello feeling, ultimately, pretty darn healthy. But we won't be renouncing our carnivorous ways any time soon.

Potato Champion

6.4 Food
6.5 Feel

With fries like this all we need is an excuse to eat them all the time

American

Food cart **$5** Price

www.potatochampion.com

Wed–Sat 8pm–3am

Bar None
Credit cards None
Outdoor dining

Hawthorne
SE 12th and SE Hawthorne
No phone

This immensely popular food cart—part of the famous late-night hawker center of food carts near the western end of Hawthorne east of the river—purveys French fries, and only French fries. They're labeled "Belgian," but they're not really Belgian in style. First of all, they're skin-on; second of all, they're less crispy than the traditional double-cooked Belgian style. This is perhaps because of the combination of large fry batches with a relatively small fryer, which forces the fries to sit in a big pile, getting a bit soggy from fry-to-fry contact, rather than cooking them in smaller batches and spacing them out enough to maintain their crispness.

These are relatively petty complaints for the friendly, flirtatious, bearded Potato Champion. First of all, mad props are bestowed upon him for the service of poutine, that Québécois specialty in which a dish of fries is sprinkled with cheese curds and drowned in beefy gravy. Here, the gravy has an unusually vinegary tinge, but it's good stuff, and poutine is one of the most popular orders amongst the cult following of foodies that descend on the cart in the wee hours. If you're not in a poutining mood, the frites sauce (dubbed "European-style mayo," and it would perhaps be most common in Holland and Belgium) is the world's most perfect topping for French fries. Props for that, too, although we wish they served our favorite, curry mayo. There are, however, numerous other mayos and sauces, some of them quite spicy. This certainly honors the Dutch-Belgian tradition.

Even if these fries aren't world-class—even if they won't transport you to Antwerp or Amsterdam, where French fries are an art form—the Potato Champion is a worthy addition to Portland's food-cart scene. These are just good, hot fried potatoes, served at a reasonable price in terrifically late hours. And there's absolutely nothing wrong with that.

Powell's Seafood

The best Chinese restaurants are next to impossible to find—and this is no exception

8.5 Food   **7.0** Feel

Chinese, Seafood

Casual restaurant   **$15** Price

Daily 11:30am–11pm

Bar Beer, wine
Credit cards Visa, MC, AmEx
Reservations Not accepted

Southeast Portland
6633 SE Powell Blvd.
(503) 775-3901

Look under the industrial awning of a little terra-cotta-colored building for the small neon sign in the window: Powell's Seafood House. It's easy to miss but it would be a shame to. This little gem is totally underrated—mostly because it's undervisited.

Which works out for you, the diner, as there isn't often a wait, the servers have time to be warm and speedy, and watching them buzz around adds to the simple room décor.

There won't be much in the way of Szechuan spice here—it's all Cantonese and Mandarin, lots of seafood like conch, prawns, crab, and lobster. Salt-and-pepper squid is fantastic, toothsome and properly crusted in seasoning. When it's available, sweet-and-sour crispy whole fried fish is not to be missed. The flaky, moist meat has a wonderful crunch to it, and it's not nearly as sweet as you might think. Manila clams with black bean sauce are also great, but you could do just as well with a hot pot. And congee is warm and filling on cold days. The best way to do it up here is with a large group so you can have a few bites of everything.

We've thoroughly enjoyed goose intestines with black bean sauce, which aren't at all texturally bizarre (of course, if you meditate on what you're eating, you'll always gag a wee bit—just dissociate). Just ignore the take-out standards like General Tso's and kung pao chicken. Stick to (naturally) the seafood, and the many vegetarian options. Don't get too excited when you see ma po tofu—there isn't nearly enough Szechuan peppercorn in this dish to make it worthwhile.

This is a delightful find that's a bit closer in to downtown Portland and the gentrified Southeast than the 82nd-Avenue agglomeration.

The Press Club

Crêpes and wine with lit mags and old movies—why would you ever leave?

6.8	9.5	7.5
Food	Feel	Wine

Sandwiches, Crêpes

Casual restaurant

$20
Price

Sun–Thu 11am–11pm
Fri–Sat 11am–midnight

Bar Beer, wine, liquor
Credit cards Visa, MC, AmEx
Reservations Not accepted
Date-friendly, live music, outdoor dining, veg-friendly, Wi-Fi

Division/Clinton
2621 SE Clinton St.
(503) 233-5656

The American café is all about coffee and pastries, and increasingly, a pleasant place to plop your laptop. The European café is a place of socializing, eating, and drinking, but almost never a workspace. By providing an airy, comfortable lounge-like space where laptops can coexist with cocktails and candlelit tables, The Press Club straddles this line with ease. Plus, it boasts Southeast Portland's most extensive selection of retail magazines and journals, from lit mags like *Tin House* to popular biker rags, and a slew of indie zines.

Large glass doors and skylights bring plenty of natural light into this high-ceilinged room, and the work of local artists hangs on the walls and changes every now and then. The free Wi-Fi invites hours of hanging out and working, and the magazines mean that dining alone in a somewhat romantic space never means feeling lonely. Local bands often play, and great old movies play once a week. Sometimes, in fact, it seems there's no reason to ever leave.

And you'll be kept plenty fueled, between Stumptown coffee and pretty good sandwiches made on breads from the excellent Pearl Bakery. There's a limited menu of sweet and savory crêpes, which are prepared carefully, neither gummy nor crunchy. A plate of decent meats and cheeses is a worthwhile companion to a glass from the surprisingly extensive wine list (which is delightfully weighted toward the cheaper, but still well-made, end). Salads are also a good bet, like a delicious version with salty slices of cured salmon atop field greens.

There are also many beers in the bottle, and okay cocktails. The vibe here is totally relaxed, within reason—you can hang out forever, but you should have the decency to be eating or drinking most of the time. We'd venture to guess that that's not going to be much of a problem.

Puerto Marquez

Celebrating Mexico's coast with an array of seafood and, of course, cerveza

Mexican

Casual restaurant

$25
Price

Daily 11am–11pm

Bar Beer, wine, liquor
Credit cards Visa, MC
Reservations Accepted
Kid-friendly

Far East Portland
1721 SE 122nd Ave.
(503) 253-6842

When Americans think of Mexican food, their minds often turn to tortillas filled with myriad meats, beans and rice, cheese, and bright salsas. The more devout followers of Mexican tradition might crave the stewed tripe in challengingly pungent menudo, the crunchy fried crickets of the Oaxacan marketplace, the gelatinous tacos de cabeza, the street-vendor sopes, or the plate of machaca, that magical combination of gamy dried beef and egg.

It's easy to forget, amidst all of these unique treasures, that along so much of the country's vast coastline, the most highly prized food of all is one of the simplest: fish. In many parts of Mexico, the ideal meal is a whole fried or grilled head-and-bones-on fish—mojarra, huachinango (red snapper), or corvina (bass), perhaps—served on a big platter, ready to be devoured. Tortillas and rice and everything else take a backseat to the sea creatures at the center of the table. It is a life-affirming celebration of the local fishermen and their spoils, a ceremony of plenty.

That's not to take away from the importance of the rest of the sea's bounty: giant raw oysters, for example, served with a squeeze of lime and a dab of hot sauce, a Mexican spin on cocktail sauce or mignonette; a cocktail of octopus, clams, or partly cooked shrimp; fish ceviche, that wondrously tender fish appetizer that gets its cure from lime and its bounce from cilantro; or the classic plate of juicy shrimp al mojo de ajo, sautéed in garlic butter.

Lest you think we digress, all of these are descriptions of dishes served at one of Portland's unsung gems, Puerto Marquez. So are camarones ahogados—raw shrimp marinated in a sauce of chile and lime, a rare treat that (to our knowledge) you'll find nowhere else in the city. Enjoy the bean dip, but otherwise, avoid the non-seafood items on the menu.

The place is really out in the middle of nowhere, so it might surprise you, given the dingy sign and parking-lot entrance, that the warm red-and-orange room does a pretty good job (by strip-mall standards) of transporting you to coastal Mexico. Soccer balls and giant Modelo cans hang from the ceiling like piñatas; long banquet-style tables look ready to accommodate groups of 15 or 20. It's fun when it's full of people, but when it's empty, it's as if someone threw a big fiesta for the 6th-graders and nobody showed up.

You should take it upon yourself to help make the room full, not empty, because the charming staff is also a pleasure. Maybe the Pacific Northwest—another place where fish is of paramount importance—is the natural melting pot for Mexican coastal culture.

Queen of Sheba

Food from the birthplace of humanity served in a slightly dingy, totally sincere place

8.7	6.5	7.0
Food	Feel	Drinks

Ethiopian

Casual restaurant

$35
Price

www.queenofsheba.biz

Sun–Wed 5pm–10pm
Thu–Sat 11am–3pm, 5pm–10pm

Bar Beer, wine, liquor
Credit cards None
Reservations Accepted
Veg-friendly

Northeast Portland
2413 NE MLK Blvd.
(503) 287-6302

Queen of Sheba is our favorite Ethiopian restaurant in Portland. Spice-filled air emanates from this hole in the wall operating out of an old converted store in a musty building. The dining rooms are strange and shabby, lit by mostly burned-out fluorescent bulbs. A few flags and painted figures on the walls attempt to brighten things up. A list of interesting cocktails is available from the quiet full bar in back: a "Greenfire Kiss," for instance, mixes brandy or tequila with serrano peppers, ginger, olive juice, and a dash of vermouth. It's unusual, and a good entry to a transportive meal.

Just about everything that is not fresh is imported from Ethiopia. The owner apparently makes yearly trips there, returning with grains, spices, and other necessary ingredients.

The injera (spongy sourdough bread) here is nice, slightly citrusy-sour, and its brightness complements the deep, spicy flavors of the food it picks up and takes to your plate in lieu of cutlery. Try a vegetarian sampler (be prepared to share—there's a lot of everything) that includes: split-pea stew with warm spices; lentil and okra stew; chickpea paste; Oregon mushroom stew; mustard greens steamed and seasoned with flax seeds; and so on.

Beef, lamb, and chicken come either as alicha—in a complex sauce of ginger, garlic, onion, fenugreek, cumin, basil, cardamom, oregano, and turmeric—or as berbere, a piquant combination of wine, cumin, clove, cardamom, turmeric, allspice, fenugreek, ginger, chili, and garlic. Neither sauce is mouth-scaldingly hot, which isn't the goal of this cuisine. Alicha is more aromatic and vivacious; berbere is slightly silkier and rich. Always dependable is doro wat, the national dish of Ethiopia—a lemon-washed chicken leg simmered in berbere and topped with a hard-boiled egg. Some meats can be a little overcooked, but never distractingly so.

Where Portland's (few) other Ethiopian restaurants tend to be more shy on flavor and quality ingredients, the dishes here achieve an excellent balance, never masking the subtleties of the flavors. The prices are hard to beat, and the whole experience is sensuous and fun.

Red Onion Thai

A tale of two Thai restaurants

8.2 Food **7.0** Feel

Thai

Casual restaurant **$30** Price

Mon–Fri 11am–3pm, 5pm–9pm
Sat–Sun noon–9pm

Bar Beer, wine
Credit cards Visa, MC, AmEx
Reservations Not accepted

Northwest Portland
1123 NW 23rd Ave.
(503) 208-2634

This city's dining scene is peppered with occasional bursts of hysteria surrounding one restaurant or another opening, reinventing itself, having a massive change in staff, or having been flying under the radar of Portland's restaurant-going population for years. Red Onion Thai is one such burst, having opened in the space that used to house MisoHapi. (And we're so happy that we don't have to deal with that over-the-top goofy name anymore.) It was met with lots of positive press, and comparisons to Pok Pok, Portland's holy grail of Thai food, were hinted at—but only in hushed tones.

Your average Thai takeout joint in America serves gloopy, sweet dishes like pad Thai, which doesn't really exist (at least in the American form) in Thailand, at least outside of tourist traps. Along Khao San Road, which is Bangkok's backpacker epicenter, you can get Nutella and banana crêpes. But that doesn't mean they're Thai.

And, what do you know, pad Thai stares right up at you from this menu. But so do a host of other interesting dishes that you don't see at your #6-lunch-special joint, especially on the "Thai Specials" menu, which you sometimes have to ask for. (The specials were previously strictly off-the-menu, but after the blogosphere spilled the beans, Red Onion wised up and printed them up.)

We like the pork-filled deep-fried squid, and pandanus-leaf chicken. Delicious, too, are larb moo (spicy salad) made with pork tongue and liver; Chiang Mai sausage; and naam prik ong (ground pork simmered with chili paste and tomato). Tom mamuang and pla trout ta krob, for instance, is a version of the classic sour-and-spicy green mango and crispy shredded catfish salad, but it's done with trout instead of catfish, and it's exquisite.

So hang out in the part of the menu that the Thai in-crowd does. It will make you so much happier.

RingSide Steakhouse

5.6	8.0	7.0
Food	Feel	Wine

An old-school steakhouse that sometimes slips into obsolescence

Steakhouse

Upmarket restaurant

$80
Price

www.ringsidesteakhouse.com

Mon–Sat 5pm–midnight
Sun 4pm–11:30pm

Bar Beer, wine, liquor
Credit cards Visa, MC, AmEx
Reservations Accepted
Date-friendly

Northwest Portland
2165 W. Burnside St.
(503) 223-1513

Northeast Portland
14021 NE Glisan St.
(503) 255-0750

The downtown RingSide is stuck mid-century. It looks like just about everything we want from an old steakhouse, dark and clubby, with deep padded booths. A large fireplace dominates the center of the room, creating an especially comforting warmth in colder, wetter months. Sardi's-style, while tuxedo-clad waiters scuttle around, seemingly unaware that the whole place smells unmistakably like mildew.

Normally, we find overdressing to be a problem in steakhouses, but these salads are practically buck-naked—which might be okay if the leaves had any natural flavor, but in the case of a Caesar, the dressing is the thing. The anchovies are a dried-out afterthought, lying sadly among plasticky shards of parmesan.

Steaks fare scarcely better. A 14-ounce New York strip is cooked to a proper medium-rare, but gets a crust that tastes more burnt than charred. Both this and a 24-ounce Porterhouse will provide more gristle than flavor.

In a move that is boldly outdated and out of touch, sides include your choice of garlic mashed potatoes (okay), baked potato (old and petrified), french fries, jasmine rice pilaf (really?), or cottage cheese (really??). For an additional charge, RingSide's "famous" onion rings are expertly cooked (they ought to be after over 60 years of practice), but the accompanying blue-cheese-and-ketchup sauce tasted, on one visit, like it had gone bad.

Unlike at El Gaucho, you won't get a zany tableside show with your bananas Foster, just a sad, withering plate of ice cream over bananas. Desserts, in general, are of the bake-sale variety.

The wine list is spectacularly ambitious, but completely unaffordable. You can get your Château Pétrus '66 for $8,500, but inexcusably the cheapest French red on the list is $49. Think domestic wines are cheaper? A quick Excel analysis reveals that the average price of a California Cab on the list is $231, and the median $210. Incredible. We do, however, appreciate the vintage Port wines and Madeiras from the 1980s and '90s, which are under $15 per glass.

We're all for preserving old-timey standards of service and décor, but RingSide just feels careless, like by including all the perfunctories, it will somehow stay alive and well. But Portland's dining scene has been growing up around these walls, and the once-mighty steakhouse is now dwarfed.

Ristretto Roasters

Not your grandmother's watery cup of joe, nor the burnt sludge of your corporate past

Coffee, Baked goods

Café

www.ristrettoroasters.com

Daily 6am–6pm
Hours vary by location

Bar None
Credit cards Visa, MC, AmEx
Outdoor dining, veg-friendly, Wi-Fi

Mississippi Ave. Area
3808 N. Williams Ave.
(503) 288-8667

Northeast Portland
3520 NE 42nd Ave.
(503) 284-6767

Ristretto roasts its own coffee every day in a vintage Probat roaster. You might have already had a cup of Ristretto coffee, if you have ever been to Bar Vendetta, Siam Society, Javarama, or any number of the other restaurants that carry it. There are now two Ristretto branches where you can have your pick of about seven or eight roasts, at any time of the day. They'll grind the beans, and drip a cup for you.

Though the location in Northeast (where they do all the roasting) is somewhat cramped, the lovely and spacious North Williams branch invites lingering with the paper. The high ceilings and exposed wood beams are rustically elegant, and the simple shapes and brown-and-white scheme remind us of a paper coffee cup. It's a great place to showcase local artwork—much of it by employees of Ristretto. The dishware is a playful, vibrant orange, and the Wi-Fi is free.

The roasts traverse South America, Central America, and East Africa; many are fair trade. Roasting is careful and studied, and coffee never tastes burnt or harsh. Complex flavors and aromas are allowed to come through in each cup—if you ever want to compare and contrast, attend one of their frequent free cuppings (like a wine tasting for coffee). Espresso drinks are also pulled well here, and the staff is obviously well trained in the art.

A nice selection of pastries by the acclaimed bakery Crema are available. So get on in there and get serious about coffee already.

Rogue Public House

Hiccup—what the hell are you looking at?

5.6	7.5	9.5
Food	Feel	Beer

American

Bar **$25**
Price

www.rogue.com

Sun–Thu 11am–midnight
Fri–Sat 11am–1am

Bar Beer, wine, liquor
Credit cards Visa, MC, AmEx
Outdoor dining, Wi-Fi

Pearl District
1339 NW Flanders St.
(503) 222-5910

We're totally wasted right now. Stop laughing, we're serious. Okay, what were we saying? Seriously, though—seriously. Listen.

Rogue is the shit. No, it is, just hear us out. We just drank, like, five of those little taster trays. No, not five tasters—five *trays* of tasters. It's, like, impossible to stop, you know? There are just so many: there's Dead Guy—the really famous one that's all hoppy and alcoholic; there's Chocolate Stout—that's all hoppy and alcoholic; there's Independence—that's all hoppy and alcoholic, too. Hey, shut up, we remember everything we had. We just don't remember what was what.

Or maybe it wasn't the beer that got us so sauced; 'cause now we're remembering we had some Rogue spirits, too. A shot of dark rum, which was hoppy and alcoholic. Nah, just kidding. It was strong, though, and thick like molasses. We had white rum, too, but it tasted like vodka—was it vodka? No, it was rum, but don't drink it by itself. Yecch!

Oh yeah, we ate…something. It was maybe soup. Or cheese. Cheese soup. Beer cheese soup, that was it! Yeah, it was okay. We think. Hey why are you asking so many questions, anyway? We know we had a burger, that's for sure. That was good. And they're made with, like, Kobe beef from some good farm or another. Hey, Kobe's a big deal, which is why Rogue lets you know it's Kobe, even though it's not from Kobe, Japan and the burger isn't really that great anyway.

We always come with a big group, and it feels like we're in an English pub, with all the wood and stuff. We mostly come for birthdays, or when somebody got dumped or fired or anything else we don't want to remember the next day. The girls that work here are pretty hot, but don't piss them off. They're total pros, which you'd have to be, serving (mostly) dudes this high-octane brew all night long. It gets you wasted enough to make all kinds of bad decisions, like bruschetta. What the hell makes a person order bruschetta in a place like this? It's stale bread topped with watery tomatoes and salt. Stuff like this drives us to drink. Another Dead Guy, please. Actually, make it a Double Dead Guy.

Russell Street BBQ

How can such a sweetly hokey barbecue joint be so divisive?

Barbecue, Southern

Casual restaurant

$25
Price

www.russellstreetbbq.com

Mon–Thu 11am–9pm
Fri–Sat 11am–10pm
Sun 11am–9pm

Bar Beer, wine, liquor
Credit cards Visa, MC, AmEx
Reservations Not accepted
Kid-friendly, outdoor dining

Northeast Portland
325 NE Russell St.
(503) 528-8224

Barbecue is one of those topics you just don't want to broach, like politics, religion, or pizza. All across America—but especially in the South—there is a whole lot of passion without much unification. Everyone has an opinion, but there's little regional confidence to help back any of it up. It's like *Lord of the Flies*, only for ribs.

Russell Street is right in the middle of this argument, with some fans and some detractors. Its supporters love its Texas classics like pimento cheese sandwiches and Frito pie, and the fact that it uses carefully raised meat that is free of hormones and antibiotics (a claim most exemplary Texas barbecue joints can't make—or don't really care to); its critics point out that the meat often feels rubbery, perhaps due to the restaurant's use of lean meat, as attested to on their menus. Beware the barbecue joint that advertises lean meat.

One thing is certain: any experienced Southern-barbecue pilgrim will balk at a menu full of grilled tofu, grilled salmon, and grilled chicken breast slathered in sauce. It does call into question the seriousness of the place as a barbecue destination. Shrimp? Not on your life, partner.

But fries are good, sides are reasonably good, and cheap as the dickens. We suspect the slew of pigs has a lot to do with its popularity. There are lots of pigs here: wood pigs, ceramic pigs, pig posters, and on and on. Red-checkered tablecloths set the mood, as does the goofy paraphernalia on the walls.

As far as the main event goes, well, it doesn't. Ribs are rubbery and not very smoky, brisket has come dry and chewy, and sauce seems to be what this place is really counting on for success. Sure, in Texas, there's sauce, but it's hardly the point—not even close.

Ruth's Chris

A Louisiana-based steakhouse chain, yes, but a loveable one

7.5	8.0	6.5
Food	Feel	Wine

Steakhouse

Upmarket restaurant

$100
Price

www.ruthschris.com

Mon–Thu 5pm–10pm
Fri–Sat 5pm–11pm
Sun 4pm–9pm

Bar Beer, wine, liquor
Credit cards Visa, MC, AmEx
Reservations Accepted
Date-friendly, Wi-Fi

Downtown
309 SW 3rd Ave.
(503) 221-4518

There's something very specific about the pleasures of a good steakhouse. You walk in knowing exactly what you want. A shrimp cocktail, perhaps, or an iceberg wedge with blue cheese dressing. An expensive steak, aged and buttery, with a big California Cabernet. It's self-indulgent capitalism, and for a long time, it was impossible to find at a chain. Enter Ruth's Chris, which got started in New Orleans in 1965, and in the years since, daringly challenged the notion that a chain restaurant had to be mediocre—and, in the process, added a nuance to the Great Chain Debate that simply could not be ignored.

Bread comes to the table fresh and warm. The chopped salad, touted as a classic, sports a little spill of fried onions on top that adds texture but steals thunder from the tasty blue cheese. Steak arrives as refreshingly rare as ordered, with a bewildering, peppery sizzle, and extra melted butter on request (do it!). Creamed spinach is like a dream, with the pepper and béchamel and spinach leaves all blending together into an irresistible pile of fatty goodness.

Being the chain that it is, you can rest assured that you'll feel equally at home at all locations. There is an equalizing dark, clubby feeling, although this decade-old branch is looking a bit worse for wear. The décor is starting to look dated, and the tacky mural along the back isn't helping. We've noticed the dining room is increasingly filled with people in shorts and sandals. Is carelessness contagious?

Even at these prices?

Saburo's

An okay neighborhood sushi restaurant that gets the job done

5.9	7.0	7.5
Food	Feel	Beer

Japanese

Casual restaurant

$30
Price

www.saburos.com

Mon–Thu 5pm–9:30pm
Fri 5pm–10:30pm
Sat 4:30pm–10pm
Sun 4:30pm–9pm

Bar Beer, wine
Credit cards Visa, MC, AmEx
Reservations Not accepted

Sellwood
1667 SE Bybee Blvd.
(503) 236-4237

In spite of Portland's amazing supply of fresh fish, too much of the sushi around town isn't up to par. With the exception of maybe one or two dishes done differently here and there, or offered uniquely, no one sushi place seems to be spectacular. Our highest-regarded Japanese places are noted for their izakaya, not their raw-fish feats.

That doesn't necessarily mean sushi is bad in this city; it's certainly not offensive. But most sushi restaurants seem to be merely banking on the popularity of the genre, which is evident in the long lists of rolls that really have nothing at all to do with sushi. At least not with what sushi can be.

Saburo is among the least remarkable of these. It's totally representative without being genuine, like the intensely colorful mural on the wall that covers all of Japan's Greatest Hits: Hokusai waves; geishas on a footbridge; a bonsai tree weeping over a river; and so forth. Consider a huge platter of equally colorful sushi, hand formed with impressive factory-like speed and efficiency; but the pieces are rather unjudiciously garnished, many with a simple sneezing of sesame seeds, and the rice barely seasoned enough to create a perfect counterbalance to the fish's flavor. Sure it's pretty to look at, but this nigiri is meant to be drowned in that grayish wasabi/soy mire we've learned to make in the absence of artful, splendid balance.

The cuts of fish here are too large and ungainly, further upsetting this balance—especially gargantuan unagi that look as though the chefs employed an entire eel in each piece. The result is an uncomfortable commitment to the overly sweet eel that would have been better tolerated in a shorter burst. Saba is lovely, however, gently garnished with a little fresh ginger and tasting fresh and maritime.

Hot dishes are no less ho-hum. Tempura is lumpy and knobby, so you wind up with more batter than steamed vegetable in each bite. But agedashi tofu is a fine umami bomb, spongy, hot, and a little crisp. It's merely serviceable. Like Saburo's.

Sahagún Chocolates

Chocovalhalla

Sweets   Market

www.sahagunchocolates.com

Wed–Sat 10am–6pm   **Bar** None   **Northwest Portland**
                          Credit cards Visa, MC, AmEx   10 NW 16th Ave.
                          Date-friendly, veg-friendly   (503) 274-7065

This little shop feels like a precious secret you really don't want to tell anyone about. It is cozy and unpretentious, with little more than a few stools at which to sit and sip cocoa on winter days.

Sahagún (pronounced saw-goon) chocolates have been sold at the Portland Farmer's Market for years, creating a frothing following of theobromine freaks. If you aren't yet among them, just pop into the shop for a sample. We promise you will walk out with the whole inventory. There just isn't a flaw anywhere in the whole display case.

Pepitapapas, a dark Ecuadorian bittersweet chocolate bark with barely toasted little pumpkin seeds, has just a hint of home-grown jalapeño for an earthy depth. Oregon hazelnuts dipped in dark chocolate give a slight crunch followed by an explosion of flavor. Candied ginger, orange, and lemon peels, dipped in chocolate, play a wonderful game between textures and flavors: bitter, sweet, and acid. "Mega Pills Morning Chocolates" puts Portland's famous Stumptown coffee inside single-origin chocolate. These are unexpectedly moist and creamy, giving with the slightest pressure, caffeine on caffeine—better than sex, or at least bad sex.

But the pièce de résistance is a caramel about the size of a large thimble inside a thin, brittle dark chocolate shell. You can't just nibble, the different ingredients need to be experienced all at once. Pop the whole thing in your mouth at once, and it explodes, sending ribbons of incredible salty/sweet/buttery caramel across your palate. A single hazelnut gives a slightly crunchy texture. One can only go so far in describing a bite of food; just let us say that it is an experience that has blown a fuse somewhere deep in our brains.

There's nothing better than finishing with a cup of Sahagún's hot chocolate, made with hormone-free milk and melted single-varietal chocolate. One time, it was made with São Tomé, a bittersweet bar that is 75% cacao, giving it a long, lingering finish and earthy depth. This isn't your typical whipped-cream-topped, powdered plotz. It is more like heaven in a cup; a quintessential chocolate experience. This place is a wonderful first-date stop; or, for that matter, third-date stop. Or totally non-date-related stop.

Sal's Famous Italian

A mid-century menu that's been making strides—the rest needs to catch up

6.5	6.0	8.5
Food	Feel	Wine

Italian, Pizza

Casual restaurant

$35
Price

www.salskitchen.com

Mon–Thu 11am–9pm
Fri–Sat 11am–10pm
Sun noon–9pm

Bar Beer, wine, liquor
Credit cards Visa, MC, AmEx
Reservations Accepted
Outdoor dining

Northwest Portland
33 NW 23rd Pl.
(503) 467-4067

Sal's Famous Italian was, for a long time, a mostly nostalgic venture. The menu was full of hearty dishes of comfort foods you may have had as a kid—that is, Southern-Italian-influenced American classics, like Caesar (actually, Mexican-influenced, but a longtime adoption not worth making a fuss over), chicken cacciatore, and fettucine alfredo. These are still here, but they're in the minority—for now, anyway.

From the outside, this little red neighborhood joint suggests checkered tablecloths, Chianti-bottles-in-wicker-basket candles, and a goateed tenor belting out "That's Amore" in the corner. But the inside is surprisingly airy, bordering on cold. There are pictures on the walls, smartly arranged and lit by ambient pendants; there's packed seating and cheap, catalogue-y furniture. Look past the serviceable "table wine" in carafes to a wine list with some surprising producers at terrifically low markups. Just because you're not in the market for a serious Italian meal doesn't mean you can't have an affordable serious Italian bottle, which this menu amply offers (along with some more avoidable domestics).

Gone are many mid-century Americana dishes like salmon over bow-tie pasta, and the like. Sal's has been making some admirable strides towards authenticity. A simple butternut-squash ravioli dish with sage and brown butter is fine, if a little on the sweet side; amatriciana is done properly with bucatini, so that the slightly spicy sauce, slow simmered with salty pancetta, garlic, and onions, leaks into each narrow tube.

Since Sal's is owned by the folks behind Pizzicato, it makes sense that pizza is offered here, a vaguely Italian-style pie with a thin crust. Although a large selection of toppings is available, you would do well to exercise restraint. The simpler versions are best, with well-performing tomato sauce and mozzarella.

Portions have shrunk since the retro days, which is a lot closer to a true Italian meal, but still here are strong flavors—and clunky execution. Dishes have come cool in places, and so has service; salumi plates taste grocery-store-bought. With one location already closed and so many better pizzerias opening up, more authentically Italian restaurants everywhere, and even a surprisingly decent, locally owned chain of pasta restaurants, Sal's might be stuck in that mid-century dilemma. It can either go fully retro-chic or tighten it up a whole lot. At this rate, checkered tablecloths and corny crooners might actually work in its favor.

Samurai Bento

Japanese food whose fame we fail to understand

4.1 Food

5.5 Feel

Japanese

Food cart

$15 Price

Daily 10am–3pm

Bar None
Credit cards Visa, MC
Outdoor dining

Downtown
940 SW Alder St.
(503) 757-8802

Samurai Bento is, admittedly, a fairly humorous moniker, but it was cleverly chosen by the proprietors of this food cart: a Google search of the name (sans any additional info like "Portland," "food cart," or "Japanese") returns this place's Yelp review as the #1 hit. An impressive feat indeed, given that those are two of the Japanese words most familiar to the non-Japanese speaker.

The name continues to worm its way into our collective consciousness by way of the many accolades posted on Samurai Bento's glossy menu. Rave reviews—some of them from prominent Japanese customers—and slick advertisements line the outside of this cart, an aesthetic that we think detracts from the whole experience of eating your food on a sidewalk. You want to feel like a pioneer at these times, not like a lemming chasing the same yakisoba off a cliff as everyone else.

More importantly, how is this place managing to get such positive endorsements? The food here is totally overrated and utterly disappointing. It's like the Asian food that a non-Asian college student would whip up in the dorm kitchen. (Sauté garlic, sauté vegetables, sauté tofu, drench in soy sauce, et voilà!)

Agedashi tofu has come improperly fried, rendering it soggy and boring; the best thing it has going for it is the gingery sauce that perks it up ever so slightly. Enormous sautéed vegetables monopolize a whole corner of your Styrofoam box; they're underseasoned, bland, and worthless. You can try your luck with the teriyaki chicken and various other meat dishes, but they, too, are plagued by the same incorrect frying techniques.

The staff, at least, are nice, but they can't rescue this food.

Sapphire Hotel

Even the dismal hotel menu and sugary cocktails can't kill this cathouse vibe

5.3	**9.0**	**8.0**
Food	Feel	Beer

Modern, Pan-Asian

Bar **$20** Price

www.thesapphirehotel.com

Mon–Fri 4pm–2am
Sat 9am–2am
Sun 9am–midnight

Bar Beer, wine, liquor
Credit cards Visa, MC, AmEx
Date-friendly, live music, outdoor dining, veg-friendly, Wi-Fi

Hawthorne
5008 SE Hawthorne Blvd.
(503) 232-6333

We love a good brothel-turned-bar. There's always this faithful recreating of sexy vibes and mystery, or at least the romanticizing of what was more likely a very sad, dangerous life (former brothels and ghost tours tend to go hand-in-hand). We love our fantasies—however off the mark—about red-scarf-draped lamps and sultry women in control, and Sapphire Hotel has that in spades. For a romantic drink or a friendly chat with Dita Von Teese, this place can't be beat.

Exotic lanterns hang overhead, barely burning, and live jazz smolders on Sundays. A weekend brunch served in the quirky lobby has a great ambience, if some questionable judgment. It's, ahem, provocative to describe meyer lemon crêpes as "topped with fresh fruit, goat cheese & blueberry catsup." And while this is much better than it sounds (what was wrong with "compote"?), ill-advised moves like this are all over these globetrotting menus, which read like they were constructed from back issues of *Bon Appetit*: salmon corn cakes topped with stone-ground mustard; sesame-crusted ahi tuna with ponzu; curried mahi-mahi with coconut rice and apple-jicama slaw.

In fact, these are exactly the sort of dishes one would find at a hotel restaurant, which is when the rose-tinted bubble bursts and you realize that's exactly where you are dining, after all. It's like the moment of clarity one might have just before engaging the services of a lady of the evening—perhaps skin contact isn't the best idea. At least some sort of prophylactic measure is called for when ordering a cheese platter described simply as including brie, Stilton, and chèvre; or an "antipasta" of marinated artichoke hearts, pickled asparagus, deli meats, and anything else you might pick up from Trader Joe's on your way into work.

Suffice it to say: the food's not the point here. And it doesn't need to be. Unfortunately, the drinks—which *are* the point here—are largely dominated by vodka, fruity juices, and sugary sweet gimmicks normally reserved for getting an under-aged girlfriend drunk. There's a good Madeira here, and much better beers, a few of which are on tap. Happy Hour is offered half the week from 10pm to midnight, and includes $1 PBR tallboys. When everyone else in town is charging three or four bucks for a regular Pabst (irony doesn't come cheap), this is one outdated move we can get behind.

Saucebox

Delicious cocktails paired with derivative,
outdated food in a self-described swank-fest

6.1	7.5	9.0
Food	Feel	Drinks

Pan-Asian

Bar

$40
Price

www.saucebox.com

Mon–Thu 4:30pm–midnight
Fri 4:30pm–2am
Sat 5pm–2am
Sun 5pm–midnight

Bar Beer, wine, liquor
Credit cards Visa, MC, AmEx
Date-friendly, outdoor dining

Downtown
214 SW Broadway
(503) 241-3393

Oh, Saucebox. What a troubling place. It's considered both a Portland classic and a has-been; it's been both a phenomenal bargain and a phenomenal disaster. It's across the street from the iconic Mary's strip club, but no one seems to make it over here to eat. Perhaps it's hard to find—the neon sign of monkeys is on an office building that, if you're trying to negotiate the traffic and find parking, might be deceiving and confusing. Or perhaps the word is out that Saucebox may have delivered once, but is now just a forgettable meal.

The place is self described as "sexy, delicious, swanky," and indeed it's all that—in a decidedly 1998 sort of way, which is also the year it was dubbed "Restaurant of the Year" by *The Oregonian*. Even amidst Portland's cocktail revolution, Saucebox cocktails—if sometimes sweet—are standing tall. This is the only place where we've seen kaffir-lime-infused drinks that actually taste like kaffir lime leaf. Hallelujah!

Also stuck in the 20th century, though, is this menu of Pacific Rim snores. The highlights, lately, have been banh mi, although that term is used loosely, as they come on ciabatta; we like a version with juicy, fatty, tasty pork belly. Green papaya salad is a competent version, but without any of the heat of the chili peppers the dish is built around in authentic Thai versions. A burger is fine, but nothing more, and its fries have come oversalted to the point of inedibility.

Udon and a white miso soup are decent, but not among the best of their kind. Spring rolls are bland, and pad Thai is an insult to even the most mushy food-court renditions around town. Whether you say it out loud or put it in your mouth, ahi tuna tataki has no ring to it whatsoever; it's not much better than the sum of its parts and relies totally on the one-dimensional version of flavors made popular by better Japanese kitchens. Happy hour is popular, perhaps because people have figured out that paying full price for this food is just tragic, but even here, we aren't feeling like it's money well spent.

All this to the tune of thumping DJ-spun music, as if there were some sort of pretentiousness challenge going on. Admittedly, there are some great spinners, but we can't in good conscience recommend combining a dance party here with a meal. And although the murals on the walls by local artist Daniel Duford are fantastic, we'd rather have Pacific Rim food at Thatch Tiki Bar, where at least the goofy cuisine isn't trying to be taken seriously. The only two remaining reasons to come to Saucebox are the creative cocktails and late-night kitchen hours.

Screen Door

A popular place for decent Portlanded-up Southern food

7.3	7.0	7.0
Food	Feel	Drinks

Southern

Casual restaurant

$35
Price

www.screendoorrestaurant.com

Tue–Sat 5:30pm–10pm; Sat
9am–2:30pm, 5:30pm–10pm;
Sun 9am–2:30pm, 5:30pm–
9pm

Bar Beer, wine, liquor
Credit cards Visa, MC, AmEx
Reservations Not accepted
Kid-friendly, outdoor dining

Southeast Portland
2337 E. Burnside St.
(503) 542-0880

Everyone everywhere loves Southern food, and Screen Door capitalizes on this human imperative in a smart, hip way. It doesn't look like much in its butter-colored cinderblock building. But the best soul food kitchens of the South look exactly like this on the outside (save for the large windows), and the interior goes for this same type of rustic simplicity with wooden tables, chairs of red and blue, and little on the walls. Again in Southern style, the patio is lovely in warm weather.

Screen Door is wildly popular at brunch, where you'll find good fried chicken and impossibly fluffy waffles, creamy-gravied biscuits, house-made bacon coated in pralines (a classic New Orleans treat), and shrimp and grits.

We love to love the menu, whose comfort-food classics like fried green tomatoes, jambalaya, and mac and cheese sound good to just about anyone. The kitchen definitely has a way with the fryer; as with chicken, fried okra is right on the money, and oysters have an ideal briny pop in a crispy, non-greasy shell. As much as we love the rotating selection of seasonal farmer's-market-vegetable-based dishes, few of these preps really shine. And trickier feats like catfish can taste quite muddy and metallic.

There's a careful selection of beers on draft, including Louisiana's Abita, and many in the bottle. Cocktails go for gentle and successful twists on classics, with some Southern playfulness. A "Blanche DuBois" gets refreshingly bitter Campari, some muddled lemon, and sweet iced tea (brewed, of course); a mint julep gets a proper cane-sugar treatment instead of icky simple syrup. All are served in correctly smaller glasses, and are priced low enough to sample around.

But a common complaint is that service is strange and standoffish. On one visit, a server dismissed the restaurant's only rosé as "gross…the whole kitchen staff agrees." Why would a restaurant willingly serve a gross wine? Intrigued, we ordered it—it wasn't bad. The server later told us that she "didn't like Chardonnay," a bizarre comment to make about a relatively neutral grape used to make some of the world's greatest wines (e.g. white Burgundy).

Chardonnays and rosés aside, a clueless staff shouldn't be advising customers on wine. Like the farmer's-market-veggie disappointment, it's another way in which Screen Door can be more about shine than substance. Now, if the shine were moonshine, then we'd be talking.

Sel Gris

It's pricey and pretentious for Portland, but the kitchen is superb

9.2	8.0	6.0
Food	Feel	Wine

Modern

Upmarket restaurant

$80
Price

www.selgrisrestaurant.com

Mon–Thu 5:30pm–10pm
Fri–Sat 5:30pm–11pm

Bar Beer, wine, liquor
Credit cards Visa, MC, AmEx
Reservations Essential
Date-friendly

Hawthorne
1852 SE Hawthorne Blvd.
(503) 517-7770

Sel Gris comes on strong with expertly executed French-inspired food, stimulating looks, and the kind of pretentious service that makes the high price tag feel more earned. We like the space for the infectious energy of its open kitchen. If you can sit at the chef's table, it's alternatively a total floorshow and an illuminating one-on-one with the chef.

The place is intimate and beautiful, but more in a seasonal-flowers sort of way than some other hotel-lobby drama queens. Your eye tends to go straight to the copper pots hanging in that dynamic kitchen at the end of the room, which makes for great conversation if you're on an awkward first date.

Dishes here are innovative in the style of Seu George covering David Bowie—there's nothing to the melody you haven't heard before, but when it's plucked on a nylon strong guitar and sung in Portuguese, you'll hear a side of "Life on Mars" you never knew was there. Take, for instance, sweetbreads. They're cooked properly crispy, as they are in most places. While they're often paired with a tart fruit component, Sel Gris' combination with a green apple butter imparts a lovely balance of richness and acid in a way that is astoundingly subtle. Another time, that job was done by a sparky tomato jam, this time hitting both sweet and spicy notes that complemented the creamy insides of the sweetbreads.

The slight pretentiousness makes its way onto the menu, as well, with items like "foie gras of the moment" (we get it, this is a chef-driven restaurant) and a salad including "sieved egg" (hold for applause). But many of these descriptions are seductive, too; the danger here, of course, is that the food may not always live up to it. A New York strip with "green garlic pommes dauphinoise," grilled ramps, asparagus, and ramp butter, the steak prep one night, was very expensive but not particularly well marbled or interesting. But homemade filled pastas are always a sure thing.

The wine list offers little of interest for under $40. There's some resourcefulness, but it favors the pricier (though very good) bottles. And for what you spend, these reds are carelessly served much too warm.

Seasonal desserts are good, and chocolates finished with a little sel gris are a nice finishing touch. Although this kitchen doesn't take a whole lot of risks, it is as consistent as any in the city.

[Editor's Note: At press time the restaurant had closed because of a fire, but was reopening soon.]

Serratto

There are few surprises, for better or for worse, at this reliable date spot

8.2	8.0	9.0
Food	Feel	Wine

Modern

Upmarket restaurant

$60
Price

www.serratto.com

Mon–Thu 11:30am–10pm
Fri–Sat 11:30am–11pm
Sun 11:30am–9pm

Bar Beer, wine, liquor
Credit cards Visa, MC, AmEx
Reservations Accepted
Date-friendly, outdoor dining

Northwest Portland
2112 NW Kearney St.
(503) 221-1195

Serratto is one solid player, from beginning to end. The rustic Mediterranean décor is sparse and chic, with a lot of warm, worn woods and precious tablecloths. It's a great date space at night, with a separate bar and lounge area, as well as a lofted lounge with couches; by day, large windows let in natural light. Service knocks it out of the park every time: knowledgeable, friendly staff excel at making diners feel welcome.

Almost as reliable is the food, which you might describe as seasonal Portland-Mediterranean: Anderson Ranch lamb meatballs in roasted garlic tzatziki, Muscovy duck with Oregon blackberry demi-glace, and the like. For a menu with such variety, the kitchen is surprisingly fluent, whatever the dish. Risotto dishes are rich and flavorful, with impossibly fresh-tasting vegetables. Homemade pappardelle with wild boar ragù is deep and satisfying.

During happy hour (daily, 4pm-6pm), the best deal is a third-pound Painted Hills burger with bacon, white cheddar, a delicious barbecue sauce, and a crispy stack of fried onions. On a good day, it's one of the best burgers in town.

The wine list is interesting and well chosen, with virtually no clunkers and some unbelievably low markups. Its main focus is Italy—not just Piedmont and Tuscany—with a surprising range in France, Spain, and the Pacific Northwest, as well. Anyone—whether a novice or a pro—will find a great and affordable bottle with ease here. There is also one of the best half-bottle selections we've seen around, so you don't have to stay married to the same wine all night.

Cocktails are less ambitious than they are capable, with a smoky, balanced mezcal margarita and a Dark and Stormy made darker and stormier by real ginger beer. Beers are just okay, mostly cheaper imports; but the small touches, like soda, tea, and fresh-squeezed juice, are impressive.

Serratto is by no means a perfect restaurant. There are the occasional missteps, like watery sauces and salting issues. And it is a bit pricey for the overall experience, which is solid but not mind blowing. But it feels good to be there, to eat there, and to drink there. No more, no less.

Shenzhen

Friends don't let friends order General Tso's from a place this authentic

8.1 Food   **6.0** Feel

Chinese, Seafood, Dim Sum

Casual restaurant   **$25** Price

Daily 10:30am–midnight

Bar Beer, wine
Credit cards Visa, MC
Reservations Accepted
Kid-friendly

82nd Avenue Area
707 NE 82nd Ave.
(503) 261-1689

This mostly Cantonese restaurant is kind of like the unassuming version of Wong's King—it sort of looks like it was a Baker's Square or Marie Callender's at one point. Fuchsia tablecloths give it a distinctly grandmotherish appeal. Shenzhen has seafood tanks, but they don't inspire as much confidence as some. They're dark and glum, implying that the seafood within is suffering from some sort of stress-related malady.

But be not afraid, this place serves delicious, authentic dishes, of which you can see pictures in the glossy, biblical menu. Of course, there's an unfortunate proliferation of boring, gloopy Americanized dishes like General Tso's and lemon chicken, but it's hard to fault the management for trying to make a good living. Barbecue duck and pork is okay, but certainly not the best you can do here. If you have Andrew Zimmern with you, you might opt for lamb intestine, but you'll be wowed by more accessible prospects. Salted fish and chicken fried rice is absolutely showstopping, transporting you to the Chinese province of Yangzhou, flanked by the muddy banks of the Yangtze River and the briny Pacific Ocean.

Also outstanding are Shenzhen's green-onion pancakes, extremely flavorful and not greasy. The seafood proves to be plenty healthy on the palate. Salt-and-pepper lobster is gorgeous. Noodle dishes like beef chow fun are good, and tofu is homemade and firm. There are also handwritten signs on the walls advertising goat and lamb dishes. Szechuan dishes like ma po tofu are not quite as spicy and peppercorny as they would be at a Szechuan restaurant, but that's sort of obvious.

Of course, Shenzhen also does a mean dim sum, with terrific, steaming dumplings and expertly cooked greens. The best way to make use of this very true-to-life Hong Kong-style eatery is to just show up hungry and with other adventurous eaters, point to signs on the wall, and don't worry about what exactly you're ordering (chances are, your Chinese-speaking server won't be able to convey it to you). Then enjoy the wonderful variety of sincere flavors of which this cuisine is capable, and vow to never again let anyone you love order kung pao.

Siam Society

More-and-less Thai dishes served in a fun,
eye-catching industrial space

7.6	9.0	7.0
Food	Feel	Wine

Pan-Asian, Thai

Casual restaurant

$40
Price

www.siamsociety.com

Tue–Thu 11:30am–2:30pm,
4:30pm–9pm; Fri 11:30am–
2:30pm, 4:30pm–10pm; Sat
noon–2:30pm, 4:30pm–10pm

Bar Beer, wine, liquor, BYO
Credit cards Visa, MC, AmEx
Reservations Accepted
Date-friendly, outdoor dining,
veg-friendly

Alberta Arts District
2703 NE Alberta St.
(503) 922-3675

Let's get this out of the way: Siam Society is not authentic Thai, nor is it
annoying, trendy fusion that falls flat by trying to fly too high. Rather, it
takes a cuisine that is already influenced by many of the worlds' cultures,
and adds its own flavor, all the while careful to keep things in balance.
This may mean, in many cases, that heat has been compromised for
effect. You can ask for chili sauce on the side.

Siam Society is located in an old power company substation, a square
blockhouse that was once a warren of little rooms filled with electrical
equipment. Its industrial past is still very much present in the architecture
of large steel beams and a high ceiling studded with skylights. Old
windows with beautiful iron shutters are still in place. With the
accompanying industrial artwork and dramatic lighting from a setting sun,
it's quite beautiful.

Prettily presented portions here are daunting, perfect for sharing family
style. For starters, calamari are exemplary, lightly battered and cooked to a
correct crispness, and infused with the subtle flavors of lemongrass and
hot peppers. Pork spring rolls are a hit, crackling crisp, and with
cinnamon, hazelnuts, and vanilla beans giving them a pleasant depth. If
they're on the menu, robust homemade sausages are a must, especially
when paired with cabbage, peanuts, and ginger.

Lard na has an impressive deep, smoky flavor from the pork, while fat
wheat noodles provide a toothsome base against bright, crisp Chinese
broccoli and mushrooms. Pad Thai might be the most insipid and
misreproduced thing in America outside of Dan Brown novels, and here
it's a little better than a food-court version. Phad kee mao, on the other
hand, is less banal, and more sophisticated, with crispy fried basil
exploding in every few bites, although the heat is too restrained.

Homemade curries tend to vary somewhat from batch to batch. Meats,
like Chinese-style pork chops, are cooked properly tender and juicy with a
wonderful sear. Sauces tend to be paired correctly, but there's neither the
excellence of a reverently followed tradition nor any mind-blowing
innovation. Same goes for the wine list, which kowtows to modern trends
and buzz varietals (we'd take advantage of the generous $10 corkage
fee); the cocktail list is just a string of more-interesting-than-usual -tinis.
Siam Society is certainly an experience, though, start to finish; when you
spend an evening here, you feel like you *did* something. That's still worth
something.

Silk

Vietnamese done totally Pearl style—if that's your thing

7.0	7.5	7.5
Food	Feel	Wine

Pan-Asian, Vietnamese

Upmarket restaurant

$40
Price

www.silkbyphovan.com

Mon–Sat 11am–3pm, 5pm–10pm

Bar Beer, wine, liquor
Credit cards Visa, MC, AmEx
Reservations Accepted
Date-friendly, outdoor dining

Pearl District
1012 NW Glisan St.
(503) 248-2172

Silk, by the owners of the successful, upscale Pho Van empire, is the Pearl's inevitable answer to Vietnamese. So it's no surprise that it's a little over the top. To one side, there's a bar with a very studied hip and trendy feel that reminds us of a W Hotel lounge. Cream-colored furnishings look brand spanking new, and the spotless walls undulate with 3D textured hangings. Similarly breezy are long, flowing curtains in brown and black, and hanging, shimmering lamps of white shells. Doesn't all this make you feel like eating Vietnamese?

But the menu isn't strictly Vietnamese; it's actually pretty pan-Asian. Pho is not the focus here—there are only two on this menu, and they're among the most dumbed-down, boring protein combos in the entire real Pho Van repertoire. Elsewhere, there are appearances from kaffir lime leaf (which appears in nearly everything), lemongrass (ditto), peanut sauce, and ginger, but ultimately this restaurant only skims the surface of the cuisines of this incredible region. Where is the soul (and heart, intestines, and blood)?

Still, dishes are plated beautifully, and the simpler the explanation, the better; a sea bass steamed in banana leaves, for instance, is moist and flaky, with a subtle flavor from scallions and ginger. But for more than $22? This premium is clearly being charged for the space, not the food. There are some decent spring rolls and vermicelli dishes here, but nothing you'd want to skip a cheaper, less fussy pho place for.

Perhaps most telling is the line of Pho-Van-branded sauces that greet you at the front, each with a picture of the chef smiling proudly, like a Vietnamese Emeril. The line-up includes a garlic-lemongrass marinade, "Creamy Peanut," and something coyly referred to as "House Special," which upon further examination reveals itself to be based on fish sauce, an indispensable element of Vietnamese cuisine. Why the camouflage? Is Pho Van afraid Americans aren't sophisticated and cultured enough to appreciate fish sauce by its real name? This doesn't inspire confidence.

You're better off coming for the discounted items during the 4–9:30pm "silky hour" (sounds kind of prurient), but only if you like sugary sweet cocktails made with Sour Apple Pucker and the like. We'd stick, instead, to a smartly chosen, terse wine list of mostly appropriate bargain wines made by some very reputable small producers—or even a brief beer selection that includes an excellent cherry lambic. Now if only we could find something to eat with it that's as exciting.

Simpatica Dining Hall

It's brunch, it's a supper club, it's a caterer—it's mighty good

9.0	9.5
Food	Feel

Modern

Upmarket restaurant

$50
Price

www.simpaticacatering.com

Fri 7:30pm–10:30pm
Sat 7pm–11pm
Sun 9am–2pm

Bar Beer, wine, liquor
Credit cards Visa, MC, AmEx
Reservations Essential
Date-friendly

Southeast Portland
828 SE Ash St.
(503) 235-1600

The phrase "dining hall" calls to mind cavernous rooms of exposed wood beams and raucous Vikings. Simpatica's room is about halfway there—voices bounce aggressively off the low ceiling and walls of this converted part of the old La Luna music club, where diners sit at long community tables. There is one seating on Friday and one on Saturday, and the menu is pre-ordained and prix fixe. No muss, no fuss, and no allergies, restrictions, or special requests (okay, vegetarians will be accommodated if you let them know in advance). You can also reserve the space throughout the week for events, which they will, of course, cater. You'll never have better wedding food.

You are in capable hands here. Fish is cooked expertly, whether breaded and fried or roasted whole. Excellent cuts of meat are cooked exactly to temperature, and technical feats like a uniform brunoise of vegetables go largely unnoticed by the public, but are murmured about appreciatively by other chefs. Handmade ravioli are cooked with great care and paired justly with sauces that don't overwhelm them, like simple brown butter with a touch of shaved truffle (never the oil). The menu, which changes weekly, is always accessible, but never dumbed down, and is a real bargain.

Perhaps it is because of this chef-driven awesomeness that the service often feels imbued with its own sense of awesomeness. Attitude is routine here. Also, a word of advice: don't try to pay the bill with more than two credit cards per table, even with a large group. It gets ugly.

Sunday brunch is exceedingly popular here, which translates to frustrating long waits. But for crispy, seasoned fried chicken and fluffy, strawberry-syrup-sticky waffles? We'll stick it out. Eggs Benedict are also spectacular, with perfectly poached eggs poised like dollops of yolky cream atop thick, sweet-salty ham. A huge order of decadent biscuits and gravy with sausage might kill you, but what a way to go.

Maybe it's just the veil of night, of wine, and of discovery, but we think the brunch is only a fraction (but a big one) as successful as the dinners. Bring a group of your food friends, the ones who will really pay attention to the flavors and notice the skill in these dishes. Just make sure they bring cash.

Slow Bar

A lively, sometimes awkward bar with a near-perfect burger

8.0	7.0	5.5
Food	Feel	Drinks

American

Bar **$25**

Price

www.slowbar.net

Mon–Fri 11:30am–2:30am
Sat–Sun 5pm–2:30am

Bar Beer, wine, liquor
Credit cards Visa, MC, AmEx
Date-friendly, outdoor dining

Southeast Portland
533 SE Grand Ave.
(503) 230-7767

This cult-following bar in a cult-following part of town is in this book for one reason: it does burgers right. But the righteous atmosphere alone justifies that cult following: fun, friendly bartenders; sultry round banquettes; dark red mood lighting; drunkards any night of the week.

There are problems, too. The music is good, but too loud. A chilly wind blows in from the door. Bar patrons huddle in their coats, yelling to each other over the soundtrack. Fondue—a nice idea—is overwhelmed by truffle oil. Ceviche—a dive bar attempting ceviche? Nah. And the fries that come with the burger are totally soggy. Some are warm, some are cold. What's up with that?

But about that burger. First, the bad news: the kitchen doesn't really honor medium-rare orders. If you want to see much pink, order "very rare"—and even then, don't expect much blood. But it's okay, because the Painted Hills beef is of excellent quality, and has enough natural flavor to carry the burger even at medium. It's juicy, and its juices seep into every crevice of the sweet, delicious bun. In the face of mild mayonnaise, butter lettuce, generally timid Gruyère (its stinkiness only comes out in about every fourth bite), and subtly flavored beef, pickle relish turns out to be a dominant flavor, and, happily, it's a flavor that works.

But here's the punch line: there are also onion rings on the burger. Putting onion rings—*good* onion rings, richly battered and carefully fried onion rings—on a burger may be the Slowburger's, and Slow Bar's, greatest stroke of genius. The batter's great crunch and the sweetness of the onion are unexpectedly wonderful. If only the kitchen would stop down the meat a notch or two, this would be one of the very best burgers in the city.

Oh, by the way, here's another theory of why it's called "Slow Bar": cocktails haven't progressed out of the Sweet Age. Even the ones with masculine names—"Cock and Bull" (Fighting Cock Bourbon and Red Bull) and "Zerkpatric," a pomegranate margarita with peppercorn-infused Sauza tequila—are sugar bombs. And what's with the lack of local beers here? Here's hoping for some fast bar evolution.

Sorabol

Come for some of the better Korean food outside the
Beave, but skip the so-so sushi

7.5 Food

7.5 Feel

Korean, Japanese

Casual restaurant

$30 Price

Daily 11:30am–11pm

Bar Beer, wine
Credit cards Visa, MC, AmEx
Reservations Accepted

Southeast Portland
7901 SE Powell Blvd.
(503) 771-5842

Sorabol isn't your typical pan-Asian restaurant. It's considered
predominantly Korean with a few Japanese conceits, like udon and sushi.

Although Sorabol is many things, it is first and foremost as a spot for
Korean barbecue. The whole layout of the restaurant hints at this fact,
with grills and smoke hoods on several tables. The lighting is warm, the
colors are dark reds and blacks, and when it's got a lively crowd (which
can happen even at 10pm on a weeknight), this can be a very fun place,
with a bar-like feeling. A large television plays Korean pop videos and
commercials. All that's missing is a karaoke machine with hilarious
"Engrish" translations of Steely Dan songs.

As is the case at many Korean restaurants, prices are ridiculously low,
and most everything comes with banchan. Pajeon and other pancakes are
wonderful. This seafood version comes brimming with fat scallop pieces,
expertly cooked squid, and shrimp. Shabu shabu is fine, but the best
cooking-at-the-table experience to be had is in the grill: bulgogi, spicy
pork, and mackerel, as wonderfully oily and umami-rich as food can get.
And it's the healthiest fish, don't you know?

As for the Japanese conceits, they're good too, but they're not near the
caliber of what you can get at their all-Japanese colleagues. In other
words: do you really want to order sushi from a place that sort of tacks it
on as a money-making afterthought? But for Korean experiences, Sorabol
serves up one of the best in Portland proper. Even if it's not quite up to
the Beaverton standard.

Southpark Seafood

7.1	7.0	9.0
Food	Feel	Wine

Decent fish and better wine in a slightly corporate setting

Modern, Seafood

Casual restaurant

$40
Price

www.southparkseafood.com

Mon–Thu 11:30am–3pm, 5pm–10pm; Fri–Sat 11:30am–3pm, 5pm–11pm; Sun 11:30am–3pm, 5pm–10pm

Bar Beer, wine, liquor
Credit cards Visa, MC, AmEx
Reservations Accepted
Date-friendly, outdoor dining

Downtown
901 SW Salmon St.
(503) 326-1300

Southpark Seafood Grill & Wine Bar is one of the places PSU students take their folks when they're in town—and it feels like that kind of place. It's benign-looking, no matter what area you hail from; there's a proliferation of mahogany and track lighting, with sort of vague corporate-looking art. It's pleasant enough to look at, but low on character. Perhaps unsurprisingly, the service is somewhat cold, as if they've been told that friendliness is too low-class for the feel they're going for. Regardless, they're efficient enough not to let Dad go too long without a fresh martini.

You'll find much more warmth in the bread full of big chunks of soft potato that's served at the start of your meal. Raw oysters are fresh enough, but come out a bit drained of their oyster liquor, suggesting perhaps a shucking problem. Instead of a mignonette, these are served with an icy cucumber granita, whose extreme temperature and slight crunch either augments the experience or is totally irritating, depending on your level of purism. Fried calamari are decent in their thick cornmeal breading, but could use less batter and a gentler fry. They're served with an oddly sweet tomato sauce that reappears on other dishes; one time, it came on the daily fish special, a fillet of steelhead trout cooked just right in the brick oven (also used for serviceable pizzas). The high temperature and quick cooking gave it excellent charred skin while keeping the inside very moist and juicy. Vegetable accompaniments like snappy green beans are cooked expertly and well salted.

Paella is competent, with the rice getting a nice integration of juices and good shrimp, but chicken breast does nothing at all for the dish. Chorizo has a good savory kick, but red pepper dominates the garlic, when what you want is for the opposite to happen. Nevertheless, it's a competent preparation of a notoriously tough dish to nail.

This also being one of Portland's first downtown wine bars, the wine list is nicely chosen and organized in a way (by style and personality) that turns out to be more helpful than other lists' methods. Bottles are also sold to take away. So thank the old man for footing the bill by snagging him a bottle of something local on the way out.

Spella Caffè

Come judge for yourself—we want to see the look on your face

Coffee

Food cart

www.spellacaffe.com

Mon–Fri 9am–4pm

Bar None
Credit cards Visa, MC, AmEx
Outdoor dining, veg-friendly

Downtown
SW 9th & Alder
(503) 421-9723

If this corner of Portland is food-cart restaurant row, then Spella Caffè is its Italian starlet, a gamine darling tucked safely into the corner by a waist-high red brick wall and a few bordering trees. The coffee here makes people absolutely crazy; they're hovering and buzzing around it at all hours, insisting to anyone who will listen that this coffee is better than much-revered Stumptown's (although few dare to say it's better than Albina Press).

There's no doubt that Spella knows coffee; it loves coffee; and it takes pride in every cup. It roasts its own beans (not on the premises, of course), and the owner is as well versed in beans as a Master of Wine is in grapes, educating customers on growing climates, soil types, and roasting procedures. All of the baristas are knowledgeable and friendly, and are masterful at pulling an espresso with unbroken crema, cappuccinos with perfect clouds of milk resting atop a whisper of tan, or just a deeply heady and complex—but not bitter—cup of drip coffee. They won't fire two pots at once, for the sake of keeping coffee as fresh as possible. Besides, waiting for coffee to brew here is a great way to commune with fellow devotees, sitting at the tiny tables around the cart.

Chai tea is also wonderful here, especially with steamed soy milk. The soy enhances the chai spices, and it's served at the proper temperature so as not to scald or mute the flavors. There are also top-quality loose-leaf teas and good pastries (but nothing to write home about). In fact, little here is phoned in: chairs are curlicued and dear; the chalkboard bears the whorls and tendrils of perfect handwriting; and the cups and saucers are painted ceramic. It's all part of the devotion Spella obviously has toward its product—a devotion we all benefit from.

Spring Restaurant

A hidden gem whose authentic stews and noodle dishes are as transportive as the strange digs

8.7	5.0
Food	Feel

Korean

Casual restaurant

$15
Price

Mon–Sat 10am–7pm

Bar None
Credit cards Visa, MC, AmEx
Reservations Not accepted

Beaverton
3975 SW 114th Ave.
(503) 626-7819

Formerly known as Umma's, Spring Restaurant is the Holy Grail of gastroventurists, that ultimate hidden gem concealed inside an Asian supermarket. This Korean dive is in a humble alcove at the top of Pal-do market, staffed by fairly crabby folks who might prefer watching their TV show to making your dining experience all you dreamed of. If you catch them on a good day, though, they might hover over you, showing you how to mix and match certain sauces and what order to eat in. Just relax and get into it.

Don't panic if you aren't well versed in Korean cuisine. There are pictures of the food, and it's impossible to go wrong, although this isn't really the place for barbecue, so you should let go of the one dish you might be most familiar with. Daeji bulgogi is good, not great, with spicy pork that isn't as sickly sweet as some other Americanized places make it. Cold, spicy noodles in bibim naengmyeon are tangy and mustardy, somehow soul-warming even though the dish isn't served hot. Wheat noodles served in a thick black soybean paste (the Chinese-influenced jajangmyeon) are fantastic, as well, resilient and rich, with tender pieces of beef.

Banchan dishes taste fresh and are of the standard order: kimchi, spicy potato, sesame-oily bean sprouts, and sausages. It's all just a little better against a backdrop of Korean-language commercials. A word of advice to food-porn junkies: be discreet with your camera here, unless you want to get yelled at by a suspicious manager. We also totally recommend getting yelled at by the suspicious manager. It just adds to the flavor of the experience.

St. Honoré

Frenchish pastries and sandwiches in a charming, if overwrought Frenchish space

6.3 Food	**9.0** Feel

Baked goods, Sandwiches, Coffee

Café **$15** Price

www.sainthonorebakery.com

Daily 7am–8pm

Bar None
Credit cards Visa, MC
Outdoor dining, veg-friendly

Northwest Portland
2335 NW Thurman St.
(503) 445-4342

If Disney were to design a French bakery, St. Honoré would be it. This is not necessarily a bad thing. This boulangerie is named for the patron saint of bakers, and his figure keeps watch over the bakery next to a large gas-fired clay oven. The space is huge with high ceilings, generous windows that open to the street, and rustic wood beams. On any day of the week, it's packed with scenesters drinking the excellent Caffè Umbria coffee on outside tables under retractable awnings (just like in Provence!). As a place to sit and absorb the vibe, it's hard to beat this balcony.

A long counter snakes through one corner, tempting with tray upon tray of pastries. Breads sit cooling in baskets on the tile walls. The pastries vary wildly in flavor. Some look beautiful but underwhelm, perhaps because they frequently use out-of-season ingredients.

Best has been a wonderful apple chiboust, with a thin crust atop a layer of cooked apples and another layer of custard, with a brûléed top. For this much money, it had better be this good. Plain croissants are chewy and butter-greasy, but the amandine is better, coming in a hailstorm of slivered nuts. "Normandy apple toast" looks great, but is flat-out dull.

Most of the sandwiches are accompanied by a simple salad of lettuce with light Dijon mustard vinaigrette. We like the croque monsieur, which has just the right amount of cheese and arrives with a light crispy brown crust. Be forewarned: a cold brie sandwich comes, in the French tradition, buttered. Trés Homer Simpson!

Organic salads are large and satisfying, but not terribly authentic and a bit on the pricey side. A roasted-red-beet salad with apples, blue cheese, walnuts, and vinaigrette over mixed greens is great, with mild, creamy cheese that beautifully counters the sweet beets and bitter walnuts.

The breads aren't cheap, nor are they the best in town. It's like something is missing on the finish. Do try to get them in the morning, or don't bother. Unless the Tour de France is on. In which case, pull up a loaf and some butter and get down with your Epcot-Gallic self.

Stumptown Roasters

A religion of coffee with a loyal following and temples everywhere

Coffee, Baked goods

Café

www.stumptowncoffee.com

Mon–Fri 6am–9pm
Sat–Sun 7am–9pm
Hours vary by location

Bar None
Credit cards Visa, MC, AmEx
Outdoor dining, veg-friendly, Wi-Fi

Downtown
128 SW 3rd Ave.
(503) 295-6144

Downtown
1022 SW Stark St.
(503) 228-2277

Belmont
3352 SE Belmont St. (Annex)
(503) 467-4123

Additional locations
and more features at
www.fearlesscritic.com

Utter the name "Stumptown" in Portland, and you'll hear gasps and sighs, maybe a little bit of moaning and the stretched-out syllables of hyperbole: *Ohhhh my gawwwwd, it's sooooo good.*

These guys are the New York Yankees of artisan coffee roasters: the name is synonymous with inarguable stat; they have a crazed following; and the naysayers even love to hate them. Stumptown coffee is sold at too many restaurants to name. It is rivaled only by a handful of others in town, and surpassed by none.

Stumptown procures its beans from Latin American, Africa, and Indonesia; all are sorted by hand, and in many cases, Stumptown works directly with the grower to make sure they have the best of their bounty. There's even a "grand cru" distinction for those harvests that Stumptown deems worthiest. Stop at one of the shops, and you can have a bag roasted to order. There's an ephemeral window for optimum roasting— what opium is to good marijuana, one of these roasts is to your usual cup. Or so the aficionados claim.

Roasting is a synergy of art and science, and these guys are mad devotees of the craft. You can watch roasting all day at the Division Street café. Heck, ask questions. They love it. Any one of these zealots can teach you how to properly brew at home, regardless of your method of choice. You might learn that by hacking your beans with a blade chopper instead of a more even burr grinder, you'll wind up with one-note, bitter, extracted coffee. Stop by the Annex, on Belmont, and you can probably pick one up, or any number of other Stumptown-approved brewing accessories.

The cafés are all minimalistic and elemental, with exposed brick, concrete or wood floors, and simple steel fixtures. The Annex is a little brighter and more utilitarian than the other location. Downtown has a good beer and wine selection. There's even one in the lobby of the hipster Ace Hotel. But nothing beats smelling the coffee roasting at Division.

Given all the hubbub, it's not unusual to receive a bit of hipper-than-thou attitude from the baristas, in spite of their pedagogical willingness. But grinning incompetence is overrated, too. Throw in a Nuvrei scone, and it's all good.

SuperDog

Hot dogs that hit the right spots even if they don't transport you to Chicago

5.1	6.5
Food	Feel

American

Counter service **$10** Price

www.superdogpdx.com

Mon–Fri 11am–7:30pm
Hours vary by location

Bar Beer, wine
Credit cards Visa, MC, AmEx
Kid-friendly, outdoor dining

Downtown
1033 SW 6th Ave.
(503) 719-4009

Downtown
1438 SW Park Ave.
(503) 243-5045

The reputation of SuperDog precedes it. This simple, friendly little hot dog joint in downtown Portland, which seats only about 20 people at a smattering of little tables and a few bar seats, has a cult following in town. The little space is frequented by solo diners, who watch ESPN on the loud front-and-center TV while enjoying their dogs. The staff is warm and wonderful, and there's even beer on tap—four beers, at last check—and homemade soups, which are just okay. The space is cheery, decked out with beer, football, and Superdog memorabilia.

But the question is: does the dog measure up? Is this just Portland hype, or is it true Chicago-style bliss?

The answer: it's mostly hype, but the dogs are still enjoyable enough. The local Zenner's double smoke in the "Portland Original Dog" is a touch too salty; as such, against our usual sensibilities, we actually prefer the simpler Nathan's frank. Good, too, are the curry wurst, the spicy Italian sausage, or the Mount St. Helens Sausage Dog, which is advertised as "very hot" but we find quite tolerable.

What's more disappointing than the meat itself is the toasted roll, which is more the size and shape of a hamburger roll than of a hot dog roll. Strangely, the bread gets chewy quickly, and sacrifices the absorbency of the simpler pale-white-bread hot dog roll that's still fashionable in Chicago. The reason Chicago-style hot dogs are served in cheapo hot dog rolls is the same reason Texas BBQ is served with Wonder bread: it seeps in more of the meat's juices.

Among toppings, cheese (good shredded Tillamook cheddar, which melts between dog and roll) is requisite. Pickled "sport peppers" are also a good idea, as is Chicago-style bright green relish. We certainly appreciate the wide range of mustards, hot sauces, and other do-it-yourself condiments. There are sliced jalapeños, there's Sriracha, there are two types of relish, and there's a crockpot of sauerkraut, which is serviceable, if a bit mushy.

We can take or leave the chili, which is mild, beefy, and cuminy, the consistency of a Bolognese sauce. And definitely leave the big, unripe slices of tomato, which make the "Chicago Style Dog" difficult to eat and much less enjoyable.

In the end, the cult following might not be justified. But few cult followings are. Just eat your dog, and don't expect fireworks.

Swagat

A reasonably priced feast for all the -vores
that may not bore (but little more)

7.2	7.0	7.5
Food	Feel	Beer

Indian

Casual restaurant

$25
Price

www.swagat.com

Daily 11:30am–2:30pm, 5pm–10pm

Bar Beer, wine, liquor
Credit cards Visa, MC, AmEx
Reservations Accepted
Veg-friendly

Northwest Portland
2074 NW Lovejoy St.
(503) 227-4300

Beaverton
4325 SW 109th Ave.
(503) 626-3000

Hillsboro
1340 NE Orenco Station Pkwy.
(503) 844-3838

This Northwest mini-chain exceeds some expectations of Indian-restaurant atmosphere and vibe, and just yaws around others. The glossy hardwood floors and exposed brick give it a bit of character, and the sans-serif menu font is avant-garde (not literally). But the office-style ceilings and big parking lot in front make the place feel suburban and a bit corporate. Try to avoid getting stuck in the expansive room in back; it's like a dungeon. Service is fine, but it seems as if the higher-ups have a certain self-importance and a noticeable favoritism towards certain customers. But if you're looking to get full on the cheap, this place won't disappoint.

Ultimately, this is more vegetarian-friendly comfort food than a rip-roaring South Indian flavor trip. Here you'll find competent renditions of aloo gobi, with very tender cauliflower and some alluring spice; palak paneer with sparse cubes of browned paneer that create an appealing textural counterpoint; and wimpy, underflavored dal that only impresses with its more-off-putting-than-usual ochre color. Upma comes off like sweetened Cream of Wheat. Not that there's anything wrong with Cream of Wheat. South Indian sambar (lentil soup-like) is excellent; it's served like a soup on the buffet, without a starch to dip in it, but its flavor is clear and present, with judicious but not overbearing coriander and bracing heat.

If ordering from the menu, try a "Swagat South Indian combo" with a masala dosa, idli, urad vada, and sambar. It's delicious, and it's deliciously priced. A lot of the stews are relatively one-dimensional, but it's a good, satisfying dimension; there's a reason people crave this stuff.

Meats are a mixed bag here. Chicken is routinely rubbery and dry, even in a buttery makhani or with a nice char from the tandoor oven. Naan is also doughy and thin, and raita is more like chunky yogurt soup than a condiment.

So, while some dishes are better than others—with little rhyme or reason—it's hard to get more satisfaction for your dollar than the $8.95 lunch buffet here. Especially if you're a vegetarian. Isn't that a nice change?

Sweet Basil

Run-of-the-mill Thai that leaves its mark—just not in the way you would like

5.9	7.0
Food	Feel

Thai

Casual restaurant

$25
Price

www.sweetbasilor.com

Mon–Thu 11:30am–2:30pm, 5pm–9pm; Fri 11:30am–2:30pm, 5pm–10pm; Sat 5pm–10pm; Sun 5pm–9pm

Bar Beer, wine, liquor
Credit cards Visa, MC, AmEx
Reservations Not accepted
Kid-friendly, outdoor dining

Northwest Portland
1639 NW Glisan St.
(503) 473-8758

Northeast Portland
3135 NE Broadway
(503) 281-8337

Although this Thai restaurant has a real following, its cuisine is pretty cookie cutter Thai-American.

Rice is molded into cutesy shapes, curry is saccharine sweet, and pad Thai is forgettable. Overcooking is a rampant problem here, as everything from scallops to shrimp to beef is rendered chewy and tough. There are some cool moves, though, like "forbidden rice," a nuttier black rice we normally only see in upscale Modern American restaurants. Of course, it's made into a star shape. Prepare for some really artful platings. Everything is scalloped and stacked and zig-zagged, but not in an outdated way; it's actually very nice.

Dine outside on the patio of the pinkish-red Broadway location if you can; it's shaded by a lanai covered with leafy vines, and the tables are actually clothed, instead of the cheap plastic or wire furniture you normally find on Thai patios. Inside, it's mad with color but cursed with perfunctory, often absent service.

At least the kitchen doesn't wuss out on spice. But offering a scale for diners to choose their desired level of heat from is pointless if everything comes out like a spice crapshoot (no pun). The level of intensity in Thai chilies can be extremely variable—cooks have to be able to tell by size, shade, and firmness how hot that pepper is going to be. Here, it seems to just throw in a certain number, and lower it for more sensitive people. But one of those things at super strength can equal four at the expected intensity. At least something on the table will be memorable.

Syun Izakaya

A sake education with a side of grilled saba—
and sushi if you've gotta have it

8.1	9.0	8.0
Food	Feel	Wine

Japanese

Casual restaurant

$35
Price

Mon–Thu 11:30am–2pm,
5:30pm–10pm; Fri 11:30am–
2pm, 5:30pm–11pm; Sat noon–
3pm, 5pm–10pm; Sun 5pm–
10pm

Bar Beer, wine, liquor
Credit cards Visa, MC, AmEx
Reservations Not accepted
Outdoor dining

Hillsboro
209 NE Lincoln St.
(503) 640-3131

Syun Izakaya is tucked into the bottom of an old library in Hillsboro that looks like the sort of musty brick building you'd find on an aging college campus. The tiny room is crowded with sake bottles (there are about 50) and a diverse clientele sitting at little tables and at a sushi counter. There are also a few tables outside in a sort of makeshift garden.

If Yuzu is an authentic izakaya that's not at all for sushi seekers, Syun is kind of its more placid, accessible opposite. It's better lit, and it's pretty well patronized by a whiter shade of pale, so the fare is less salted-and-dried cuttlefish and more miso-marinated cod. Not that there's anything wrong with miso-marinated cod. What you get here is spot-on flavor, no pretense, and a quirky setting in which to enjoy it all.

What you won't find is a ho-hum attitude. There's passion behind this operation. One night, the sushi chefs handed out an amuse-bouche of surprisingly tender, tinny-sweet geoduck clams. Grilled mackerel is ridiculously good (when isn't it?), all oily and charry. Marinated pork belly, also charred a bit on the grill, is tender, juicy, and deeply porky. We understand the desire to put raw, fresh fish in your mouth, but if you're here for sushi rolls, you're just completely missing the point. Stick to nigiri and expand your horizons with small plates (which people tend to refer to, kind of annoyingly, as "Japanese tapas").

There are a few Korean conceits here, as well, which is pretty typical of the izakaya genre in the Pacific Northwest. Don't bother with the perfunctory, weird grape wine selection—this is a sake bar. While you're here, get off that hot crap you might have been drinking (it's served hot for a reason; same reason bad beer is served at subzero temperatures), and try some delicate, complex cold sake. A handy guide on the back of the sake list gives an introductory lesson in the different degrees of seimaibuai. Take advantage of this educational opportunity—one that is, no doubt, more fun than the studies that once went on in this space.

Tabla

Is this just a charming neighborhood joint, or is it one of the city's best restaurants?

9.2	9.5	9.0
Food	Feel	Wine

Modern

Upmarket restaurant

$45
Price

www.tabla-restaurant.com

Daily 5pm–9pm

Bar Beer, wine, liquor
Credit cards Visa, MC, AmEx
Reservations Accepted
Date-friendly, outdoor dining

Northeast Portland
200 NE 28th Ave.
(503) 238-3777

After a few years of ups and downs, it seems that Tabla has finally come into its own—its marvelous transformation is as exciting as anything that's happened in Portland's recent culinary memory.

It's always been a pleasant place, bright and airy, with a large open kitchen in the back. A chef's counter puts you in the center of the action; out of the way, there's a private party space, and additional tables stretch down the sidewalk.

A prix-fixe three-course dinner (at press time, a gift to the city at $24) is a fantastic introduction to the menu and can be paired with a great selection of food-loving, carefully made wines selected by a passionate, knowledgeable, and patient sommelier. The waitstaff is also quite helpful and friendly. A handful of house cocktails play on the nostalgic, and there are exciting craft brews on draft.

These people get it, and you really have to dig to find fault. On one visit, Galician-style octopus was surprisingly tender for its large, meaty pieces. It could have used just a touch more olive oil, but smoked paprika was an alluring, simple touch. A rich "flan" of delicata squash was stellar, slightly sweet and texturally wonderful, with delicious maple brown butter. There's great use made of local ingredients here: Tails and Trotters' pork rillette has come pan fried, soft and indulgent, with green beans, mustard crème fraîche, and pickled chard stems.

Homemade pastas have recently included lovely mushroom-and-sherry agnolotti with pickled chanterelles; ravioli stuffed with ricotta and a poached egg paid homage to an Emilia-Romagna dish, bursting with warm yolky goodness when cut into. Pappardelle in a sugo of well-braised pork was wonderfully flavorful, if a little watery.

But the kitchen's finest hour comes with proteins. Duck confit has had crackly, delicious skin, while the meat inside is moist and pulled easily from the bone. Oregon albacore came in a forest of coriander, roasted red pepper, pine nut agrodolce, minted yogurt, and couscous. It was a sensory stunner that somehow didn't overwhelm the fish. Overcooking fish is a pitfall of which this kitchen has amazingly almost never been guilty.

There's a rare combination of both innovation and deftness here that, at last, edifies Tabla beyond its humble neighborhood-restaurant status. For now, at least, it's one of Portland's best.

Tábor

Just try and say "schnitzelwich" without smiling

8.2 Food **7.5** Feel

Czech

Food cart **$10** Price

www.schnitzelwich.com

Mon–Fri 10am–3pm

Bar None
Credit cards None
Outdoor dining, veg-friendly

Downtown
SW 5th St. at Stark St.
(503) 997-5467

We had a difficult time selecting which food carts to include in this book. It was stupid hard. There are so many notable choices, most of which we hope to one day include on fearlesscritic.com. Until then, we've chosen the best and most high-profile carts, as well as those selling the most unique foods. Tábor's (pronounced "Taah-bor") adorable, highly conspicuous raspberry-and-lime-colored cart fits both profiles. It's part of the growing, makeshift restaurant row downtown, and is one of the best-loved lunch spots for people who work in the area.

There's a sense of permanence at this cart (which is really more of an Alpine hut in Technicolor), with its array of tables and chairs, faux-granite counter, and homey kindness. People line up for the whimsical-sounding schnitzelwich, a gut bomb that pits soft, warm ciabatta from Grand Central Bakery against crusty, breaded, and tender pork loin with a peppy paprika spread, horseradish, sautéed onions, and romaine lettuce. It's an irresistible order, the textures and flavors yielding to each other like a dream—yet it renders you completely incapable of movement for several hours, like a snake digesting a whole rabbit.

Vegetarians will love a sandwich of fried Muenster cheese, with mayonnaise and romaine. It's every bit as filling as the schnitzelwich (and, we're sure, just as artery-hardening). For something lighter but still hearty, goulash is a faithful rendering, with either ciabatta for dipping, or homemade spätzle dumplings (noodles, if available), and more of the ubiquitous paprika. Spätzle also delights with Polish kielbasa and sauerkraut with "other secrets"—perhaps paprika?—and sour cream; the kielbasa snaps slightly and gives way to a juicy, porky interior and the sour, tart elements combine to remind you why this is one of the world's favorite comfort foods.

Finish up with some fluffy dumplings filled with seasonal fruit, like plums, apricots, or strawberries and topped with a sort of sweet "cottage cheese." One order includes three child's-fist-sized dumplings, so take them back to the office and use them to bribe coworkers to keep supervisors away while you nap.

Tanuki

Okinawan-style good times rooted in raucous tradition

7.3	8.0	8.0
Food	Feel	Wine

Japanese, Korean

Casual restaurant

$35
Price

www.tanukipdx.com

Tue–Sat 4pm–9:30pm

Bar Beer, wine
Credit cards Visa, MC
Reservations Not accepted
Outdoor dining

Northwest Portland
413 NW 21st Ave.
(503) 241-7667

Tanuki is a shape-shifting Japanese spirit creature that, according to Shinto folklore, travels from sake shop to sake shop, tricking owners into accepting his useless leaves as money, while he imbibes, eats, and philanders to his fill. He's basically the Japanese version of Bernie Madoff. What's not to love?

This party animal promises good times inside the tiny place, which looks exactly like a take-out café. Tables are so cheap they might as well have come from Taco Bell. It's cute, cozy, and frustrating; there are probably all of 15 seats in the place—half are at the counter. As tempting as it would be, don't come with a group larger than four, ever. Let Tanuki be your company.

Whoever you bring, you will be eating and drinking fairly delicious stuff. It's rare to see a Japanese menu that changes seasonally, let alone one that uses local ingredients. And it's great to see things like soondae outside a serious Korean restaurant. This isn't the classic Korean blood sausage—it's more of a boudin noir. Nothing wrong with that.

Dried, shredded squid is an addictive bar snack: sweet, spicy, and salty. House-made pickles are fine, as is kimchi—the menu will be quick to remind you this is all humble, spicy, salty bar food.

But that doesn't preclude disappointment (unless you've already had a lot of sake): natto, fermented soybeans over rice with raw egg, sounds terrific, but is very boring, with little flavor. Okinawan pork belly, however, is some of the kitchen's best work.

Come nightfall, Tanuki turns into a raucous, dark bar with excellent sakes and debauchery. Understand this fact, have plenty of sake, and you'll learn to put up with the hassles—the cramped quarters, the occasional attitude.

There are nightly specials, like Tuesday night pork belly discounts, and $5 noodles on Thursdays. On Wednesday and Saturday nights, Tanuki shows Japanese films (of both the classic and culty genres), which just plain rules. Every city in the States needs a few of these.

Taquería Los Gorditos

Mediocre tacos in a half an hour—we just don't get the fascination, even if it *is* a food truck

Mexican

4.9	3.5
Food	Feel

Food cart | **$5** Price

Mon–Sat 9am–8:30pm

Bar None
Credit cards None
Outdoor dining, veg-friendly

Division/Clinton
SE 50th & SE Division
(503) 875-2615

Taquería Los Gorditos enjoys extreme popularity. We don't know if it's because people love the underdoggish food truck; if it's because of the kitschy Southwestern mural; or if it's because there's an attempt to cater to vegans and vegetarians. Whatever it is, we don't get it. The tacos are just not that good.

Service is absurdly slow, and it can take up to half an hour or more to get your tacos at busy times. We've seen the process hundreds of times all over the world: meat on the griddle, meat off the griddle, tortilla, tortilla, onions, cilantro, and here you go. Grab a lime wedge on your way out. It's a process that normally takes seconds and tastes significantly better. So who has the patience for this sort of wait when it's not justified by good tacos?

Though it sounds disconcerting, there is something to the soyrizo—it makes up in fat and salt what it lacks in animal protein—but the carne asada tacos are disastrously dry. At one visit, we asked first for lengua, then cabeza, both on the menu...and both were out of stock. Al pastor has been the least of evils, reasonably seasoned, decent, competent, basically average. Tortillas are okay, but no more.

The crowd is made up of families, hipsters, and Joe the Plumbers, all eating on the covered deck. And we want to share their enthusiasm—some of our highest-rated eateries have been food trucks. Would these tacos taste better if they came out in a decent amount of time? Why do all these folks continue to come when there are much better tacos down the road at ¿Por Qué No? We can't say for sure, although we're sure soyrizo has something to do with it.

Taquería 7 Estrellas

The best tacos in the Portland area, where you least expect them

9.0 Food
4.5 Feel

Mexican

Casual restaurant

$15 Price

Daily 8am–10pm

Bar None
Credit cards Visa, MC
Reservations Not accepted

Tigard
12198 SW Main St.
(503) 747-0864

Those iconic hand-painted signs, the signals of regional authenticity, decorate the expanses of cheap-looking glass that separate this unknown, underappreciated Mexican restaurant from the Tigard strip-mall parking lots that surround it. "Estilo Jalisco," says one of the paintings—indicating the style of Mexico's Jalisco state, home to Guadalajara, where the torta ahogada (drowned sandwich)—listed on the menu here as "hogada"—is king. It's served on a bolillo (baguette-ish roll), stuffed with chunks of juicy roast pork, and bathed in a spicy tomato-and-chile broth. The torta ahogada is like a hot Mexican version of French dip, and this is one of the only places in the United States where we have seen it on a menu.

No less impressive are the 7 Estrellas tacos. It is rare that we say this, but every single one on the menu is outstanding, built around some of the best tortillas in the Portland area, light, fluffy, and a touch sweet. Seven stars stand out in the firmament of fillings. Birria de res (slow-stewed beef) has a lovely, aromatic baking-spice quality to it. Tacos de cabeza have that gelatinous loveliness we seek in head cheese. Small shrimp are fried, yet of a remarkable lightness and sweetness; tacos de pescado (fish) are thickly battered, and look heavy—yet the flaky, moist, bright white fish flesh balances out the richness of the batter, as in an excellent English fish and chips. Lengua (tongue) is unusually meaty, al pastor has great depth, and carnitas are meltingly tender. Order an assortment, and they'll come in one big platter of deliciousness, strewn with onions and cilantro and lime, a celebration of Mexico's many meats.

Tortas beyond the ahogada, made from fresh bread and high-quality produce, are also a great way to go. Chiles rellenos, enchiladas, and other more ubiquitous Mexican-American preps are also well executed, and you can get them stuffed with those same delicious fillings. We've enjoyed a carne asada platter, and an excellent pork tamal. Still, tacos are really the star of the show.

You might as well call ahead and order take-out (which is easier if you speak Spanish), because there is nothing to like about the room, whose ten or so tables have a suburban-pizzeria quality to them. The staff is friendly, but food can take an extremely long time to come, even when the restaurant is almost empty. But such is the cost, perhaps, of serious tacos, seriously prepared to order; you can pass the time with Mexican sodas and such. The truth, uncomfortable as it may be, is that this unsung taquería off Route 99 is better than any Mexican restaurant in the city of Portland.

Tara Thai

A standard take on recognizable dishes made much more palatable by its homey digs

6.7 Food

8.0 Feel

Thai

Casual restaurant

$25 Price

www.tarathainorthwest.com

Mon–Thu 11am–9pm
Fri 11am–10pm
Sat noon–10pm
Sun noon–9pm

Bar Beer, wine, liquor
Credit cards Visa, MC, AmEx
Reservations Accepted
Date-friendly, outdoor dining

Northwest Portland
1310 NW 23rd Ave.
(503) 222-7840

"Tara Thai" is probably one of the five most common Thai restaurant names in America. Considering that so much American Thai food consists of a standardized menu of dishes that seem to have been identically dumbed down by some central Thai-food-dumbing-down authority, which may work in conjunction with the FDA's cook-meat-to-180-degrees terrorists, having such a common name doesn't inspire confidence.

What does set Tara Thai apart is its absolutely charming renovated house, which sits on a leafy residential street. Cranberry-colored wall-to-wall carpeting, antiques, and vaguely Thai-looking artwork make this restaurant feel as if you'd just stepped into someone's parlor for dinner. The walk upstairs to another dining room is eerie, as if you might accidentally walk in on someone napping in their bed. As you might expect, the staff is completely friendly and hospitable—one common feature of Thai restaurants that we're thankful for. The wooden deck outside is a gorgeous place to sit in nice weather, shaded by a rambling oak.

But that's where the distinctions end. The menu is full of the same, sugary, mundane standards that fill the menus of most Americanized Thai places; dishes that have a much more thrilling and complex basis in their native land, but have been distilled to their most obvious and intense components. Pad Thai, for example, is capable of an exquisite balance of salty dried shrimp, sour vinegar, spicy chilies, and sweet, pungent fish sauce. But here, as is so often done, the dish is already made too sweet, then defaced further by the overcooked, bland meat of your choice, relying on a squirt of lime to keep it from being cloying.

Instead, stick close to the Northern Thai/Lao specialties on this menu, like a citrusy, spicy larb whose ground pork is a little overdone, but whose flavors are much more complex and interesting than the curries offered here. Or som tam (green papaya salad), whose searing sour-spicy freshness makes it a staple in virtually all Thai households.

It's difficult to call out Tara Thai on falling away from the integrity of true Thai recipes, because virtually everyone else is doing it. Of those, Thai Tara is no worse and no better. But Pok Pok has shown Portland that more is possible. When will the rest catch up?

Tastebud

Farm-fresh ingredients and anything you can toss into a wood-fired oven

7.0	8.0	7.5
Food	Feel	Beer

Pizza

Casual restaurant **$30** Price

www.tastebudfarm.com

Thu–Sun 5pm–10pm

Bar Beer, wine
Credit cards Visa, MC, AmEx
Reservations Not accepted
Date-friendly, outdoor dining,
veg-friendly

Southeast Portland
3220 SE Milwaukie Ave.
(503) 234-0330

These days, making a pizza is like running for office. It's not good enough to have a wood-fired oven: this guy imports his from Naples. But this one over here is the only one to get above 800°. Then the upstarts come, touting coal as the new deal. The truth is, none of these methods is guaranteed to make a great pizza—that's still up to the maker. A beautiful black, blistering sear is still the product of the marriage between humans and fire.

Tastebud first came on the scene at the farmer's markets using seasonal, fresh ingredients. They're out there every week selling pizzas baked in a mobile wood-burning oven, and other items. We've had a salad with fresh, interesting veggies, but leg of lamb comes overcooked, underseasoned, and totally dry. Wood ovens alone don't make superior food.

So how does the crust measure up? It's quite puffy, much thicker than the wafer-thin crusts at Ken's, properly blistered and a little chewy. But when loaded with Tastebud's generous, rich toppings, these already formidable crusts can become real belly burdens.

The restaurant is located near the Aladdin Theater, and looks more like an elegant osteria than a pizza joint. There are communal tables, arrangements of fresh flowers, pictures of the old country, and a patio shaded by some trees and vines with an ambient fountain.

Combinations change with the harvest, and some are better balanced than others. One particularly successful version saw roasted peaches paired with house-made pancetta, creamy mascarpone, and peppery arugula. Fennel sausage is a rightfully popular choice, and is best with just tomato and mozzarella. But some combinations, like morel mushrooms and zucchini, have been bland. Appetizers are strangely oily, no matter what they are, and fruity desserts baked in the oven have systematic crust problems. Bagels are rock hard—in this case, just because you have a wood-fired oven doesn't mean you should use it. The wine selection is better than at most pizza joints, but there's a reason Italians prefer beer with their pie; here the beer choice is right on, local-minded, with Hair of the Dog and others on draft.

More than anything else, Tastebud's incredibly fresh ingredients and seasonal combinations are what make it a worthy contender. This crust may not be for everyone, but diversity is a good thing.

Teardrop Lounge

Kneel before Pernod

7.3	9.0	9.5
Food	Feel	Drinks

Modern

Bar **$35**
Price

www.teardroplounge.com

Mon–Sat 4pm–2am

Bar Beer, wine, liquor
Credit cards Visa, MC, AmEx
Outdoor dining

Pearl District
1015 NW Everett St.
(503) 445-8109

Falernum, cassis, orange flower water, Herbsaint, and tepache. They were standard ingredients back in the day, but you don't see them much anymore. Instead, we have banana rum, blueberry vodka, Red Bull, and DeKuyper's Sour Pucker; ingredients to make boring, horrendously sweet drinks on the cheap—a bottom-line-driven trough of swill just palatable enough to keep tabs open.

But there's been a breathtaking resurgence of long-lost drinks with exotic names like Dog Hair, Jerusalem's Between the Sheets, and Death in the Gulf Stream—drinks that require true craftsmanship and study, not just an assembly line, to layer the contrasting flavors and textures a cocktail can (and should) have.

The bartenders at Teardop, some say, are zealots of this cause. It's fitting, then, that the spartan room of cinder-block walls, exposed wood-beam ceiling, and centrally placed island bar feels like a sanctuary built by devoted ascetics. A window wall and skylight let in natural light, should you be lucky enough to start drinking before dark.

A raft of small-batch artisanal liquors is decoration enough for the legions of believers who assemble around the bar to watch the creations of drinks like "Smoke & Mirrors," in which a fresh canary melon is muddled with light rum and hibiscus water, then poured into a glass whose rim is crusted in chipotle salt. Or a "Batida Apasionada," where fresh passion fruit is peeled before your eyes and muddled with cachaça, coconut water, lime, organic cane sugar, and finished with a quick grate of whole nutmeg. Even a prosaic Mai Tai reaches new heights with house-made falernum, a floral digestif redolent with almond, orange, and spices.

A terrific range of sakes can be drunk alone or as the basis of a sangría that is a refreshing mix of seasonal fruit, Hakutsuru sake, Oregon Pinot Gris, brandy, and spices. Chopsticks are provided to pick out slices of sake-poached peaches and berries. The sangría is a steal at only $4 during the daily 4pm-7pm happy hour.

There are also nearly 20 beers here, including microbrews, Belgian, and well-loved imports. As seems to be the norm for ambitious cocktail programs, though, the wines are perfunctory and underwhelming, not at all chosen with the same passion and awareness as the other imbibables.

Small plates of fusiony, competent culinary concoctions are in service to the cocktail program: gazpacho (a little flat and dull); duck confit with sherry-thyme escabeche (fine, if a touch overcooked); ahi tataki with mango and coconut rice (okay, fresh-tasting); and hoisin-marinated chicken drummettes (addictive, simple). After all, man cannot live on falernum alone.

Ten01

This trendy restaurant has re-emerged as one
of the Pearl's star tables

8.7	8.0	8.0
Food	Feel	Wine

Modern

Upmarket restaurant

$70
Price

www.ten-01.com

Mon–Thu 11:30am–10pm
Fri–Sat 11:30am–10:30pm

Bar Beer, wine, liquor
Credit cards Visa, MC, AmEx
Reservations Accepted
Date-friendly, outdoor dining

Pearl District
1001 NW Couch St.
(503) 226-3463

This restaurant's striking appearance precedes it. In places, the ceiling
soars three floors, with dramatic light fixtures drawing the eye skyward.
Endless lattices of windows overlook the street, and the dining room is
open and airy. We also applaud the creative and attractive use of
recyclable materials. Cork is used to keep the noise level reasonable, even
with a full house. The walls are all tans and yellows, very neutral and easy
on the eyes.

Like many upmarket Portland restaurants, the kitchen at Ten01 has had
its ups and downs in recent memory. Happily, though, the latest trend has
been up and up. Innovative platings like sockeye salmon with summer
beans, cauliflower purée, red sorrel, cherry tomato, and black olive oil
have shown great finesse. A salad of delicious heirloom tomatoes and
Ancient Heritage feta with Banyuls vinaigrette drew out the late-summer
sweetness from the fruit and balanced it expertly with the cheese's salt.
And roast chicken, the litmus test of a professional kitchen, has come out
perfectly cooked and seasoned, earthy from chanterelle, richly matched
with a bed of creamy polenta.

We've also really enjoyed our recent lunches at Ten01, when the
kitchen breathes a bit more easily, and turns out simpler things at simpler
prices (including a bargain three-course prix-fixe). A sensational chicken-
liver mousse, for instance—made with sherry and served in a glass, with
the consistency of parfait—paired beautifully with slices of expertly grilled
baguette and the lilting sweetness of fig jam. A roast-pork sandwich with
celery-root slaw has also demonstrated great balance.

More disappointing has been a tartare of pine nuts, cocoa nibs,
amarena cherry, juniper, and arbequina olive oil; it was a sweet, chunky,
unrefined, preparation that seemed less than the sum of its parts. Risotto
with summer squash, zucchini, and grana padano has also withered in its
own shadow, underseasoned and overcooked.

For us, the bar scene is much more fun than the main dining room.
Cocktails can come improperly muddled and insipid, but the wine list
offers a tour of exciting, well-made, sometimes culty bargains from the
Old World (along with some less thrilling options from the New World).
There is a broad range of half bottles and verticals, and markups are
pretty reasonable.

In short, it's a pleasure to report that the high dinner prices are once
again justified at what has long been one of the city's most high-profile
restaurants.

Thatch Tiki Bar

Portland ambition meets mid-century
Americana kitsch

5.7	9.0	7.5
Food	Feel	Drinks

Hawaiian, Pan-Asian

Bar **$30**
Price

Daily 4pm–11pm

Bar Beer, wine, liquor
Credit cards Visa, AmEx
Date-friendly

Northeast Portland
2733 NE Broadway
(503) 281-8454

Who doesn't love a tiki bar? That 1960s Americana kitschy-fabulous image just pops into everyone's head so clearly. Whether you've been to Disneyland's Polynesian Resort, San Francisco's Tonga Room, or the iconic Bahooka in the suburbs of Los Angeles—or even if you've only glimpsed a tiki bar in a ridiculous romantic comedy involving a disastrous Club Med getaway—you will feel a familiar tinge upon walking into this hilariously fun room.

Although it looks totally unassuming from the outside, the inside bursts through the door like a cracked-passionfruit, lava-colored lighting emanating from dangling puffer-fish bodies and tortoise-shell-like lamps. A wooden bridge spans a dribble of water from shell fountains, and leaves modern Portland utterly behind you, freeing you up to make all kinds of bad decisions, so long as they're served out of a large goblet with several decorative umbrellas.

Take a seat in a space-age orange booth underneath some bamboo and fake-grass thatching (naturally) and beneath the watchful eye of tiki carvings (complete with phallic-worship detail), and order something out of a coconut, or something fruity—it's allowed here. There will be no judgment if bitters aren't your thing and you never understood the rye resurgence. There will only be Blue Hawaiians, Mai Tais, Fog Cutters, Tiki Punches, and Singapore Slings. The outside world still belonging to Portland, however, these cocktails will go above and beyond the call of fruity duty, with blue Curaçao and orgeat, expert balance, and some signature creations. And you know you want a flaming bowl of tropical fruit and liquor. You came this far, so why not? But you've gotta share between three people. Did we mention it's a bowl? Of liquor?

The food is similarly authentic to the era, but it's done a bit better than you'd expect. Crab Rangoon is just silly, but when these deep-fried wonton wrappers are filled with real crab in addition to the cream cheese, they get a little serious. Groups absolutely must order the pu-pu platter, which consists of egg rolls, fried shrimp, and other vaguely Chinese-Polynesian finger foods, with a little hibachi grill in the middle for cooking meat skewers. Dipping sauces go beyond quotidian teriyaki with coconut and ginger elements. Okay, we admit it, the food's not really very good. But...it's fun to say. Pu-pu. Really, it's fun to do anything here.

Thistle

Bargain hunters and foodies: there's gold in this here wine country

9.2	9.0	9.0
Food	Feel	Wine

Modern

Upmarket restaurant

$60
Price

www.thistlerestaurant.com

Tue–Sat 5:30pm–10pm

Bar Beer, wine
Credit cards Visa, MC
Reservations Essential
Date-friendly

McMinnville
228 NE Evans St.
(503) 472-9623

This brilliant little restaurant is well worth the trip out to McMinnville. You'll even enjoy getting lost in the old downtown area, as the sign (off the main road) is a little obscured. Inside, it feels warm and friendly, as if you're over to a family's house for dinner. This husband-and-wife team with the big-city pedigree started this place as an adventure in mid-2009, bringing unprecedented sophistication to this cute little wine country town. There are very few tables, and reservations are absolutely essential, even on a random weekday. The décor is sparse and minimalist, but in a totally cozy, European country bistro sort of way.

A chalkboard lists what the chef is cooking up that night, and you can watch him prepare your food in a flurry of fire and knives from a bar seat. The menu changes frequently, but we've flipped over duck liver parfait in a Lillet gelée. It was cold, luscious, and sublime. Chilled cucumber soup with mint, lime, and chili flake was like a walk around the park before dinner. Seasonal fresh oysters—one time creamy, full-bodied little guys from Netarts Bay—come with a nearly perfect, non-intrusive Champagne mignonette.

A handful of main dishes are available on any given night, so you'll need to be open and receptive (do you question your grandmother when she tells you what's for dinner?). Even the mains that aren't mind-blowing are still expertly made. Homemade gnocchi with chanterelles, tomato, and sheep's cheese have just the right texture. We've enjoyed Alaskan sablefish (black cod) with meaty lobster mushrooms, corn, and green chilies, and a grass-fed beef flatiron steak, ideally seared and served with duck-fat potatoes, broccoli, and hollandaise. The steak is a fattier cut than usual, yielding more flavor than the quotidian cut generally does.

And what a spectacular wine list. If you're into wine, talk to the staff and let them know you're really into trying something more obscure. In this way, we've been treated to an off-the-list 2001 Rolly Gassmann Auxerrois from Alsace for only $30, a fleshy white full of peaches and gravel that you would normally have to sift through an endless, marked-up-to-hell Vegas list to find. And here, we paid retail for it. Man, how we love the thrill of the hunt.

3 Doors Down Café

It gets most things right...but that's only a small part of what it's trying to do

7.1	8.5	8.5
Food	Feel	Wine

Modern

Upmarket restaurant

$45
Price

www.3doorsdowncafe.com

Tue–Thu 5pm–9:30pm
Fri–Sat 5pm–10pm
Sun 4pm–9pm

Bar Beer, wine, liquor
Credit cards Visa, MC, AmEx
Reservations Not accepted
Outdoor dining

Southeast Portland
1429 SE 37th Ave.
(503) 236-6886

It's hard to say whether it's the folksy name, the lighting warm enough to flatter even the weakest of chins, the advantageous location on the edge of one of Portland's hippest neighborhoods, or the bargain-priced happy-hour menu that sustains the cult following of 3 Doors Down Café.

Whatever it is, this effortlessly artsy, eternally popular restaurant seems to have its shtick down. At a recent visit, we were most impressed by an unexpected and welcome cranny of the beverage program: a flight of hard ciders from Normandy's Eric Bordelet. Cider is one of the most underrated of alcoholic drinks, and to taste three different versions—all more or less dry—from some of its most hallowed grounds of production is a special treat. The wine list is also interesting and broad across Europe, the cocktail list nostalgic and better than average.

Wonderful slices of big, crusty bread start things right, but the globetrotting menu is wrought with the sorts of embarrassing cross-continental misunderstandings (not to mention misspellings) that can occur when you try to speak too many languages at once. Although the kitchen's work is clearly competent, the lack of focus is preventing this restaurant from rising to the top tier.

An Anaheim chile, for instance—a special on a recent visit—was stuffed with jack cheese, dipped in an ethereally light egg batter, and expertly fried, but the tomato sauce in which it was bathed was...well...just tomato sauce, and lime crème fraîche had little detectable lime. The execution was so good that it was frustrating, because an additional layer of spice complexity could have really taken this dish to the next level—and that layer of complexity might be possible if the restaurant were to develop real expertise in Mexican cuisine instead of trying to be Italian, French, Spanish, and Japanese as well.

A pasta called "tortiglione" (a form of rigatoni, really), is also executed well and cooked ideally al dente, but plagued by another underperforming recipe: an overrich sauce that's a bit too chunky, too heavy with cream, weighed down by unappetizingly gray sausage. All that said, the dish still manages to taste good. Starches are what these chefs do best, after all, whether orecchiette or risotto or that lovely bread.

However successful the formula has been for 3 Doors Down, we just can't heartily recommend a restaurant that offers to grind black pepper from a great big mill onto your pasta with tomato sauce. Sometimes it's best to refrain from knocking on the doors of so many cuisines and try to master just one.

The Tin Shed

Its success truly does lie in the journey, not the destination

5.6	9.0
Food	Feel

Vegefusion, American

Casual restaurant

$30
Price

www.tinshedgardencafe.com

Daily 7am–10pm

Bar Beer, wine, liquor
Credit cards Visa, MC
Reservations Not accepted
Kid-friendly, live music, outdoor
dining, veg-friendly

Alberta Arts District
1438 NE Alberta St.
(503) 288-6966

How retro-fabulous to see the Calypso font used for a legitimate, three-dimensional sign instead of on an office flyer for a rummage sale! If the Harry Belafonte spirit doesn't seize you with the signage, the faux-lean-to design will. This is a restaurant made out of corrugated aluminum: you're in for more wackiness than you can shake a sugar cane at.

The interior and patio follow through with hippie eclectica and tatted-up servers with purple streaks in their hair. (Or are those customers?) It's exactly what you'd expect from a restaurant with a purple-and-green website. The mission statement? "To cook really tasty food in a warm and unpretentious environment, and to have authentic interactions with our guests." And it succeeds in exactly that.

The goodwill here is best typified by a summertime weekly open-air market in which you can buy local produce while sipping cocktails, and novice gardeners can get tips on growing their own. Terrific local artists are on display here, and art shows are held once a month (advertised on flyers using Calypso?). Movies are shown weekly in the garden, and local bands play in the summer. For charity. Seriously, where's Tin Shed's arts endowment?

All this and food, too. Not just food, but a philosophy. Free-range meats, organic and shade-grown coffee, hormone-free dairy. None of this is surprising, given that 1) this is Portland and 2) Tin Shed acts the part in every other way. Yet in a move that's above and beyond, the kitchen's vegetable scraps are composted.

At the end of the day, unfortunately, all this good energy amounts to pretty mediocre food. What else would you expect from a place that serves, in addition to a kids' menu, a dogs' menu? For bipeds, it's not-bad black-bean tacos and nachos, fresh-tasting salads, really decent burgers (specify medium-rare for best results), and serviceable pastas with inventive compositions (smoked salmon, mushrooms, capers, sweet onion, and roasted red peppers) and hilarious names ("Phyllis Diller"). The latter can be overwrought with sauce, but are satisfying.

Breakfast is better, with some innovative dishes and others we just don't see enough of elsewhere: potato pancakes, Monte Cristos, and some scrambles that make vegetarianism actually sound appealing to us. Tin Shed's ethic and sincerity is catching, and its detectable in every dish, whether expertly executed or (more often) just adequately.

As for the dogs' menu, our dog loved it. But he also loves his own shit.

Toro Bravo

Consistent crowds and kvelling press—it's
tough being the top tapas game in town

7.8	7.0	8.0
Food	Feel	Drinks

Spanish

Upmarket restaurant

$45
Price

www.torobravopdx.com

Mon–Thu 5pm–10pm
Fri–Sat 5pm–11pm
Sun 5pm–10pm

Bar Beer, wine, liquor
Credit cards Visa, MC, AmEx
Reservations Not accepted
Date-friendly

Northeast Portland
120 NE Russell St.
(503) 281-4464

Spanish nights are long and vibrant; a night out begins more like a food tour and marathon party fueled by filling, cheap tapas that vary from bar to bar. Toro Bravo is Portland's most finely realized version of this, with one caveat: a lot of your night will be spent not partying or eating, but rather waiting for a table. No reservations are accepted, and the wait even on weeknights is often more than an hour. For this, two points are deducted from the feel rating.

In its turn-of-the-century building next to the Wonder Ballroom, this restaurant relative fills its airy space night after night with people, capitalizing on the relative lack of legitimate Spanish tapas options in town. The fiery orange-red walls and ceiling, plank-wood tables, and small, intimate touches like a fully stocked bookshelf in the reception area create a homey, yet convivial atmosphere that feels like the real thing.

Yet the kitchen doesn't turn out entirely faithful renditions of Spain's diverse dishes. Some minor liberties are taken, but they feel pragmatic, not flippant. A simple affair like grilled ramps (playing on the Catalonian tradition of barbecuing spring onions) is impressive, with a lovely char-and-garlic flavor that balances out some of the richer dishes. Seared scallops come expertly grilled, one time with tomatoey, peppery romesco. Lamb is excellent, as are boquerones (fresh marinated anchovies), and fried croquettes are not at all greasy, with a distinct fresh-cod taste.

But tortilla española, the common unifying dish of Spain, is noticeably weak; the egg and potatoes are routinely overcooked. We've had disappointingly mushy squid's-ink pasta with egg and dissociated grilled greens.

Toro Bravo has paella and fideua (where thin noodles are used in lieu of rice) with seasonally changing ingredients like whole clams in shell, duck sausage, and vegetables. While the former transcends the sum of its parts, making for an ultimate textural and flavorful experience, the latter is simply oversalted and under-saffroned.

The wine list is focused and competent, and red and white sangrías (the white is only available in the summer) are available by the glass and pitcher; these are not too dry nor too sweet, and filled with fresh seasonal fruit and sherry. We also love the creative cocktails, which give proper respect to Campari. And while the tapas and vibe here are quite good at evoking those of Spain's enviable nightlife, we have absolutely no idea what motivates people to wait an hour to eat at this decent restaurant when Portland has so many better ones with no wait at all.

Tube

Now eating vegan can be grungy cool
instead of frumpy hippie

5.3	7.5	7.5
Food	Feel	Drinks

Vegefusion

Bar **$15**
Price

Daily 5pm–2:30am

Bar Beer, wine, liquor
Credit cards Visa, MC
Date-friendly, veg-friendly

Old Town Chinatown
18 NW 3rd Ave.
(503) 241-8823

We don't know if this Old Town bar is cooler than you, dear reader, but it's definitely way cooler than *us*. The joint is like a grungy biker bar...but a grungy biker bar Portland-style, which means vegan, indie-emo-rocker, cutting-edge cool. A DJ station sits prominently in the middle of the main bar area, pumping everything from hip-hop to loud scenester jams to the Beatles. Every inch of the bathrooms, and the corridor leading up to them, is lined with graffiti. And don't bother trying to lock the bathroom door. Tube is just that comfortable with its sexuality.

To add to the effect, the "Tube" logo on the front door and throughout the restaurant is done up in that ironic Old English font, Mara-Salvatrucha-style. The furniture, though, is more '70s than '00s, with glowing wall panels and strange bunny art. All of this is shrouded in near-darkness, which seems somehow appropriate given the vibe of the music and the crowd. Given all the atmospheric hijinks, the staff is surprisingly friendly: no indifferent shrugs or holier-than-thou attitude here. That said, you're definitely part of the outgroup if you're not part of the ingroup. Everyone seems to know everyone else here, and if you're not part of that everyone, you might feel left out.

The beer is an embarrassment to this beer town: there's nothing on tap, and mostly garbage in the bottle (e.g. skunked Miller). Better, on Wednesdays, are the $4 Monopolowa and $4 Jim Beam specials. Speaking of specials, the daily happy hour, during which cheap food flows freely from the kitchen, runs a liberal 5pm–10pm.

The menu centers on dishes (hot dog, ham-and-cheese sandwich, and so on) that can be made in versions either vegan or non-vegan. What the vegan preps lose in meaty flavor, they make up in vegetable-oil grease. For example, the "muffin" ($3 during happy hour) isn't bad, if you focus your mental energy on the chipotle, pickled pepper, and margarine fat on the english muffin—which rivals any diner's—instead of the decidedly non-ham-tasting ham or the gluey fake cheese. Then there's vegan spaghetti and meatballs, "turkritos," vegan tacos, tofu scrambles. None of it is good, but most of it is fine, if paired with a bit of selective attention. And all of it is similarly not very healthy. But that's hardly the point at this late-night musical dive.

After all, in its pure form, veganism is a philosophical stance, not a diet. And it's a philosophical stance that we—like Tube, in its grungy, glorious wisdom—don't practice but do admire.

23Hoyt

This "gastro-tavern" does neither particularly well

5.3	6.5	8.0
Food	Feel	Wine

Modern

Upmarket restaurant

$60
Price

www.23hoyt.com

Mon–Sat 11:30am–10:30pm
Sun 5pm–10pm

Bar Beer, wine, liquor
Credit cards Visa, MC, AmEx
Reservations Accepted
Date-friendly, outdoor dining

Northwest Portland
529 NW 23rd Ave.
(503) 445-7400

There is something rather sterile about this two-storied, modern establishment. Located on gentrified 23rd Street, the restaurant reflects the neighborhood's lack of originality. Patio tables are nice for people-watching, and the seats at the bar are comfortable, but the black-and-white motif is dull rather than stimulating-minimalist, and leaves the place feeling rather cold, despite the welcome attempts at bringing nature inside.

Likewise, we just can't get excited about this food, which the restaurant dubs "gastro-tavern" fare (cribbing from *Bon Appétit* to describe itself). It implies a much warmer, cozier vibe than what you get here. Rather, this is really just a straightforward American restaurant that neither pushes the envelope nor benefits from a particularly adept execution. One really irritating example is the burger, which, diners are routinely told, they can only have medium-well. Either this place is run by an ex-Health Department supervisor, or the kitchen is trying to disguise some shady meat. Either way, the burger doesn't enjoy the same gooey, juicy, charred goodness you'd get from a hamburger stand's typically medium-well version. Fries are soggy, salads are a bit wilted, and pasta is gummy.

Not everything is disappointing at 23 Hoyt. Roasted chicken is appropriately moist and juicy, with great flavor throughout, not just on the skin. Steaks are cooked well (not literally, thankfully), but a greasy lamb shank once left a bizarre petrol flavor in our mouths, with none of the good gamy lambness that you'd expect. Even a prosaic Caesar has none of the anchovy that could make this salad even remotely worthwhile.

For a "gastro-tavern," the beer selection is lacking, but for most other kinds of restaurants, it would be pretty decent. There are a few drafts and more in bottle from local craft beers to Czech giants. The wine list has a few interesting, food-loving bottles peppered throughout an otherwise solid but mainstream selection. A Gamay blend from the Franco-Swiss-Italian wonderland Valle d'Aosta is the sort of wine that makes us want to order all kinds of food, just to see the interplay. At these prices, you certainly could afford to. Just don't rely on the food to hold up its end of the deal.

Typhoon!

A sugary romp through America's old-school-Asian faves

4.9	7.5
Food	Feel

Pan-Asian, Thai

Casual restaurant

$40
Price

www.typhoonrestaurants.com

Mon–Thu 11:30am–2:30pm, 4:30pm–9pm; Fri 11:30am–2:30pm, 4:30pm–10pm; Sat 12:30pm–3pm, 4:30pm–10pm; Sun 12:30pm–3pm, 4:30pm–9pm

Hours vary by location

Bar Beer, wine, liquor
Credit cards Visa, MC, AmEx
Reservations Accepted
Date-friendly, outdoor dining, veg-friendly

Downtown
410 SW Broadway
(503) 224-8285

Northwest Portland
2310 NW Everett St.
(503) 243-7557

Beaverton
12600 SW Crescent Way
(503) 644-8010

If Typhoon! sounds like a wacky Broadway musical from the 1960s celebrating the antics of WWII servicemen in the Pacific Islands, you're not far off. The restaurant, which purports a Thai heritage, is designed around mid-century America's idea of Southeast Asia. Perhaps most American of all, there's this crazed focus on providing as many products for consumers as you can fit under one restaurant roof: gift certificates; catering; and even Typhoon!'s own brand of wok.

The egalitarian message spreads to the menus, which is a veritable food court unto itself: "Pacific Rim sandwiches"; "Mongolian BBQ"; bento boxes; Vietnamese noodle soups; Chinese-American take-out classics; and (eep!) sushi—all marketed under different names, but prominently featuring the "Typhoon!" name, so you don't mistakenly think this came from actual Vietnamese, Japanese, or Chinese restaurants.

And for all the restaurant's fuss about its Thai executive chef and posted information about the foods of Thailand, renditions are faithful only to trends. They're trenditions. Larb has none of the ground pork that's so brilliant on this limey, hot salad—only your choice (yours, the experienced Thai chef) of chicken, tuna, or shrimp. And these are not the tiny, dried shrimp that you could reasonably expect to find in Thai food—they're big, bland shrimp like you'd find blackened on an Applebee's Caesar salad. Pad see ew's noodles are overcooked to the point of soupiness, with the same sweet sauce the kitchen drowns everything in.

Even the "Chef's Specialties" nervously genuflect before middle-American palates. A duck curry with pineapple and grapes substitutes sweetness for a clove-curry intrigue, masking the flavor of the overcooked (we're guessing not wild) duck without complementing it.

There are some neat features, like an extensive selection of loose-leaf teas and vegan and gluten-free menus. But in a city with Pok Pok and even Siam Society, why would anyone come here?

The answer may lie in the vast, cozy, and swanky atmospheres of its branches. An even-swankier new conceit has opened downtown called, awkwardly, Bo Restobar. We would have reviewed it but, honestly, we feel like we just did.

Urban Farmer

Sample pricey flights of beef in a post-modernist urban pasture

7.6	8.0	9.0
Food	Feel	Drinks

Steakhouse, Modern

Upmarket restaurant

$110
Price

www.urbanfarmerrestaurant.com

Mon–Thu 6:30am–3pm, 5pm–10pm
Fri 6:30am–3pm, 5pm–11pm
Sat 11am–3pm, 5pm–11pm
Sun 11:30am–3pm, 5pm–10pm

Bar Beer, wine, liquor
Credit cards Visa, MC, AmEx
Reservations Accepted
Date-friendly

Downtown
525 SW Morrison St.
(503) 222-4900

On the eighth floor of The Nines hotel, in an atrium courtyard that is airy and bright by day and darkly sexy at night, is the hippest steakhouse in the city. Although Urban Farmer's swanky décor feels decidedly PR-slutty—like NYC's Soho Grand, where you stand a very good chance of spilling your Corpse Reviver on an It-girl—the nature-meets-architecture theme does make for good eye candy: antler chandeliers; pickling jars as accessories; and what appears to be sorghum growing healthily between the booths. It's like a celebrity's theme park devoted to Portland's farm-to-table movement.

The central problem here is that to capitalize financially on what Portland represents, in such a dramatic way, is...well...very un-Portland. This is easily the most overpriced restaurant in the city, with steaks that shatter the $50 ceiling, and even, in one case, the $75 ceiling. That's downright insulting. We're not in Vegas or St-Tropez.

You can choose from corn-fed beef, grass-fed/grain-finished beef (it helps it get that familiar beefy flavor Americans can't do without), and all grass-fed. American wagyu gets its own category, despite the fact that it should, technically, fall within the grain-fed category.

And if you can swing it, do try the incredible, mouth-melting wagyu at an equally incredible, wallet-melting price. This kitchen does great justice to these wonderful, quality meats. Strawberry Mountain NY Strip is available dry-aged for 21 or 42 days. In a world where steakhouses have historically been one of the largest customers of the industrial meat complex, it's nice to see a focus on provenance. But at what prices!

Of course, you don't have to get steak. A special one night of beans baked with duck and sausage, rather like a cassoulet, was pretty underwhelming. Some small plates feel gimmicky, like Dungeness crab crêpe with shaved snap peas and lime that turns out no better than your average crab cake.

The wine list is overpriced and not at all interesting—in that way, it really does resemble a steakhouse. Instead, explore the cocktail program; both classics and twists are done very well. Better yet, enjoy the cocktails in the spectacular top-floor bar, Departures, complete with views and exquisite cruise-ship theming. A "Moonshiner Boilermaker" gets house-made moonshine with a teacup chaser of...cold tea. It's fun, like Urban Farmer, and maybe just as equally meant to be a sporadic thing.

Uwajimaya

A clean, attractive place to find all your Japanese needs—for a price

Groceries, Japanese, Seafood

Market

www.uwajimaya.com

Mon–Sat 7am–10pm
Sun 9am–9pm

Bar Beer, wine
Credit cards Visa, MC, AmEx
Veg-friendly

Beaverton
10500 SW Beaverton Hillsdale Hwy.
(503) 643-4512

Uwajimaya began as a family-owned market in Tacoma that provided down-home meals for the many Japanese people drawn to Washington's shores for work in the fishing and timber industries. Today, its flagship store is in Seattle's Chinatown, and has stretched out to consume a few city blocks with residential and retail units in the Uwajimaya Village. The unstoppable juggernaut hit Beaverton in the late '90s, and every now and then, rumors of its plans to invade Portland's Old Town Chinatown are bandied about town, to mixed reactions.

On the one hand, the store is lovely, with much less of the distinctive, challenging squid-and-tripe smell that other Asian markets tend to possess. (It's not a Pan-Asian market—this is strictly Japanese.) And while it's cheaper to get your goods at Fubonn Supermarket, Uwajimaya's selection of products is of generally superior quality. Plus, service is much friendlier and more helpful. Shelves are well stocked, and there are none of the chaotic boxes and plastic wrappings lying around that you often see at Fubonn. Did we mention that it's a bit more expensive over here? Well, it will show, thank goodness. You'll find top-notch Japanese chef's knives and hundreds of brands of Japanese noodles. You'll find bulk frozen ikura (smelt roe), and you can choose your nori from dozens.

You'll see it in the tanks of live, healthy-looking seafood; the attractive selection of meats, which includes locally raised, hormone-and-antibiotic-free beef and chicken; and in better-quality housewares. The sake selection is absolutely fantastic—better than at any wine or liquor store in the greater Portland area.

We never, ever sanction sushi from a grocery store—even at gourmet fancy-pants places. It's so often just a bland, pointless rendition of nigiri and maki, and here it's only slightly better. The grab-and-go udon is actually quite passable, but what's actually delicious is the food at the excellent Hakatamon (reviewed separately). That store can be entered directly from the supermarket.

There are things here that you'll find almost nowhere else in the US, like a huge Japanese-language bookstore. There's something a little cold and corporate about Uwajimaya. But we look at it like this: sometimes you want the heart-racing thrill of uncertainty and discovery in your Asian vacation. For everyone else, there's Uwajimaya.

Hakatamon

Authentic, simple Japanese soups and sushi
served with little fuss or aplomb

9.1	6.5	7.5
Food	Feel	Wine

Japanese

Casual restaurant

$30
Price

www.uwajimaya.com

Mon–Sat 11:30am–11pm

Bar Beer, wine
Credit cards Visa, MC, AmEx
Reservations Accepted

Beaverton
10500 SW Beaverton-Hillsdale Hwy.
(503) 641-4613

Hakatamon hunkers darkly inside (and sort of next to) the Uwajimaya supermarket, where its sprightly lime-green walls only sort of distract you from the grungy surroundings. This tiny space gets packed and noisy with a mixed crowd of Anglos and Japanese-speaking diners, which livens up the atmosphere. Still it's a bit too mall-like for a nice, relaxing dinner. For an authentic Japanese lunch, though, it can't be beat.

Despite the bustle, service is good and the staff accommodating, although you might have to wait a bit at peak times. Gluten-free folks are offered wheat-free tamari, which they can put on very fresh sushi to their hearts' content. The cuts are beautiful, the right balance between satisfyingly thick and delicately thin, with silky yellowtail belly and a sweet, buttermilky uni that rivals the very best. Rice is seasoned just right to set off the flavors and textures of the fish—just a dab of soy sauce is all you'll need.

Don't miss out on other terrific, authentic dishes like hiya yako, where wonderful homemade tofu cubes are topped with bonito shavings and scallions with fresh ginger; fresh, chewy udon noodles; or magically deep tonkotsu ramen, Kyushu-style, the broth cloudy and unusually complex from cooking a pork bone for 12 hours. Here, as with other ramen preps, the noodles are wonderfully bouncy and not a second overcooked.

There is a pretty good selection of hard-to-find sakes and the usual beers in bottle, but again, you might find yourself more impressed at lunch than at dinner. Not that we're suggesting you should only drink sake and beer at dinner. Not by a long shot.

Vault Martini

A Tale of Two Cocktail Bars

6.4	2.5	7.0
Food	Feel	Drinks

Modern

Bar **$35** Price

www.vault-martini.com

Mon–Wed 4pm–1am
Thu–Sat 4pm–2am
Sun 4pm–midnight

Bar Beer, wine, liquor
Credit cards Visa, MC, AmEx
Date-friendly, outdoor dining

Pearl District
226 NW 12th Ave.
(503) 224-4909

Vault is a dramatically Iron-Curtainish space where even the restrooms are beautiful (although the wallpaper is somewhat seizure-inducing). People flock to this spot to see and be seen. Gay, straight, young hipster, old money, new money, lawyer, advertising exec, nervous Internet date—they're all here. Huge windows provide great people-watching on the street, and a fireplace fills the lounge with warmth on cold afternoons.

The draw here is a list of more than 40 variations on the martini, mostly vodka-based drinks that do their best to cover the taste of alcohol. When they succeed, the results can be interesting, but they're rarely sublime. Compared with the alchemy taking place at another Pearl District cocktail lounge, Teardrop—along with cutting-edge cocktail bars over the East Side—Vault feels gimmicky and trite. Most of the drinks are candyish and mass appealing, as opposed to revelatory. Vodka with cilantro, fresh mint, and lemon-lime syrup tastes good, but it won't stop any conversations. Vault's #1 seller, a habanero martini, leaves a long, burning finish, but little material for contemplation.

It's hard to argue with a seasonal fresh cantaloupe -tini, especially on a warm day, but cocktails are capable of so much more than this, as is increasingly evidenced by the more nostalgia-driven programs springing up all over town. Not only is Vault's approach becoming outdated, but the drinks can be inconsistent, depending on who is making them and how busy they are. Infusions also vary with the day—one time, the habanero vodka brandished a herniating heat; another time, it was wimpy.

There is a selection of better-than-bar food that is serviceable: salads; flatbread pizzas; various panini and wraps. None of it is craveworthy, nor especially inspired by the drinks, unlike the food at Teardrop. But then, if you're here, you probably don't mind much.

Understaffing is a constant problem here, as evidenced by the numbers of people we've seen leave without being served (or, sometimes, without paying). What is completely inexcusable, beyond that, is the indifferent-at-best, hostile-at-worst attitude of the staff. We've rarely seen service this consistently obnoxious in Vegas, Soho, Paris, or anywhere else.

Veritable Quandary

7.3	9.5	6.5
Food	Feel	Drinks

An old establishment that's full of charm, but not full of culinary genius

Modern

Upmarket restaurant

$45
Price

www.veritablequandary.com

Mon–Fri 11:30am–3pm, 5pm–10pm
Sat–Sun 9:30am–3pm, 5pm–10pm

Bar Beer, wine, liquor
Credit cards Visa, MC, AmEx
Reservations Accepted
Outdoor dining

Downtown
1220 SW 1st Ave.
(503) 227-7342

This is...ahem...a verit...okay, a very difficult restaurant to write about. In fact, it is one of Portland's most difficult. We say this because there is so very much to like about the place. In the front of the narrow old building, full of quirk and creak, is one of the city's most enjoyable pubs. Exposed brick isn't "found"; it's been here all along. The fans, suspended from the high, cheery wooden ceilings, spin in a gracious Creole sort of way.

You may love or hate the name, but what's not in dispute is that Veritable Quandary is a pub in the old sense of the word, a publick house, a community gathering place that binds the old and new Portlands, the shipping and the hipping, the bikers and the bicyclists. Regulars are acknowledged by name, and served well-executed, classic stiff martinis. And in spite of the good local beer lineup and lively bar scene, the food is not a mere afterthought, even if it's not always successful.

That central quandary is whether to take the place seriously as an upscale restaurant. Clearly that aim is there, too; the back rooms, behind all the pubbing, are more formal, dimly lit places of tablecloths and after-dinner coffees. There's a crowded open kitchen full of shouts and clanks, which always seems barely out of the weeds around its peak time of about 6:30pm (it's an older crowd).

The clear competence of that energetic kitchen—and the employment of local ingredients and pleasures as wild sturgeon, rabbit pâté, and poached-egg-and-lardons salad—make it even more of a mystery why the menu would attempt to cover every continent on Earth.

There is real skill in executing on some of those ideas, however scatterbrained they may seem. A poblano pepper stuffed with chorizo and cheddar gains complexity from a sauce of fruit and dried red chile—like a sweetened-up mole—and crumbled queso fresco. The poblano was lightly battered and expertly deep-fried, attaining a crunch that's frequently missing from the egg coating of often-soggy chiles rellenos at more authentic Mexican spots, yet its lightness preserved the almost metallic acidity of the pepper. The dish was a pleasant surprise, even with its useless sprinkle of field greens.

But then there are the recipes that are doomed from the start, like a grilled-chicken-breast sandwich with sun-dried tomato, artichoke and onion relish, feta, and spinach, and pasta salad. There are the sometimes-soggy fries, and the fact that the delicious Ken's brown bread is sometimes left to get stale. But order carefully—or, hey, just order a beer—and you are certain to be charmed by this legendary local.

Vincenté's Pizza

Good, comforting pizza in a fun, late-night space—aaay!

5.8	8.5	8.0
Food	Feel	Beer

Pizza

Casual restaurant

$20
Price

www.vincentesgourmetpizza.com

Mon–Sat 11am–midnight
Sun noon–midnight

Bar Beer, wine, liquor
Credit cards Visa, MC, AmEx
Reservations Not accepted
Delivery, outdoor dining,
veg-friendly

Hawthorne
1935 SE Hawthorne Blvd.
(503) 236-5223

Vincenté's (according to the spelling on their sign) hails from the mid-'90s, a time before gourmands began fetishizing Neapolitan-style pies and Brooklyn pizza geeks using promises of "coal-fired" and "wood-fired" to allure zealots. That is, it's just okay, overly cheesy in that very American way, and heaped upon with gourmet ingredients.

Some of those gourmet ingredients sure are delicious; lamb sausage is one of our favorites. But has anyone been up for a "Spicy Thai pizza" since En Vogue broke up? Nevertheless, the crust is pretty crunchy, and pretty doughy. Don't expect too much from salads, like a Greek that sometimes has off notes.

We like Vincenté's fun atmosphere. It's a big space, and more refined than you'd expect from a pizza joint, with an adjoining, slightly pubby room that stays lively later. We really like the warm lighting and the easy casual vibe. Plus, you can eat here later than almost anywhere else. Here, they serve good beers on draft and can actually answer questions about them. Upstairs, you can play pool; outside, there are benches for comfortable seating on nice nights.

Okay, we've just gotta ask: what's up with the accent on the final "e" in Vincenté? When you spend that much on signage, shouldn't you make sure it makes sense? At this rate, you'd pronounce it "Vinchent-ay!" like you're the Fonz.

Not that there's anything wrong with sounding like the Fonz. Word has it, he's cool.

Vindalho

Indian-influenced dishes served in an equally evocative architectural stunner

7.9	8.5	7.5
Food	Feel	Wine

Indian

Upmarket restaurant

$60
Price

www.vindalho.com

Tue, Wed, Thu, Sun 5pm–9pm
Fri–Sat 5pm–10pm

Bar Beer, wine, liquor
Credit cards Visa, MC, AmEx
Reservations Accepted
Date-friendly, outdoor dining,
veg-friendly

Division/Clinton
2038 SE Clinton St.
(503) 467-4550

This fun, colorful, two-story space has a lot of drama and flair. The architecture makes for a more visually stimulating experience than at Vindalho's gargantuan, vapid sibling restaurant Lauro Café. Interesting shadows are cast on the mango-colored walls by geometric art installations. Perhaps most stunning is the artful range hood in the open kitchen, where you can watch the cooking if your date isn't doing it for you. A large door rolls up in nice weather.

The menu bills itself as "spice route cuisine," and the mostly Indian-influenced menu does stretch now and then into Indonesia and the Middle East. Don't miss the specials, which are usually quite good. Of these, chicken pakoras have been terrific—creamy coriander-spiced chicken is wrapped in a coconut shell and deep fried. Samosas are made with seasonal ingredients to complement the potato base, and have a light, non-greasy dough. They're expertly fried.

Lamb kebabs in fenugreek cream are cooked to tenderness in the tandoor. Goan-style mussels get a marvelous sweetness from coconut milk, although the finish falls a bit flat. Pork vindalho is one of the best things on the menu, tender and moist, with a tangy and fragrant sauce and a long, spicy finish. A dash of balsamic vinegar gives the saffron basmati rice a piquant, yet balanced undertone. That said, we don't know why the dish is topped with onion rings.

There are about eight chutneys at Vindalho, which you can (and should) try as a sampler of three for $5. These include a wonderful peach-and-fennel flower, a properly made cucumber-mint raita, a tangy red onion-and-date, a tamarind, and a sweet tomato chutney. Each gives the dishes a whole other dimension of flavor, perhaps making up for the lack of more authentically penetrating spices within.

The beer list includes four or five changing taps of local microbrews, and a few more in bottle from here and abroad. The wine list is well chosen, with helpful suggestions for pairings. This isn't the most spicy, authentic Indian food around, but sometimes that's not what you're looking for.

In the end, you'll appreciate the creativity and capable execution of these dishes, just as you'll appreciate the artfulness of the design here.

Vita Café

The meat's the only thing that's faked in this cute, fun, and sincere café

7.0	8.0	7.5
Food	Feel	Wine

Vegefusion

Casual restaurant

$25
Price

www.vita-cafe.com

Mon–Fri 9am–10pm
Sat–Sun 8am–10pm

Bar Beer, wine, liquor
Credit cards Visa, MC
Reservations Not accepted
Kid-friendly, veg-friendly, Wi-Fi

Alberta Arts District
3023 NE Alberta St.
(503) 335-8233

This lively Alberta-hip café is often polled as being among the city's best for vegetarian and vegan options (although it does serve a small amount of free-range, hormone-and-antibiotic-free meat, as well). You get the best sense of its popularity in the early evenings, when there's quite a crowd of hip young families. The buzz is partly due to the fact that kids can eat from a $1 menu every day from 5–7pm, so if you have them, this is a spectacular deal; if you don't, this is a spectacular pain in the ass. Nevertheless, the crowd dies down as the night wanes.

With so many exciting scenes in town that are vegetarian- and vegan-friendly, Vita has some stiff competition. But Vita shines by night with good cocktails made with fresh, organic local juices.

And some of the world's truly most exciting, good-value wines are being made by Rudolph-Steiner worshippers planting deer bladders under the full moon and refusing to use chemical pesticides and fertilizers; the result is some wonderfully character-driven biodynamic bottles, a few of which show up on this list.

Aside from a free-range beef burger and some wild salmon, the bulk of the menu is devoted to simply substituting tempeh and tofu for meat in traditionally meaty dishes, especially burgers. If you're going to be vegan, why spend your time eating fake burgers? There are so many cuisines that make wonderful work of vegetables and legumes—namely South Indian and Middle Eastern. Vita makes a serviceable hummus platter and a benign Thai coconut soup, but we'd still rather go to an Indian restaurant than eat any of this…or a "fakin" BLT. Until they figure out how to make this not taste like floor jerky, we'll pass.

Brunch is popular and includes more omnivorous dishes using free-range eggs. The airy space and kelly-green walls have a sort of cheering effect, and Bloody Marys (here made with no actual blood or people) are strong. If you prefer nursing a hangover with nutritious scrambles full of tofurkey and fake bacon to slurping a broth of tripe and beef tallow, at least Vita gives you some palatable options.

Vivace

A charming, quaint spot for coffee and crêpes without much fuss—for better or worse

4.8	7.0
Food	Feel

Sandwiches, Crêpes, Coffee

Café **$15** Price

Mon–Thu 7am–10pm
Fri 7am–11pm
Sat 8am–11pm
Sun 8am–10pm

Bar Beer, wine
Credit cards Visa, MC
Outdoor dining, veg-friendly, Wi-Fi

Northwest Portland
1400 NW 23rd Ave.
(503) 228-3667

In a renovated Victorian-style house, Vivace warms the soul with coffee and crêpes. It's nicely decorated with comfortable chairs, couches, and a great patio space. The only problem can be squeezing into one of these spaces, as it does get crowded, and this isn't really a hostess-and-reservation kind of place. Channel your inner Viking and claim a seat, then growl at anyone who comes too close.

The sandwich board listing the available crêpes is in a hokey Comic Sans font (yes, we're obsessed with fonts), which tells you almost everything you need to know about the vibe here. It's cute but not cutting-edge, competent but not mind-blowing.

For instance, some savory crêpes come with mozzarella cheese. Who puts a cheese that bland in a crêpe? The fillings don't get much more exciting, with what appears to be deli ham, flavorless chicken, spinach, tomatoes, and mushrooms. That's it. The most exciting ingredient is walnuts, and nearly all of it relies on pesto for flavor. The crêpes themselves are properly made with buckwheat flour and are smooth as a baby's butt, but there's no crispy edge to them.

Sweet crêpes are made well with all-purpose flour, have some good spotting, and are jammed full of delicious Nutella and banana, but then doused in totally pedestrian aerosol-textured whipped cream. A simpler honey and butter crêpe is good (get it sans whip), but raspberry jam is just that: raspberry jam. What, no compote? Like we said, this isn't that kind of place.

Stumptown coffee is served, but made this haphazardly, it could be from anywhere. There are some lovely little designs drawn in the latte foam, so there's that. Smoothies are made from frozen fruit. Beers in the bottle are kind of knee-jerk, as is the wine list, which only specifies grape varietals (as if that tells you anything—ever had a Pinot Noir from Amador County, CA?), and not producers or regions.

We struggle to understand Vivace's eternal popularity; it is our duty to respectfully dissent.

Voodoo Doughnut

The star attraction of Portland's culinary freak show: Maple Bacon
Doughnut

Baked goods, Sweets   Counter service

www.voodoodoughnut.com

24 hours   **Bar** None   **Downtown**
Hours vary by location   **Credit cards** None   22 SW 3rd Ave.
                            Date-friendly, veg-friendly (503) 241-4704

Northeast Portland
1501 NE Davis St.
(503) 235-2666

Voodoo and doughnuts: neither was invented in America, but both have
risen in the pop culture here as magnificently alluring concepts that go
together surprisingly (super)naturally. Doughnuts can be quite a religious
experience, especially in the twilight hour of their birth. And like spiritual
objects, doughnuts can be filled with almost whatever you wish: jelly,
cream, peanut butter…NyQuil.

Voodoo Doughnut is open late in an area near Chinatown that's
populated by bars, strip clubs, and hot dance spots, which is part of the
beauty of the place. Buy an extra doughnut for one of the many homeless
people hanging around—they are an integral part of Voodoo's ambience
(and it's good juju).

You can rent out the Pepto-pink space to get married in a non-
denominational "Intentional Commitment Ceremony." Or just come for a
wild, perverse doughnut trip. Okay, so the NyQuils are no longer available
(apparently it upset the FDA—who knew?), but you can load up for the
bachelorette party with a "Cock-n-Balls" (cream filled, naturally), indulge
your inner child on one covered in Froot Loops and Cap'n Crunch, or act
out anger issues with a brilliant Voodoo doll doughnut, which squirts red
jelly from a pretzel stick protruding out of its plump belly, a look of
absolute misery iced on its face.

But no first-time visit is complete without a maple bacon doughnut. It
is, as it sounds, strips of crispy bacon atop maple-glazed fried dough. It's
sick and wrong and it has to be done. Novelty aside, we prefer a "Butter
Fingering" (who doesn't?), a chocolatey devil's food that's vanilla glazed
and covered in crushed Butterfingers. There's even a selection of vegan
donuts.

Ideas are constantly bandied around the shop, and special orders of
gag-gift doughnuts are taken. But whatever gross thing you can think
of—Jägermeister doughnuts, oyster-shooter doughnuts—Voodoo's
already been there and done that.

The Waffle Window

A magic portal onto a world in which Belgian waffles are a vehicle for everything

8.2 Food **7.5** Feel

Baked goods, Sandwiches

Counter service **$10** Price

www.wafflewindow.com

Sun–Thu 8am–5pm
Fri–Sat 8am–9pm

Bar None
Credit cards Visa, MC, AmEx
Kid-friendly, outdoor dining,
veg-friendly

Hawthorne
SE 36th Ave. and Hawthorne
Blvd.
(503) 239-4756

This is the era of the waffle. Flavour Spot's got the waffle-as-taco stance down, and the Little Blue Waffle Wagon has found success serving as an impromptu dessert for Pok Pok diners. Perhaps the most well loved of them all, The Waffle Window is a wee portal cut into the side of Bread and Ink Café. Its Liège-style waffles (the dense, sweet version most often found in Belgium) are served open faced, rather than folded, and come in both sweet and savory preps. Neither will be any good for you, so just throw caution and glycemic indexes to the wind when you come here.

The waffles are made well, a little crisp on the edges and fluffy within. And if it's too cold outside, the nice folks will let you eat them in the café.

The ooey-gooiest choice here—which you will have to split, as there ain't no way you're getting this baby down by yourself—is a Guittard-chocolate-dipped beauty that would be better with a skosh of sea salt to make it more of a soft, very fine chocolate-covered pretzel. Liège waffles get a bit of pearl sugar (harder, larger grains of white sugar that give a crunchy pop of sweetness). The phenomenon works best in a "Plain Pearl" with lemon. It's also hard not to love a glistening, Oregon strawberry coulis with whipped cream, even though the cream tastes like the thinner, milkier aerosol stuff.

Theoretically, you could eat a lunch- or dinner-type waffle here, like a "Farm Fusion," and excellent combination of chèvre, roasted red bell peppers (which aren't the slimy, overrated sort we normally see on sandwiches), grape tomatoes, spinach, and sautéed mushrooms. We'd hesitate to call this a healthier waffle, but it does have some nutritional value and is much more complex, with earthy, creamy, and tart flavors going on. But it doesn't get much better than a pork product in a waffle, and here you have a few options: add peppered bacon on a "Farm Fusion"; have the bacon with brie, basil, and excellent homemade peach jam (our favorite, although you have to redistribute the ingredients to get the best bites); or Black Forest ham with melting Gruyère and Jarlsberg cheeses, and your choice of rhubarb-rosemary ketchup or maple syrup.

Why choose? We'll take both, and switch off bite after bite.

Westcafé

We'll make it easy for you: live jazz, brunch, and happy hour

4.9	7.5	7.5
Food	Feel	Drinks

Modern

Casual restaurant

$35
Price

www.westcafepdx.com

Mon–Fri 11:30am–2pm, 4pm–9pm
Sat 4pm–9pm
Sun 10am–2pm

Bar Beer, wine, liquor
Credit cards Visa, MC, AmEx
Reservations Accepted
Date-friendly, live music, outdoor dining, Wi-Fi

Downtown
1201 SW Jefferson St.
(503) 227-8189

Westcafé reminds us of that one firework that shoots into the sky with all the others, but never explodes. It is perhaps burdened with trying to be so many things to so many people: a casual restaurant, a jazz lounge, a happy hour haunt, a brunch café. It's a huge space, decorated in a concerted attempt at looking upscale. But too many unfortunate catalog-looking furnishings and textiles are employed for Portland street cred. The service is absolutely un-corporate, though—it's sincere, personable, and knowledgeable in a way that suggests talent, not a training full of platitudes and threats, is behind their success.

That happy hour is quite happy, with generous hours, funny bartenders, and seasonal cocktails that evoke a few of the classics and, yes, a little of that boring, outdated –tini scene, as well. Sazeracs are dumbed down with simple syrup; and good luck finding the word "bitters" on this list. Still, most cocktails are made decently, and food is discounted pretty heavily, which is nice.

Perhaps owing to that lack of focus (the menu changes from bar to lunch to dinner somewhat haphazardly; there isn't the sense that dinner has an intentional style), dishes are mostly unchanging and tend to be underwhelming. A grilled artichoke-heart-and-prawn skewer is somehow bland, despite the good amount of char on it; chicken skewers are better, tender and spicy. "Moroccan" chicken with apricots is goofy and much too sweet. Hilariously, mains come with "a whisper of salad." The modesty is unwarranted, however, as these salads are a bit larger, perhaps a smidge. Crab-and-corn cakes are okay, but their accompanying mango sauce is overwrought and outdated. Really? Mango?

Brunch is fine, but nothing special. Basically, this is nothing we haven't seen done better elsewhere, and generally long ago—but even then, it wasn't that interesting. It seems better suited to people on their way to or from the Portland Art Museum, or to those who adore the live smooth jazz that plays on Saturdays. At just above a whisper.

Whiffies Fried Pies

Delicious fried pies in the wee hours—when just about anything would be delicious

Baked goods

Food cart

www.whiffies.com

Tue–Sat 8pm–3am

Bar None
Credit cards None
Outdoor dining

Hawthorne
SE 12th and SE Hawthorne
(503) 946-6544

As a purveyor of fried pies, this food cart—part of the Hawthorne hawker center that stays open practically all night, catering to the post-bar crowd—gets the job done, and serves (or rather, calls out your name and extends a hand from the window bearing your pie) with a smile.

The best part of the Whiffies pie is the first bite into that deep-fried pie batter. It's very batter-y. It makes you think of the state fair. It's light to the touch, yet deliciously fatty to the chew. It's just what it should be. It's even superior to the fried batter that encased the old-school McDonald's apple pies—before some point in the 1990s when Mickey D's sold out like suckers and started baking their apple pie instead of frying it. And we don't take a statement like that lightly.

Our favorites among the offerings are blueberry and cherry, although each tastes a bit over-syrupy, as canned or jarred blueberries tend to. Savory pies—for which we had high hopes—undershoot expectations; there's something overwhelming about the influx of proteins and fats; the fried batter is better balanced by fruit. Culinary perfection this is not. But at 2am, stumbling out of a bar, is that really what you're after?

The Whole Bowl

A mish-mash of ingredients, topped off with the world's most addictive sauce

7.0 Food

6.5 Feel

Vegefusion

Food cart

$5 Price

www.thewholebowl.com

Mon–Fri 11am–3pm
Hours vary by location

Bar None
Credit cards None
Outdoor dining, veg-friendly

Downtown
SW 9th and Alder
(503) 757-2695

Pearl District
1100 NW Gilsan St.

Hawthorne
4411 SE Hawthorne Blvd.
(503) 757-2695

Two carts—one downtown and one in the Pearl—plus a standing location and a roving truck make up this mini-franchise. (It's a mini-franchise by Portland standards, at least.)

But stationary or mobile, the Whole Bowl sets off some alarms for us. Our first impression is that this is a joke—vegefusion at its worst—and we have the lowest of expectations. These bowls are a *lot* of stuff thrown together, and it's a lot of stuff from a lot of different food cultures. Then again, this place seems pretty popular; there's almost always a queue, no matter the time, no matter the location.

So, what does happen when you throw together brown rice, beans (red and black), avocado, salsa, black olives, sour cream, cheese, and cilantro?

Not a whole lot.

It's the addition of the Tali sauce that's key, that ties the whole dish together, and that bumps the Whole Bowl bowl up to tasty status. Named after the owner, it's a lemony, garlicky concoction, made from a secret recipe. It's somewhat akin to aïoli. If we had to guess, we'd venture to say that there's a bit of curry powder or turmeric in the mix.

But, oh, is that sauce good. It takes an unbelievably dense and filling bowl and elevates it. Even the black olives don't seem out of balance, and the cilantro seems to be working in overdrive.

You can't go wrong by adding some hot sauce, and there's a big array to choose from: Tapatío, Mae Ploy sweet chili, Sriracha, Cholula, and Aardvark habanero. Our vote is with Cholula, whose vinegary flavor adds another dimension, although the Aardvark has a lovely kick.

But, no matter what, it's the Tali sauce that steals the show.

Whole Foods Market

The show-stopping foodie and wine-geek wonderland to end all arguments

Groceries

Market

www.wholefoodsmarket.com

Daily 8am–10pm
Hours vary by location

Bar Beer, wine
Credit cards Visa, MC, AmEx
Veg-friendly

Pearl District
1210 NW Couch St.
(503) 525-4343

Southeast Portland
2825 E. Burnside St.
(503) 232-6601

Northeast Portland
3535 NE 15th Ave.
(503) 281-3173

Whole Foods is the homegrown health-food market gone national—a hippie, food-obsessed Austin, Texas boy made good. It is no small praise for the American consumer—a glimmer of hope?—that Whole Foods has been such a success story. This is not just because the stores are gorgeous (but they are); the produce, cheese, and seafood are all beautifully displayed, and the overall experience is quite simply overwhelming, in part because there is just so much to choose from.

But Whole Foods has chosen wisely—with one eye on the environment and another on good taste. Its scope is so vast that the global research magic happens behind the scenes, leaving the shopper more choice than ever—but the right kind of choice.

Sprinkled throughout most stores are several mini-restaurants and buffet stations, which display seafood, sandwiches, barbecue, pizza, sushi, salads, "living foods," and more. Foods from around the world (sometimes different parts of the world at different times of day) can be boxed up or plated, eaten inside or outside or taken home. Wander around until something piques your interest, but find it fast before sensory overload completely incapacitates you.

Equally staggering—yet chosen with magnificent care—is the wine section. It is an operation that's equally concerned with quality, savings, and supporting independent, small, sustainable producers—yet also gently exerting enough influence on the buy side that they get the best prices from producers and reflect those savings back to the customer. It's like having a brutally honest, personal expert wine agent represent you in the marketplace, and find you the best deals.

It is hard to pick out a few deli items to mention from amongst all the options, but we do love the creamy, rich lobster bisque, with its gentle Southwestern heat. Satisfying pizza, available by the whole pie or slice, boasts fresh toppings, a nicely thin crust, and you can get some interesting vegetarian combinations like artichoke hearts, tomatoes, Kalamata olives, spinach, and goat cheese. Don't miss the cannoli—the shells are dense and toasty, the filling is light, and they are adorned with dark chocolate and pistachio. And the cheese department is legendary not just for carrying an incredible range of small-production cheeses, but for the care with which they keep them.

Not bad for a trip to what was once just a healthy grocery store down in Austin, Texas.

Wildwood

With a reverence for all things local and natural, this longtime favorite still rocks

8.6	8.5	9.0
Food	Feel	Drinks

Modern

Upmarket restaurant

$70
Price

www.wildwoodrestaurant.com

Mon–Thu 11:30am–2:30pm, 5:30pm–9:30pm; Fri–Sat 11:30am–2:30pm, 5:30pm–10pm; Sun 5pm–9pm

Bar Beer, wine, liquor
Credit cards Visa, MC, AmEx
Reservations Accepted
Date-friendly, outdoor dining

Northwest Portland
1221 NW 21st Ave.
(503) 248-9663

Wildwood is to local eating what Neil Young was to grunge. About 15 years ago, it was cutting-edge, using local produce and meats before they came with their own pamphlets. But like Young, it's not at all out of date either, even next to all these rebellious, tattooed upstarts taking the local eating thing to newer, wilder heights.

Fresh from a sort-of-recent renovation, Wildwood is spacious and airy, with clean lines and—naturally—a sort of sylvan feeling from all the wood surfaces, off which voices aggressively bounce when the place is crowded. (That seems to happen even during lazy weekday lunches.) A large open kitchen is a focal point—it perfumes the air with baked dough and smoked shellfish.

The menu changes frequently, and is riddled with the names of local farms and ranches. A salad of Creative Growers' gem lettuce is simply dressed with retro-tastic green goddess dressing, a spot-on complement to the romaine-like leaves. There's always a stone-fired pizza of some kind listed among the starters—one recent version featured bacon and heirloom tomatoes. Using fresh tomatoes on pizza can be problematic, though, as it leads to a soggy center; couple that with the copious amounts of cheese, and it's a gooey mess—albeit a nicely flavored one. One of Wildwood's unchanging signature dishes, skillet-roasted Totton Inlet mussels, come in an oily sun-dried tomato, saffron, and garlic broth that is rich and deep, and made fresh from a bit of lemon. The mussels are plump and exquisite, even if the dish is a little pricey for what it is.

Lamb crépinette has been among the best dishes we've had in town, with braised, shredded lamb meat rolled into a ball and fried in butter to a very dark brown, then served on a buttery roll with a rich mix of corn and white beans. Though a heavy dish, it is executed with just enough balance to make it not cumbersome. Albacore salad is like the tuna salad of your dreams, fresh and summery-tasting. Dungeness crab cakes are also very good, crusted with potato and served on a salad of fennel, radish, cucumbers, and almonds with a light aïoli.

Desserts are just as capable and fun, and small-production cheeses from the Pacific Northwest make an ideal companion to a hefty number of wines from some of the region's better producers. It's no small thing, in a city full of chefs rocking out offal and obscure regional preps, for Wildwood to still be as relevant as ever.

Wing Wa BBQ King

What you see is what you should get

7.4	5.0
Food	Feel

Chinese, Dim Sum

Casual restaurant

$20
Price

Daily 9am–10:30pm

Bar Beer
Credit cards Visa, MC
Reservations Not accepted

82nd Avenue Area
2788 SE 82nd Ave.
(503) 771-1848

Wing Wa BBQ King looks totally legit. It's got all the traits of a classic Chinatown winner: a name that is steeped in hyperbole; more Chinese characters than English on its signage; a random invitation to play video lottery; and street-side windows that, if you peer through them, show off the golden, glistening bodies of ducks and pigs hanging in the back of the joint.

The room is drab and a bit grungy. You'll have little desire to sit here, even just while you wait for your barbecue to go.

As you might have guessed, the Cantonese barbecue and roast meats at Wing Wa are its best work. Period. Not some of its best. Its best. As in, don't venture off the path. Normally, if there's a greaseboard featuring specials in Chinese, we insist you go for it, no matter what it is. And you can gloss over the majority. Just point and insist to your friendly but doubtful server that you want it, even if it's the innards of a sea dragon. But here, you will be likely disappointed by anything but the barbecue.

Ignore the enormous menu and dim sum carts (especially if the restaurant is slow); Wing Wa is the "BBQ King," remember? Order half a duck, hacked up and served with sticky rice and sweetish sauces. Or nibble juicy pork off its bones and cartilage.

Delicious.

Wong's King Seafood

An enormous, popular dim sum spot that serves up
seconds-old seafood from the cleanest tanks ever

7.6	7.0
Food	Feel

Chinese, Seafood, Dim Sum

Casual restaurant

$45
Price

www.wongsking.com

Mon–Fri 10am–11pm
Sat–Sun 9:30am–11pm

Bar Beer, wine, liquor
Credit cards Visa, MC
Reservations Accepted
Outdoor dining

82nd Avenue Area
8733 SE Division St.
(503) 788-8883

Wong's King Seafood is infinite. We're pretty sure there's a wormhole lurking in here, somewhere between the meticulously kept seafood tanks and the bathrooms. How else could you explain the endless numbers of servers, dishes, customers being processed per day, per hour, per minute?

The place is spotless, with crisp, white tablecloths. A smartly attired waitstaff moves with almost-military precision. Despite its overwhelming size, this Cantonese restaurant fills up frequently because of its inordinate popularity.

The dim sum variety is large, and the carts are refreshed frequently. The staff is very knowledgeable and, unlike at many places, doesn't hesitate to help you with your selections. Shrimp and pork dumplings in light wrappers are delicious and fragrant. Congee (rice porridge with flavorful bits of pork) is also great, as are char siu bao (barbecue pork buns).

Lunch specials are inexpensive and good. Light little crab puffs, which actually taste like crab, might be the best in Portland. But the standard lunch mains are not nearly as delicious as they used to be. We've had them inedibly vinegary. Here, as everywhere, you're definitely better off avoiding the Chinese-American stuff. The kitchen seems more careful with seafood and more exotic (traditional) dishes.

Dinner is more reliable, with a tome-like menu of rather condescending pictures. Chicken and duck are cooked beautifully, with an extremely crispy skin that crackles when you bite into it. Unfortunately, the meat beneath can be a bit bland—use sauce. For hot pot, firepots of stock are delivered steaming to your table, waiting to be plied to your liking with thinly sliced meats and fresh vegetables.

But what you ought to do is look to those tanks for your dinner. Abalone is unusually tender and silky; one excellent rendition is served thinly sliced with mushrooms. Scallops with XO sauce are expertly cooked, juicy and flavorful; the same goes for salty-spicy prawns. Salt-and-pepper squid is also aptly done, crunchy and hot.

We find Wong's to be a little overhyped, but stick to the live seafood and you won't be disappointed. This place definitely has that ostentatious thing going on—the display of shark fins and such. It's tacky but authentic. What more can you ask of Portland Cantonese cuisine?

World Cup Coffee

Coffee

Café

www.worldcupcoffee.com

Daily 9am–11pm
Hours vary by location

Bar None
Credit cards Visa, MC, AmEx
Date-friendly, kid-friendly,
veg-friendly, Wi-Fi

Pearl District
Powell's Books
W. Burnside St.
(503) 228-4651

1005

Northwest Portland
1740 NW Glisan St.
(503) 228-4152

Beaverton
Powell's Books
3415 SW Cedar Hills Blvd.
(503) 228-4651

When World Cup began roasting in 1993, Portland wasn't quite the coffee mecca that it is today. World Cup was one of the first operations in town to source estate coffees directly from abroad (Central and South America), and thus one of the pioneers of Portland's coffee revolution.

By the time the first World Cup coffeeshop opened at 18th and Glisan in 1999, the revolution was well underway. Ten years later, these guys still roast their own beans; their coffee, organic tea, and espresso drinks continue to do justice to the prestigious Portland appellation—and continue to support sustainable coffee growing.

The original location, which is blessed with giant windows, good light, and great street scenes, is as popular as ever. They do sandwiches, pastries, and such, but naturally, the focus is on the coffee. The baristas here take their work incredibly seriously, and they're formidable players in the best-design-on-the-cappuccino-froth game.

But the single best thing about World Cup is its location inside Powell's City of Books, the largest new/used bookstore in the world. (There's also one inside the Beaverton Powell's.) If the marriage between bookstores and coffeeshops was made in heaven, this one is a trip directly there.

The prospect of browsing the book selection—3,500 subsections, and more than 1,000,000 books—and sitting down for a cup of delicious Portland coffee is an offer that's simply too good to refuse, which is what draws people in here by the boatload. Although Borges' Library of Babel was but a thought experiment, this place comes closer to acting it out than any other establishment in human history.

In short, everybody in Portland has a cup of coffee at the World Cup in Powell's, sooner or later. *Everybody*. It's an icon of the city, an essential experience.

Yakuza Lounge

Cool Japanese fusion food—maybe a little too cool, like the neighborhood

7.0	8.0	8.5
Food	Feel	Drinks

Japanese

Upmarket restaurant

$60
Price

www.yakuzalounge.com

Wed–Sun 5:30pm–10pm

Bar Beer, wine, liquor
Credit cards Visa, MC, AmEx
Reservations Accepted
Date-friendly, outdoor dining

Alberta Arts District
5411 NE 30th Ave.
(503) 450-0893

This self-described "Japanese pub" is actually the most ambitious entry of all from the restaurant group that has taken the corner of 30th and Killingsworth by storm—Beast, Fats, DOC—and turned it into the so-called "Fox-Chase Addition," a neighborhood that aims to extend the gentrification of Alberta Avenue to the north. It's a really enjoyable space to inhabit for an evening, and it's a great date place, too: expanses of sleek wood, hanging pots and pans, flowing curtains, warm recessed lighting, avant-garde murals, and garagelike window panels onto a bustling street corner.

Yakuza's minimalist, trendy, casually elegant vibe is backed by an extremely complex (and hardly publike) cuisine, which is far broader in focus than the normal izakaya—both in the sense that raw fish is emphasized, and in the sense that the menu is more pan-Asian than Japanese. A salad of Japanese cucumber, avocado, togarashi, sesame, and sugar-vinegar sushi-rice dressing—plays somewhere between an upmarket seaweed salad and Korean banchan; it's a bit sweet, more than a bit salty, and very intense. So is "mentaiko spaghetti" (jalapeño, smelt roe, squid's-ink noodles, and sherry). So is a lot of the menu.

Sometimes the sweetness goes a bit far, as in mackerel that's glazed with miso and sugared up with sweet mustard vinaigrette. But other times it's just right, as in sweet-and-sour red cabbage that's served with pork cheek that's first braised and then panko-breaded and fried. It feels like a reference to Czech or Hungarian pork-and-cabbage plates.

Sushi rolls are pleasurable enough, but yellowtail sashimi, which comes with a salad of herbs and daikon (radish), jalapeño oil, and ponzu sauce, comes off as a late-1990s Nobu derivative. More interesting is a plate of tuna carpaccio, chives, black peppercorns, and ponzu that play off two subtly sweet elements: silky sea urchin and "white soy ponzu." Salt and sugar—sound familiar?

Craft cocktails employ ingredients like basil, fresh carrot juice, muddled ginger, and pink peppercorns to great effect. A "sugar snap" cocktail really distills the grassy flavor of snap peas to great effect; the vodka and lime are merely treble notes. The sake list is short but effective. There's an argument to be made for utilizing Yakuza as a place to go for a before-dinner cocktail and snack, rather than zigzagging your way through a whole meal.

Yummy Yummy Seafood

Cantonese that's earned both of its yummies

8.0	**5.5**
Food	Feel

Chinese, Seafood

Casual restaurant

$35
Price

Mon–Thu 8am–2am
Fri–Sun 11am–11pm

Bar Beer, wine
Credit cards Visa, MC
Reservations Accepted
Kid-friendly

82nd Avenue Area
2745 SE 82nd Ave.
(503) 517-9992

"Yummy." What is it with this word lately? It seems to pop up everywhere you look, staring out at you like a perky, lollipop-licking first-grader. Don't get us wrong, lollipop-licking first-graders are cute, but it's creepy when grown women (and, shudder, men) talk like one. Not only does it sound annoying, it means absolutely nothing. A Twinkie can be "yummy," if by "yummy" it means it makes you think "yum." So, then, can a beautifully seared pork belly. Hey, describing food in 400 words or less is a postmodern pain in the ass. But regressing is never the answer (unless you're Pee-Wee Herman).

The neon sign in Chinese characters (reading, naturally, "Yummy Seafood") looks hilarious laid over what appears to be the shell of a former KFC (which has very yummy biscuits). Inside, it's often empty, except when there's a special occasion, which is what the place looks like it's set for—a very authentic touch among Chinese seafood restaurants. It's not unusual to have to interrupt the staff watching television to get something, but we admit that we kind of love that. It makes us feel like we've slipped into a Hong Kong hole in the wall.

On the menu you'll find good renditions of traditional Cantonese and often-controversial delicacies like abalone, sea cucumber, shark's fin, and bird's nest—but they're not always available. We will refrain from moral judgment here, but their presence is a good signal, anyway, for authentic Chinese cuisine. Fried pork ribs are delicious and garlicky, but succulent lamb is even better; as is a kick-ass version of cold jellyfish salad, as spicy and gelatinous as it should be. Tripe rocks the house, and being Cantonese, this kitchen also does a great job with salt-and-pepper shrimp (shell-on) and squid. Fish straight from the tank done up in faithful Cantonese style. In short, this is one of the top Chinese tables in Portland. Fried homemade tofu is delicious, properly crispy. Skip the stir-fried noodles, which are greasy and underwhelming, with none of the crispy qualities indicative of a good, hot fire.

Yuzu

In a region of great izakayas, this is the very best

9.2	8.5	7.5
Food	Feel	Wine

Japanese

Casual restaurant

$40
Price

Mon–Sat 6pm–midnight

Bar Beer, wine
Credit cards Visa, MC, AmEx
Reservations Essential
Date-friendly

Beaverton
4130 SW 117th Ave.
(503) 350-1801

Don't come here looking for sushi—this is an exciting array of Japanese bar/street food: beef tongues and tofu and fish cakes (oh my!). Izakaya is all the rage in the Pacific Northwest, and this humble Beaverton spot, hidden in a strip shopping center, is perhaps the foremost practitioner of the art in Oregon.

It's tiny and green, with one open kitchen, a few bar seats, and just a few more tables. Get there early; by opening time at 6pm, there are already people waiting for a seat, and it stays packed (mostly with Japanese people) until closing. Coming as a large group (with reservations) works great, too.

Just don't bring anyone picky or with obnoxious food prejudices. Yuzu serves up an amazing bowl of stewed pig intestines; wonderful braised pork belly; breaded and fried kobe katsu (like a deep-fried hamburger, really); and a codfish liver mousse that's sultry, salty, and wonderful. Even edamame are way above average, with more soybean flavor than salt. For best results, stick to fatty pork and innards, although the kitchen does a nice job with deep-fried fish as well. Expect to order about three or four small plates per person.

Ramen preps are very good, although the noodles are not handmade. It's all about the broth, which is deeply meaty and lively with ginger. Skewered meats have a great char and fat marbling. The sake selection is wide, if lacking a bit on the lower end. There are some treasures in here, though. There are only two draft beers (yes, one is Sapporo), but we doubt anyone much minds.

Whether you're in Beaverton or not, Yuzu is worth the trip—remember to reserve in advance, or you'll be sitting at the bar. Just please don't call it "Japanese tapas." We have to stop the madness somewhere.

Zell's An American Café

Get your fill of eggs, eggs, and more eggs at this comfy spot

7.0 Food **8.5** Feel

American

Casual restaurant

$20 Price

Mon–Fri 7am–2pm
Sat–Sun 8am–2pm

Bar Beer, wine, liquor
Credit cards Visa, MC, AmEx
Reservations Not accepted

Belmont
1300 SE Morrison St.
(503) 239-0196

Sometimes a place has such a great neighborhood vibe, such an obvious, easy appeal—which is the point of a restaurant, when all is said and done—that it starts to matter less and less what's on the plate, as long as it's serviceable.

Zell's is one of these establishments. Walk in, and you're welcomed like family. Jazz and sunlight stream in. You and your party suddenly become your best selves. A cup of drip coffee becomes an elixir; a simply country biscuit, sweet and buttery, seems somehow life-affirming. And the egg, that symbol of rebirth and renewal, becomes the subject of a certain hero worship. This Sunday (or Saturday—or Tuesday, for that matter) brunch rebirths your day, renews your mood.

That hero worship extends to the menu, which is so egg-centric that they have to label a section of it "not eggs." Traditional eggs Benedict is extremely popular and, as the French might say, it's correct, with well-executed hollandaise and eggs that aren't over-poached. We like the Benedict less with baked salmon, which fights with the hollandaise instead of touching it up with a slightly salty, slightly chewy counterpoint, as Canadian bacon does.

The specials board is often where it's happening—or, at least, where it's most interesting, because much of the breakfast-lunch menu is extremely predictable in that upscale-diner sort of way. A "Reuben scramble"—a special at one visit (and one of several riffs on the legendary Reuben we've seen in Portland this year)—was just fine, no better. Its vinegary sauerkraut gave a surprising pop to the soft eggs, but the bread could have been toasted a bit more, its gruyère more carefully melted. A slather of mayo seemed unnecessary, and the sandwich was too thick and unwieldy to eat. The eggs inside the sandwich were soft enough, and the cute little diced potatoes nicely home-fried, but it wasn't clear that we wouldn't rather be eating a plain old Reuben.

Or, for that matter, just a plate of those eggs and home fries, side of sausage, buttered toast. It's what Zell's does best—aside from warming the heart.

Ziba's Pitas

This food truck from the Balkans purveys meat pie, spinach pie—and total uniqueness

6.9 Food **7.0** Feel

Bosnian

Food cart **$5** Price

www.zibaspitas.com

Mon–Fri 10:30am–3:30pm

Bar None
Credit cards None
Outdoor dining, veg-friendly

Downtown
SW Alder St. & SW 9th Ave.
(503) 473-9372

When in a new country and unable to speak the language, you can charm the natives with your cooking. At least that's what Ziba has done for the last half-decade, from a food cart sandwiched between other food carts in the makeshift "restaurant row to go" between Powell's and the Central Library. Ziba has clearly assimilated during that time: in a very anti-Eastern-European and pro-Portland touch, the cart is supremely vegetarian-friendly.

Pita here is really burek ("Ziba's Pitas" rolls off the tongue better than "Ziba's Burek"), based on a buttery phyllo-dough pastry crust and wrapped around meat and other fillings. They're vaguely similar to Malaysian roti murtabak. The "pitas" are made fresh each morning, rolled out thin, with either eggs, cheese, and sour cream; cottage cheese, eggs, and spinach; or ground meat, zucchini, and cheese. They're then cooked, like a pie, and served with a little refreshing cucumber salad with sour cream.

Spinach and cheese is a good preparation, but the meat version is even better, succulent and a little spicy. At off-hours, however, the crusts are microwaved to heat them up, which takes away considerably from the texture of the dough, making it soggier than it should be. Ajvar, a treat of puréed red bell pepper and eggplant, will haunt your dreams for days. There are also delicious, moist meatballs (here called cufte).

A refreshing yogurt sauce is drizzled over everything, but it's sometimes too much. You can ask for the sauce on the side to be safe. A combo plate lets you have any two halves of a pita-pie or a half a pita and an order of ajvar. If you can walk here from work, even better—you will want to take a nap on your desk otherwise.

Go, enjoy some of this nice lady's food, and make her feel as welcome as she makes you feel. Ah, food. The universal language.

Fearless Critic
Index

Notes